Ingwersen's Manual of Alpine Plants

Ingwersen's

Manual of Alpine Plants

Will Ingwersen V.M.H.

First edition published 1978 to commemorate the fiftieth
anniversary of the establishment of W. E. Th. Ingwersen Ltd.

This edition published 1986 by
Collingridge Books
an imprint of Newnes Books
a division of The Hamlyn Publishing Group Limited

First published in the USA in 1986 by:
Timber Press
9999 S.W. Wilshire
Portland, Oregon 97225

ISBN 0–88192–026–6

Printed in Yugoslavia

CONTENTS

A SHORT HISTORY OF BIRCH FARM NURSERY

Although the nursery now celebrates its Golden Jubilee, the story actually began in the very early years of this century, when Walter Ingwersen, born of Danish parents in Hamburg, came to England after a period spent in gaining experience in Continental nurseries, and established his own alpine plant nursery in Croydon.

The business flourished until the first World War, which eventually forced its closure. Walter Ingwersen then spent a period as war service in charge of the rock garden department at the Wisley Gardens of the Royal Horticultural Society. After the war he spent several years in partnership, first with the late Clarence Elliott at the famous Six Hills Nursery in Stevenage and, later, with the late Gavin Jones at Letchworth.

When seeking a site upon which to establish again his own nursery, he visited the late William Robinson, at Gravetye Manor, with whom he discussed his desire to set up in business, specialising in alpine plants. Robinson immediately offered him the lease of Birch Farm, a small farm on the estate with an Elizabethan house and several acres of land.

After Robinson's death the estate passed to the Forestry Commission, from whom Will and Paul Ingwersen eventually purchased the property in 1969.

INTRODUCTION

This Manual makes no pretence to be a botanical treatise. It is more a gathering together, between two covers, of information previously scattered through countless pages of books, periodicals and catalogues. Within the limits imposed by my own imperfect knowledge, I have endeavoured to attain a sufficient degree of accuracy of names and descriptions. For mistakes and inaccuracies — and some there will assuredly be — I accept full and sole responsibility. To the many who have so willingly responded to my appeals for information I express my sincere gratitude. In particular I am grateful to Chris. Brickell and Dr. Martin Rix, the Director and Botanist respectively of the Wisley Gardens of the Royal Horticultural Society for my frequent calls upon their wisdom.

I believe that a Manual such as this will be helpful to those interested in alpine plants, remembering always that it has been written by one who may perhaps lay some claim to being a dedicated plantsman, but who is not a botanist in the true sense of the word, although a modicum of botanical knowledge must have been accumulated during a lifetime spent among plants, and close associations with those who are acknowledged authorities.

Before deciding upon the title of this volume I hesitated over the word 'Alpine'. So many of the plants described are not, strictly speaking, alpines, that it might be thought misleading. I eventually decided to use the word in its loose sense of implying plants appropriate to rock gardens and alpine houses. Even then I admit to having allowed myself considerable latitude.

To produce such a work as this has been my dream for many years and this, our 50th anniversary, seemed a very appropriate time to stop thinking about it and get on with the job! To compile it has been a long, often exhausting, but always rewarding task. It has also been a very humbling occupation and I emerge from two years of research, seeking help and advice, and writing, with a healthy appreciation of my own ignorance.

Gardeners are frequently at odds with botanists over the changes in the names of plants. Although I sometimes find myself with a foot in both camps, in general I stand firmly among the gardeners. Where a name has become familiar by long usage I commonly retain it, whilst at the same time indicating what the correct name should be, hoping thus to please both the pedant and the dilettante. In certain cases I have accepted the latest ruling, but, again, quote also the more familiar appellation.

7

It is our intention that the Manual should be used in conjunction with our annual catalogue, which will appear each year in an abbreviated form. All plants described in the Manual, of which we have available stocks to include in our catalogue, will be listed and priced, but not described. In the case of such families as Aubrieta Phlox, Helianthemum, etc., of which there are so many named cultivars and hybrids, the name of the variety will be followed by a colour description.

Many plants which will be in our annual catalogue will not appear in the Manual. For these there will be the necessarily brief description which, unfortunately, economy now dictates. Bulbs, with certain exceptions, are excluded from the Manual, as are Heathers and Conifers although some which are truly rock garden shrubs are included, shrubs are also excluded. In any case I did not wish to become involved in deciding what was, or was not, a shrub!

In its original conception it was envisaged that there would be coloured illustrations in the Manual, but, as time proceeded and costs escalated it became evident that the idea of illustrations must be abandoned. I admit that I accepted this decision with some relief. The few pages of illustrations which could have been included at a reasonable cost would not have been helpful. To illustrate it fully would necessitate a very high price. I hope, therefore, that your imaginations, coupled with my descriptions, will convey with sufficient clarity a picture of the plants.

The name of each genus is immediately followed by its Natural Order, printed in italics. After this, where known, comes the derivation of the generic name. For much of this latter information I am deeply indebted to the great knowledge of Dr.W.T. Stearn of the British Museum, from whose book on the subject I have shamelessly cribbed.

To the botanically minded reader I apologise for the absence of given authorities after each specific name. As I have said already, this is not a botanically orientated book and it is written by a gardener for gardeners.

Of the many omissions in the pages of the Manual I am all too conscious. I began with the intention of including only plants which are definitely in cultivation but, as time passed, the temptation to include a number of plants which I knew would not be easily obtainable became irresistible. Even so, in some of the splendid amateur collections and in botanical gardens there must be plants which ought to be here, but are not.

It is my experience that any book about plants is out of date immediately it is published and I have no doubt that, in a few years time, a new edition of this Manual will be essential — although I may not be here to write it. I can only hope that all of you who buy and use the Manual will forgive its shortcomings and accept it as the culmination of a long life spent in loving and trying to know something about alpine and other hardy plants.

In my old-fashioned way I have given all measurements in feet and inches, feeling sure that older readers would feel more at home with them. A metric conversion table is included for the benefit of the younger generation and those who have already adopted, and adapted themselves, to the metric system. General cultivation instructions will be found on a separate page.

Finally, it is now fifty years since my late father, Walter Ingwersen, one of the great plantsmen of his day, began to make Birch Farm Nursery a Mecca for lovers of alpine plants. (A brief history of the nursery is written on another page.) I was a young man then, fired by his boundless enthusiasm and proud to be his right-hand man. Since his death in 1960 I have endeavoured to continue in the way he would have wished, with the able assistance of my half-brother Paul and our loyal nursery manager, George Henley who has been our friend and standby since the earliest days. I would also extend thanks and appreciation to our printers, Dunnsprint of Eastbourne, for the interest and care they have given to the production of the Manual.

CULTURAL ADVICE

To have given cultural advice after every plant would have increased the bulk of the Manual so substantially, and would have been so pointless that, with the exceptions of instances where individual treatment has seemed advisable, I have avoided detailed instructions, and offer instead these general suggestions.

Unless otherwise stated the plants described will be contented in any well-drained garden soil which is adequately supplied with humus and an open, sunny position. If it is desired to make up a standard compost for alpine plants an excellent medium can be composed of a mixture of two parts loam, or good top-spit garden soil, one part leafmould, or fine-grade moss peat and one part sharp sand or fine grit, all parts by bulk. A generous dusting of bonemeal to the heap of ingredients before mixing will provide all the fertiliser necessary. Do not use stable manure for alpines. Unless otherwise stated the plants will not object to alkaline soil.

Where a plant is said to be suitable for a peat garden, this it is assumed will be constructed with peat blocks and the beds and terraces filled in with a mixture which is at least 50% moss peat, the remaining 50% being a mixture of equal parts lime-free soil and sharp sand or fine grit. A peat garden should be positioned in a place which either has a cool north aspect, or is lightly shaded, but not overhung by trees. If the garden should be on a slope and the soil alkaline, the peat garden ought to be at the top and not at the bottom of the slope, otherwise there could be a dangerous infiltration of lime-laden water.

An alpine house, in the proper sense of the word is a specially made structure, of low pitch, with more ventilators than in a conventional greenhouse, ideally on both sides of both roof and staging. Other houses can be adapted by the addition of extra ventilators. To those who wish to have the real thing we strongly recommend the firm of C.H. Whitehouse Ltd., Buckhurst Works, Frant, Nr.Tunbridge Wells, Kent, who construct a greenhouse specifically designed for alpine plants and whose workmanship is impeccable.

ACAENA. *Rosaceae*. From the Greek *akaina*, a thorn, because of the spines on the calyces of these plants.

A large family of, mostly, carpeting plants, native to New Zealand with some outliers in S. America and Polynesia. They are invasive but ornamental and possess considerable garden value. They should never be planted near to less vigorous plants, which they might smother. They ask for nothing more than open, sunny positions and will flourish in the poorest of soils. Useful for crevices between paving stones they may also be employed as ground-cover for considerable areas. The small, inconspicuous flowers are carried in rounded, closely-packed heads and are often accompanied by decorative, brightly coloured spines. Confusion exists regarding the nomenclature of some of the cultivated species and not all authorities may agree with the accuracy of some names here used.

— **adscendens.** Although a carpeting species, this is not as prostrate as some. Its stems may rise to a height of 9 in. in a tumbled mat of tangled stems clothed with blue-grey, toothed leaves. As I know the plant the flower-heads are creamy-green in colour. New Zealand and the Falkland Islands.

— **buchananii.** A good carpeter with pea-green leaves in dense, low mats and bristly flower-heads of yellowish-brown. New Zealand.

— **glabra.** This is not so prostrate as some but is a valuable carpeter. The leaves and stems are without hairs and the flower-heads are without bristles but are ornamented by red calyces of the small flowers. New Zealand.

— **glauca.** Prostrate and to be valued for its silky-haired leaves of soft grey-blue. New Zealand.

— **microphylla.** Possibly the most popular of the cultivated species for the sake of its prostrate mats of bronzed foliage and burr-like heads of flowerlets armed by scarlet bristles. There is some confusion in gardens between this plant and its variety 'Inermis' and in many cases they appear to be synonymous. New Zealand.

- **novae-zealandiae.** Of the provenance of this species there can be no doubt. It is allied to, but a slightly coarser plant than *A. sanguisorbae*. A vigorous spreader making mats of leaves clothed in silky hairs and with purple, spiny flower-heads.

- **sanguisorbae.** Similar to the above-named species but more prostrate and also possessing purple flower-heads. New Zealand.

  Other names which may be occasionally encountered are *A. splendens* from Chile, which is said to be resplendent with silver hairs, an upright-growing species named *A. pumila*, and any of the following should be worth growing – *abyssinica, laevigata, pinnatifida, ovalifolia* and *magellanica*, the last two named from S. America.

ACANTHOLIMON. *Plumbaginaceae.* From the Greek words *akantha*, a thorn, and *limonium*, sea-lavender, to which plant it is related.

A large genus containing upward of 100 species of tufted, evergreen perennials with sharply-pointed rigid leaves, natives of Greece and eastward through Syria to Tibet. Few of the species are in cultivation, although many are highly desirable. They all relish dry, sunny positions in sharply drained soil. Resentful of root disturbance they are slow-growing and, once established should be left alone. The rarer species from hot mountain-slopes in the Middle East, if obtainable, are best treated as alpine house plants unlikely to relish our uncertain winter climate in the open. Summer flowering.

- **acerosum.** From Anatolia. Hard cushions of spiny, blue-grey leaves form the foundation for 6 in. slender sprays of white flowers. It may be encountered under the erroneous name *A. pinnardii*.

- **androsaceum.** See *A. echinus*.

- **cilicicum.** Cilicia. Very tufted and silvery-grey needle-like leaves. Like all the species, the small flowers are enclosed in papery bracts which, in this case, are pink.

- **creticum.** From Greece and the Island of Crete. Some authorities agree that this is only a form of *A. echinus*, which it closely resembles, but is denser and more compact and the few-flowered spikes are very short, carrying flowerlets surrounded by chaffy calyces of white, veined with purple.

- **echinus.** (androsaceum.) This Cretan cushion plant appears to vary considerably but what might be considered the type forms mounded hummocks of spiky leaves and carries spikes of flowers enclosed in white, pink veined chaffy cups.

- **glumaceum.** Whereas most of the species here described are, as I said in the introduction, best regarded as alpine house plants unless special provision can be made for them outside, this is definitely 'everyman's acantholimon'. It will flourish in any open, sunny position as long as the soil is well drained. Deep green cushions of narrow leaves, less spiny than in most species, are surmounted by short sprays of pink flowers. It can be found on Mt. Ararat and in

Russia and has been grown in British gardens since 1851, but had to wait until 1960 before receiving its well-deserved Award of Merit.

— **hohenackeri.** A native of the Eastern Caucasus. I rather doubt if this species ramains in cultivation. I grew it for some years but it finally collapsed during a severe winter, and as it never favoured me with flowers I am uncertain what colour they should be. It is very dense and compact in habit and the needle-like leaves are glaucous-blue and studded with whitish lime spots.

— **kotschyi.** Another very dense and tufted species, from the Cilician Taurus, and Mt. Berytagh in particular. Its leaves are broader than most and markedly blue-green in colour. The very short stems carry a few pink flowers.

— **libanoticum.** Characteristically mounded in habit and the short stems are clothed at the base with recurved dead leaves of previous years. It comes from Lebanon and carries rather long spikes of white-bracted flowers, the outside of the papery cup veined with purple.

— **lycopodioides.** An extremely desirable species from Kashmir and northward to the Karakorum where it grows at great elevations and forms tight masses like a Cassiope studded with 2 in. spikes of pink flowers in a white cup. I doubt if it is at present in cultivation, but wish that it were.

— **melananthum.** On recent visits to Iran I have seen several handsome species of acantholimon collected in the dry mountain areas, from where comes this worthy plant. Its short, rather broad leaves overlap to form dense pads of blue-grey. The flowers are almost stemless, may be pink or white and sit in a deep purple cup.

— **pinnardii.** See *A. acerosum.*

— **venustum.** This shares with *A. glumaceum* an amiability which enables it to be more often encountered in gardens than most of the species in this beautiful, but comparatively little known genus. It comes from the Cilician Taurus, was first introduced in 1873, and, according to the records, was given a First Class Certificate in the same year, which throws some doubt on the date given for its introduction. Needle-like leaves of grey-green form rather lax cushions which display to great advantage the long, arching sprays of pink-bracted flowers. It is much happier in an alpine house than in the open.

The above list is far from complete. Reference books and Floras may tempt you with many more names. I am hopeful that recent explorations in Iran and Afghanistan may produce a few more with which we may experiment in gardens. Their propagation is far from easy. They do not strike readily from cuttings and seldom provide fertile seeds. Layering an old plant by filtering into it sandy, peaty soil may result in a plant so treated being divided into a number of rooted pieces eventually.

As a nomenclatural footnote I observe that the new *Flora Europaea* has returned to *A. androsaceum* its specific rank, but I find this an aggravating publication, very upsetting to reactionary diehards like myself.

ACANTHOPHYLLUM. *Caryophyllaceae.* From the Greek *akantha,* a thorn, and *phyllos,* a leaf, referring to the spiky foliage.

This is a small genus, related to Dianthus and only modestly represented in gardens. When obtained they should be given hot, dry positions or grown in the alpine house.

— glandulosum. From the rocky slopes of Iranian mountains, on their hot, southern sides, where it grows in company with *A. grandiflorum,* both forming spiny cushions, concealed at blossoming time by innumerable short-stemmed flowers, which might be white, pink, or even purple.

— spinosum. The plant sometimes encountered under this name in gardens I believe to be correctly *Dianthus noeanus,* which see.

ACERIPHYLLUM. *Saxifragaceae.* From the similarity of the leaves in shape to those of the sycamore *(Acer pseudo-platanus).*

— rossii. As far as I am aware this Korean plant is the only species in its genus; references to it are few and far between. It was shown to the Alpine Garden Society in 1934, and given a Botanical Certificate but was then wrongly named *A. borisii.* In nature, it appears to inhabit ledges on moist cliffs where it forms clumps of thick rhizomes from which rise quite large, glossy leaves and 6 to 9 in. stems carrying umbels of white flowers. I have found it to be hardy in a cool position. It can be increased by division, or from seeds and is spring-flowering.

ACHILLEA. *Compositae.* The name honours the Greek hero Achilles, who was taught in his youth the healing properties of this plant by his tutor Chiron the Centaur.

A large race of sun-loving plants, varying from tall border plants to tiny carpeting kinds ideally suited to rock gardens, crevices in paving or walls. None of them is difficult to grow, they ask only for sunny positions and any good, well drained soil. They may live longer and certainly flower more freely in soil which is poor rather than rich.

— abrotanoides. A pleasant species from the Eastern Alps with ash-grey foliage felted with fine hairs and strongly aromatic. Clusters of white flowers are carried on 6 to 9 in. stems.

— ageratifolia. (A. serbica. Anthemis aizoon.) From Greece. The narrow, silver leaves are deeply toothed at the margins. The quite large white flowers are carried on leafy stems 4 to 6 in. in height.

— ambigua. A plant which appears to be as ambiguous as its name suggests. According to most text books it is a form of *A. millefolium,* the common Yarrow, but, as I have always known it, it is a neat 4 to 6 in. hummock of silvery leaves with rather uninspiring white flowers.

— argentea. This is yet another species concerning which authorities

14

disagree. According to some it is synonymous with *A. clavenae*, others give it specific rank. I have always regarded the two as distinct and value *A. argentea* for its mats of silver filigree foliage and flowers like small, very pure white marguerites on short stems.

— atrata. A species common in the European Alps which is usually damned with faint praise, but it has its uses as a neat carpeter, especially when grown under starvation conditions on a sunny scree and one need not be discouraged by Reginald Farrer's typical, and inimitable, description of a plant for which he had no liking. He says of *A. atrata*, and I quote: 'It has the carriage of a Camomile and a clustered head, on a stem of 6 in. or so, of large flowers which are, unfortunately, of a grubby and world-soiled white, indescribably unalluring, with a sad bad eye of dirty darkness'.

— aurea. This is a not unattractive species forming low mats of emerald-green feathery foliage and bearing flat umbels of yellow flowers on 6 in. stems. It is surpassed, and has been largely superseded by *A. a.* 'Grandiflora', a magnificent form discovered many years ago by my late father on Mt. Olympus in Greece. The ferny foliage is grey-green and the flowers are richer in colour and carried in larger heads on 9 in. stems.

— X barbeyana. As far as I can discover, and regrettably, this is not at present in cultivation and references to it are not easy to discover. I believe it to be of Grecian origin, and a hybrid of undisclosed parentage, and it is said to have gloriously silver foliage in neat tufts with heads of white flowers on 3 to 4 in. stems.

— brachypylla. See *A. monocephala.*

— chrysocoma. A good plant from Dalmatia, not unlike *A. tomentosa* in character, but with a dense coating of fine hairs giving a grey sheen to the very aromatic foliage. Golden flowers in compact heads on 6 in. stems.

— clavenae. A distinct species from Eastern Europe, with oval, irregularly toothed, intensely silver leaves and 6 in. stems bearing heads of white flowers. Although *A. argentea* is said to be no more than a synonym for this species there are certainly two distinct plants in cultivation.

— clypeolata. In the mountainous regions of Eastern Europe this tends to take the place of our native Milfoil, or Yarrow, *A. millefolium*. It makes mats of hairy, pinnatifid leaves and bears heads of, usually, white flowers but they may occasionally be a rather dingy shade of pink.

— compacta. (*A. sericea.*) From the Balkans. Silkily hairy grey-green foliage and dense, fastigiate corymbs of mustard-yellow flowers on 9 in. stems.

— dacica. Botanically this plant hovers on the verge of being an Anthemis. It is rather coarse with good heads of white flowers on 9 to 12 in. stems.

— fraasii. This European species has been unjustly condemned by some writers. Although the flowers are of little value, it is a handsome foliage plant, forming foot-high mounds of filigree silver. It should be cut to the ground periodically to maintain the desirable neatness and tidyness of habit.

— **grandiflora.** A Caucasian species which is really too large for the rock garden. Although introduced early in the nineteenth century it has never become a common garden plant. Foaming masses of cream-white flowers which cut well.

— **grisebachii.** Probably of garden origin, and may be a hybrid of unknown parentage. Handsome silver foliage and heads of pure white flowers on 4 in. stems.

— **herba-rota** (or **erba-rotta**). From Central Europe and with the habit of *A. atrata*. The foliage is strongly aromatic and the white flowers are carried in loose corymbs on 6 to 9 in. stems.

— **holosericea.** Although not an aristocrat this species is well worth growing, if only for the sake of its silver, finely dissected foliage and the bold heads of yellow flowers on 9 in. stems are not without virtue. It comes from Thrace and Macedonia.

— **huteri.** European Alps. Mounds of aromatic grey foliage and heads of snow-white flowers on short stems.

— **integrifolia.** This is probably a form of *A. clavenae*, it differs in lacking the toothed leaf margins. The white flowers have large and conspicuous ray-florets.

— **X jaborneggii.** This hybrid between *AA. clavenae* and *moschata* is reasonably intermediate between the parents in appearance but the foliage lacks the silver charm of *A. clavenae*. The white flowers are carried in loose heads on short stems.

— **X kellereri.** One parent of this hybrid was undoubtedly *A.clavenae*, the other has not been identified. It is a good plant, with finely cut, very silvery foliage and good white flowers on 6 in. stems.

— **X 'King Edward'.** An excellent hybrid raised almost simultaneously by two people many years ago. One raiser gave it this name, the other labelled it *A. X lewisii*, but the former appeared to have priority. The parents were *AA. tomentosa* and·*argentea* and the marriage resulted in a delightful dwarf plant with flat carpets of grey-green leaves and lemon yellow flowers in small clusters on 4 in. stems.

— **X kolbiana.** This resulted from crossing *A. clavenae* with *A. umbellata* and gave a plant with grey, pinnatifid leaves and corymbs of white flowers on short stems.

— **leptophylla.** A little known and rather obscure N. African species with very aromatic foliage and corymbs of small yellow flowers.

— **X lewisii.** See *A. X* 'King Edward'.

— **millefolium.** The species itself does not claim admittance to gardens, but *A. m.* 'Borealis', from Alaska and the Aleutians should be garden-worthy, if obtainable. The heads of flowers are richly pink, over dark green foliage. It varies in height and the dwarfest forms would seem to be the most desirable.

— **monocephala.** (*A. brachyphylla.*) Doubtfully in cultivation, and origin uncertain, but it sounds a pleasant species offering prostrate mats of moss-like, silvered shoots with large white flowers on 6 in. stems.

— **moschata.** This species from Italy and the Engadine is exceptional in the genus in displaying a preference for light shade, which provides conditions better suited to its soft green rather rosetted foliage. It has no startling beauty but pleases in a quiet way. The loose corymbs of flowers carried on short stems have yellow disc florets and white ray florets.

— **X obristii.** A hybrid of dubious parentage, similar in some ways to *A. X. huteri*, but of loose habit.

— **nana.** Probably the smallest of the alpine achilleas. Native of the European Alps at considerable elevations. Nice, aromatic, grey-green pinnate foliage but worthless flowers of dirty white.

— **X prichardii.** A garden-hybrid of uncertain parentage but a nice dwarf plant with semi-double white flowers on 6 in. stems.

— **pseudopectinata.** A rather handsome species from the Balkans with finely-cut silver leaves and richly golden flowers in compound corymbs on stems which may reach 10 in. in height.

— **pyrenaica.** Not an exciting plant, from the Pyrenees. It, too, is fairly tall, its stems reaching a foot or so in height and bearing heads of small white flowers.

— **rupestris.** From Southern Europe. Compact rosettes of green, almost untoothed leaves and neat corymbs of flowers on short stems. The ray florets are white and those of the disk greenish-white.

— **serbica.** See *A. ageratifolia.*

— **sericea.** *See A. compacta.*

— **setacea.** An uncommon species from Greece which is well spoken of but is probably not in cultivation. Of rather loose habit it carries, on lax stems, many soft yellow flowers.

— **tomentosa.** Native to Europe and N. Asia, this is probably the best-known alpine achillea in gardens. Its ferny, softly hairy leaves grow in dense, prostrate mats which are decorated by flat heads of yellow flowers on 6 in. stems.

— **X trautmannii.** A hybrid from Silesia between *AA. pyrenaica* and *tomentosa.* Of no considerable garden value it bears, on rather tall stems, corymbs of yellowish flowers.

— **umbellata.** Dwarf tufts of oval, lightly serrated silvery leaves and loose heads of white flowers on 6 in. stems. It is a native of Greece and there is a recorded form, 'Argentea' which differs only in having even more silvery leaves.

— **X wilczekii.** A garden hybrid between *A. ageratifolia* and the taller, non-alpine *A. lingulata.* Handsome masses of loose silver-grey rosettes composed of saw-edged leaves and rather drooping corymbs of white flowers. 6 to 9 in.

Achilleas are, generally speaking, late spring and summer flowering,

17

but some of them will flower on into the late summer months. The species can be increased by seeds or division. The hybrids, being sterile, must of course be divided or grown from cuttings.

ACHLYS. *Berberidaceae.* Named for a Greek goddess of hidden places, probably an allusion to the woodland habitat of members of this genus.

A small genus of woodland plants requiring shade and cool, preferably lime-free soil. They are unassuming plants but not without interest and charm.

- japonica. Creeping rhizomes from which rise green leaves divided into three, and slender 9 in. spikes carrying many small white flowers in early summer. Japan.
- triphylla. From Western N. America and similar in general appearance to the Japanese species. The foliage has the same fragrant properties possessed by our native woodruff, *Asperula odorata*, and can be dried by hanging in bunches. Both species are propagated by division or by raising them from seed.

ACIPHYLLA. *Umbelliferae.* From *akis*, a point, and *phyllon*, a leaf. The segments of the leaves are very sharply pointed.

A race of interesting, if not startlingly beautiful plants from New Zealand and other parts of Australasia. It is questionable if they really come within the scope of this Manual. Some of them attain a height of 6 ft. and more and even the dwarfer kinds are dubiously hardy, although they will survive in an alpine house. Of the forty or more species only a very few have been cultivated in Britain outside botanical garden collections. They are plants which must be positioned carefully and handled with caution as most of them terminate their stiff, narrow leaves with iron-hard, needle-sharp spines. They appear to prefer a fairly light, sandy soil but present no serious cultural difficulties. Propagate by seed. It is pointless for me to compose a list of names of plants which are rarely available, but any of the dwarfer species which might be obtained are sure to provide considerable interest. The excellent book: 'New Zealand Alpine Plants' written by A. E. Mark and Nancy M. Adams, is sure to inspire interest in New Zealand alpines. It is lavishly and splendidly illustrated and contains a comprehensive list of Aciphyllas, as well as all the other exciting New Zealand alpines we all long to grow.

ACORUS. *Araceae.* From *akoros,* a name used by Theophrastus for a plant with an aromatic rhizome.

A small genus, containing only two species. With *A. calamus,* the Sweet Flag, we need not be concerned, but the species described below, and particularly its two forms, are of interest to alpine gardeners. Moist soil is needed for their well being. The Sweet Flag is native to Asia and America and was introduced into Europe by 1557, and is recorded as naturalised in Britain by 1660.

— gramineus. Stiff, narrow, grass-like leaves in dense tufts up to 10 in. in height. Of no great garden value, but desirable in the forms 'Pusillus' and 'Variegatus'. The former is a miniature, no more than 2 in. in height and is amusing at the edges of small pools or in a cool nook. The latter grows to a height of 6 in. or so and the foliage is striped green and white.

ACTAEA. *Ranunculaceae.* Latin name derived from the Greek *aktea,* Elder-tree, from a supposed resemblance of the foliage to that of the Elder.

A small genus of plants which are not really alpines but herbaceous perennials. However, they are frequently listed in alpine plant catalogues and are not out of place in shady areas of a fairly large rock garden, or in its immediate environment.

— spicata. Britain to Scandinavia and Japan. Woody stems up to 18 in. in height carry green leaves divided into several leaflets. Terminal and axillary spikes carry numerous inconspicuous flowers, which are followed by glossy black berries. The following, although usually listed as species, are in reality little more than forms of *A. spicata. A. alba* bears white, or pale pink berries; *A. erythrocarpa* has red fruits and there is a sub-form, 'Leucocarpa' with white berries. *A. rubra* has deep red berries.

ACTINELLA (ACTINEA). *Compositae.* From the Greek *aktis,* a ray.

— acaulis. This is a rare but rather undistinguished composite from Colorado. Dwarf tufts of grey, spoon-shaped leaves form the foundation for tall stems carrying rayless yellow buttons. It will expect to be given a dry, sunny position.

Listed in obscure textbooks are numerous Actinella names, but few, if any, are cultivated and not many are garden-worthy and several are no more than forms of *A. acaulis.* The genus is also sometimes confused with, and may be synonymous with, the genus *Actinea. Actinellas grandiflora* and *scaposa* are sometimes encountered in gardens and have quite good flowers and attractive foliage.

19

ADENOPHORA. *Campanulaceae.* From the Greek *aden*, a gland, and *phoreo*, to bear. A sticky nectary surrounds the base of the style in the flowers of Adenophora.

A genus separated only by minor botanical details from Campanula. They are mostly fairly tall, and blossom in the summer. Any good garden soil suits them well enough and they are sun-lovers but will tolerate light shade. They are mostly mountain-dwellers in nature and are found in Siberia, China and Japan with a few outliers in Europe.

— bulleyana. W. China. Stems up to 3 ft. branching terminally. Clusters of deep lavender bells, individually about 1 in. long.

— chinensis. See *A. sinensis.*

— communis. See *A. lilifolia.*

— confusa. (A. farreri.) China. Stiffly erect tall stems, heavily leafed. Lightly branched panicles of deep blue bells.

— diplodonta. Yunnan, W. China. Tall, pubescent stems and leaves hairy beneath. Flowers may be in racemes, panicles or in pairs, bell-shaped and coloured white to pale lilac.

— farreri. See *A. confusa.*

— lamarckii. Siberia and the Altai. 2ft. leafy stems and long racemes of pale blue flowers.

— lilifolia. (A. suaveolens. A. communis. A. liliflora.) Stout stems up to 4 ft. clothed with serrate leaves and panicles of white, or blue-white fragrant flowers. Central Europe and Siberia.

— megalantha. Glabrous stems up to 2 ft. racemes of 2 in. long bell-shaped deep blue flowers. W. China. A form with white flowers exists.

— nikoensis. Japan. Only a foot or so in height and spikes of pale blue flowers.

— ornata. W. China. Variable in height from 2 to 4 ft. Panicles of purple-blue flowers.

— palustris. E. Asia. Broadly bell-shaped flowers of light blue on 3 ft. stems.

— polymorphia. Russia to Japan. A variable species, widely bell-shaped flowers varying from violet to purple.

— remotiflora. Japan. 2ft. stems carrying racemes or panicles of narrow, bell-shaped violet-blue flowers.

— sinensis. (A. chinensis.) China. Foot-high stems and narrow racemes of blue flowers.

— stricta. Japan. The short stems are clothed in white hairs on the upper parts. Dense spikes of violet-blue flowers.

— suaveolens. See *A. lilifolia.*

— takedai. Japan. Rather weak stems up to 2 ft. and bell-shaped violet-blue flowers.

— tashiroi. Japan. Quite dwarf, 5 to 10 in. Violet-blue flowers either few to a spike or solitary.

ADESMIA. *Leguminosae. A*, without and *desmos*, a bond, referring to the stamens being free.

A considerable genus of evergreen shrubs and herbs native to S. America. Few if any are at present in cultivation but *A. salicornoides* has been collected and introduced from Patagonia from time to time. It is very dwarf, with foliage as fleshy as that of a sedum and pea-shaped flowers of, one assumes, yellow.

ADONIS. *Ranunculaceae.* The classical Greek name for this plant.

Hardy herbaceous perennials — and some annuals. Not really alpine plants but often grown on rock gardens. They thrive in sun or light shade in any good, ordinary soil. They can be increased by seeds or by division in the early spring as soon as growth begins. They are spring and summer flowering.

- amurensis. Manchuria and Japan. May flower as early as March. Crowded tufts of deeply segmented leaves and golden flowers on stems which vary in height from 9 to 18 in. It is a variable species and in Japan there exist many selected forms with white, rose, red or striped flowers.
- pyrenaica. Pyrenees. Deeply cut foliage and many yellow flowers on short stems in June and July.
- vernalis. Europe. Tufts of multifid leaves, the lower ones reduced to little more than scales and large yellow flowers on 9 in. stems in March and April.
- volgensis. Russia. Like a more robust, larger-flowered *A. vernalis* with branching stems.

AETHIONEMA. *Cruciferae.* Origin of the name is uncertain.

An invaluable race of dwarf, shrubby plants, all avid sun-lovers and ideal for hot, dry positions on the rock garden, or for crevices in sunny walls. They are lime-lovers but will tolerate neutral soil. Flowers are carried abundantly from early summer onward. Propagate by seeds or by cuttings made from soft growth tips before flower buds are formed.

- armenum. Armenia. Dense bushlets. Stems clothed with small, narrow leaves. Pink flowers in terminal racemes.
- cardiophyllum. Cappadocia and Armenia. Six-inch bushlets with rigid and unbranching stems and small, grey-green, heart-shaped leaves. Clusters of rose-pink flowers.
- cordatum. Lebanon. A 9 in. shrub with small, heart-shaped leaves and racemes of small sulphur flowers.

- **coridifolium**. (A. jucundum.) Asia Minor. Erect woody stems up to 9 in. glaucous foliage and rounded heads of rose-lilac flowers.
- **'Warley Rose'**. A splendid selection, or possibly a hybrid, which occurred many years ago in the then famous garden belonging to the late Ellen Willmott at Warley in Essex. It is an invaluable compact shrublet, as handsome as a daphne when sheeted with its rich rose-pink flowers. It received an Award of Merit as *A*. 'Warley Hybrid' in 1913 and a selected form, which was named *A*. 'Warley Ruber', was similarly honoured in 1928. Both forms still exist in gardens.
- **creticum**. (A. ovalifolium.) Dwarf tufts of tangled stems clothed with very glaucous leaves and capitate racemes of small, soft rose flowers. From Southern Europe and by some considered to be only a variant of *A. saxatile*.
- **diastrophis**. Asia Minor. Similar to, but slightly taller and looser in habit than *A. pulchellum*.
- **gracile**. From Carniolia. Dwarf and shrubby, with slender, leafy branches up to 9 in. or more and terminal racemes of purplish flowers.
- **graecum**. Greece. A neat little bush with unusually large rose-pink flowers.
- **grandiflorum**. Lebanon and Iran. This very beautiful plant was first introduced in 1879 and has long been a garden favourite. It was given the coveted Award of Garden Merit in 1938. The 12 in. bushes of loosely branched stems carry innumerable terminal racemes of warm pink flowers from May until August.
- **iberideum**. Eastern Mediterranean and Asia Minor. Mats of grey-green leaves become obscured in summer with multitudes of white flowers in small terminal racemes.
- **jucundum**. See *A. coridifolium*.
- **kotchyi**. The provenance of this nice dwarf species is uncertain, but E. Europe or the Middle East would be a fairly safe bet. It is now a rarity in cultivation. Very dwarf, neat bushes and rich pink flowers.
- **oppositifolium**. Greece and the Lebanon. Very dwarf, with rather fleshy leaves and small heads of pink flowers.
- **ovalifolium**. See *A. creticum*.
- **persicum**. This name is sometimes encountered but the plant it identifies is probably either *A. iberideum* or *A. saxatile*.
- **pulchellum**. Asia Minor and Iran. Ranks with *A. grandiflorum* for beauty. Low, mounded bushes of grey-green leaves obscured when flowering by clouds of crowded racemes of blossoms of coconut-ice-pink.
- **rotundifolium**. This must be the plant usually grown under the name *Eunomia rotundifolia*. It comes from Syria and is a dainty plant, best cared for in an alpine house or a choice nook in a stone trough or sink garden. The almost prostrate stems are clothed with rounded, grey-green slightly fleshy leaves and end in heads of comparatively large white, or gently pink-flushed flowers.

— saxatile. S. Europe and Algeria. Although the R.H.S. Dictionary of Gardening describes this species as an annual, in other text books it is said to be a good perennial and my own experience agrees with this. Not a very tidy plant, it has 9 in. rather sprawling stems which end in heads of small, but nicely pink flowers.

— schistosum. Asia Minor. Varies in height from a few inches to a foot. The large flowers are of a good rich pink, carried on an imbricated raceme. There used to be a very fine form of this species, named 'Dixcroft Variety' with extra large and more richly coloured flowers, but I have not seen it for many years now.

— stylosum. Lebanon. Seldom more than 4 in. in height and the bearer of heads of good rose-pink flowers.

— theodorum. I have always been mystified by this plant, for which I can discover no provenance. It differs only very slightly, if at all, from a good form of *A. grandiflorum*.

— trinervium. Iran. Dwarf, woody shrublet with heads of quite large white flowers. Dubiously in cultivation at present.

AGOSERIS. *Compositae.* From the Greek *agon*, a cluster, and *seris*, Chicory. The genus is related to Chicory.

A small family of N. American plants of no startling garden value, easily grown in any reasonably good soil and full sun.

— cuspidata. (Troximon cuspidatum.) Tufts of lanceolate leaves, varying from 4 to 10 in. in length and often with crimped and white-woolly edges. Yellow flower heads on 12 in. stems in summer.

— glauca. (Troximon glaucum.) Similar in general appearance but the tooth-edged leaves lack the woolly margins.

— major. This is a tall annual, with golden flowers.

— subalpina. Is little more than an alpine Hawkweed. The yellow flowers are not without attraction but it could become a weed.

— villosa. This I have not seen, but Dwight Ripley, who knew about plants, described it as 'a handsome dandelion'!

AJUGA. *Labiatae.* The origin is obscure, possibly a variant of *Abiga*, the old Latin name.

A genus of some thirty or more species, widely distributed over temperate regions. The common Bugle, *A. reptans*, is a native of Britain and selected clones of it are cultivated and used extensively for ground-cover. The most desirable quality of such clones is in their foliage, which displays a variety of variegation and, in some, leaf colour as brilliant as in some tropical house plants. They are mostly too invasive for rock gardens but have their uses beneath trees and shrubs, where they appreciate the cooler, more shady conditions.

- alpina. See *A. genevensis.*
- australis. (A. grandiflora.) Introduced from Australia in 1882. Slightly hairy leaves in low mats and 6 in. stems carrying whorls of blue flowers. I have not seen this and believe that it may not be completely hardy.
- brockbankii. *See A. genevensis.*
- chamaepitys. This annual species, an occasional British native, differs from most species in having yellow flowers spotted with red. It also departs from the family custom in liking dry, chalky soil and sunny situations.
- chia. Another departure from the norm with yellow, purple-striped flowers on foot-high stems. It comes from E. Europe.
- genevensis. (A. alpina.) This has the characteristic creeping habit and its whorled flowers, on 6 to 9 in. stems may be blue, white or pink. The clone named 'Brockbankii' is dwarfer and has flowers of deep, clear blue.
- grandiflora. See *A. australis.*
- metallica 'Crispa'. See *A. pyramidalis.*
- orientalis. A species from E. Europe with woolly leaves and short spires of blue flowers. It likes a drier, sunnier spot than most ajugas.
- ovalifolia. It was the late Kingdon Ward who found, and introduced this species from Tibet. I am not at all sure that it remains in cultivation. He wrote well of it and said that its pyramidal spike of leaves, partially concealing the long, narrow, tubular violet-purple flowers, was attractive.
- piskoi. This is another species we would dearly like to see reintroduced from its native Greece, for it carries on its 9 in. flower spikes, blossoms of good size and pink in colour. It, with *A. chia* and *A. ovalifolia* would form an interesting and desirable trinity of unusual ajugas in any garden.
- pyramidalis. A European species and an occasional British native. Spreads freely by stolons and displays erect, 9 in. pyramidal spikes of whorled blue flowers. The curious plant usually seen under the name *A. metallica* 'Crispa' is claimed to be a form of *A. genevensis.* It makes dense tufts of small, dark leaves with heavily crimped margins. It is not a good 'doer' and often dies out unless it is frequently lifted, divided and replanted in fresh soil. A plant which is curious rather than beautiful, but it never fails to attract admiration.
- reptans. One does not admit the common Bugle to gardens except in the wildest corners, where it is an acceptable ground-coverer, but in its selected clones it has considerable value as long as it is remembered that they are all vigorous, spreading plants able to usurp a considerable area, however decoratively they may do so. All will flourish in almost any soil and appreciate at least partial shade and will take full shade if necessary. They all grow as prostrate mats spreading by leafy stems which root as they go.

'Burgundy Glow' is one of the best, the leaves are patterned in purple, bronze and gold. It will take more sunlight than other clones and colours better in stronger light. 'Multicolor' has bronzed variegated foliage and is the same plant as the one sometimes listed as 'Rainbow'. 'Pink Elf' is very dwarf and free flowering and has short spikes of pink blossoms. 'Purpurea' (sometimes 'Atropurpurea') has dark red-purple leaves and the foliage of 'Variegata' is silver and green.

— vestitum. See *Scutellaria macrochlamys.*

ALCHEMILLA. *Rosaceae.* The origin of the name is obscure. It is possibly the Latinised version of an Arabic name.

There are thirty or more species of Alchemilla distributed through Asia, America and Europe. They are low-growing, perennial herbaceous plants. The flowers are, as a rule, of no particular value, but the foliage is often decorative. *A. vulgaris,* the common Ladies Mantle, is a British native. They are tolerant of a wide range of soils and situations and in no way difficult to grow under normal garden conditions. Not many of them qualify as alpine plants.

— alpina. Neat tufts of fairly broad leaves which are 5- to 7-foliate, green above and glistening silver on the underside. Short-stemmed corymbs of greenish flowers are unimportant in comparison with the pretty leaves. A good plant for a cool, rocky chink. It is an occasional British native.

— alpestris. This is probably a form of *A. vulgaris,* but a dwarfer plant with garden value. It occurs sparingly on the higher slopes of Snowdonia.

— conjuncta. A species to be found at high altitudes in the Swiss Alps. It is used as a pain-killer according to local lore but has no particular garden value.

— **ellenbeckii.** From Kenya. Neat, compact and attractive.

— fissa. A smaller version of *A. vulgaris* widely distributed in Europe.

— glomerulans. A native of Britain and the high mountains of Europe. Rounded, silky-haired leaves, notched at the lobed edges and dense clusters of greenish flowers on foot-high stems.

— hageniae. A rare species from the mountains of E. Africa. It is not unlike *A. mollis,* but more compact and the leaves are greener with more acutely pointed lobes. I have not seen it in flower but they are not highly spoken of and are the habitual greenish-yellow.

— major. This is probably only a garden name, applied to strong forms of *A. vulgaris* and/or *A. mollis.*

— pentaphylla. A species commonly found in the Pyrenees. The leaves have heavily fringed lobes and the clustered small, yellow-green flowers are carried in dense corymbs.

— pyrenaica. A not dissimilar species, also from the Pyrenees and insufficiently distinct or beautiful for detailed comment.

— sericea. This Caucasian species is like a rather more robust *A. alpina* and, were it available, would be well worth growing.

ALCHEMILLA — *continued*
- X **splendens.** *(A. alpina x A. vulgaris.)* An interesting and not unworthy hybrid of low stature with leaves silvery beneath.

ALECTORURUS. *Liliaceae.* From *alectryon*, a cock, and *urus*, a tail. A reference to the arching panicle.

A monotypic genus of one Japanese species from mountain woodlands.
- **yedoensis.** (Anthericum yedoense.) From a thick rootstock rise tufts of long and narrow leaves and fairly tall stems bearing panicles of bell-shaped flowers. I have not seen the plant in flower and am confused by opposing descriptions, one of which says the flowers are white, and the other pink. This plant is related to, and has been synonymous with, both Anthericum and Bulbinella.

ALKANNA. *Boraginaceae.* The Arabic name.

A genus of some forty or more species, natives of Mediterranean regions and the Near East. Few are in cultivation or worth growing, and fewer still qualify as rock garden plants.
- **incana.** This is an exceptional species. It is endemic to Turkey, where it dwells in rock crevices and screes. From basal tufts of grey-green, roughly bristly leaves rise short, stiff stems carrying several deep blue flowers. A good plant, but not easy to grow and even more difficult to obtain. If acquired, it should be treated austerely in full sun, or kept in the alpine house.

ALLARDIA. *Compositae.* Presumably named in honour of E. J. Allard, of the Cambridge Botanic Garden, *c.* 1904.
- **tomentosa.** A rare and exceedingly handsome plant. A native of the Western Himalayas, it remains fitfully in cultivation since its introduction many years ago by Mr. B. O. Coventry, author of that excellent book 'Wild Flowers of Kashmir', in which, unfortunately, he does not mention Allardia, although it is to be found in Kashmir.

  The plant is deciduous and, from woody basal shoots rise, in the spring, handsome, ferny, silvery-grey pinnatifid leaves of considerable size, forming a lacy silver mound of great beauty. So far the plant has refused in cultivation to bear what are described as large daisy-shaped blossoms with pink rays and a yellow disk rimmed with brown. It should be given alpine house treatment and grown in large, deep pots or pans in gritty, but humus-rich soil.

ALLIUM. *Liliaceae.* From the classical Latin name for garlic.

This immense genus, containing upward of 300 species widely distributed throughout the temperate regions of the Northern Hemisphere is very diverse, ranging from such giant species as *A. siculum*, handsome and desirable, but too large for any self-respecting rock garden, to tiny tufted plants eminently desirable. It has its rogues too; there are those who have reason to regret planting such a lovely but rampagious species as *A. moly* in any but the wildest of wild gardens. Some species, such as the common onion in its many manifestations, are definitely bulbous, others have stems which are thickened or modestly bulbous at their bases. It is not an easy genus to handle in the context of this Manual. Many which are desirable rock garden plants are by no means 'alpine'. Those described, sometimes of necessity briefly, by no means exhaust the supply of Alliums, but all those best suited to the rock garden or its environs have been included. For details of some of the more recent introductions from Iran, Afghanistan, Beluchistan and neighbouring countries I am indebted to Brian Mathew's invaluable book on Dwarf Bulbs.

For including some of the definitely rampant kinds I make no apology. Warned of their ability to spread they can be used to good effect in suitable places and many a garden would be less beautiful because of their absence. Generally speaking, Alliums are easy to grow and tolerant of most soils. Only those newer introductions from the Middle East may need the protection of an alpine house, or of a special bulb frame where winter cover can be provided.

Although bulbs, as such, are, generally speaking, excluded from this Manual, as I felt that they demanded separate and detailed attention, some bulbous plants will obviously have to be included, of which this partially bulbous genus is an example. That we still have other good Alliums with which to become acquainted I am firmly convinced, especially after seeing some of the species collected in Iran and Afghanistan by Professor Wendelbo and now being grown in the Aryamehr Botanic Garden in Iran.

Nothing would have been easier than to fill many pages of this Manual with names and descriptions of Alliums galore, many of them obviously desirable rock garden plants. As it is, I may have included too many, but it is an important, if rather neglected genus. I know that some which I have included are either not in cultivation or rare and difficult to obtain, but there is always the hope that some reader may be inspired to go and do some collecting!

— **acuminatum.** Western States of N. America. Many-flowered umbels of rose-pink flowers on 9 in. stems.

— **akaka.** From Iran, Iraq, Turkey and the Caucasus. Best in a bulb frame. Very few leaves and an umbel almost at ground level of flowers varying from white to shades of pink.

— albopilosum. See *A. christophii.*

— amabile. (A. mairei. A. yunnanense.) From Yunnan. Fibrous rhizomes and tufts of fine leaves. Inflorescence up to 6 in. with a few-flowered umbel of reddish-purple flowers, the segments often spotted internally.

— anisopodium. From China and Siberia. A dwarf, not very important species having umbels of small, campanulate white flowers.

— azureum. See *A. caeruleum.*

— beesianum. (sikkimense.) From Western China. Clumps of small fibrous rhizomes and slender, erect, 6 to 9 in. stems carrying pendant umbels of bright blue flowers. One of the most desirable rock garden species.

— bigelovii. From New Mexico and Arizona. May need some winter protection. Sparse, narrow, twisted leaves and short-stemmed umbels of white flowers, irregularly marked with carmine.

— brandegei. From Western N. America. On a very short scape, sometimes not rising above the leaves, are many-flowered umbels of rose-purple flowers.

— breweri. See *A. falcifolium.*

— caeruleum. (azureum). From Russia and the Near East. Perhaps a little tall for most rock gardens, but a nice plant. On stems which can attain 18 in. appear densely-flowered umbels of small, but very bright, clear blue flowers, which are occasionally accompanied by a few scattered bulbils. This viviparous characteristic is displayed by many alliums.

— **callumischon.** (haemostictum.) From Greece and Crete. Not especially beautiful but valuable as it flowers in the autumn. On short stems it carries papery-petalled white or soft pink flowers, the segments marked with deeper colour.

— carinatum. European. On stems up to 15 in. high are lax umbels carrying 15 to 20 small, bell-shaped reddish-violet flowers, often with bulbils appearing among the flowers.

— caspicum. A recent introduction from Afghanistan and the USSR. Best given bulb frame or alpine house treatment until more is known of its needs. Stems up to 9 in. bear many-flowered umbels of white or soft pink flowers with long, exserted stamens.

— cernuum. N. America. The 9 in. stems have a curious 'bend' at the apex giving the effect of a pendulous umbel, which is counteracted by the flower pedicels turning upward. Rounded flowers varying in colour from white through shades of pink to reddish-purple.

— christophii. (A. albopilosum.) From Iran and Turkestan. Really too large for the rock garden, but such a handsome species that I cannot leave it out. On tall, naked stems are carried massive, globular umbels containing myriads of flowers coloured metallic blue-purple. The dried flower heads are much in demand for winter decorations.

— circinatum. From dry hills on Crete. Very small, with short, 3 in.

stems carrying small heads of white, pink-striped flowers. Not spectacular, but worth growing.

— crenulatum. Western N. America. Common in the Olympic Mountains of Washington State. Very dwarf, with neat umbels of rose-red flowers on 4 in. stems. It has, so far, been disappointing in cultivation but should be persisted with.

— cristatum. Western N. America. From the round bulbs rise 4 in. stems carrying small umbels of light pink flowers, each segment with a central vein of deeper colour.

— cyaneum. (purdomii.) From Western China. Tufts of very narrow leaves and 6 in. stems bearing heads of cobalt-blue flowers with exserted stamens. Small and neat enough for a sink or trough garden.

— 'Dasystemon'. See *A. kansuense.*

— cyathophorum 'Farreri'. The type species does not appear to be in cultivation but this form is a charming pygmy. From fibrous rhizomes rise tufts of narrow leaves and short stems carrying crowded umbels of wine-red flowers. It will spread readily but can be controlled by removing the seed heads.

— dioscoridis. See *A. siculum.*

— falax. To be found in the Pyrenees and probably no more than a rather undistinguished form of *A. senescens.*

— falcatum. Western N. America. The sickle-shaped leaves are distinct and interesting and short scapes carry umbels of large, deep violet-blue flowers.

— falcifolium. (breweri.) Short, rather grey, sickle-shaped leaves and 4 in. stems on which appear umbels of flowers varying from pink to wine-red. From California and deserving of a warm and sunny position.

— flavum. From Southern and Eastern Europe. A very variable species. For the rock gardener the most desirable form is undoubtedly *A. f.* 'Minus' which bears straw-yellow flowers on a very short scape in a rather scattered umbel. For a hot, dry position.

— forrestii. Originally collected in China by George Forrest, in the Lichiang Range and probably one of the many good plants he introduced not now in cultivation. On stems varying in height from 6 to 12 in. it carries umbels of claret-red flowers and would be a most desirable acquisition.

— glaucum. See *A. senescens* 'Glaucum'.

— hirtifolium. From Iran and said to be very handsome, but tall. On 3 ft. stems are seen large globe-shaped heads of mauve-purple flowers. Too large for most rock gardens.

— humile. From Kashmir. A nice, dwarf, white-flowered species, which grows in company with *A. semenowii*, which see.

— kansuense. (cyaneum 'Dasystemon'.) From Western China and very similar to *A. beesianum*, but with smaller blue flowers in a more upright umbel.

— karataviense. Turkestan. Rather large for a small rock garden but a handsome and spectacular species. The leaves, usually two per bulb, are long and wide and grey-blue in colour. On sturdy 9 to 13 in. scapes are carried globular heads of grey-lavender flowers. It is decorative in both foliage and flower.

— loratum. From Kashmir. Only about 3 in. high with clusters of cream-white flowers. Doubtfully in cultivation, but a charmer.

— mairei. See *A. amabile.*

— microscapum. This was collected on the 1966 Albury, Cheese and Watson expedition to Turkey and may or may not be still in cultivation. It was said to be a species new to science and is one for which I unfortunately lack a description.

— mirabile. Western N. America. A tiny species with pendant, snow-white bell-shaped flowers on very short stems.

— mirum. A recent introduction which, if obtained, should be cared for in a bulb frame or the alpine house. It comes from Afghanistan and displays two, rather plantain-like, purplish leaves and has a spherical umbel of white to purple flowers, each segment marked with a dark stripe.

— moly. South-Eastern Europe. This is one of the species about which I gave a warning in the introduction to the genus Allium. Lovely though it is, with golden flowers on 9 to 12 in. stems, it is capable of becoming a considerable nuisance and is not easy to eradicate once firmly established in the wrong place. It must be used as a plant for semi-wild situations.

— montanum. See *A. senescens.*

— murrayanum. This seems to be a slightly dubious name covering a plant from Western N. America and having umbels of bright pink flowers on 6 to 8 in. stems. It is said to be useful for colonising in light shade.

— narcissiflorum. (pedemontanum.) Northern Italy and Southern France. A delightful species forming dense tufts of fibrous-covered rhizomes. It is very definitely one of the most beautiful of dwarf alliums and is well placed in a sunny position on the rock garden. The bell-shaped, wine-red flowers are borne in pendant umbels on 6 in. stems.

— neapolitanum. From Mediterranean regions and may be slightly tender in cold districts. On the 10 in. stems are loose, many-flowered umbels of pure white flowers. It is a good cut-flower and bunches of it are frequently seen in markets in parts of Europe. A variant from Albania named *A.n.* 'Breviradium' has been described but it differs little from the type.

— neoanum. A rare and distinct species from Iran, Turkey and Syria of which little is yet known in cultivation. It should be given the shelter of a bulb frame or alpine house. Curious umbels shaped like shuttlecocks stand on 6 to 10 in. stems and carry narrow-petalled pink flowers.

— olympicum. From Turkey. This was in cultivation fairly recently but

ALLIUM — *continued*

seems to have disappeared, I hope only temporarily, for it has handsome rounded umbels of pink and crimson flowers on quite short stems.

— oreophilum ostrowskianum (A. ostrowskianum.) From Turkestan and one of the very nicest dwarf alliums. From small, round bulbs rise tufts of narrow leaves at ground level and on 4 to 6 in. scapes are carried many-flowered umbels of broad petalled carmine-red flowers. The most richly-coloured form is the cultivar named 'Zwanenburg'.

— ostrowskianum. See *A. oreophilum ostrowskianum.*

— paniculatum. Southern Europe. Fairly tall stems and an umbel of small white flowers. A pleasant but not spectacular plant.

— paradoxum. Caucasus. A fairly tall species with waxy white flowers. Travellers in the Caucasus report buying its bulbs in the markets and using them for culinary purposes.

— pedemontanum. See *A. narcissiflorum.*

— platycaule. California. A very attractive dwarf species with a liking for a warm and sunny exposure. On short stems it carries a large umbel — from 50 to 80 flowered — of good pink blossoms.

— pleianthum 'Particolor'. Endemic to one area in the State of Nevada, U.S.A. The recumbent scapes end in umbels of pale pink flowers striped with red. The blossoms are curiously closed at the mouth. It should be provided with a warm and dry position.

— pulchellum. Similar to, and sometimes thought to be a form of *A. flavum*, the significant difference being the umbels of violet-purple flowers. From South and South-East Europe.

— purdomii. See *A. cyaneum.*

— roseum. From Mediterranean regions. Stems up to 15 in. carrying large umbels of bright pink flowers, the broad segments being marked with a stripe of deeper colour.

— schubertii. From Syria and Israel. A curious and striking species asking for a warm and sunny position. Very large umbels of pale rose-pink flowers are carried on scapes which vary from 12 to 18 in. in height. The individual flowers are borne on pedicels varying from 2 to 8 in. in length.

— semenowii. A species from Kashmir with good yellow flowers on short stems.

— senescens. (glaucum, montanum.) Widely distributed in Europe. Narrow leaves in dense tufts and clustered flowers in umbels on 6 to 8 in. stems. The colour varies from pale to deep pink, or almost purple.

— glaucum. This differs from the type in its often spirally twisted stems and in even denser heads of more narrowly bell-shaped flowers. There is confusion over its name, some authorities referring it to *A. angulosum.*

— siculum. (dioscoridis.) Rather tall for the rock garden, but a highly desirable species. On 3 ft. stems appear loose umbels of large campanulate flowers of the strangest blue-green colour, each segment having a maroon stripe. The bells are almost square in shape. It is

31

native to France, Sicily and Italy and is also to be found on the island of Sardinia. This species, together with the rather similar *A. bulgaricum* should probably now be referred to the genus Nectaroscordum.

— sikkimense. See *A. beesianum*.

— stellatum. Western N. America. A not very distinguished species bearing heads of small pink flowers on 9 to 12 in. stems.

— stocksianum. A recent introduction from Afghanistan and Beluchistan where it grows on exposed stony slopes. It will almost certainly appreciate alpine house protection during our winters. Narrow, acutely coiled basal leaves and short-stemmed umbels of from 15 to 20 rose-violet flowers.

— stracheyi. From the Karakoram and very doubtfully in cultivation, but highly desirable. A few long, narrow leaves subtend a slender 9 to 12 in. stem which carries a globose umbel of small, bell-shaped deep reddish-purple flowers.

— thomsonii. From Kashmir and Tibet and similar to *A. stracheyi*, and similarly rare in cultivation.

— triquetrum. Native and included because it has a pretty flower, but it is a species against which a warning is needed for it can become a weed. Relegate it to a semi-shady place in the wild garden where it can grow into dense colonies of leaves and triangular stems a foot high carrying few-flowered umbels of quite large, pendant, bell-shaped fragrant white flowers, each segment with a green stripe.

— unifolium. A N. American species and misnamed, since the leaves although few in number are rarely if ever confined to one. It is one of the nicest of the N. American species with many-flowered, rather lax umbels of large, campanulate flowers of bright rose-pink on stems up to a foot in height.

— ursinum. The common British, also European and Asian, wild garlic, or Ramsoms, and under no circumstances to be introduced into gardens, lovely though it may seem when seen *en masse* in the wild.

— victorialis. Tufts of netted rhizomes and leafy stems up to a foot in height carrying dense umbels of white flowers. Not a sensational beauty but worth a place in a cool corner. E. Europe and the Himalaya.

— wernleum. I have been unable to trace the *locus natalis* of this species, but it was grown, and described by the late Sir William Lawrence, a great plantsman, as a worthy plant, dwarf, with blue flowers.

— woronowii. Zinaida Artiushenko is a Russian botanist to whom we owe thanks for many descriptions of plants from the Caucasus, but I wish she had provided a description of the flowers of this species, which she briefly mentions as having glaucous ribbon-shaped leaves — and says no more!

— yunnanense. See *A. amabile*.

— zebdanense. If a sheltered nook is available this Mediterranean

ALLIUM — *continued*

species should be given a trial, if obtainable. The large, white bell-shaped flowers are carried erect, on 9 in. stems. It also has a faint but pleasant scent.

Maybe I have not dealt too generously with such a large genus, containing so many plants of good garden value. It is perhaps unfortunate that the characteristic family odour acts as a black mark against all the members of the tribe, but few of them are offensive unless roughly handled. By no means all of those I have described are easily obtainable, but all of them have been in cultivation, and could be again even if they are temporarily absent.

ALOPECURUS. *Graminiae.* From the Greek *alopekouros*, grass like a fox's tail.

— lanatus. Several species of Alopecurus are the Foxtail grasses of British meadows and wastelands and are not invited into gardens, although *A. pratensis* 'Aureus' is sometimes used in carpet bedding. *A. lanatus* is a tufty little Spanish grass with hoary grey leaves and is attractive in a warm, dry and sunny position and may be trusted not to become a nuisance and there is a bonus of beauty when it carries on short stems the flower heads, which are small, white woolly bundles.

ALSINE. See ARENARIA and MINUARTIA.

ALSTROEMERIA. *Amaryllidaceae.* Named in honour of Baron Claus Alstroemer (1736-1794), a friend of Linnaeus.

Only the fact that there are species of Alstroemeria in S. America which would delight the heart of any rock garden enthusiast persuades me to include the genus in this Manual. If we could obtain, and persuade to grow, for example, *A. pygmaea*, there would be much rejoicing. It is actually in cultivation, although fitfully and possibly temporarily.

ALTHAEA. *Malvaceae.* From the Greek *althaia*, a cure, an allusion to the use of some species in medicine.

These are not exactly alpine plants and have no specific place here, with the possible exception of *A. kurdica*, which, if it were introduced from Iran, where it grows on the dry slopes of the Zagros mountains, might be persuaded to endure where the climate is not too severe and a warm, sun-baked position assured.

ALYSSOIDES. *Cruciferae.* Meaning "like an alyssum".

— utriculatum. From S. Europe. A foot-high perennial with yellow flowers very much like those of the wallflower. It is hardy and modestly attractive, but not long-lived.

ALYSSUM. *Cruciferae.* From the Greek *a*, not or against, and *lyssa*, rage or madness. This herb was sometimes thought to be a specific against madness and rabies.

The genus Alyssum consists of eighty or more species of annual and perannial herbs or sub-shrubs. Some species are now placed by botanists in distinct genera, including the well-known *A. saxatile*, which some authorities contend should be *Aurinia saxatilis*. As a hardened reactionary I retain the names to which common usage has accustomed us, with the exception of some with white flowers, which must be sought under PTILOTRICHUM and SCHIVERECKIA. They are all avid sun-lovers and tolerant of any reasonably good soil as long as the drainage is good. In general they are spring and early summer flowering. The distribution of the genus geographically is wide and they are to be found in Europe, Asia Minor eastward to the Caucasus, Iran, Siberia and N. Africa. All are yellow-flowered.

— alpestre. From Mediterranean regions and cultivated since 1777. A tiny, tufted shrublet with grey leaves, flowers in small, unbranched racemes.

— amamum. See *A. sphacioticum.*

— arduinii. A species from mid-Europe, very close to *A. saxatile*, but with flowers in a smaller, dense corymb.

— armenum. From Cilicia and similar to *A. montanum* in habit but the hoary leaves are clothed in stiff, starry hairs.

— atlanticum. Atlas Mountains and the Caucasus. Tufted habit and small, grey, hairy leaves. Quite large flowers in a dense corymb.

— bornmuelleri. See SCHIVERECKIA *bornmuelleri* in addenda.

— borzeanum. From the lowlands of Bulgaria and the Black Sea coast. It makes an attractive low mound of glaucous foliage but is not especially attractive in flower.

— chalcidicum. Said to be similar to *A. markgraffii*, which see and doubtfully in cultivation.

— condensatum. From Syria. Usually less than 6 in. high with woody stems and softly hairy leaves and racemes of rather lemon-yellow flowers.

— corymbosum. S.E. Europe. Dwarf, rather spreading stems but a good plant with richly golden flowers.

— creticum. Crete. Up to a foot in height with entangled, woody stems and silver-grey foliage. Flowers in rather loose corymbs.

- cuneifolium. Mediterranean regions. A rare species, probably not in cultivation now, but said by the late Dwight Ripley, who knew his plants, to be worth growing. It makes dwarf mats of silver-grey hairy leaves and on radiating stems carries dense heads of small flowers.
- diffusum. A rather uncertain name. Plants so identified are probably *A. montanum.*
- edentulum. See *A. gemonense.*
- gemonense. (edentulum. petraeum.) From Austria. Like a smaller, more compact *A. saxatile* with flowers which are individually larger.
- halimifolium. See PTILOTRICHUM *halimifolium.*
- idaeum. Crete. A neat and desirable species with woody, quite prostrate stems dressed with small, silvery-green leaves and heads of soft yellow flowers. Gritty soil and sun — a good scree plant.
- lagascae. See PTILOTRICHUM *purpureum.*
- lanceolatum. A species found and described by Admiral Furse when collecting in the Hindu Kush, but doubtfully in cultivation. Said to grow densely in crevices and to have small grey leaves and heads of pale yellow flowers on 2 to 3 in. stems.
- lapeyrousianum. See PTILOTRICHUM *lapeyrousianum.*
- leucadeum. Shores of the Adriatic. Collected in 1937 by Dwight Ripley, this splendid alyssum is probably not in cultivation at the present time, but it ought to be. It will demand a warm and sheltered position, or a place of honour in the alpine house. The leaves resemble those of *A. saxatile,* but the flowers are much larger, the petals deeply notched and it blossoms without stint during January and February.
- longicaule. See PTILOTRICHUM *longicaule.*
- markgraffii. Albania. Up to one foot in height, with narrow, hairy leaves and quite large flowers in dense panicles.
- mildeanum. See *A. stribrnyi.*
- moellendorfianum. E. Europe. Another species which comes close in appearance to *A. montanum* but is sufficiently distinct for garden purposes — if and when obtainable.
- montanum. Central and S. Europe and the Caucasus. Can be prostrate, or up to 6 in. with grey, hairy leaves and the heads of soft yellow flowers are fragrant. A distinct form, with yolk-yellow flowers, *A. m. ssp. brymii* is to be found in the mountains of Yugoslavia.
- olympicum. Greece. A charming, very dwarf species seldom exceeding 3 in. with neat grey leaves and globose heads of flowers.
- orientale. Crete. A sub-shrub up to one foot in height with handsome corymbs of flowers over the grey-leaved bushes.
- ovirense. See *A. wulfenianum.*
- persicum. A species which extends into W. Asia. I have not seen it but it is described as a sub-shrub slightly more than a foot in height with heads of large flowers.
- petraeum. See *A. gemonense.*

- podolicum. See SCHIVERECKIA *podolica*.
- pulvinare. Bulgaria and Greece. A desirable species, if only it were obtainable. Dense, silver-leaved cushions with heads of lemon-yellow flowers on 3 to 4 in. stems.
- pyrenaicum. See PTILOTRICHUM *pyrenaicum*.
- repens. (trichostachyum.) E. Europe and the Caucasus. Perhaps rather too tall for most rock gardens as it can grow to 18 in. or more, but there are dwarfer forms. Fine rich golden flowers.
- reverchonii. See PTILOTRICHUM *reverchonii*.
- rochellii. See *A. wulfenianum*.
- rupestre. See PTILOTRICHUM *rupestre* in addenda.
- saxatile. From E. Europe, and a favourite in British gardens since 1710. It occurs in numerous forms as named clones. The type plant forms bold clumps of hoary grey-green leaves and displays great masses of golden flowers in dense corymbs. The following are the best known clones. 'Citrinum', flowers lemon-yellow. 'Compactum', condensed habit. 'Plenum', fully double flowers. 'Tom Thumb', usually no more than 3 in. tall. 'Dudley Neville', out of alphabetical order but distinct, with orange-buff coloured flowers. There is also one with variegated foliage which appeals to collectors of curiosities but lacks any real garden merit.
- scardicum. Greece. Ash-grey leaves, covered in starry hairs and dense heads of rather pale yellow flowers.
- serpyllifolium. From Spain and also found on Mt. Cenis. Close to *A. alpestre* but even smaller.
- sphacioticum. (amamum.) Crete. Dubiously in cultivation but some plants cultivated as *A. amamum* are possibly this species. Dense, foot-high clumps of softly hairy grey-green leaves and sulphur-yellow flowers.
- spinosum. See PTILOTRICHUM *spinosum* in addenda
- stribrnyi. (mildeanum.) Balkans. Variable in height from a few inches to one foot. Probably not at present in cultivation.
- tortuosum. E. Europe and first introduced in 1804 but now a rarity. Slender woody stems in contorted tangles and small corymbs of soft yellow flowers.
- transylvanicum. A subspecies of *A. repens* similar in general appearance, but usually more compact.
- trichostachyum. See *A. repens*.
- troodii. From Cyprus. A tiny shrublet with stiff, erect branches and glaucous leaves. The large flowers are richly golden. A handsome dwarf especially if given a spartan diet.
- utriculatam. See ALYSSOIDES *utriculatum*.
- wulfenianum. (rochellii. ovirense.) Quite prostrate, the trailing woody stems dressed in small grey leaves and adorned by small heads of good yellow flowers. A native of S. Europe.

AMARACUS. There was an attempt to separate some species of Origanum from that genus and include them in the genus Amaracus, but I am thankful to note in the new *Flora Europaea* that the older, and well known generic name has been retained, so, for Amaracus, see ORIGANUM.

AMMOCHARIS. *Amaryllidaceae.* From the Greek *ammos,* sand, and *charis,* grace or beauty.
Rather doubtfully included in this Manual as they are bulbous and, as regards the S. African species, unlikely to be hardy, but it seems possible that *A. heterostyla* from Mount Elgon in Kenya might be growable. It is described as having fragrant white flowers decorated by a red stripe.

AMPHORICARPUS. *Compositae.* From the Greek *amphoreus,* a two-handled vase, and *karpus,* a fruit. From the shape of the fruit.
— **neumayeri.** Dalmatia. From rather woody, creeping rhizomes rise woolly stems with pointed leaves, cobwebbed with hairs on the upper sides. One or two heads of purple flowers are carried on each fairly tall stem in summer. It will like well drained soil and full sun.

ANABASIS. *Chenopodiaceae.*
— **aretioides.** A rarity from Morocco which, if obtained, will demand semi-desert conditions, where it might form dense, hard cushions of tough, whitish to olive-green spherical and spine-tipped leaves. The flowers are small and inconspicuous.

ANACYCLUS. *Compositae.* A shortened form of the Greek *Ananthocyclus,* from *an,* without, *anthos,* a flower, and *kuklos,* a ring — but don't ask me why!
— **depressus.** So well known has this delightful daisy from the Atlas Mountains become under this name that I hesitate to employ what I believe may be its correct identification as *A. pyrethrum var. depressus.* I merely record it as a probability if absolute botanical accuracy is desired. From a carrot-like root radiate prostrate stems carrying finely cut leaves ending in wide, many-rayed composite flowers, the ray florets being white on the upper side and crimson beneath and the central disk of florets yellow. The crimson of the unopened flowers, and the white of the expanded ones contrast excitingly with the grey-green ferny foliage. One may also encounter *A. atlanticus* and *A. maroccanus,* which seem to be no more than slight variants on the same theme. The N. African habitat of this good plant would immediately suggest that it relishes a sunny position

in soil which is sharply drained and that it might resent a really wet winter, although it appears to be unharmed by low temperatures.

ANAGALLIS. *Primulaceae.* Possibly from *anagelao*, to delight, or it may be a Greek plant name.

This small genus is widely distributed over the world, only a few having garden value. *A. arvensis* is a well-loved annual British native, better known as Scarlet Pimpernel, or Poor Man's Weather Glass. It also occurs with red and blue flowers, but is seldom if ever cultivated. Reference to Engler's 'Pflanzenreich' in the section *Primulaceae* reveals a list of species of considerable length, but many of them are annuals, and others, although possibly desirable garden plants, are not in cultivation.

— alternifolia. S. America. White or pink flowers adorn prostrate tufts of glossy foliage. As a point of identification it differs from other species in having alternate leaves.

— breweri. See *A. linifolia.*

— caerulea. Is a form of *A. arvensis.*

— collina. See *A. linifolia.*

— crassifolia. The rounded, tiny, slightly succulent leaves are tightly packed in two rows on the huddled, prostrate stems. The small, round flowers are usually white, but may vary to soft pink. It can be found in Portugal, Sardinia, and has also been reported from N. Africa.

— filiformis. From S. America and related to *A. tenella.* Very dubiously in cultivation. A typically botanical description to which I have access gives no indication of the colour of the small, campanulate flowers! It will, if obtained, probably share the liking of *A. tenella* for a moist position.

— fruticosa. See *A linifolia.*

— grandiflora. See *A. linifolia.*

— linifolia. (fruticosa. grandiflora.) Widely spread in the warmer, sunnier areas of Europe and into N. Africa. A superb, but sometimes short-lived perennial but easily perpetuated by seeds or cuttings. The semi-trailing, rather woody stems form tangled mats a foot or more in width which disappear for weeks on end during the summer beneath the wealth of large deep gentian-blue flowers. *A. linifolia* should be regarded as an aggregate species and varietal rank given to the several variants, such as *breweri*, blue, *collina*, red flowers, *phillipsii*, extra large blue flowers, *monellii*, which may well be the same as *linifolia*, and 'Sunrise', which was given an Award of Merit in 1970 and is like an even more splendid *collina*. Most of these forms appear to be less reliably perennial than the type and should be propagated vegetatively from time to time to ensure their survival.

— meyeri-johannis. A S. African species, but from Kilimanjaro, near the eternal snows, and should be hardy, if only we could get it.

Farrer rhapsodised about it. The prostrate stems are crowded with small fat leaves in two rows and the pearl-white flowers sit facing upward along the stems and amidst the leaves.

— **monellii.** See *A. linifolia.*

— **phillipsii.** See *A. linifolia.*

— **serpens.** This is one of the plants we would very much like to have from the Abyssinian mountains and for which I lack a clear description, although I believe it to be close to *A. tenella.*

— **tenella.** This is our native Bog Pimpernel, to be found in marshy areas in many parts of Britain. In cultivation the star turn is the especially fine clone collected in Dorset and identified as *A. t.* 'Studland'. On prostrate mats of fresh green leaves adorning tangled stems sit myriads of almost stemless clear pink, honey-scented flowers.

— **willmoreana.** See *A. linifolia monellii.*

ANAPHALIS. *Compositae.* The ancient Greek name for another of the 'Everlastings'.

A small genus of, mostly, fairly tall herbaceous perennials, better suited to the flower border than to the rock garden, but the one species described below is dwarf. They are all sun-loving, summer flowering and tolerant of most soils.

— **nubigena.** Tibet and Yunnan. Both the 9 in. stems and the narrow leaves are felted with soft silver-grey hairs. Heads of white, papery flowers.

ANARTHROPHYLLUM. *Leguminosae.*

— **desideratum.** This exciting plant from Patagonia, which has been called the 'Scarlet Gorse', has been introduced on several occasions, but retains only a fitful hold on cultivation. Like other desirable rarities from the same region we do not yet seem to have fathomed its needs in gardens. It makes huddles of spiny grey leaves, up to a foot in height and covered in the spring with upstanding scarlet or orange flowers, but those who have grown it to flowering age are few in number. It will demand open, sunny rock ledges, or a place in the alpine house.

ANCHONIUM. *Cruciferae.*

— **billardieri.** From the Lebanon. Branching stems carry loose racemes of purple flowers in the manner of a fairly dwarf, rather lax wall-flower.

— **elichrysifolium ssp. persicum.** Dubiously in cultivation, although it has been fairly recently collected in Turkey. It has been enthusiastically described as having tufts of silver leaves and heads of very

ANCHONIUM — *continued*

fragrant golden flowers. Both species, if obtained, will undoubtedly ask for a warm position in sharply drained soil.

ANCHUSA. *Boraginaceae.* From the Greek *ankousa*, Alkanet.

Most of the plants in this genus are hardy herbaceous perennials and do not fall within the scope of this Manual. There is, however, one species greatly admired and desired by alpine gardeners.

— caespitosa. This pygmy species from the high mountains of Crete forms dense, compact tufts of narrow, deep green, rather rugose leaves with undulate margins, rising from a deep-delving and stout root. Each rosette of leaves is centred in the spring by a cluster of almost stemless, gentian-blue flowers. It is usually grown in deep pots or pans, but it also flourishes in the open in gritty soil and full sun and is tolerant of either alkaline or acid conditions. A very different species, *A. angustissima* has unfortunately been much confused in gardens with the true *A. caespitosa.*

ANCYLOSTEMON. *Gesneriaceae.*

— concavus. There appears to be no little botanical confusion between the genera of this section of the family *Gesneriaceae*, which include *Roettlera, Tremacron, Didissandra, Briggsia, Oreocharis* and *Ancylostemon. A. concavus* was exhibited in London in May 1941, when it received an Award of Merit. The ramonda-like rosettes of light green crinkled leaves produce flower stems each bearing a few tubular yellow flowers. Native to Yunnan, it grows there on the trunks of the trees or on mossy boulders and always in shade. It should be given alpine house treatment, in similar soil to that which would be provided for ramondas and haberleas.

ANDROMEDA. *Ericaceae.* Named by Linnaeus after the mythological maiden who was chained to a rock as an offering to a sea-monster and rescued by Perseus.

Most of the plants previously included in this genus have now been removed to other genera, notably PIERIS. Only two species remain and both are valuable dwarf shrubs for lime-free soil and cool, or semi-shaded positions.

— glaucophylla. (A. polifolia angustifolia.) From N. E. America. Dwarf, with erect stems and narrow leaves which differ from those of *A. polifolia* in being white tomentose on the undersides. Pale pink pitcher-shaped flowers are borne in terminal clusters in late spring or early summer. There is a form, 'Latifolia' which is a looser, rather straggling shrub with broader leaves.

— polifolia. A native of Central and Northern Europe, including

Britain, this is the Bog Rosemary of bogs and damp places. In gardens it is easily pleased by peaty soil and is indeed one of the most appropriate dwarf shrubs for a peat garden. In its typical form it can attain 18 in. in height and many alpine gardeners prefer one or other of the more compact-growing forms. The wiry stems are adorned by many hard leaves which appear narrower than they actually are as the margins are recurved. The pink, bell-shaped flowers are carried in compact clusters at the tips of the wiry branches during May and June. In addition to the named clones, such as 'Compacta', 'Major' and 'Minima', there is a charming variant with pure white flowers.

ANDROPUS. See the genus NAMA.

ANDROSACE. *Primulaceae.* From the Greek *aner*, a man, and *sakos*, a shield, a name used by Dioscorides for another plant.

A large genus, distributed widely throughout Europe and in Asia and N. America, containing some of the most exciting, desirable and beautiful alpine plants. Their needs are so various that it is not possible to generalise upon the cultivation, but it can be assumed, unless otherwise stated in the individual descriptions, that they will like full sun, open, gritty soil and are not difficult to grow. There is a minority of really choice high alpine species which should be regarded as alpine house plants. By referring to standard text books and monographs it would have been possible to fill several additional pages with species which, however desirable, are not at present, and unlikely to be in the foreseeable future, in cultivation or commerce. These I have shamelessly omitted. They are all spring and early summer flowering.

— **acaulis.** See *A. septentrionalis.*
— **aizoon.** From China and the Himalaya. Neat rosettes of rather leathery leaves with mucronate margins. Umbels of rich pink flowers on foot high stems.
— — **coccinea.** (A. bulleyana.) From Western China with flowers of richer colour than the type.
— — **himalaica.** (A. himalaica.) From Kashmir, with rose-pink flowers.
— **albana.** An annual species from the Caucasus. Dense rosettes of small leaves and crowded umbels of flowers, which are commonly white but might be pale pink on 6 to 9 in. stems.
— **alpina.** (glacialis.) From high altitudes in the European Alps. A choice and lovely species from alpine screes but one which has never yielded happily to the tenderest care given to it in gardens. Described by Farrer as 'The royal rose-pink splendour of the highest shingles', it captivates the heart of all who see it, and breaks the heart of those

who try to grow it! Even the provision of the lime-free conditions it chooses in nature, in humus-rich detritus and plenty of moisture at the roots seldom spells success. Mats of softly hairy leafy shoots and, in nature, myriads of clear and startling pink flowers create a picture which should tempt only the most obdurate optimist.

— arachnoidea. See *A.villosa.*

— X aretioides. (A. X bruggeri.) A rare natural hybrid between *A. alpina* and *A. obtusifolia.* Growable, and forms tiny humps of soft stems and leaves crowned with almost stemless rose-pink flowers. For the scree, a stone sink or trough or the alpine house and best in lime-free soil.

— argentea. See *A.vandellii.*

— armeniaca. A rather undistinguished annual species from Persia and Armenia, with white flowers on a tall, leafy scape.

— brevis. See *A. charpentieri.*

— brigantiaca. See *A. carnea.*

— X bruggeri. See *A. X aretioides.*

— bulleyana. See *A. aizoon.*

— carinata. A desirable-sounding species which is described as coming from the Colorado Rocky Mountains, particularly on the famous Pike's Peak, but I have not seen it and the colour of its flowers is omitted in all references I have consulted.

— carnea. (A. reverchonii.) Widely distributed in the European Alps and a popular, easily grown plant. Tufts of tiny, dark green, awl-shaped leaves and small heads of pink, or occasionally white, flowers. There are several named forms, all desirable. *A. c. brigantiaca*, with soft white flowers comes from the Cottian Alps, *A. c. eximea*, a robust version of the type, from the French Alps, as does *A. c. halleri.* From the Pyrenees comes the finest form, *A. c. laggeri* with larger flowers of pink with a yellow eye. There are also several versions of delightful hybrids between *A. carnea* and *A. pyrenaica*, most of which have never been officially named, but are extremely desirable alpine house, or stone trough plants making the neatest of domed clusters of tiny rosettes, studded with small flowers in several shades of pink. One which has been named 'Pink Gin' and was first distributed from Jack Drake's Nursery in Scotland, is particularly good.

— caucasica. See *A. raddeana.*

— chaixii. There has been endless confusion between this species and *A. lactiflora* and *A. septentrionalis.* The latter can be assumed to deserve specific rank — just, but the former is probably synonymous with this species, *A. coronopifolia* also no more than a slight variant. A not very common species, it is to be found in the Western and Maritime Alps of Europe. It is dwarf and carries pink or white flowers in loose heads on stems of unequal length.

— chamaejasme. Distributed in the turf of European alpine meadows. It is a plant which likes to be closely associated with others and is an excellent companion for *Gentiana verna*, which has similarly companionable tastes. Softly hairy, silvery-grey, pointed leaves form tiny rosettes above which stand short stems bearing heads of flowers, white when they first expand, but changing to rose-pink with a central yellow eye as they age.

— **charpentieri**. (A. brevis.) A rare inhabitant of limited areas in the Italian Alps. Short, but soft, lax stems carry rosettes of blunt leaves, felted with fine hairs. The short flower stems are equally downy and each carries one rose-red flower. It is not one of the easiest, but will yield to blandishments if these include gritty soil not lacking in humus. It is usually given alpine house treatment but will succeed, if not too much exposed to winter wet, in a scree or in a sink or trough garden.

— **chumbyi**. See *A. primuloides*.

— **ciliata**. This choice rarity from the Pyrenees has been known as a form of *A. pubescens*, but should be accorded specific rank. The flat leaves, hairless except at the margins, mound into neat humps. On each short stem appear one or two rose-pink, yellow-throated flowers.

— **coccinea**. See *A. aizoon*.

— **coronopifolia**. See *A. chaixii*.

— **cylindrica**. This too, has been erroneously referred to as a form of *A. pubescens*. From the Central Pyrenees. The tiny, downy leaves build into crowded grey-green rosettes topping the dead leaves of previous seasons. The almost stemless flowers are white, or, occasionally, very pale pink. It is one of the group which asks for, and deserves, very special care in a scree or the alpine house.

— **delavayi**. From Yunnan, and a species which it would be very desirable to have in cultivation. It belongs to the same aristocratic group as *A. pyrenaica*, *A. pubescens*, *A. cylindrica*, etc., and would be a plant for alpine house treatment. Densely crowded rosettes of downy, wedge-shaped leaves form small domes which are surmounted by white or pink flowers.

— **elongata**. From Middle and Eastern Europe and Asia. Rosettes of lanceolate, sessile leaves and 3 to 4 in. stems bearing loose heads of starry white flowers.

— **X escheri**. A rare natural hybrid between *A. obtusifolia* and *A. chamaejasme*. Close mats of crowded rosettes. It is very free-flowering, producing in April a flush of wide-petalled white, yellow-eyed flowers and often follows this with a second display later in the summer. The flowers are carried in umbels on stems usually not more than 1½ in. high.

— **filiformis**. Probably not in cultivation, and equally probably, not very exciting. It is described as having rather small white flowers carried on short stems over rosettes of roundish, toothed leaves. It occurs in Russia, Siberia and, surprisingly, also in Western N. America.

— **foliosa**. This species from the Himalaya is only dubiously in cultivation, *A. strigillosa* usually doing duty for it in gardens. The smooth nonhairy leaves form tufts rather than proper rosettes and the 9 in. stems bear clusters of lilac flowers.

— **gaudinii.** See *A. X heeri.*

— **geranifolia.** A species from N. India and Tibet and very different in appearance to the European species with their tightly clustered rosettes. Scalloped, rounded and softly hairy leaves form loose tufts from which rise slender, wiry stems to a height of several inches carrying loose heads of pink flowers. The stems may eventually bend over to touch the soil, where they will form roots and become separate individuals.

— **glacialis.** See *A. alpina.*

— **globifera.** A somewhat obscure plant from Himalaya, probably close to *A. villosa* and bearing small, pale pink flowers.

— **halleri.** See *A. carnea.*

— **hausmannii.** From the limestones of the Austrian Dolomites and a delightful cushion-forming species with soft pink flowers on short stems. Give it gritty soil and a choice position or grow it in the alpine house.

— **hedraeantha.** Clustered rosettes of blunt, smooth leaves and umbels of reddish-violet flowers on short stems. Not too difficult out of doors, but worthy of the alpine house or a nook in a stone trough.

— **X heeri.** (A. gaudinii.) A rare natural hybrid between *A. alpina* and *A. helvetica,* and usually easier to grow than either parent, but still demanding, and deserving, special care. Inch-high domes of densely clustered hairy stems and tiny narrow leaves provide a setting for stemless pink flowers.

— **helvetica.** From high places in the European Alps, usually on limestone. The tiny leaves are densely coated with fine grey hairs and the rosettes they form crowd into domed hummocks on which rest stemless white, yellow-throated flowers. It is a difficult plant, needing great care with the watering can and is definitely for the alpine house.

— **himalaica.** See *A. aizoon.*

— **hirtella.** From the Central Pyrenees and another of the high alpine species demanding extra care. It has been regarded as a variety of both *A. pubescens* and *A. cylindrica,* but has every right to specific rank. It resembles a compact form of the already pygmy *A. pubescens* and the stemless flowers are usually white but can be a very pale pink.

— **X hybrida.** This is a recorded, but slightly dubious natural hybrid between *A. helvetica* and *A. pubescens* and is said to be intermediate in appearance between the parents.

— **imbricata.** See *A. vandellii.*

— **jacquemontii.** See *A. villosa.*

— **lactea.** An easy, pleasant but not exciting species from alpine meadows of Europe, especially at the Eastern end. Underground stems form loose mats of rosettes of smooth leaves and 4 to 6 in. stems each carry a few milk-white, yellow-eyed flowers.

ANDROSACE — *continued*

 — **lactiflora.** See *A. chaixii.*

 — **laggeri.** See *A. carnea.*

 — **lanuginosa.** A Himalayan species of great garden value and a popular plant for occupying narrow crevices and chinks from which its trailing, silver-leaved stems can descend. A rather cool aspect is likely to be appreciated. Axillary scapes carry heads of good pink flowers. The variety 'Leichtlinii' differs only in bearing white flowers with a pink or yellow eye.

 — **lehmannii.** From Nepal where, at considerable elevations it forms inch-high mats of narrow leaves covered in white, or occasionally pink flowers.

 — **macrantha.** An Armenian species and usually rather short-lived but easily raised again from seeds. Rosettes of narrow, deeply-toothed leaves and umbels of white flowers on 3 to 4 in. stems.

 — **mathildae.** From the Italian Alps. Tufts of rosettes of small, smooth and shining leaves and white flowers on short stems.

 — **maxima.** A small, rather oddly named species from Mediterranean regions and Turkey. Small, oblong, toothed and softly hairy leaves form loose rosettes above which are umbels of white or rose coloured flowers on 3 to 4 in. stems.

 — **microphylla.** See *A. mucronifolia.*

 — **mucronifolia.** From the Himalaya and notably in Kashmir. Prostrate tufts covered with very short-stemmed white, sweetly scented flowers.

 — **muscoidea.** A rarity from the Himalaya. Cushions of imbricated rosettes carpeted with white flowers, which become pink after fertilisation. This probably explains why it is described in some text books as being pink-flowered.

 — **obtusifolia.** From the Apennines. Loose clumps of rosettes of rather spoon-shaped leaves, slightly hairy at the margins and 6 in. stems each carrying a few short-stalked white flowers.

 — **occidentalis.** From N. America. Rosettes of softly hairy leaves, lightly toothed and short scapes carrying many, rather small white flowers.

 — **ochotensis.** (A. tschuktschorum.) A jewel of a plant from Alaska which, alas, appears not to be in cultivation. It is described as offering compact mounds of congested rosettes smothered in bright pink flowers.

 — **pacheri.** See *A. wulfeniana.*

 — **X pedemontana.** A natural hybrid between *A. carnea* and *A. obtusifolia.* It was found in Piedmont and the narrow leaves have wavy margins and white flowers with an orange eye are borne on slender stems 4 to 6 in. high.

 — **primuloides.** (A. sarmentosa.) A Himalayan species represented in gardens by many named clones, mostly seen under the umbrella of the synonym. It is doubtful if the type species exists in cultivation but has been replaced by the several selected and named clones which are such popular rock garden plants. In all of them the small, acutely hairy leaves are gathered into rounded, almost sempervivum-like rosettes to form dense, prostrate mats and the flowers, in varying shades of pink to red, are carried in many-flowered umbels on stems varying in height from 4 to 6 in. There is no point in minutely describing the cultivars, but seek them under such names as 'Chumbyi', 'Salmon's Variety', 'Watkinsii' or 'Yunnanensis'. A cultivar which is in circulation as 'Galmont's Variety' is, I am sure, no more than an incorrect rendering of 'Salmon's Variety', which was raised by the late Mr. Salmon, author of a Flora of Surrey. All the forms of *A. primuloides* flourish in open, sunny positions and gritty soil but are not too fond of a very wet winter and under conditions of prolonged rain appreciate some light protection.

— **pubescens.** From the Pyrenees. Ash-grey, hairy leaves clustered in thickly packed rosettes forming neat domes, each rosette centred by a short-stemmed, pearl-white flower. Needs extra care and dislikes winter wetness.

— **pyrenaica.** From the Pyrenees and one of the most accommodating of its particular, rather temperamental section, but best regarded as an alpine house plant. The tiny green, pointed leaves are felted with grey, fine hair and form minute rosettes which are crowded into the neatest of rounded hummocks. Each of the wee rosettes produces one neatly rounded white, yellow-eyed flower and the entire cushion may disappear beneath the wealth of blossom.

— **raddeana.** (A. caucasica.) Rosettes of smooth, rather fleshy leaves lightly toothed near the tips and rose-pink, yellow-eyed flowers on short scapes, perhaps 6 in. tall. From the Caucasus.

— **reverchonii.** See *A. carnea.*

— **rotundifolia.** From N. India. Rounded to kidney-shaped smooth leaves, lobed at the edges and many-flowered umbels of pink flowers on 6 in. stems.

— **sarmentosa.** See *A. primuloides.*

— **selago.** From the Himalaya and would be an exciting alpine house species were it available. Thick, dense tufts of overlapping, triangular leaves with hairy margins. Rich purple flowers on very short stems.

— **sempervivoides.** From Kashmir and Tibet. Sempervivum-like rosettes of overlapping, smooth green leaves and short scapes carrying several good pink flowers. Easy in any gritty soil and full sun.

— **septentrionalis.** (A. acaulis.) Annual, or occasionally biennial. From the Alps of Europe. Small rosettes of lance-shaped, slightly downy, toothed leaves and flower stems varying from in height 6 to 12 in. with stiff, erect stalks carrying white, or sometimes pink-flushed flowers.

— **spinulifera.** A species from Central China and Yunnan sometimes erroneously described as *A. spinosa.* The rather long, linear leaves terminate in a spiny tip and overlap so densely as to form, when young, an almost globular rosette. On stems of 6 in. or so are carried heads of purple flowers.

— **strigillosa.** Quite large leaves densely felted with hairs and with an acute, almost spiny tip and umbels carrying several purple flowers on 9 to 12 in. stems.

— **tibetica.** A stoloniferous species from the Himalaya with grey, softly hairy leaves, slightly fleshy and with ciliate margins. Erect, 3 in. scapes carry heads of pink flowers. It is a variable species in its habit of growth, sometimes almost as loose as *A. lanuginosa* and at other times as rosetted as *A. primuloides.*

— **tschuktschorum.** See *A. ochotensis.*

— **vandellii.** (A. argentea. A. imbricata.) It goes very much against the grain to revert to this name after we have come to know and love one of the most beautiful cushion androsaces so well under one or other of its synonyms, but the name *vandellii* appears to have precedence. It comes from granite cliffs in the Central and Southern Alps, where it makes dense cushions of rosettes of white-felted leaves which disappear at times beneath countless stemless, rounded, yellow-eyed flowers. It demands the utmost care if grown in the open, to protect it from winter wet, but is not at all difficult when grown in pots or pans in an alpine house.

— **villosa.** From the Alps of Europe and also from Asia. At the ends of wiry, often red stolons are clustered tufts of small grey-green leaves, the whole growing into small mats over which are carried small heads of rounded flowers which are usually white, or might be pale pink with a reddish eye. They are also fragrant. It is an easy plant to grow in a sunny, gritty scree. An enticing form of the type is *A. arachnoidea* from the Eastern Alps. It is more compact and more silvery and occurs on the limestone summits of the Karawanken Mountains. On very short scapes it displays neat heads of white, pink-eyed flowers. *A. jacquemontii* comes from the Himalaya and is clothed in russet hairs and the flowers are rose-pink.

— **vitaliana.** See the genus DOUGLASIA.

— **wardii.** From China and Tibet. Loose rosettes of long-petioled leaves and corymbs of cherry-pink flowers, probably not now in cultivation although it received a Preliminary Commendation in London in 1940.

— **watkinsii.** See *A. primuloides.*

— **wulfeniana.** (A. pacheri.) Locally abundant in the Eastern Alps. Mats of rosettes of pointed, slightly hairy green leaves and deep pink flowers on short stalks. Treat with some care, but not too difficult.

— **yunnanense.** See *A. primuloides.*

— **zambalensis.** A rarity from Nepal and probably not at present in cultivation. A cushion plant adorned with stemless white flowers, each with a pink or yellow eye.

ANDRYALA. *Compositae.* The meaning of the name is obscure. A small genus of perennials mostly from Mediterranean regions and avid sun-lovers in any good garden soil. Only one of the species is appropriate to rock gardens.

— **agardhii.** A dense sub-shrub of congested growth with dark, much branched stems ending in crowded tufts of narrow, very silvery leaves. Solitary yellow flower-heads appear in June and July. It seldom attains more than 9 in. in height.

ANEMONE. *Ranunculaceae.* The name is commonly thought to have derived from the Greek *anemos*, the wind, but this is almost certainly a misconception. It is said by W. T. Stearn — and there is no greater authority — to be a corrupted Greek word borrowed from the Semitic and referring to the lament for the slain Adonis, or Naaman, whose scattered blood produced the blood-red *Anemone coronaria.*

The members of this large genus are native to the cooler parts of the Northern Hemisphere, with a few outliers in S. America and S. Africa. It is difficult to be arbitrary in the choice of those I can include as appropriate for the rock garden and I propose to allow myself some licence, although some which readers might expect to find have been excluded simply because they are so positively 'unalpine'. Their cultural needs vary so much that generalisations are not really practicable, but it can be assumed that, unless stated to the contrary in individual descriptions, they can be grown under ordinary garden conditions with no special requirements as to soil or situation. As with the genus androsace, it would have been possible to fill several pages with descriptions of species not in cultivation. Most of these have been omitted, but a few crept in as they are so obviously desirable and may, one day, be cultivated.

— **acutipetala.** See PULSATILLA *alpina.*
— **albana.** See PULSATILLA *pratensis.*
— **alpina.** See PULSATILLA *alpina.*
— **altaica.** A dainty little species from Japan and Siberia. It resembles a glorified Wood Anemone *(A. nemorosa).* On 6 in. stems it displays large, many-rayed flowers of white, veined with soft blue lines. It asks for the same cool treatment one would give to *A. nemorosa.*
— **angulosa.** See the genus HEPATICA.
— **antucensis.** This comes from Chile and would seem to be a nice plant, again in the likeness of *A. nemorosa.* Now that there are collectors working in S. America we may see this properly introduced to cultivation.
— **apennina.** Southern Europe. Although usually classified among bulbs, this species grows from a tuberous rhizome. It, and its several forms are spring-flowering and like cool, or semi-shaded positions in any

48

good, well-drained soil. The type bears blue flowers similar to those of *A. nemorosa*, but there are named clones with white, pink and double flowers which it is unnecessary to enumerate here as they are well described in bulb catalogues.

— **baicalensis.** From cylindrical rhizomes spring deeply cleft leaves and on stems which vary in height from 6 to 12 in. are solitary or twin white flowers, the sepals softly hairy on the outside. It likes cool or partially-shaded positions, but will take full sun if necessary.

— **baldensis.** A rarity from Southern and Eastern Europe. It runs underground in alpine pastures and emits tufts of dark green, finely shredded leaves. The solitary flowers are of goodly size, white, and backed with blue with a good golden eye. It is curiously averse to cultivation and should be tempted by a rather earthy scree mixture in full sun.

— **biflora.** From Kashmir, and rather needlessly condemned by Farrer. It can present twin flowers of rather dingy red on 6 in. stems, but there are forms which are well worth growing.

— **blanda.** The mountain anemone of Greece and E. Europe. It is not unlike *A. apennina*, growing from a tuberous rhizome with more fleshy leaves divided into three or more leaflets. The flowers may be deep blue, paler blue, mauve, white or pink according to the particular clone. It requires similar conditions to those suggested for *A. apennina*, and the numerous clones are described and listed in most bulb catalogues. One of the very best blues is *A. b.* 'Atrocaerulea', and *A. b.* 'Radar' is quite startling with red, white-centred flowers of large size.

— **borealis.** See *A. parviflora*.

— **caerulea.** From Siberia and doubtfully in cultivation. It can be likened to the Wood Ginger, *A. ranunculoides*, but the flowers are not yellow, but misty blue. It should be given, if obtained, woodland conditions.

— **cernua.** See the genus PULSATILLA.

— **cylindrica.** From N. America, and rather too tall for most rock gardens, but a handsome plant with divided, silky-haired leaves and heads of large greenish-white flowers on stems up to 2 ft. tall.

— **demissa.** From N. India and China. A good plant in the likeness of *A. narcissiflora* with leaves divided into wedge-shaped lobes and branching, foot-high stems carrying large white flowers which are stained reddish-mauve on the reverse. For full sun and gritty soil.'

— **drummondii.** This plant, in N. America takes the place of the European *A. baldensis*, which it closely resembles.

— **flaccida.** From mountain woodlands in Japan. From creeping rhizomes rise coarsely-toothed leaves which are almost fleshy in texture and 12 to 15 in. stems carrying large, pure white flowers.

— **halleri.** See the genus PULSATILLA.

— **hepatica.** See the genus HEPATICA.

— **X lesseri.** A hybrid of garden origin between *A. multifida and A.*

sylvestris. Although perhaps rather tall for most rock gardens this is such a good plant that space should be found for it. On 12 to 15 in. erect stems are carried heads of many sizeable flowers of glowing deep pink to red. Any sunny position and ordinary soil.

— lithophila. A N. American species from damp positions. Possibly not in cultivation but should be, for its 4 to 6 in. stems carry starry soft blue flowers.

— magellanica. From Chile and Patagonia. An easy plant which does not always receive the praise it deserves. Although not of startling beauty it carries good heads of cream-white flowers on 6 in. stems over tufts of deeply divided, hairy basal leaves. There is a form in cultivation, rather ambiguously referred to as 'Major', which is identical except that it is more robust in all its parts.

— montana. See the genus PULSATILLA.

— narcissiflora. A widely distributed species, being found in Europe, N. America and Asia. It is very variable in height, the flower stems ranging from 9 to 18 in. The palmate, deeply lobed and toothed leaves appear in tufts from which rise the stems carrying umbels of white, cream or pink-flushed flowers. There is a form, *A. n.* 'Villosa' which has particularly hairy leaves. Sun and gritty soil provide all it needs.

— nemorosa. This is our well-loved native Wood Anemone, cultivated in the form of several named clones. It has long, thin, woody rhizomes from which rise deeply cleft leaves in loose clusters. Of the numerous garden forms some of the best are *A. n. allenii* with soft blue flowers, *A. n.* 'Alba' (or 'Grandiflora' or 'Alba Major') with large white flowers, *A. n. robinsoniana* with very large powder-blue flowers, *A. n.* 'Alba Plena', white and double and *A. n.* 'Vestal' which fills the centre of its white flowers with a cluster of staminoid filaments.

— obtusiloba. From the Himalaya, and a beautiful plant, sometimes referred to as the 'Blue Buttercup of Kashmir'. Loose tufts of palmate, hairy, lobed leaves form the foundation for spreading, branching stems carrying large, circular flowers which, in the form commonly cultivated as 'Patula', are soft blue. In nature it is found with flowers of white, cream and violet colour. It likes full sun and gritty soil, and blossoms for a long summer period.

— occidentalis. See the genus PULSATILLA.

— palmata. From S.W. Europe. From a tuberous rootstock spring small, rounded, lobed leaves and stems up to 6 in. high carrying several yellow, slightly cup-shaped flowers. There also exist white-flowered forms. It will need a warm, sheltered position in gritty, but humus-rich soil.

— parviflora. (A. borealis.) From N. America and Siberia and would be a good plant to have if it were in cultivation, which is doubtful. The leaves are wedge-shaped, with scalloped margins and, on short stems appear large, solitary white flowers tinted with blue at the base of the petals.

ANEMONE — *continued*
- **patens.** See the genus PULSATILLA.
- **pratensis.** See the genus PULSATILLA.
- **pulsatilla.** See the genus PULSATILLA.
- **raddeana.** From Japan and sounds attractive. It grows from creeping rhizomes with three-parted leaflets on long-petioled leaflets. The flowers are described as white, with a purple hue.
- **ranunculoides.** From Europe and the Caucasus. A woodland plant. From thin, horizontal rootstocks rise divided, toothed leaves and bright yellow, usually solitary flowers in early spring. There are several variants, *A. r.* 'Pleniflora' is double, *A. r.* 'Superba' has bronzed leaves and larger flowers and a very small form with thicker rhizomes and narrow, sharply toothed leaves has been distinguished as *A. wockeana.*
- **reflexa.** From Siberia and Korea. Not beautiful but an interesting species related to *A. nemorosa,* the greenish-white sepals reflex so sharply that, according to Farrer, 'they form globes with the wrong side out'.
- **rupicola.** The rootstock of this Himalayan and Chinese species is a woody rhizome. The leaves are deeply divided and lobed and foothigh, branching stems carry large white flowers tinted purple on the outsides. It likes a not too hot position in any good ordinary soil.
- **sulphurea (or sulfurea).** See PULSATILLA *alpina.*
- **sylvestris.** The Snowdrop Anemone, from Europe and Turkestan. A running rootstock produces quantities of hairy, deeply cut and toothed leaves and 12 in. stems carrying loose heads of slightly drooping fragrant white flowers. There is a rare form with double flowers and a selected form, *A. s.* 'Spring Beauty' with much larger flowers. For cool, gritty soil and not a baking hot position.
- **tetrasepala.** A version of *A. narcissiflora* from the Himalaya but with four instead of the usual five sepals.
- **thalictrioides.** See ANEMONELLA *thalictrioides.*
- **trifolia.** A delightful cousin of *A. nemorosa* and, in its most beautiful form from woodlands around Misurina, it displays flowers of soft, clear blue, rather like those of a Hepatica over leaves resembling those of *A. nemorosa.*
- **trulliiflora.** If only we could possess this condensed version of *A. obtusiloba,* which comes from the high Himalaya, it would be assured of a welcome if only for the sake of its rich golden flowers.
- **tschernjaewii.** A recent introduction from Kashmir. The shiny leaves have few divisions and large white or pink flowers sit on 4 in. stems.
- **vernalis.** See the genus PULSATILLA.
- **wockeana.** See *A. ranunculoides.*

ANEMONELLA. *Ranunculaceae.* A diminutive of Anemone, which the plant resembles.
- **thalictrioides.** (Anemone thalictrioides. Thalictrum anemonoides.

51

ANEMONELLA — *continued*

Syndesmon thalictrioides.) This is the only species in the genus and it is native to N. American woodlands. A frail beauty which rambles gently in peaty soil and light shade. Sprays of tiny, thalictrum-like leaves and loose umbels of white or soft pink flowers on 6 in. stems in spring.

ANEMOPSIS. See the genus HOUTTUYNIA.

ANISOTOME. *Umbelliferae.* From the Greek *anisos*, unequal, and *tome*, cut. An allusion to the manner in which the edges of the leaves are cut in plants of this genus.

This small genus is confined to New Zealand and some sub-arctic islands where they grow in alpine and sub-alpine regions. Few are in cultivation and any obtained should be given alpine house treatment or a position in an earthy scree.

— **aromatica.** Loose rosettes, or tufts, of finely divided deep green leaves and umbels of small, aromatic white flowers on 9 to 12 in. stems.

— **imbricata.** Dense domes of crowded dark green leaves cut as finely as the frond of a fern. The umbels of greenish-white flowers are comparatively insignificant, but it is worth growing as an interesting cushion plant.

ANOGRA. See the genus OENOTHERA.

ANOMATHECA. See the genus LAPEIROUSIA.

ANTENNARIA. *Compositae.* From the Latin *antenna*, the yard of a sailing ship. The pappus of the flower is supposed to resemble the antennae of a butterfly.

A genus of, mostly, grey or silver-leaved plants widely distributed in temperate regions, including Europe and America, both north and south. It is largely *A. dioica* and its forms which are cultivated as small ground-covers for the rock garden but there are other species worthy of consideration if available.

— **alpina.** An almost prostrate stoloniferous creeper with green leaves and small heads of rather inconspicuous flowerlets. From the mountains of N. America.

— **aprica.** N. America. Very similar to *A. dioica*, white flowers.

— **candida.** See *A. dioica* 'Minima'.

- canescens. From the ice-bound mountains of Greenland and closely related to *A. alpina.*
- carpathica. From the European Alps. Varies from 1 to 6 in. in height, leaves grey with fine hairs. Similar to *A. dioica.*
- chilensis. From Chile, Similar in many ways to *A. dioica*, with white or faintly pink flower heads on 2 to 3 in. stems.
- dioica. (tomentosa.) Europe, Asia and N. America. The most commonly grown species and an easy spreader in any soil. It is useful as a carpeter for small bulbs, or as a unit in an alpine lawn. Mats of grey leaves and short erect stems carrying small heads of whitish flowers. There are several named varieties. 'Hyperborea' has leaves woolly on both surfaces and pinkish flowers. 'Minima' is a condensed version of the type, and 'Rosea' has flowers of quite a rich pink.
- geyeri. From California and Oregon. A woody base and tufts of thick, grey, woolly leaves. Flower heads tipped rose or ivory white.
- hyperborea. See *A. dioica.*
- media. N. America and British Columbia. Silver-grey mats and heads of off-white flowers on short stems.
- neglecta. N. American. Grey carpets, flowers white or pale pink.
- nitida. N. America. Almost lichen-like mats of silver leaves and tiny heads of white or pinkish flowers on very short stems.
- plantaginifolia. From N. America. Mat-forming, tufts of grey-green leaves and not very conspicuous flowers on 6 to 9 in. stems.
- posildii. Sweden and Greenland. A rather insignificant species, hardly worth cultivating. Mats of grey leaves and very small flower heads.
- tomentosa. See *A. dioica.*

ANTHEMIS. *Compositae.* The Greek name for the Chamomile, *A. nobilis.*

A genus of 80 or more species widely distributed in Europe, Asia and N. Africa. Many are not garden-worthy, and of those which are grown several are hardy perennial border plants. They are all sunlovers.

- abyssinica. This species has been mentioned as coming from the mountains of Kenya. Unfortunately, the late Dr. R. Seligman, for whose knowledge I had great respect, does not describe the colour of the flowers in the only reference to it which I can discover. He only tells us that it was prostrate and infers that it was attractive.
- aizoon. See ACHILLEA *ageratifolia.*
- barbeyana. This, too, sounds a desirable plant. It comes from the Alps of Aetolia and forms cushions of fine-cut silky-silvery foliage with white daisies in clusters on short stems.
- barrelieri. From the Apennines. Rosettes of finely dissected grey leaves and white flowers on 6 in. stems.

ANTHEMIS — *continued*

- **biebersteinii.** (A. rudolphiana.) From the Caucasus. Tufts of silvery, filigree-fine leaves and richly golden flowers on 9 in. stems. Best in rather poor, gritty soil.
- **boveana.** A Moroccan species making small bushes of green leaves on woody stems, about 6 to 9 in. high. Many heads of bright yellow flowers.
- **carpatica.** (A. styriaca.) Southern Europe. Low mats of irregularly cut green leaves and large white 'Marguerite' flowers on 9 in. stems.
- **cassia.** From Syria, and probably not in cultivation, and perhaps a little tall for most rock gardens as its large white flowers are carried one to each 18 in. stem over clumps of narrow, silvery-silky leaves.
- **chia.** An annual species from Eastern Europe provides green carpets studded with short-stemmed white daisies.
- **cupaniana.** Although this Italian species may be thought over-large for the rock garden, I cannot ignore it. Foaming masses of grey, aromatic foliage may spread over a yard or more and are decorated from spring until late in the autumn with large white daisy flowers, one to each long stem.
- **hauschnechtii.** I am not at all sure about this plant. Text books insist that it is an annual from Syria, but as I have known it and grown it for many years, it forms perennial mats of filigree silver leaves with short-stemmed rich golden flowers.
- **macedonica.** See *A. montana.*
- **montana.** (A. macedonica.) A very variable species from Eastern Europe, of which several sub-forms and variants have been noted. Typically it makes dwarf mats of small green leaves and many white flowers.
- **nobilis.** It might be thought that the common Chamomile has no place in a Manual of Alpine Plants, but it should be recorded that there is a form with double white flowers which, although invasive, is not without attraction. Then of course there is the invaluable, non-flowering clone named 'Treneague' which is so useful as a ground-coverer and for making small lawns.
- **pedunculata.** The species hails from Morocco, and is not exciting, but a recently introduced variety, *A. p.* 'Tuberculata' promises to be a useful rock garden plant for hot, dry places. Neat dwarf, grey-leaved bushlets are covered with white, golden-eyed daisies of substantial size for many summer weeks.
- **rudolphiana.** See *A. biebersteinii.*
- **styriaca.** See *A. carpatica.*
- **tigrensis.** From East Africa in the Aberdare Mountains. Described as a conspicuous plant with inch-wide white flowers over mats of deeply divided green leaves.
- **tricolor 'Artemisioides'.** This comes from Cyprus and is to be valued only for its foliage. It grows at considerable elevations and the leaves are felted with soft and silky hairs. The type species, which grows at lower elevations is not hardy, but would be a better garden plant if it were.

ANTHERICUM. *Liliaceae.* From the Greek *antherikon,* the name of the asphodel.

A genus of more than one hundred species, natives of Europe, America and Tropical Africa. The majority of them are not hardy but among the European species are several valuable garden plants — mostly too tall for the average rock garden but commonly included in catalogues among alpine plants. They are sun-lovers and flourish in any good garden soil and flower in late spring and summer.

- algeriense. See *A. liliago.*
- angustifolium. To be found on Mt. Elgon in Kenya and probably not in cultivation. I know little of it except that it should bear white or pinkish flowers.
- boeticum. Probably synonymous with *A. liliago.*
- curviscapum. Another of the E. African species and said to have almost prostrate flowers. There is every chance that these E. African species would be hardy and it would be interesting to have them introduced.
- eccremorrhizum. Comes from the Peruvian Andes and is yet another species that would meet with a warm welcome and we might then discover what it looks like, which Dora Stafford fails to tell us in her writings of her expeditions to the Andes.
- humboldtii. This also comes from the Peruvian Andes and I can only repeat my comments relating to *A. eccremorrhizum.*
- humile. A dwarf species from Abyssinia which ought to be, but is not, as far as I can discover, in cultivation. It has a few flowered raceme of large bell-shaped white flowers on quite short stems.
- liliago. (A. algeriense. Phalangium liliago.) The dainty St. Bernard's Lily of alpine meadows in the European Alps. Tufts of narrow leaves 12 in. long and racemes of from ten to twenty lily-like flowers of glistening white on 15 to 18 in. stems.
- liliastrum. See PARADISEA *liliastrum.*
- racemosum. Must be *A. ramosum,* which see.
- ramosum. (Phalangium ramosum.) Farrer fittingly describes it as 'a haunter of sub-alpine rocks'. Tufts of rather frail, almost grasslike leaves and, in late summer, many elegant, branching stems bedecked with starry white flowers.
- subpetiolatum. Yet another of Mt. Elgon species, for which a detailed description is lacking.
- yedoense. See ALECTORURUS *yedoensis.*

ANTHYLLIS. *Leguminosae.* The ancient Greek name for this plant.

A genus of sun-loving herbs and shrubs, natives of Central and Southern Europe. Well suited to any average garden soil, summer flowering.

- alpestris. See *A. vulneraria.*

ANTHYLLIS — *continued*

— **aurea.** From the Balkans. Mat-forming, with grey leaves and globular heads of golden flowers.

— **dinarica.** This name appears on the pages of the invaluable Bulletins of the Alpine Garden Society, without a description, and is one for which I can discover no authority.

— **erinaceae.** See ERINACEA *anthyllis*.

— **fulgurans.** Another name for which I lack authority. It is recorded obscurely as being Corsican, where it is said to occur near the coast in spiny mounds.

— **hermanniae.** A Mediterranean shrub up to 2 ft. or more in height. Tangled, tortuous stems form rounded bushes, the branches becoming spiny at the tips as they age. In gardens the more desirable plant for rock gardens is *A. h.* 'Compacta', which is a highly desirable, yellow-flowered bushlet of little more than 1 ft.

— **jacquinii.** See *A. montana*.

— **montana.** European Alps from the Pyrenees to the Apennines. Stems woody at base forming loose, foot-high bushes. The branches end in rounded heads of red or red-purple flowers. A subspecies, *A. m. jacquinii* is found in the East Alps, and there is a cultivated form *A. m.* 'Rubra' with flowers of rich red.

— **podocephala.** According to the *Flora Europaea* this is synonymous with *A. polycephala*, but the late Dwight Ripley, for whose botanical knowledge I had the greatest respect, insists that they are distinct, and I follow his ruling. *A. podocephala* comes from Spain and is a handsome small shrub, smothered in summer with woolly yellow pompons.

— **polycephala.** This species creeps out of Europe and is found in the Riff Mountains of N. Africa, whence it was introduced in 1936. The pinnate leaves are covered with silvery, silky hairs and the stems terminate in small heads of yellow pea-flowers. For the alpine house or a warm and sheltered niche in the open.

— **ramburei.** From Spanish mountains. Rather loose bushes of woody stems clothed in lightly hairy pinnate leaves. The rounded heads of yellow flowers become reddish as the blossoms age.

— **serpentinicola.** See *A. vulneraria*.

— **tetraphylla.** From Portugal and also recorded from Morocco. A neat dwarf, only a few inches high with sparse foliage in rosettes and loose heads of purple flowers.

— **vulneraria.** This is the Ladies Fingers of our British countryside, but it is a vast and polymorphic species, widely distributed in a multitude of subspecies and forms. The *Flora Europaea* lists between twenty and thirty subspecies, which it would be pointless to elaborate upon. The type is seldom cultivated, but *A. v.* 'Coccinea' (*A. v. dillenii*) has good red flowers, as does *A. v.* 'Rubra'. *A. v.* 'Serpentinicola' is a Grecian subspecies said to have merit.

ANTIRRHINUM. *Scrophulariaceae.* From the Greek *anti*, like, and *rhis*, a nose, or snout. A reference to the characteristic shape of the flowers.

The common Snapdragon, *A. majus*, is usually grown as an annual or biennial, and is employed for bedding out and does not concern the rock garden (regrettably, some dwarf strains have been recommended as 'suitable for rock gardens'). A few species which are permissible and like warm, dry situations, are described below. They need no special composts, but the drainage must be good. Spring and summer flowering.

- **asarina.** See the genus ASARINA.
- **barrelieri.** From Spain and Portugal. It varies in height from one foot upward and is too tall for small rock gardens. The handsome flowers of pink and yellow are carried in erect racemes.
- **chrysothales.** Endemic to limestone hills in Morocco, for which a clear description is lacking, but is well spoken of.
- **glutinosum.** See *A. hispanicum.*
- **grossii.** From Central Spain. Only dubiously in cultivation, but a handsome species which might well be hardy. It is dwarf and grows in narrow rock crevices. The woody stems carry many large white flowers having a purple stripe on the lip.
- **hispanicum.** A Spanish species which, according to some authorities is synonymous with *A. latifolium*, but the *Flora Europaea* makes the latter a distinct, but much taller species. Foot-high bushes carry loose racemes of flowers which may be white, pink or purple, with a yellow palate. *A. h.* subsp. *glutinosum* is a neat, compact plant with soft yellow flowers and narrow red stripes on the palate.
- **latifolium.** See mention under *A. hispanicum.*
- **molle.** From the Pyrenees. Dwarf, woody bushlets with slightly sticky stems and leaves and racemes of white and yellow flowers.
- **orontium.** An annual, and now referred to the genus *Misopates.*
- **sempervirens.** From the Pyrenees. A more or less prostrate plant with tangled, woody stems. The white flowers are striped with lilac and the palate is yellow.
- **speciosum.** This must be *Galvesia speciosa*, a scarlet-flowered, antirrhinum-like plant, certain not to be hardy, as it comes from Southern California.
- **tortuosum.** From Mediterranean regions and probably too tall for most rock gardens. On branches up to 2 ft. high it carries purple flowers on short, crowded racemes.

AOTUS. *Leguminosae.* From the Greek *a*, without, and *otos*, an ear, an allusion to the lack of appendages on the calyx found in the related genus *Pultenaea.*

- **villosa.** A Tasmanian plant, probably not in cultivation, but to be desired for the sake of its short sprays of yellow pea flowers.

57

APHYLLANTHES. *Liliaceae.* From the Greek *a*, without, and *phyllon*, a leaf, and *anthos*, a flower. The flowers are carried on leafless, rush-like stems.

— **monspeliensis.** This, the only species in its genus, inhabits hot hill and mountain sides in Mediterranean regions. It is hardy, in a suitable situation and sharply drained soil. Tufts of rush-like stems and inch-wide clear blue flowers carried terminally amidst chaffy bracts on 4 in. stems in summer. It has been cultivated since 1791.

APINELLA. *Umbelliferae.*

— **frigida.** A small umbellifer from Greece. Compact tufts of glabrous pinnatisect leaves and short-stemmed umbels of green-white flowers. Dubiously in cultivation, but if obtained would ask for an open, sunny position and a spartan diet.

APLOPAPPUS. See the genus HAPLOPAPPUS.

AQUILEGIA. *Ranunculaceae.* From the Latin *aquila*, an eagle, from the form of the petals.

A large genus of decorative plants widely distributed over temperate regions of the northern hemisphere, with one or two outliers in S. Africa. Easily grown, with the exception of one or two slightly temperamental high alpine species, they relish any good garden soil and sunny positions and are spring and summer flowering. Tall kinds better suited to flower beds and borders are omitted from the following selection, as well as many of the multitudinous names which can be found in text books and catalogues, to say nothing of the Bulletins of the Alpine Garden Society. Many such references are of obscure plants, or kinds which differ little from others. Apart from being thoroughly amoral, hybridising all too easily, aquilegias afford full opportunity to botanical 'splitters'.

— **adantoides.** This is synonymous with *A. eximea*, which is itself probably no more than a sub-form of *A. formosa*.

— **akitensis.** See *A. flabellata*.

— **alpina.** This is the charming blue Columbine of the European Alps. Unfortunately it seldom breeds true from seed and does not increase readily by vegetative means and is, therefore, seldom seen true in gardens. At its best it carries large blue, or blue and white flowers on foot-high stems.

— **amaliae.** From Greece, and a lovely plant, not dissimilar to *A. alpina*.

— **arctica.** Is no more than *A. formosa*.

— **barnebeyi.** A recently introduced species from North-Western Colorado, with blue-green leaves and long spurred flowers of pink and yellow. It may yet prove to be synonymous with *A. rubicunda*.

— **bertolonii.** (A. reuteri.) Although usually regarded as a species this may be a form of *A. pyrenaica*, from the Eastern Alps. 4 in. stems each carry one large blossom of rich blue, with a prominent hooked spur.

— **brevistyla.** A rather undistinguished American species with small, short-spurred cream and blue flowers.

— **buergeriana.** A Japanese species, carrying on rather tall stems yellow flowers flushed sometimes with purple.

— **caerulea.** The State Flower of Colorado and a handsome plant with large blue and white flowers on 12 to 15 in. stems. It, too, seldom breeds true and forms and hybrids with individual names abound. It is probable that the plant grown as *A. helenae* rightly belongs here.

— **canadensis.** An infinitely variable American species which, as it is also only too eager to fraternise with any other aquilegia within wind or bee-range, is difficult to typify. The flowers may be red and yellow, or all yellow, or almost all red.

— **cazorlensis.** One of the several good plants which are endemic to the Cazorla district of Spain. A neat dwarf, with blue flowers, seldom, alas, seen in cultivation.

— **dichroa.** A rather obscure species from Spain, variable in height with blue and white flowers.

— **discolor.** From Spain and a delightful dwarf species, seldom exceeding 4 in. in height with elegantly poised soft blue and cream flowers over tufts of finely-cut leaves.

— **ecalcarata.** See the genus SEMIAQUILEGIA.

— **einseleana.** From the European Alps, the Dolomites in particular. On 9 to 12 in. stems are carried quite large violet-blue flowers.

— **elegantula.** A N. American species allied to *A. canadensis*, but sufficiently distinct to merit specific rank. On short stems it carries red flowers lacking the yellow overtones of *A. canadensis*.

— **flabellata.** (A. akitensis.) There seems to be some confusion in gardens regarding this species. It is Japanese and the type is described as being fairly tall, with stems varying from 9 to 18 in., and flowers which are purple-blue — rarely white. In gardens the most universally popular variant is the plant known as *A. f.* 'Nana Alba', which is a waxy-grey-green-leaved pygmy with thick petalled cream-white flowers.

— **formosa.** (A. arctica.) This is really an aggregate species showing wide variations, most forms being too tall for the average rock garden. It is an American plant with a wide distribution and commonly bears red, or red and yellow flowers. It seems at times to more or less merge with *A. canadensis*.

— **glandulosa.** When seen in its true form this species from the Altai Mountains is quite magnificent. A guide to its verity exists in the earliest stages, as its seeds are dull, whereas other aquilegias have shiny, glossy seeds. On 15 in. stems are carried bold flowers of blue and white. The variety *jucunda* is dwarfer, with even larger flowers.

If the typical non-shiny seeds are obtained it breeds true.

— **helenae.** See *A. caerulea.*

— **hinckleyana.** A very desirable American species which does not appear to be in cultivation. It should bear golden flowers on fairly tall stems. The spurs of the flowers are conspicuously long, recalling those of *A. longissima*, which, owing to its height of about 2 ft., is omitted from this Manual.

— **jonesii.** This rare species from the Rocky Mountains of N. W. America is the delight and despair of alpine gardeners. It can be grown, with little difficulty, especially when given alpine house treatment, but is reluctant to flower with any freedom. I believe this to be an inborn characteristic, for I have walked through great colonies of it in the wild and noted that only a percentage of the many hundreds of plants were blossoming. From little tufts of grey-green leaves rise stems of about 3 in. each carrying one large, short-spurred blue flower — if you are lucky!

— **jucunda.** See *A. glandulosa.*

— **kitaibelii.** A European species, the leaflets slightly hairy above and below and 12 to 15 in. stems carrying nodding, blue-violet or red-violet flowers.

— **laramiensis.** A rare American species which appears to breed true from seed. It inhabits granite outcrops and has short-spurred cream-white flowers. It is reported as having the curious character of being a neater, more compact plant in gardens than it is in nature.

— **macrantha.** I suspect this of being the same as *A. micrantha*, described in the Bulletin of the Alpine Garden Society. It is an American species of no particular virtue, with sticky leaves and small pink and yellow flowers.

— **micrantha.** See *A. macrantha.*

— **nivalis.** A plant from Kashmir about which there remains some doubt. Some authorities refer it to *A. jucunda*, others to *A. fragrans*. It appears to be sparingly in cultivation and may, in time, be properly identified, although little has been seen of it since it received a Preliminary Commendation in 1962. A correction was published in Bulletin No. 38 of the Alpine Garden Society which does, to some extent, clarify the position of this very handsome plant. The large, deep blue, dark-centred flowers are carried on short erect stems.

— **ottonis.** A good species from Greece, with large blue and white flowers on erect, foot-high stems.

— **pyrenaica.** From the Pyrenees — with one station as a garden escape recorded in Britain. On fairly tall stems appear many blue, or lilac-blue flowers.

— **reuteri.** Correctly *A. bertolonii*, q.v.

— **rubicunda.** See *A. barnebeyi.*

— **saximontana.** This is one of the charming dwarf American species. Typically it carries the short-spurred blue and white flowers on 3 to 4 in. stems, but it may grow a little taller in gardens.

- **scopulorum.** A delightful pygmy American in the likeness of *A. jonesii*, but with slightly larger, very 'blue' leaves and large blue flowers on 3 in. stems. To maintain the really dwarf habit it should be given the spartan treatment of a stony scree. From Nevada comes *A. s.* 'Perplexens', which may carry flowers of red, blue, white or red and white, blue and white, or even, occasionally, yellow.
- **sibirica.** From Siberia in 1806, but seldom seen. About a foot in height, it carries on each stem many quite large lilac and white flowers.
- **X stuartii.** This is a hybrid of garden origin and doubtful parentage, but a good garden plant, if perhaps a trifle large for most rock gardens. The large flowers are blue and white and are not unlike those of *A. glandulosa.*
- **viridiflora.** From Siberia and China. Fragrant green and maroon flowers on foot-high stems. Unusual and desirable.

ARABIS. *Cruciferae.* The origin of the name is obscure.

A large genus widely distributed over the Northern hemisphere with a few species in S. America. The genus contains many weeds and a number of good rock garden and alpine house plants. I include a few of the more robust kinds, such as *A. caucasica* (A. albida) because of their great value for growing in sunny walls along with alyssums and aubrietas. In general, they are of the easiest culture, sun-lovers and spring and summer flowering. The pages of a modern flora of Japan reveal the names of several species which might well be valued, but they are not in cultivation and are, therefore, excluded from the following pages.

- **albida.** See *A. caucasica.*
- **alpestris.** European Alps. Tufts of leaves fringed and edged with hairs. White flowers on 6 in. stems.
- **alpina.** Widely spread in Europe, including Britain, on the mountains of Skye. Rosettes of leaves adorned with star-shaped hairs and short or tall stems carrying clusters of white flowers.
- **androsacea.** An enticing alpine cushion plant from the Cilician Taurus. The densely tufted leaves are felted with fine grey hairs. White flowers in short racemes on 2 in. stems. Worthy of alpine house treatment, but will grow well outside in gritty soil.
- **aubrietioides.** From the Cilician Taurus and can be described as a neater, more compact *A. alpina* with clean pink flowers.
- **blepharophylla.** A N. American species and rather short-lived, but easily raised from seed. Tufts of stiff leaves margined by hairs and heads of flowers which may be pink, rose-purple, or white, on 4 to 6 in. stems.
- **bryoides.** From Greece. Hoary tufts of softly hairy tiny leaves and white flowers on inch-high stems. It, and the even more compact

and silkily hairy *A. b.* 'Olympica' are excellent alpine house plants.

— **carduchorum.** See DRABA *gigas.*

— **caucasica.** (A. albida.) Distributed from S.E. Europe to Persia and grown in Britain since 1798. A variable plant, it is grown and liked best in its several named clones, which may carry white, pink, or red flowers, and there is a fine form which is white and double.

— **ciliata.** Pyrenees. Similar to *A. alpestris* but without hairs.

— **collina.** Italy. A rather obscure species, with pink flowers and apparently of little garden value.

— **conringioides.** A little-known species from the Atlas Mountains of N. Africa. Rather loose habit and mauve flowers.

— **cypria.** Endemic to the Island of Cyprus. It has white flowers but little garden value.

— **erubescens.** From the Great Atlas and sounds as if it might be nice, if obtained. It should have round, rather succulent leaves and short stems bearing mauve flowers.

— **ferdinandi-coburgii.** A species from Macedonia, forming mats of grey-green leaves which become green in winter, and white flowers on short stems. It is most commonly grown now in the clone 'Variegata' which is valuable as a compact foliage plant with green and white foliage.

— **hirsuta.** A biennial species from Europe, America and Asia growing to 2 ft. or more with greenish-white flowers of little garden value.

— X **kellereri.** A garden-raised hybrid between *A. bryoides* and *A. ferdinandi-coburgii.* Cushions of ash-grey leaves and heads of white flowers on short stems.

— **lucida.** A mat-forming plant introduced from Hungary in 1790, with green leaves and white flowers. A more garden-worthy plant is *A. l.* 'Variegata', well worth growing for its beautifully variegated foliage.

— **lyallii.** From N.W. America and Canada. It carries pink flowers on foot-high stems.

— **nutans.** See *A. pumila.*

— **petraea.** See CARDAMINOPSIS *petraea.*

— **praecox.** See *A. procurrens.*

— **procurrens.** (A. praecox.) From S.E. Europe. A useful carpeter with spreading, leafy stems from which rise foot-high stems carrying quite large white flowers. Will grow in light shade.

— **pumila.** (A. nutans. A. stellulata.) European Alps, often in damp places. Mats of oval, sometimes toothed leaves and 6 to 9 in. stems carrying heads of white flowers.

— **purpurea.** Endemic to the Island of Cyprus. Similar to *A. aubretioides* but a smaller, neater plant.

— **scopoliana.** Eastern Alps. Not an excitement but a neat alpine with white flowers on 4 in. stems.

— **serpyllifolia.** From sub-alpine rocks in the Pyrenees. Mat-forming, white flowers on short stems.

— **soyeri.** Another species from the Pyrenees, where it occurs together

ARABIS — *continued*

with two, similar, sub-species. White flowers on 6 to 9 in. stems.

— stellulata. See *A. pumila.*

— stricta. Very smooth and shining leaves in low mats and white flowers on short stems. From the Pyrenees.

— sturii. Botanically the name is uncertain and I cannot trace the provenance of the plant going under the name in gardens, but it covers a neat, dark green tuffet of small leaves with large white flowers on 3 in. stems.

— sundermannii. A plant which originated from the Royal Gardens of Bulgaria in 1912, and almost certainly a hybrid. A neat cushion-forming plant with good white flowers on very short stems.

— wilczeckii. Probably a hybrid, but I can trace no authentic record of its provenance. It makes dense tuffets of stiffly hairy leaves and carries white flowers on short stems.

ARCTERICA. *Ericaceae.* From *arktoos,* northern. A monotypic genus of one species, found in Japan and Kamtschatka, sometimes included in the genus PIERIS.

— nana. A prostrate shrublet usually less than 4 in. in height. The thin, woody stems bear glossy, deep green leaves in pairs or in whorls of three. Cream-white, urn-shaped flowers are produced in terminal clusters during the spring. Cool shade and lime-free soil.

ARCTOMECON. *Papaveraceae.* From *arktos,* a bear, and *mekon,* a poppy.

A small genus of probably only three species, two of which occur in the State of Nevada and one in Utah. As they inhabit gypsum deserts they are unlikely to achieve the popularity in British gardens which their beauty undoubtedly merits.

— californicum. In spite of the specific epithet this species does not occur in California, being found only in Nevada. Tufts of blue-green leaves emit smooth, tall, leafless stems, each carrying a corymb of golden poppy flowers. Another species, *A. merriamii,* is said to be even more beautiful, carrying singly large pure white flowers. The third species, *A. humilis,* is possibly the most lovely of the three, being only about 6 to 8 in. tall and carrying umbelliform racemes of large white flowers.

ARCTOSTAPHYLOS. *Ericaceae.* From *arktos,* a bear, and *staphyle,* a grape. Bears are said to eat the fruits.

A genus of twenty or more species, mostly tall shrubs but with a few prostrate members which are valuable ground-covering evergreens for lime-free soil. They thrive in light shade or sun. Two species are found in Europe, the remainder inhabit N.W. America, Mexico and Central America. There is confusion in the nomenclature of the few prostrate species commonly grown.

— **alpina.** See *Arctous alpinus.*
— **californica.** Although there is a plant bearing this name in cultivation the name appears to lack authority and it is probably *A. nevadensis* or a similar species.
— **canadensis.** This, too, may be a misnomer for another prostrate species.
— **hookeri.** A Californian species forming wide mats of shining, evergreen leaves on trailing woody stems. It seldom exceeds 4 in. in height and displays several white, pink-flushed bells on the tips of the shoots in spring.
— **X media.** A hybrid between *A. columbiana* and *A. uva-ursi* growing as a foot-high bush and carrying white, urn-shaped flowers.
— **myrtifolia.** From California. Quite prostrate and having typical white bell-shaped flowers.
— **nevadensis.** Another prostrate Californian with white flowers in small panicles, followed by red berries.
— **nummularifolia.** Similar to *A. myrtifolia.*
— **pumila.** From the warmer parts of California and not as hardy as it might be. Dull green leaves, white or soft pink bells and brown fruits. Very dwarf.
— **uva-ursi.** Native to Scotland, N. Britain and Ireland, as well as N. Europe, Russia, Japan, Greenland and N. America. A creeping alpine evergreen shrub with white, pink-tinted flowers and red berries.

ARCTOUS. *Ericaceae.* Closely related to ARCTOSTAPHYLOS.
— **alpina.** (Arctostaphylos alpina.) Rare British native in the north and also found in N. Europe and Asia and from Greenland to the mountains of New Hampshire in the U.S.A. A deciduous shrublet of only a few inches. Bright-green, toothed leaves and terminal clusters of a few urn-shaped, white, pink-flushed flowers followed by black berries. Lime-free soil and cool conditions.

ARENARIA. *Caryophyllaceae.* From the Latin *arena,* sand, an allusion to the fact that many of the family grow in sandy places, thus the common name of Sandwort.

There exists no little confusion between the genera Arenaria, Alsine and Minuartia and I make no promise that absolute accuracy has been achieved here. Authorities disagree to an extent which leaves a mere gardener bewildered. It would have been no problem to have included more names, but many of them would have been mere duplications, or would identify plants so near to other species that only a botanist would care to differentiate between them. More names of species not in cultivation could also have been included, several of them with tempting descriptions, but it seems pointless to include plants which are not, and are unlikely to be, available in the foreseeable future. Even so, a number of those described below will not be readily available.

Arenarias are mainly spring and early summer flowering, and sun lovers, to be grown in any good, well-drained soil. Some of the high alpine cushion-forming species will naturally be given V.I.P. treatment in an alpine house or a gritty scree. They may be increased by division, cuttings or from seeds.

— **acerosa.** From Anatolia and, if it were in cultivation, would be extremely desirable. It resembles a miniature *A. ledebouriana*, tuffets of fine grey leaves and large white flowers of solid substance on short stems.

— **aculeata.** From N.W. America and said to be a glaucous, aromatic mat with good white flowers.

— **aggregata.** (A. capitata.) From S. France and Italy. Rather loose grey-green mats of foliage and many-flowered heads of white flowers on reasonably short stems.

— **arduinii.** See MINUARTIA *graminifolia*.

— **aretioides.** This is also ALSINE *aretioides* and MINUARTIA *aretioides*. Dense tufts and stemless white flowers.

— **armeriastrum.** A Spanish species and worthwhile. Tufts of grey-haired stems and leaves and short-stemmed heads of white flowers. A smaller and congested version, *A. a.* 'Frigida' is to be found in the southern Spanish Sierras.

— **balearica.** From the Balearic Islands. A mere film of tiny bright green leaves and myriads of white flowers dancing on inch-high stems. For a cool, moist position. It will grow over the face of porous rocks.

— **banatica.** See MINUARTIA *setacea*.

— **bertolonii.** A neat, glossy-leaved mat from the Maritime Alps, Corsica and Sardinia, with good white flowers on short stems.

— **biflora.** From the European Alps. Prostrate, with rather fleshy, tiny leaves and short-stemmed white flowers.

— **caespitosa.** See SAGINA *glabra*.

— **capitata.** See *A. aggregata*.

— **caroliniana.** From N. America, especially in the Pine Barrens of New Jersey. Cushions of dark green leaves and starry white flowers.

— **cephalotes.** From Russia. A curious species with tufts of stems rather woody at the base and clad with tightly adpressed leaves. Sessile heads of white flowers.

— **cerastifolia.** Mats of fine stems with very narrow leaves and white flowers on short stems. From the Pyrenees.

— **ciliata.** Europe, including Britain, to N. America and the Arctic. Mats of creeping, branching stems and umbels of quite sizeable white flowers on 6 in. stems. The form 'Hibernica' can be found on Irish limestones and is said to be distinct.

— ciliolata. From Sikkim, and should be good, if we could get it. Loose mats of hairy stems and leaves and large, solitary white flowers.

— compacta. From N. America. Tuffets of downy leaves and solitary white flowers.

— cretica. From Crete, and a desirable tuft of tiny leaves and several large white flowers on very short stems. On Mount Olympus in Greece can be found *A. c.* 'Stygia', a plant of loose, trailing habit and many small white flowers.

— decussata. See *A. tetraquetra.*

— densa. See *A. gracilis.*

— dianthoides. Almost certainly not now in cultivation, but extremely desirable. From Azerbaijan and form prickly rosettes of grey-green leaves from which rise 12 in. stems carrying heads of large white flowers.

— dyris. From Morocco. Hard, neat tufts of leaves and short-stemmed white flowers.

— erinacea. From hot, dry Spanish mountains. Grey scabs of tightly congested leaves studded with stemless white flowers.

— filifolia. See *A. graminifolia.*

— foliosa. From the Himalaya. Loose tufts of narrow-leaved stems and long-stalked cymes of white flowers.

— franklinii. (A. hookeri) From Western N. America. Narrow leaves and dense heads of white flowers on tallish stems.

— gothica. A rare and occasional native of British limestones. Often annual or biennial, but attractive, forming tiny tufts of glossy, dark green leaves and surprisingly large almost stemless white flowers of solid substance.

— gracilis. (A. densa.) Europe. Creeping stems. White flowers.

— graminifolia. (A. filifolia.) Eastern Europe and on to Kamtschatka. Erect, 9 in. stems and narrow, grey-green leaves and racemes of small, white flowers. More to be valued for foliage than blossom.

— grandiflora. Europe and N. Africa. Wide mats of smooth, bright green leaves and white flowers on loosely branching 9 in. stems.

— gypsophilioides. Another species from the Near East which would be desirable. Leafy stems carry panicles of white flowers having yellow-green, black-pointed sepals.

— hookeri. See *A. franklinii.*

— huteri. Mats of creeping, leafy stems and short stems bearing two or three white flowers. European Alps.

— koriniana. From the Orenburg Desert, wherever that may be! A good cushion plant with grassy leaves and white flowers on 6 in. stems.

— laricifolia. By some authorities now referred to Minuartia, but I retain the more familiar name. Loose tufts of fine green leaves and several starry white flowers on 6 in. stems. A good crevice plant. From the European Alps.

— **ledebouriana.** From Armenia. Another excellent crevice plant with grey-green, narrow leaves in dense tufts and short-stemmed cymes of good white flowers.

— **linnaei.** See SAGINA *saginoides.*

— **lessertiana.** A spiny cushion from the Middle East which would be very desirable if available. Foot-high stems carry large white flowers, and there is said to be an even more entrancing form in the Iranian Alps, *A. l.* 'Minor', which is a very compact version of the type.

— **lithops.** (*A.* pulvinata.) As the specific epithet indicates (it derives from the Greek *lithos,* a stone), this is a tight, dense, hard cushion from Spanish mountains with stemless white flowers and would be as highly cherished as the softer *A. tetraquetra.*

— **longifolia.** From Siberia and Russia. Tufts of very narrow leaves and cymes of funnel-shaped white flowers on fairly tall stems.

— **montana.** From the Alps of Central and Southern Europe and a good garden plant, excellently employed to cascade from narrow crevices with trailing grey-green stems and leaves, the whole mat shrouded in early summer with clouds of large, pure white flowers. An especially fine form is marketed as *A. m.* 'Grandiflora'.

— **musciformis.** See *A. polytrichoides.*

— **nevadensis.** Since this is an annual Spanish species of little merit, the plant which masquerades under its name in gardens must be *A. tetraquetra* 'Granatensis', which see.

— **norvegica.** An annual or biennial species, an occasional British native and extending to the far north of Europe. Of little merit but sometimes grown in screes for the sake of its lax tufts of green leaves and small white flowers.

— **obtusiloba.** A N. American species, not to be confused with the European annual *A. obtusiflora,* which is not worth garden space. Lax tufts of grassy leaves and many white flowers on 6 to 9 in. stems.

— **parnassica.** See MINUARTIA stellata.

— **pestalozzae.** From the mountains of interior Turkey, discovered, I believe, by Dr. Peter Davis. A condensed huddle of tiny rosettes with many white flowers, but dubiously in cultivation.

— **pinifolia.** Usually referred to the genus Alsine, but its provenance and the accuracy of its name appear doubtful. The plant cultivated makes loose tufts of grassy leaves adorned by many white flowers on 6 in. stems.

— **polytrichoides.** (*A.* musciformis.) From the Himalaya, and would be treasured if we had it. It should grow in the form of tight huddles of rigid, pale green leaves starred by stemless white flowers.

— **pulvinata.** See *A. lithops.*

- **pungens.** Another desirable Spaniard forming 6 in. mounds of prickly, spine-tipped leaves with white flowers either solitary or in several-flowered cymes on 9 in. stems.
- **purpurascens.** From the Pyrenees and Spanish mountains. A mat-forming plant which departs from the traditional white flowers of the genus and bears many short-stemmed soft purple flowers.
- **recurva.** Although not recorded in *Flora Europaea* this should be a good species from the Pyrenees with rather thick leaves in close tufts and white flowers on short stems.
- **rigida.** From the Ukraine and the Black Sea area. It does not inspire much enthusiasm by reading the botanical descriptions but might be of interest by virtue of its tufts of rigid stems and leaves.
- **rosanii.** A doubtful name, sometimes listed under Alsine, but the plant as known in gardens is an emerald cushion studded with stemless white flowers.
- **rotundifolia.** There seems to be no botanical reason for separating this from *A. biflora*, but, to the gardener's eye it is sufficiently distinct. Soft mats of rounded leaves and quite sizeable white flowers on short stems.
- **sajanensis.** From Western N. America and Siberia. 4 in. tufts of green leaves on rather rigid stems and good white flowers.
- **saxatilis.** Siberian. Rather woody stems which root as they run to form low mats, and many-flowered racemes of, presumably, white flowers.
- **sedoides.** This is probably more correctly *Cherleria sedoides*, native to the Outer Hebrides where it forms wide cushions, with stemless greenish-yellow flowers.
- **steveniana.** From Armenia, and related to *A. graminifolia*, but not such a worthy plant although similar in appearance.
- **stygia.** A species from Greece making downy, slightly sticky mats studded with white flowers of no striking beauty.
- **tetraquetra.** (A. decussata.) From the Spanish Sierras and related to *A. erinacea*. A most desirable cushion plant for screes or alpine house. Crowded grey-green tiny leaves in four-angled array and stemless white flowers. The variety 'Granatensis' (A. nevadensis) is even more condensed.
- **triflora.** A name of dubious authenticity, but a pretty enough plant from the Pyrenees with stems carrying one to four white flowers over mats of smooth leaves.
- **uliginosa.** A rarity confined to a small area in Teesdale, and correctly *Minuartia stricta*. Of no great garden value and too rare to be collected.
- **verna.** See MINUARTIA *verna*.

AREQUIPA. *Cactaceae*. From the name of the Peruvian city near which the type species grows.

Although it is not the purpose of this Manual to include Cacti, this plant is so resistant to frost that it is worth a trial if obtainable.

— **leucotricha.** Clumps of globular cylinders covered with long spines. From the centre of each globe spring funnel-shaped scarlet flowers. Grow in an alpine house or a very warm, sheltered position outside in sharply gritty soil.

ARETHUSA. *Orchidaceae.* Named for Arethusa, a wood nymph who, pursued by a river god was changed by Artemis into a fountain, an allusion to the habit of the plant.

— **bulbosa.** This dainty orchid, once common in the Pine Barrens of New Jersey, has been collected almost to the point of extinction. Those who are successful with terrestrial orchids may like to attempt it in a shady place in a mixture of loam, sand, peat and sphagnum, but it is not an easy plant to grow. In June it emits 9 in. stems, each carrying one large rose-purple fragrant flower.

ARETIA. See DOUGLASIA.

ARISAEMA. *Araceae.* From the Greek *aris*, or *aron*, arum, and *haima*, blood, used in the sense of 'relationship', i.e. akin to Arum. There are more than one hundred known species of Arisaema, mostly Asiatic, but with a few in tropical Africa. I do not propose to deal exhaustively with the genus, but shall include a few which are, even if sometimes sparingly, in cultivation and available to those who have an interest in Aroids, not necessarily noted for their beauty, but with a fascination all their own which many find irresistible. Those mentioned may be regarded as hardy and like to be grown in soil rich in humus and, generally speaking, in cool conditions. Those who seek more detailed information may find some sixty or more listed in Ohwi's splendid *Flora of Japan.*

— **atrorubens.** See *A. triphyllum.*
— **candidissimum.** From W. China. Probably the most commonly grown species and undeniably one of the most beautiful and desirable. It will take a more open and sunny position than most. From large, flattish tubers rise, rather late in the spring, large, handsome, 3-foliate leaves. The 'flower' is a wide, white, pink and green striped hooded spathe sheltering the phallic spadix typical of the genus.
— **consanguineum.** From the Himalaya. Curious rather than beautiful. The leaves are divided into numerous leaflets. On tall stems appear the green and red-brown spathes, each with a long 'tail'.
— **flavum.** Himalayan. Deeply divided leaves, a yellow spathe and the blade, or spadix, purple with green veins.

- **japonicum.** From Japan. Of the typical two leaves the lower one is larger than the upper. The hooded spathe is purple, or green, with white stripes in the form 'Viridens'.
- **purpureogaleatum.** Whence cometh this strange plant I do not know, but it is probably Himalayan. It makes occasional appearances in British gardens and displays a deep purple-black hood from which depends a slender tail almost a foot in length.
- **ringens.** From sea-coast woodlands in Japan. The bold hood may be green or deep purple.
- **ruwenzoricum.** From the Mountains of the Moon in E. Africa, and might just be hardy in an alpine house. Green and white striped spathes with an elongated tip.
- **sazensoo.** See *A. sikokianum.*
- **sikokianum.** (A. sazensoo.) From Japan. A striking plant with deep purple spathes striped with green and white.
- **tortuosum.** Kashmir and other Himalayan areas, and has been described as 'a green-flowered curiosity', which is fair comment, but it does appeal, with its crinkled leaves and the long brown tails which hang from the spathe.
- **triphyllum.** (A. atrorubens.) A N. American species. Its broad spathe is green outside striped with purple-brown lines within. It has been grown in Britain since the middle of the seventeenth century.

ARISARUM. *Araceae.* From the Greek name, *arisaron*, for *Arisarum vulgare.*

Of the three species only one is of genuine interest to rock gardeners.
- **proboscideum.** From the European Alps. Sometimes called the Mouse-tail Plant and especially fascinating to children but also well liked by adults to whom floral beauty is not the be-all and end-all of gardening. From small tuberous rhizomes spring innumerable spear-shaped leaves on 4 in. stems. In early spring multitudes of long-tailed spathes, olive-green above and whitish beneath, appear to plunge into the foliage like hordes of long-tailed mice. For a shady spot or a north aspect in any soil.

ARISTOLOCHIA. *Aristolochiaceae.* From the Greek *aristos*, best, and *lochia*, childbirth. The shape of the flower recalls the human foetus in the correct position prior to birth.

The genus is a large one, consisting of, mostly, shrubs, many climbing. Only one species is likely to interest alpine gardeners.
- **sempervirens.** From Crete, whence it was introduced in 1727. Not hardy everywhere, but can be grown outdoors in dry soil and a sheltered position. Prostrate, flexous stems set with heart-shaped, pointed glossy green leaves and curiously-shaped 'Dutchman's pipe' purple-brown flowers.

ARMERIA. *Plumbaginaceae.* Latinised form of the old French name *armoires* for a cluster-headed dianthus.

A large genus of sun-loving plants of which some are better fitted for the flower-border than the rock garden. Of the dwarfer kinds there are far more names than plants in cultivation and I have made an admittedly arbitrary choice of those which could find a place in this Manual. To deal in depth with the genus would demand far more space than can be spared here and would also involve the unravelling of a number of botanical tangles, which I feel unqualified to attempt.

— **alpina.** This I have always known as a tidy green hummock with heads of pink flowers on 4 to 6 in. stems, and regarded as a European species. Some authorities now regard it as synonymous with *A. montana,* and the *Flora Europaea* appears to treat it as a sub-species of a sub-species of *A. maritima.* In my old-fashioned way I still call it *A. alpina.*

— **allioides.** This is possibly rather tall for most rock gardens, but it is a handsome species from Spain with globose heads of white flowers on more than foot-high stems.

— **X caesalpina.** A spontaneous hybrid between *AA. caespitosa* and *alpina,* and intermediate between the parents. The flowers may vary in colour from a very soft to a deep pink and, whereas most armerias are spring-flowering, this pretty mule will blossom continuously throughout the summer.

— **caespitosa.** See *A. juniperifolia.*

— **cantabrica.** From the Pyrenees. Green tufts and large heads of rose-pink flowers on 4 to 6 in. stems.

— **cineria.** From Portugal. Narrow, upstanding leaves and hairy flower stems carrying heads of pale pink blossom. There is a form, 'Pubigera', with very hairy grey-green foliage, but otherwise similar.

— **corsica.** I am sure this has no right to a specific name and is only a colour form of *A. maritima,* but it is so well known under this name that I retain it. The flowers are of a curious shade of brick-red, quite distinct from any other form of the common Thrift.

— **elongata.** A Portuguese species, perhaps rather tall for the rock garden, but handsome when carrying its long-stemmed heads of rose-purple flowers.

— **girardii.** See *A. setacea.*

— **juncea.** See *A. setacea.*

— **juniperifolia.** One of the best-loved alpine Thrifts. It comes from Spain and makes tight hummocks of congested narrow dark green leaves studded with almost stemless heads of pink flowers. It has produced one or two notable garden forms, of which the best is that known as 'Bevan's Variety', discovered in the wild by the late Dr. Roger Bevan.

— **laucheana.** See *A. maritima.*

— **maritima.** Our British native Sea Pink, or Thrift, has provided

71

several splendid rock garden plants which are easily grown, colourful and very popular. They all grow into wide, dark green mats of thread-fine leaves and carry, on short, erect stems, large heads of flowers. The best of them are 'Alba', white; 'Laucheana', rich pink; 'Merlin', soft pink; and 'Vindictive', rich glowing red. There was once a form which turned its foliage to gold in the winter months, but this seems to have disappeared.

— montana. From the Alps of Europe and similar to, but sufficiently distinct from the plant which I insist upon retaining as *A. alpina*, and have described under that name.

— multiceps. A Corsican species of merit, with the habit of *A. maritima* and heads of individually large white flowers.

— setacea. (A. juncea.) According to the latest classification this may be *A. girardii*, it has borne a multiplicity of names, but remains a choice dwarf species from the Alps of Europe, particularly in the south, with rose-pink flower heads on 4 in. stems.

— splendens. The name is a slight misnomer, for this is of but modest beauty. It comes from Spain and has heads of purplish flowers on short stems above congested tufts.

— welwitschii. A rarity from Portugal of compact habit and heads of flowers which may be white or pink.

— wilkommii. According to the *Flora Europaea* this Portuguese pygmy should be *A. humilis* subsp. *humilis*. Ignoring such accuracy I remember it under this name when collected many years ago by my late father as a neat, dark-leaved tuft with short-stemmed clusters of rich pink flowers, and wish that I still had it.

ARNICA. *Compositae.* The derivation of the name is obscure, but this is the classical name for the genus.

A small genus with species to be found in Europe and N. America. Few are dwarf enough, or suitable for the rock garden. I describe only a limited number, but several more names can be found in lists of N. American perennial herbs. *A. montana* definitely, and most other species probably, are lime-haters. They all grow easily in full sun and good soil and may be propagated from seed or division. Summer flowering.

— alpina. From N. America and, for those with alkaline soil, the alternative to the European *A. montana*, for it will tolerate lime. Rosettes of rough, broad leaves and 15 in. stems carrying quite large, solitary yellow flowers.

— lessingii. From N. America, 9 in. stems carrying nodding yellow flowers.

— louiseana. N. American and somewhat similar to *A. lessingii*, but with flowers of deeper yellow.

— montana. The Alps of Europe where it is plentiful in sub-alpine meadows. Rosettes of hairy, oval leaves and tall stems carrying the large, richly golden flowers.

— **nana.** Of the provenance of this species I am ignorant. It was shown in 1935 at an Alpine Garden Society exhibition and described as a new plant, but seems to have disappeared since then. If it is as dwarf as its specific epithet implies, it should be worth seeking.

ARONICUM. Plants bearing this generic name are now referred to the genus DORONICUM.

ARRHENATHERUM. *Graminiaceae.* From the Greek *arren*, male, and *anther*, a bristle. The male flowers are furnished with awns.

— **elatius 'Bulbosum Variegatum'.** It is with some trepidation that I include this invasive grass, but, in a position where it cannot become a nuisance, it serves a useful purpose with tufts of handsomely variegated foliage. The type is a British native, also occurring in other parts of Europe, in N. Africa and W. Asia.

ARTEMISIA. *Compositae.* Named in honour of Artemis, the Greek goddess of chastity.

A large genus of shrubs, sub-shrubs, herbaceous perennials and annuals, mostly aromatic and sun-loving. In distribution they are European, American and Asian. The numbers really suitable for rock gardens are limited and some included below may err on the side of being too large. They all have merit as foliage rather than flowering plants.

— **alpina.** See *A. caucasica.*
— **arctica.** A dwarf species from the Olympic Mountains of the State of Washington. Desirable but dubiously available. Grey-leaved mats.
— **assoana.** Prostrate, spreading silver-leaved and delightful. From mountain regions in Central Spain.
— **baumgartenii.** (A. villarsii.) 4 in. tufts of downy grey leaves and unexciting downy flower-heads. From Southern and Central Europe.
— **campestris.** From the European Alps. Foot-high humps of aromatic grey-green leaves.
— **canescens.** I can find no authority for this name, and no longer possess the plant, but when I grew a plant so-called, it was a tumbled mat of filigree silver up to 12 in. in height.
— **caucasica.** (A. alpina.) From Armenia, and another prostrate, spreading, woody stemmed plant with silver-grey leaves.
— **frigida.** From N. America and Siberia. Really a sub-shrub with low tufts of woody stems and leaves covered with silky down. 18 in.

stems carry heads of what are said to be yellow flowers, but I have not seen it in blossom.

— **genipii.** See *A. spicata.*

— **glacialis.** European Alps. Prostrate stems and tufts of silvery, silky leaves.

— **granatensis.** From Spain, and greatly to be desired. Travellers anywhere within reach of the Sierra Nevada please look for its carpets of silver leaves.

— **lanata.** (A. pedemontana.) Central and Southern Europe. Foaming cushions of glistening silver foliage.

— **laxa.** See *A. mutellina.*

— **mutellina.** (A. laxa.) Central and Southern Europe. Only a few inches high, except for the 8 in. flower spikes — which can advantageously be removed — and decorative with silver-grey leaves.

— **nitida.** European and not exciting, but a reasonably attractive grey-green tuft to tuck into a crevice or grow in a Tufa rock.

— **pedemontana.** See *A. lanata.*

— **petrosa.** This is similar to and possibly synonymous with *A. baumgartenii.*

— **pygmaea.** From the State of Nevada and notable for its close cushions of green, not silver, leaves.

— **rupestris.** A European species with pinnate green leaves which are strongly aromatic. It may be anywhere from 6 to 15 in. in height.

— **schmidtiana.** From Japan and too tall for most rock gardens, but the form in cultivation as *A. s.* 'Nana' is a treasure. Rounded rosettes of glistening filigree silver form prostrate mats which never fail to delight.

— **scopulorum.** From Colorado and should be desirable if it were available. Dwarf and silvery.

— **spicata.** (A. genipii.) European Alps. Woody stems clothed with white hairs and silver leaves. Usually no more than 6 in. high.

— **spinescens.** A 9 in. shrub from Western N. America which has, by some authorities been shunted into the genus Picrothamnus. Divided leaves felted with white hairs.

— **stelleriana.** From N.E. Asia and Eastern N. America, and naturalised in one small area of Cornwall. Magnificent mounds of silver foliage, not to be planted too close to smaller plants.

— **vallesiaca.** Strongly aromatic foliage. Prostrate habit, good silver ground cover for full sun.

— **villarsii.** See *A. baumgartenii.*

ARTHROPODIUM. *Liliaceae.* From the Greek *arthron,* a joint, and *podion,* little foot. The pedicels are jointed in the middle.

A small genus of a few species confined to their distribution to Australasia. They succeed in good loam soil to which generous amounts of peat or leafsoil have been added and a sunny exposure.

Propagate by seeds or division of old plants. Spring and summer flowering.

- **candidum.** From New Zealand. Tufts of narrow, grass-like leaves and slender, 9 in. stems carrying forked racemes of white flowers.
- **cirrhatum.** Not dissimilar to the above and also from New Zealand, but a more robust and taller plant. The flower stems can attain 18 to 24 in.
- **millefoliatum.** Tasmanian. From the tufts of grassy leaves spring wiry 6 to 9 in. stems bearing several white or soft lilac flowers.

ARUM. *Araceae.* From *aron*, the Greek name for these poisonous plants.

Mostly grown for their handsome foliage and also for the brightly coloured fruits which some species carry in dense racemes. They will colonise freely in cool or woodland conditions and seem to prefer a soil which is heavy rather than light and is moisture-retentive.

- **corsicum.** See *A. pictum.*
- **creticum.** Nearly all rules have exceptions and *A. creticum* is a handsome species from Crete which prefers, in Britain at any rate, to grow in an open, warm and sunny position. From its stout tubers spring typical arum leaves and flowers with a wide, handsome, clear yellow spathe.
- **italicum** 'Marmoratum'. This is the handsome foliage plant usually offered as *A. i.* 'Pictum', and is much in demand by flower arrangers. It is in leaf by late December with fine, arrow-shaped leaves streaked and marbled with white and yellowish-white. The rather dowdy flower spathes are followed by brilliant red fruits. S. Europe to N. Africa.
- **'Pictum'.** See *A. i. 'Marmoratum'.*
- **pictum.** (A. corsicum.) Deeply cordate green leaves and green spathes marked white. Spain and Corsica.

ASARINA. *Scrophulariaceae.* The Spanish vernacular name for an Antirrhinum.

- **procumbens.** (Antirrhinum asarina.) From Southern France. A trailing plant with sticky stems and softly hairy grey-green leaves and large white 'Snapdragon' flowers tinted with yellow and red. For a cool position, good in a shady wall, spring and summer flowering.

ASARUM. *Aristolochiaceae.* The Latin and Greek name for these plants.

A small genus of interesting plants, lacking floral beauty but with good foliage. Useful for cool corners in the rock garden or for colonising in the shade of trees and shrubs.

- **canadense.** From Eastern N. America and Canada and grown in Britain since 1713. Low tufts of glossy, kidney-shaped leaves springing from a creeping, rhizomatous rootstock and curious, brown, bell-shaped flowers typical of the genus and usually hidden by the leaves.
- **caudatum.** Large heart-shaped leaves and reddish-brown flowers. From California.
- **europaeum.** Europe, and naturalised in a few localities in Britain. Leaves kidney-shaped, often with waved margins, glossy deep green. Dull brown, drooping, inconspicuous flowers.
- **hartwegii.** California. Large and handsome leaves and typical dark coloured bell-shaped flowers. There is a form with white flowers.

ASPERULA. *Rubiaceae.* A diminutive of *asper*, rough. An allusion to the rough stems.

A sizeable genus, natives of Europe, Asia and Australia, of which a few are suitable for rock gardens or alpine houses. They are spring and early summer flowering, prefer positions which are not hot and dry, but exposed to good light. Propagate by division, seeds or cuttings.

- **arcadiensis.** There is considerable confusion between this Grecian species and *A. suberosa*, also from Greece and, frankly, I hesitate to differentiate between them although I believe the plant most commonly cultivated to be *A. suberosa*, which see.
- **asperrima.** A species from the Spanish Sierras, rather tall growing but I am unaware of the flower colour.
- **athoa.** See *A. suberosa*.
- **boissieri.** A species very near to *A. nitida*. It comes from Greece and the stemless flowers may be pink or, occasionally, yellowish.
- **cynanchica.** (A. montana.) An occasional British native, known as Squinancy wort. Weak stems with whorls of small leaves and terminal corymbs of pink or white flowers. Grow in shade.
- **gallioides.** (A. glauca.) Mid-Europe. Small leaves in whorls on 6 to 9 in. stems. Flowers white or pink. Grows on dry hills.
- **glauca.** See *A. gallioides*.
- **gussonii.** In gardens this species from Sicily is often thought to be synonymous with *A. nitida*, but the two should be distinct, even if similar. Dense dwarf tufts of dark, tiny leaves and stemless, sessile heads of flesh-pink flowers. A very good scree plant, and flourishes in Tufa.
- **hexaphylla.** From the Maritime Alps. Loose, floppy cushions of lax stems ending in clusters of starry pearl-pink flowers.
- **hirsuta.** From the Atlas Mountains of N. Africa, and seen at its best in the form *A. h.* 'Longiflora'. Low mats of soft aromatic foliage and fragrant pink flowers.

— **hirta.** From the Pyrenees. Mats of short, lax roots with whorls of smooth green leaves and many clusters of rose-pink, starry flowers. It spreads modestly by means of underground running stems.

— **lilaciflora.** Mediterranean regions and a nice, dwarf, cushion-forming plant with clusters of pink flowers. Its most desirable manifestation is seen in *A. l.* 'Caespitosa' which is condensed into a prostrate pad of foliage, often obscured by the rich pink flowers.

— **lutea.** From Greece and Crete, the best form being *A. l.* 'Alpina', with small yellow flowers among the hoary leaves on the short, ascending stems.

— **montana.** See *A. cynanchica.*

— **nitida.** As said in the description of *A. gussonii,* the two species are often confused in gardens. From the Bithynian Olympus. Short, densely leafed stems tangle into close mats adorned with clusters of pink flowers.

— **odorata.** See *Galium odoratum.*

— **pendula.** From crevices on Spanish mountains. Short stems with whorls of small leaves, green above and hoary beneath. Small pink flowers all the way along the stems.

— **pontica.** From Turkey and Iran and similar to the preceding, but with longer leaves.

— **rupestris.** From Sicily, and described as similar to, but slightly less of an aristocrat than, *A. suberosa.* Probably, if found, best in the alpine house.

— **suberosa.** (A. athoa.) Regarded by many as the gem of the race. It comes from Greece and resents winter wet and we see it at its lovely best when grown in an alpine house. Flat mats of hairy grey leaves smothered in clusters of pink, tubular flowers.

— **taurina.** From S. Europe and a foot high. Erect stems with typically whorled leaves and axillary clusters of white flowers.

— **thessala.** From Greece, and sounds very desirable. Low mats covered with bright pink flowers.

ASPHODELUS. *Liliaceae.* The Greek name for the true asphodel. Most of the species in this handsome family are too large for rock gardens, with the exception of the one species described below.

— **acaulis.** A treasure from the Atlas Mountains of N. Africa. Prostrate clusters of long, narrow leaves centred in the spring or early summer by an almost stemless corymb of funnel-shaped, flesh-pink flowers. Give it a warm, sheltered position, or grow it in the alpine house in deep pots to accommodate the lusty roots.

ASPLENIUM. *Polypodiaceae.* From the Greek *a*, not, and *splen*, the spleen. A reference to the traditional virtue of these ferns in afflictions of the spleen and liver.

Ferns, as such, do not figure prominently in this Manual, but a few of those which are indispensable for the rock garden are included. They are admirably adapted for tucking into cool crevices.

— **adiantum-nigrum.** A British native and a most attractive Spleenwort. The fronds of shining green have a thick texture. It appreciates shade.

— **fontanum.** Although occasionally found wild in Britain, is not a true native, it comes from the central and southern mountains of Europe. A neat, dwarf fern with narrow fronds which are dark green above, pale green beneath. From the western Mediterranean. A charming dwarf fern with glandular, sticky fronds with divisions definitely scalloped.

— **ruta-muraria.** British native. The 2 in. fronds are deeply cut into narrow, grey-green pinnae. The Wall-rue Spleenwort may not be a beauty, but it never fails to charm.

— **septentrionale.** Native of Britain. Tiny, leathery fronds, deeply cleft.

— **trichomanes.** The Maidenhair Spleenwort is one of the nicest small ferns for rock gardens. The fronds have black stems and many opposite pairs of pinnae. A British native.

— **viride.** Also a native of Britain with small fronds of oval green pinnae.

ASTELIA. *Liliaceae.* From the Greek *a*, without, and *stele*, a pillar. Some species are epiphytic, depending upon others for support.

A small genus, mostly confined to New Zealand. Certainly not generally available, but I include a few which would be desirable alpine house plants if obtainable. Those described grow in subalpine scrub and pasture land, often in damp conditions.

— **graminea.** Tufts of narrow leaves, male flowers maroon, female ones greenish. Bright orange berries follow the flowers.

— **nervosa.** Probably synonymous with *A. cockaynei.* Tufts of narrow leaves up to 2 ft. in length. The heads of flowers may be obscured by the foliage, but the clusters of orange-red fruits are prominent.

— **petriei.** Bold clumps of broad, long, pointed leaves, silvery beneath and heads of greenish flowers followed by orange fruits.

— **skottsbergii.** Like a smaller version of *A. petriei.*

ASTER. *Compositae.* From the Latin *aster*, a star. An allusion to the shape of the flower.

This enormous genus presented no small problem in the context of this Manual. I have been hard-put to decide whether to put in all that could possibly be considered suitable for rock gardens, or should I be selective? Finally, when confronted by many enticing descriptions of species unlikely to be obtainable, I decided to be selective. Even so, some are included which may be over-large for small rock gardens — but most rock gardeners also have a flower border. For others we may yet have to await their introduction — or re-introduction. All those listed may be regarded as sun-lovers, likely to be content in any good and well drained soil. Generally speaking they flower from early summer onwards.

— acaulis. From the high Andes of S. America and said to be dwarf and very beautiful. I include this, and one or two other Andean species in the hope that one or other of the expeditions which now reach up into those delectable mountains may send home seeds.

— alpigenus. See *A. pulchellus*.

— alpinus. From the European Alps and one of the most deservedly popular rock garden asters. Spreading tufts with rather narrow leaves and large purple, gold-centred flowers carried singly on 9 in. stems. There is a good albino, and some selected clones, one of which, *A. a*. 'Beechwood' is outstandingly beautiful.

— bellidiastrum. See BELLIDIASTRUM *michellii*.

— diplostephioides. The original plant, introduced from Sikkim in 1882, appeared to differ little from *A. subcaeruleus*, but subsequent introductions in 1949, by Ludlow and Sherriff from Bhutan, appear to be distinct. It is a good purple, golden-eyed aster with bold flowers on rather tall stems.

— ensifolius. See INULA *ensifolia*.

— falconeri. From Kashmir and would seem to be eminently desirable if obtainable, with very large flowers with narrow rays of violet-blue surrounding a golden-yellow disk.

— farreri. Usually said to be closely allied to *A. diplostephioides*, but Farrer says in his field notes, and I quote: "The most glorious Aster of the year, a towering, touzle-headed person of a thousand narrow rays of richest violet flopping from a central disk of vermilion-orange." Even allowing for Farrer's known exaggerations, one wonders if we have the true plant in gardens?

— flaccidus. (*A. purdomii*.) From N. China and allied to *A. alpinus*. More hairy leaves and slightly taller stems differentiate it from the European species.

— forrestii. See *A. soulei limitaneus*.

— heterochaeta. Again similar to *A. alpinus*, from the Altai Mountains, the Himalaya and Tibet. Large, solitary, short-stemmed flowers of rich violet-blue.

— himalaicus. From Sikkim. Hairy stems and leaves and narrow-rayed purple-blue flowers. Varies from 6 to 15 in. in height.

— likiangensis (or *lichiangensis*). From Yunnan and again one wonders if we have the best form in cultivation. Collectors' original praises

79

are not upheld by the plants we see in gardens. It comes somewhere in the *A. diplostephioides* group, with, too often, rather dowdy purple flowers on 12 in. stems.

— natalensis. From the Drakensburg Mountains of S. Africa, and hovers uneasily between the genera Aster and Felicia. It is, perhaps rather surprisingly, completely hardy and runs about modestly to form mats of grey-green, hairy leaves surmounted by clear blue, golden-eyed daisy flowers on 4 to 6 in. stems. It appreciates a warm, sunny position and, essentially, well drained soil.

— oreophilus. A Chinese species and variable. In its best forms it should be attractive, dwarf and bear purple-blue flowers on short stems. In gardens it often disappoints by being gawky and too tall for the rock garden.

— pappei. One feels that this S. African shrublet ought really to be a Felicia — which it well may be, but it is now so well known as an aster that I describe it here. Not hardy everywhere or always, it is so easily propagated from seeds or cuttings that it is always worth a gamble for the sake of its summer-long displays of clear blue daisy flowers on rounded, 12 to 15 in. bushes.

— pulchellus. (Aster alpigenus. OREASTRUM alpigenum.) From the mountains of Wyoming and sounds desirable. Tufts of narrow leaves and 6 in. stems each carrying one large purple-blue flower.

— purdomii. See *A. flaccidus*.

— pygmaeus. There are occasional mouth-watering references to this species from the Canadian Arctic and it is described in Porsild's 'Illustrated Flora of the Canadian Arctic Archipelago' as having creeping rhizomes producing lilac flowers with a dense, white, woolly involucrum.

— pyrenaeus. Handsome in sub-alpine meadows of the Pyrenees, but its two-foot stems are too tall for most rock gardens, even for the sake of the lilac-blue flowers carried in corymbs.

— scopulorum. Botanists of its native N. America have consigned this species to IONACTIS alpina. Wherever it finally settles, were it available, it would be desirable. Tufts of ash-grey, very hairy leaves and 6 in. stems each carrying one large violet-blue flower.

— souliei limitaneus. Having obeyed the authorities and referred *A. forrestii* to this spot, I have a guilty feeling that I should have followed my inclinations towards common usage and retained the better-known name for such a good plant. From Tibet and Yunnan, with large violet-purple flowers, orange-disked on fairly tall stems.

— stracheyi. From the Himalaya. Prostrate tufts of leaves and short stems bearing narrow-rayed, soft lilac-blue flowers.

— subcaeruleus. The provenance, as well as the validity of this plant is uncertain. It is confused in gardens with *A. diplostephioides* but, as we know it, is a mat-forming plant with solitary, pale-blue flowers on 15 in. stems.

— tibeticus. The Himalaya and Tibet. Resembles *A. alpinus* in habit.

The bright blue flowers have narrow rays and may be carried singly or in twos and threes.

— **vahlii.** Having seen several comparatively worthless plants under this name, I cannot believe that they were the true species from S. America and the Falkland Islands, which should resemble *A. alpinus* in habit with large purple-blue flowers.

— **xylorrhiza.** This species from Idaho has been in cultivation but appears to have disappeared — one hopes only temporarily — for it is a dwarf with good flowers shading from lavender to violet.

— **yunnanensis.** The provenance is obvious and this good plant bears large flowers with broad, clear-blue rays on short stems. There are cultivated forms or hybrids which are handsome, but too tall for the rock garden.

ASTERANTHERA. *Gesneriaceae.* From the Latin *aster*, a star, and *anthera*, anther.

The anthers are joined in a star-like manner.

— **ovata.** It is debatable whether this Chilean shrub should find a place in this Manual, but many alpine gardeners grow it in pans in their alpine houses, and it is hardy out of doors in protected places, in woodland, lime-free soil and a cool or north aspect. It will climb or scramble, given the opportunity, is evergreen with small, leathery dark green oval or rounded leaves, toothed at the margins, and tubular, rich red flowers in high summer.

ASTERISCUS. *Compositae.*

— **maritimus.** From Morocco and dubiously hardy, but worth attempting in a warm, sunny and sheltered spot, or, more satisfactorily, in the alpine house. It should probably be referred to the genus ODONTOSPERMUM. Short-stemmed golden flowers appear in profusion over prostrate tufts of leaves.

ASTILBE. *Saxifragaceae.* From the Greek *a*, without, and *stilbe*, brightness, a reference to the dullness of the leaves of the type species.

A genus of a few species found in Asia and the U.S.A., and many garden forms, clones and hybrids. Not many are dwarf enough for the rock garden, but those which are suitable are very desirable, and like to be given cool soil and a not too hot position and are propagated by seeds or division. Summer flowering.

— **chinensis.** The type plant was introduced from China in 1892 and can grow to a height of at least 2 ft., but the form 'Pumila' is the one liked by rock gardeners. It carries thick spikes up to 9 in. high of mulberry-red flowers crowded in a dense raceme.

- X 'Crispa'. Under this name shelter several named hybrids, probably claiming *A. simplicifolia* as one parent. They are all dwarfs, with curiously restricted and crinkled foliage and short spires of flowers ranging in colour from white to deep pink. Three names to be found in catalogues are 'Gnome', 'Perkeo' and 'Kobald'.

- glaberrima. For several years a dainty little astilbe has been in circulation and considerable demand. It came from Japan and is known both as *A. g.* 'Saxosa' and *A. g.* 'Saxatilis'. It would appear that neither name is valid and that it should be correctly *A. japonica* 'Terrestris', but it is now so familiar to us under the invalid name that I retain it. A perfect miniature, it forms neat tufts of finely dissected bronzed leaves and carries elegant 6 in. sprays of small pink flowers.

- simplicifolia. The type is Japanese, but is rarely grown, its place in gardens being taken by an ambiguous selection of so-called forms, of which the best known is *A. s.* 'Rosea'. This is the dwarfest and most suitable for the rock garden, growing to a height of rather less than one foot, with elegant plumes of small rich pink flowers over dainty foliage. A particularly good hybrid is named 'Willy Buchanan'. like all the plants which originated in the Scottish garden of that great plantsman, it is excellent. Crimson-tinted dissected foliage and sprays of creamy-white flowers on 9 in. stems. It, too, may have come from *A. simplicifolia.*

ASTRAGALUS. *Leguminosae.* The Greek name for some leguminous plants.

Widely distributed over the Northern Hemisphere, mostly in temperate regions, are more than one thousand species of Astragalus. Of the few which are either suitable or available for the rock garden, all are avid sun-lovers, not difficult to grow, but bitterly resentful of any root disturbance once established. There are many others which might prove more temperamental, but are greatly to be desired if only they could be introduced. Propagate by seeds or by cuttings. Summer flowering.

The pages of Farrer, Sampson Clay and the indices of the Alpine Garden Society's Bulletin contain so many names that one is in despair to decide what to include or what to omit. Owing to their almost complete unavailability I have taken the coward's way out and omit almost all.

- alpinus. Northern Europe, including Britain. A prostrate plant branching from the base with woody stems and leaves of many leaflets. Purple-blue flowers in short, cylindrical racemes.

- danicus. Also occasionally British, and sometimes identified as *A. hypoglottis.* Somewhat similar in appearance to *A. alpinus.* Flowers violet-blue with a yellow-white base, in dense oval heads. A form is known in which the flowers are wholly cream-white.

ASTRAGALUS — *continued*
— hypoglottis. See *A. danicus.*

ASTRANTIA. *Umbelliferae.* The derivation of the name is obscure, but may be an allusion to the star-like flower heads.
A small genus of hardy perennial plants, natives of Europe and Asia. All but one are too tall for the rock garden.
— minor. Europe, cultivated since 1686. 6 to 9 in. stems with lobed, sharply toothed leaves. The small flowers are white and are surrounded by white involucral bracts as is common to the family. A neat but not gaudy plant for cool soil and a sunny position.

ASTROCARPUS. *Resedaceae.* From the Greek *astron*, a star, and *karpos*, a fruit. A reference to the shape of the fruits.
A genus of possibly only two species. Hardy and not fussy as to soil or situation.
— sesamoides. Distributed from Italy to Portugal. 9 in. stems rise from rosettes of narrow leaves and carry small clusters of white flowers. Flowers from spring until autumn.

ASYNEUMA. *Campanulaceae.* Derivation of the name unknown. A small genus closely related to both CAMPANULA and PHYTEUMA, and of little interest to rock gardeners. Of the eighteen or so species, natives mostly to S. Europe, few are in cultivation, or particularly desired.

ATHAMANTA. *Umbelliferae.* After Mount Athamas, in Sicily, where some species of the genus are to be found.
Two species, *A. cretensis*, from Crete, and *A. macedonica*, from the Balkans, are occasionally seen in cultivation. They are not traffic-stoppers, but have pleasant low mounds of silvery, deeply-dissected foilage and carry clusters of fragrant cream-white flowers. They will both appreciate a hot, dry situation in full sun and sharply drained soil and would be likely to suffer without protection during a long, cold and wet winter. They make good specimen plants in an alpine house.

ATRACTYLIS. *Compositae.* Derivation uncertain.
— caespitosa. A small, thistle-like plant from high in the mountains of Algeria. The flowers are of little value, but the narrow, spine-toothed leaves are sometimes webbed over with fine grey hairs and gathered into curled rosettes. Give it warmth and sunshine if obtained.

ATRAGENE. See the genus CLEMATIS.

AUBRIETA. *Cruciferae.* Named in honour of Claude Aubriet
(1668-1743), a French botanical artist.
There are a dozen or more species of Aubrieta, distributed over a
wide area extending from Sicily to Iran. Few of them are cultivated
except in botanical gardens or in the collections of avid collectors.
Their great garden value is found among the many forms and
hybrids, most of which probably arose from selected seedlings of
A. deltoidea, with the possible admixture of one or other of such
species as *AA. erubescens, kotschyi, libanotica* and *olympica.* It
would be pointless to append in this Manual a long list of garden
names; all of which can be found adequately described in alpine
plant catalogues. I shall content myself with brief descriptions of a
few of the species. The garden forms are all spring-flowering and
lovers of sun and lime. They benefit from being cut back hard
after flowering and are invaluable for an early display, especially
when grown in walls or crevices between stones in the rock garden.
Strains of mixed seedlings are often offered, but the best results
are achieved by selecting named forms. They can be increased by
division or by cuttings, but do not come true from seed. In many
catalogues they may still be found under the erroneous spelling
Aubrietia.
  — deltoides. From Sicily to Asia Minor. Tufts of wedge-shaped, toothed
    roughly hairy leaves. Variable in colour of flowers from lilac to red-
    purple.
  — kotschyi. Tufted habit, roughly hairy green toothed and wedge-
    shaped leaves and flowers white to soft lilac. The mountains of
    Iran.
  — libanotica. Lebanon. Close tufts of grey-green leaves and short, few-
    flowered racemes of flowers which are variable in colour.
  — olympica. From Asia Minor and usually a dwarf tuft, but can
    develop taller stems. Leaves only slightly toothed, soft purple
    flowers.

AURINIA. See the genus ALYSSUM.

AZORELLA. *Umbelliferae.* From the Greek *a,* without, and
zoraleos, scaliness, but the derivation is slightly dubious.
There is much confusion as to the correct placing of Azorella, most
authorities now incline to include them in the genus BOLAX and,
I have dealt with them under that name, which see.

BABINGTONIA. See the genus BAECKIA.

BACCHARIS. *Compositae.* From Bacchus, the god of wine. It is supposed that the roots were sometimes used to add a spicy flavour to wine.
A genus of American plants, mostly shrubs or trees, but with some herbs. Only one species seems to fall within the scope of this Manual, and of this, little seems to be known in cultivation.

— magellanica. A dwarf shrub for which I can find no valid description, except that it comes from the southern tip of the American continent and flowers at Christmas-time.

BAECKIA. *Myrtaceae.* Named for Abraham Baeck, Swedish physician and a friend of Linnaeus.
A genus of evergreen shrubs, mostly Australian.

— camphorosmae. (Babingtonia camphorosmae.) A neat shrub, less than 2 ft. in height with crowded, rounded leaves on the short branches. Racemes of clustered, small white or pink flowers. It will relish a warm protected position.

BALAUSTION. *Myrtaceae.* Derivation uncertain.

— pulcherrimum. A prostrate, evergreen shrub from Western Australia with waxy scarlet bell-shaped flowers. Rare in cultivation and will need care and a warm, sheltered situation and probably with a preference for peaty, lime-free soil.

BALLOTA. *Labiatae.* The Greek name for black horehound, one of the species of this genus.

— **pseudodictamnus.** This Cretan sub-shrub is maybe a little large for most rock gardens, but it is frequently grown by alpine gardeners for the sake of its mounded 12 to 15 in. bushes of entangled stems clothed in rounded leaves densely felted with white wool. The white, purple-flecked flowers are carried on 18 in. stems in many-flowered whorls during the summer. There is another species, *B. saxatilis*, which might be a good rock garden plant, but it comes from Upper Galilee and is unlikely to be very hardy.

BALSAMORRHIZA. *Compositae.* Rather obscurely derived from *Balsamina* (Impatiens) and *rhiza*, a root.

— **hookeri.** From Central N. America. From a tuberous root rise rosettes of white-haired leaves and solitary heads of yellow composite flowers on stems varying from 4 to 12 in. tall. Any good soil and full sun.

BARBAREA. *Cruciferae.* Known in ancient times as the Herb of St. Barbara.

— **vulgaris.** An occasional British native and far from being an alpine plant, but the form with double yellow flowers on 15 in. stems is sometimes grown and appreciated, and *B.v.* Variegata has handsome rosettes of green leaves marbled with cream blotches.

BARTSIA. *Scrophulariaceae.* Named in honour of the Prussian botanist, John Bartsch.

— **alpina.** A native of European Alps and occasionally found on British mountains. Not very distinguished, but worth growing for the sake of its purple flowers, carried between purplish bracts in short spikes. *B. spicata*, from the Pyrenees, is similar, but rather taller.

BAUERA. *Baueraceae.* Named in honour of Franz and Ferdinand Bauer, Austrian botanical artists of note.

— **rubioides.** From Tasmanian mountains. At low elevations it is a tall shrub, but in an alpine environment becomes a prostrate, twiggy shrub with wiry stems and opposite, trifoliate leaves. Quite large flowers, resembling those of the dog rose are carried on single stems in clusters at the ends of the branches. The white or pink petals surround a central disk of yellow stamens. It will need care, warmth and probably lime-free soil.

BELLIDIASTRUM. *Compositae.*

— **michelii.** (Aster bellidiastrum.) European Alps. Like an enlarged and robust common daisy. The ray florets of the inch-wide white flowers may be flushed with pink.

BELLIS. *Compositae.* From the Latin *bellus*, pretty.

Although they occasionally make an appearance on rock gardens, the forms of *B. perennis*, the common daisy, have no proper place there. In a more appropriate position I like dainty little soft pink 'Dresden China' and its albino counterpart, 'White Pearl'. I can live without the monstrous 'Double Daisies' used for bedding, but am amused by the *B. p. prolifera*, the curious Hen and Chicken Daisy, which carries a ruff of leaf rosettes around the flower head. If you grow any of the forms of *B. perennis*, it is worth remembering that they benefit from being lifted, divided and replanted into new soil every other year.

— **caerulescens.** See *B. rotundifolia.*

— **rotundifolia** 'Caerulescens'. From N. Africa. Similar in appearance to *B. perennis*, but the ray florets are fewer, broader and soft blue in colour.

— **sylvestris.** From southern France. Looser growing and taller than *B. perennis.* The flower heads often droop and the tips of the white ray florets are crimson.

BELLIUM. *Compositae.* From *Bellis*, daisy.

Only technical botanical differences separate this genus from Bellis.

— **crassifolium.** From Corsica and Sardinia. Not exciting, but a daisy worth growing. Rosettes of rather thick, glossy leaves and whitish-yellow flowers on 6in. stems.

— **minutum.** *(B. rotundifolium.)* Completely prostrate pads of tiny leaves and white daisies on inch-high stems. Good for paving. From the Levant.

— **rotundifolium.** See *B. minutum.*

BERARDIA. *Compositae.* Named in honour of M. Berard, a professor of chemistry at Montpelier.

— **subacaulis.** From W. Europe and the only species in its genus. It is said to be difficult to grow. Rosettes of large, very woolly leaves centred by a head of white flowerlets.

BERBERIS. *Berberidaceae.* The Latinised form of the Arabian name for the fruits.

Of this large and important family, very few indeed can be considered rock garden plants and it is with slight misgivings that I include even the few mentioned below.

- empetrifolia. From Chile and Patagonia. Given plenty of space this low-growing, spreading species is very ornamental. It may grow to 18 in. in height and spread over a generous square yard. Evergreen, with small, dark green leaves on the arching branches, yellow flowers and black berries.
- X stenophylla 'Corallina Compacta'. A neat, rounded bush seldom exceeding a foot in height. Evergreen, coral-red buds expanding to yellow flowers. .This is the plant sometimes listed as *B. irwinii* 'Corallina Compacta'. *B. X. irwinii* and its cultivars are now all referred to *B. X. stenophylla.*
- 'Nana'. A compact shrub with golden flowers.
- thunbergii 'Atropurpurea Nana'. Neat, low, rounded bushes with rich purple foliage and usable as a dwarf rock garden shrub.

BERGENIA. *Saxifragaceae.* Named for Karl August von Bergen (1704-1760), one-time professor at Frankfurt.

I stretched a point by including Berberis in this Manual, but, although many rock gardeners grow Bergenias (sometimes called Megasea), they are neither alpine nor really fitted for the rock garden, with the possible exception of *B. stracheyi*, which can keep itself to a height of 6 to 9 in., comes from the Western Himalaya and carries pink flowers in March. It has a good alpine form in *B. s.* '*Alba*' whose snow-white flowers are effectively displayed against the bronzed leaves.

BERTEROA. *Cruciferae.* Named for Carlo Giuseppe Bertero (1789 -1831), Italian physician and botanist, drowned at sea during a voyage from Tahiti to Chile.

A small genus allied to, and sometimes included in, ALYSSUM. Seldom grown, but the two undernoted species may sometimes be encountered. Treatment as for Alyssum.

- incana. Europe to Eastern Asia. Tufts of narrow leaves grey with fine hairs and a dense raceme of white flowers on short stems.
- mutabilis. Armenia and Transcaucasia. Narrow, sharply pointed leaves and loose racemes of white flowers on 9 in. stems.

BESSEYA. *Scrophulariaceae.* Derivation unknown.

A rather obscure genus closely related to, and sometimes included in SYNTHYRIS. Natives of W. N. America.

— alpina. Clumps of leathery, scalloped leaves and short spires of purple-blue flowers.

— arizonica. Clumps of rounded, scalloped leaves and rather long, slender racemes of purple flowers.

BETULA. *Betulaceae.* The Latin name for this genus.

— nana. This is the only species applicable to rock gardens. Native of Britain and other northern temperate regions, it makes a straggling low bush of entangled stems. The Scottish 'Glengarry' form is distinct, and there is a microform from Norway which never exceeds a few inches in height.

BIARUM. *Araceae.* A name used by Dioscorides for a related plant.

A small genus of tuberous rooted herbs, mostly native to Mediterranean regions and hardy in light shade and well nourished soil rich in humus. They do not have beautiful flowers, but have the same strange attraction possessed by so many aroids.

— carratracense. From Spain, with short, spathulate leaves and flowers with an ephemeral pink spadix which is followed by clusters of red berries.

— davisii. Discovered on Crete by Dr. Peter Davis. Oval leaves with undulating margins rest in clusters on the ground and, in the autumn, appear erect, tiny arum flowers of pinkish-brown, with the broad spathe hanging over a short spathe. It dispenses a powerful and decidedly unpleasant odour when in blossom.

— tenuifolium. Common in Mediterranean regions with chocolate coloured flowers which appear before the leaves.

BIEBERSTEINIA. *Geraniaceae.* Named in honour of the sonorously entitled Friedrich August Frieherr Marschall von Bieberstein (1768-1826), author of the *Flora Taurico-Caucasica* and other botanical works.

— odora. From the Altai Rounded, pinnate leaflets, deeply toothed and racemes of yellow flowers on foot-high stems in spring. Probably best in the alpine house.

— orphanidia. Greece. 12 to 18 in. stems rise from a tuberous rootstock. Hairy pinnatisect leaves and clusters of two or three pink flowers in a dense spike. Hardy, but will appreciate a well-chosen, sheltered position.

BISCUTELLA. *Cruceriferae.* From the Latin *bis*, twice, and *scutella*, a small flat dish. An allusion to the form of the seed pods.

A small genus of little horticultural importance with the possible exception of the species described below.

— frutescens. Spain and Morocco. Large rosettes of scalloped, velvety leaves and fairly tall stems bearing clouds of golden flowers. A cliff dweller demanding austerity and full sun.

BLETIA hyacinthina. See BLETILLA *striata*.

BLETILLA. *Orchidaceae*. A diminutive of BLETIA, another genus of terrestrial orchids, which it resembles.

— striata. (Bletia hyacinthina.) A Chinese near-hardy terrestrial orchid for light shade and soil rich in humus. Foot-high stems carry racemes of large rose-purple flowers in mid to late summer. There is also a rare and lovely form with pure white flowers.

BLUMENBACHIA. *Loasaceae*. Named in honour of Johann Friederich Blumenbach (1752-1840), professor of medicine at Göttingen.

— hieronymi. S. America. Trailing habit and light green leaves which are covered with stinging hairs. Starry white flowers with five petals which curve, partially concealing the scarlet centre of the blossom. Not long-lived, but seeds freely and asks for a warm and sheltered position.

BOLAX. *Umbelliferae*. Derivation obscure.

— gummifera. This has also been known as *Azorella caespitosa* and *A. glebaria*. The two genera are greatly confused. Iron-hard hummocks of congested rosettes composed of hard, leathery, green leaves. The minute yellowish flowers are carried in stemless umbels in the centre of the rosettes. For stony, sunny screes or the alpine house. Not a floral beauty, but a fascinating cushion plant, from the Falklands Islands, Magellan and Chile.

BOLOPHYTA. See the genus PARTHENIUM, in addenda.

BONGARDIA. *Berberidaceae*. Named in honour of August Gustav Heinrich Bongard (1786-1839), a German botanist who worked extensively in Russia.

— chrysogonum. The only species in its genus and native to Syria and Iran. A curious and rather beautiful plant with a tuberous root from which spring leaves of many leaflets, green, marked with reddish-purple. Foot-high stems carry loose and graceful panicles of quite large golden flowers in spring. Hardy if given protection from too much winter wet, and light, sandy soil.

BORAGO. *Boraginaceae.* Derivation uncertain, but probably from the Latin *burra*, a hairy garment, an allusion to the hairy leaves.

— laxiflora. The only species really admissible to a rock garden, and even this is frowned upon by some who find its modestly invasive habits annoying. From Corsica, forming lax tufts of coarsely hairy leaves and lax, branching stems carrying gentian-blue flowers throughout the summer. About a foot or a little more in height and seeds itself freely.

BOYKINIA. *Saxifragaceae.* Named in honour of Dr. Samuel Boykin (1786-1846), an American botanist.
A small genus, native to N. America and Japan, of which only the one species described below is seriously sought after by rock gardeners.

— jamesii. One of the famous plants of Pike's Peak in Colorado. Squat tufts of kidney-shaped, rather leathery, coarsely-toothed leaves and 6 in. stems carrying racemes of carmine-crimson flowers in early summer. Often sparse flowering in cultivation, and should be grown in austere conditions. A cool crevice or the alpine house, preferably but not essentially, in lime-free soil.

BRACHYCOME. *Compositae.* From the Greek *brachys*, short, and *kome*, hair.
A genus of Australasian plants (with one species in Tropical Africa), few of which are of an alpine character, but one or two are drifting in from the Australian mountains. They prefer dry, sunny positions and sharp drainage. Summer flowering. Propagate by seeds.

— nivalis. Dwarf and tufted with soft foliage and short-stemmed white or soft blue daisy-shaped flowers.

— rigidula. Low clumps of glossy, divided leaves and lavender daisy flowers on 3 in. stems.

— scapigera. Neat tufts of toothed leaves and wiry stems of 6 in. or so carrying white flowers.

BRACHYTROPIS. See the genus POLYGALA.

BRAYA. *Cruciferae.* Named in honour of Count Francisci Gabrieli von Bray (1765-1831), a German botanist.

- alpina. European Alps. Crowded rosettes of slightly toothed leaves and short stems carrying dense corymbs of white flowers which flush purple as they age.
- pinnatifida. Pyrenees. Fragrant white flowers in a dense raceme on short stems. Both species easily grown in gritty soil and sun.

BRIGGSIA. *Gesneriaceae.* Named for Munro Briggs Scott (1889-1917), a botanist at Kew Gardens from 1914 to 1917;
A small but exciting genus offering a challenge to the skilled cultivator and best regarded as plants for the alpine house or cool greenhouse. Few are in cultivation. They come from China, the Himalaya and Yunnan. Conditions agreeable to Ramondas offer the best chance of success.
- agnesiae. Has been described as one of the best of the many good plants brought from Yunnan by George Forrest. Rosetted hairy leaves, silver above and tawny beneath and large crimson flowers singly on slender 3 in. stems.
- amabilis. See. *B. kurzii.*
- forrestii. Large rosettes of green leaves and purple flowers, sometimes in pairs.
- kurzii. (B. amabilis.) Flat rosettes ot coarsely hairy green leaves and large, foxglove-shaped flowers which may be white, yellow or orange.
- longifolia. Similar to the above but the yellow flowers are flushed with purple and crimson at the margins.
- musicola. First found in Bhutan, growing on the mossy trunks of pine trees. Rosettes of pale green leaves with an overlay of silvery hairs. Soft yellow flowers loosely carried on arching stems.
- penlopii. Apple-green leaves in ramonda-like rosettes. Tubular deep yellow flowers marked with orange in the throat.

BROSSARDIA. *Cruciferae.* Derivation unknown.
- papyracea. A rare plant from Kurdistan, probably not in cultivation, but should be acquired. Dwarf habit and curving stems carrying terminal racemes of purple flowers. A form with white flowers has also been recorded.

BRUCKENTHALIA. *Ericaceae.* Named in honour of Samuel and Michael von Bruckenthal, Austrian noblemen.
I have deliberately excluded the genera CALLUNA and ERICA from this Manual. To deal with them competently would demand a separate volume and they are lengthily and adequately described elsewhere. I include Bruckenthalia because it is such a useful dwarf

shrub with which to bridge the gap between the flowering periods of heathers.

— **spiculifolia.** The only species in its genus and a native of S.E. Europe and Asia Minor. It demands the lime-free soil chosen by most of the *Ericaceae* and is easily grown in conditions which please heathers. 6 to 9 in. compact bushes and crowded terminal racemes of bell-shaped pink flowers from May to July.

BRUNONIA. *Goodenoviaceae.* In honour of Robert Brown (1773-1858), a famous Scottish botanist.

— **australis.** A delightful plant from Australia and Tasmania. From mats of grey and woolly leaves rise 9 in. stems carrying sky-blue flowers. Grow in gritty, humus-rich soil and a warm position.

BRYANTHUS. *Ericaceae.* From the Greek *byron*, a moss, and *anthos*, a flower.

— **gmelinii.** (B. musciformis.) From Japan and Kamtschatka. An evergreen, mat-forming plant for lime-free soil and a shaded or cool, north-facing position. Wiry, interlaced stems and tiny narrow leaves and short racemes of pink, bell-shaped flowers in spring and early summer. Increased by cuttings or seeds.

— **musciformis.** See *B. gmelinii.*

BRYOCARPUM. *Primulaceae.* A monotypic genus, allied to SOLDANELLA and found in Sikkim, Bhutan and Tibet. Although not uncommon in nature, it has proved difficult to grow and may not now survive in cultivation.

— **himalaicum.** A deciduous plant resting during the winter as a bud from which, in the spring, unfold a few long leaves, pale green above and grey-green beneath. Pendant, purple-blue soldanella-like flowers are carried singly on slender, hairy stems about 6 in. tall.

BUPHTHALMUM SALICIFOLIUM. *Compositae.* From the Greek *bous*, an ox and *ophthalmos*, an eye, in allusion to the appearance of the flower. Low, bushy habit and many heads of yellow flowers.

BUPLEURUM. *Umbelliferae.* From the Greek *boupleuros*, meaning ox-rib, a name for another plant.

— **angulosum.** From the Pyrenees. Tufts of long, narrow leaves and stems up to a foot high carrying umbels of small flowers surrounded by yellow-green bracts.

— **falcatum.** Pyrenees. Stiff, foot-high stems and heads of attractive yellow flowers and bracts.

BUPLEURUM — *continued*

- gramineum. See *B. petraeum.*
- multinerve. See *B. nipponicum.*
- nipponicum. (B. multinerve). Japan. Leafy, foot-high stems and umbels of yellow-green, cup shaped flowers.
- petraeum. (B. gramineum). Dense tufts of grassy leaves and 6 to 8 in. stems bearing umbels of small yellow flowers. Central Europe.
- ranunculoides. European Alps. Variable in height from 6 to 18 in. Narrow, stem-clasping leaves and umbels of up to ten yellow-green flowers.

There are several other species, but there is so much family similarity that they do not deserve separate descriptions. Whilst possessing no great floral beauty, the Bupleurums none-the-less always attract attention.

CAIOPHORA. *Loasaceae.* From the Greek *kaios*, a burn, and *phoreo*, to bear. An allusion to the stinging hairs of these plants. Most, if not all of the members of this S. American genus have now been transferred to the genus BLUMENBACHIA, which see.

CALAMINTHA. *Labiatae.* From the Greek *kalos*, beautiful, and *minthe*, mint.

A genus of, mostly, aromatic shrubs and herbs, natives of northern temperate regions, a few of which are appropriate rock garden plants for sunny positions in any good and well drained soil.

— alpina. Freely branching tufts about 6 in. high or less, with whorls of purple flowers in spring and summer.

— candidissima. From Oran, and best in the alpine house. Woolly white leaves on foot-high stems and cymes of pink flowers surrounded by green calcyes.

— grandiflora. Like an enlarged version of *C. alpina*, of which some authorities consider it a variety. Loose racemes of reddish-purple flowers on 6 to 9 in. stems in winter.

— mimuloides. From California, and perhaps a little tall and possibly tender for the rock garden. It breaks the family traditions by bearing large, bright orange flowers amidst oval, strongly aromatic leaves on 18 in. stems.

CALANDRINIA. *Portulacaceae.* Named in honour of Jean Louis Calandrini (1703-1758), professor of philosphy at Geneva.

A genus closely related to LEWISIA and needing some care with the watering can and should be regarded as alpine house plants. Neither of the two described species is long-lived and should be regularly re-propagated from seeds. Early summer flowering.

— caespitosa. S. America. Trailing stems and fleshy leaves and flowers of vivid violet-magenta.

CALANDRINIA — *continued*

— **umbellata.** From the S. American Andes. Narrow, softly hairy leaves on semi-procumbent stems and brilliant crimson-magenta flowers.

CALCEOLARIA. *Scrophulariaceae.* From the Latin *calceolus*, a slipper, an allusion to the shape of the pouched flowers.

A very large genus, mostly natives of South America, with outliers in Central America and one or two in New Zealand. Those described below as being suitable for rock gardens or alpine houses will appreciate cool, humus-rich soil and protection from burning sunlight. They are increased by division or cuttings, or from seeds. Spring and summer flowering.

— **acutifolia.** This is so similar to *C. polyrrhiza* that it could well be considered synonymous, and as such I treat it here. From the Argentine and Patagonia. Modestly creeping, with slightly hairy leaves on slender rhizomes and many axillary, solitary flowers of rich yellow, dotted with reddish-purple. 9 to 12 in.

— **arachnoidea.** The densely white-woolly stems and leaves are so vulnerable to winter wet that this Chilean species should be regarded as an alpine house plant. Few-flowered panicles of purple-red flowers on fairly tall stems.

— **biflora.** Another Chilean plant with rosettes of soft, toothed leaves and corymbs of yellow flowers on 9 in. stems.

— **cymbiflora.** From Chile and said to prefer a hot and dry situation and to resemble an improved *C. acutifolia* (polyrrhiza). Dubiously in cultivation.

— **darwinii.** Although not an 'alpine' — it comes from the Straits of Magellan — this species is one of the excitements of an alpinist's life! Seldom very long-lived, definitely temperamental and only too apt to be decimated by red-spider mites, it nevertheless remains a popular plant. It should be sheltered from bitter winds and given rich but gritty soil and divided or propagated from seeds at regular intervals — it can also be rooted from cuttings. Branching rhizomes carry tufts of toothed, dark green leaves and the large, solitary flowers, borne on 4 in. stems, are yellow-brown with an astonishing bar of pure white across the pouch.

— **fothergillii.** From Patagonia and the Falkland Islands and similar in many ways to *C. darwinii.* The leaves are more hairy and the flowers smaller, less vividly coloured although in the same tonal range. There now exist several hybrids between the two species and only time will prove if they are better garden plants.

— **pinifolia.** From Chile and Argentinia. Almost shrubby, but very compact, probably best in the alpine house. Small leaves densely packed on short stems and 9 in. stems carrying lax clusters of small yellow flowers.

— **polyrrhiza.** See *C. acutifolia.*

96

— **tenella.** From Chile. A prostrate plant with creeping stems which root as they run. Tiny bright green leaves and several small, pouched yellow flowers on 2 in. stems.

CALLIANTHEMUM. *Ranunculaceae.* From the Greek *kallos*, beauty, and *anthemon*, flower.

A small genus of alpine plants closely related to RANUNCULUS. They relish treatment in exposed, gritty screes or as alpine house plants. Spring flowering.

— **anemonoides.** (C. rutifolium.) Thin tufts of leaves deeply cut into narrow segments. Short stems carry flowers which may be more than 1 in. in diameter. Broad white petals, sometimes pink outside, surround a central orange ring. European Alps.

— **angustifolium.** From the Altai, and dubiously in cultivation. Twice pinnatifid leaves and large, shapely, pure white flowers on short stems.

— **cashmirianum.** From Kashmir, where it is endemic. White flowers on short stems appear before the deeply cleft, ground-hugging leaves.

— **coriandrifolium.** European Alps. Long-stalked, grey-green leaves cut into several leaflets and large, saucer-shaped white flowers.

— **farreri.** China. Once collected by Farrer and a plant which should be reintroduced. Low tufts of glaucous, divided foliage and large flowers, described by Farrer as being of a melting china-blue.

— **kernerianum.** From the Eastern Alps. Not unlike *C. anemonoides*, but with reddish leaf-stems and narrow-petalled white flowers often flushed with lilac.

— **rutifolium.** See *C. anemonoides.*

— **sajanense.** From Central Siberia and. if not in cultivation, certainly ought to be. Blue-grey dissected leaves and short-stemmed white or soft lilac flowers.

CALLIRHOE. *Malvaceae.* Named in honour of the daughter of the Greek deity Achelous, a river god.

— **involucrata.** Very definitely not an alpine, but sometimes grown on rock gardens, in the hottest, driest possible situation. From the central U.S.A. and produces far-spreading, ground-hugging stems clad in deeply cleft leaves along the length of which appear large, cup-shaped flowers of brilliant crimson-magenta in colour.

CALLUNA. *Ericaceae.* Excluded for the reasons stated in the description of *Bruckenthalia spiculifolia.*

CALTHA. *Ranunculaceae.* From the Latin name for a plant with yellow flowers — possibly Calendula.

It is with slight hesitation that I include the genus Caltha, but a recent introduction from Australia, plus the fact that many alpine pools and streams in gardens are adorned by clumps of our native *C. palustris* and its handsome double-flowered form induced me to find space for these moisture-loving, spring-flowering plants.

- biflora. N.W. America. Dwarf tufts of leaves similar to those of a smaller *C. palustris* and white flowers, sometimes with a flush of soft blue on the petals.
- introloba. From the mountains of Australia. A new introduction which is already much admired and will become increasingly popular as it becomes more widely distributed. Low tufts of curious, arrow-shaped leaves and almost stemless flowers which may be white, or some shade of lilac-blue or soft purple. It appears to be hardy, but is at present usually given alpine house treatment in moisture-retentive soil.
- novae-zelandiae. Prostrate tufts of small, glossy leaves and stemless greenish-yellow flowers. New Zealand.
- obtusa. Another New Zealander with curious upturned leaf-lobes and large, presumably yellow flowers on short stems.
- palustris. Our beloved Marsh Marigold needs no description from me. It should be planted at the water's edge so that splendid rich yellow, single or double flowers can be reflected, like the image of Narcissus, in the water below.
- scaposa. From Sikkim, dwarf, and brilliant in the spring with heads of golden flowers.

CALYPSO. *Orchidaceae.* Named in honour of the nymph Calypso daughter of Atlas.

- borealis. See *C. bulbosa.*
- bulbosa. (C. borealis.) Although terrestrial orchids are by no means widely represented in this Manual, I must find room for this, the only species in its genus. Native of various highlands in the Northern Hemisphere, it grows in shady places in leaf-detritus and moss. The 4 in. stems thicken at the base to become almost pseudo-bulbs. There is usually one broad, veined leaf and the solitary flowers are coloured rose and brown with a bright yellow crest on the lip. Spring or early summer flowering and needs care.

CALYPTRIDIUM. *Portulacaceae.* Derivation possibly, if obscurely, from the Greek *kalyptra*, an extinguisher.

- umbellatum. (Spraguea multiceps. S. umbellata.) From north-western America, where it grows at high altitudes in stony detritus. Related to Lewisia, it makes prostrate rosettes of small, fleshy leaves from which radiate stems, each terminating in a head of fluffy pink papery bracts enclosing the tiny flowers, like the foot of a kitten and explaining its local name of "Pussy-paws". Give it lime-free soil and grow it in an alpine or cold greenhouse.

CAMPANULA. *Campanulaceae.* Diminutive of the Latin *campana,* a bell, in allusion to the shape of the flowers.

This is one of the very large genera which presents something of a problem as far as this Manual is concerned. To deal comprehensively with the known species of Campanula suitable for alpinists which have been, are, or may be available, would occupy more space than even this very complete Manual could spare. I have, therefore, omitted a number which are unlikely to be obtainable, kept descriptions in general to a minimum, and, in the case of species such as *C. carpatica,* of which there are numerous cultivars, have been very brief. With the exceptions which will be noted in individual descriptions, Campanulas are sun-lovers, easily grown in any ordinary, good, gritty soil. They mostly flower in mid- and late-summer, and are increased by seeds, division and cuttings.

— abietina. From rocky ridges in the Carpathian Alps. A short-lived species which should be divided and replanted every two or three years. Rosettes of bright green, narrow leaves and branching foot-high stems carrying purple flowers of open star-shape.

— allionii. (C. alpestris.) From the European Alps. A plant for very gritty soil or scree conditions, in which it will spread by underground stems, emitting here and there tufts or rosettes of narrow, slightly hairy leaves. The 2 to 3 in. stems each carry one large purple-blue flower. It is variable in colour and white forms are not unknown, and a notable form with pink flowers received an Award of Merit under the clonal name *C. a.* 'Frank Barker' in 1930.

— alpestris. See *C. allionii.*

— alpina. From the Eastern Alps and the Tyrol, and apt to be short-lived unless it is grown hard in very gritty soil. Allied to *C. barbata,* it is much dwarfer than that species, forming flat rosettes of leaves from a deep taproot. The stiffly erect 6 in. stem carries a pyramidal raceme of lavender bells.

— ardonensis. See *C. tridentata* group.

— arvatica. From Spanish mountains, and a gem. In nature it is usually saxatile, but in cultivation it runs freely in gritty scree soil. It forms mats of small leaves which may be notched or smooth at the edges. From each rosette springs a stem of about 3 in. carrying several star-shaped, upturned flowers of rich violet-blue. There is also a handsome form with pure white flowers.

— aucheri. See *C. tridentata* group.

— barbata. European Alps, including Norway. Not a long-lived plant, but is easily increased from the plentiful seeds and often self-seeds. In nature it is, more often than not, found on granitic formations, but it does not object to alkaline soil. From a deep tap-root rise rosettes of narrow, roughly hairy leaves, from the centre of which erupts an erect, foot-high almost leafless stem carrying several pendant bells, bearded on the inside. White-flowered forms often appear among the seedlings.

— bellardii. See *C. cochlearifolia.*

— bellidifolia. See *C. tridentata* group

— betulaefolia. A saxatile species from Armenia. Tufts of smooth, wedge-shaped, pointed leaves, toothed at the edges from which radiate semi-procumbent stems carrying elegant clusters of large flowers varying in colour from almost white to soft pink with buds which are almost wine-red. Although hardy, it is seen at its best in an alpine house.

— X 'Birch Hybrid'. A cross between *C. portenschlagiana* and *C. poscharskyana,* and intermediate in appearance between the parents. A robust, free-flowering and handsome plant.

— caespitosa. From the Alps of E. Europe and, in general appearance, not unlike *C. cochlearifolia,* but it does not run from the root as that species does. From the deep tap-roots spring neat tufts of leaves, pointed at each end and lightly toothed on the margins. The 4 to 6 in. stems terminate in loose clusters of pendant blue bells, noticeably constricted at the mouth of the flower.

— calaminthifolia. From Crete and several of the Greek islands. It is perennial, but short-lived, producing from a tap-root prostrate rosettes of hairy, radiating stems clothed in ash-grey, crenulate leaves. Terminally and in the leaf axils appear many soft blue flowers. The stems are very brittle and it resents winter wet and should be regarded as an alpine house plant.

— carnica. See *C. linifolia.*

— carpatha. See *C. tubulosa.*

— carpatica. From the Carpathians, and originally introduced in 1774, The type plant is seldom seen outside of a Botanic Garden, but the several named forms and hybrids which appear beneath the umbrella name of *C. carpatica* are invaluable rock garden plants, showy, and easy to grow. Habitually they all make strong tufts of long-stalked, glossy, slightly cordate leaves. The erect flowers stems varying in height according to kind from 6 in. to a foot or more and carry large flowers of open bell shape and varying in colour from white through shades of blue to rich purple. Any representative alpine plant catalogue offers a choice of the best kinds. One distinct and desirable form is *C. c. turbinata,* which is very dwarf and carries just one large, upturned bell on each short stem.

— cashmiriana. From the Himalaya. A saxatile species delighting in narrow crevices into which it plunges its woody tap-root. From the crown radiate several procumbent zigzagging stems with light green, softly hairy leaves. The stems branch and carry several large pale

100

blue bells. The broad calyx-lobes form a 'saucer' in which each flower rests. Probably best in an alpine house.

— cenisia. A lime-hater from the heights of Europe's Alps, and an excitement to those who are fortunate enough to see it in the wild, but an exasperation to those who try to please it in cultivation. It can be grown, with care, and provision of very, very gritty, lime-free soil in pots and pans, kept rather dry during the winter, but with ample moisture in spring and early summer. Thread-like runners emit small rosettes of tiny, rounded, glaucous leaves and funnel-shaped flowers of a curious slate-blue colour. A white form has been recorded — and indeed grown — for it received an Award of Merit in 1914.

— choziatowskyi. From the mountains of Russian Armenia and a choice, but rare species. From thick, creeping rootstocks rise tufts of small, thick, dentate leaves and erect, flexible, branching 6 to 9 in. stems carrying numerous funnel-shaped flowers of rich purple-blue.

— cochlearifolia. (C. pusilla.) This delightful and ever-popular plant has also been known as C. bellardii and C. pumila. It also, and wrongly, sometimes appears labelled *C. caespitosa*, but that is a distinct species, q.v. The thin roots run freely underground forming spreading colonies of tiny, shining green leaves above which, on 3 in. stems dangle innumerable fairy-bells ranging in colour from pure white to soft lavender and blue. Several forms have been selected and named, and may be identified as 'Miss Willmott', 'Miranda', 'Mist Maiden', etc.

— collina. An old garden plant, introduced from the Caucasus in 1803. A boldly handsome campanula forming tufts of long-stalked, ovate cordate dark green leaves, toothed at the edges and softly hairy. Erect, 15 in. stems carry an abundance of funnel-shaped deep purple-blue bells.

— dasyantha. See *C. pilosa*.

— elatines. From cliff faces in the Cottian Alps. From a thick rootstock spring rosettes of small, ivy-shaped leaves with scalloped margins. The stems and leaves can be softly hairy or quite smooth. The long, procumbent flower stems are brittle, and branch at the ends to carry star-shaped blossoms of violet-blue.

— elatinoides. Closely related to *C. garganica* and comes from a limited area in the Maritime Alps of Italy. Tufts of grey-green hairy leaves emit rock-hugging stems which carry along their length clusters of purple-blue flowers in the leaf axils.

— ephesia. A splendid, but monocarpic species from Anatolia. Best grown in deep pots or pans in an alpine house. Bold rosettes of lyrate, hairy grey leaves take some years to reach maturity, at which time a bold central stem emerges, sometimes more than one foot in height. The large tubular flowers are carried singly on short scapes from the axils of the stem leaves. The colour is a soft, clear blue. Renew it from seed when it has flowered and perished.

— excisa. A lime-hating species from a limited area of the European Alps, where it inhabits rocky crevices and screes, running underground and sending up 3 in. thin, wiry stems clad in smooth, narrow leaves, each stem bearing one slightly pendant, blue flower displaying the characteristic punched-out hole at the base of the lobes from which it derives its name. It appears to tire quickly of a particular area and benefits from fairly frequent division and replanting in fresh soil.

— fenestrellata. See *C. garganica*.

— formaneckiana. Another handsome monocarpic species which must be renewed from seed after it has flowered. It comes from Macedonia and was first introduced in 1931. It is a crevice-lover forming splendid rosettes of symmetrically arranged crinkly, downy-grey leaves. From the centre of each rosette eventually arises an erect rigid, leafy stem to a height of possibly 2 ft. From the leaf axils, on long pedicels, spring large, tubular flowers, usually white, but occasionally flushed blue or pink. Best in the alpine house.

— fragilis. From the Italian Alps. From woody rootstocks rise tufts of long-stalked leaves, coarsely-toothed and of a glistening green colour. Many branched, semi-prostrate stems carry quantities of mid-blue flowers. It is more often grown in the alpine house, but will succeed in a narrow, warm crevice outside. It is very definitely a lime-lover.

— garganica. A variable species from both sides of the Adriatic. The type has been known in gardens since 1832 and it is grown in several of its slightly differing forms, which are sufficiently distinct whilst having a general family resemblance. All of them are splendid wall and crevice plants with rock-hugging radiating stems which carry abundances of the star-shaped flowers. There is a good albino, and an old, but still good cultivar named 'W. H. Paine', with rich-blue, white-centred flowers. *C. istriaca*, so called, also belongs here, but is correctly *C. g.* 'Hirsuta'. Another good form is *C. fenestrellata*, sometimes listed as *C. g. erinus*.

— X 'G. F. Wilson'. This good old garden plant resulted from hybridising *C. pulla* with *C. carpatica turbinata*. It was raised many years ago but retains its vigour and desirability. It makes neat tufts of leaves sometimes rather yellow-green in colour and bears large bell-shaped flowers on short stems.

— glomerata. This is a native species and of no real garden value but for rock gardens *C. g.* 'Acaulis' is a desirable pygmy. It carries almost stemless clusters of purple-blue flowers.

— X 'Hallii'. This is said to be a hybrid between *C. cochlearifolia* 'Alba' and *C. portenschlagiana*, a parentage of which I have always been slightly dubious. Nonetheless, it is a charming dwarf of tufted habit with many white bells on 4 in. stems.

— hawkinsiana. It is unfortunate that this rare and beautiful species from Greece never obtained a firm roothold in cultivation. It makes fleeting appearances and is always coveted, but it is more often absent than present. It grows in screes of serpentine and schist and radiates from its central rootstock rather straggling, prostrate shoots with rounded, blue-green, fleshy leaves. The flowers are wide-open bells of dark blue with an even darker veining in the petals. Unfortu-

102

nately the plant is given to collapsing without warning and those fortunate enough to possess it should root a few cuttings periodically as an insurance

— **X haylodgensis.** A hybrid between *C. cochlearifolia* and *C. carpatica* with yellow-green foliage and lax, short stems carrying many double blue flowers.

— **hederacea.** See *Wahlenbergia hederacea.*

— **herzegovinensis.** A treasure from Herzegovina forming neat little bushlets in the limestone crevices in which it delights to grow. Slender, wiry 4 to 5 in. stems carry rich lilac, erect starry flowers. There is a particularly precious form, *C.h.* 'Nana' which seldom exceeds 2 in. in height and is very free-flowering.

— **hostii.** See *C. rotundifolia.*

— **hypopolia.** From the Caucasus, and a very distinct, if sometimes shy-flowering species. Tangles of trailing stems are furnished with long, narrow grey-green leaves. The stems terminate in branching stems which carry singly flowers narrowly bell-shaped and light blue in colour. For a sunny scree or the alpine house.

— **imeritina.** It is doubtful if the true Caucasian species is in cultivation, its place usually being taken by an impostor. It should form tufts of rather oval leaves from which rise 9 in. stems adorned with many bells of rich purple-blue.

— **incurva.** (C. leutweinii.) A monocarpic species from Greece. Rosettes of long-stalked ovate leaves, softly hairy and yellowish-green in colour. From the rosette come both prostrate and ascending stems, the upright ones attaining 15 in. in height, carrying very large, rather bulging bells of lavender-blue. In general appearance it can be likened to a dwarf Canterbury Bell.

— **isophylla.** From Italy and not reliably hardy in any of the several cultivated forms, but able to survive in an alpine house if the winter is not too severe. I hesitate to enlarge upon a species which is unsuited to rock gardens and is more popular as a plant for hanging baskets.

— **istriaca.** See *C. garganica.*

— **jenkinsae.** See *C. rotundifolia.*

— **kemulariae.** From Transcaucasia. From a running rootstock rise tufts of shining green cordate and serrate leaves on long petioles. The foot-high, freely branching stems carry mauve-blue flowers of open bell-shape and goodly size.

— **X kewensis.** A hybrid between *C. arvatica* and *C. excisa* and intermediate in appearance between the parents. A choice dwarf plant.

— **kolenatiana.** From regions in the Caucasus and monocarpic or, at best biennial. It is a sub-alpine plant not unlike *C. sarmatica* without the ash-grey leaves and with rigid, erect foot-high stems bearing one-sided racemes of quite large, violet-purple bell-shaped flowers.

— **lasiocarpa.** From Japan, and, occasionally, the Rocky Mountains of N.W. America. Neat tufts of smooth, rather rounded leaves with slightly jagged edges. The 3 in. stems each terminate in one shapely bell of clear blue. A good albino has been seen but is a rarity. Grow it in scree or the alpine house.

— leutweinii. See *C. incurva.*

— lanata. (*C. velutina.*) From Greece and Bulgaria and usually monocarpic. In nature it is commonly a crevice plant forming basal tufts of hairy, heart-shaped leaves, coated with soft grey hairs. A tall, branching stem carries many pale-yellow, rather waxy bells similar in shape to those of the Canterbury Bell *(C. medium).*

— linifolia. Widespread through the European Alps. In appearance it much resembles *C. rotundifolia,* but differs in several botanical details, and the narrow stem-leaves are usually softly grey-haired. The flowers are usually of a rich purple-blue colour and it is a desirable, if variable plant, for the flower colour can vary to pale blue and almost white. The plant commonly grown as *C. scheuchzeri* is no more than a form of this species, carrying its flowers singly on the slender stems. A particularly fine Spanish variant, encountered as *C. s.* 'Covadonga' should also shelter beneath this umbrella. It has profusions of narrow, deep royal-purple bells on lax, 6 in. stems.

— loreyi. See *C. ramosissima.*

— macrorrhiza. From the Maritime Alps of S. France and again similar to *C. rotundifolia,* but it is a crevice-loving species with neat tufts of small, glossy, rounded leaves, and erect 9 in. stems carrying many of the purple-blue bells.

— mirabilis. A spectacular, but monocarpic species from the Caucasus. It takes several years to attain flowering size. From the wide rosettes of flat, fleshy oval leaves rise eventually single central stems of a foot or so in height carrying alternate leaves from the axils of which spring clusters of erect, stalked campanulate flowers of soft lilac-blue. It is a magnificence which is easily raised again from seed when the rosette has blossomed and died. Best in an alpine house.

— 'Miranda.' See *C. cochlearifolia.*

— morettiana. A rare and beautiful saxatile species from the Tyrol and Dalmatia. It should be given full alpine house treatment in gritty soil, wedged between small stones. Tufts of tiny, ivy-shaped leaves, felted with fine grey hairs, emit short stems each carrying one large, broadly funnel-shaped bell of violet-blue. There is also a desirable albino. It is one of the choicest alpine species.

— muralis. See *C. portenschlagiana.*

— nitida. See *C. persicifolia.*

— X 'Norman Grove'. A hybrid of doubtful origin sometimes said to be between *C. isophylla* and *C. stansfieldii* (itself already a hybrid). Short, erect stems carry flowers of light purple-blue.

— orbelica. From the Balkans. From basal tufts of narrow leaves rise fairly tall, leafy stems each carrying a lilac-blue bell-shaped flower.

— oreadum. A Grecian species of great merit and equal rarity. It is one of most intensely and determinedly saxatile of campanulas and relishes being wedged into minute crevices between limestone rocks.

Rosettes of broad, softly downy leaves on long footstalks and a central spike with procumbent, branching stems carrying great numbers of violet-purple flowers. Grow it in an alpine house.

— pallasiana. See *C. pilosa.*

— patula. A short-lived species, native to Britain and Central, Southern and Northern Europe. Tall, slender stems carry funnel-shaped purple-blue flowers. It is graceful and decorative.

— pelia. Another monocarpic Thessalian for the alpine house. Rosettes of grey hair-coated lyrate leaves and radiating, prostrate stems at the base of an erect one, all carrying in the leaf axils tubular flowers of clear pale blue.

— persicifolia. A tall-growing species for herbaceous borders and of interest to rock-gardeners only in its curious microform variously identified as *C. nitida* and *C. planiflora.* Tiny huddled rosettes of dark green, deeply crinkled leaves foster short, stiff erect stems bearing blue or white open bell-shaped flowers. When and where this Mendelian recessive occurred is uncertain. If seeds of it are saved and sown they produce nothing but pure *C. persicifolia.*

— petraea. From S. France and Italy. Often only of biennial duration. Rosettes of roughly hairy leaves green above but grey beneath. Foot-high erect stems terminate in heads of small off-white, sometimes yellowish, flowers. It is interesting but cannot be described as beautiful — unless the beauty be in the eye of the beholder!

— X 'Peter Nix'. A hybrid of dubious parentage which has made a recent appearance. It is vigorous and floriferous and displays light blue harebells on 9 in. stems.

— petrophila. From the Caucasus, where it inhabits cool, moist crevices at great elevations. Clusters of rosettes of ovate leaves, sometimes three-toothed at the tip harbour wiry, prostrate stems carrying each from one to five large purple-blue flowers.

— pilosa. (C. pallasiana.) From Alaska, the Aleutians and Japan. A stout root is crowned with a rosette which emits short stolons ending in similar rosettes of leaves. The flowering rosettes carry erect, 3 in. stems bearing several flowers of open bell-shape and light blue in colour. It is a very variable species and there is a form in cultivation identified as *C. p. dasyantha,* which differs little from the type but usually carries only one flower on each stem.

— piperi. A delightful species, endemic to the Olympic Mountains of the State of Washington and a determined haunter of minute rock crevices. Give it alpine house treatment and a sparse, lime-free diet in confined conditions. Running roots emit neat rosettes of smooth, tiny, dark green leaves, pointed at the tip. Slender inch-high stems carry one or two large, stalked deep purple-blue flowers with conspicuous scarlet anthers.

— planiflora. See *C. persicifolia.*

— portenschlagiana. (C. muralis.) A Dalmatian species, grown and loved for countless decades. Probably the most popular and widely grown alpine campanula. It flourishes in sun or light shade, remains full of vigour and is consistently free flowering. Leafy mats become obscured by innumerable panicles of deep blue flowers carried on short, semi-procumbent stems. It is also a splendid wall plant. A form with slightly larger flowers is sometimes listed as *var.* 'Bavarica'.

— **poscharskyana.** This rampagious but lovely species was introduced from Eastern Europe by my late father in 1933. In some ways it resembles a much more vigorous, long-stemmed *C. garganica.* It forms tangled mats of long, horizontal stems richly clothed in rounded, toothed, cordate leaves and innumerable loose, axillary racemes of starry, lavender-blue flowers obscure the whole plant for weeks on end. It admirably clothes rough walls or areas of poor soil.

— **pseudo-raineri.** A doubtfully authentic name which covers a probable hybrid, possibly between *C. carpatica* 'Turbinata' and *C. raineri.* Wide salver-shaped blue flowers singly on 2 in. stems.

— **pulla.** From the Eastern Alps and an attractive species which runs below ground to form pleasant colonies. It is a sun and lime-lover with small, glossy, ovate leaves. Plentiful 4 in. stems rise and carry solitary pendulous bells of luminous purple.

— **X pulloides.** A pleasant hybrid between the previous species and *C. carpatica* 'Turbinata'. It has a similar running habit but bears larger, more erect flowers of lighter blue on 6 in. stems.

— **punctata.** From Siberia and Japan. It is probable that plants grown as *C. nobilis* may be identical with this species. Probably too tall for the average rock garden, but a handsome plant carrying on 18 in. stems several pendant, large, tubular bells of cream-yellow, speckled within with purple-red markings.

— **pusilla.** See *C. cochlearifolia.*

— **raddeana.** From the limestones of Transcaucasia. A running species forming tufts of triangular, cordate, dark green and glossy leaves toothed on the margins. On 9 to 12 in. stems are carried showers of pendant, deep violet-blue flowers. It benefits from fairly regular division and replanting in fresh soil.

— **raineri.** A lover of limestone from the Italian Alps. In nature it is usually a crevice plant with a woody rootstock from which spring tufts of small, ash-grey almost stemless leaves. The erect 3 in. stems carry normally one large open bell, but occasional stems carry two blossoms. There is a rare and rather lovely form with pure white flowers, and another variant is *C. r.* 'Hirsuta' which has extra hairy foliage.

— **ramosissima.** (C. loreyi.) Although little more than an annual this is well worth growing. A native of Asia Minor and S. Europe, it forms a loose, leafy bush about 8 in. and the erect, wiry stems carry individual flowers of star-shape, goodly size and violet-blue petals often white at the base.

— **rhomoboidalis.** A wild garden rather than a rock garden plant from sub-alpine areas of Europe. Two-foot stems carry smooth or slightly hairy sessile leaves and terminate in heads of slightly pendant purple-blue flowers.

— **X rotarvatica.** A very pleasing hybrid between *C. rotundifolia* and *C. arvatica* which inherits the easy constitution of the former parent, coupled with the starry, bright blue flowers of *C. arvatica* on 4 to 5 in. stems.

— **rotundifolia.** A widely distributed species, being found throughout the temperate and even the sub-artic regions of the Northern Hemisphere, and a much-loved British native. It is the 'Bluebell' of Scotland and the Harebell of British meadows and hedgerows. An immensely variable species it is cultivated in several of its selected forms. One of the best of these comes from the Olympic Mountains of the State of Washington and is identified as *C.r.* 'Olympica'. Two well-known campanulas mostly referred to as *C. hostii* and *C. jenkinsae* probably belong here in what should really be regarded as an aggregate species. The former has large blue bells on 9 in. stems and the latter is of similar habit but blossoms are white.

— **rupestris.** A species from Greece which some authorities describe as perennial, but garden experience usually proves it to be monocarpic. It should be grown in an alpine house or cold frame, where it makes handsome rosettes of grey, hairy, lyrate leaves from which spring semi-procumbent branching stems carrying several erect, tubular bells of lilac-blue. Save and sow seeds as an insurance.

— **sarmatica.** From the Caucasus forming low clumps of downy grey, rather crinkled leaves, toothed at the margins. On foot-high stems it carries one-sided racemes of pendant grey-blue bells. Raise it from seed and expect a few rather nice albinos among the seedlings.

— **sartori.** Another Grecian monocarp for the alpine house. Neat rosettes of dentate, slightly hairy cordate leaves. Short, branched stems carry funnel-shaped flowers, usually white but occasionally flushed with pink. It is a crevice-haunting plant for stony soil and a sparse diet and is possibly happier without lime.

— **saxifraga.** See the *C. tridentata* group.

— **scheuchzeri.** See *C. linifolia.*

— **spathulata.** A good perennial from the mountains of Greece. A somewhat tuberous root emits tufts of crenate leaves on thin petioles and foot-high branching stems carry many stalked flowers of violet-blue. A form identified as *C. s. giuseppii* has more prostrate stems and distinctly hairy foliage. There is also confusion between this species and names such as *CC. spruneriana* and *sibthorpiana.*

— **X stansfieldii.** An old garden hybrid of somewhat dubious parentage, but possibly *C. carpatica* x *C. tommasiniana*, although *C. tommasiniana* x *C. waldsteiniana* has been suggested. Mats of small, rather hairy leaves and ascending, branched 4 in. stems slightly pendant, violet-blue cup-shaped flowers.

— **steveni.** From the Caucasus, and near to *C. abietina* and, like that species, benefits from regular division and replanting. From the stoloniferous roots rise rosettes of smooth, slightly serrate leaves on long petioles and from these again rise leafy stems of variable height, but usually about 9 to 12 in. carrying lilac-blue, funnel-shaped flowers, commonly singly but occasionally in a few-flowered raceme.

— thyrsoides. An exception in a family of almost universally blue, purple or white flowers, this European species carries fragrant, straw-yellow flowers on a thick, erect spike about 1 ft. high. The long, narrow leaves are bristly with short, stiff hairs. It is monocarpic but is easily raised from seed. There is a form from E. Europe, *C. t.* 'Carniolica', which is slightly taller and bears flowers of creamy-white.

— tommasiniana. From the mountains of Istria, where it is locally abundant. Thick perennial rootstocks emit thin, wiry stems up to 4 in. which branch and carry many very narrow, pendant bells of lavender-blue.

— tridentata. This is really a collection of several closely related and similar plants, mostly from the Caucasus. It should really be regarded as a group containing *C. ardonensis*, *C. aucheri*, *C. bellidifolia*, *C. saxifraga* and *C. stenophylla*. They all, from thick, almost carrot-like roots form clusters of rosettes of rather broad leaves, mostly slightly hairy and sometimes lightly toothed at the margins or tips. From the clusters of rosettes spring decumbent stems each carrying one large open bell-shaped flower. The colour varies in intensity of shades of violet and purple-blue.

— tubulosa. (C.carpatha.) A Cretan monocarpic for alpine houses. It makes rosettes of rather thick leaves felted with grey hairs and decumbent stems from the leaf axils of which spring short, often branched stems carrying erect tubular light blue bells either singly or in small groups.

— turbinata. See *C. carpatica*.

— X tymonsii. Said, rather incredibly, to be a hybrid between *C. carpatica* and *C. pyramidalis*. Little evidence of the latter species is evident in this short-stemmed (6 in. at most) plant which carries on stiff, erect, branching stems wide-mouthed bells of purple-blue.

— valdensis. This is really no more than a form of *C. linifolia* with very grey, softly hairy foilage.

— velutina. See *C. lanata*.

— vidalii. From the Azores and differs from most campanulas in being of a shrubby habit. It is dubiously hardy and should be grown in an alpine house. The woody stems, branching from the base, are clothed in thick, fleshy leaves, coarsely toothed. The flowers, carried in terminal racemes, are waxy-white with a ring of bright orange in the centre.

— waldsteiniana. From rocky crevices in Dalmatia. Thick rootstocks produce many wiry, 4 in. stems with narrow, toothed leaves. Each stem ends in a cluster of erect, star-shaped violet-blue flowers.

— zoysii. From the Eastern Alps and a treasure — if you can protect it from the slugs who like it as much as we do. It should be given a very gritty soil rich in lime, or grown in a narrow crevice. Tufts of

CAMPANULA — *continued*

tiny, glossy, short-stalked leaves above which appear short erect stems each carrying several clear blue flowers of curious shape, the mouth of the narrow bell being crimped and puckered.

CAMPHOROSMA. *Chenopodiaceae.* From the Greek *kamphora,* camphor, and *osme,* an odour. The plant is camphor-scented.

— **monspeliaca.** Too tall for most rock gardens, and best suited to warm maritime gardens, or as a specimen small shrub in the alpine house. Evergreen, heath-like bushes up to 18 in. with crowded softly hairy grey tiny leaves. The rather inconspicuous flowers are carried in small axillary clusters in summer.

CARDAMINE. *Cruciferae.* From the Greek name for a plant of the cress family.

A genus containing some 50 species of annual or perennial herbs, few of which have rock garden interest. The exceptions are described below. Recent classification places several species of DENTARIA in the genus Cardamine, but we adhere to the more familar naming and Dentarias should be sought in their proper alphabetical sequence.

— **latifolia.** A very handsome plant from the Pyrenees, but too large for most rock gardens. It delights in moist soil where it makes bold, leafy tufts from which rise 15 to 18 in. stems carrying heads of large lilac-pink flowers in early summer.

— **pratensis.** This is the Cuckoo Flower or Lady's Smock of our own meadows and, although a pretty plant is too weedy for gardens. There is, however, a good form with fully double soft pink flowers on 9 in. stems which is very desirable.

— **trifolia.** A nice dwarf species for a cool, partially shaded position. It comes from the European Alps. Tufts of trifoliate leaves and small heads of white flowers on 4 to 6 in. stems in spring.

CARDAMINOPSIS. *Cruciferae.* From Cardamine and the Greek *opsis,* like.

— **petraea.** (Arabis petraea.) From Europe, including Britain. Tufts of small, leaves, the basal ones pinnatifid, the upper ones entire and heads of small white, or occasionally pink-flushed flowers on 3 in. stems. in spring.

CARDUNCELLUS. *Compositae.* A diminutive of Carduus.

A small genus of sun-loving prickly herbs, mostly natives of Mediterranean regions.

— **caeruleus.** Too tall for most rock gardens, but a handsome thistle with heads of blue flowers on 18 in. prickly-leaved stems. From Spain, Greece and Crete.

— **duvauxii.** From Morocco and a handsome, 9 in. thistle with spiny, white-edged deep green leaves and branching stems carrying large heads of bright blue flowers.

— **pinnatus.** From Sicily and N. Africa. Handsome prostrate rosettes of pinnate leaves, the segments spiny at the tips. In the centre of the rosette is a short-stemmed head of blue flowers.

— **rhaponticoides.** From Morocco and introduced comparatively recently by Mrs. Robert Lukin. It occurs in Algeria and in both the Great and the Middle Atlas mountains. It makes large, flat rosettes of long, tapering leaves edged with spiny hairs and the footstalk is stained purple. The inflorescence is a large, stemless central boss of small bright blue flowers.

CAREX. *Cyperaceae.* The classical Latin name for the genus.

Few of the 600—plus species of Sedge find a place in the rock garden, but there are one or two exceptions, not noted for their floral beauty, but attractive nevertheless. For cool, moist positions

— **atrata.** The Black Sedge is a native of Europe, including Britain. It makes neat tufts of stiff, grassy leaves and carries small, rounded, almost black flower-heads on 4 in. stems.

— **baldensis.** Another European species which makes tufts of narrow leaves and displays cream-white flower heads on short stems.

— **firma.** This tiny sedge is widespread throughout the Alps of Europe but it is the form with cream margins to the stiffly tufted narrow green leaves which is the more desirable. As *C.f.* 'Variegata' it received an Award of Merit in 1971. It should be given careful treatment in gritty, but humus-rich soil as it can be curiously temperamental. It is more likely to succeed in an alpine house than in the open.

CARLINA. *Compositae.* A medieval name derived from Carolus, (Charles), referring to the tradition that Charlemagne used the root of this thistle to cure a plague which prevailed in his army.

— **acaulis.** The alpine thistle of Europe which has been grown in British gardens since 1640. Clusters of pinnatifid leaves and large, short-stemmed or stemless whitish flower heads.

— **racemosa.** A species found in Morocco. It grows about a foot high with freely branching stems and carries attractive yellow flower heads.

110

CARMICHAELIA. *Leguminosae.* Named for Capt. Dugald Carmichael (1722-1827) who appears to have lived to a ripe old age, and introduced many good plants.

A genus of about 35 or more species of shrubs, all but one native to New Zealand. They are hardy but only two are really acceptable rock gardens plants. They like an open, well drained soil and a sunny position.

- — **enysii.** Dense 6 to 9 in. hummocks of interlaced flat green branches and almost leafless. Flowers solitary, or a few together, Flowers lilac-pink.
- — **monroi.** Dubiously in cultivation here, but ought to be. A low-growing shrublet with the flattened stems typical of the genus — they take the place of conventional leaves — and many small, white and violet flowers.

CASSIOPE. *Ericaceae.* Cassiope was the mother of Andromeda in Greek mythology, hence the name for a genus related to *Andromeda.*

A small but fascinating genus of heath-like, lime-hating shrublets from mountainous and Arctic regions of the Northern Hemisphere. They are very hardy but should be found a cool position; a north aspect is ideal. Shade is not essential, or even desirable, if the cool conditions can be otherwise provided.

- — X 'Bearsden'. A garden hybrid of uncertain parentage, but probably *C. fastigiata* x *C. lycopodioides.* It was selected from a number of seedlings by that great plantsman, the late W. C. Buchanan and named after the little town near Glasgow in which he spent most of his life. Intermediate in appearance between the supposed parents it is a vigorous and floriferous.
- — 'Beatrice Lilley'. See *C. lycopodioides.*
- — X 'Edinburgh'. A hybrid between *C. fastigiata* and *C. tetragona.* This good hybrid occurred spontaneously in the Edinburgh Botanic Garden. Compact bushes up to a foot in height, the stems only slightly branching. The tightly imbricated leaves are margined with silver hairs. At the tips of the branches occur crowded racemes of white, urn-shaped flowers.
- — **ericoides.** From Arctic Russia and dubiously in cultivation. It is described as having very fine foliage, fringed and bristly, and white, three-lobed bells.
- — **fastigiata.** From the Himalaya. A dwarf bush up to 9 in. with erect, square stems densely clothed with tiny imbricated green leaves. Flowers carried singly in the leaf axils, white and bell-shaped.
- — X 'George Taylor'. A hybrid between *C. wardii* and *C. fastigiata.* The plant leans towards *C. wardii* in appearance but has taller, stouter, noticeably four-angled stems, the shining, imbricated dark green leaves sparingly adorned with white hairs. The short-stalked white bells are carried at the tips of the branches.

- **hypnoides.** A native of Arctic and sub-Arctic regions of Europe and N. America, and although it was introduced to Britain in 1798, has never taken kindly to cultivation and is the despair of ardent gardeners. Almost moss-like tufts of hair-fine leaves on prostrate, slender stems and solitary bell-shaped flowers on inch-high red stems and a bright red calyx.

- X **'Kathleen Dryden'.** A fine hybrid of unknown parentage, although it is suspected that *C. lycopodioides* is one parent. A few main shoots grow upright but all the laterals are horizontal, forming a mat of interlaced, sturdy stems. The white, urn-shaped flowers, with slightly 'pinched' mouths are carried on arching pedicels.

- **lycopodioides.** From the Aleutian Islands to Japan. Mats of entangled stems clothed with scale-like leaves and white bells with scarlet inch-high pedicels and a red calyx. One of the best of the genus. 'Beatrice Lilley' is a desirable, even more compact form.

- **mertensiana.** N. America, from California to Alaska. Upright, foot-high stems and sombre green, scale-like leaves. Cream-white bells singly on short pedicels at the tips of the branches.

- X **'Muirhead'.** A hybrid between *C. wardii* and *C. lycopodioides*. Loose, upright bushes of about 6 to 8 in. White bells with hairy, coral-pink pedicels. There also exists a clone which is much dwarfer but otherwise similar.

- **myosuroides.** From Burma and Yunnan and not at present in cultivation, although it has been grown in the past from seeds collected by Kingdon Ward. Mat forming, with tightly imbricated leaves and white bells on short stems.

- **palpebrata.** Also from Asia, recorded from Burma and China but not in cultivation. Said to be prostrate, with leaves not imbricated but placed at right angles to the stems.

- **pectinata.** Said to be one of the gems of the genus, which we await with impatience to be introduced from its native Burma or Tibet. Said to be intermediate in appearance between *C. wardii* and *C. fastigiata*, its leaves fringed with white hairs and with large white bells.

- X **'Randle Cooke'.** This is *C. wardii* crossed with *C. fastigiata* and is a robust plant growing 6 in. tall. The semi-prostrate shoots turn up towards the tips and have the whipcord appearance of those of *C. lycopodioides*. The white bells are crowded at the tips of the branchlets.

- **rigida.** Said to come from Japan, but Ohwi, in his monumental Flora of Japan mentions only *C. lycopodioides*. This is similar in appearance to that species, but the innumerable flowers of waxy white are carried on shorter, less brightly coloured pedicels.

- **selaginoides.** From Tibet. Erect, much-branched stems dressed with densely imbricated leaves fringed with white hairs. White bell-shaped flowers pendant on long, hairy, green pedicels and red calyces.

- **stelleriana.** (Harimanella stelleriana.) Along the Pacific coast of N. America northwards to the Aleutians, Alaska and Japan. A tiny mat-forming shrublet not unlike *C. hypnoides* in appearance, but with tiny leaves at right angles to the stems. Red buds at the tip of each stem expand into ivory-white bells backed by red calyces.

— tetragona. From Arctic and sub-Arctic Europe and N. America. Erect, quadrangular shoots with dark green leaves and ivory-white bell-shaped flowers slightly constricted at the mouth.

— wardii. From Tibet and one of the gems of the genus. Erect, slightly branching stems clothed in four rows of imbricated leaves which are fringed with fine white hairs. The large white bells appear in the axils of the leaves and are borne on short pedicels. It spreads modestly by means of underground running stems.

CASTILLEJA. *Scrophulariaceae.* Named for the 18th century Spanish botanist Domingo Castillejo.

A race of handsome, but almost ungrowable parasites from N. America and one in N. Asia. Their beauty lies in the brilliantly coloured bracts which surround the inconspicuous flowers. Occasional unexpected successes lead to further attempts to cultivate them but they are unlikely ever to become good garden plants and it is pointless to describe the numerous species in detail.

CATANANCHE. *Compositae.* From the Greek *katanangke*, a strong incentive. It was used as a love-philtre.

— caespitosa. A rarity originally introduced from the Atlas Mountains by E. K. Balls, and lately reintroduced. Rosettes of long, narrow grey leaves, pronged at the tips and short-stemmed flowers of pale yellow in the spring. For the alpine house and gritty soil.

CATHCARTIA. *Papaveraceae.* Named in honour of John Fergusson Cathcart (1802-1851) an amateur botanist.

— villosa. The only species in its genus, native to the Himalaya and first introduced in 1850. Not long-lived but easily raised from seed and succeeds in sun and any good, fairly light soil. Rounded, lobed and cordate, softly hairy leaves and showy yellow 'poppy' flowers carried singly on 12 in. stems in June.

CEANOTHUS. *Rhamnaceae.* From the Greek name *Keanothus*, used to identify a spiny plant in no way related to Ceanothus.

A race of handsome and popular shrubs, mostly natives of California. Only one species qualifies for inclusion in this Manual.

— prostratus. A spreading, prostrate, woody shrub hardy except during exceptionally severe winters and will survive even these if grown in a warm and sheltered position. The clusters of small flowers which appear at the tips of the shoots are commonly blue, but white and lavender forms have been recorded.

CELMISIA. *Compositae.* Named after Celmisios, son of the Greek nymph Alciope.

A large genus of Australasian plants, mostly natives of New Zealand. Several species are grown with varying success. On the whole they seem to succeed better in the north of Britain than in the south. I do not propose to deal with the genus in any great depth and shall mention only those more commonly cultivated, although study of a New Zealand Alpine Plant Flora suggests many species we would desire to have. Their degree of hardiness varies and they should be given warm, sheltered positions where possible, in well cultivated and nourished soil.

— argentea. For the sunny scree or an alpine house. Congested tiny tufts of narrow, silver-haired leaves and stemless white flowers at the tips of the shoots.

— bellidioides. The easiest of all to grow. Flat mats of dark green leaves and white daisy flowers on 3 in. stems in spring and summer.

— coriacea. Bold tufts of long, narrow silver-haired leaves. Large white, densely woolly flower heads on tall stems.

— gracilenta. Clusters of very narrow whitish leaves and characteristic, inch-wide white flowers on lax stems.

— hectori. Mat-forming with crowded, narrow, silver leaves and broad-rayed white flowers on 3 in. stems.

— longifolia. From Tasmania. Tufts of grassy, grey-green leaves and golden-eyed white flowers, one on each 9 to 12 in. stem.

— ramulosa. Small, grey-green leaves on what is almost a sub-shrub of little height and the typical white daisy flowers of the genus.

— sessiliflora. Mats of needle-fine grey leaves and short-stemmed white flowers. Best in an alpine house.

— spectabilis. One of the giants of the genus. Long, wide, pointed and grey leaves matted with buff tomentum beneath and large white flower heads on 15 to 18 in. stems.

— traversii. Dark green leaves with brown edges and very large and imposing white flower heads.

— walkeri. (C. webbii.) Mounds of rather narrow, leathery, grey-green leaves and smallish white flowers carried on 12 to 15 in. thin and wiry stems.

— webbii. See *C. walkeri.*

CELSIA. *Scrophulariaceae.* Named in honour of Olof Celsius (1670-1756) Professor of theology at Uppsala.
- **acaulis.** There are thirty or more species of Celsia spread from the Mediterranean regions through Abyssinia and eastward to India, but only this one is suited to the rock garden or alpine house. Introduced to Britain from Greece in 1938, it forms a neat tuft of rough, narrow, toothed green leaves and displays clusters of stemless, yellow, verbascum-like flowers in the centre of the rosettes. Gritty soil, sun and propagate by seeds or root-cuttings.

CELSIOVERBASCUM. *Scrophulariaceae.* A bi-generic hybrid whose name is made of a composition of the names of the parent genera.
- **'Golden Wings'.** It was in 1947, or thereabouts, that Mr. H. C. Pugsley began hybridising Verbascums, his work resulting in some valuable garden plants. This bi-generic hybrid resulted from crossing *Celsia acaulis* with *Verbascum spinosum.* Both species grow on Crete but there is no record of a natural hybrid between them. This excellent plant forms stubby 9 in. bushes of erect, woody stems carrying a great many clear yellow flowers in dense racemes over a long summer period. A good alpine house plant or for a sunny nook outside.

CENTAUREA. *Compositae.* From the Greek *kentauros*, centaur.

There are at least 500 known species of Centaurea, annual, biennial or perennial herbs, all but three natives of the Old World and those three American. Not many of them appeal to rock gardeners but the best of the few which might are described below. They are all easily grown in any good soil and full sun and increase from seeds or division. I cannot promise that all those mentioned are easily obtainable.
- **achteroffii.** This delightful species was introduced from the Balkans by my late father many years ago but I doubt if it still exists in cultivation. It makes silver rosettes of spoon-shaped leaves, flat on the ground, each rosette centred by large, stemless purple-blue corn-flowers. If obtained it would relish a very gritty scree or the alpine house.
- **argentea.** Endemic to Crete. Deeply cut leaves felted with white hairs. The flowers, carried on short, hard stems, are yellow. It is unlikely to be hardy outside an alpine house.
- **parolinii.** Equally desirable and equally scarce, from the mountains of Turkey. Mat-forming, with Struwelpeter heads of golden flowers, their necks surrounded by a collar of radiating spines.

115

CENTAUREA — *continued*

- **pindicola.** This Grecian species is still around in the gardens of a few enthusiasts. It runs below ground, emitting rosettes of grey leaves with undulating margins, on which sit almost stemless white cornflower blooms. Similarly for scree or alpine house.
- **pulchra.** From Kashmir and perhaps on the large side, but a handsome plant with large, globose, bright purple flowers on foot-high stems in late summer.
- **simplicaulis.** From Armenia, and makes good rock garden ground cover for small bulbs. Dark green leaves, white beneath, rest on the ground and the mauve flowers appear on 6 in. stems and are often followed by nice fluffy seed-heads.
- **stricta.** From Eastern Europe. I omitted *C. montana* because of its height, but this resembles it but is only about 6 in. tall. Silvery lanceolate leaves and axillary and terminal blue flower heads.

CENTAURIUM. *Gentianaceae.* From the Greek *centauros*, the half-man-half-horse of mythology. Chiron the Centaur is said to have cured a wound in his foot by using this herb.

- **scilloides.** (C. portense. Erythraea diffusa. E. massonnii.) Europe, including Britain. Three-inch tufts of small, rounded, shining green leaves and clear pink flowers on short stems in spring and summer.
- **portense.** See *C. scilloides.*

CERASTIUM. *Carophyllaceae.* From the Greek *keras*, a horn, an allusion to the shape of the seed capsule.

A race of many weeds and a few good rock garden plants. Easily grown in sunny positions and any good soil, spring and summer flowering. Increase by seeds or division or cuttings.

- **alpinum.** Europe, including Britain. A mat-forming, grey-green plant useful for ground-cover. Cymes of small white flowers on 3 in. stems.
- **glaciale.** See *C. uniflorum.*
- **lanatum.** (C. villosum.) Similar to *C. alpinum* but more densely covered with grey-hairs. A good and useful carpeting plant with sizeable white flowers on short stems.
- **uniflorum.** (C. glaciale.) European Alps. Tufts of bright green leaves and large white flowers in two and threes on short stems. A good scree plant.
- **villosum.** See *C. lanatum.*

I have deliberately ignored *C. tomentosum*, commonly known as Snow-in-summer because of its deserved reputation as a thug and a strangler. Even so, there are places which it can harmlessly adorn with its sheets of grey leaves and snowfields of flower.

CERATOSTIGMA. *Plumbaginaceae.* From the Greek *keras*, a horn and *stigma.*

There is a hornlike excrescence on the stigma of the flower.

- **plumbaginoides.** (Plumbago larpentae.) Not an alpine, but often planted on rock gardens, where it is very decorative. An herbaceous perennial, it runs below ground with woody roots which emit wiry, foot-high stems carrying green leaves which adopt rich autumn tints and, in late summer, many gentian-blue flowers. It likes a warm position and sharply drained soil. Increase by cuttings or division.

CHAENORRHINUM. See the genus LINARIA.

CHAMAECYTISUS. See CYTISUS *purpureus.*

CHAMAELIRIUM. *Liliaceae.* From the Greek *chamai*, dwarf, and *lirion*, a lily.

- **luteum.** From N. America and the only species in its genus. From a tuberous root spring neat rosettes of bright green, slightly fleshy leaves and 12 to 18 in. stems carrying slender racemes of cream-white flowers in summer. North aspect or light shade in moisture-holding soil.

CHAMAEPERICLYMENUM. See CORNUS *canadensis.*

CHEIRANTHUS. *Cruciferae.* The derivation is obscure.

- **cheiri** 'Harpur Crewe'. This is the only wallflower included in this manual, apart from some closely related species of Erysimum. It is not, of course, an alpine plant in any sense of the word, but it grows on many rock gardens and is deservedly popular for the sake of its rounded bushes covered in summer with clusters of yellow, sweetly fragrant double flowers. Better in soil which is poor rather than rich and likes all the sun it can get.
- **linifolius.** See Erysimum linifolium.

CHERLERIA sedoides. See ARENARIA *sedoides.*

CHEVREULIA. *Compositae.* Derivation unknown.

- **stolonifera.** From Bolivia. A more or less prostrate perennial with branching stems and rounded, untoothed leaves and yellow flower heads on short stems in summer.

117

CHIASTOPHYLLUM. *Crassulaceae.* From the Greek *chiastos*, crosswise, and *phyllon*, leaf, referring to the pairs of opposite leaves.

— **oppositifolium.** (Cotyledon *oppositifolia.* Cotyledon *simplicifolia.*) Fleshy, rounded, coarsely toothed leaves on 4 to 6 in. stems carrying pendant, branched racemes of golden flowers. Delightful in a cool crevice, late spring and summer flowering.

CHIMAPHILA. *Pyrolaceae.* From the Greek *cheima*, winter weather, and *phileo*, to love.

— **umbellata.** Widespread distribution in Eastern N. America, North and Central Europe, N. Asia and Japan. A lime-hater best pleased in a peat bed or in the alpine house in peaty soil. Whorls of dark green, evergreen leaves on short stems and small umbels of greenish-white or slightly pink flowers in mid- to late summer.

CHIOGENES. *Ericaceae.* From the Greek *chion*, snow, and *genos*, offspring. An allusion to the snow-white berries.

— **hispidula.** N. America and Japan. The only species in its genus. For peaty, lime-free soil and shady or cool conditions. Evergreen, creeping aromatic plant with small, ovate leaves backed with rusty hairs. White bell-shaped flowers solitary in the leaf axils, followed by glistening white berries. Spring flowering.

CHRYSANTHEMUM. *Compositae.* From the Greek *chrysos*, gold, and *anthos*, a flower.

In this large genus of popular garden and greenhouse plants there are not many alpine or rock garden plants. The few which are appropriate are described below and may be regarded as hardy and summer flowering. Some species entitled to inclusion are occasionally confused with genera LEUCANTHEMUM, TANACETUM and PYRETHRUM and I admit to personal doubts as to where some of them really belong.

— **alpinum.** (Pyrethrum alpinum.) European Alps. Tufts of small, deeply cut leaves and large white golden-eyed daisy flowers on semi-procumbent stems in summer. A good scree plant but usually not long-lived in gardens, so save and sow seeds occasionally.

— **arcticum.** (C. sibiricum.) From Alaska and Japan. Foot-high stems carry large white flower heads, the ray florets sometimes flushed pink, in June/July.

— **argenteum.** From the Orient and, if grown austerely, makes a good silver carpet with solitary white flower heads on quite short stems.

— **depressum.** From the Atlas mountains. Dwarf, and rock loving. Mats of finely-cut greyish leaves and long-stemmed white daisies with crimson buds.

- **haradjanii.** See *Tanacetum densum* 'Amanii'
- **hispanicum.** From Spanish mountains and very desirable — if dubiously resistant to winter-wet. It resembles a very silvery-leaved, golden-flowered *C. alpinum*, and there is a form, *C.h.* 'Sulphureum' with blossoms of soft sulphur-yellow. Perhaps best in an alpine house.
- **montanum.** (Leucanthemum montanum.) European Alps. A neat and tifted plant with small, fleshy, toothed leaves and inch-wide, yellow-centred flower heads on very short stems.
- **radicans.** From Spanish mountains and resembles — and may only be a form of, *C. hispanicum*. The flowers are yellow, or deeper gold and often show purple colouring at the base of the ray florets.
- **sibiricum.** See *C. arcticum*.
- **tomentosum.** From Corsica and very similar to *C. montanum*, with hairy, pinnate foliage.

CHYSOGONUM. *Compositae.* From the Greek *chrysos*, golden and *gonu*, a knee. The flowers are commonly carried at the nodes.

- **virginianum.** From N. America and the only species in its genus. An herbaceous perennial with procumbent, leafy stems. The leaves are ovate and bluntly toothed. The yellow flowers are freely produced during May and June. It prefers a not too hot and dry position but is a sun-lover.

CICERBITA. (LACTUCA) *Compositae.* The Italian name, of medeval origin, for sow-thistle, but now applied to a genus of blue-flowered plants allied to LACTUCA.

- **tenerrima.** From Morocco. A frail, prostrate plant with grey foliage and pale blue chicory-flowers on short, branching stems. For a warm, sunny position and not long-lived, so save and sow the seeds as an insurance.

CICHORIUM. *Compositae.* The Latinized version of an Arabic name.

A small genus containing such edible plants as Chicory and the Endive. Only one species is of interest here.

- **spinosum.** From Greece, Spain and Sicily. Intricate thorny hummocks only a few inches high of woody branches. From the intricacies of the tangled stems peer cheerful little chicory-flowers of intense blue during the summer. It asks for, and deserves, alpine house treatment, and likes hot, dry conditions and care with the watering can.

CISTUS. *Cistaceae.* With some hesitation I am omitting the genus Cistus from this manual apart from a brief reference. They really fall into the classification of shrubs, although several of the smaller kinds are grown on rock gardens. Reference to our price lists will provide brief descriptions of those we offer and for more detailed information there is no better source than Hillier's magnificent Manual of Trees and Shrubs.

CLAYTONIA. *Portulacaceae.* Named in honour of John Clayton (1686-1773). An Englishman who worked largely in Virginia, he was once described as 'the greatest botanist in America'.

A small genus, related to LEWISIA. The few appropriate species are described below. Probably happiest in lime-free soil and full sun, or in the alpine house. Spring and early summer flowering.

— asarifolia. From the Olympic Mountains of the State of Washington. Usually grows in rather moist, stony soil. Loose clusters of white flowers on short stems. Probably not long-lived.

— australasica. From Australia and New Zealand. Quite prostrate and spreads by running underground stems. Almost stemless white flowers.

— nivalis. Mountains of N.W. America. A crevice lover in nature but happy in cultivation if given the same treatment accorded to Lewisias. Loose tufts of narrow, fleshy leaves and bright rose-red flowers on short stems. The most desirable species but should be kept in an alpine house.

CLEMATIS. *Ranunculaceae.* The Greek name for various climbing plants.

Of this very large genus of herbaceous, woody and climbing plants only one species really qualifies for admission here.

— alpina. Native to Europe and N. Asia, and first introduced in 1792. It was at one time known as *Atragene alpina* because of slight botanical differences, but has now been classified as a species of Clematis. It is conventionally a climber, but can be used to great advantage in places where it can sprawl over large rocks or clamber into adjacent low bushes. The flowers, carried singly on short stems, appear with the young foliage in the spring. The four sepals are powder-blue centred by spoon-shaped petals of similar colouring. The rather similar *C. macropetala*, from China and Siberia, introduced first in 1910, or thereabouts, is rather more robust, with large flowers, the sepals powder-blue and the centre of each flower filled with petal-like segments, the outer ones blue, the inner ones white. Not quite so suitable for a rock garden, but an extremely beautiful plant.

CLINTONIA. *Liliaceae.* Named for Governor De Witt Clinton (1769-1828), of New York.

A small genus of woodland plants from Asia and N. America. They relish sandy peat and light shade or a cool north aspect and are ideal for peat gardens or the alpine house. Spring flowering.

- alpina. From the Himalaya. In its dwarfest form a desirable plant, with white flowers in loose racemes on stems which vary between 9 in. and 24 in. in height.
- andrewsiana. From California, and rather tall for most rock gardens. Bell-shaped, rose-red flowers in umbels followed by blue berries on two-foot stems.
- borealis. N. American, with yellow-green flowers in small umbels on 12 in. stems. It is curious rather than beautiful.
- uniflora. N. America. Six-inch stems carry solitary white flowers which are followed by porcelain-blue berries.

COCHLEARIA. *Cruciferae.* From the Latin *cochlear*, a spoon, referring to the shape of the basal leaves.

- alpina. The alpine scurvy-grass is unlikely to cause any great furore, but it is a rare native on British mountains. Basal rosettes of cordate, lobed or entire leaves and racemes of small white flowers on semi-procumbent stems in spring.

CODONOPSIS. *Campanulaceae.* From the Greek *kodon*, a bell, and *opsis*, resembling, a reference to the shape of the flowers.

A small genus of mostly perennial herbs with fleshy, slightly tuberous roots, found from the Himalaya to Japan. Some are convinced climbers, others tend to scramble through any convenient support. Easily grown in light soil and sunny positions, propagate by seeds. Mid to late summer flowering.

- bulleyana. Rather lax, leafy stems rising from a tuberous root and carrying bells shaped like a Chinese lantern and of a clear pale blue colour.
- clematidea. The long, frail, leafy stems will scramble up convenient supports and carry bells of soft blue delicately pencilled in deeper colour.
- convolvulacea. (C. tibetica.) From the Himalaya, and deserves alpine house treatment. Its slender, climbing stems need the support of light twigs as they rise from the tuberous root. The large blue flowers are of open bell-shape and very beautiful. Equally lovely is the form with pure white flowers. This handsome albino originated among a batch raised from wild collected seed and was given an Award of Merit in 1967, the type plant was similarly honoured in 1952.

121

— dicentrifolia. From Nepal and dubiously in cultivation, although it was said to grow well in the gardens at Keillour Castle in Scotland at one time. A slender scrambler with dark blue flowers tessellated inside with white.

— forrestii. See *C. convolvulacea.*

— lanceolata. Was once known as *Campanula lanceolata.* From China. A twiner with tuberous roots and purple stems. Bell-shaped flowers pale lilac outside and violet within.

— macrophylla. A rarity, possibly not now in cultivation, with yellowish bells on slender stems which appreciate light support.

— meleagris. From fleshy roots rise rosettes of rather wrinkled, acutely pointed leaves and 9 to 12 in. stems terminating in one or two large, bell-shaped flowers of a curious shade of greenish-yellow. As with many species the greatest beauty lies within the bell, which is striped with chocolate lines.

— mollis. From Tibet. The leafy, ascending stems carry rather beautiful bells of pale blue. The leaves are dressed in grey hairs and, unlike some species which emit a slightly foetid odour when handled, this is odourless.

— ovata. The plant usually grown under this name is probably not the true species. It comes from the Himalaya and has slender, semi-erect, hairy stems carrying almost sessile, pointed leaves. The pale blue bells are borne singly at the end of each stem. The inside of the bell is purple-veined with a basal blotch of almost black surrounded by a green zone.

— purpurea. Doubtfully in cultivation. In Nepal it grows on standing dead tree trunks in dense forests and would probably not be easy to please. The bells are described as deep, clear claret colour and it sounds desirable.

— tangshen. A twiner which will scramble to a height of several feet given support and hang out pale blue bells from the frail, leafy stems.

— thalictrifolia. Another desirable, but dubiously obtainable Nepalese. On each 18 in. leafy stem it carries a curiously waisted bell with an open mouth. The colour is a clear, soft blue.

— tibetica. See *C. convolvulacea.*

— vinciflora. A frail but lovely twiner which asks for a few twigs to support its leafy stems. Large, wide open flowers of clear, deep blue.

— viridiflora. A twiner with bells of soft green, marked inside with purple.

COMARUM. *Rosaceae.* From the Greek *komaros,* a name for the Arbutus, or strawberry tree, but transferred to *Comarum palustre* on account of the strawberry-like fruiting heads.

- **palustre.** (Potentilla comarum.) Closely related to Potentilla and an occasional British native. Known as the Marsh Cinquefoil, it likes a moist position. The pinnate leaves are green above and grey beneath and grow in tufts, from which rise foot-high stems carrying small, purple brown flowers terminally and in the axils in summer.

CONANDRON. *Gesneriaceae.* From the Greek *konos*, a cone and *andron*, anther. The appendages of the anthers are united in a cone around the style.

- **ramondioides.** A monotypic genus from Japan, allied to Ramonda. Can be grown in cool crevices outside but is happier in an alpine house. Large, crinkled leaves, shining green in colour and short-stemmed cymes of lilac-purple, orange-centred flowers. Increase by seeds, division or leaf cuttings.

CONVALLARIA. *Liliaceae.* From the Latin *convallis*, a valley. from its common habitat.

I hesitated before including Lily of the Valley in an Alpine Plant Manual, but it is so well loved, and appears on so many rock gardens that I could not deny its right to be here, however 'unalpine' it may be.

- **majalis.** There is only one species in the genus, but it exists in a number of variable forms. It is too well known to require description. Collectors may seek the form with soft pink bells, or another with double flowers. A third variant carries its bells in tight clusters and yet another has golden striations in the foliage. These markings are not consistent and may disappear one year, only to reappear the next and almost always vanish temporarily after replanting. There is also a robust form known as 'Fortin's Giant'.

CONVOLVULUS. *Convovulaceae.* From the Latin *convolvo*, to twine around.

A large genus of herbs, sub-shrubs and shrubs, widely distributed in temperate and sub-tropical regions and abundant around the Mediterranean. Few are rock garden or alpine house plants and I dare not recommend the rampagious, rampant but lovely *C. althaeoides*, which can be as vicious a weed as the common bellbine, a fault which damns it in spite of its lovely pink flowers. They are all avid sun-lovers, and spring and summer flowering.

- **boissieri.** A name sometimes given to *C. nitidus*, which see.

— cantabricus. S. Europe. A deciduous shrublet from 6 to 12 in. in height with green leaves adorned by silvery hairs. Each flower-stem carries up to four good pink flowers.

— cochlearis. From Greece and the Balkans. Not an easy plant to grow and best in the alpine house. Hard pads of intensely silver leaves and very short-stemmed large white, funnel-shaped flowers. Appreciates austerity.

— cyprius. From Cyprus. Small bushes of hard stems clothed in silver leaves and many funnel-shaped white flowers on stems just above the foliage.

— holosericeus. From Albania. Low, slowly spreading mats of silver leaves on woody stems and many almost stemless white flowers of satiny texture. Definitely an alpine house plant.

— lanuginosus. From Spain, S. France and Morocco. Erect stems, up to a foot in height. Narrow, intensely silver leaves and heads of white, pink-striped flowers.

— lineatus. From Spain and similiar to *C. holosericeus*. A glamorous mat-forming plant with gleaming silver leaves and clusters of pure white funnel-shaped flowers. Keep it in an alpine house or a choice corner in a stone sink or trough garden in very gritty soil.

— mauritanicus. From N. Africa. In a warm, sunny, protected niche this may be grown out of doors. Its trailing stems are dressed in softly hairy green leaves and the wide open flowers are blue, with a white throat.

— nitidus. (C. boissieri.) Another of the delightful Spanish species forming silver mats and carrying large, short-stemmed white funnels of satiny texture. It is not always free-flowering but will blossom if given austere treatment.

COPROSMA. *Rubiaceae.* From the Greek *kopros*, dung and *osme*, smell, an allusion to the fetid smell of some members of the genus when bruised.

A genus of trees and shrubs, largely native to Australasia. They are unisexual with sexes on different plants. Only one species is really appropriate for rock gardens.

— petriei. Dense three-inch mats of entwined stems with small, pointed, more or less hairy leaves and inconspicuous flowers followed by attractive round berries which may be almost white, or purple-blue

COPTIS. *Ranunculaceae.* From the Greek *kopto*, to cut. A reference to the deeply cut leaves.

A small genus widely spread over northern temperate and Arctic regions. Happiest in cool, moist, preferably lime-free soil and a north aspect or light shade. Ideal peat garden plants. Spring flowering.

COPTIS — *continued*

- **asplenifolia.** From N.W. America and Japan. About 12 in. high, foliage pinnatifid and toothed, few-flowered scapes of white blossoms.
- **quinquifolia.** Japan. Neat, palmate leaves in low tufts from which rise short stems carrying white, anemone-like flowers.
- **trifolia.** Japan, and cool regions of the Northern Hemisphere. Low tufts of dark green, trifoliate leaves and white, cup-shaped flowers on three-inch stems. Hardy, easy and delightful.

COREOPSIS. *Compositae.* From the Greek *koris*, a bug, and *opsis*, like. The seeds are thought to resemble a bug or tick.

- **rosea.** The only member of this family of, mostly, herbaceous perennials which falls within the scope of this Manual. It comes from Eastern North America. Farrer rhapsodies about it, but in reality, although a pleasant enough little plant, it is far from exciting. A virtue is that it flowers in the late summer, when its small pink marguerites on 9 in. stems over filmy foliage are acceptable. Full sun and any good soil, and increase by division.

CORIS. *Primulaceae.* A name used by Dioscorides.

A genus of only two Mediterranean species. For warm, dry positions and even then not completely hardy during really severe winters. Sandy, peaty soil.

- **hispanica.** Leafy sub-shrub of up to 1 ft. in height with ascending, leafy branches and racemes of soft lilac flowers in summer.
- **monspeliensis.** A dwarfer species with rather leathery small leaves and short, dense racemes of lilac or rose flowers.

CORNUS. *Cornaceae.* The Latin name for the Cornelian Cherry, *C. mas.*

Few of the Cornels find a place in the rock garden, but two species are excellent peat garden inhabitants although one of them is far from easy to please. They demand lime-free soil and cool conditions.

- **canadensis.** (Chamaepericlymenum canadense.) The creeping Dogwood comes from N. America and runs underground to form dense carpets of rounded, leathery dark green leaves. The clusters of small inconspicuous flowers are surrounded by four conspicuous white, petal-like bracts. Berries bright red and holly-like.

- **suecica.** A rare native of Northern Britain, also found in Arctic Europe, Asia, America and Japan. Creeping roots send up annual woody stems a few inches high with leathery, oval leaves. The small flowers are again surrounded by handsome white bracts followed by globose red berries. It is usually found to be difficult to establish.

125

CORONILLA. *Leguminosae.* Diminutive of the Latin *corona*, a crown. A reference to the umbels of flowers.

A race of tall and dwarf shrubs, lovers of hot, exposed and sunny places in sharply drained soil, late spring and summer flowering.

— **cappadocica.** From Asia Minor. A prostrate herbaceous perennial with leaves divided into many leaflets, rounded and toothed. Large yellow flowers in umbels.

— **emerus.** The Scorpion Senna from Central and S. Europe is too large for rock gardens but there is known a dwarf form, found in the Dolomites which makes low mats of dark green angled branches and compound bright green leaves. Golden flowers in pairs decorate the ends of the short stems, displaying a conspicuous, erect, hooded standard.

— **glauca.** This, too, is overlarge for most rock gardens, but there is a form, *C.g.* 'Pygmaea' which seldom exceeds 18 in. and is a desirable dwarf, golden-flowered shrub. Like the type it can be cut in cold winters.

— **minima.** From S.W. Europe. Procumbent stems forming low and tangled bushes covered in summer with umbels of fragrant yellow flowers. It should not be grown in cold, exposed positions.

— **varia.** A rampant species which cannot be mentioned without a warning of its capabilities in spreading far and wide. Given ample space it makes a riotous tangle of leafy stems and carries multitudes of pink and white flowers in large umbels.

— **viminalis.** Comes from N. Africa, and should be a good shrub, even if a trifle large. It sprawls and hangs out large trusses of white and lilac-blue flowers. It would need a warm and protected position.

CORTUSA. *Primulaceae.* Named in honour of Jacobi Antonio Cortusi (1513-1593) Director of the Botanic Garden at Padua.

A genus of but two species of primula-like plants demanding cool, moisture retaining soil and a north aspect or light shade. Spring flowering. Increase from seeds.

— **matthioli.** From mountains in Europe and Asia. Heart-shaped, softly hairy leaves in low tufts and 6 to 9 in. stems carrying one sided umbels of pink, pendant bell-shaped flowers.

— **semenovii.** From Turkestan. Similar to but slightly more robust than *C. matthioli* and with yellow flowers. Desirable, but dubiously in cultivation.

CORYDALIS. *Papaveraceae.* A Greek word meaning a lark. The flowers have spurs like those of larks.

A genus of some twenty or more species, some with tuberous roots, natives of temperate regions in the N. Hemisphere. Their requirements are too diversified to be covered by any general comments.

- aitchisonii. From the Hindu Kush, and very beautiful. It is sparingly in cultivation. Prostrate mats of glaucous, lobed, blue-grey leaves and large golden flowers on short stems.
- ambigua. From Japan. From a globular tuber spring pairs of divided leaves with rounded leaflets. On short stems appear terminal racemes of flowers with typical upturned spurs. The colour may be blue, purple or white.
- angustifolia. From Caucasus and Iran. Much divided leaves springing from a tuberous root and flesh-pink or white flowers in short racemes on 6 in. stems.
- bracteata. From the Altai mountains in Siberia. Grey, dissected leaves grow from a tuberous root and short stems carry dense racemes of pale yellow or creamy white flowers, the lower lip of each blossom being extended into a substantial lip.
- bulbosa. (C. cava.) Widespread from N. Europe to the Balkans. Tuberous roots hollowed on the upper surface. Leaves cut into wedge-shaped segments and short racemes of purple flowers.
- cashmiriana. From the Himalaya. One of the most beautiful species. It grows well out of doors, especially in the north of Britain and is also a delightful alpine house subject. Finely cut, blue-green, almost fernlike leaves make low tufts from which rise 6 in. stems carrying flowers of an almost indescribable glacier-blue. It is a capricious plant, succeeding here and failing there for no apparent reason but worth any effort to please.
- caucasica. From the Caucasus. Tuberous roots and small, deeply dissected leaves. Lax racemes of either cream-white or rose-purple flowers with an expanded lower petal.
- cava. See *C. bulbosa.*
- cheilanthifolia. Bold tufts of fernlike leaves and foot-high stems carrying dense racemes of yellow flowers. From China, and desirable.
- crassifolia. From Kashmir. Thick and leathery kidney-shaped grey leaves and short, densely clustered heads of soft purple flowers.
- diphylla. From the Himalaya. Loose tufts of dissected grey leaves rise from a tuberous root and 6 in. stems carrying lax racemes of flowers with white, purple-tipped petals with a spur having a pronounced upward tilt.
- marschalliana. From Russia and Iran and sometimes regarded as a sub-species of *C. bulbosa.* Deeply cut grey-green leaves and 9 in. stems bearing racemes of creamy yellow, or occasionally purple flowers.
- nobilis. From Siberia, and a striking and hardy plant. Its thick, fleshy roots resent disturbance once established. Deeply dissected foliage and stout, foot-high stems carrying spherical racemes of yellow flowers which are darker at the tips of the petals and display dark anthers.
- rutifolia. Found in rocky, often damp places in Crete, Turkey and Pakistan. Both flower and leaf stems creep underground horizontally

from the tuberous root, emerging in tufts here and there. Short stems carry lax racemes of flowers varying in colour from white, tipped with purple, to deep purple. Likes to be kept rather dry when dormant.

— solida. From Northern Europe, the Balkans and Asia Minor. Rather like a more slender *C. bulbosa* but displaying a characteristic scaly bract on the stems at ground level. The short, dense racemes of flowers may be white or purple-pink.

— transsilvanica. A great rarity, best kept in the alpine house. Not unlike *C. solida* in general appearance but with flowers on the short, erect racemes of terra-cotta pink. The origin is obscure, and forms are now appearing with mauve-purple flowers.

— wilsonii. From China and a handsome plant. Almost fernlike glabrous foliage and erect 12 in. stems carrying racemes of canary-yellow flowers.

This does not complete the tale of Corydalis but lists those likely to be obtainable from time to time. It is more than probable that current explorations in the Middle East and Asia Minor may introduce to us several more very desirable species.

COTONEASTER. *Rosaceae.* From the Latin *cotoneum*, quince and — *aster*, a suffix indicating a resemblance. From the similarity of the leaves of some species to those of the quince.

Although shrubs, as such, are excluded from this Manual, it seemed impossible to exclude a few of the very dwarf cotoneasters which are such ideal inhabitants of the rock garden.

— adpressus. From China. Very dwarf, making wide mats of congested. woody stems clothed in tiny, leathery green leaves which adopt rich autumn tints and are then accompanied by red, holly-like berries.

— buxifolius. From S.W. India. Dense, dwarf huddles of tangled stems and dull green leaves which show off the red berries.

— congestus. (C. pyrenaicus.) A creeping, woody evergreen forming mounds of small blue-green leaves. Berries bright red. From the Himalaya.

— dammeri. (C. humifusus.) From China. Quite prostrate and most useful as ground-cover beneath and between tall shrubs, but also has its uses on the large rock garden. Long trailing stems clad in evergreen foliage and fruits of sealing-wax red. There is a form *C. d. radicans*, which is even smaller.

— humifusus. See *C. dammeri.*

— microphyllus. From China and the Himalaya. Glossy-leaved evergreen with woody stems in tangled mats and large, globular scarlet berries. *Var. cochleatus* is even more prostrate with bright green rather broader leaves and *var. thymifolius* has tiny, glistening green leaves.

— pyrenaicus. See *C. congestus.*

COTULA. *Compositae.* From a Greek word meaning a small cup. The bases of the leaves of some species form cups.

A race of invasive but useful carpeting plants, mostly natives of the S. Hemisphere. Of the many species I describe only the few likely to appeal for use as ground-cover in the rock garden, or for planting in the cracks between paving stones, for which purpose they are ideally suited. Their flowers are unimportant but they can be esteemed for their pretty foliage.

— potentillina. The creeping stems are adorned by deeply pinnatifid green leaves.

— reptans. Carpeting, with pinnate, sometimes softly hairy leaves.

— squalida. Mats of deeply cut, often bronzed green leaves.

COTYLEDON. See the genera CHIASTOPHYLLUM and ROSULARIA.

CRASPEDIA. *Compositae.* From the Greek *kraspedon*, a fringe, an allusion to the feathery pappus.

— uniflora. Native to Australia, New Zealand and Tasmania. Perennial herb with stems and leaves coated densely with woolly grey hairs. 9 to 12 in. stems carry globular heads of closely packed small yellow flowers in summer. Best as an alpine house plant.

CRASSULA. *Crassulaceae.* A diminutive of the Latin *crassus*, thick. An allusion to thick, fleshy leaves of these plants.

There is really but one species hardy enough to be grown in the open, but I include one tender species which is very often esteemed as an alpine house specimen. The 300 or more known species are mostly natives of S. Africa with a few outliers in other tropical areas.

— milfordae. See *C. sedifolia.*

— sarcocaulis. Like a tiny gnarled tree. The erect, woody stems carry small, fleshy, pointed narrow leaves and terminate in cymes of crimson buds which expand into pink flowers. In very favoured situations it will survive out of doors.

— sedifolia. (C. milfordae.) From the Drakensberg mountains of Basutoland. Close, dense pads of congested rosettes of tiny bronzed, fleshy leaves and heads of small white flowers on 1 in. stems in summer. A good sink or trough plant for a sunny position.

CREMANTHODIUM. *Compositae.* From the Greek *kremao*, to hang, and *anthodium*, flower-head, referring to the pendant flower-heads.

A small genus of plants from India, Tibet and China. Not very easily grown but may succeed in soil rich in humus and cool situations. Late summer flowering.

— delavayi. Stems and the long, narrow leaves partly cobwebbed with fine white hairs and drooping heads of yellow flowers.

— farreri. Of similar habit to the preceding but the pendant flowers are more globular, white at first, changing as they age to claret.

— reniforme. Dwarfer than the two preceding species and neat in habit with the characteristically pendant flowers of clear yellow.

— sherriffii. A rare and refined species. The pendant florets are nearly an inch in length, white when first expanded but slowly changing, first to pink and then to deep red.

CRENULARIA. *Cruciferae.*

— eunomyoides. A rarity from the Cilician Taurus and happiest in the alpine house. Sparse branches clothed with small, grey, fleshy leaves form loose 6 in. bushlets and the stems terminate in clusters of small pink flowers. It is apt to collapse without warning and a reserve should be maintained from seeds or cuttings, which root easily. Summer flowering.

CREPIS. *Compositae.* From the Greek *krepis*, a boot, but why, is obscure.

— aurea. From the European Alps. Tufts of dandelion-like leaves and heads of orange-bronze flowers on short stems in summer.

— incana. From Greece, and an aristocrat in a sometimes rather weedy race. Rosettes of narrow, notched leaves grey with soft hairs. Stiffly branching foot-high stems carry myriads of pink hawkweed flowers over a long summer period.

— pygmaea. From Mediterranean regions. Lyrate leaves clothed in white hairs and heads of small yellow flowers on short stems.

CROWEA. *Rutaceae.* Named in honour of James Crowe (1750-1807) an English surgeon.

— exaltata. From Australia. Stiff, slender stems forming a low bush with narrow leaves. Bright pink flowers in profusion over a long summer period. For the alpine house.

CRUCIANELLA. See the genus PHUOPSIS.

CRUCKSHANKSIA. *Rubiaceae.*

Rarities from the Southern Andes of S. America, seldom success-fully grown but infinitely desirable. There appears to be no recipe for success and ample scope for experiment, were the material with which to experiment available.

- glacialis. (Oreopolus citrinus.) Found at sea levels in Magellan, which one might expect to presuppose a tolerance of winter-wet. Rosettes of smooth, thick, grey-green leaves gathered into hummocks. Bright yellow flowers sit on inch-long corolla-tubes instead of stems, and are said to be fragrant.
- macrantha. From alpine scree beds in Patagonia. A stout rootstock sends out slender stems to form mats of small rosettes of grey, partly rounded leaves. The yellow, starry flowers are carried on long corolla-tubes.

CUNILA. *Labiatae.* The Latin name for one of the mints.

- mariana. See *C. origanoides.*
- origanoides. (C. mariana.) An aromatic herb from Eastern N. America forming foot-high mounds of leafy stems surmounted by heads of pink or purple flowers in late summer, when extra colour is useful on a sunny place in the rock garden.

CYANANTHUS. *Campanulaceae.* From the Greek *kyanos,* blue and *anthos,* a flower.

A small genus of desirable, alpine herbaceous perennials natives of Central and Eastern Asia. They like sunny, open positions in gritty soil rich in humus. They appreciate plenty of moisture if accompanied by perfect drainage. Summer flowering and possibly happiest in lime-free soil although they will tolerate some alkalinity. Only those likely to be occasionally available are listed, but any species obtainable at any time is worth growing.

- integer. See *C. microphyllus.*
- lobatus. The species most widely cultivated, and one of the best. From a thick root rise many stems which radiate to form rounded pads clothed densely in lobed leaves and terminating in a single, large rich blue flower. A form with pure white flowers is known and there are geographical variations which have been identified under such names as *C. insignis* and *C. farreri.*
- microphyllus. (C. integer.) Slender, leafy, prostrate stems radiate from a central crown to form wide mats on the perimeter of which rests a circle of the purple-blue, funnel-shaped flowers which terminate each shoot.
- sherriffii. One of the gems of the race and comes from high, dry zones

131

in Tibet. The early stems are thickly clothed in silvery hairs, which become sparse as the growths elongate, eventually ending each in a single, rather tubular light blue flower, bearded in the throat — as are the blossoms of most other species. It is seen at its best when grown in an alpine house and is a rather risky proposition outside.

CYATHODES. *Epacridaceae.* From the Greek *kyathodes*, cup-like, an allusion to the cup-shaped, toothed disk of these evergreen shrubs.

A small genus of heath-like Australasian shrubs demanding lime-free soil and cool conditions. Ideal peat-garden plants. Some species are occasionally included in the genus LEUCOPOGON.

— **acerosa.** Although this New Zealand shrub is capable of growing to a height of 15 ft. or more, there are dwarf alpine forms which are suitable for the rock garden. One such form makes a compact bush 15 to 18 in. high with woody stems clothed in dark green, heath-like leaves. The white, bell-shaped flowers are axillary and are followed by white, pink or dull red berries. Possibly more correctly known as *C. juniperina.*

— **colensoi.** Erect, stiff stems dressed with tiny grey-green leaves. The small axillary flowers are white and are followed by luscent white berries. It will grow to a foot or more in height.

— **empetrifolia.** Prostrate, heath-like plant with massed slender, wiry stems and cream-white flowers in the leaf axils. Succulent red or white berries.

— **ericoides.** See LEUCOPOGON *ericoides.*

— **fraseri.** See LEUCOPOGON *fraseri.*

— **pumila.** A prostrate New Zealander with matted stems, and small white flowers followed by glistening red fruits.

CYCLAMEN. *Primulaceae.* The Greek name for these plants.

The needs of these popular rock garden and alpine house plants are diverse and generalisations as to cultivation would be useless. Some like shade, others relish full sun, some are hardy, others demand winter protection. The subject of their proper classification remains controversial and I have taken as my authority the excellent Monograph prepared by the late Doris Saunders and published by the Alpine Garden Society. All species develop from tubers which undergo a period of dormancy, varying according to their periods of growth and flowering. The purchase of tubers which have been lifted and dried should be avoided where possible.

- africanum. From Algeria, and botanically close to *C. hederifolium*. The tuber is flattened and usually slightly concave above and has a flaking, corky skin. The leathery leaves are large and of variable shape with only occasional markings on the upper surface. The flowers, sometimes faintly fragrant, are large and light or dark pink in colour, at the base of each petal is a crimson patch. Too tender for outdoor cultivation but a good alpine house species. Autumn flowering.

- alpinum. There remains some doubt as to the validity of this name, the plant having obvious affinities with both *C. cilicium* and *C. coum*. The rounded leaves have hastate markings above and are red beneath. The rose-pink petals of the flowers are twisted, propeller-wise, and stand out horizontally and each petal has a dark crimson blotch at the base. There is usually a distinct honey fragrance. Spring flowering.

- balearicum. From the Balearic Isles and S. France. The tuber is flattened and the roots spring from the centre of the base. Leaves narrow, pointed and toothed, marbled with silver, the lower surface crimson. The small white flowers are faintly pink-veined and fragrant. It is a spring-flowering shade lover best kept in the alpine house.

- cilicium. From S.W. Turkey. The flattened tuber has a grey-brown skin and the roots emerge from the centre of the base. Spoon-shaped leaves varying in size and marking. The hastate markings give a freckled appearance to the foliage. The underside is usually, but not consistently, red. Small flowers with long, pointed petals and varying in colour from near-white to rose-red. From the basal crimson blotch on the petals extend faint pink lines. Autumn flowering and fragrant.

- coum.This should really be regarded as a complex of slightly varying forms, a number of cyclamen grown under various names can be included in this group. The group has a wide distribution through E. Europe, the Caucasus, Asia Minor and into Iran, The rounded tuber has a thin, dark skin and the roots spring only from the base. The foliage is extremely variable, from entirely green to green marbled with silver. In form the leaves may be round or kidney-shaped. The under surface may be red, green or mottled. The flowers have short petals and vary in colour from near-white to deep crimson but always with a red or purple blotch at the base of the petals. Winter and spring flowering.

- creticum. From Crete. The tuber is flattened in shape. Leaves like those of *C. repandum*, but much smaller, cordate, pointed and with a jagged margin. The flowers are a little larger than those of *C. balearicum*, white, with a flush of soft pink and are faintly violet-scented. Spring flowering and not reliably hardy.

- cyprium. From Cyprus. The rounded tuber has a rough grey skin and is often flattened on both surfaces, roots grow from the base, sometimes acentrally, Small olive-green leaves with light green patterning, carmine-red beneath. The fragrant flowers may open soft pink but become pure white and there is a V-shaped purple blotch at the base of the petals. Autumn flowering, best in the alpine house.

- europaeum. See *C. purpurascens.*

133

— graecum. Widely distributed in Mediterranean regions and common on the mainland of Greece, with local variants on the Greek Islands. It grows in woodland or in the shade of bushes and is dubiously hardy in Britain, asking, and deserving alpine house treatment. Globular tubers with a corky skin and long fleshy roots emerging from the base of the tuber. The foliage is superbly marked but so variable that no description would be adequate. The flowers may be soft rose or deep pink with two plum-purple blotches at the base of the petals from which veins of pink run almost to the tips of the petals. Autumn flowering.

— hederifolium. (C. neapolitanum.) The most popular of all hardy cyclamen and invaluable for colonising. The tubers are rounded, often flattened above and the roots emerge from the top and the side. No two tubers produce leaves of identical shape or marking but are patterned in an infinitely varying degree of silver markings on the sombre green base colour. The large rose-pink flowers appear in the autumn and there is also a delightful albino, very rare in the wild but not infrequent among seedlings in cultivation.

— libanoticum. From the Lebanon, where it is now extremely rare. Not hardy, but one of the most beautiful of all cyclamen species. The tubers are rounded and slightly flattened and roots emerge from the base. The leaves are lobed, usually blue-green with distinct hastate patterning and beetroot-red beneath. The flowers have large, broad, pointed petals of clear rose-pink and appear in February and March.

— mirabile. From Turkey, where it was first discovered in 1906 but disappeared from cultivation until it was re-introduced in the 1960's. The plant resembles *C. cilicium* and flowers at the same period. The upper surface of the leaves is dull green, with a zone of pink or silver marbling. The characteristic pink markings are inconstant and often disappear as the foliage matures. The soft pink flowers have small purple blotches at the base of the petals. It may eventually be proved that this and *C. cilicium* are no more than segregates of one variable species.

— neapolitanum. See *C. hederifolium.*

— parviflorum. From Turkey, and not very easy to please. It probably asks for cool and moist conditions. The tuber is small and round and the leaves uniformly dull green. The not very conspicuous flowers are lavender-pink in colour with deep purple basal blotches on the petals. It flowers at about the same time as *C. coum.* to which species it is evidently related.

— persicum. There is a persistent refusal of uniformity evident in most species of cyclamen and nowhere is this character more evident than in *C. persicum*, which is the plant from which plant breeders have evolved the range of large-flowered florists' strains which are such popular pot and house plants. The type comes from the Eastern Mediterranean where it is widely distributed. The tuber is round and covered with a corky skin and the fleshy roots emerge from the sides and base of the tuber. The leaves are infinitely variable in size, shape and markings and the flowers, equally variable, from white to deep pink, appear in the early spring and are often sweetly scented. It must be regarded as no more than half-hardy and even in the alpine house should be protected from frost.

— **pseud-ibericum.** From Turkey and Asia Minor. The flattened, globular tuber has roots emerging only from the base and dark green, pointed leaves with some light marbling and a reddish reverse. Large lilac or magenta flowers with a white band surrounding the mouth of the corolla tube and a chocolate blotch at the base of each petal. It flowers in early spring and is usually fragrant.

— **purpurascens.** (C. europaeum.) From limestone areas of the European Alps. The tuber is rounded or irregular in shape and has a brown, slightly corky skin. The circular leaves are green with white patterning which may be faint or distinct. The short-petalled rose-pink or carmine flowers are strongly scented. Summer flowering.

— **repandum.** From Corsica, Sardinia and other Mediterranean areas. A woodland plant in nature with rounded tubers and roots emerging only from the base. The broad, cordate leaves taper swiftly to an acute point and have toothed margins and a silvery patterning. The flowers, some of which are scented, appear in the spring and have long, slightly twisted elegant petals of carmine-red. There is an attractive albino. Although not as hardy as *C. hederifolium*, it may be grown outside in sheltered positions.

— **rohlfsianum.** From Libya with a limited distribution in rocky places. It is not hardy but survives with ordinary alpine house care. The tuber may be very large and is often of a curiously distorted shape and is covered with a corky skin. It is unusual in that there are growing points all over the tuber and it can be increased by carefully cutting it into fragments, each of which must possess a growth point. The large, broad leaves are usually bright green, patterned with silver surfaces. The large pink flowers have acutely pointed and slightly twisted petals and appear in the autumn. A thorough baking during the dormant period is essential.

CYMBALARIA. *Scrophluariaceae.* From the Greek *kymbalon* or Latin *cymbalum*, a cymbal, referring to the leaf shape of some species.

The species described below are more frequently found under the name LINARIA, from which genus they have been removed.

— **aequitriloba.** (Linaria aequitriloba.) Although rampant, this is a delightful scrambler for walls or the crevices between paving stones. Tiny ivy-shaped leaves and myriads of purple-pink flowers in summer. From S. Europe.

— **hepaticifolia.** (Linaria hepaticifolia.) Another prostrate spreader, harmless in narrow crevices and delightful with small, kidney-shaped greyish leaves and lavender flowers with darker tips in summer. From Corsica.

— muralis. (Linaria cymbalaria.) The ordinary Kenilworth Ivy is too rampant for any but the wildest places but there is a nice miniature *C.m.* 'Nana Alba' which is neat and tidy and spangles its mats of green foliage with white, yellow-throated flowers all summer.

— pallida. (Linaria pallida.) A creeper which likes moist soil. Tiny rounded leaves and lavender flowers in summer.

CYPRIPEDIUM. *Orchidaceae.* From the Greek *Kypris*, Venus and *pedilon*, a slipper.

These beautiful hardy terrestrial orchids are in perpetual demand but are lamentably scarce in cultivation and the wise restrictions on their collection in the wild will make them even more difficult to obtain until someone discovers the secret of propagating them from seed or by some modern method of vegetative increase.

— acaule. (C. humile.) From N.W. United States. Large, solitary, pouched flowers of reddish-purple. Flowers in May-June and relishes being kept dry after flowering and likes an acid soil.

— arietinum. N. United States and Canada. The solitary flowers have sepals and petals greenish-brown with a red, white-veined lip. May flowering.

— calceolus. The British native, now almost extinct in Britain, but widespread in Europe. Several red-brown and yellow flowers with narrow, twisted petals. Spring flowering and lime-loving.

— candidum. N. America. Neat and dwarf, greenish-brown sepals and petals and a white lip, or pouch. Flowers in early summer.

— cordigerum. From the Himalaya. Sepals and petals white, yellow or green, lip white, with purple markings. Early summer flowering.

— debile. Japan. Small flowers with light green sepals and petals and a white pouch. Spring flowering.

— guttatum. From N. America, Russia and Siberia. A beautiful species with white flowers blotched with rose-purple markings. Likes shade and to be kept dry when dormant. Spring and early summer flowering.

— humile. See *C. acaule.*

— japonicum. Japan. Solitary flowers, the sepals green, and red-spotted, petals and lip white, stained crimson. Summer flowering.

— macranthon. Tibet and Siberia. Large, solitary rich purple flowers with an inflated pouch. May-June flowering.

— montanum. (C. occidentale.) N. America. Flowers brownish-purple with a white lip spotted crimson. Summer flowering.

— occidentale. See *C. montanum.*

— parviflorum. From N. America and closely resembles *C. calcelous.*

— pubescens. N. America. Large flowers with yellow-brown sepals and petals and a soft yellow pouch. Grows up to 18 in. Summer flowering.

CYPRIPEDIUM — *continued*

- **reginae.** (C. spectabile.) One of the most beautiful N. American species. Sepals and petals white, often rose-flushed and an inflated rich rose-pink pouch. Summer flowering.
- **spectabile.** See *C. reginae.*
- **yatabeanum.** Japan. Allied to *C. guttatum.* Sepals and petals yellow-green and a purple lip. Early summer flowering.

Several of the above species of Cypripendium are occasionally available but even if obtained patience will be needed as they resent being moved and may take some time to re-establish.

CYTISANTHUS. *Leguminosae.* See the genus ECHINOSPARTIUM.

CYTISUS. Leguminosae. From the Greek *kytisos*, used for several kinds of leguminous shrubs.

A large race of deciduous and evergreen shrubs and small trees. Although shrubs in general are excluded from this Manual it is fitting that several which are dwarf and admirable for use on rock gardens should be included. This is a sun-loving race easily grown in any well drained soil. Summer flowering.

- **ardoinii.** (Genista ardoinii.) Maritime Alps. Dwarf deciduous shrublet with quantities of yellow flowers which may be solitary or in axillary clusters.
- **X beanii.** A hybrid between *C. ardoinii* and *C. purgans* which occurred spontaneously at Kew in 1900. A semi-prostrate shrub with long sprays of golden flowers.
- **decumbens.** (C. prostratus.) No more than 6 in. high with sparsely hairy branches with small clusters of yellow flowers carried on the previous year's shoots. From S. Europe.
- **demissus.** (C. hirsutus demissus.) From Greece. Low and spreading deciduous shrub with grey-haired stems. The yellow flowers are carried in small clusters in terminal leaf axils and are adorned by a chocolate-brown keel.
- **hirsutus demissus.** See *C. demissus.*
- **hispanicus.** See GENISTA *hispanica.*
- **X kewensis.** A hybrid between *C. ardoinii* and *C. multiflorus*, raised at Kew in 1891. A deciduous, procumbent shrub up to a foot in height. Flowers cream-white or soft yellow.
- **pilosa.** See GENISTA *pilosa.*
- **procumbens.** (Genista procumbens.) A leafy, 18 in. shrub with slender, arching shoots, hairy when young and cylindrical racemes of yellow flowers.
- **prostratus.** See *C. decumbens.*
- **purpureus.** (Chamaecytisus purpureus.) A low, deciduous shrub from the European Alps. Purple flowers in loose sprays. There are some colour variants, including an albino and one with flowers of lavender-blue.

DALIBARDA. *Rosaceae.* Named in honour of Thomas Francois Dalibard, (1703-1779), a French botanist.

A monotypic genus containing one species best suited for lime-free soil and a shady, sheltered position.

- **repens.** From E. North America. A creeping plant with hairy stems and heart-shaped leaves and two or three white flowers on each short scape. It is related to RUBUS.

DAPHNE. *Thymeliaceae.* The Greek name for the bay tree, or laurel, *Laurus nobilis,* later transferred to this genus.

An important genus of some 30 or more species of evergreen and deciduous shrubs, widely distributed in Europe and Asia. Although most of them will tolerate alkaline soil, they seem to prefer lime-free conditions, but there are a few lime-loving exceptions. The taller growing kinds have been excluded from this Manual, with one or two exceptions of species which are of value for larger rock gardens, or even on smaller ones for the several years which will elapse before they outgrow their welcome.

- **alpina.** (D. candida.) Widely distributed in the Eastern Alps and invariably on limestone formations. Although not one of the most decorative species it makes a neat deciduous shrub up to 18 in. in height. The young growths are softly downy with narrow, alternate, grey-green leaves. The white, fragrant flowers are carried in terminal heads and are followed by red or orange fruits. Spring flowering.
- **arbuscula.** (D. cneorum var. abientina.) Originally introduced from the Carpathian mountains. A semi-prostrate, evergreen shrub forming mats of interlaced branches. The alternate, leathery, shining green leaves are grooved and slightly hairy beneath. The dense terminal clusters of very fragrant flowers are normally pink, but vary from almost white to deep rose-pink. Hardy, and also a splendid alpine house plant.

138

DAPHNE — *continued*

- australis. See *D. collina.*
- blagayana. From limestone areas in S.E. Europe. A dwarf evergreen shrub whose far-flung stems are almost leafless and benefit from being covered with leafy soil, or flat stones. It prefers a not-too-hot position and soil rich in humus. The terminal heads of crowded, tubular, cream-white flowers are intensely fragrant and appear in early summer.
- candida. See *D. alpina.*
- cneorum. (D. odorata.) A variable, but always beautiful species widespread from Central and Southern Europe to Russia. A freely branching, evergreen and partially trailing shrub, often known as the Garland Flower and universally popular. It flowers in spring and occasionally again in early autumn. The fragrant pink flowers are borne in dense terminal heads with immense freedom. It relishes an open, sunny position in essentially well-drained soil on either alkaline or acid soil and appreciates an annual top dressing of leafy soil to cover the stems, which become bare in time. *D. cneorum var. abietina* is a synonym of *D. arbuscula.*
- collina. (D. australis.) A plant of uncertain origin, and probably more correctly merged with *D. sericea,* but it is so well known and popular under this name that it is retained for the sake of common-usage. It is a compact evergreen, able to make a domed-shaped bush up to 18 in. in height. The shining, green, leathery leaves are pubescent beneath. The fragrant, rose-purple flowers are carried in terminal clusters in early summer.
- glomerata. From Turkey and the Caucasus. It is unfortunate that this splendid plant has not taken kindly to cultivation, where it lingers but fitfully in a few collections. It would seem essential to provide it with cool, humid conditions and a loose, peaty or leafy soil lacking lime. It is a dwarf, evergreen shrub, spreading by underground suckers — if you are lucky! — with glossy, leathery, shining dark green leaves clustered at the ends of the branches. Thirty or more cream-white, very fragrant flowers are gathered in terminal clusters from May to July.
- jasminea. From Greece. There are at least two very distinct forms of this highly desirable species, the most desirable from the alpinists point of view being the form from Delphi, which is quite prostrate. The other is an erect bush up to 18 in. in height. I will concentrate on the dwarfer form, which should be given alpine house treatment. It forms intricate mats of woody stems dressed with small, blue-grey leaves. The white or cream flowers, often red or purple on the outside of the tube, are very fragrant and are carried in heads of two or three and are followed by red fruits. It likes full sun and very sharp drainage in gritty soil and should be grown in pots or pans deep enough to accommodate the deeply delving woody roots.
- odorata. See *D. cneorum.*
- oleoides. From S. Europe and Asia Minor. A grey-green bush up to a foot or a little more in height with terminal heads of cream-white

139

fragrant flowers which are followed by orange, fleshy berries. It flowers in early summer and relishes a sunny position in well nourished soil.

— **petraea.** (D. rupestris.) The *creme de la creme* of alpine shrubs. From a limited area of the Southern Alps of Europe, where it inhabits crevices in limestone cliffs. For scree beds or crevices in the rock garden, for holes in tufa rocks, or for the alpine house, in gritty, limy, humus-rich soil. It is very slow-growing and most of the best plants in cultivation are of the 'Grandiflora' clone, and grafted onto another species of daphne. The woody branches tangle into intricate huddles to form dense, low, rounded hummocks, almost totally obscured in late spring by countless heads of tubular, rich pink remarkably fragrant flowers.

— **retusa.** From China, and only creeps in here because of its desirability, and because it is sufficiently slow-growing to qualify as a rock garden shrub. An evergreen shrub with erect, branched stems and pointed, narrow, leathery dark green leaves. Terminal, many-flowered clusters of rose-purple flowers emit a sweet fragrance and are followed by red, globose fruits.

— **rupestris.** See *D. petraea.*

— **sericea.** From Crete, and, as stated in the description of *D. collina*, much confused with that species. My own experience has been that *D. sericea* makes a taller, more erect bush with rose-purple fragrant flowers in terminal heads followed by fleshy orange fruits.

— **striata.** From the European Alps and resembles a prostrate *C. cneorum*. The woody stems radiate horizontally to form a tangled mat adorned with small, narrow evergreen leaves. The stems end in small heads of closely packed pink, fragrant flowers carried in early summer. It likes a peaty, gritty soil and a position which is not sun-baked.

— **X thauma.** A natural hybrid between *D. petraea* and *D. striata*. First found by Reginald Farrer on the Cima Tombea in 1911. Loose, low bushes of woody stems and small dark green leaves are adorned by clusters of pink flowers with tubes of richer colour. Flowers in spring and early summer. Should succeed in conditions rather less austere than those chosen by *D. petraea.*

DAVALLIA. *Polypodiaceae.* Named for Edmond Davall (1763-1789), Swiss botanist of English origin.

Although ferns play only a minor part in this Manual I could not exclude the one species of Davallia described below. It is an excellent alpine house plant and has proved hardy in the open in this cold corner of Sussex for many years. It relishes a cool position in soil rich in humus and does well in a peat garden.

— **mariesii.** From Japan and the only hardy Hare's-foot fern. From the creeping, hairy rhizomes spring many erect fronds in spring, deeply dissected and dark bronze-green in colour. Height about 9 in.

DEINANTHE. *Saxifragaceae.* From the Greek *deinos*, wondrous, and *anthe*, a flower.

Woodland plants from China and Japan asking for lime-free, peaty soil, light shade and protection from cold winds. Late summer flowering. There are but two species in the genus.

- **bifida.** Deciduous. Roughly crinkled, toothed leaves and terminal clusters of white flowers on 9 in. stems.
- **caerulea.** A little taller than *D. bifida*, but otherwise similar except for the colour of the flowers, which is a delicate violet-blue.

DELPHINIUM. *Ranunculaceae.* The Greek name *delphinion* is derived from the word *delphis*, a dolphin, an allusion to the shape of the flowers of one annual species.

Few delphiniums qualify for inclusion here but those suitable for a rock garden are described briefly. They ask only for any good soil and open, sunny positions, except if otherwise stated in individual descriptions.

- **brunonianum.** From Afghanistan to China. Kidney-shaped, softly hairy, musk-scented foliage and short, loose racemes of large, pale-blue to purple flowers on 12 to 15 in. stems in summer.
- **cashmirianum.** From the Himalaya. Lobed, hairy leaves and rather tall stems carrying corymbs of azure-blue to deep violet flowers.
- **muscosum.** A choice species introduced from Bhutan in 1949, which has only dubiously persisted in cultivation. Hairy, deeply dissected leaves and short, branching stems on which appear the solitary, large flowers varying in colour from light blue to deep violet-blue. The petals are edged with soft hairs and there is a tuft of white or yellow hairs in the throat of the blossom. It seldom exceeds 6 in. in height. Alpine house.
- **nudicaule.** A short-lived perennial from California. Loose panicles of red or orange flowers on short, branching stems in summer.
- **pylzowii.** From China. Softly hairy palmate leaves and several violet-blue flowers on each 9 to 12 in. stem in summer.
- **tatsienense.** From Szechwan. Perhaps a little tall for the average rock garden but an elegant, easy plant with corymbs of violet-blue, orange-bearded flowers in early summer.

DENDROSTELLERA. *Thymeliaceae.*

- **lessertii.** Probably not in cultivation, but a desirable cousin of the daphnes and certain to require alpine house treatment as it inhabits desert areas in the Elburz mountains of Iran. Dwarf shrub with heads of small cream, fragrant flowers.

DENTARIA. *Cruciferae.* From the Latin *dens*, a tooth, an allusion to the toothlike scales on the roots.

Modern classification places several species of DENTARIA in the genus CARDAMINE, but, as stated in the prefix to that genus, I retain the more familiar naming. Deciduous perennials for cool north aspects or light shade in well drained humus-rich and moisture-retentive soil. Spring flowering.

— **bulbifera.** A native of Europe, including Britain. Books will tell you that it has pinnate leaves and large purple flowers. In practice it seldom does more than bear clusters of bulbils in the uppermost leaf axils on the foot-high stems.

— **digitata.** From S. Europe. Leaves deeply cut and toothed and purple flowers on 18 in. stems.

— **enneaphylla.** From the Eastern Alps where it grows in sub-alpine woodlands. Deeply cut foliage and pendant sprays of pale yellow flowers.

— **pinnata.** European. Leaves pinnate with pointed segments and flowers which may be white or pale purple. About 12 in.

— **polyphylla.** E. Europe. Whorls of pinnate leaves. One of the best with slightly pendant, campanulate pale yellow flowers carried in heads well above the foliage on 15 in. stems.

DIANTHUS. *Caryophyllaceae.* From the Greek *dios*, divine and *anthos*, a flower.

An important genus of importance for the rock garden and alpine house, but abounding in hybrids, many of which although highly desirable, are often of confused parentage and defy classification. I make no apology for excluding many of these and devoting most of my limited space to the species and natural variants. With a few exceptions they are lime lovers, and should be given open, sunny positions. They are summer-flowering. The genus really needs a monograph and can be given scant justice here. In 1949 I wrote a book entitled 'The Dianthus', which was reasonably comprehensive. It is out of print but can usually be obtained from second-hand bookshops, and we do occasionally have spare copies to offer.

— **alpester** (alpestris) See *D. furcatus.*

— **alpinus.** European Alps. One of the alpine glories of the race in its best forms. Prostrate mats of narrow green leaves and huge, rounded flowers with wide, overlapping petals of rose-crimson on 2 to 3 in. stems. It is subject to attack by the Carnation Fly, *Hylemyia brunnescens*, a few crystals of paradichlorbenzene placed round the base of the plants in March and August will repel the egg-laying flies. It likes leafy, gritty soil. A form named 'Adonis', if it still exists, has extra large salmon-pink flowers which change as they age to pearl-white. There is also a good albino.

DIANTHUS — *continued*

- **androsaceus.** See *D. pinifolius.*
- **arboreus.** From the Mediterranean and shrubby, capable of growing to a height of about 18 in.. It must have a warm, sunny, sheltered position or be grown in an alpine house. The stout, erect stems carry narrow, long grey-green leaves and the branching stems erupt into heads of showy pink flowers from midsummer onward.
- **arenarius.** From N. Europe, and rather similar to *D. squarrosus* but looser growing and slightly taller. The white flowers have cleft petals and are very fragrant.
- **aridus.** From Greece and E. Europe. Not very decorative, but of interest as it is one of the few species bearing yellow flowers. The colour is not as rich as that of *D. knappii* but it has potential value as a parent. It has bare, rather lanky stems and should be grown among other plants to conceal this defect.
- **armeria.** This is the Deptford Pink and is one of the very few British species. It also extends throughout Europe and into the Caucasus. The foot-high stems carry heads of small pink flowers. Its garden value is not high.
- **arvernensis.** This origin of this excellent dianthus is somewhat shrouded in mystery. Some authorities deny it specific rank and consider it a hybrid between *D. monspessulanus* and *D. seguieri* (sylvaticus) but this I have never believed. It is more likely to be a form of *D. gratianopolitanus* (caesius) from the Auvergne mountains of France. It is a mat of grey foliage adorned by myriads of shapely rich pink flowers on short stems, and there is a delightful albino with pure white flowers.
- **barbatus.** Not an alpine, but it has been cultivated since 1573 and is the origin of the colourful Sweet Williams which are such popular bedding plants. Its only interest for alpinists lies in one or two hybrids, notably 'Napoleon III' and 'Dr Dangar', which are dwarf, leafy plants with bold heads of deep crimson-red flowers. Unfortunately both seem to have flowered themselves to a regretted death. Should either be discovered it demands rich soil, great care and frequent propagation by cuttings.
- **biflorus.** From Greece, and it has been said that it should remain there, but I have a liking for the twin flowers of coppery-red carried on stems which are just too long. It produces little other than flower stems and is not easy to keep going.
- **X boydii.** This is one of the admissible hybrids — if obtainable. One of its parents was undoubtedly *D. alpinus* and it may well be of the same parentage as *D. X calalpinus.* It has the habit of *D. alpinus* and carries its large, rounded bright pink flowers on 2 in. stems.
- **brachyanthus.** Authorities have consigned this plant to various other species from time to time and the verity of its name remains in doubt. It comes from Spain and is sufficiently variable to add to the confusion of its nomenclature. Above the neat, dark green hummocks of its narrow leaves appear many small, but shapely pink flowers on 6 in. stems.

— caesius. See, regrettably, *D. gratianopolitanus.*

— X calalpinus. This is a natural hybrid between *D. alpinus* and *D. callizonus* and is a gem. It is intermediate in appearance between the parents and should be prized in a choice position and very gritty but not impoverished soil and propagated regularly from cuttings.

— callizonus. A choice species from the Carpathians and one of the most beautiful. In general appearance it is not unlike *D. alpinus*, but the short-stemmed flowers are larger, lavender-pink in colour and each blossom has a prominent purple, white-flecked central zone. A cool, gritty scree and frequent top-dressings of fine soil provide what it needs but it is not the easiest dianthus to keep alive and happy.

— carthusianorum. A species from the Alps of Europe which has been continuously in cultivation since the 16th century. It is variable and the heads of frankly magenta flowers may be poised on stems of a foot or 3 ft. in height. It is not one of the beauties of the race but the fact that it has survived in gardens for 400 years proves that it must be found desirable.

— cinnabarinus. A Grecian species of rather gawky habit. If the true plant can be obtained it is worthwhile for the sake of the cinnabar-red flowers, but it is too often represented by some less worthy plant. It should be planted amongst other plants so that the rather ungainly stems are at least partially concealed.

— cruentus. From the Balkans, and similar to *D. carthusianorum* but with bright crimson flowers.

— deltoides. The Maiden Pink and an occasional native. It is extremely variable and forms with flowers of varicus shades of pink to pure white occur among seedlings. Several clones have been selected and named and the best of these, with very dark green foliage and red or crimson flowers are 'Flashing Lights', 'Wisley Variety' and 'Bowles's Variety'.

— erinaceus. A rare species from Asia Minor. It forms prickly cushions and, on short stems carries flowers singly, or in pairs of rose-red with fringed petals. It demands a hot, dry position and is not very fond of winter wet.

— freynii. Probably only a form of *D. glacialis*, but too well known under the specific name for this to be abandoned. It comes from the Balkans and makes neat, low tufts of narrow, grey-green leaves which disappear in summer beneath the innumerable small, soft pink flowers carried on inch high stems. It is a splendid sink or trough plant.

— frigidus. The plant encountered in gardens under this name is no more than a high alpine form of *D. sylvestris* condensed in habit and with large and richly coloured flowers.

— fruticosus. It grows on Crete and also in Greece and is a bushy, rather shrubby species not unlike *D. arboreus* in appearance but of denser, more compact habit. On short flower stems it bears corymbs of deep pink, non-fragrant flowers. It must have a warm and sheltered position.

- furcatus. (D. alpester. D. alpestris.) From alpine meadows of European Alps. It resembles *D. sylvestris* but the 9 in. stems carry several large, rather nodding flowers of deep rose-red. They are fragrant, and the petals are fringed, although not so deeply cut as those of *D. sylvestris.*
- gallicus. A native of sand dunes in Northern France and definitely not an alpine plant but worthy of a place on any rock garden. It is not unlike *D. deltoides*, with short, narrow leaves which are hairy at the base and fragrant, pink, fringed flowers. It is a good crevice plant.
- glacialis. From the Eastern Alps and has been regarded as a lime hater but it does not object to alkaline soil in cultivation, Resembling *D. alpinus* in some ways, it makes a deep tap-root and forms low tufts of dark green leaves, which are broad, blunt and glossy. The large, carmine-pink flowers are carried singly on short stems. There is a good albino which almost always breeds true from seeds.
- graniticus. Occurs on granite rocks in S. France and closely resembles *D. deltoides*, but with shorter, dark green leaves and clusters of small, bright pink flowers.
- gratianopolitanus. (D. caesius.) It is unfortunate that laws of priority insist upon changing the name of the Cheddar Pink, so well known in gardens as *D. caesius*. A rare native, it also occurs throughout Western and Central Europe. It is a variable species and is represented in gardens by many similar but slightly divergent forms and some hybrids. In its most typical manifestation it forms low mats of grey, narrow leaves over which hover many flowers of deep rose-pink and fine fragrance on 4 to 6 in. stems. It has been too ruthlessly collected from its station on the Cheddar rocks and should be respected as a rare native.
- haematocalyx. From the Thessalian Olympics and a treasure, forming cushions of sharply pointed grey leaves from which rise 9 to 12 in. stems carrying sprays of purple-red flowers the petals of which are backed cinnamon-yellow. There are two distinct forms also in cultivtion, one, *D.h. pruinosus*, is of laxer habit and usually carries but one flower on each stem. *D.h. alpinus* is the best of all, making dense tufts with short-stemmed large flowers carried singly.
- inodorus. See *D. sylvestris.*
- jacquemontii. A desirable species from Kashmir only dubiously in cultivation. It should make dense tufts of narrow leaves and carry white sweet-scented flowers on short stems.
- juniperinus. A rare species from Southern Europe and almost shrubby in habit, forming foot-high bushes of ascending stems clothed in hard, spiny leaves. The branching stems carry heads of soft pink flowers from mid-summer on into autumn. Give it plenty of sunshine.
- kitaibelii. The true plant is a gawky weed unworthy of garden room. The plant sometimes grown under this name is probably *D. petraeus.*
- knappii. From Eastern Europe. Although it is cursed with an untidy, gawky habit of growth, and is not long-lived, often flowering itself to death, this species is noteworthy for its flowers of clear yellow,

carried in clusters at the tips of straggling stems. It comes true from seed, which should be regularly saved as it seldom makes adequate growth from which cuttings can be made.

— **langeanus.** From S.W. Europe. Very neat tufts of narrow leaves rising from a woody stock and solitary carmine-red flowers on less than inch-high stems.

— **microlepis.** From the mountains of Bulgaria and happiest in lime-free soil. It makes neat, circular tufts of tiny grey leaves and carries many small, clear pink, almost stemless flowers.

— **monspessulanus.** Grows in stony alpine meadows from Portugal to Yugoslavia. Of tufted habit it carries many deeply fringed, large flowers of lavender-pink or almost white and sweetly fragrant on erect, foot-high stems. In the Eastern Alps occurs the form *D.m. sternbergii,* which is dwarfer, with even larger flowers of rich rose-red.

— **musalae.** From the high mountains of Bulgaria and sometimes said to be a form of *D. microlepis,* but surely worthy of specific rank. Grow it in conditions of austerity and it will make hard cushions of tiny grey-green leaves which it conceals beneath glowing red flowers carried on inch-high stems.

— **myrtinervis.** When first introduced many years ago this was thought to be a microform of *D. deltoides,* but it now has, and deserves, specific rank. It is another plant demanding austere treatment to induce the typical dense habit, with cushions as tight and hard as those of *Silene acaulis,* covered by myriads of almost stemless bright pink flowers. Given luxury treatment it becomes loose, lax, and disappointing.

— **neglectus.** See *D. pavonius.*

— **nitidus.** A small species from the Carpathians forming neat tufts and cushions of bright green leaves and inch-high stems carrying almost black buds which expand into fragrant pink flowers of goodly size.

— **noeanus.** I scarcely know where to include this good plant. I referred it here from Acanthophyllum but, if the truth were told, it is probably a sub-species of *D. petraeus.* However, to avoid further confusion for gardeners I leave it under this well known name. It is a tufted plant from Bulgaria with many fragrant white flowers on 9 in. stems.

— **pavonius.** A popular species under its better known but invalid name of *D. neglectus.* It usually inhabits lime-free soils and is common in the Eastern and South-Eastern Alps. Low pads of thin, pointed leaves form the base from which spring the short stems carrying large flowers, varying in colour from pale to deep pink, but always with the characteristic buff colouring to the backs of the petals.

— **petraeus.** From the Balkan Peninsula and a variable species. The most typical forms make cushions of narrow leaves and produce thin, leafless stems of about 6 in. each carrying one small white flower with evenly notched petals. There is an attractive double-flowered form and, according to some authorities, the plant which I have described under *D. noeanus* should be a sub-species of this.

- pindicola. According to the latest classifications this is another sub-species of *D. haemetocalyx* from Eastern Europe. Tiny tufts of sharply pointed broad grey leaves and rose-red flowers with a buff reverse to the petals carried on short, stiff stems.

- pinifolius. (D. androsaceus.) A cushion-forming plant from Greece with compact huddles of narrow, grass-like grey-green leaves and 2 to 3 in. stems each carrying several rose-red flowers. It gives of its best when accorded a somewhat spartan diet.

- X roysii. A hybrid of uncertain parentage, but undoubtedly claiming *D. pavonius* (neglectus) as one parent. It grows like a robust *D. pavonius* and has very large flowers with wide, overlapping petals of rich rose-pink. The petals show the buff reverse characteristic of *D. pavonius.*

- scardicus. From mountain pastures in the Eastern Alps. Domed cushions of narrow, pointed green leaves and short stems carrying dainty pink flowers.

- seguieri. From the Pyrenees and Italy and late flowering. A rather tall plant usually found growing amongst herbage. Clusters of magenta flowers on 15 to 18 in. stems.

- simulans. It is not proven that this is a true species, but it is in gardens under this name. It came from the Graeco-Bulgarian frontier mountains in 1933 and forms dense tufts of grey, spiny leaves which are hidden beneath the wealth of short-stemmed rose-red flowers in early June. A fine scree or trough plant.

- spiculifolius. From the Carpathians and similar to *D. petraeus*, and may indeed be no more than a subspecies of that plant.

- squarrosus. From Russia and Siberia. Mats of deep green, rather spiny foliage and 9 in. stems carrying deeply, fringed and slashed pure white flowers with an intense fragrance. One of the nicest species and easily grown.

- sternbergii. See *D. monspessulanus.*

- strictus. A good species from S.W. Asia, but there is no little confusion in gardens as to which plant should bear this name. It has been grown as *D. integer* and as *D. strictus brachyanthus.* I remain uncertain as to the rights of the matter but the plant I have forms mats of grey-green leaves and has flowers of deep pink on short stems.

- suendermanii. The plant grown under this name in gardens forms mats of green, narrow leaves and bears white or cream flowers with overlapping petals on 6 in. stems. By some authorities the name is quoted as a synonym of *D. petraeus*, from which this plant differs.

- superbus. Throughout Europe and into Northern Asia. This grand old plant has been known since the 13th century. Not the tidiest of species it is apt to sprawl into wide cushions of lax stems with broad leaves and long branching stems carrying sprays of intensely fragrant lavender-pink, green-eyed flowers whose petals are deeply cut and fringed into segments as narrow as those of our wild Ragged Robbin *(Lychnis flos cuculi)*.

— sylvestris. (D. inodorus.) In spite of its name which indicates a sylvan environment this species invariably inhabits open, sunny positions in the European Alps. Bold tufts of grassy foliage from which emerge arching stems carrying many rounded, rose-pink flowers with notched petals. It is variable in colour and the best forms should be selected.

— versicolor. From Russia and an unusual and rather exciting species. In general appearance it is not unlike *D. pavonius* (neglectus) but the large flowers, carried on 6 in. stems open pure white and slowly change to buff-pink. Later still they become deep pink in colour and in the height of its late-summer season it presents a chequered appearance of white, pale and deep pink flowers all expanded together.

DIAPENSIA. *Diapensiaceae.* The Classical Greek name adapted by Linnaeus.

A small and very select genus of rather difficult plants for lime-free soil and very careful alpine house cultivation. Their distribution is in Asia, N. America and N. Europe. Spring and summer flowering.

— himalaica. From the Himalaya. Close, dense mats of tiny leaves studded with almost stemless bright pink flowers.

— lapponica. (D. obtusifolia.) Occurs over the whole range of the genus and was recorded as a British native in Inverness in 1951. Dense prostrate tufts with rounded, greenish-white flowers on inch-high stems. The Asiatic variant, *D.l. obovata* is similar and appears to be more tolerant of cultivation.

— obovata. See *D. lapponica.*

— obtusifolia. See *D. lapponica.*

The two other Himalayan species, *D. purpurea*, and *D. wardii*, although extremely desirable appear to be entirely out of cultivation.

DIASCIA. *Scrophulariaceae.* From the Greek *di*, two, and *askos*, a sac. The flowers have two spurs.

A genus of S. African annual and perennial herbs, few of which are hardy.

— cordata. Mats of more or less prostrate leafy stems from which rise 6 to 9 in. flower stems carrying short racemes of terracotta-pink. Summer flowering, for warm positions in any good, well-drained soil. It appears to be very hardy, as does the hybrid between it and the annual *D. barberae*, grown as *D. X* 'Ruby Field', which is rather taller, very floriferous and has flowers of rich salmon-pink.

DICENTRA. *Papaveraceae.* From the Greek *dis*, twice, and *kentron*, a spur. The flowers have two spurs.

This is a genus which places me in a slight quandary. Of the twelve or more species, natives of Asia and N. America, few really qualify as rock garden plants, although listed in most alpine catalogues. I shall content myself by describing only the dwarfer species best suited to alpine houses and rock gardens. Such kinds as *D. eximea*, *D. formosa*, *D. spectabilis* and *D. oregana* are more in the realm of herbaceous perennials.

- canadensis. From N. America. About 6 in. tall, with glaucous, finely cut foliage and short racemes of white, short-spurred, typically lyre-shaped flowers in May. Tiny tuberous roots, grow in gritty soil in the alpine house or in a cool choice position outside.

- cucullaria. From N. America and similar to but dwarfer than *D. canadensis* with pretty, deeply cut blue-green leaves springing from the small tubers. Flowers white, yellow-tipped in spring.

- nobilis. From Korea and I know it only by a brief description. It is probably too tall for most rock gardens but the golden flowers make it sound desirable — if it is in cultivation, which I doubt.

- peregrina. The delight, and too often the despair of alpine plant enthusiasts who delight in the aristocrats of the alpine world. It comes from Japan and the plant originally introduced was named *D.p.* 'Pusilla' but it is a slightly variable species and Ohwi, in his monumental *Flora of Japan* states that it should be correctly just *D. peregrina.* Low tufts of finely dissected blue-green leaves and short stems each carrying several soft pink lyre-shaped flowers in spring. Give it gritty soil not lacking in humus, grow it in the alpine house and hope for the best.

Mention should be made of the 'Rokujo Hybrids' raised in America by the late Professor Marion Ownbey. They are the results of hybridising *D. peregrina* with several of the American species and the results are a series of very handsome plants of fairly dwarf stature, having ornamental foliage and flowers of varying shades of pink and soft red.

DICLIS. *Scrophulariaceae.*

- bambuseti. From E. Africa and dubiously in cultivation. A carpeting plant from open highland forests with heads of white flowers.

DICRANOSTIGMA. *Papaveraceae.* From the Greek *dikranos*, two-branched, plus *stigma.*

- lactucoides. From the Himalaya. Tufts of spreading, rather dandelion-like leaves, blotched towards the midrib. The branching, foot-high stems carry many large rich yellow flowers in summer. Likes a not too

149

hot position in any good soil. This species has been confused in gardens with the much taller, Chinese species *D. franchetianum*, which is little more than a biennial.

DIDISSANDRA. *Gesneriaceae.* From the Greek *di, dis,* twice two, and *ander,* stamens.

Disagreement between botanical 'splitters' and 'lumpers' has caused much confusion between the genera DIDISSANDRA, OREOCHARIS and BRIGGSIA, to say nothing of ANCYLOSTEMON, ROETTLERA and TREMACRON. None of them is easy to grow, all demand alpine house conditions and some are barely hardy, but they are very beautiful plants, rare in cultivation but worth any effort to obtain and grow.

— grandis. Rosettes of Ramonda-like leaves, dark green touched with bronze, and umbels of tubular, violet-blue flowers. The stems and calyces are felted with brown hairs. From Yunnan, where it grows on shady rocks. Spring flowering.

DIELSIOCHARIS. *Cruciferae.*

— kotschyi. From the mountains of Turkey and Iran. A humped cushion-plant which grows among the Dionysias, and mimics them. Sheets of short-stemmed yellow flowers. If obtained should be sheltered in an alpine house and given the treatment one would accord to the choicest Draba — a genus which it closely resembles.

DIGITALIS. *Scrophulariaceae.* From the Latin *digitus,* a finger. The flowers are like the fingers of a glove. The common name Foxglove undoubtedly derives from 'Folk's-glove'.

The twenty or more species are widely distributed in Europe, N. Africa and Asia. Many are, of course, herbaceous plants for flower beds and borders, even some of the few described below may be so positioned.

— ambigua. See *D. grandiflora.*
— davisiana. From Turkey, 18 in. stems carrying racemes of bronze-yellow flowers.
— dubia. A Spanish species with short stems of about 9 in. rising from rosettes of downy leaves. Flowers soft purple-pink. Slightly tender and not very long-lived.
— grandiflora. (D. ambigua.) From sub-alpine Europe. Tufts of large, hairy leaves and tall racemes of yellow flowers closely netted with brown veins.
— mariana. A rare Spanish species which, in gardens, has been confused with another Spanish species, *D. obscura.* The true plant has leaves densely felted with white tomentum. Flowers purple.

DIGITALIS — *continued*

  — obscura. From Spain. A low sub-shrub with leathery leaves and short
    racemes of orange-red flowers. It asks for, and deserves, care and a
    warm dry situation.

DIMORPHOTHECA. *Compositae.* From the Greek *dis*, twice,
morphe, a shape, and *theka*, fruit. There are two kinds of achenes
found in the same fruiting heads of these S. African plants.

  — barberiae. The only species with any pretension to hardiness and even
    so not reliably so. Rock gardeners are more likely to appreciate it in
    the dwarfer, hardier form known as *D. b.* 'Compacta'. Tufts of narrow,
    rather leathery aromatic leaves over which hover short-stemmed large
    daisy flowers of rosy-purple all summer. Sandy soil and full sun.

DIONYSIA. *Primulaceae.* From Dionysos, the earlier Greek name
for Bacchus.

A fascinating genus confined in its distribution to the mountains of
the Middle East and Southern U.S.S.R. There are now nearly 40
known species, several of which are in cultivation, some firmly
established, others more tentatively sampling the conditions and
environment we have to offer them. They mostly occur on limestone, in very dry conditions. They are spring and early summer
flowering and demand alpine house conditions and careful cultivation. The injudicious use of the watering-can has caused many
tragedies. A detailed description of the known species would be out
of place here, especially as many of them are not yet available, but
there is an excellent Monograph on the genus, written by Mr. C.
Grey-Wilson and published by the Alpine Garden Society.

  — aretioides. From the Elburz mountains of Iran. First discovered in
    1770 but not introduced to cultivation until 1959. It is one of the less
    difficult and most beautiful of the species. Dense cushions·of packed
    rosettes of softly hairy leaves, lightly toothed at the upper margins.
    From each rosette springs an almost stemless yellow flower. It is a
    variable species and selected forms have been given clonal names —
    viz. *D.a.* 'Gravetye' and *D.a.* 'Paul Furse'. Like all the Dionysias I
    have so far grown it is very happy in Tufa rock.
  — bryoides. From the South of Iran, first collected in 1842 but not
    established in gardens until the sendings of 1966, which appear to be
    settling down. Dense green cushions of congested rosettes carried on
    columnar stems. Long-tubed pink flowers. It is likely to prove one of
    the less amenable species.

- **caespitosa.** From Iran. Of densely tufted habit with tiny, lightly-haired leaves overlapping on the short stems. The flower stem, variable in height up to 2 in. carries a few-flowered umbel of rich yellow flowers.

- **curviflora.** First introduced by Paul Giuseppi in 1932 and now well established in cultivation. More recent introductions appear to be more free-flowering than the original form. Dense, compact huddles of rosettes of green or grey-green leaves and many solitary pink flowers with a yellow eye.

- **janthina.** From Iran, and not to be confused with *D. ianthina*, which is a synonym of *D. curviflora*. Dense, very compact, silvery-grey cushions. The pink, yellow eyed flowers are solitary and sessile. Spasmodically in cultivation, it appears to demand very dry conditions, especially during the winter.

- **michauxii.** From S. Iran and first collected in 1783. Reintroduced in 1932 and again in 1966. It forms dense rounded pads of stems clothed in scale-like overlapping leaves. The yellow, long-tubed flowers are solitary and sessile. It is difficult and demands very dry conditions and appears to resent root disturbance once established. Repotting should only be undertaken when absolutely necessary.

- **tapetodes.** Distributed from the Southern U.S.S.R. through Iran and into Afghanistan. Tufted cushions of short stems clothed in overlapping leaves. Long-tubed yellow flowers on a very short scape. Usually inhabits shady cliffs of limestone or dolomite. Variable, especially in the foliage.

- **teucrioides.** The only Turkish endemic species. Introduced in 1867 and it is only too willing to give up the ghost without warning. The habit is loose and tufted, the branches dressed with oblong, toothed leaves and with soft, fine hairs. The short, erect scape carries an umbel of up to three yellow flowers.

The garden history of Dionysias is only now being written and there is much experimenting to be done before we are assured of success with these captivatingly lovely and exciting plants and it is reasonably certain that some of the more intractable species will continue to present a problem as challenging as that posed by *Eritrichium nanum*, that other coy inhabitant of high places.

DIOSCOREA. *Discoreaceae.* Named in honour of Pedanios Dioscorides, first-century Greek physician and herbalist and compiler of *Materia Medica.*

- **pyrenaica.** More correctly *Borderea pyrenaica*, but I adhere to the better-known name. From the Pyrenees and the only non-tropical Yam. It has no beauty but is an interesting plant to grow. From a very large tuber spring trailing stems clothed in heart-shaped green leaves and with inconspicuous small yellow-green flowers in summer. The genus Borderea was named in honour of Henry Bordere (1825-1889) student of the Pyrenean flora.

DIOSPHAERA. *Campanulaceae.*

It seems probable that all the diosphaeras will eventually be included in the genus TRACHELIUM but, sticking to my loyalty to 'common-usage' — and also, I admit, taking the coward's way out I am leaving those which have become well known as Diosphaeras under this name, but take a look at TRACHELIUM too.

— asperuloides. From the banks of the River Styx and a treasure for the alpine house. The short, frail stems are dressed with tiny soft green leaves and the plant forms a symmetrical cushion which disappears in the spring or early summer beneath myriads of small, powder-blue starry flowers. Grow it in Tufa and gritty soil, guard the use of the water-can and give it a gentle hair-cut after it has flowered.

— dubia. This, certainly, should be known as *Trachelium rumellianum*, but let it rest here for the nonce. Low tufts of green, serrated leaves and clusters of deep blue flowers in midsummer. From Greece and Bulgaria and best in the alpine house, although it will succeed in a crevice in a stone sink or trough.

— jacquinii. Rather similar to the preceding, from Crete but of rather looser habit and with larger leaves.

— tubulosa. From Syria. It flowers late, often in November, and is not unlike *D. dubia* in general appearance and the tubular flowers are white. Best in the alpine house.

DODECATHEON. *Primulaceae.* From the Greek *dodeka*, twelve, and *theos*, god, The name given by Pliny to a plant, probably the primrose, which was under the care of twelve gods.

A genus confined to N. America of which several species and clones are in cultivation. They enjoy conditions similar to those accorded to moisture-loving primulas and are summer flowering. Increase by seeds or division. There is no little confusion in the nomenclature of the plants grown in gardens. Apart from albinos, the colour range throughout the genus is confined to variations from pale rose-madder to crimson and carmine. They all carry flowers with swept-back petals which gives them the vernacular name of Shooting-Star and the leaves are mostly inclined to be fleshy with entire, or occasionally slightly, toothed margins and the flower stems range in height from 9 in to 15 in.

— alpinum. About 12 in. flowers reddish-purple with a yellow tube and a purple ring in the throat.

— clevelandii. A taller species with very pale green leaves, irregularly toothed and umbels of red-purple flowers, yellow at the base and with deeper purple markings in the throat.

— conjugens. Variable in colour but commonly rosy-pink.

— cusickii. Rich purple, yellow-throated flowers, about 9 in.

- dentatum. Cordate, toothed leaves and lax umbels of white flowers with dark, exserted anthers. A striking plant.
- frigidum. Varies from an inch or two to 12 in. in height. Few flowered umbels of purple-violet flowers.
- hendersonii. (D. latifolium.) About 12 in. Flowers violet with yellow anthers.
- jeffreyi. Distinguished by its unusually large leaves. One of the taller species with many-flowered umbels of reddish-purple flowers having purple stamens.
- latifolium. See *D. hendersonii.*
- latilobum. Up to 12 in. Few-flowered umbels of cream-white flowers with reddish-purple anthers.
- macrocarpum. Few to many lilac-purple flowers on 12 in. stems.
- meadia. The best known species in gardens, and one of the tallest. Many rosy flowers with white bases to each umbel and reddish-yellow anthers.
- pauciflorum. See *D. pulchellum.*
- pulchellum. (D. pauciflorum.) Also, occasionally, but wrongly, D. integrifolium. 9 to 12 in. with pale lilac flowers in loose umbels. The flowers have a purple, wavy ring in the throat. Of exceptional beauty, is one named 'Red Wings' which bears crimson flowers on 12 in. stems and has been described as the handsomest of all dodecatheons.
- tetrandrum. Similar to *D. jeffreyi.* The purple flowers have a ring of yellow spots in the throat.
- uniflorum. Dubiously in cultivation. It is said to be a 2 in. pygmy but I have not seen it in flower.

DONATIA. *Donatiaceae.* Named for Vitalianus Donati of Padua.

- novae-zelandiae. This is one of those captivating alpine cushion-plants from New Zealand which we so ardently desire, but seldom see in our gardens. Dense, hard, green cushions of small, thick and glossy leaves. Stemless white flowers with fleshy petals stud the cushions.

DONDIA. See the genus HACQUETIA.

DORONICUM. *Compositae.* Derivation uncertain.

A small genus of, mostly, herbaceous perennials of which only a very few are appropriate to rock gardens. They are easily grown plants in any good garden soil and sunny places, and are spring-flowering.

- cordifolium. See *D. cordatum.*
- columnae. See *D. cordatum.*

- cordatum. (D. cordifolium. D. columnae.) From Europe and W. Asia. From a running, fibrous root spring tufts of heart-shaped green leaves and large golden many-rayed flowers on 6 in. stems.
- glaciale. From the Alps of E. Europe. Stems of 12 in. clad in narrow, toothed leaves and yellow flower-heads.

DOUGLASIA. *Primulaceae.* Named for David Douglas (1798-1834) Plant Collector for the Horticultural Society of London.

This genus has always hovered uneasily between the genera PRIMULA, GREGORIA, ARETIA, ANDROSACE and DOUGLASIA and the modern botanical thinking is likely to include it in yet another genus, VITALIANA, but I stubbornly adhere to common-usage. It is a small family distributed partly in Europe and partly in N. America, mostly cushion-forming plants for sunny screes or the alpine house, or to grow within the confines of stone sinks and troughs. They are spring and summer flowering, increased by seeds, cuttings or division and although, not difficult, demand that little extra care and attention which they so richly deserve.

- arctica. Closely related to *D. montana* but of looser habit. From Arctic N. America.
- dentata. From N. America, particularly in the Cascade Mountains. Loose tufts of lax, ash-grey rosettes of small, spoon-shaped leaves which are irregularly toothed at the tips. One inch stems carry scapes of violet flowers.
- laevigata. Dense pads of small-leaved green rosettes and few-flowered heads of rose-red flowers on very short stems. N. American and there are geographic variants of additional merit, those from the Fraser River and the Columbia River areas being particularly noteworthy.
- montana. From N. America. Forms mats of small, glabrous leaves and is smothered with many almost stemless pink flowers. An alpine form, *D.m. biflora* is said to be an improvement, and easier to grow.
- nivalis. From British Columbia. Rather loose tufts of hairy stems and leaves with flesh-pink flowers on short scapes.
- primuliflora. See *D. vitaliana.*
- vitaliana. (D. primuliflora.) From the mountains of Spain and Central Europe. Carpets of small, grey-green leaves and yellow, fragrant flowers. The form *D.v. praetutiana* is of denser habit with more silvery foliage, and is commonly more free-flowering.

DRABA. *Cruciferae.* The classical Greek name *drabe* was for a cruciferous plant, possibly *Cardaria draba.*

There are more than 250 species of Draba widely distributed over Europe, Asia and America. Many of them have little or no garden value, others rank among the choicest alpine aristocrats. Sheer lack of space forces me to be selective but I feel that this is excusable in a family containing so many members of only botanical interest — and sometimes not even that. No praise, however, is withheld from the gems of the race which fittingly adorn the most hallowed alpine houses.

— acaulis. From the Cilician Taurus and as tight and compact in its green cushions as an Aretian Androsace. Almost sessile heads of golden flowers sit tightly over the leaves which are felted with fine, silky hairs. Like all the species it is spring flowering, and requires careful alpine house treatment in very gritty soil.

— aizoides. A tufted plant from the mountains of Europe and also rarely in Britain. Narrow, rigid, bristle-tipped green leaves in rosettes and rather shrill yellow flowers on 2 in. stems. Not one of the best, but worth having.

— aizoon See *D. lasiocarpa.*

— alpina. Really a group of similar plants mostly confined to Arctic regions. All are densely rosulate, with stems clothed in stellate hairs, the yellow flowers are carried on short stems in small, dense heads.

— breweri. N. America. Low cushions and white flowers in heads on short stems.

— bruniifolia. From the Caucasus. Loose tufts of narrow, hairy leaves and corymbs of golden flowers on 4 in. stems. The subspecies *kurdica* from Turkey, if it were obtainable, might be a better, dwarfer plant.

— bryoides. From the Caucasus. Dense, rounded cushions of tiny green leaves and golden flowers several to a head on inch-high, threadlike stems. The variety *imbricata* is even smaller and more compact.

— crassifolia. From Arctic Scandinavia. Low tufts of bristly leaves and heads of pale yellow flowers on very short stems.

— dedeana. Spain and the Pyrenees. Dense tufts of small, wide, bristle-tipped leaves and crowded corymbs of white flowers on 2 to 3 in. stems. It is a variable species and there exist several named forms of little importance.

— densifolia. From N. America. Dubiously in cultivation but a splendid cushion-forming plant having sheets of almost stemless yellow flowers.

— dicranoides. See *D. rigida.*

— gigas. (Arabis carduchorum.) From Armenia and hovers uneasily between the two genera. Dense tufts of rosetted leaves with quite large white flowers on inch-high stems.

— hispanica. As the name implies, a Spanish species. Close tufts of softly hairy leaves and several pale yellow flowers in each corymb held on 2 in. scapes.

— hoppeana. (D. zahlbruckneriana.) From the Alps of Europe. Close tufts of leaves with bristly margins and stemless pale yellow flowers.

— incana. A short-lived species and a rare British native. Tufts of very hairy leaves and heads of small white flowers. More interesting than beautiful.

- lasiocarpa. (D. aizoon.) Carpathians and E. Alps. Rather like a looser and more robust *D. aizoides* but with smaller pale yellow flowers in a loose raceme.
- mollissima. From the Caucasus and one of the gems of the race for the alpine house. Usually not difficult but temperamental and can collapse with little warning. Domed hummocks of soft stems and tiny leaves which disappear in spring beneath countless small heads on short stems of soft yellow flowers. Grow in gritty soil not lacking in humus, and water with discretion, especially in winter.
- oreadum. From Morocco, and a neat cushion with small heads of good white flowers on short stems.
- polytricha. From E. Europe and Armenia. Neat rosettes in symmetrical array forming tight, mounded hummocks which become almost pyramidal. The alpine house and perfect drainage and great care in winter watering spell success and a fine display in spring of the myriads of heads of golden flowers carried on frail 2 in. stems. Occasional rosettes will die. Remove them and replace with a small stone to keep the cushion tight.
- pyrenaica. See PETROCALLIS *pyrenaica*.
- rigida. (D. dicranoides.) From Armenia. Small, neat, rounded hummocks and thread-like stems 2 in. high carrying corymbs of yellow flowers. For *D. rigida* 'Bryoides' see *D. bryoides* 'Imbricata'.
- X salomonii. Probably a hybrid between *D. bruniifolia* and *D. dedeana*. Near to the latter in habit and appearance but with yellow flowers.
- stylaris. Probably only a northern form of, and similar to, *D. incana*.
- zahlbruckneriana. See *D. hoppeana*.

DRACOCEPHALUM. *Labiatae*. From the Greek *draco*, a dragon, and *cephale*, a head. From the shape of the flowers.

A family of summer-flowering annual and perennial herbs, natives of Europe and temperate Asia. The few suitable for rock gardens are not widely cultivated but are worthy of more attention. Easily grown in any good soil and sunny positions. Only brief mention will be made of those not usually available, or of lesser merit.

- argunense. From Japan. Has been variously described as having white or blue flowers. They should be blue-purple in spikes on 9 to 12 in. stems.
- bullatum. From China. Rich blue flowers on 12 in. stems.
- calophyllum.
- forrestii. From China and similar to, if not identical with the plant grown as *D. calophyllum*. Foot-high spikes of deep purple-blue flowers.
- grandiflorum. From Siberia. Stems 6 to 9 in. high carry oblong spikes of large tubular blue flowers.

- **hemsleyanum.** One of the most decorative species, introduced from Tibet by Kingdon Ward. Like a dwarf shrub, with greyish, hairy leaves and slender foot-high spikes of clear gentian-blue flowers.
- **isabellae.** China. 18 in. stems and racemes of blue flowers.
- **nutans.** From Russia. 12 in. stems carrying whorls of purple-blue flowers in slightly drooping racemes.
- **ruyschianum.** A European species and rather tall. The stems can reach 2 ft. Whorls of purple-blue flowers.
- **wendelboi.** From the Hindu Kush and dubiously in cultivation, but ought to be as it is a beauty with spikes of cobalt-blue flowers.

DRACOPHYLLUM. *Epacridaceae.* From the Greek *drakon*, a dragon, and *phyllon*, a leaf. The leaves of some species resemble those of the Dragon Tree, *Dracaena draco.*

A genus of Australasian shrubs or small trees, of which possibly only *D. muscoides* falls within the compass of this manual, or would, if it were in cultivation. Moss-like tufts of creeping stems dressed with tiny leaves and white flowers carried singly and stemlessly at the tips of the branches.

DRAPETES. *Thymeliaceae.* A small genus of New Zealand alpines of which the only species at present cultivated here appears to be *D. dieffenbachii.* This forms low tufts of procumbent stems clad in grey-green, scale-like leaves, the shoots terminating in small clusters of white flowers in spring. It responds well to careful alpine house treatment in gritty but not impoverished soil. *D. lyallii* is a desirable, cushion-forming species which would be a welcome addition.

DROSOPHYLLUM. *Droseraceae.* From the Greek *drosos*, dew, and *phyllon*, a leaf. The leaves carry drops of glutinous fluid to entrap insects.

- **lusitanicum.** From S.W. Europe and N. Africa and the only species in the genus. Not an alpine, but amusing to grow in an alpine house. Woody stems and narrow, recurved leaves covered with stalked glands carrying the sticky fluid which entraps the insects upon which it partly feeds. Handsome golden flowers in summer.

DRYAS. *Rosaceae.* From the Greek *dryas*, a wood nymph, to whom the oak was sacred. The leaves of *D. octopetala* are like tiny oak leaves.

DRYAS — *continued*

A small genus of prostrate sub-shrubs from mountainous areas in the N. Hemisphere. Spring and summer flowering, for full sun.

— drummondii. From N. America. Woody stems and leaves similar to those of *D. octopetala* but slightly more wedge-shaped. Bell-shaped, nodding yellow flowers which seldom expand fully, carried singly on erect 4 to 6 in. stems.

— integrifolia. See *D. octopetala*.

— lanata. See *D. octopetala*.

— octopetala. Europe, including Britain. The well-loved Mountain Avens. A trailing, woody evergreen with small, dark green, oak-like leaves and large white flowers on short stems. Slightly distinct forms exist in *D.o. integrifolia* with leaves scarcely toothed, *D.o. lanata*, with softly hairy foliage and *D.o.* 'Minor', a compact form.

— X suendermannii. A natural hybrid between *D. octopetala* and *D. drummondii*, The flowers, yellow in bud are white when expanded, and usually slightly pendant.

DRYMOPHILA. *Liliaceae.*

— cyanocarpa. An Australian woodland plant varying in height from 6 to 18 inches. The solitary white flowers are pendulous and are followed by large blue, or occasionally white, berries. It may or may not be fully hardy.

DRYPIS. *Caryophyllaceae.* From the Greek *drypto*, to tear, because of its sharp spines.

A monotypic genus from limestone rocks in Dalmatia. Asks for a warm, dry, sunny position in the open, or for the alpine house.

— spinosa. A low, dense bushlet with woody stems and many awl-shaped leaves ending in sharp spines. Dense corymbs of pink or white flowers in summer.

DUCHESNEA. *Rosaceae.* Named in honour of Antoine Nicolas Duchesne (1747-1827), French horticulturist.

— indica. (Fragaria indica.) From Korea. A trailing herb with branches which root as they run, three-parted leaves and yellow flowers followed by edible, strawberry-like fruits.

EBENUS. *Leguminosae.* From the Greek word *ebenos*, apparently of Egyptian origin, a name used for another leguminous plant.

- cretica. From the Grecian Archipelago. Evergreen shrub up to 15 in., the young stems and the leaves felted with silvery hairs. Globose heads of purple flowers in summer. For a hot, dry situation or the alpine house.
- sibthorpii. From Greece, where it grows up to 2 ft. high, but if kept prostrate by starvation or pruning, makes a delightful low, silver-leaved shrub with spherical heads of red-purple flowers in summer. Must be kept hot and dry or in an alpine house.

ECHINOSPARTUM. *Leguminosae.* From the Greek *echinos*, a hedgehog, and Spartium, another leguminous genus.

A group of plants now removed from the genus GENISTA and given generic rank. They come from hot, dry places in the mountains of Spain and Portugal and should be treated accordingly.

- horridum. (Genista horrida.) A compact, very spiny shrub making humped domes of spine-ended stems with a few three-foliate leaflets and small terminal heads of bright yellow flowers in summer.

Also to be seen in the wild, but seldom grown, are *E. boissieri* and *E. lusitanicum* and its subspecies *barnadesii*. They are of similar habit and appearance, differing only in botanical details.

EDRAIANTHUS. *Campanulaceae.* From the Greek *hedraios*, sitting, and *anthos*, a flower. The flowers are sessile in a cluster at the growth tips.

There has been, still is, and I fear always will be, much confusion between the genera EDRAIANTHUS and WAHLENBERGIA. One of the main distinctions is that the flowers of Edraianthus are carried in clusters and those of Wahlenbergia singly. Irrespective

160

of botanical accuracy I shall list them under the names by which they are best known to gardeners, with cross-references where these seem desirable. They like sunny positions and gritty soil and should really be regarded as plants for screes, stone sinks and alpine houses.

— **bosniacus.** I am not sure if this is a good name, but it appears in gardens and is a tufted plant with narrow leaves and good heads of large pale blue bell-shaped flowers.

— **caudatus.** (E. dalmaticus.) Rosettes of narrow leaves and erect, 4 to 6 in. stems carrying heads of violet-blue flowers.

— **dalmaticus.** See *E. caudatus.*

— **dinaricus** Another uncertain name, and it may even be a Wahlenbergia as it usually carries its large, open bell-shaped flowers singly on short stems over clumps of narrow-leaved rosettes.

— **graminifolius.** Like all the species, this is a native of Mediterranean regions and is similar in many ways to *E. caudatus,* but with rather longer leaves, bristled with short hairs and clusters of purple flowers on 6 in. stems.

— **kitaibelii.** Even more robust than *E. graminifolius* with green, lightly toothed leaves and purple-blue flowers in clusters.

— **niveus.** A rarity from Jugoslavia which may not have persisted in cultivation but is eminently desirable. Low tufts of needle-fine green leaves and large, white, upturned flowers on short stems.

— **pumilio.** One of the gems of the race and a splendid scree or trough plant. Neat, small tufts of narrow, grey-green leaves on which rest upturned funnel-shaped flowers of violet-blue.

— **serbicus.** Several closely similar species seem to have acquired names relating to the geographic distribution and this is one which differs only in minor details from others, such as *E. caudatus, E. graminifolius* or *E. kitaibelii.*

— **serpyllifolius.** See the genus WAHLENBERGIA.

— **tenuifolius.** A narrow-leaved, tufted plant, again with a close similarity to other species. The violet-blue flowers often have a whitish base.

— **wettsteinii.** Another rarity from Jugoslavia. From a central rosette of narrow leaves spring leafy stems carrying at their apex clusters of mauve flowers.

ELMERA. *Saxifragaceae.*

— **racemosa.** Unfortunately it is doubtful if this plant is now in cultivation but I write this in order to correct an error on my part in the Bulletin of the Alpine Garden Society for September 1938, where, on page 215 *E. racemosa* is illustrated as *Boykinia heucheriformis.* It is a neat, bronze-leaved, summer-flowering plant with creamy bells in short spikes on 9 in. stems.

EMPETRUM. *Empetraceae.* The Greek *empetron*, from *en*, on, and *petros*, a rock.

- nigrum. N. Temperate Zone, including Britain, N. and S. America and Asia. A creeping plant with reddish young stems, tiny leaves, pink bells and black globose berries. For peaty, lime-free soil.

ENCELIOPSIS. *Compositae.* 'Resembling an Encelia', another race of Composites. The derivation of Encelia, rather dubiously, is from *eychelion*, a little eel, from the shape of the seeds.

In the limestone areas of S. Nevada are several species of Enceliopsis which sound desirable garden plants but are dubiously in cultivation and might prove difficult if obtained, but look out for *E. nudicaulis*, and *E. argophylla*. Both have large, golden-rayed flowers and the latter has oval leaves plated with silver hairs.

EOMECON. *Papaveraceae.* From the Greek *eos*, the dawn and *mekon*, a poppy.

A monotypic genus from China for cool positions. Summer flowering.

- chionantha. Spreads by underground running roots. Leaves wide and cordate, slightly fleshy and grey-green. Loose panicles of large, handsome white flowers on 12 in. stems.

EPIGAEA. *Ericaceae.* From the Greek *epi*, upon, and *gaia*, the earth, a reference to the creeping habit.

A small genus of creeping evergreen shrubs requiring lime-free soil and protection from full sunlight. Spring and early summer flowering.

- asiatica. From Japan. Prostrate, hairy, rooting stems and blunt, rounded leathery, leaves. Terminal or axillary clusters of white or pink bell-shaped flowers, slightly fragrant.
- X 'Aurora'. A hybrid between *E. asiatica* and *E. repens* and intermediate between the parents.
- gaultherioides. (Orphanidesia gaultherioides.) A rare and beautiful plant from the Black Sea area. Prostrate, spreading, hairy stems and leathery green leaves. Large, sessile, cup-shaped, soft pink flowers in few-flowered racemes from the terminal leaf-axils. Demanding absolute shade. Not easy, but worth any effort to please.
- repens. From N. America. Similarly prostrate and evergreen and a definite lover of shade. Flowers in terminal or axillary clusters, urn-shaped and white or soft pink in colour.

EPILOBIUM. *Onagraceae.* (Sometimes *Oenotheraceae.*) From the Greek *epi*, upon, and *lobos*, a pod. The petals surmount the pod-like ovary.

A genus widely distributed in temperate areas of both the northern and southern hemispheres. There are some weeds in the race but also many good garden plants. They are sun-loving and succeed in any good, well-drained soil.

- alpinum. See *E. anagallidifolium.*
- anagallidifolium. (E. alpinum.) Weedy, but not unattractive and unlikely to become the pest that some of the naughty species can be. An occasional British native. Leafy 6 to 9 in. stems carry racemes of rose-red flowers in spring and summer.
- antipodum. See *E. crassum.*
- brevipes. From New Zealand. Glossy, thick, reddish leaves and ascending, branching stems carrying white or pink flowers in summer. Seldom exceeds 9 in.
- X 'Broadwell Hybrid'. A hybrid between *E. kai-koense* (if that is a proper name?) and *E. glabellum.* Pretty, bronzed leaves and funnel-shaped cream, pink-flushed flowers for most of the summer. 9 in.
- chlorifolium. New Zealand. Woody, foot-high stems with leaves which are often bronze-green carry several large, cream-white flowers over long periods. It resembles a rather larger-flowered *E. glabellum.*
- crassum. (E. antipodum.) Creeping, branching stems and fleshy leaves, often reddish on the undersides. White or pink flowers on short stems in summer. From New Zealand.
- dodonaei. From the European Alps and often said to be synonymous with *E. fleischeri*, but they are distinct species. *E. dodonaei* is too tall for most rock gardens, carrying its rose-red flowers in a lax inflorescence on tall stems in spring and summer.
- fleischeri. European Alps. Leafy 12 in. stems bear corymbs of slightly pendant rose-red flowers in summer.
- glabellum. New Zealand. An invaluable, long-flowering plant whose stems are adorned by glossy, often slightly bronzed leaves and carry loose, elegant heads of funnel-shaped cream-white flowers.
- kai-koense. Said to come from New Zealand, but this is a pretty little species concerning whose provenance and name I am dubious. It is a rather frail plant with slender stems up to 6 in. bearing numerous pink or almost white flowers in summer.
- latifolium. From N.W. America, where it usually grows in moist meadows. On 15 to 18 in. stems it displays large, magenta-red flowers during the summer months.
- luteum. Another N. American species with pale yellow flowers in few-flowered clusters on 15 in. stems.
- nummularifolium. A pretty little pest from New Zealand, which, since its introduction has spread zealously over the whole country. One may admire its shining, coppery tiny leaves on creeping stems and white flowers on 2 in. stems, but it can become an ineradicable weed.

163

- **obcordatum.** From California, and apt to suffer during severe winters. On 6 in. stems it carries glaucous green leaves and many showy, bright-rose-purple flowers from June until August.
- **pedunculare.** Another New Zealander to beware of. It is prostrate and obstreperous and displays many small white or pink flowers on slender 3 in. stems all summer.
- **pycnostachyum.** New Zealand. Semi-woody stems, unbranched and about 9 in. tall. Numerous large white flowers appear at the ends of the stems.

EPIMEDIUM. *Berberidaceae.* The Greek name *epimedion* for a very different plant.

A valuable genus of herbaceous perennials widely distributed in the temperate regions of the Old World. They spread by means of creeping rhizomes and grow in any reasonable soil with a partiality for light shade. They are handsome both in foliage and in flower. The blossoms appear in the spring and are better enjoyed if the old dead leaves are cut away before the flower stems grow too tall.

- **alpinum.** Southern Europe, and widely distributed in sub-alpine woodlands. Loose panicles of 15 to 20 flowers on 9 in. stems. Outer sepals greyish, speckled red, inner ones crimson, petals yellow.
- **colchicum.** See *E. pinnatum.*
- **diphyllum.** From Japan and one of the dwarfest species, seldom exceeding 6 in. Bifoliate leaves and many small, white, uncharacteristically non-spurred white flowers in loose panicles.
- **grandiflorum.** (E. macranthum.) From Japan, Manchuria and Korea. A boldly handsome species, very variable in the colour of its flowers, which may be white, pale yellow, deep rose or violet. Several selected forms exist under clonal names and all are good. It will grow to 18 in. under good conditions.
- **hexandrum.** See VANCOUVERIA *hexandra.*
- **macranthum.** See *E. grandiflorum.*
- **musschianum.** See *E. X youngianum.*
- **X perralchicum.** This name really covers a group of hybrids between *E. perralderianum* and *E. pinnatum colchicum.* They variously show themselves as intermediate between the parents.
- **perralderianum.** From N. Africa. Handsome trifoliate leaves, bright green tinted reddish-brown. Flowers yellow, in a loose raceme on 12 to 15 in. stems.
- **pinnatum.** From parts of the Caucasus and N. Iran (Persia). Handsome foliage of many leaflets. The naked 15 in. stems carry loose peduncles of yellow flowers with short petals, brown spurs and protruding stamens. It is variable and *E.p. subspecies colchicum* has bolder foliage, is sometimes evergreen and the yellow flowers are larger.

- **pubigerum.** Europe, Transcaucasis and Asia Minor. Leaflets of the bold foliage glaucous and pubescent beneath. The many-flowered racemes carry yellow flowers, the inner sepals soft pink or white. It can grow to nearly 18 in.

- **X rubrum.** *E. alpinum* x *E. grandiflorum*. Resembles a larger, and more brightly coloured *E. alpinum*.

- **sagittatum.** From China. Good foliage and tall stems, up to 18 in., carrying compound heads of small flowers, the petals brownish-yellow, the inner sepals white.

- **X versicolor.** A group of garden hybrids between *E. grandiflorum* and *E. pinnatum subspecies colchicum* and more or less intermediate between the parents in appearance.

- **X warleyense.** *E. alpinum* x *E. pinnatum subspecies colchicum*. Neat green, spiny-toothed foliage and loose heads of flowers with coppery-red outer sepals and yellow petals, with red-streaked spurs.

- **X youngianum.** *E. diphyllum* x *grandiflorum*. Again covering a group of plants with white or rose-red flowers. The forms *niveum* and *roseum* are of special merit, the former in particular being a charmer with snow-white flowers poised in butterfly grace.

EQUISITUM. *Equisitaceae.* From the Latin *equus*, a horse, and *seta*, a bristle.

Many gardeners spend many fruitless hours trying to rid their gardens of the common Horsetail, *E. arvense*. The only admittable species is briefly described below. It has no beauty but is of interest to collectors of plant oddities and it behaves itself.

- **scirpioides.** From Scandinavia. Mats of inch-high, leafless green stems. Makes good ground cover in a moist position.

EREMOSTACHYS. *Labiatae.* From the Greek *eremia*, a desert, and Stachys, another genus.

Few of the species are suitable for rock gardens, but one or two rarieties from the Hindu Kush suggest themselves as desirable — if obtainable. They will demand hot, dry situations, or alpine house treatment.

- **acaulis.** On stems a few inches tall appear heads of rich golden flowers.

- **badakshanica.** A recent discovery with woolly white foliage and a cob-webbed raceme of pink and white flowers.

ERICA. Excluded for reasons as stated in BRUCKENTHALIA and CALLUNA.

ERIGERON. *Compositae.* A name given to a Composite by Theophrastus.

A large race, of world-wide distribution. It would be all too easy to fill many pages of descriptions of all the dwarf species, but a good many are of but slight garden value and I have forced myself to be selective. By and large they are easily grown in gritty soil and sunny positions and spring and early summer flowering.

- alpinus. See *E. borealis.*
- atticus. See *E. villarsii.*
- aurantiacus. A trifle large for most rock gardens but easy and handsome, with bright orange flower heads on foot-high stems. From Turkestan.
- aureus. A gem from the mountains of N. America. Dense, low tufts of spoon-shaped leaves clothed in grey, fine hairs and solitary rich yellow flowers of substantial size on 2 in. stems all summer. Grow in a choice scree, sink garden or the alpine house.
- basalticus. Endemic to the State of Washington in the USA. A choice rarity which grows on cliffs of black basalt which form an admirable back cloth to its clear white daisies, carried on short stems over tufts of cleft leaves.
- X 'Birch Hybrid'. A natural hybrid which occurred in cultivation between *E. aureus* and *E. flettii.* Intermediate between the parents in appearance and with cream-yellow flowers on 4 in. stems.
- borealis. (E. alpinus.) From Northern Europe and a rare native of Britain in alpine areas. Crowded tufts of softly hairy leaves and purple-rayed, yellow-centred daisies on 4 to 6 in. stems.
- compositus. (E. multifidus.) Tiny tufts of hairy leaves, lobed, and cut again into segments. Pale blue or almost white daisies on 3 in. stems. From Western N. America.
- eriocephalus. This is sometimes, but I believe erroneously, said to be synonymous with *E. uniflorus*, a European species. A native of Arctic N. America and has hairy leaves and stems and white flowers which become lilac on 6 in. stems.
- flabellifolius. See *E. trifidus.*
- flettii. From the Olympic Mountains of N. America. Tufts of grey-green leaves and more than inch-wide white daisies on 4 to 5 in. stems. A fine scree, trough or alpine house plant.
- frigidus. From Spanish mountains. Like a three-inch *Aster alpinus* with softly hairy grey leaves. For scree, trough or alpine house.
- humilis. From the far north of N. America. Densely hairy leaves and stems and white and purple daisies on 3 in. stems.
- leiomerus. N.W. America. Glabrous leaves, entire and small lavender-violet flowers on very short stems.
- mairei. From Morocco. A modest but dainty species making neat tufts of grey-green leaves with rosy-purple daisies on very short stems.
- mucronatus. (Vitadenia triloba.) A weed, but a lovely one. A Mexican plant which has industriously spread itself all over Europe.

It is splendid in the cracks of walls and seeds about freely. In flower the whole summer its bountiful daisies show a profusion of colour varying from white to deep pink. Its thin, woody, branching stems grow to a height of 6 to 9 in.

— multifidus. See *E. compositus.*

— nanus. A rarity from N.W. America. Tufts of upright, narrow leaves and wide-rayed lavender-violet flowers on 4 in. stems. For the alpine house or a stone sink.

— pinnatisectus. From Colorado. Tufts of almost fernlike foliage and large mauve daisy flowers on 6 to 9 in. stems.

— pygmaeus. From the Sierras of N. America. A tiny plant with good purple flowers on 3 in. stems.

— radicatus. From the Rocky Mountains of N.W. America. It resembles a slightly taller and more robust *E. leiomerus.*

— simplex. From N. America and not unlike a dwarf, white-flowered *Aster alpinus.*

— trifidus. From N. America. It can be compared to *E. compositus* but has slightly thicker, almost fleshy leaves and white to pale lilac flowers on very short stems.

— tweedyi. A rare species from N. America. The leaves are densely felted with fine white hairs and the plant looks rather like a tuft of some species of ERIOGONUM. I have not seen it in flower and have no record of their colour.

— unalaschkensis. From Scandinavian mountains and into the Arctic. The short stems carry flowers surrounded by a collar of dark mauve hairs.

— uniflorus. Central Europe and Scandinavia. It has been reported as a British native but the record is of dubious authenticity. Closely resembles *E. borealis* (alpinus) but with white ray-florets which later become purple-blue

— villarsii. Probably more correctly *E. atticus.* Europe. 12 in. stems carry heads of many purple flowers.

ERINACEA. *Leguminosae.* Resembling a hedgehog.

— anthyllis. (E. pungens.) The only species in its genus. From Spain and the Pyrenees, and also from N. Africa. Dome-shaped mounds of rigid, intricately branched, spine-tipped stems, the young shoots softly silky-hairy. The few leaves quickly fall. Many clusters, almost resting on the stems, of violet-blue flowers in spring. Likes a hot, dry position or the alpine house.

— pungens. See *E. anthyllis.*

ERINUS. *Scrophulariaceae.* The Greek name *erinos,* used by Discorides for another plant, later transferred to this genus.

— **alpinus.** A small genus, mostly from S. Africa, but this one is native to the mountains of Western Europe, and has become naturalized here and there in Britain. A pretty, tufted plant for walls and chinks with small terminal corymbs of flowers which may be lavender-pink, white or carmine-red. It seeds modestly. It is never more than an inch or two in height and is a desirable commoner.

ERIOGONUM. *Polygonaceae.* From the Greek *erion*, wool, and *gony*, a knee. The stems are downy at the nodes.

A large, interesting and often beautiful genus, mostly natives of Western N. America. Few of them are cultivated and they are not particularly easy, being particularly resentful of winter wet. The few that are cultivated, with one or two exceptions, are grown in alpine houses, preferably in gritty, lime-free soil although they are not entirely calcifuges. A few which are, or have been, in cultivation are described below.

— **acaule.** One of the gems of the genus, forming tight 'buns' of congested white woolly leaves with heads of yellow flowers tucked in amidst the foliage. Sure to demand an alpine house.

— **caespitosum.** Mats of felted silver leaves and heads of yellow flowers which redden as they age.

— **crocatum.** Haunts rocky crevices in S. California and is one of the most handsome of the race. Almost black stems carry ovate leaves felted with silver hairs. On 6 to 9 in. stems appear heads of canary-yellow flowers.

— **depressum.** Grows on the petrified lava flows of volcanic areas in the State of Idaho. Pads and humps of congested silvery foliage over which are short-stemmed heads of cream-yellow flowers. A form named *nivale* is in cultivation and is, if possible, even more silvery and compact.

— **jamesii.** Wide mats of leathery green leaves and umbels of cream-yellow flowers on 6 in. stems.

— **ovalifolium.** Low mounds of intensely white woolly leaves and heads of lemon-yellow flowers on short stems in abundance. One of the choicest and certainly an alpine house plant.

— **subalpinum.** One of the easy ones which flourishes in the open in a sunny position. Much like *E. umbellatum* in habit but with cream flower heads which become rosy with age.

— **torreyanum.** Tufts of leathery green leaves and umbels of soft yellow flowers on 6 in. stems.

— **umbellatum.** Leathery, grey-green leaves in rosettes and yellow flower-heads, on 6 to 9 in. stems.

Eriogonums are summer flowering and perusal of the pages of the Bulletins of the Alpine Garden Society will reveal many more names, most of which are coveted, but seldom if ever available in cultivation, and likely to prove temperamental if they were. Some of them come from alkaline desert areas and enjoy conditions difficult, if not impossible, to duplicate here.

ERIOPHYLLUM. *Compositae.* From the Greek *erion*, wool, and *phyllon*, a leaf .

— **caespitosum.** See *E. lanatum.*

— **lanatum.** (E. caespitosum. Bahia lanata.) Tufts of green, sometimes entire but usually deeply-cut leaves and many heads of yellow flowers on 6 to 9 in. stems in summer. An easy, pleasant, but not exciting plant.

ERITRICHIUM. *Boraginaceae.* From the Greek *erion*, wool, and *thrix*, hair. The leaves are softly hairy.

As much has been written and said about *E. nanum* as of any alpine plant. It has been referred to as the gardeners' classic failure perhaps rather an extreme statement, since some good cultivators have grown it quite successfully — for a time, but no one will deny that it is never seen in cultivation in the beauty it displays in its native haunts.

— **aretioides.** Probably synonymous with *E. elongatum*, which see.

— **argenteum.** Dense tufts of silver-haired leaves in rosettes and short stems carrying heads of intensely blue flowers. Definitely an alpine house plant, as are all but one of those here described. From N.W. America.

— **elongatum.** (E. aretioides.) Another of the N. American high alpine versions of our European *E. nanum*. Pads of grey-haired leaves and heads of rich blue flowers on short stems.

— **howardii.** Again a N. American high alpine in the category of *E. nanum*. Although always certain to be temperamental and demanding special care, it has been proved that these American species are more amenable to cultivation than our beautiful but aggravating European species.

— **nanum.** As seen high in the European Alps this is one of the most supremely beautiful of all alpine plants, reflecting in its sheets of azure, yellow-eyed flowers the colour of the skies above. There is no guaranteed recipe for success in growing it, this depending upon individual skills, and each will have his own ideas.

— **pauciflorum.** This, and its subspecies *sajanense* grows in Central Siberia and sounds like another jewel in the eritrichium crown. Tufts of silky, silvery hairy leaves grow in rocky crevices and are adorned by typically caerulean-blue, golden-eyed flowers. I am sure it is not at present in cultivation.

— **strictum.** From the mountains of Asia, and very distinct. Its long, narrow, silver-grey leaves in tufts and 4 to 6 in. stems carrying sprays of clear, soft blue flowers. It may be correctly a form of *E. rupestre* and it has also appeared in gardens labelled CYNO-GLOSSUM *wallichianum*. Like all the species, it is spring flowering.

169

ERODIUM. *Geraniaceae.* From the Greek *erodios*, a heron. The carpels resemble the head and beak of a heron.

A genus related to GERANIUM which contains many valuable rock garden plants. They are mostly natives of Asia Minor and Mediterranean areas and are consistently sun-lovers of easy culture. They flower from spring onwards.

— **absinthoides.** From S.E. Europe and Asia Minor. Foliage deeply cut and grey-green. Loose heads on 6 to 9 in. stems of pink or almost white flowers. The variety *amanum* comes from Syria and has silvery foliage and pink veined white flowers.

— **amanum.** See *E. absinthoides.*

— **carvifolium.** From Spain. Pinnatisect leaves and foot-high stems carrying sprays of rich pink flowers.

— **chamaedrioides.** (E. reichardii.) An old garden favourite, originally from Majorca in the 18th century. Mats of small, toothed, dark green leaves and white, pink-veined flowers on one-inch stems all summer. It is less commonly grown than the variety with pink flowers and a semi-double counterpart.

— **cheilanthifolium.** From Spain and N. Africa. Deeply divided leaves in low tufts, usually green but sometimes grey-green to almost silver. Sprays of pink flowers marked with deeper coloured veins. In gardens it has frequently been confused with *E. trichomanifolium.*

— **chrysanthum.** From Greece, and a beautiful species. Dense tufts of filigree silver foliage from which rise foot-high branching stems carrying heads of large, sulphur-yellow flowers. The sexes are carried on separate plants, the plant bearing male flowers being less beautiful than the female, but if seed is desired, both sexes must be present.

— **corsicum.** From Corsica and Sardinia, where it grows in rock crevices at sea level and is often washed by the salt sprays of the Mediterranean waves. For sunny crevices in the open, or for the alpine house. Tufts of downy, grey, gently scalloped leaves and pink flowers veined with deeper colour on short stems. A selected form with especially richly coloured flowers is cultivated as *E.c.* 'Rubrum'.

— **daucoides.** From Spain. Rosettes of deeply cut, hairy leaves and few-flowered heads of pink flowers.

— **gruinum.** From the Mediterranean and, although of little more than annual duration, I include it for the sake of its beauty. Low tufts of deeply cleft leaves, every lobe again deeply scalloped. The naked, foot-high stems carry singly a large, rich violet, dark-eyed flower.

— **guttatum.** Tufts of slightly lobed and toothed leaves and 6 in. stems carrying sprays of white flowers, the two upper two having a dark spot at the base. S.W. Europe.

— **macradenum.** From the Pyrenees. Aromatic, pinnate leaves and sprays of pale violet flowers, the two uppermost marked with a deep purple spot.

— **manescavii.** From the Pyrenees and really too large for most rock gardens but very handsome where there is space for an 18 in.

wide rosette of segmented green leaves and 15 to 18 in. stems carrying large, rich red-purple flowers.

— petraeum. From S. France and Spain. Tufts of softly hairy, segmented leaves and 6 in. stems bearing several flowers of soft pink, gently veined with deeper colour.

— reichardii. See *E. chamaedrioides.*

— supracanum. Flat rosettes of grey-green dissected foliage and 6 in. stems carrying clear pink flowers. From the Pyrenees.

— trichomanifolium. From the Lebanon. Tufts of soft green, downy, dissected leaves, resembling, as the name suggests, those of one of the spleenworts. 9 in. stems carry loose heads of unspotted pink flowers, the petals veined with deeper colour.

Hybrids between various species of Erodium are frequent, and often create some confusion when they incline in appearance towards one or other of the parents. Few of them have been authoritatively named, but *E.X kolbianum* is a hybrid between *E. supracanum* and *E. macradenum* and *E.X wilkommianum* is *E. cheilanthifolium* crossed with *E. macradenum.* A supposed hybrid between *E. macradenum* and *E. chrysanthum* has been distributed under the name E.X 'Sara Francesca'.

In the new *Flora Europaea* several name changes have been authorised, but I have adhered to the well known names under which the plants have become familiar to gardeners.

ERPETION. See VIOLA *hederacea.*

ERUCASTRUM. *Cruciferae.* Resembling *Eruca.*

— nasturtiifolium. (E. obtusangulum.) A short-lived perennial from S.W. Europe. Rosettes of deeply divided leaves and racemes of yellow flowers. An easy, sun-loving, pleasant but not exciting plant.

ERYNGIUM. *Umbelliferae.* The Greek name, *eryggion*, for *E. campestre.*

A family of, mostly, herbaceous perennials, containing a few species suitable for the rock garden or alpine house. Sun-loving and summer-flowering.

— alpinum. Perhaps more suited to a flower border than a rock garden, but it inhabits European sub-alpine meadows and is appreciated on large rock gardens. Glossy leaves heart-shaped and deeply toothed and ascending 18 to 24 in. stems carrying heads of small flowers subtended by blue bracts which appear spiny but are actually soft to the touch.

— bourgatii. From the Pyrenees and again, a tall plant, its stems, up to 2 ft. in height bearing ovate heads of small flowers with purple-blue bracts.

— glaciale. From Spain and described in the R.H.S. Dictionary as being from 3 to 6 ft. high. This should be disregarded as it is a dwarf with rigid, woody stems and hard, spiny leaves. The globose heads of soft blue or almost white flowers are surrounded by a crown of silver-grey thorns. For the alpine house.

— maritimum. Our native Sea Holly, and not an easy plant to grow. Give it very sandy soil and full sun and never disturb it once established. Thick, spine-edged, lobed silver-grey leaves and rounded heads of very pale blue flowers with the usual attending spiny bracts. It seldom exceeds 9 in. in height.

— spinalba. From dry, stony places in Mediterranean regions. Lobed leaves deeply toothed and foot-high stems carrying ovate heads of whitish flowers.

ERYSIMUM. *Cruciferae.* From the Greek *eryo*, to draw, or *erysimon.* Some species are said to cause blisters.

A genus closely related to, and in part confused with CHEIRANTHUS. Widely distributed in N. Temperate Zones. Many species are annual or biennial but a few are easily grown, valued rock garden plants. Full sun and any good soil. Spring flowering. The names I have included are by no means guaranteed. *Flora Europaea*, for example, totally ignores *E. alpinum* and provides for it no synonym. Where there is doubt I have used the name by which a plant has become familiar to gardeners.

— alpinum. From Europe, including Scandinavia. Fragrant sulphur-yellow flowers in neat heads on 6 in. stems. It has been met with as *Cheiranthus alpinus* and is one of the probable parents of the garden hybrid known as *Cheiranthus* 'Moonlight'. *Cheiranthus* 'Pamela Purshouse' is yet another of its supposed children.

— bocconei. Comes from the Atlas Mountains and appears not to be in cultivation. It is a crevice plant said to bear heads of lemon-gold flowers on short stems.

— capitatum. From coastal regions of California and Oregon and resembles a dwarf wallflower with dense spikes of fragrant, primrose-yellow flowers. It was given an Award of Merit in 1938 and I am not sure that the same plant persists in gardens.

— helveticum. (E. pumilum.) European Alps. Neat tufts and 3 in. stems carrying heads of fragrant yellow flowers.

— kotschyanum. Asia Minor. Tufts of pale green leaves and short-stemmed heads of large, fragrant, orange-yellow flowers.

— linifolium. (Cheiranthus linifolius.) Spain. On leafy, 9 to 12 in. stems are racemes of cool lilac flowers.

— pulchellum. From Asia Minor, and has from time to time appeared in catalogues as *E. rupestre.* Mustard-yellow flowers on foot-high stems.

— pumilum. See *E. helveticum.*

— wilczeckianum. Another desirable species from N. Africa which does not seem to be in cultivation. It should offer fragrant tufts of yellow flowers on short stems.

ERYTHRAEA. See the genus CENTAURIUM.

ESCALLONIA. *Saxifragaceae.* Named for Senor Escallon, a Spanish traveller in S. America.

A genus composed of shrubs and small trees of which only one, a pygmy form of a tall species, is appropriate to rock gardens.

— rubra 'Pygmaea'. The type is a tall shrub, a native of Chile and this dwarf is a witch's broom which originated in Ireland, and would be more properly known as *E.r.* 'Woodside'. It forms a neat, rounded bush and bears many small rose-crimson flowers in summer. It is apt to revert and the errant shoots should be removed as soon as they are apparent.

EUNOMIA. *Cruciferae.* From the Greek *eu*, good, and *nomos*, order. The leaves are opposite and the seeds twin.

— oppositifolia. From the Caucasus, Armenia and Turkey. It may be that this ought to be referred to the genus AETHIONEMA but it is in cultivation under this name. Even so it remains a rarity for the alpine house or a sink or trough garden. Wiry stems clothed in blue-grey, fleshy, circular leaves and ternimating in heads of lilac-pink flowers during the spring.

— rotundifolia. See AETHIONEMA *rotundifolium.*

EUONYMUS. Although certain forms of *E. fortunei*, and possibly *E. farreri* are more or less prostrate shrubs and are frequently planted on rock gardens. I have excluded them from this Manual considering that they do not really qualify for inclusion, especially as space is at a premium.

EUPHORBIA. *Euphorbiaceae.* Supposed to have been named for Euphorbus, physician to the King of Mauretania.

A vast genus, containing more than 1,000 species, ranging from annual herbs to stout herbaceous perennials, trees, shrubs and even succulents. I can fittingly include only two, both of them avid sun-lovers and one which needs to be planted with caution as it can become a weed, even though of undeniable beauty.

— cyparissias. From Europe, and commonly known as the Cypress Spurge. It runs below ground, emitting countless erect, leafy stems less than one foot in height and terminating in heads of greenish-yellow flowers and bracts. It is attractive, but not to be trusted near less vigorous neighbours.

173

— myrsinites. From S. Europe. Snakelike, trailing woody stems radiate from a central crown and are dressed with spirals of narrow, pointed fleshy leaves. The branches end in large heads of yellow bracts and flowers during the summer. It is seen at its best trailing over the face of a sunny wall or over a sunny boulder.

EURYOPS. *Compositae.* Rather dubiously derived from *euryops*, having large eyes, a supposed reference to the conspicuous flowers of some species.

A race of S. African evergreen shrubs of which only one species is dwarf enough, or hardy enough, for inclusion in this Manual.

— **acraeus.** (E. evansii.) From the Drakensberg mountains. A rounded bush up to 15 in. in height with woody stems carrying many narrow silver leaves and crowned in summer with many bright yellow composite flowers on short grey stems. It was at one time sheltered in alpine houses but proves hardy and is more likely to survive in the open.

— evansii. See *E. acraeus.*

FELICIA. See ASTER *pappei*.

FESTUCA. *Gramineae*. A Latin word meaning a grass stalk.

A large genus of annual and perennial grasses, a few of which are of great value for tucking into crevices and odd corners in the rock garden. They are, of course, grown principally for their foliage. Their flowers, which are occasionally quite decorative, are seen usually during June and July.

- alpina. Alps of Europe. 4 in. tufts of bright green foliage.
- crinum-ursi. See *F. eskia*.
- eskia. From the Pyrenees. From a creeping rootstock rise dense, sometimes foot-high tufts of cylindrical, glaucous leaves.
- glacialis. Central Europe and Spain. Neat tufts of fine grey-green leaves. One of the dwarfest and tidiest and useful for associating with alpines that enjoy companionship.
- glauca. See *F. ovina*.
- novae-zelandae. A New Zealand tussock grass with short, hard, needle-like leaves.
- ovina. A wide European distribution. For rock gardens the varieties 'Glauca' and 'Tenuifolia' are the most desirable. The former is handsomely blue-grey and the latter has much thinner, narrower and softer leaves.
- punctoria. From Greece. A real hedgehog with stiff, acutely pointed quills.
- rubra. (F. viridis.) Loose tufts of dark green, flat or rolled leaves, up to a foot in height.
- viridis. See *F. rubra*.

FICUS. *Moraceae*. The Latin name for *Ficus carica*, the edible fig. There is just one of the 600 or more species of Ficus, mostly from the tropics, which is admissible in an alpine plant collection and is sometimes grown in alpine houses.

FICUS — *continued*

- **pumila.** (F. repens.) From China and Japan. A small-leaved, creeping and climbing plant of which the form 'Minima' is occasionally grown in shallow pans, or, in favoured localities, in shady corners out of doors. It makes a prostrate mat of interlaced stems clothed in small, rounded, thick, veined dark green leaves.
- **repens.** See *F. pumila.*

FORSTERA. *Donatiaceae.* Named for one of the Forsters, father and son, who accompanied Cook as botanists on his second voyage to New Zealand.

- **sedifolia.** A trailing sub-shrub from sub-alpine regions in New Zealand. Branching stems, at first procumbent and later erect clothed in sessile, overlapping, glossy leathery green leaves. Slender stems rise from among the terminal leaves, each carrying one quite large, six-petalled white flower. For the alpine house if obtainable.

FRANKENIA. *Frankeniaceae.* Named for John Frankenius (1590-1661) Professor of Botany at Uppsala.

A genus of usually prostrate evergreen plants, native to sea-coasts in temperate and sub-tropical regions. Those listed are easily grown in light soil and sunny positions. They are summer flowering.

- **corymbosa.** From Morocco and in effect a slightly larger edition of our native *F. laevis.*
- **hirsuta.** Also from Morocco and forming mats of deep green leaves covered when blossoming with deep red flowers.
- **laevis.** A neat carpeter, native to Britain, carpets of green, tiny leaves and flesh-pink flowers in profusion.
- **palmeri.** From California, and of more upright habit than most of the species. Wiry, red-tinted stems and pure white flowers.
- **thymifolia.** (F. reuteri.) Spain. Creeping stems clothed in grey-haired leaves and rose-pink flowers in innumerable tiny stemless clusters.
- **reuteri.** See *F. thymifolia.*
- **webbii.** From Spain, short, erect stems and white flowers just flushed with pink.

FUCHSIA. *Onagraceae.* Named for Leonhart Fuchs, (1501-1566) German physician and herbalist.

Understandably, I hesitated before including the genus Fuchsia in this manual, but the one species I describe is so often grown in alpine houses and is so nearly hardy that I relented.

- **procumbens.** From New Zealand. A trailing plant with small, rounded, rather fleshy leaves. On the stems sit erect, tubular flowers of orange, purple and green and these are followed by large red-purple fruits.

FUMANA. *Cistaceae.* From the Latin *fumus*, smoke, an allusion to the grey stems and leaves.

— **nudiflora.** See *F. procumbens.*

— **procumbens.** (F. nudiflora.) From the Pyrenees. A 9 in. sub-shrub with heath-like leaves and large yellow flowers like those of a helianthemum. For a warm, dry position or the alpine house. Summer flowering.

GALACITES. *Compositae.* From the Greek *gala*, milk. The veins of the leaves are milk-white.

— tomentosa. From N. Africa. Foot-high branching stems carry white-veined and white-backed leaves and heads of soft purple flowers in summer. For a warm, dry and sunny position.

GALAX. *Diapensaceae.* From the Greek *gala*, milk, Probably an allusion to the white flowers of the only species in the genus.

— aphylla. See *G. urceolata.*

— urceolata. From Eastern N. America. A handsome evergreen for peaty, lime-free soil in partial shade or a north aspect. From a modestly creeping rootstock spring wiry, 9 to 12 in. stems carrying large, rounded, leathery, glistening green leaves which become bronze in winter. In June/July it offers slender racemes of crowded small white flowers.

GALIUM. *Rubiaceae.* From the Greek *gala*, milk. The yellow bedstraw, *G. verum*, has been used in cheese-making to curdle the milk.

A large genus, mostly weedy, widely distributed in temperate regions and on mountains in the tropics. Numerous names will be found in Floras and text books, but few are of particular value for the rock garden. Such species as *G. caspitosum*, *G. ephedrioides*, *G. jungermannioides*, and *G. tolosanum* would be worth having, if obtainable, but the only worthy species likely to be is described below.

— **odoratum.** Our native and well-loved Woodruff valuable for ground cover beneath shrubs. Too well-known to require describing apart from a reminder that its stems and leaves when dried and enclosed in small bags are deliciously aromatic.

— olympicum. From Mediterranean regions. Neat, soft tufts of tiny, brilliant green leaves, less than one inch high and smothered in summer with short-stemmed loose heads of wax-white flowers. A particularly compact and desirable form, *G. aretioides*, comes from the Cadmus.

178

GAULTHERIA. *Ericaceae.* Named for Jean Francois Gaultier (1708-1756), also called Gaulthier, French physician and botanist of Quebec.

A large genus of evergreen, lime-hating shrubs, widely distributed in N. America, the Magellan region, the Himalaya, E. Asia, Australia, Tasmania and New Zealand. They vary from tall bushes down to ground-hugging shrublets, a few of which are described below. Early summer flowering.

- adenothrix. From Japan. A creeping shrub forming tangled mats of hairy, reddish-brown stems clothed in small, leathery dark green leaves. The flowers, solitary in the upper leaf-axils, are white flushed-pink and are followed by hairy red fruits.
- humifusa. From N.W. America. Compact habit and rounded leathery leaves with lightly waved margins. The urn-shaped pink flowers are followed by red berries.
- miqueliana. From Japan. Bushes up to a foot in height with bright green leaves. The white, bell-shaped flowers are followed by white or soft pink edible fruits. (They taste like toothpaste!).
- nummularioides. From the Himalaya. Prostrate, spreading stems with a double rank of ovate, bristly leaves. The white, urn-shaped flowers tend to be hidden in the foliage but the following blue-black fruits are conspicuous.
- procumbens. One of the easiest and also one of the best. It is the Partridge Berry of N. America and creeps by underground stems to form dense, low carpets of glossy, dark green leaves among which gleam the white, or sometimes pink-flushed flowers. The red, holly-like berries show vividly in the late summer and autumn.
- pyrolifolia. See *G. pyroloides*.
- pyroloides. (G. pyrolifolia.) From the Himalaya. Very dwarf, forming mats of woody stems dressed with thick, reticulated leaves. Pink, urn-shaped flowers and blue-black fruits.
- tricophylla. From China and the Himalaya and a gem. Four-inch cushions of smooth green leaves. The solitary flowers vary from white to deep pink and are followed by turquoise-blue berries.

GENISTA. *Leguminosae.* The Latin name used by Virgil and from which the Plantagenet Kings and Queens of England took their name, *planta genista.*

A large and valuable genus of, mostly, deciduous trees and shrubs, varying from plants only a few inches high to tall bushes and even small trees. In nature they are confined almost exclusively to Europe but a few reach the borders of Western Asia. They are essentially, as a family, sun-lovers and succeed in any well drained soil. Botanically the genus is closely allied to CYTISUS and CHAM-AESPARTIUM, into which families some species are now placed.

179

GENISTA — *continued*

With certain exceptions I retain the older and better known generic names, which I am sure will be approved by gardeners and frowned upon by botanists. They are summer flowering.

— ardoinii. See CYTISUS *ardoinii.*
— dalmatica. See *G. sylvestris.*
— delphinensis. This may be a very dwarf and compact form of *G. sagittalis*, which itself, having been sometimes known as *Genistella sagittalis*, is now removed to the genus CHAMAESPARTIUM. I retain the familar name for this neat, prostrate shrub with crooked, winged, zigzagged shoots and golden flowers. It comes from the Pyrenees.
— hispanica. From S.W. Europe and in its typical form, too tall for most rock gardens. There is in gardens a form known as *G.h.* 'Compacta' which does not exceed a foot in height and provides a sheet of golden flowers.
— horrida. See ECHINOSPARTIUM *horridum.*
— januensis. From Italy and eastward to the Balkans. Usually prostrate but sometimes semi-erect. Bright golden flowers carried singly in the terminal leaf axils of the arching stems.
— lydia. From the Balkans and Western Asia Minor. An invaluable, if rather robust shrub forming rounded domes up to 2 ft. in height and more in diameter, sheeted with bright yellow flowers.
— pilosa. Widely distributed in Europe and an occasional British native. Tangled mats of semi-procumbent stems mounding up to a foot in height. The cultivar *G.p.* 'Procumbens' is the most valuable for rock gardens as is absolutely prostrate and clings affectionately to rock surfaces which it sheets with golden flowers.
— pulchella. See *G. villarsii.*
— sagittalis. Although this now belongs correctly in the genus CHAMAESPARTIUM I retain the more familiar name. From Central and S.E. Europe. Prostrate mats of stems edged with membranous wings. Leaves very few, and scattered. Terminal racemes of closely packed golden flowers.
— sylvestris. (G. dalmatica.) From Eastern Europe. Dense tufts of thin, angular hairy and spiny stems. Leaves few, erect terminal racemes carry bright yellow flowers. It seldom exceeds 6 in. in height.
— tinctoria. This is the well-known Dyer's Greenweed of gravelly areas in Britain and through Europe to Siberia. The type is seldom cultivated but there are good cultivars which are invaluable. *G.t.* 'Plena' is dwarf with, many petalled golden flowers and *G.t.* 'Royal Gold', although tall, with erect stems up to 2 ft., is richly coloured.
— villarsii. This is correctly *G. pulchella* but I retain the name by which it has become a familar and valued rock garden plant. From S.E. France. Mats no more than an inch or two in height of tangled, hairy stems and many solitary yellow flowers in the terminal leaf axils.

GENTIANA. *Gentianaceae.* Named for King Gentius of Illyria, c. 500 B.C., who is reputed to have discovered the medicinal properties of the roots of the yellow gentian, *G. lutea*, from which a tonic bitters is still made.

A large genus of vast importance to the alpine gardener. Among the 400 or more recorded species are many invaluable garden plants, and others, tall and leafy which, although of interest to collector, have little garden value. Most of these I shall either ignore or dismiss with a brief reference, leaving the maximum space for the more desirable kinds. There are Monographs on the genus which can be consulted for descriptions of species not included in this Manual. Their cultural needs are too varied for a generalised statement and will be dealt with individually. There are gentians for spring, summer and autumn flowering. It can be accepted as a rule that all the autumn flowering Asian species and their hybrids and cultivars are definitely lime-haters.

— acaulis. The provenance of the plant which has been grown for centuries in gardens under this name is uncertain and has been the subject of endless speculation and argument. Most authorities now regard *G. acaulis* as a group name, covering a number of geographical forms, similar, but distinct enough to merit individual recognition. On the authority of *Flora Europaea* I shall treat them as such and they will be found in their proper alphabetical sequence. The plant which has so long been known as *G. acaulis* has also been the subject of no little argument in connection with its behaviour. It is easy to grow in any open, sunny situation and good garden soil, but in some gardens it will flower, whereas in others it seldom displays a blossom. It even misbehaves over limited areas and a completely illogical, but often satisfactory answer to the problem is to move it, even a yard at a time, until a position is discovered of which it approves. There is a form with white, green-throated flowers, and another, named 'Caelestina' with blossoms of Cambridge-blue.

— affinis. From N. America and Canada. Its leafy stems rise to a foot or more in height and in the axils of the topmost leaves occur a few blue, narrowly funnel-shaped flowers. It is not a beauty.

— alba. Another N. American species, and equally without garden value. The lusty stems, set with pairs of leaves can attain two feet in height and end in terminal clusters of greenish-white flowers.

— algida. Dubiously in cultivation. It comes from Siberia, China and Japan. Tufts of short, spoon-shaped leaves emit erect stems up to 9 in. tall carrying at the tips several stalked white flowers speckled with purple-blue markings. It flowers in August and would be worth having.

— alpina. In the *acaulis* group, and to be found in the Pyrenees, the Savoy and in the Swiss Alps. Neat rosettes of small leaves, blunt at tips and short-stemmed flowers of deep, clear blue. A beautiful plant and usually very free-flowering.

— altaica. From Siberia. Leafy shoots from lax rosettes and the stems end in a solitary flower of deep blue and funnel-shaped. It is a good plant, flowering in the spring but has not always proved easy to keep.

— amoena. From the Sikkim Himalaya and may not now be in cultivation, although it has been grown. It is autumn-flowering and will probably prefer lime-free soil. Mats of overlapping leaves emit several longer stems which carry rather bell-shaped flowers, white or flesh coloured with longitudinal blue markings.

— andrewsii. From N.E. United States and Canada, where it grows in damp soil in woodlands. On foot-high, leafy stems it carries several clusters of deep blue flowers which seldom expand fully, a habit which has given it the vernacular name of Closed Gentian.

— angulosa. See *G. verna.*

— angustifolia. In the *acaulis* group. From the limestone Alps of Western Europe. Rosettes of narrow, dull green leaves and tubular flowers of sky-blue. One of the best of the group and free-flowering.

— arethusae. See *G. hexaphylla.*

— asclepiadea. The well-loved Willow Gentian, found in slightly varying forms from mid-Europe eastward into Asia Minor and the Caucasus. The graceful, arching, leafy stems reach at least two feet in height and in the axils of the opposite leaves are clusters of blue flowers, marked inside with purple spots and lighter coloured stripes. It flowers from July until the autumn, and there is a handsome albino form, as well as several named forms which do not differ materially from the type. It appreciates light shade.

— bavarica. An alpine gem from the European Alps. Tufts of rounded, small, yellow-green leaves and 4 to 6 in. stems carrying saucer-shaped deep blue flowers in spring. It demands careful scree or alpine house treatment in gritty, humus-rich soil.

— bellidifolia. From New Zealand and, with Antipodean contrariness, it forsakes the family tradition of having blue flowers. From a strong, deep root rise many stems forming rosettes with fleshy, spoon-shaped dark green leaves. The 6 in. erect stems carry loose clusters of saucer-shaped white flowers, the petals marked with dark veins. It enjoys lime-free gritty soil, and flowers in summer.

— bigelovii. From N. America and akin to *G. affinis* and equally without garden value. The tall, leafy stems carry clusters of small, whitish, purple-tinged flowers.

— bisetae. From Oregon and not unbeautiful. The 18 in. leafy stems carry solitary purple-blue flowers of reasonable size in July and August.

— brachyphylla. From high up in the European Alps and a gem, not very easy to grow. It should be given high quality scree treatment or grown in the alpine house. It resembles a smaller, more compact *G. verna* and the saucer-shaped flowers are deep azure blue in colour. Spring flowering.

— burseri. From the Pyrenees and the Western Alps, and no great beauty. The leafy stems can attain more than 2 ft. in height and the leaves are large and coarse. The greenish-yellow flowers are carried in whorls in the leaf axils during July and August.

— cachemirica. From Kashmir, and often confused in gardens with *G. loderi*. Rosettes of small, ovate leaves from which rise purple-tinted, semi-procumbent stems carrying from one to three bell-shaped clear blue flowers, striped with yellowish markings. Late summer and autumn flowering.

— calycosa. From Western N. America. Erect, foot-high stems clothed in paired leaves and carrying a solitary, bell-shaped blue flower in late summer.

— clusii. In the *acaulis* group. Central and Eastern Alps and the Carpathians. One of the largest flowered and longest-stemmed of the group, distinguished by the unusual length of the calyx-lobes. Of all the variations in the group this approaches nearest to the garden plant we know as *G. acaulis*.

— corymbifera. Another of the white-flowered New Zealanders. Its erect stems are said to attain twenty inches but I have never seen it so lanky. The stems rise from rosettes of narrow, dark green leaves. The dark stems handsomely set off the clusters of bell-shaped white, purple-veined flowers which appear in August.

— crassicaulis. A large, coarse plant from Yunnan and Szechwan and really not worth garden room. Clusters of small, greenish-white flowers are fortunately almost concealed by the upper leaves.

— cruciata. From Mid-Europe to Siberia, Turkestan, the Caucasus and Asia Minor, and best left there, for its small blue flowers are concealed in coarse and unlovely foliage on tall, leafy stems.

— dahurica. From a deep root rise leafy stems carrying one or two tubular purple-blue flowers in August. It will not stop any traffic, but is not undesirable for an odd corner.

— decumbens. From the Himalaya, Mongolia and Siberia. One of the least coarse of the coarse gentians. From rosettes of narrow leaves rise stems at first prostrate but later ascending. The purple-blue flowers appear terminally and in the leaf axils in August.

— depressa. From considerable elevations in Nepal and Sikkim. Mats of rosettes from which spring the stems carrying the solitary flowers tubular-bell-shaped and greenish-blue in colour. A distinct and beautiful plant, rare in cultivation but not difficult if obtained. It flowers in mid to late summer.

— dinarica. In the *acaulis* group. Restricted to small areas in Bosnia and the Carpathians. It is near in appearance to others of the *acaulis* group, but the blue flowers are unspotted.

— excisa. There appears to be no difference between this and *G. kochiana*, also of the *acaulis* group.

— farreri. Discovered by Reginald Farrer and Bill Purdom in Kansu-Tibet in 1914. I doubt if the original introduction exists in cultivation, its place having been taken by seedlings and hybrids, none of which has quite the exciting luminous Cambridge-blue colouring. It is autumn flowering, and, although it belongs to the group of Asian lime-hating species, is slightly more tolerant of lime than others.

— favratii. From the European Alps, the Caucasus and Iran. *Flora Europaea* classifies it as a subspecies of *G. brachyphylla*. A low, tufted plant with small, broad leaves and short flowering stems terminating in solitary deep blue starry flowers. It is happy in a limestone scree and is spring-flowering.

— fetisowii. From Siberia, Turkestan and China. It is similar to, but less attractive than *G. decumbens*.

— freyniana. From Asia Minor, and resembles a rather more frail *G. septemfida*, with which species it has been confused in gardens. On upright, leafy stems it carries, either singly or in small clusters, blue or purple-blue flowers in August and September.

— frigida. From Western Europe. Tufts of narrow basal leaves, thick in texture with lightly waved margins. The leafy, 9 in. stems carry terminally single tubular flowers which are yellowish, striped on the outside with blue. It flowers in late summer.

— froelichii. From the limestone Alps of Austria. From lax, leafy rosettes spring sideways short stems each carrying one bell-shaped flower of soft, unspotted blue in August.

— gelida. From Asia Minor, the Caucasus and Iran. Leafy stems up to 12 in. without a basal rosette. It comes within the *septemfida* group but has few flowers to a head and they are pale yellow, produced in July and August.

— georgei. From Yunnan and has been claimed as one of the most beautiful gentians, but it is doubtful if it is at present in cultivation. From basal rosettes of long, narrow leaves rise short stems, each bearing one large, bell-shaped flower of deep, clear blue, sometimes striped with narrow green lines. It will expect lime-free gritty, humus-rich soil and should flower in September and October.

— gilvostriata. From Burma and Tibet. Tufts of prostrate stems ending in small rosettes with short stems each carrying one funnel-shaped sea-blue flower, striped pale blue on the inside and with purple-blue dotting. It is a distinct and delightful gentian, probably happiest in gritty, lime-free soil and flowering in the autumn.

— glauca. Widely distributed, not only in Asia, but in N. America. It is dubiously in cultivation although it did exist from seeds I collected many years ago in the Rockies. From neat tufts of basal rosettes rise 4 in. stems with a few leaves. In the axils of the leaves and terminally, are carried the pale blue flowers, paler inside than out, during July.

— gracillipes. (G. purdomii of gardens.) From China, collected by Purdom and originally mistakenly named after him. From a central rosette of long and narrow leaves erupt several lax stems clothed in pairs of leaves. The stems branch and each branchlet carries one narrowly bell-shaped purple-blue flower in mid to late summer. Happiest in lime-free soil.

- **grombczewskii.** From Turkestan, and not worth garden room, which is just as well, for who could pronounce its name? Coarsely-leaved tall stems and heads of small not quite yellow flowers.

- **hexaphylla.** When first sent home from Kansu in 1914 this species was mistakenly named *G. arethusae.* It is a lovely and distinct species sending up many short stems clothed in whorls of tiny leaves, looking more like a species of Galium than a gentian. The stems grow to a length of 4 to 6 in. and each carries one pale blue flower with broad deeper blue bands on the outside and green markings within the corolla. It flowers in July and August and needs lime-free soil. It is now a rarity in cultivation.

- **hopei.** See *G. trichotoma.*

- **imbricata.** See *G. terglouensis.*

- **kesselringii.** From Turkestan. From basal rosettes ascend a few 9 in. stems carrying off-white flowers with lines of purple dots on the outside of the corolla. It is closely related to *G. decumbens* and of no considerable garden value. It flowers in late summer.

- **kirishima rindo.** See *G. scabra.*

- **kochiana.** In the *acaulis* group. This is now stated by *Flora Europaea* to be *G. acaulis!* I leave it to the botanists to wrangle over. It is most commonly found in non-calcareous areas of the European Alps and should be given lime-free soil. Descriptively it falls within the usual pattern of this group, with large flowers on 2 to 3 in. stems of deep azure blue.

- **kurroo.** From Kashmir and the N.W. Himalaya at high elevations. It has been fitfully in cultivation for many years but has never secured a strong root-hold in gardens, more's the pity, for it is a handsome plant. From a basal rosette of long and narrow leaves spring stems, at first procumbent but later sharply ascending and carrying terminally and in the leaf axils long, narrowly bell-shaped flowers of clear blue, whitish and with green spottings in the throat. It likes a well-fed scree and flowers in the late summer. At least one prominent member of the Alpine Garden Society regularly distributes its seeds, which are reluctant to germinate.

- **lagodechiana.** From the Caucasus, and I am doubtful if the true species is in cultivation. It is closely akin to *G. septemfida* and a form of that species usually takes its place. It can be likened to a frailer *G. septemfida* and should carry but one — or rarely two — flowers at the apex of each leafy, 9 in. stem in mid to late summer.

- **lawrencei.** From Siberia, whence it was introduced in 1905. From a definite central rosette it sends out 6 in. stems clothed with pairs of narrow leaves and ending in a solitary flower. The blossom is long and tubular, of turquoise-blue, whitish inside and with several bands of deeper blue on the outside of the corolla. It somewhat resembles *G. farreri* and it flowers in July and August.

- **linearis.** From N.W. America and Canada. Not one of the most ornamental of the gentians, but worth growing. It flowers in early autumn and prefers a lime-free soil. On erect, leafy stems of a foot or so are carried clusters of narrowly funnel-shaped blue flowers.

— loderi. From Kashmir. On the short stems, at first procumbent but later ascending, appear solitary bell-shaped flowers of good blue, showing well against the foliage which has a silvery sheen on the green colouring. It flowers from July until late August and has been confused with *G. cachemirica*.

— lutea. Widely distributed in the European Alps. A giant of the race with stems ascending to 3 ft. or more. The basal leaves are very large and broad becoming smaller as they ascend the robust stems. In the axils of the leaves are clusters of pale yellow flowers. It is a stately plant with good 'architectural' value. It relishes good, deep soil and a sunny position, and flowers in mid-summer. Once established it should not be disturbed.

— makinoi. From Japan and a distinct and worthy plant. It makes no basal rosette but sends up leafy, erect stems to a height of about 12 in. The lower leaves are scale-like, becoming larger towards the top of the stems, which carry terminal heads of pale blue flowers marked with deeper spotting. It flowers in late summer and should be provided with lime-free soil and appreciates extra humus.

— newberryi. From California. Small rosettes and short stems carrying pairs of narrow leaves and terminating in, usually, single flowers of pale blue. A nice plant for a cool position and lime-free soil, flowering in August.

— nipponica. A temperamental and not especially beautiful species from Japan. Of loose, branching habit with thick-textured leaves and purple-blue flowers in late summer. Give light shade and leafy soil.

— olivieri. From the Orient and Asia Minor and dubiously in cultivation, but well worth growing. Rosettes of spoon-shaped leaves and flowering stems at first procumbent but later ascending and ending in a cyme of several deep blue, bell-shaped flowers in late June and July. It relishes a warm and fairly dry position.

— ornata. From Nepal and now a rarity in gardens. In some ways it can be likened to a more compact, shorter-stemmed *G. sino ornata*, forming a small basal rosette from which radiate short, leafy stems ending in solitary deep blue flowers, whitish inside and bands of purple with cream margins on the outside. It flowers from August onward and should be given lime-free soil.

— pannonica. From Middle and Eastern Europe. Not a beauty but with a certain appeal where there is space for a robust leafy gentian with stems up to 18 in. tall. Whorls of flowers appear in the upper leaf-axils and are brownish-purple spotted with darker colouring. It flowers in late summer.

— parryi. From alpine zones in Colorado, New Mexico and Utah. Foot-high stems set with pairs of ovate, glaucous leaves. Clusters of purple-blue flowers terminate the stems. It prefers lime-free soil and is autumn-flowering. In gardens forms of *G. septemfida* are sometimes seen under this name.

- **phlogifolia.** Probably only a form of *G. cruciata* from Transylvania and of only slightly greater garden value. The leaves are less coarse and the flowers a trifle larger.

- **pneumonanthe.** In one or other of its several forms the Marsh Gentian is widely distributed over Europe and extends into Asia and the Caucasus. As a British native it is occasionally found on open moorland in moist places. Upright, leafy shoots ascend from basal rosettes with blue, tubular flowers sitting singly in the leaf axils, from mid to late summer. Of particular merit is the form from Styria which has stems up to 15 in. tall and larger flowers of rich, deep blue.

- **porphyrio.** This inhabits the pine barrens of New Jersey and is as temperamental as other rarities from the same locality, notably the Pixie Moss, *Pyxidanthera barbulata.* On tall stems clothed with thick, fleshy leaves are terminal, solitary flowers of brilliant blue. A moist situation in humus-rich, lime-free soil would appear to offer the best chance of success.

- **prolata.** A neat and desirable species from Sikkim and Bhutan. Mats of short shoots without a central rosette, the shoots ending in narrowly tubular bells of good blue, the outside banded with purple and cream. The flowers do not expand widely. It is lime-hating and late summer flowering.

- **przewalskii.** From China and Tibet, and the difficulty of pronouncing its name can be surmounted by not growing it, for it has no great merit as the 9 in., leafy stems each carry a few whitish or yellowish flowers faintly streaked with blue in late summer and autumn.

- **pumila.** From the limestone of S.E. Europe and resembles a small, rather loose-growing *G. verna*, with flowers of azure-blue during July and August. It is not easily pleased but may succeed in a gritty limestone scree or the alpine house.

- **punctata.** From alpine and sub-alpine meadows of the European Alps. From deeply delving tap-roots spring 18 in. stems clothed in pairs of leaves ending in clusters of yellow, purple-spotted flowers during July and August.

- **purdomii.** See *G. gracillipes.*

- **purpurea.** From alpine pastures in Europe. It is one of the strong-growing meadow gentians having tall, leafy stems ending in several upright, reddish-purple bells, yellowish within and with green stripes on the outside. It flowers in mid to late summer and is one of the better of the coarse gentians.

- **pyrenaica.** Success seldom attends attempts to please this charming little species. It is found in the Pyrenees, again in the Carpathians and then in the Caucasus, Turkish Armenia and Iran. It usually inhabits moist, peaty situations, where it forms low mats of crowded shoots, several of which carry singly the deep violet-blue flowers during May and June.

- **rigescens.** From dry, stony slopes in Western China. Foot-high purple-brown stems carry many pairs of leaves and end in clusters of sessile flowers, with a few blossoms set in the upper leaf-axils. The colour ranges from reddish-purple to purple-blue, with green spots inside the flower. It flowers in October and is more desirable than it may sound.

— saponaria. From N. America and Canada. Erect, leafy stems carry flowers in the upper leaf-axils and also a terminal head of several blossoms. The blue flowers do not expand fully, but close their mouths like those of *G. andrewsii*. It appreciates lime-free soil and light shade and is summer-flowering.

— saxosa. From New Zealand and characteristically white-flowered. A very delightful plant with short, dark stems and rosettes of small very dark green leaves and 4 in. flower stems carrying cymes of flowers with purple-brown veining on the white corolla segments. Full sun in the scree or for the alpine house or sink garden. It usually flowers in July and August.

— scabra. Northern Asia, including Japan. A variable species with erect, foot-high stems on which the leaves are arranged in pairs. In the leaf-axils and terminally are the bell-shaped blue flowers, often heavily spotted inside. The variety *buergeri* has larger flowers of deeper blue, and the plant sometimes grown as *G. kirishima-rindo*, but correctly the variety *saxatilis* of *G. scabra* is quite impressive, with long, semi-trailing stems and large, sapphire-blue flowers. It is a late-flowering species.

— scarlatina. Although it is not in cultivation mention must be made of this S. American species, which has been grown and flowered in gardens and would be welcomed, together with other exciting species with red or reddish flowers from the Andes.

— sceptrum. From N.W. America and Canada, where it inhabits moist places in open woodlands. Erect stems up to 18 in. and clusters of two or three flowers set in the leaf-axils and terminally during August. The colour is deep blue and it can be regarded as one of the hand-somest of the American species. It will appreciate light shade but does not demand a bog.

— septemfida. A very variable species extending from the Caucasus through Asia Minor, Iran and Turkestan. It could be called 'every-man's' gentian, for it flourishes in almost any soil or situation without fads or fancies. It forms low domes of leafy stems which end in large heads of bell-shaped blue or purple-blue flowers. It can be relied upon to be permanent and beautiful. Summer flowering. Several named forms are in cultivation and one of special vigour, size and richness of colour is *G.s.* 'Cordifolia'. As stated in the description of that species it too often takes the place of *G. lagodechiana*.

— setigera. From damp places in California. Semi-rosettes of rounded leaves and spreading stems up to 12 in. tall. Up to four flowers at the end of each shoot in August, purple-blue, clearer blue at the base of the lobes. Lime-free soil pleases it best.

— sikkimensis. From the Himalaya. A mat-forming species with short stems and pairs of rather broad leaves of dark and glossy green. The stems end in a cluster of flowers surrounded by a circle of leaves. The rather tubular flowers are blue, with a white throat. Grow it in lime-free soil and expect it to flower in July and August.

— sikokiana. A Japanese species close to *G. scabra* in appearance with blue or purple-blue flowers in mid to late summer.

— sino-ornata. In spite of its absolute insistance upon lime-free soil this splendid Chinese gentian remains a top-favourite and any nurseryman who grows or sells it knows it for a constant 'best seller'. Dense mats of procumbent stems clothed in narrow green leaves disappear in the autumn beneath countless azure-blue trumpets. It benefits from regular division and replanting in March/April. There are one or two variants. One which flowers a month earlier than the type is known as 'Praecox', the 'Brin form' has longer, slender shoots which will scramble up into any adjacent bush and there is a good albino.

— stragulata. A species from Yunnan which has maintained a precarious root-hold in cultivation since its first introduction in 1914. Mats of short shoots with oval, dark green leaves and short, trailing stems ending in several very narrow tubular flowers which do not fully expand. The colour is deep blue. Lime-free soil in full sun and it should flower in July and August.

— straminea. From Tibet and China and not a beauty, only likely to interest a collector. Rosettes of large leaves and foot-high stems carrying clusters of straw-yellow or greenish-white flowers in late summer.

— stylophora. This might be thought of as a Himalayan counterpart of the European *G. lutea*. It is said to attain a height of five to six feet in nature. Long-stalked yellow flowers are carried terminally and in the leaf-axils of the stately stems during July and August.

— terglouensis. (G. imbricata). From the Southern and Eastern Alps of Europe. Tiny mats of green leaves and deep blue flowers like those of *G. verna.* It relishes a gritty limestone scree and usually flowers in July.

— tibetica. From Tibet, and best left there. A robust, leafy plant with heads of greenish small flowers.

— trichotoma. (G. hopei.) Dubiously in cultivation, but ought to be. From China and was given an Award of Merit in 1923 as *G. hopei.* Tall, slender stems with clusters of flowers terminally and in the upper leaf-axils. Narrowly tubular in shape the colour is clear blue. Lime-free soil, flowers in July.

— triflora. It is doubtful if this Siberian species is at present in cultivation, which is unfortunate, because it is a good, autumn-flowering plant which would be welcomed. The erect stems of about one foot carry leaves in pairs with flowers in the upper leaf axils and a terminal cluster of deep, or purple-blue blossoms with white on the outside and of goodly size.

— tubiflora. This is really a warning, for there is a coarse, leafy plant grown under this name which is not worth garden space. The true species, if available, should be a tufted plant of no more than an inch or two in height, with spoon-shaped leaves and solitary, inch-long flowers of clear blue. It comes from the Himalaya and is very desirable and should require lime-free soil, and flowers in the autumn.

— veitchiorum. When first introduced from China this was thought to be a form of *G. ornata*. It was, in fact, given an Award of Merit in 1909 as *G. ornata* but was later renamed *G. veitchiorum*. It makes basal rosettes of narrow, blunt-ended, dark green leaves, from which radiate spreading stems, which branch, each branch carrying one funnel-shaped flower of deep royal blue. It needs lime-free soil and flowers from August onward.

— verna. The ever-popular spring gentian has an enormously wide distribution, being found in Europe (including Britain), Asia Minor, the Caucasus, Turkestan, Siberia and Mongolia. There are many forms of the species, including one, much desired, with yellow flowers. The most commonly cultivated form is *G.v. angulosa* with fine flowers of deep azure-blue on short stems in the spring. It grows well in humus-rich, gritty soil and full sun and is a lime-lover but will tolerate acid soils. It is sometimes short-lived and should be regularly replaced by young plants grown from seed.

— waltonii. A robust species in the *G. decumbens* group and resembling that species. It comes from Tibet and forms distinct rosettes of quite large leaves and carries flowers in the leaf-axils of the semi-erect stems and also terminally. The colour varies from deep blue to purple or even magenta. It flowers in the late summer.

— walujewii. A species from Turkestan only likely to attract the collector as it has little garden value, with leafy, robust stems carrying cymes of yellowish flowers in August.

GENTIANS (HYBRID).

There are multitudes of hybrid gentians, especially among the lime-hating, autumn-flowering Asians. They come and they go; many are raised, named and distributed only to disappear again. The best of them have persisted and should be listed, but I do not propose to give descriptions. Following will be found an alphabetical list of those most likely to be encountered, with the actual or supposed parentages, which will provide an indication of their habit and appearance and needs.

— X 'Alpha'. This, and *G.X* 'Omega', were raised on Jack Drake's nursery in Inverness-shire and are probably of *G.X hexa-farreri* parentage.

— X 'Apollo'. A hybrid between *G.X* 'Inverleith' and *G. ornata*, recently raised by H. Bawden in Devonshire.

- X 'Bernardii'. Of dubious parentage, but probably either *G. sino-ornata* X *G. veitchiorum*, or the reverse parentage. It has been around for many years but did not receive its Award of Merit until 1970.
- X 'Carolli'. *G. farreri* X *G. lawrencei*.
- X 'Christine Jean'. Parentage unknown to me. Fine rich purple flowers with a purple sheen on the corolla.
- X 'Coronation'. Raised in 1953 with *G. farreri* as the only known parent.
- X 'Davidii'. *G. prolata* X *G. lawrencei*.
- X 'Devonhall'. *G. ornata* X *G. farreri*. Received a First Class Certificate in 1936 and persists as a good plant.
- X 'Edina'. *G. ornata* X *G. prolata*.
- X 'Elizabeth Brand'. A seedling from *G.X* 'Macaulayi'.
- X 'Farorna'. *G. farreri* X *G. ornata*.
- X 'Fasta Highlands'. *G. farreri* X *G.X* 'Stevenagensis'.
- X 'Glendevon'. *G. ornata* X *G. sino-ornata*.
- X 'Hascombensis'. Said to have been a hybrid between *G. lagodechiana* and a good form of *G. septemfida*. It seems to have disappeared from cultivation.
- X 'Hexa-farreri'. *G. hexaphylla* X *G. farreri*.
- X 'Inez Weeks'. A seedling from *G.X* 'Hexa-farreri'.
- X 'Inverleith' *G. veitchiorum* X *G. farreri*. A fine hybrid, given the Award of Merit in 1952.
- 'Kidbrooke Seedling'. A vigorous form of *G.X* 'Macaulayi'.
- 'Kidora' *G.X* 'Kidbrooke Seedling' X *G. ornata*.
- X 'Kingfisher'. Said to be a selected seedling from *G.X* 'Macaulayi'.
- X 'Macaulayi'. *G. sino-ornata* X *G. farreri*. One of the oldest and still one of the best hybrids. The form 'Wellsii' has flowers of paler blue.
- X marcailhouana. A hybrid between *G. lutea* and *G. burseri*, originally found in the Pyrenees by Wilhelm Schacht and probably no longer in cultivation.
- X 'Midnight'. A seedling from *G.X* 'Inverleith' with deep royal-blue flowers.
- X 'Omega'. See with *G.X* 'Alpha'.
- X 'Orphylla'. *G. ornata* X *G. hexaphylla*.
- X 'Orva'. One of the best garden hybrids. *G. ornata* X *G. veitchiorum*.
- X 'Stevenagensis'. A hybrid between *G. sino-ornata* and *G. veitchiorum*, raised by the late Frank Barker.
- X 'Susan Jane'. A seedling raised from *G.X* 'Inverleith'.
- X 'Veora'. *G. veitchiorum* X *G. ornata*.
- X 'Vorna'. Similar parentage to *G.X* 'Veora' with flowers of deep Prussian-blue.
- X 'Wealdensis'. *G.X* 'Hexa farreri' X *G. veitchiorum*.

GERANIUM. *Geraniaceae.* The classical Greek name, from *geranos*, a crane, an allusion to the long beak of the carpels.

A large family, widely distributed over temperate regions of the world. They vary from small alpine plants to tall-growing herbaceous perennials and only those fitted for rock gardens or alpine houses are included here, and even so, I admit that some which I have described are marginal cases. A long standing devotion to the entire family makes exclusion of any a matter of some difficulty. Generally speaking the cultural needs are simple. If good garden soil, well drained and an open position can be given they will thrive. Particular instances requiring different treatment will be dealt with in individual descriptions. They are spring and summer flowering, often extending their blossoming over a long period. It is scarcely necessary in a Manual such as this to mention that the hardy species here described have nothing whatever to do with the so-called 'Scarlet Geraniums', which are correctly Pelargoniums.

— 'Appleblossom'. See *G. cinerium.*

— argenteum. From the mountains of Central and Eastern Europe. Tufts of silky-haired silver leaves no more than 3 to 4 in. high, the foliage deeply cleft, and pink flowers, the petals veined with deeper colour, on short stems in spring. It likes very gritty soil and full sun. A good scree plant. There are selected forms with more richly coloured flowers which have been given clonal names.

— atlanticum. See *G. malvaeflorum.*

— 'Ballerina'. See *G. cinerium.*

— candicans. This Chinese species is one of the border-line cases which possibly should have been excluded, for it is a sprawling plant, taking up a good deal of space and too large for a small rock garden. It likes a modicum of shade and will then spread its straggling, leafy stems and display a summer-long succession of cup-shaped white flowers, rose-flushed in the centre.

— cataractarum. Of the persuasion of *G. robertianum,* our native Herb Robert, from Spain but with flowers thrice the size of our native weed and with central bosses of orange anthers.

— cazorlensis. From Spain, and probably a subspecies of *G. cinerium* forming neat tufts of densely caespitose leaves and carrying small, white, pink-veined flowers.

— celticum. Botanists would probably decree that this should be regarded as a form of *G. robertianum* but it is so distinct from that species that I have no hesitation, rightly or wrongly, in retaining for it specific rank. It originated in Ireland and has been described as 'the sweetest tiny weed that could be admitted to the rock garden'. Tiny tufts of light green leaves as deeply cut as parsley form a backing for constellations of pure white starry flowers throughout the summer. It is short-lived but seeds modestly and will happily colonise any cool, lightly shaded position. It loves to grow in rock crevices.

- **cinerium.** From the Pyrenees and a true alpine of easy culture for sun and gritty soil. Neat mounds of deeply-cut grey-green leaves on thin stalks, above which flutter quite large, cup-shaped flowers of various shades of deep pink, the petals usually pencilled with veinings of deeper colour. There is known a good albino form. Outsmarting its Pyrenean cousin is the subspecies *subcaulescens*, usually grown as a species which is a superb plant carrying a long succession of rich crimson, dark-eyed flowers on trailing stems. Also now in circulation are two plants, possibly hybrids, one named 'Ballerina', with ash-grey leaves and lilac-pink flowers veined with purple, and 'Apple blossom', of similar habit with clear pale pink flowers.

- **collinum.** From Russia and E. Europe. A confused species which has been referred to *G. donianum* and to various other species. Even now the position is not clear. It should be a 6 in. plant with moderately divided foliage and good flowers of some shade of pink or purple.

- **dalmaticum.** From Jugoslavia and Albania. This small plant has been described as a microform of *G. macrorrhizum* and if one thinks of that species reduced to 4 inches one has a fair picture of *G. dalmaticum*. The glossy leaves take on rich autumn tints and the front-facing rounded pink flowers are extremely attractive. There is an albino the petals of whose flowers are usually just faintly flushed with pink. Easy in any good soil and full sun.

- **donianum.** See *G. collinum*.

- **farreri.** I retain this name although it has been referred, possibly wrongly, to *G. napuligerum*. From high in the Chinese mountains and an extremely desirable small rock garden or alpine house plant. Tufts of grey-green leaves and large, cup-shaped flowers of soft and tender pink, their beauty enhanced by clusters of soot-black anthers.

- **grevilleanum.** From the Himalaya and, in its high alpine form a good rock garden plant with creeping stems bearing kidney-shaped, hairy leaves and large pale rose flowers, the petals often marked with conspicuous deep purple spots.

- **kotschyi.** From Russian Armenia and related to *G. tuberosum*. From small, round corms rise anemone-like leaves and 6 in. stems carrying branching heads of soft purple flowers with cleft petals veined with deeper colours. It dies down by mid-summer and is seen no more until the following spring.

- **lancastriense.** See *G. sanguineum*.

- **lucidum.** This is a native of Britain, and a weed, but may be allowed to colonise a cool wall or shady nook with its tufts of glossy leaves and small pink flowers on red stems. The leaves take on rich autumn tints.

- **macrorrhizum.** Much as I would have liked to enlarge upon this species and its several good forms I feel that it is not really a rock garden plant and must, albeit unwillingly, exclude it from this Manual.

- malvaeflorum. (Or malviflorum.) (G. atlanticum.) From the Atlas mountains. A curious, tuberous-rooted plant which awakes from a summer sleep in the early autumn, when it produces anemone-like leaves and foot-high stems carrying blue flowers of fair size. It relishes a sort of Maquis habitat on dry, stony soil.
- napuligerum. See *G. farreri*.
- procurrens. A prostrate, ground-covering species from the Himalaya, invaluable for carpeting between shrubs and trees. Glossy foliage and many rose-purple flowers in late summer.
- pylzowianum. From Tibet, and a pleasant little wanderer that spreads below ground, forming chains of tiny tubers from which spring the finely dissected leaves and 3 in. stems carrying cup-shaped flowers of clear pink. It is an excellent inhabitant of alpine lawns and mingles happily with other plants which it is too frail to smother.
- renardii. Introduced in 1935 from the Caucasus mountains by my late father, Walter Ingwersen. Clumps of rounded, velvety leaves, their matt surfaces deeply marked with embedded veins. On short erect stems appear clusters of pastel-lavender flowers with violet pencillings on the petals. It is seen at its best under conditions of some austerity.
- sanguineum. Widely distributed in Europe, including Britain, and in W. Asia. The typical plant is scarcely a rock garden inhabitant, but the prostrate-growing form, *G.s.* 'Lancastriense' is highly desirable and a very popular, easily grown, long-flowering plant making spreading mats of dark green leaves ornamented by many short-stemmed salmon-pink flowers of immaculate shape.
- sessiliflorum. From S. America and Australasia. Dense mats of grey-green leaves among which nestle almost stemless small white flowers. The variety *nigricans* is similar but for the leaves which are almost chocolate-brown in colour and lend more importance to the white flowers. There was a recorded hybrid between this species and *G. traversii*, which seems, most unfortunately, to have disappeared from cultivation.
- stapfianum. The plant in cultivation under this name may well prove to be no more than a distinct form of *G. pylzowianum*. The most commonly encountered form is *G.s.* 'Roseum', and it is like a slightly more robust *G. pylzowianum* with slightly larger flowers of deeper pink. It shares the modestly running habit of that species.
- subcaulescens. See *G. cinerium*.
- traversii. From New Zealand and its hardiness is suspect. Deeply cut green leaves with a silver sheen and white flowers. The form 'Elegans', which has been grown as the type, has clear pink blossoms. It is here and I should perhaps place *G. X* 'Russell Prichard', a notable hybrid between *G. traversii* and *G. endressii*. The whole summer through this valuable plant adorns its low mounds of lush foliage with myriads of crimson-red flowers.
- tuberosum. From S. Europe, with tuberous roots and many-lobed leaves, from among which spring hairy, 9 in. stems carrying 'chintzy'

purple-violet flowers in May. After this it soon dies down to rest until the following year.

- **wallichianum.** Typical *G. wallichianum* from the Himalaya just misses being a good garden plant, but its failure to be a complete success is compensated for by *G.w.* 'Buxton's Blue', a seedling which appeared many years ago in the garden of the late E. C. Buxton of Bettws-y-Coed. It is a sprawler, demanding ample space in light shade for its long, leafy stems. In late summer and on into the autumn it bears innumerable large, saucer-shaped flowers of Nemophila-blue with a white centre.
- **webbianum.** This may not be a valid name, and the plant is of dubious origin, but it is worth growing and resembles *G. argenteum*, with tufts of very silvery foliage and flowers of amaranth-rose on 4 in. stems.

GEUM. *Rosaceae.* The classical Latin name, used by Pliny.

A genus of numerous species widely distributed throughout temperate regions of the world. Mostly herbaceous perennials for the border, but a few are desirable rock garden plants, spring and summer flowering, for open, sunny positions in any good soil.

- **montanum.** Alps of Europe. Rounded, softly hairy leaves form dense tufts, from which rise short, erect stems carrying large, rich yellow flowers. There is a form, *G.m.* 'Maximum', collected in the Eastern Alps, which is of special magnificence, with extra large flowers on slightly taller stems.
- **reptans.** One of the glories of Europe's non-calcareous mountains. From the loose rosettes of pinnatifid leaves spring long, red strawberry-runners which form rosettes of leaves at the tips and root down to spread the colony. Carried singly on 6 to 9 in. stems are large, rounded golden-yellow flowers, followed by heads of seeds with long silvery awns. It demands a diet of at least 50% stones, mixed with plenty of coarse humus.
- **rossii.** (Sieversia rossii.) From Alaska and a good plant, infrequent in gardens. Deeply cleft, rather hairy leaves and large yellow flowers on 9 to 12 in. stems.
- **uniflorum.** From New Zealand, where it forms wide, low mats in moist places and carries solitary white flowers on 3 in. stems. May not be completely hardy.

GLAUX. *Primulaceae.* A Greek name used by Dioscorides for another plant.

- **maritima.** A monotypic genus, native to North temperate regions and to coastal areas of Britain, where it grows in grassy salt marshes. Worth growing as a prostrate, matting plant with quite pretty pink flowers on very short stems in spring and early summer.

GLOBULARIA. *Globulariaceae.* From the Latin *globulus*, a small round ball, from form of the flower heads.

A small genus of Mediterranean plants for dry, sunny positions, summer flowering.

- aphyllanthes. See *G. punctata.*
- bellidifolia. See *G. meridionalis.*
- cordifolia. Mountains of Southern and Central Europe. Woody mats and tiny, dark green leaves notched at the tips. Round heads of many small blue flowers on short stems.
- incanescens. Italian Alps. Sparsely-leaved dwarf sub-shrub with glaucous leaves and terminal globular heads of blue flowers.
- majorcensis. This is probably correctly *G. cambessedesii* from the Balearic Islands, and one of the *G. vulgaris* group. Good heads of deep blue flowers on tall stems above rosettes of wide green, rather leathery leaves.
- meridionalis. (G. bellidifolia.) Mats of entangled woody stems and tiny dark green, usually un-notched leaves, heads of rich blue flowers on short stems. From Europe and W. Asia.
- nana. See *G. repens.*
- nudicaulis. Mountains of Spain and Portugal. From basal tufts of leathery green leaves rise almost leafless, 6 to 9 in. stems carrying round heads of blue flowers.
- orientalis. Tortuous, spreading and ascending branches with heads of blue flowers in a loose spike. From N. Syria.
- punctata. (G. willkommii. G. aphyllanthes.) Widely distributed in Europe and Russia. Rosettes of rounded, leathery leaves and heads of small blue bell-shaped flowers on 9 to 12 in. stems.
- repens. (G. nana.) Rather like *G. cordifolia* but even smaller, making dense, compact mats of tiny, leathery leaves on tangled woody stems. Round heads of deep blue flowers on inch-high stems. S.W. Europe.
- stygia. From Greece. Creeping woody stems rooting at the nodes and also spreading by subterranean stolons. Flower heads like those of *G. cordifolia* but larger.
- trichosantha. From the Balkans. Basal leaves usually 3-toothed at tips. Leafy 9 in. stems carry prominent heads of bright blue flowers.
- vulgaris. European Alps. Bright blue flowerheads on 9 in. stems.
- willkommii. See *G. punctata.*

GNAPHALIUM. *Compositae.* From the Greek *gnaphalion*, a softly downy plant used to stuff cushions.

A genus of herbs and sub-shrubs widely distributed throughout the world but, as at present known in cultivation, of little importance to alpine gardeners, although some of the New Zealand alpine species such as *G. nitidulum* or *G. mackayi* would certainly create a modest furore could we but obtain them. *G. leontopodium* is a synonym of the Edelweiss, *Leontopodium alpinum.*

GOODENIA. *Goodeniaceae.* Named for Dr. Samuel Goodenough (1743-1827), Bishop of Carlisle and an enthusiastic amateur botanist.

— radicans. See SELLIERA *radicans.*

GRATIOLA. *Scrophulariaceae.* From the Latin *gratia*, pleasantness, an allusion to the medicinal uses of these herbs.

A small genus, related to Mimulus, some perennial and tall, others annual. Moist positions in the rock garden would presumably please *G. ramosa*, 9 in. tall with white flowers from Spring until late summer, and *G. virginiana*, flowers yellow and white, on 6 to 9 in. stems in late summer. Both come from N. America and do not seem at present to be in cultivation in Britain.

GREGORIA. A synonym of DOUGLASIA.

GUNNERA. *Gunneraceae.* Named for Ernst Gunnerus (1718-1773), Norwegian Bishop and botanist, author of a flora of Norway.

Most of the gigantic-leaved plants which so handsomely adorn many of our gardens under the name of *G. manicata* are, in fact, the very similar species *G. chilensis.* Neither is of interest to alpine gardeners, but there are a few mat-forming species, such as *G. arenaria* and *G. dentata*, both from New Zealand, and *G. magellanica* from S. America which are of interest as ground-hugging carpeters for moist places. They are all slightly suspect as regards absolute hardiness.

GYPSOPHILA. *Caryophyllaceae.* From the Greek *gypsos*, gypsum, and *philos*, loving.

Most of the 50 or more species are lime-lovers.

— aretioides. From the mountains of Iran. A fascinating cushion plant forming iron-hard pads of congested minute rosettes of tiny, leathery, dark green leaves occasionally studded with stemless white flowers. In the Caucasus is found *G.a. caucasica*, an even tighter, harder pincushion. Best in the alpine house in gritty soil.

— cerastioides. From the Himalaya. Three in. tufts of soft leaves and white pink-veined flowers in loose corymbs all summer. 'Cooper's Variety' is a fine form.

— fratensis. See *G. repens.*

— nana. This Cretan species, although only dubiously in cultivation, is a neat cushion studded with short-stemmed pink flowers. Probably best in an alpine house.

— repens. From the European Alps and usually grown in one or other of its selected forms or clones. The flowers of the type may be white or pale pink. *G.r.* 'Rosea' displays mats of good pink flowers, *G.r.* 'Fratensis' is neater and dwarfer and rich pink whilst *G.r.* 'Monstrosa' (possibly a hybrid) is much more robust with grey foliage and sprays of white flowers.

— tenuifolia. From the Caucasus. Rosettes of smooth foliage and 4 in. stems carrying sprays of pink flowers. Rather like a condensed and refined *G. repens* in habit.

HAASTIA. *Compositae.* Named for Sir Johann Franz Julius von Haast (1824-1887), government geologist, who collected many plants in New Zealand.

A small genus of alpine cushion plants endemic to New Zealand. They are not at all easy to grow and must be given tender care in an alpine house if obtained.'

- **pulvinaris.** Tightly packed, woolly, buff-coloured cushions of crowded branches with closely overlapping tiny leaves. The small heads of yellow flowers scarcely emerge from the pads of rosettes. Treat with all the respect given to an Aretian Androsace, even so, it is seldom long-lived in cultivation.

HABERLEA. *Gesneriaceae.* Named for Carl Constantin Haberle (1764-1832), professor of botany at Budapest.

A small genus, related to RAMONDA and native to the Balkans. They prefer the same conditions given to Ramondas, i.e., cool, north-facing or shaded crevices and are spring and early summer flowering.

- **ferdinandi-coburgii.** Probably only a form of *H. rhodopensis*, from which it differs only in having rather larger flowers, more open-mouthed with richer frecklings of gold in the throat of the tubular blossom.
- **rhodopensis.** Rosettes of wide, hairy leaves with toothed margins and drooping umbels of flowers on short stems, in colour soft lavender-lilac. There is also a handsome albino with pure white flowers in the shape of H. 'Virginalis'.

HACQUETIA. *Umbelliferae.* Named for Balthasar Hacquet (1740-1815), Austrian writer on alpine flowers.

- **epipactis.** (Dondia epipactis.) From the Alps of Europe and the only species in its genus. Like a tiny, rosetted Astrantia with three-foliate leaves in low tufts and heads of golden flowers set on a dainty frill of green leaves. Only a few inches in height and flowers in earliest spring in cool positions.

HAPLOCARPHA. *Compositae.* From the Greek *haploos*, single, and *karphe*, a scale.

— ruepellii. This weedy but pretty plant appeared in many catalogues for some years as a species of Landtia. Flat rosettes of toothed leaves, green above and silvery beneath and stemless yellow composite flowers with black anthers in summer. It runs about and should be given plenty of room in poor soil.

HAPLOPAPPUS. *Compositae.* From the Greek *haploos*, single and *pappos*, pappus.

A genus of shrubs and perennials, mostly from N. and S. America. Summer flowering.

— coronopifolius. Foot-high evergreen bushes of dark, leathery, narrow leaves and many golden flower heads on short stems. It is similar to, and may be synonymous with *H. lyallii.*

HARIMANELLA stelleriana. See CASSIOPE *stelleriana.*

HEBE. *Scrophulariaceae.* Named in honour of Hebe, the goddess of youth, cup-bearer to the gods.

A genus of Australasian shrubs allied to and much confused with Veronica. A representative few of those suitable for rock garden or alpine house are briefly described below.

— buchananii. Rounded hummocks of entangled stems clothed in small, glossy, shining green leaves. The most desirable manifestation is found in *H.b.* 'Minor', which is extremely small, neat and compact. There are very occasionally small white flowers.

— X 'Carl Teschner'. A hybrid between *H. elliptica* and *H. pimelioides.* An excellent 6 in. shrublet with abundant racemes of violet-blue, white-throated flowers in summer. A selection named 'Colwall' is tighter and dwarfer and the young growth is red in the spring.

— epacridea. Like a prostrate conifer, the trailing stems clad in scale-like leaves. Short terminal racemes of white flowers in summer.

— pinguifolia. Bushes of grey-blue foliage and white flowers up to 18 in. in height. *H.p.* 'Pagei' is dwarfer and more desirable, forming low mats of grey foliage and giving sheets of white flowers.

— tetrasticha. Tiny huddled bushes of four-angled stems clothed in green, scale-like leaves. White flowers are occasionally produced.

HECTORELLA. *Hectorellaceae.* Named for Sir James Hector (1834-1907), New Zealand botanist of Scottish origin.

— caespitosa. The only species and endemic to New Zealand. A highly desirable but dubiously obtainable cushion plant. Short, fleshy branches end in rosettes of glabrous leaves, each rosette offering several white flowers. Plants are unisexual and the orange stamens of the male flowers make them more attractive than those of the female blossoms. Definitely for the alpine house in very gritty soil.

HEDERA. *Araliaceae.* The Latin name. Ivy was sacred to Bacchus and was intimately connected with his revels.

Few of the ivies contend for places in the rock garden, although some of the smaller-leaved kinds can be used as ground cover.

— helix. This is the common ivy, and the clones 'Congesta' and 'Conglomerata' are slow-growing, congested pygmies admirably adapted for planting where they can grow close against a rock or boulder. They are even admissible in a large stone sink or trough.

HELIANTHEMUM. *Cistaceae.* From Greek *helios*, the sun, and *anthemon*, a flower.

A race of sun-loving, easily grown dwarf shrubby plants of which the most universally grown and popular for the rock garden are the innumerable named forms found under the umbrella of *H. nummularium.*

— alpestre. This is correctly a subspecies of *H. oelandicum* but I retain the better known name. It comes from Central and Southern Europe and is a neat, small leaved shrublet, with golden flowers. Especially small leaved and prostrate is *H.a.* 'Serpyllifolium'. Spring and summer flowering.

— lunulatum. From the Maritime Alps of France and Italy. Nine in., grey-leaved bushes and many small but showy yellow flowers in summer.

— nummularium. Beneath this banner dwell the multitudes of named clones, hybrids and cultivars which make such a brilliant contribution to spring and summer colour in the rock garden. It is pointless to name and describe them in detail, their colours are given in any good catalogue of rock garden plants. Clip them over hard after flowering and they will remain neat and be long-lived and, if so treated, will very often give another, later display of blossom.

— tuberaria. See TUBERARIA *lignosa.*

HELICHRYSUM. *Compositae.* From the Greek *helios*, the sun and *chrysos*, golden.

A large genus of more than 300 species, distributed widely in the

Old World, with the greatest concentrations in S. Africa and Australasia. They vary from tiny cushion plants to tall shrubs. Many are not hardy but there are some excellent rock garden and alpine house plants among them. Mostly summer flowering, they appreciate warm, sunny positions and sharply drained soil.

— **acuminatum.** From Australia. A 9 in. bush with leaves edged with fine hairs. The albino form seems to be the one in cultivation, with brilliant white flowers.

— **bellidioides.** Although the RHS Dictionary tells us that this is half-hardy, and should be given alpine house treatment, it has been grown as a perfectly hardy plant for many years. Prostrate mats of branching stems, tiny grey-green leaves and solitary, terminal white flower heads make it an attractive and easy ground-coverer.

— **confertum.** This S. African species is more wisely grown in an alpine house. It is a neat, dwarf evergreen with woolly leaves on white woolly stems with terminal white everlasting flowers enclosed in a scaly, golden-brown involucre.

— **coralloides.** From New Zealand and a much cherished plant, usually grown in the alpine house but hardy out of doors, especially if tucked into a Tufa hole. Gnarled silver and green bushes of upright, branching stems dressed with scale-like, overlapping leaves showing the edges of a white wool packing beneath. Small heads of yellow flowers sometimes decorate the growth tips.

— **frigidum.** From the highest Corsican mountains. For the alpine house, or in the open if it can be given protection from winter wet. Tiny tufts of silver stems and leaves and quite large white everlasting flowers which persist for many summer weeks.

— **grandiceps.** See LEUCOGYNES *grandiceps.*

— **leontopodium.** See LEUCOGYNES *leontopodium.*

— **marginatum.** See *H. milfordae.*

— **milfordae.** (H. marginatum.) From S. Africa, and hardy in a sunny scree. Flat pads of crowded silver-leaved rosettes and large, conical, crimson-backed buds which expand into round white everlasting flowers on 2 in. stems in summer.

— **milliganii.** From Tasmania. Rosettes of pale green, slightly hairy leaves and short-stemmed large flowers of glistening white. For a choice scree or the alpine house.

— **orientale.** From S.E. Europe. Foot-high bushes with white woolly leaves and heads of white flowers, the involucral bracts straw-yellow. Hardy in all but exceptionally cold areas.

— **plumeum.** A comparative newcomer from New Zealand. It can be likened to *H. coralloides* reduced in size and softer and 'fluffier' in all its parts. A must for the alpine house or sink or trough garden.

— **retortum.** Tangled tumbles of grey stems set with irridescent silver leaves. A fine alpine house plant.

— **selago.** From New Zealand and cultivated in its typical form of a

9 in. bushlet of erect stems, and a major and minor form. The leaves are small, pointed, scale-like and closely overlapped, showing a thin margin of white felt. Flower heads small and yellow. For stone sinks or the alpine house.

— tumida. From New Zealand. Tangled grey-green whipcord branches and has small, powder-puff heads of pale yellow flowers on the tips of the stems. It will grow to a foot or more, best in an alpine house.

— virgineum. From the Balkans, Wide, silver woolly leaves and 9 in. stems carry fat buds enveloped in shell-pink bracts, later opening into large white everlasting flowers. A splendid alpine house plant.

HELIOSPERMA. *Caryophyllaceae.* From the Greek *helios*, the sun and *sperma*, a seed, from the shape of the seeds.

A small genus of tufted herbs from E. Europe. Only two seem to have been generally cultivated, *H. micranthum* and *H. pusillum*, both with quite nice pink, silene-like flowers.

HELIPTERUM. *Compositae.* From the Greek *helios*, the sun and *pteron*, a wing. A reference to the plumed pappus.

— albicans 'Alpinum'. From Australia and apparently hardy. Tufts of white leaves and 9 in. stems carrying white, orange-centered everlasting flowers in summer. Give it a warm and sunny position.

— anthemioides. Also Australian and also hardy. Frail, upright stems clad with small, pointed leaves and ending in pure white, papery flowers. 9 in. summer.

HELLEBORUS. *Ranunculaceae.* Greek *helleboros*, the name of the Lenten Hellebore, *H. orientalis*.

Although many alpine gardeners are fond of hellebores and grow them in their gardens, they do not really qualify for inclusion in this Manual, with the possible exception of *H. niger*, the ever popular Christmas Rose, which, in any case, is surely too well known to need any description here?

HELONIAS. *Liliaceae.* From the Greek *helos*, a marsh — a chosen habitat of these plants.

— bullata. The only species in the genus and a native of N. America. From dense tufts of long, narrow leaves rise 12 to 15 in. stems in spring, carrying dense racemes of pink flowers. Although a bog-lover from choice it will grow well enough in a cool position and moisture retentive soil.

HELONIOPSIS. *Liliaceae.* From *Helonias* and *opsis*, resemblance. A small genus, similar in many ways to the preceding, from Japan and Formosa, and asking for similar treatment. The three species most likely to be encountered in gardens — albeit not as frequently as they deserve to be — are *HH. breviscapa, japonica* and *umbellata* and there is a general similarity in their appearance. They all form strong clumps of fairly narrow, pointed leaves and carry their pink flowers in spring on slender, 12 to 15 in. stems in short, dense racemes.

HELXINE. See the genus SOLEIROLIA.

HEPATICA. *Ranunculaceae.* From the Greek *hepar*, the liver. A double allusion to the shape and colour of the leaves. According to the Doctrine of Signatures they would be good for complaints of the liver.

Formerly known as *Anemone hepatica*, these are well-loved spring flowers for shady positions. They are definitely lime-lovers, widely distributed in Northern Temperate Zones.

— acutiloba. From Canada and N. America and similar in most ways to the European *H. nobilis*.

— angulosa. See *H. transsilvanica*.

— X media. A natural hybrid intermediate between the parents, *HH. nobilis* and *transsilvanica*.

— nobilis. (H. triloba.) Tufts and clumps of three-lobed leaves and myriads of starry blue flowers. There is a pretty albino, and, in the past, there were forms with double blue, pink or white flowers. These are now great rarities, to be treasured and cossetted if obtained. Widely spread through Europe, Asia and America.

— transsilvanica. (H. angulosa.) From E. Europe and larger in all its parts than *H. nobilis* but otherwise similar. In 1916 the late Ernest Ballard, of Michaelmas Daisy fame, crossed selected forms of *H. nobilis* and *H. transsylvanica* and, from the resulting seedlings selected and propagated one exceptionally fine plant with very large, intensely blue flowers. This subsequently, in 1938, received an Award of Merit and also the Reginald Cory Memorial Cup as the best deliberate hybrid between two species exhibited that year. It is identified as *H.X media* 'Ballardii' after having been originally named *H.* 'Trilosa'.

— triloba. See *H. nobilis*.

HERACLEUM. *Umbelliferae.* From the ancient Greek name *Heracleon*, Hercules.

These giant cow-parsleys have no place in the rock garden, but the genus contains one pygmy which is quite fascinating. The glossy-green, deeply cleft leaves form low tufts, over which are carried umbels of small pink flowers on 4 to 6 in. stems in early summer. Seek for it as *H. minimum* 'Roseum' but I am unaware of its provenance.

HERNIARIA. *Caryophyllaceae.* From *hernia*, a rupture, for which the plant was once supposed to be a cure.
- **glabra.** From Europe (including Britain), Asia and N. Africa. Of use as a green carpeter forming flat mats of bright green tiny leaves. Flowers inconspicuous. It appreciates a situation which is not too hot and dry.

HERPOLIRION. *Liliaceae.*
- **novae-zelandae.** From the mountains of Australia, Tasmania and New Zealand. From a short rhizome rise tufts of grassy leaves. The flowers are large, almost sessile and may be blue or white. It flowers in the summer and would seem to prefer a position where the soil was moist rather than dry.

HESPEROCHIRON. *Hydrophyllaceae.* From *hesperos*, western and *Chiron*, Chironia.
A small genus of curious and attractive plants, native to Western N. America.
- **californicus.** Short, thick roots and clusters of succulent leaves. The flowers, carried singly on short stems are widely saucer-shaped and pure white, with some dark striping on the petals.
- **pumilus.** Similar in appearance to the above but the flowers may be white, pink, or soft lavender in colour. Both species die down very quickly after flowering in early summer and are not seen again until the following spring. Grow them in gritty, preferable lime-free soil in the alpine house.

HEUCHERA. *Saxifragaceae.* Named in honour of Johann Heinrich von Heucher (1677-1747), Professor of Medicine.
Heucheras are normally regarded as plants for the flower border but there are a few alpine species well suited to the rock garden. They are all natives of N. America, from Mexico to the Arctic Circle, and are summer flowering and easily grown.
- **bracteata.** Dense tufts of lobed, kidney-shaped leaves and close spikes of cream-white flowers on foot-high stems.

- **glabella.** Similar in habit and appearance but with distinctly yellow-cream flowers.
- **racemosa.** A neat miniature from N.W. America with rounded, slightly lobed rather dark-green leaves and short stems carrying racemes of creamy flowers.

HIERACEUM. *Compositae.* The classical Greek name *hierakion* for several Mediterranean composites; possibly from *hierax*, a falcon (The common name for Hieraceum is Hawkweed).

In general a weedy race, but a few species are admissible and desirable. It is an enormous family, one known Monograph on the genus running to several volumes! For those which are garden-worthy provide open, sunny positions in any good soil. Spring and summer flowering.

- **aurantiacum.** Europe, and naturalized here and there in Britain. Commonly known as 'Grim the Collier', it is weedy but allowable in a not too choice position for the sake of its heads of fiercely orange-scarlet flowers on 12 in. stems.
- **pannosum.** From the Eastern Mediterranean and dubiously in cultivation. In nature it is found tucked into limestone crevices, where it forms tight tufts of silver-haired leaves. Six in. stems carry large heads of yellow flowers.
- **peletarianum.** From the Pyrenees and, if it is not still in cultivation, worth introducing, and growing in starvation conditions to maintain its neat, dwarf habit. In rich soil it becomes coarse. Large heads of lemon-yellow flowers on short stems at its best.
- **villosum.** Central Europe. A variable species but in all its forms making rosettes of intensely shaggy leaves covered in silver hairs and carrying yellow flower heads on foot-high stems.

HIPPOCREPIS. *Leguminosae.* From the Greek *hippos*, a horse, and *krepis*, a shoe. Referring to the shape of the seed pods.

- **comosa.** This is the common wild Horse-shoe Vetch and, though a pretty weed, not to be grown in choice companionship. The form known as 'E.R. Janes'. is a garden-worthy selection forming prostrate mats of tangled leafy stems and sheeted in spring and early summer with yellow flowers.

HOLCUS. *Graminiae.* The Greek name for Sorghum, one of the millet grasses.

- **mollis.** A Native grass, only admissible, and then with caution, in the form with silver and green variegated leaves. It ramps but makes a quite handsome mat of decorative foliage.

HOMOGYNE. *Compositae.* From the Greek *homos*, similar and *gyne*, female.

A small genus of three species, rather unnecessarily damned by Farrer as 'a dingy little family'. They usefully fill cool corners. They are all European. Spring and early summer flowering.

- alpina. Small tufts of evergreen, leathery, kidney-shaped, slightly toothed dark green leaves and disks of purple flowers on short stems.
- discolor. Similar in most respects but its leaves are silvery on the undersides.
- sylvestris. Very similar to *H. alpina* but the leaves are more definitely lobed.

HORMINUM. *Labiatae.* The Greek name for sage, to which this · plant is related.

- pyrenaicum. The only species in its genus, from the Pyrenees to the Tirol. Ramonda-like rosettes of rough, toothed leaves and whorls of purple-blue flowers on 6 to 9 in. stems in summer. Forms occur with pinkish flowers and an albino has been recorded. Any good soil and an open position. Not a five star plant on a cognac rating, but worth growing.

HOUSTONIA. *Rubiaceae.* Named for Dr. William Houston (1695-1733), a Scottish surgeon, also an artist and botanist.

- caerulea. The dainty Bluetts of N. America. A delightful, spring flowering plant for light shade, where it will spread into loose mats of 3 in. stems with tiny, glossy leaves and innumerable soft blue, 4-petalled flowers. The form usually cultivated is a selection of richer colour made by the late F.W. Millard, and bearing his name.

There are several other species of Houstonia, all American, but they are scarcely in cultivation, although *H. rubra*, in particular, sounds very desirable, if it could be obtained.

HOUTTUYNIA. (Anemopsis). *Saururaceae.* Named for Martin Houttuyn (1720-1794), a Dutch naturalist.

- cordata. The only species in its genus. It comes from E. Asia and is, in nature, apparently, a semi-aquatic. In gardens it shows no aversion to any not too dry soil in semi-shade and can, indeed, become something of a pretty nuisance as it spread rapidly by underground stems. The erect stems which spring from the roots are clad in broad, alternate, pointed dark green leaves and terminate in a close head of small white flowers. There is a form with fully double flowers which is possibly more desirable than the type. Handle it gently for the leaves exude a positively disgusting odour when bruised. Spring flowering. 9 to 12 inches high.

HUGUENINIA. *Cruciferae.* Derivation obscure.

— tanacetifolia. (Sisymbrium tanacetifolium.) From the Alps of Europe. Loose tufts of segmented, pinnatifid leaves and showers of yellow flowers on 12 to 15 in. stems in summer. Easy and pretty but not an aristocrat.

HUTCHINSIA. *Cruciferae.* Named in honour of Ellen Hutchins (1785-1815), an Irish botanist of note in her time.

— alpina. Mountains of Central and Southern Europe. A tiny tufted perennial for cool positions with small, pinnatifid leaves and clusters of starry white flowers on 2 in. stems in summer. The subspecies *auerswaldii* is similar but has leaves of darker green and slightly larger flowers.

— auerswaldii. See *H. alpina.*

HYDRANGEA. *Saxifragaceae.* From the Greek *hydor*, water, and *aggos*, a jar. The fruits are cup-shaped.

— 'Pia'. Perhaps no hydrangea should find a place in this Manual, but this branch sport of *H. hortensia* is a pygmy which is sometimes employed as a rock garden shrub (but not, I confess, by me) 6 to 9 in. rounded bushes and heads of pink flowers in summer.

HYDROCOTYLE. *Umbelliferae.* From the Greek *hydor*, water, and *kotyle*, a small cup.

From the shape of the leaves of *H. umbilicus.*

— moschata. From New Zealand but naturalized in Ireland, Prostrate mats of small, rounded, glossy leaves. Flowers quite inconspicuous but a neat carpeter for moist shady places.

HYLOMECON. *Papaveraceae.* From the Greek *hyle*, a wood and *mecon*, a poppy.

— japonicum. It is probably correct that this Japanese woodland plant should now be named *Chelidonium japonicum*, but I adhere to the name by which it is well known in gardens. As Hylomecon it is a monotypic genus but as Chelidonium it becomes one of several in a genus. An herbaceous perennial with elegant, pinnate leaves and poppy-like yellow flowers of good size on 12 in. stems in early spring.

HYMENOXIS. *Compositae.*

— grandiflora. (Rydbergia grandiflora.) From N. America. Rosettes of densely hairy pinnate leaves from which rise 9 in. stems carrying large, rich golden daisy flowers in summer. For hot, dry positions.

HYPERICUM. *Guttiferae.* From the Greek *hyper*, above, and *eikon*, a picture. The plant was supposed to keep evil spirits at bay. The flowers of some species were placed above images to ward off evil at the ancient midsummer festival of Walpurgisnacht, now the feast of St. John, hence St. John's Wort.

A large and widely distributed genus of herbs, sub-shrubs and shrubs, of which several of the dwarfest kinds are greatly valued as rock garden plants and a few of special merit are worthy of alpine house culture. All those described below are sun-lovers and succeed in any good, well-drained soil unless otherwise stated in their descriptions. In general they are summer and early autumn flowering.

- **aegypticum.** From the Mediterranean coasts and islands, and not entirely hardy, but, as a dwarf, evergreen shrub, makes a fine specimen in an alpine house. The grey-green leaves are crowded on the erect, round stems which carry solitary yellow flowers at the ends of short twigs. Although introduced in 1787 it is seldom seen, possibly because of its tenderness.

- **balearicum.** This species from the Balearic Isles is, like *H. aegypticum*, not entirely hardy and should be regarded as another dwarf evergreen shrub, seldom exceeding a foot in height, for the alpine house. Its rounded, rather leathery leaves are curiously covered with wart-like growths. The flowers are solitary, yellow and carried terminally on the rigid, erect shoots.

- **buckleyi.** A rare N. American species confined to a limited area in the mountains of Carolina and Georgia. It is semi-woody and deciduous, forming 9 in. rounded tufts of angled stems. Several bright yellow flowers terminate each shoot. Good for a sheltered nook in the rock garden or for the alpine house.

- **cerastoides.** (H. rhodopeum.) From Turkey and the Balkans, and early flowering, often blossoming in May. Procumbent mats of tangled stems with evergreen, hairy leaves and clusters of bright yellow flowers springing freely from the terminal leaf axils.

- **confertum.** A semi-herbaceous species from Syria and Cyprus and rather tender. Leafy stems ending in terminal cymes of crowded yellow flowers.

- **coris.** From S. Europe. A distinct dwarf evergreen shrublet of some 6 to 9 in. The tiny leaves are arranged in whorls on the wiry, erect stems and the golden flowers appear in axillary clusters during June and July. It is a definite lime-lover.

- **cuneatum.** From Asia Minor and Syria. It is slightly tender and the stems are extremely brittle and its most appropriate position is in an alpine house. Spreading, thin, brittle red stems with small, rounded leaves with waved margins and dotted on the surface with dark markings. Small yellow flowers in leafy racemes from April to July.

- **elegans.** From Central Europe and Siberia. Upright, foot-high stems, dark-spotted and slightly winged. Cordate, stem-clasping leaves and terminal panicles of yellow flowers with dark anthers.

209

— empetrifolium. From Greece and adjacent islands, cultivated since 1788. It is evergreen and grows to a foot or more, but is most often grown on rock gardens in the form *H.e. oliganthum* (H.e. 'Prostratum') which is quite prostrate with spreading woody stems and profusions of rich yellow flowers. It likes, and is worthy of, a sheltered, warm and sunny position. A severe winter in a cold garden can be fatal.

— ericoides. An alpine house treasure from Spain and N. Africa. Now very rare in cultivation but deserves reintroducing. Tiny heath-like bushes with wiry, densely-leaved stems and terminal clusters of yellow flowers in May. Forms have been collected which are entirely prostrate. In nature it haunts hard limestone crevices.

— fragile. From S.E. Europe. A 9 in. sub-shrub with small, smooth, oval leaves and terminal cymes of yellow flowers.

— humifusum. Mats of prostrate or semi-erect stems and oval leaves often edged with black dots. Flowers solitary or in few-flowered terminal cymes, yellow, sometimes flushed with red. It is a British native but well worth garden space.

— kotschyanum. From Asia Minor and Syria. Tufts of softly hairy grey-green stems and leaves and cymes of yellow flowers forming a loose panicle.

— nummularium. Sprawling, leafy stems and quite large yellow flowers, sometimes solitary, occasionally in clusters. European Alps.

— olympicum. (H. polyphyllum.) The plant grown in gardens as *H. polyphyllum* can only be regarded as a possibly slightly varying form of this species. From S. Europe, Syria and Asia Minor. Low, mounded bushes or erect stems densely clothed with small, pointed leaves and terminal cymes of large, rich golden-yellow flowers. A splendid garden plant.

— orientale. From Asia Minor. An erect, 9 to 12 in. sub-shrub with yellow flowers in small terminal clusters.

— polyphyllum. See *H. olympicum.* There may be a true *H. polyphyllum*, but it does not appear to be in cultivation.

— repens. The plant grown under this name in gardens may well prove to be more correctly *H. linarioides*, but I retain the better known name for the time being. It is often unfortunately confused with *H. reptans*, a very different, and a better plant. From Asia Minor, of rather tufted habit with small leaves and longish cymes of small yellow flowers.

— reptans. From the Himalaya. Absolutely prostrate with slender, leafy stems ending in large, solitary rich golden-yellow flowers. A fine plant, worthy of a sunny spot in gritty but not impoverish soil.

— rhodopeum. (rhodopaeum.) See *H. cerastoides.*

— richeri. From Central, Southern and Eastern Europe. Varies in height from 6 to 18 in. Erect, slightly winged stems, densely clothed in smooth leaves edged with black dots. Dense terminal clusters of small yellow flowers.

— rumeliacum. From the Balkans and, in its dwarfest forms, desirable, but in some forms it attains 18 in. or more. Clusters of yellow flowers, black-spotted, in elongated panicles.

— **tomentosum.** From S. Europe and N. Africa. A dwarf sub-shrub with tomentose stems and leaves and loose terminal clusters of small yellow flowers.

— **trichocaulon.** From Crete. Neat, prostrate evergreen with small, hard leaves and many crimson buds expanding into golden flowers.

— **yakushimanum.** From Japan — presumably, although not mentioned in Ohwi's comprehensive Flora of Japan. One of the smallest species. Creeping carpets of frail stems and small leaves and yellow, starry flowers which are succeeded by red seedheads.

HYPOCHOERIS. *Compositae.* A name used by Theophrastus for this, or a related genus.

— **uniflora.** From the Tatra Mountains. Rosettes of tufted, toothed, hairy leaves and yellow flower heads on short stems in summer. For a warm, sunny position.

HYPSELLA. *Campanulaceae.* From the Greek *hypselos*, high, a possible allusion to the habitat of the type species in the Andes.

— **longiflora.** See *H. reniformis.*

— **reniformis.** From Chile, and has been much confused in gardens with a plant of similar appearance, *Selliera radicans.* A carpeter for cool places, with rounded, rather fleshy leaves and small, Lobelia-like pink and crimson flowers, almost stemless.

IBERIS. *Cruciferae.* Greek *iberis*, indicating a plant from Iberia.

A genus of sun-loving, easily grown plants for spring and summer flowering. They are widely distributed in S. Europe and W. Asia and several of them are valuable rock garden plants.

— **aurosica.** Although described by some books as an annual, *Flora Europaea* assures us that it is perennial. It inhabits the European Alps and makes small, neat tufts of foliage, with dense corymbs of white, or mauve-flushed flowers.

— **candolleana.** See *I. pruitii.*

— **correaefolia.** This is really nothing but an inferior form of *I. sempervirens.*

— **garrexiana.** This, too, is but a version of *I. sempervirens.*

— **gibraltarica.** From Gibraltar and N. Africa. Although it has been cultivated in Britain since 1732, it is often not the true species which is seen but a form of *I. sempervirens.* It should be a 9 in. evergreen with dark, narrow, slightly wedge-shaped leaves toothed at the apex, and with heads of quite large, white, mauve-flushed flowers.

— **granatensis.** See *I. pruitii.*

— **jordanii.** Although given specific rank by some authorities, *Flora Europaea* refers this to *L. pruitii.*

— **jucunda.** See *I. tenoreana.*

— **minima.** There is no authority for this name and the plant which bears it can only be a miniature form of *I. sempervirens* — but is none the less desirable.

— **petraea.** See *I. saxatilis.*

— **pruitii.** The latest classification of the genus refers to this Mediterranean species several others which have been grown under such names as *I. candolleana. I. granatensis* and *I. jordanii.* It should possibly be regarded as a blanket name covering several similar plants, of low, tufted habit with heads of white flowers, in some cases flushed with mauve.

— **pygmaea.** Another apparently invalid name for a compact form of *I. sempervirens.*

IBERIS — *continued*

- saxatilis. (I. petraea.) From Central and Southern Europe. A neat little bushling seldom exceeding 6 in. with corymbs of white flowers, sometimes tinged with purple.
- semperflorens. From Italy and Sicily and too tall for most rock gardens, but where there is space in a warm corner for a shrub up to 2 ft. in height with corymbs of white, mauve-flushed flowers, worth a trial, but it may succumb to a hard winter.
- sempervirens. From Southern Europe. Various forms of this species are the most popular and widely grown members of the genus. They exist under several clonal names, such as 'Little Gem' and 'Snowflake' and all offer perennial displays of pure white flowers in abundance. There is a form with double flowers which is scarcely worth bothering with, and another, equally unworthy, with variegated foliage.
- tenoreana. (I. jucunda.) There is doubt as to the authenticity of this name. It is yet another which *Flora Europaea* refers to *I. pruitii*, but the plant bearing the name in gardens is so distinct that I retain the name, or its synonym. It makes 3 to 4 in. mats of evergreen leaves covered in early summer with innumerable heads of white, often mauve-flushed flowers.

ILEX. *Aquifoliaceae.* From the Latin name for the holm oak, *Quercus ilex.*

- crenata 'Mariesii'. One may wonder how a holly comes to be included in a Manual of alpine plants, but this pygmy is such an enchanting tiny shrub that it demands inclusion. It is very slow growing indeed, known specimens of 80 years or more being less than 2 ft. in height. The type comes from Japan but I do not know the provenance of this clone although it is said to have been first distributed by Veitch's nursery about 1879. Rigid, erect stems are clothed with tiny, rounded, leathery, dark green leaves. Inconspicuous flowers are followed by glossy black berries. Ideal for stone troughs and sink gardens.

INULA. *Compositae.* The Latin name for these plants.

A large genus of, mostly, tall herbaceous perennials with a few dwarf species appropriate to the Manual. Unless otherwise stated they grow well in any good soil, are sun-lovers and summer flowering.

- acaulis. From Asia Minor. Prostrate tufts of hairy, toothed leaves and almost stemless golden flower heads. Best given rather austere treatment in gritty soil or scree.
- attica. From the Eastern Mediterranean. The flowers have no great value but it is worth growing in hot sun or the alpine house for the sake of its rosettes of small, ovate, toothed leaves which are covered densely with a white tomentum.

- **candida.** From rocky crevices in S. Europe and definitely a very beautiful plant. Equally definitely it is for the alpine house. The wide leaves are so dazzlingly white with a pelt of fine hairs that it cannot be expected to tolerate a typical British winter in the open. Over the handsome rosette are slender spikes also coated with white hairs, of small, but clear yellow flowers in spring and early summer.
- **ensifolia.** Came from the Caucasus and has been with us for the better part of 200 years. Not exciting, but a useful and easy plant with erect 9 in. stems carrying several yellow flowers in late summer.
- **heterolepis.** From Turkey and only introduced in 1949. It received an Award of Merit in 1956, but remains a rarity. It is another for the alpine house. Its woody stems end in rosettes of thick, velvety leaves. The undersides are netted with white veins. The procumbens stems carry orange-yellow flower heads in midsummer, consisting of disk-florets surrounded by a white-felted involucre.
- **limonifolia.** From Greece, and a splendid foliage plant forming dense tufts of plushy silvery leaves. The flowers are unimportant. For the alpine house.
- **maletii.** From Morocco and dubiously in cultivation. I have not seen the plant but believe it to make a decorative display of ragged yellow flowers on reasonably short stems.

From Greece also come *I. serpentinica* and *I. subfloccosa.* I doubt if either is in cultivation at present, but they would appear to be desirable alpine house plants, not dissimilar to *I. attica.*

IONACTIS *alpina.* See ASTER *scopulorum.*

IONOPSIDIUM. *Cruciferae.* From the Greek *ion,* violet, and *opsis,* like.

- **acaule.** In general I am not in favour of annuals on the rock garden, but this dainty, tiny Portuguese plant is an exception. It offers 2 in. tufts of crowded lilac flowers over a long summer period. A colony in a sunny place in the rock garden is attractive and it is admirably adapted for sowing in the crevices between paving stones.

IRIS. *Iridaceae.* Named for the Greek goddess of the rainbow.

This enormous genus has made a major contribution to our gardens but we are here concerned only with the dwarfs which are appropriate to the alpine garden. Bulbous species and forms are excluded from this Manual.

- **arenaria.** See *I. flavissima.*
- **attica.** See *I. pumila*

IRIS — *continued*

- **balkana.** See *I. reichenbachii.*
- **bracteata.** From N. America. Few-leaved tufts of thick, leathery glossy green leaves and 6 to 9 in. stems bearing bract-like leaves and ending in two flowers which are yellow, conspicuously veined with brownish-purple. Spring flowering.
- **chamaeiris.** A species from South-Eastern France and North-Western Italy. It is an extremely variable plant and, in gardens, is much confused with *I. pumila.* It is spring-flowering and very dwarf, seldom exceeding 4 to 6 in. One of its finest manifestations is found in *I.c.* 'Campbellii', which has large flowers of deep indigo-blue.
- **cristata.** From N. America. This is one of the best of all really dwarf rock garden irises. It makes tangled mats of slender rhizomes ending in tufts of small, narrow, pointed leaves. The flowers, usually in pairs are lilac and orange and the falls have a conspicuous white crest. It relishes a cool position in gritty, humus-rich soil and flowers in May. There is a rare, but very lovely albino form.
- **ensata.** A variable species from temperate Asia. The stems may be a few inches or a foot in height. The flowers, usually in small clusters, may be white, lavender or deeper blue and are carried in early summer.
- **flavissima.** (I. arenaria.) From the Balkans to Siberia. Creeping rhizomes have tufts of small, typically iris-like leaves and the 4 in. stems carry several bright yellow, orange-bearded flowers in spring.
- **gracilipes.** From mountain woodlands in Japan and demands, and deserves, a selected position in light shade with soil rich in humus. The branching slender stems, up to 10 in. tall, carry rather flat, lilac flowers strikingly orange-crested. It flowers in the spring and should only be transplanted at that time, never in autumn or winter.
- **graminea.** From Central and Southern Europe, and possibly also from the Caucasus. It is unfortunate that this, quite pretty, dwarf species has the habit of partially concealing its blossoms among the dense tufts of narrow leaves. The fragrant flowers are white, veined with purple and yellow and appear in early summer.
- **innominata.** From N. America, mainly Oregon. It was only in 1935 that the yellow-flowered form of this delightful iris became known in this country and made an immediate conquest. The original form with golden flowers veined brown and buff remains the most valued, but it varies considerably from seed — and, possibly, hybridisation, and produces a wide range of blossoms which appear in various subtle 'art' shades. It flowers in spring and early summer, makes wide tufts of hard, narrow leaves and carries the flowers singly on 6 to 9 in. stems. Moisture retentive soil, gritty but rich in humus please it best and it is a sun-lover in my experience, although some text books advise half-shade.
- **kumaonensis.** From the Himalaya. In growth it resembles a miniature *I. unguicularis* and the almost stemless flowers, borne in spring, are light purple, veined and mottled with darker colour. It is rare in gardens but is not difficult in well-drained soil and full sun.

- lacustris. Formerly regarded as a variety of *I. cristata* this, one of the smallest of irises, has now achieved specific rank. It is found on the shores of the Great Lakes in N. America and makes a mat of slender rhizomes. Its flowers are similar to those of *I. cristata*, carried on inch-stems, and it requires similar treatment.

- mellita. From the Balkans, and similar to *I. pumila*. Seldom more that 3 in. tall it has flowers of smoky-brown or yellow-brown, veined with reddish and purple lines. The variety 'Rubromarginata' has its leaves edged with red.

- minuta. Known only as a cultivated plant from Japan. It grows well enough, forming almost prostrate mats of small leaves, but is shy-flowering. The flowers are yellow, marked with soft brown. On the roots are curious nodules, similar to those carried by many legum-inous plants.

- pumila. From Europe and Asia Minor and represented in gardens mainly by numerous forms and hybrids with flowers of various col-ours. It is an easily grown, spring and summer-flowering plant form-ing dense mats and blossoming freely in any good soil and full sun. A nice, very dwarf iris grown as *I. attica*, and judged worthy of an Award of Merit in 1951, is no more than a geographic form of *I. pumila*. It has soft yellow flowers, tinged green and veined with brown lines.

- reichenbachii. Similar to, and may be regarded as the Balkan version of *I. chamaeiris*. There are yellow-flowered forms and others with smoky-purple flowers, one of the best of these being sometimes grown as *I. balkana*.

- rubromarginata. See *I. mellita*.

- ruthenica. From E. Europe, Turkestan and China. A rare and dis-tinct iris not more than 9 in. tall. The flowers are shaded with purple on a white ground and the standards are a deeper colour. It is not dif-ficult to grow but should be handled only when in full growth during spring or early summer.

- stylosa. See *I. unguicularis*.

- tectorum. The roof iris of Japan, but probably originally a native of China. Broad, ribbed leaves and branching stems carrying flat flowers of rich purple-blue, the falls mottled with deeper colour and a jagged white crest. There is also a form with wholly white flowers except for the crest, which is yellow. It is shallow rooting and appreciates a good summer ripening. There are several known hybrids between this species and other bearded irises.

- unguicularis. It is probably wrong to include the winter-flowering Algerian iris in this Manual, but it is such a universal favourite that I claim space for it. Grown against a warm wall it provides innumer-able lavender flowers from November until spring and these, picked in bud, are highly valued for indoor decoration. There are many named forms of this excellent plant, varying in colour from pure white to deep lavender. It is best left undisturbed to grow into matted clumps but, if it must be moved, this should be done in April if possible.

- urumovii. From Bulgaria and related to *I. graminea*. Tufts of glaucous, almost blue-grey leaves, long and narrow and tending to overtop the twin flowers which resemble those of *I. graminea*, the falls veined and spotted with blue on a white ground.
- verna. N. America. Rather like an *I. pumila*, but without the bearded falls. Lilac-blue flowers with an orange band on the falls. It appears to like moist, peaty soil and light shade, and flowers in the spring.

ISOPYRUM. *Ranunculaceae.* From the Greek *isos*, equal, and *pyros*, wheat. The ancient Greek name for a Fumaria, probably transferred to this genus because of a similarity in foliage.
- thalictrioides. From Europe. A shade-loving, creeping perennial with much divided leaves, the leaflets lobed and toothed. Nine in. stems carry nodding white flowers in spreading panicles during March-April. Cool conditions in light shade and woodland soil. For other plants once in this genus see the genus PARAQUILEGIA.

JABOROSA. *Solanaceae.* The Arabic name for the allied Mandrake.
- **integrifolia.** From S. America. A perennial plant which creeps underground, but not invasively and emits large, oval, fleshy green leaves on short stalks and offers quite large, bell-shaped white flowers on short stems in summer. It relishes a light, well-drained soil and a warm position. A really severe winter might cause it distress.

JANKAEA. *Gesneriaceae.* Named in honour of Victor de Janka (1837-1890), Hungarian student of the flora of the Danube region.
- **heldreichii.** The only species in this genus which is closely allied to Ramonda and Haberlea. A native of the mountains of Greece, notably on Mt. Olympus. It resembles a Ramonda in its rosettes of rugose leaves, but these are heavily felted with silver hairs. The short stems carry several bell-shaped crystalline-blue flowers in spring. It is a rare gem and not very easy to please. Out of doors it should be in a narrow cleft between rocks in humus-rich soil but it is seen at its best in the alpine house.

JASIONE. *Campanulaceae.* The Greek name for another plant, given by Theophrastus to the Convolvulus.

A small genus of perennial and annual plants, native to temperate Europe, including Britain, and also in Mediterranean regions. Only two species are generally grown in rock gardens, but one or two others would be desirable if obtainable.
- **jankae.** A tufted plant from E. Europe with narrow, roughly hairy leaves and naked foot-high branching stems carrying spectacular heads of deep blue flowers in summer.
- **perennis.** From W. Europe. Rather similar to the above, but with unbranched, slightly shorter stems and globose heads of not quite so blue flowers in spring and summer.

J. amethystina from Spain and *J. humilis* from the Pyrenees are blue-flowered 4 in. dwarfs which would be welcome.

JASMINUM. *Oleaceae.* The Latin version of the Persian name *yasmin* for these fragrant plants.

A very large genus of climbing, trailing or erect shrubs, only one of which qualifies for a place in this Manual.

- **parkeri.** From N.W. India. An enticing dwarf shrub forming foot-high domes of entangled woody twigs clothed with small, dark green pinnate leaves. Short-stemmed yellow flowers in summer. Slightly tender and worthy of a sheltered position or the alpine house.

JEFFERSONIA. *Berberidaceae.* Named in honour of Thomas Jefferson (1743-1826), President of the United States 1801-1809, a patron of Botany with a deep interest in horticulture.

A genus of only two species, one from N. America and the other from Asia.

- **binata.** See *J. diphylla.*
- **diphylla** (J. binata. Podophyllum diphyllum.) From N. America. Rounded grey-green leaves deeply cleft into two lobes, on wiry stems. Solitary, inch-wide white flowers on 9 in. stems in early spring. Give light shade and woodland soil.
- **dubia.** (Plagiorhegma dubia.) From Manchurian woodlands. Rounded, lobed, glaucous leaves often tinted with violet on thin, wiry stems and solitary, cup-shaped clear blue flowers more than an inch in diameter. Spring. Grow in gritty but humus-rich soil in the open or in the alpine house.

JEPSONIA. *Saxifragaceae.*

A rather obscure race of tuberous-rooted Saxifragas containing three species, natives of N. America. It is doubtful if they are in cultivation in Britain, but if obtained, they should be treated as acid-soil plants. They flower in the autumn with loose panicles of white or pinkish flowers on short stems. Little is known about their needs in gardens and they should, in the first instance, certainly be given VIP treatment in the alpine house.

JOVIBARBA. One of the divisions of the genus SEMPERVIVUM, which see.

JUNCUS. *Juncaceae.* The classical Latin name for the bullrush.

- **effusus 'Spiralis'.** A curious form of the common wild rush. Its 18 in. stems are twisted into symmetrical corkscrew shapes, It is an oddity for those who like plant abnormalities. It is not invasive, making a dense tuft in moist soil.

JURINEA. *Compositae.* Named in honour of Louis Jurine (1751-1819), Professor of Medicine.

A race of not highly meritorious herbaceous perennials and sub-shrubs, of which the undernoted species might be of interest for the rock garden. They are sun-loving and summer flowering.

— depressa. From the Caucasus. Tufts of lyrate leaves and blue, thistle-like flower heads on 6 in. stems.

— humilis. From N. Africa. Pinnate leaves and purple thistle-heads on short stems.

KALMIOPSIS. *Ericaceae.* Kalmia and *opsis*, like, from its resemblance to Kalmia.

A genus of only one species, native to Western N. America. It demands lime-free soil but will endure full, but not scorching sun.

- **leachiana.** An enticing and very beautiful dwarf shrub of comparatively recent discovery — it was introduced here for the first time about 1935. Foot-high, rounded evergreen bushes of woody stems clothed in small, dark green, leathery leaves and short terminal racemes of open bell-shaped rich pink flowers from March to May. Since its original discovery one or two slightly divergent forms have been found, notably one named 'Lepiniec', which appears to be more easily pleased.

KELSEYA. *Rosaceae.* Named for Harlan P. Kelsey (1872-1958), a nurseryman, Massachusetts.

A monotypic genus related to PETROPHYTUM, native to restricted areas in N. America.

- **uniflora.** A rare and precious cushion-forming plant for the alpine house or a choice nook between rocks in a trough or sink garden. Although really a shrub it forms densely imbricated domes of crowded stems dressed in tiny, leathery silkily-hairy leaves. The stemless small flowers are white, flushed with pink and appear in the spring and early summer. It requires austere treatment, jammed between small pieces of rock in gritty soil, preferably, but not essentially lime-free.

KERNERA. *Cruciferae.* Named for Johann Simon von Kerner (1755-1830), professor of botany at Stuttgart.

- **alpina** and *K. saxatilis* are two rather insignificant little mountain crucifers from the alps of Europe. Their white flowers on short stems do not make much of a show but they are often sympathetically regarded as easily grown cushions for odd nooks in the rock garden, they also make useful ground cover for small alpine bulbs.

LACTUCA. *Compositae.* From the Latin *lac*, milk, because of the milky sap.

A large genus of annual and perennial herbs, very few of which fall within the scope of an alpine plant Manual. The few which are of rock garden interest are listed below. They are all perennial, easily grown sun-lovers and summer flowering.

— **macrorrhiza.** From the Himalaya. Rosettes of leaves of various shapes, some lyrate, some rounded and lobed. The purple-blue flowers are carried in a loose corymb on stems varying from 9 to 15 in.

— **perennis.** From S. Europe and too tall for any but a large rock garden. Tall stems dressed in pinnatifid leaves and corymbose panicles of light blue flowers.

— **tenerrima.** From S. Europe and N. Africa. Loose rosettes of deeply segmented leaves and slender, branching stems of about 9 to 12 in. carrying heads of many small blue flowers.

LAGENOPHORA. *Compositae.* From the Greek *lagenos*, a flask and *pherein*, to bear. The involucres are shaped like a flask.

A small race of not terribly exciting composites, natives of Australia, New Zealand and S. Asia. The few species described are worth growing although not of resplendent beauty. Summer flowering, sun and gritty soil.

— **cuneata.** From New Zealand. Rosettes of small, green, notched leaves and naked 6 in. stems carrying a fluffy head of small white flowerlets without ray florets.

— **forsteri.** From the Antarctic. Mat-forming with small rosettes and 3 in. stems carrying fuzzy white flower-heads.

— **pinnatifida.** Perhaps the best of the three. From New Zealand. Mats of rosettes composed of bronze-green leaves and small heads of white flowers all summer on stems which vary from 3 to 6 in.

LAPEIROUSIA. *Iridaceae.* Named in honour of Baron Phillipe Picot de la Peyrouse (1744-1818), French botanist and author of a flora of the Pyrenees.

— laxa (Anomatheca cruenta.) Although bulbs in general are excluded from this Manual, this pretty little plant is an exception for which I must find a space. Wild in eastern tropical and South Africa, usually in moist places, but surprisingly hardy in this country. Flat fans of small, iris-like leaves and stems, either branched or unbranched of about 4 to 6 in. carrying many inch-wide red flowers with deeper markings in the throat of the blossom. There is also a white-flowered form. The flowering period is from mid-June until late August.

LAPHAMIA. A genus of alpine American composites, several of which have been tantalisingly described by the late Dwight Ripley in the Bulletins of the Alpine Garden Society. None of them appears to be in cultivation at present, and they would undoubtedly present problems of cultivation if they were.

LATHYRUS. *Leguminosae.* The Greek name *lathyros*, for pea or pulse.

Several plants previously included in the genus OROBUS are now included in this large genus of climbing and herbaceous perennials, a few of which are sometimes grown on rock gardens. Those listed below are all sun-lovers, and spring and early summer flowering. They present no cultural problems.

— albo-roseus. I have a suspicion that this is a form of *L. vernus*, but it is commonly given specific rank, which I retain here. On the 15 to 18 in. stems are many bicoloured flowers of pink and white.
— aurantiacus. See *L. luteus aureus.*
— luteus. From Europe, and too tall for most rock gardens, but the variety 'Aureus' is dwarfer and has rich orange-yellow flowers.
— niger. Europe, including Britain — probably as an original escape. Leafy 18 in. stems and flowers of deep purple.
— vernus. A neat plant, widely distributed in Europe forming 9 in. tufts of leafy stems with many vetch flowers of red and purple.

LAURENTIA. *Campanulaceae.* Named for M. A. Laurenti, an Italian botanist of the 17th century.

— michelii. From Spain. Doubtfully in cultivation but would be a nice plant for a moist, cool corner where it could display its pale blue flowers in summer on 4 in. stems.
— tenella. From S. Europe. A neat and tiny carpeter with rosettes of small leaves and short, slender stems carrying china-blue and white

flowers, one to each stem. It, too, appreciates light shade and moisture and both species are apt to die out if not lifted and replanted every so often.

LAVANDULA. *Labiatae.* From the Latin *lavo*, to wash, from its use in soaps and toiletries.

Lavenders are not really for the rock garden with the possible exception of a condensed form of *L. spica*, usually offered as *L. vera* 'Nana', of which there is a form with white flowers as well as the purple-flowered type.

LEIOPHYLLUM. *Ericaceae.* From the Greek *leios*, smooth, and *phyllon*, a leaf, referring to the glossy foliage.

— buxifolium. From Eastern N. America. A dwarf, evergreen, lime-hating shrub of variable habit. In the wild it may be prostrate or erect up to two feet or more. The form generally cultivated is usually around one foot in height. The small, oblong, leathery dark green leaves clothe the woody stems, and crowded terminal clusters of pink flowers appear in May and June. There are two named varieties, *hugeri* and *prostratum*, neither of which differ appreciably from the type. A fine shrublet for the peat garden or alpine house.

LEONTICE. *Berberidaceae.* From the Greek *leon*, a lion, from a fancied resemblance of the leaves to the print of a lion's foot.

— altaica. See BONGARDIA *chrysogonum*.
— chrysogonum. See BONGARDIA *chrysogonum*.
— leontopetalum. From Greece. Leafy, 18 in. stems and long, terminal racemes of bright yellow flowers in early spring. It likes a sunny, dry position.

LEONTOPODIUM. *Compositae.* The classical name *leontopodion*, meaning lion's foot, for another plant transferred to this genus.

— aloysiodorum. See *L. haplophylloides.*
— alpinum. (Gnaphalium leontopodium.) The ever popular and beloved Edelweiss, surely too well known to need a detailed description of its tufts of narrow, grey-green leaves and clustered flower heads which seem to have been cut out of grey flannel. Not showy, but always fascinating and very easily grown in sunny positions and any good soil. Spring flowering. There are several named geographical forms which are mostly inferior to the typical European plant. There are, however, at least two condensed and very precious forms of *L. alpinum*

from Eastern Europe, *L.a. crassense* and *L.a. nivale*, which are as rare in gardens as they are in nature. They have intensely silvery furry leaves and short-stemmed flower heads of immaculate whiteness. They should be treasured in alpine houses if obtained.

— **haplopylloides.** (L. aloysiodorum.) From the Himalaya. The whole plant is strongly lemon-scented. Star-shaped compound heads of grey-white flowers on 9 in. stems. Spring flowering.

LEPIDIUM. *Cruciferae.* From the Greek *lepis*, a scale, from the shape of the pods.

— **nanum.** From the alkaline flats of the State of Nevada, and not an alpine, but demanding alpine plant treatment and with every characteristic of a high alpine cushion plant. It is the only one of its genus worth growing and boasts no floral beauty. It makes dense, hard, tight cushions of minute rosettes of tiny leaves closely packed into a hump. The flowers are inconspicuous. It is not easy and presents a challenge to those who like to pit their skill against intractable plants. Give it scree treatment and use the water-can with modesty.

LEPTARRHENA. *Saxifragaceae.*

Reginald Farrer, with typically cryptic rudeness, dismisses all Leptarrhenas as worthless dowds, but the species listed below is not without merit for its foliage.

— **amplexifolia.** (L. pyrolifolia.) From N. America and Canada. From stout rhizomes rise bold tufts of large, leathery, glossy green leaves, topped by heads of admittedly rather dingy small white flowers. A good ground cover plant for cool places in preferably lime-free soil.

LEPTORRHYNCHUS. *Compositae.*

A genus of Tasmanian composites of which *L. nitidus* and *L. squamatus* are useful prostrate ground-coverers. Both have yellow button heads of flowers, the former having dark green foliage and the latter leaves of grey-green and slightly hairy.

LEPTOSPERMUM. *Myrtaceae.* From the Greek *leptos*, slender, and *sperma*, seed, referring to the shape of the seeds.

A genus of Australasian shrub, some of doubtful hardiness, few of which, other than the two described below, are of interest to alpine gardeners.

— **humifusum.** (L. scoparium 'Prostratum'.) From Tasmania. A reliably hardy, low spreading shrub with reddish stems and small, thick leaves. The branches are studded in summer with many small white flowers.

— scoparium 'Nanum'. A miniature, forming rounded, foot-high bushes of dark wiry stems and dark green leaves and with many deep red flowers in summer. For the alpine house — only hardy in the open in exceptionally favourable conditions.

— scoparium. 'Prostratum'. See *L. humifusum*.

LESCHENAULTIA. *Goodeniaceae.* Named for Louis Theodore Leschenault de la Tour (1773-1826), French botanist and traveller. A genus of very ornamental, heathlike shrubs from Australia and Tasmania, of which at least two of the dwarfest, *L. biloba* and *L. formosa* would be of value as alpine house shrubs. The former has blue flowers and those of the latter are said to be red, but they are very dubiously in cultivation in Britain.

LESPEDEZA. *Leguminosae.* Named in honour of the Spanish Governor of Florida, Vincente Manuel de Cespedes. c. 1790.

— repens. From the E. United States. Trailing woody stems clothed with trifoliate leaves and loose spikes of violet-pink flowers in the late summer.

LESQUERELLA. *Cruciferae.* Named for Leo Lesquereux (1805-1889), Authority on American fossil botany.

— condensata. From N. America. A curious plant with tufts of yellowish, fleshy leaves and short, radiating, branching stems carrying the small flowers which are exceeded in beauty by the globular yellow pods which succeed them. Rarely in cultivation and best given alpine house treatment in gritty, lime-free soil.

LEUCANTHEMUM. *Compositae.*

Most of the species formerly in this genus are now referred to the genus CHRYSANTHEMUM but a few, all from N. Africa, remain here. They are sun-lovers for open places on the rock garden, or for the alpine house.

— atlanticum. Lusty clumps of dark green leaves over which hover large, snow-white daisy flowers. It will not enjoy a cold, wet winter in the open. The variety *gelidum* is much dwarfer, carrying its huge white flowers on 3 to 4 in. stems effectively over the shining dark green foliage.

- **catananche.** Perhaps too robust for small rock gardens, but a grand plant where there is space for a sub-shrub up to 18 in. and with a similar spread of leafy branches terminating in beige-coloured daisies with a red central zone.
- **hosmariense.** One of the most valuable introductions for the rock garden of recent years. The woody, prostrate stems carry trifoliate, softly hairy leaves of intense silver and there is a summer-long succession of snow-white, golden-eyed daisies of substantial size on 6 to 8 in. stems. Even before the flowers open the involucre of silver, black-edged bracts is handsome. It well deserves the Award of Merit given to it in 1958.
- **montanum.** See CHRYSANTHEMUM *montanum.*

LEUCERIA. *Compositae.* From the Greek *leucheres*, white. Some species are coated with white hairs.

Two desirable species from Patagonia would be welcomed to our alpine houses. *L. hahnii* and *L. lanata* are similar in appearance, forming rosettes of stems and leaves felted densely with white hairs. The fragrant flowers, which may be white or pink, are held in an involucre of white felted bracts. Although they grow in very exposed places, open to constant wind and heavy rain, they are unlikely to succeed in the open in Britain.

LEUCOGYNES. *Compositae.* From the Greek *leukos*, white and *eugenes*, noble.

The two species in the genus both come from New Zealand and are coveted alpine house plants and may also be grown in the open, under widely differing conditions. I have seen them flourishing in peat beds and equally happy in an exposed, gritty scree.

- **grandiceps.** (Helichrysum grandiceps.) Tufts of long, narrow, pointed leaves, leathery in texture and covered with a tomentum of white hairs on both surfaces. The small yellow flowers are closely packed in terminal clusters and are surrounded by woolly white bracts.
- **leontopodium.** (Helichrysum leontopodium.) Very similar in appearance to the previous species and with similar needs.

LEUCOPOGON. *Epacridaceae.* From the Greek *leukos*, white, and *pogon*, a beard, an allusion to the sometimes white-bearded corolla lobes.

- **ericoides.** (Cyathodes ericoides.) Australasian. A heathlike shrub described as making tall bushes, but as seen in our gardens a dwarf shrublet with many small, white, tubular flowers in short axillary clusters on the stems. For light shade and peaty soil. Summer flowering.

— fraseri. (Cyathodes fraseri.) A prostrate, heathlike shrub with small, pointed leaves closely set on the erect, 6 in. stems. The cream white flowers are solitary in the leaf axils and fragrant and are followed by small, juicy and edible berries. For similar conditions to the above and also summer flowering.

LEUZIA. *Compositae.* Named for Joseph Phillipe Francois Deleuze (1753-1835), a friend of the great botanist de Candolle.

— conifera. From S. Europe. Tufts of narrow leaves and scabious-like purple flowers on 9 in. stems in July and August. For full sun and any good soil.

LEWISIA. *Portulacaceae.* Named in honour of Captain Meriwether Lewis, leader of the Lewis and Clark expedition, the first coast-to-coast crossing of the American continent.

A very important family for the alpine garden and becoming increasingly and deservedly popular. They are spring and summer flowering, and although sometimes said to be lime-haters, experience has proved that they will tolerate a considerable degree of alkalinity. Should the soil be very chalky additional humus in the form of lime-free compost, leafsoil or fine-grade moss-peat will usually provide conditions in which they will grow well enough. Generally speaking they dislike being planted on the flat and should be set in rock crevices, or on a sharp slope if grown in the open. Most of them relish a drying-off period after they have flowered. Lewisias are greedy feeders and should be given a rich, but gritty and sharply drained soil mixture. They also benefit, it pot grown, from fairly frequent repotting into new compost, an operation which can be carried out soon after they have flowered, shaking the roots free of old soil and removing dead and decaying leaves. Those described below do not comprise an exhaustive list of the known species and hybrids, but is widely representative. For much of the information I am indebted to the excellent Monograph on the genus written by Roy Elliott, and published by the Alpine Garden Society. The genus is confined in its distribution to N. America.

— brachycalyx. A deciduous species with a thick caudex. Rosettes of fleshy, glaucous green leaves and central clusters of short stems each carrying one large, white flower in early spring. Forms occur with a faint pink flush on the petals.

— cantelovii. A rare evergreen species with a restricted distribution. From the characteristic thick caudex spring rosettes of broad, leathery, sharply toothed leaves. The 15 in. wiry stems, branching at the top, carry loose panicles of light pink flowers, the petals veined with deeper colour. Its main flowering period is spring but it blossoms spasmodically throughout the summer.

— columbiana. A widely distributed species with some geographical variants. From the thick and fleshy roots rise tufts of narrow, flat and fleshy leaves. On 12 in. stems appear loose panicles of flowers which may be bright or pale pink or almost white. It is normally spring flowering but may blossom spasmodically through the summer. The plant grown as *L.c.* 'Rosea' must be regarded as a garden cultivar. It has flowers of deeper, purer pink than the type.

— congdonii. A Californian species, evergreen, with rosettes of dark green, entire leaves, less fleshy than in other species, the erect, unbranching stems carry some leaves and panicles of rose-pink flowers in spring.

— cotyledon. Into the maw of this widely distributed and variable species must disappear the plants severally grown under such names as *L. heckneri, L. howellii, L. finchae, L. purdyi, L. mariana* and others. It is a locally variable species which would appear to have had a dominating hand in a great many of the strains and hybrids now grown. The thick, strong caudex produces a handsome rosette of long, broad, fleshy leaves with untoothed margins. The 12 in. stems carry many-flowered panicles of white, rose-tinted or salmon-pink flowers, the petals often striped with deeper colour. It is spring flowering. The two most strongly marked divergences are *L.c.* 'Heckneri' whose leaves are distinctly toothed with pink to deep rose flowers, striped with deeper coloured markings. *L.c.* 'Howellii' has narrower leaves often slightly incurved and distinctly waved and crinkled at the margins. The flowers are rich rose-pink in colour.

— disepala. Rare in nature and even rarer in cultivation. Deciduous and not unlike a smaller *L. rediviva.* From the short, thick caudex spring tufts of very narrow, fleshy leaves. The short stems each carry one large flower varying in colour from almost white to deep pink. It flowers in the spring and quickly becomes dormant thereafter.

— kelloggii. A rare deciduous species with the usual thick, fleshy caudex and a few spatulate, reddish-green basal leaves. The reddish stems are short and carry singly large, many-petalled flowers of creamy-white, sometimes pink-tinted. Spring flowering and quickly dormant.

— leana (sometimes written as *leeana.*) Widely distributed in California and Oregon. From the thick root rise many fleshy, grey-green leaves, circular in transverse section. Several wiry, 9 in. stems carry many-flowered panicles of flowers which may be magenta-pink or almost white, veined red. It flowers from June to August and seldom, if ever, hybridises.

— maguirei. Discovered in 1945 and apparently endemic to its area of South-Central Nevada. It is deciduous, with fleshy, narrow leaves and the short stems carry, in spring, from one to three white or soft-pink flowers. In nature it is said to grow in loose limestone soil. It closely resembles *L. rediviva.*

— **nevadensis.** A widely distributed deciduous species. The few narrow leaves which spring from the thick caudex have only a brief life. The stems, shorter than the leaves, carry one or two white, green-veined flowers in early summer.

— **oppositifolia.** Deciduous. The narrow, fleshy, shining green leaves are arranged in pairs on the underground stem, only the upper parts showing above ground. The 6 to 9 in. stems bear umbels of several pearl-white or pale pink flowers in early spring, centred by clusters of creamy stamens.

— **pygmaea.** Deciduous and widely distributed. Many narrow, fleshy leaves form at ground-level right above the thick root. The stems are very short and each one carries from one to three white or pink many-petalled flowers in spring and early summer. Like so many of the deciduous lewisias it dies down quite quickly after flowering.

— **rediviva.** Deciduous and widely distributed. A very popular and lovely species. The short, thick root, edible (when the bitter bark is removed!) emits clustered, narrow, glaucous fleshy leaves which wither as the plants blossom. The short stems carry large, solitary flowers with rose-coloured or white petals in spring. There is a form, *L.r.* 'Minor', of particular note and another, with richly coloured flowers named *L.r.* 'Winifred Herdman' is sometimes grown.

— **sierrae.** A rare and very tiny species, dubiously in cultivation. Deciduous, with a short, thick caudex and short, scanty, fleshy leaves. On very short stems, barely emerging from the soil are from one to three small, white, pink-veined flowers. Summer flowering.

— **triphylla.** A deciduous, widely distributed species which, instead of the usual lewisia caudex makes a deeply-buried rounded corm, from which rise a few narrow leaves and 4 in. stems carrying several very small white or pink flowers. An interesting but not showy species.

— **tweedyi.** The glory of the genus from the Wenatchee mountains of Washington and the Walathian mountains of Canada. From the stout root come clusters of large, fleshy leaves and stems of equal length carrying large, wide-petalled flowers of almost indescribable colour in a suffusion of yellow, pink and apricot. Selected forms carry deep rose-red flowers and an albino has been occasionally recorded. It is spring-flowering and very definitely relishes a drying-off period after flowering.

— **hybrids and strains.** Concerning these a detailed descriptive list would be tedious and non-productive. Notable strains, such as the 'Birch Hybrids', raised on this nursery, and Jack Drake's 'Sunset Strain' have achieved wide popularity and notoriety. Some hybrids and selections have been given names but the tale of the lewisias has yet to be told in full, and there are sure to be many more good garden lewisias produced in the future. Already it is clearly evident that new colour breaks are widening the kaleidoscope of colours found in the various strains. There are plants with rich yellow and orange flowers and some extremely good ones with large blossoms of solid white-ness. Two especially notable named hybrids are *L.X* 'George Henley', a short-stemmed, free flowering plant which produces its brick-red flowers in abundance from early spring until October, and *L.X* 'Rose Splendour' with massed large flowers of rich, clear rose-pink. The latter is fertile and is tending to become a strain as the seedlings show considerable variation in tint. *L.X* 'Trevosia', which first occurred many years ago in the garden of the late Dr. P. Giuseppi, is a splendid lewisia with long sprays of salmon-red flowers.

LIABUM. *Compositae.* Derivation obscure.

— **ovatum.** From the Andes of Peru. Rosettes of glossy, dark green leaves and stemless yellow dandelion-flowers, measuring more than 2 in. in diameter. The plant withers as soon as the flowers finish but within a short time regenerates with new green leaves. It is but doubt-fully in cultivation

LIBERTIA. *Iridaceae.* Named for Marie A. Libert (1782-1863), a Belgian botanist.

A small genus of plants found in Australasia and S. America, form-ing clumps of iris-like leaves. Most of them are too large for small rock gardens, although both *L. grandiflora* and *ixioides* from New Zealand are often grown where there is space for the bold clumps of foliage and tall stems carrying racemes of white flowers. More suitable is *L. pulchella*, which is found in Tasmania, Australia, New Zealand and on summits of a range of mountains in New Guinea. Tufts of short, narrow leaves emit 9 in. stems carrying loose clusters of snow-white flowers in summer. They all appreciate open, sunny positions in any good garden soil.

LILIASTRUM. See the genus PARADISIA.

LILIUM. *Liliaceae.* The Latin name, akin to the Greek *leiron*, the madonna-lily.

It might be thought that lilies have no place in an alpine plant Man-ual, but there are just a few which qualify for inclusion, although it irks me to exclude some of the lovely mountain lilies like *heldreichii, jankae, bulbiferum croceum* and *pyrenaicum.*

— **duchartrei.** (farreri.) The Marbled Martagon lily was discovered by Pere David in China about the year 1869 but does not appear to have appeared in cultivation until introduced by Wilson in 1903. It failed to survive and we owe its presence to the collections of Reginald Farrer about 1918. It was then regarded as a new species and named *L. farreri* but differs in no way from *L. duchartrei.* It is stoloniferous

231

and runs underground, forming new bulbs at the end of the runners. which emit stems 2 to 3 ft. tall carrying up to a dozen fragrant flowers with recurved segments. The flowers are white, spotted and streaked with purple. It likes a cool position in moist soil.

— **farreri.** See *L. duchartrei.*

— **macklinae.** Discovered by Kingdom Ward in Manipur, a small Indian state on the northern borders of Burma, in 1946. Very close to, and much resembling a Nomocharis, this has proved a valuable dwarf lily for the rock garden. The 18 in. stems carry many large drooping, bowl-shaped flowers. The colour is white, flushed with pink or soft purple.

— **pomponium.** This lovely lily from the Maritime Alps is a very old garden inhabitant, having been described by Clusius and Parkinson early in the 17th century. The stiff, rigidly erect purple stems are dressed with narrow, silver-edged leaves and terminate in loose heads of pendant turkscap blossoms of sealing-wax red. I would like to describe it as fragrant, but the odour it emits is, in fact, faintly unpleasant.

LIMONIUM. (Statice) *Plumbaginaceae.* From the Greek *leimon,* a meadow, an allusion to the habitat of some species in salt meadows. A large genus of annual and perennial herbs and sub-shrubs, a few of which are desirable plants for the rock garden and alpine house. They will grow in good ordinary soil and are sun-lovers.

— **asparagoides.** From Algeria and Morocco and a very rare and very lovely plant demanding alpine house treatment. It received an Award of Merit in 1938, is not in commerce and is occasionally seen in specialists collections. From a woody rootstock rise a few spoon-shaped basal leaves, which quickly wither, and elegant, arching stems thickly set with infinitely fine cladodes instead of leaves. Each long stem ends in a panicle of loose sprays bearing innumerable tiny bright purple flowers during the late summer. It is a plant of infinite grace and beauty.

— **bellidifolium.** A native of Europe, including Britain, where it inhabits dry areas in salt marshes. Not very exciting but worth growing for its tufts of blunt-ended, leathery leaves and short sprays of pinkish, papery florets.

— **caesium.** From Spain and, although usually described as being hardy, is probably best kept in an alpine house. This, too, is a rarity, but is occasionally available. It received a well deserved Award of Merit in 1951. From a woody rootstock rise rosettes of rounded basal leaves and branched stems subdivided into many small branchlets bearing pyramidal spikes of small pink flowers during July. The papery flowerlets retain their beauty for many weeks.

- cancellatum. From Greece and coastal rocks of the Adriatic. A neat tuft of dark green, leathery leaves and short, thin sprays of pinkish flowerlets. Hardy and easy, if slow growing.
- cosyrense. From rocky areas in Mediterranean regions. A 4 in. miniature with leathery, dark green, spoon-shaped leaves and short spikes of pink flowers in summer. Hardy.
- gougetianum. From the Balearic Isles and similar to the two preceding species but slightly taller.
- reticulatum. I am not certain if this is a valid name, but it covers a distinct, dwarf Limonium with tufts of leathery, blue-green spoon-shaped leaves and 9 in. sprays of lavender flowerlets. It appears to be quite hardy.
- sinuatum. From Greece and Portugal. Tangled mats of sinuous stems and dense spikes of white or soft violet flowers, or pinkish, changing to purple as the flowerlets dry off.

LINARIA. *Scrophulariaceae.* From the Greek *linon*, flax, because of the flax-like leaves.

A large genus, widely distributed throughout the Western Hemisphere, mostly in temperate regions. Included are some plants which have been regarded as CYMBALARIA and CHAENORRHINUM. Those described are all sun-loving and succeed in any good ordinary, well-drained soil and full sun.

- aequitriloba. See the genus CYMBALARIA.
- alpina. A short-lived perennial, native of the European Alps. Tiny tufts of whorled, blue-grey leaves on trailing stems and orange and violet toadflax flowers in racemes all summer. Sow seed frequently to ensure survival.
- anticaria. A rare and lovely saxatile species from Spain, possibly not in cultivation. Fairly tall, erect stems clothed with oval, glaucous leaves and racemes of white flowers so heavily pencilled with fine coloured lines as to appear mauve.
- cymbalaria. See CYMBALARIA *muralis*.
- faucicola. An annual or short-lived perennial from Spain. Similar in appearance to *L. alpina* but the violet-mauve flowers lack the colour contrast of that species.
- glacialis. Also from Spain and a lovely plant. Not unlike *L. alpina* but with extra glaucous leaves and flowers of luminous deep lavender entirely unmarked with yellow. Perennial but often short-lived.
- glareosa. (Chaenorrhinum glareosum.) A Spanish species which hovers uneasily between the two genera. Prostrate stems and a rather sprawling habit and few-flowered racemes of quite large violet and yellow flowers. Best in the alpine house.
- hepaticifolia. See the genus CYMBALARIA.

233

— maroccana. From N. Africa and of little more than annual duration, but well worth growing for the sake of its brilliantly coloured flowers. It is variable and hybridises readily and numerous forms or hybrids have been given cultivar names. The flower colour ranges from white, to yellow and blue and deep red. It is usually between 6 and 9 in. in height, and is summer flowering.

— nivea. A Spanish species not unlike our native *L. vulgaris*, but dwarfer and with white flowers touched gently with purple on the lip.

— origanifolia. A European species which also moves restlessly between Linaria and Chaenarrinum. *Flora Europaea* places it in the latter genus but I leave it under the better known name. Leafy, 6 in. stems carry loose racemes of flowers of rich purple with a paler throat.

— pallida. See the genus CYMBALARIA.

— peloponnesiaca. (sibthorpiana.) From Greece, and probably too large for most rock gardens. Racemes of yellow, spurred flowers on tall stems.

— platycalyx. A dwarf Spanish species with bright yellow flowers.

— repens. Widely distributed in Europe. A pretty weed but inclined to be spreading and invasive. Racemes of white or pale lilac flowers on quite tall stems.

— sibthorpiana. See *L. peloponnesiaca*.

— supina. A variable European species, possible best regarded as a group with geographical variations. Usually dwarf, fine-leaved and with yellow flowers. There is a fine Spanish version, *L.s.* 'Nevadensis' with reddish-purple and maroon coloured flowers.

— tristis. A European and N. African species with a host of variants. The best of these received an Award of Merit in 1968 under the name *L.t.* 'Toubkal', which has latterly been corrected to *L.t.* 'Lurida'. Best grown in the alpine house as a concession to its warmer, N. African habitat, it has the habit of *L. alpina* but its flowers, in loose racemes, are weirdly attractive in their colouration of yellowish-grey, veined on the lip and spur with red-purple and bearing two large velvety patches of dark purple on the mouth.

LINNAEA. *Caprifoliaceae.* Named for and by Carl Linnaeus, the eminent Swedish botanist.

A genus of only one species, to be grown in shade or a cool, north aspect in peaty, lime-free soil.

— borealis. The well loved twin-flower of our own northern woodlands and widely distributed in the colder parts of the northern hemisphere. Prostrate stems forming entangled mats and twin, bell-shaped flowers of delicate pink carried on 2 in. stems in spring and early summer. There is an American version, *L.b.* 'Americana' which has slightly larger flowers of deeper pink.

LINUM. *Linaceae.* From *linon*, the ancient Greek name used by Theophrastus.

A large family of sun-loving annual or perennial herbs and shrubs. Widely distributed in temperate regions but rarely found in the tropics. Those appropriate to this Manual like any good, well-drained soil and are highly valued and decorative plants.

— alpinum. See *L. perenne.*

— antolicum. See *L. hirsutum.*

— arboreum. From Crete. A foot-high, shrubby plant with woody stems and leaves of thick texture. Golden flowers in clusters during May and June.

— aretioides. I am doubtful if this exquisitely beautiful Linum still exists in cultivation. If not it is a 'must' for re-introduction from the few Turkish mountains on which it grows. It is essentially an alpine house plant. On tiny woody trunks sit rosettes of small grey leaves, crowded into tight hummocks. In the centre of each rosette sits a stemless clear yellow flower of size and substance. In nature it grows on limestone screes.

— austriacum. From the Austrian Alps. Erect, tall stems and heads of clear blue flowers. It is usually seen in gardens in the form of the subspecies *collinum* which is slightly dwarfer, with flowers of deeper blue.

— bungei. Dubiously in cultivation, but a nice flax from Turkey. Dwarf, and the blue flowers have a clear white eye.

— caespitosum. A desirable plant, resembling a condensed *L. arboreum.*

— campanulatum. From S. Europe and not unlike *L. arboreum*, forming foot-high bushlets smothered with corymbs of golden flowers.

— capitatum. Another woody species from S. Europe and Asia Minor. Dense heads of yellow flowers on 9 to 12 in. stems.

— chamissonis. From Chile, and not in cultivation as far as I know. It should be of shrubby habit, about 12 in. tall and bear heads of orange flowers.

— collinum. See *L. austriacum.*

— doerfleri. Of dubious specific rank. Like *L. caespitosum* it differs only from *L. arboreum* in being of more condensed habit.

— elegans. (iberidifolium.) Best in the alpine house. From Greece and Asia Minor. Woody stems and low tufts of glaucous, rather fleshy leaves and short-stemmed cymes of large rich yellow flowers. A very desirable species and rare in cultivation.

— flavum. From Central and Southern Europe, extending northward to Russia. Erect, rather woody stems to a foot or more and branched heads of yellow flowers.

— X 'Gemmell's Hybrid'. A cross between *L. elegans* and *L. campanulatum* raised in a Scottish nursery in the 1940's. Domes of fleshy, grey-green leaves and short stems each carrying several large, golden-yellow flowers. A most elegant and beautiful plant for sunny screes or sink and trough gardens, or for the alpine house.

— **goulimyi.** There appears to be some doubt as to the correctness of this name but, as described by Dr. Rechinger from plants seen in Greece it is close to *L. leucanthum*, but a larger plant with good white flowers.

— **hirsutum.** (L. anatolicum.) From S. Europe and Asia Minor. Tall stems carrying heads of large, blue, white-eyed flowers. Its form, or sub-species *anatolica* grows on gypsum formations in Turkey and is semi-shrubby with erect, foot-high stems and grey leaves. The large flowers are clear pink in colour.

— **iberidifolium.** See *L. elegans*.

— **kingii.** Almost certainly not in cultivation. *L. kingii var. sedoides* is described by Dwight Ripley as being a handsome plant with stiff stems, blue-grey, pointed leaves and good heads of clear yellow flowers. It comes from the State of Nevada in N. America.

— **leucanthum.** From Aegean regions. As shrubby as the yellow-flowered species but with fine white flowers.

— **maritimum.** From coastal regions in S. Europe. Like a dwarfer *L. flavum*.

— **monogynum.** From New Zealand. Semi-shrubby habit with erect stems, a foot or more in height and corymbs of pure white flowers. It asks for, and deserves, a sunny, protected position.

— **montanum.** This is really no more than a subspecies of *L. perenne*, which it closely resembles.

— **narbonense.** From Spain, Portugal and Mediterranean regions. A tall, graceful and handsome blue-flowered flax, seen at its best in several named clones, such as 'Six Hills Variety', 'Peto's Variety' and 'Gentianoides'. The slender, arching stems clothed in small leaves carry an abundance of large, slightly funnel-shaped rich blue flowers.

— **nervosum.** From S.E. Europe northward into Russia. Slender, tall, stems, hairy at the base and loose panicles of large blue flowers.

— **olympicum.** Very dubiously still in cultivation. From the Bithynian Olympus. Prostrate stems and softly hairy pointed leaves and sprays of campanulate lilac-pink flowers veined with deeper colour. For the alpine house if obtainable.

— **perenne.** A European species with 12 to 18 in. stems carrying heads of blue flowers. The subspecies *anglica* is a British native but it is seen at its best in the subspecies *alpinum*, which has larger flowers of clear blue.

— **salsoloides.** See *L. suffruticosum*.

— **sedoides.** An American species, well spoken of in the wild but said not to be over-handsome in gardens. It has yellow flowers and I doubt if it is cultivated in Britain at present.

— **suffruticosum.** From Spain, Italy and France. Most highly valued in the alpine garden in the form *salsoloides*, and the even more prostrate *s.* 'Prostratum', which forms flat carpets over which are carried large white flowers veined with lilac lines.

- syriacum. From Palestine, and would probably require winter protection. I know little of it except that it is dwarf and shrubby, and has yellow flowers.
- tenuifolium. From Central and Southern Europe. Slender, erect stems and flowers which vary from pink to almost white.
- X 'Waterperry'. This hybrid resulted from back-crossing *L.X* 'Gemmell's Hybrid' to *L. elegans.* It is even dwarfer than 'Gemmell's Hybrid' with pale green leaves. The small yellow flowers are abundantly produced on short stems and have wide, overlapping petals.

LIPPIA. *Verbenaceae.* Named for Augustin Lippi (1678-1701), Italian botanist.

A family of herbs and shrubs, natives of N. and S. America and Africa, only two of which really come within the compass of rock gardening.

- canescens. From S. America. A creeping plant ideal for growing in crevices between paving stones, or for flat ground cover through which small alpine bulbs can grow. The stems, which root as they run have small, fresh green leaves and are adorned by small heads of lilac or pink, yellow-throated flowers in summer.
- nodiflora. From the Southern United States. A looser, slightly taller plant than the preceding. The semi-trailing stems have rough, trifoliate leaves, deeply toothed above the middle. The globose heads of white or purple flowers are carried axillary peduncles in summer. It is not hardy in wet, cold soil.

LISSANTHE. *Epacridaceae.* From the Greek *lissos*, smooth, and *anthos*, flower. A reference to the glabrous limb of the corolla.

A small family of Australian and Tasmanian shrubs, closely related to CYATHODES and LEUCOPGON.

- strigosa. Australia and Tasmania. A prickly hump of tangled, woody branches up to a foot in height, smothered in spring with small, white, heather-like flowers, followed by white or pink berries. It will want a sheltered position in peaty soil and light shade.

LITHOPHRAGMA. *Saxifragaceae.* From the Greek *lithos*, a stone, and *phragma*, a fence.

A small family of N. American, mostly woodland plants, closely related to TELLIMA and at one time included in that genus. They like peaty soil and light shade. Only one species appears to be cultivated here.

— parviflora. The roots consist of grain-like bulblets or small tubers, from which rise slender, 6 in. stems with hairy, soft green leaves and heads of starry, soft pink or almost white flowers in spring and early summer.

LITHOSPERMUM. *Boraginaceae.* From the Greek *lithos*, a stone, and *sperma*, seed, in allusion to the hard, nut-like seeds.

A race of herbs and dwarf shrubs, natives of Mediterranean regions, but with a few outliers in Asia and N. America. *Flora Europaea* appears to have abandoned the genus Lithospermum with the exception of one species, *L. officinale*, which does not concern us here and those in which rock gardeners are likely to be interested are now in the genus LITHODORA. I retain the older, and better known generic name with the exception of a few which are more appropriately placed in the genus MOLTKIA. Botanically minded readers may note, and, if they prefer, use the new title. Whatever may have happened to the American species they are here retained as Lithospermums.

— canescens. This is one of the N. American, yellow-flowered species. It has never settled happily to cultivation in this country but we should persevere, as with the other American species. I have never persuaded it to do more than produce rather weak, straggling shoots, ending in clusters of orange-yellow flowers which promise more than they ultimately give. Lime-free gritty soil and a sunny position seem to be required for even a small measure of success.

— diffusum. (Lithodora diffusa.) From S.W. Europe. The type is seldom grown, but the named clones 'Heavenly Blue' and 'Grace Ward' have long been among the most popular rock garden plants. The former clone has more or less been superseded by 'Grace Ward', which is an even richer blue and possesses the vigour which the older plant is losing after countless generations of vegetative propagation. Lime-free soil and full sun produce the conditions necessary to attain the wide mats sheeted with caerulean flowers for long summer periods.

— X froebelii. See the genus MOLTKIA.

— fruticosum. (Lithodora fruticosa.) A 12 in. shrublet from S. Europe with narrow, revolute leaves white-haired beneath and terminal cymes of blue flowers in summer.

— graminifolium. See MOLTKIA *suffruticosa.*

— X intermedium. See MOLTKIA *X intermedia.*

— oleifolium. (Lithodora oleifolia.) From the Pyrenees. A wanderer, emitting from underground stems tufts of rounded, greyish hairy leaves and cymes of flowers, often pink in bud but opening light blue. Summer.

— petraeum. See MOLTKIA *petraea.*

LITHOSPERMUM — *continued*

- prostratum. See *L. diffusum.*
- purpureocaeruleum. This native species is of no particular garden merit and is now referred to the genus BUGLOSSOIDES.
- rosmarinifolium. (Lithodora rosmarinifolia.) From Italy, and spectacular on the Isle of Capri, but not quite hardy. Dwarf bushes of dark green, evergreen leaves and cymes of rich blue flowers in summer. For a hot, dry sunny crevice or the alpine house.
- zahnii. (Lithodora zahnii.) From hot rocks in Greece. Tidy, evergreen dwarf bushes, leaves coriaceous and greyish, and few-flowered cymes of blue or whitish flowers.

LOASA. *Loasaceae.* Origin obscure.

A race of mostly annual and biennial plants from S. America. Several species have been cultivated from time to time, but they are scarcely rock garden plants, The fact that their leaves are densely covered with stinging hairs does not add to their popularity although their flowers, axillary or in racemes and white, yellow or red in colour do not lack beauty. Grow them in a cold greenhouse, or in very warm and sheltered positions outside, and handle them with care — and gloves!

LOBELIA. *Campanulaceae.* Named for Mathias de l'Obel (1538-1616), Flemish botanist and physician to James 1.

A large genus, widely distributed and ranging from the tiny L. linnaeoides, described below, to the giant lobelias of S. Africa.

- linnaeoides. (Pratia linnaeoides.) From New Zealand. Absolutely prostrate. The frail stems creep at ground level and carry tiny, rounded, toothed dark green leaves and small white and purple flowers. Cool, peaty and gritty soil.
- minitula. From S. Africa and almost certainly not in cultivation. As small as *L. linnaeoides* and with stemless blue and white flowers.
- syphilitica. From N. America. The type is too tall for the rock garden but *L.s.* 'Nana' is occasionally grown there. It makes low bushes of light green leaves and has short racemes of pale blue flowers in late summer. It likes moistish soil and is not very long-lived.

LOISELEURIA. *Ericaceae.* In honour of the lengthily named Jean Louis Auguste Loiseleur-Deslongchamps (1774-1849), a botanist-physician.

- procumbens. (Azalea procumbens.) The only species in its genus. From alpine and arctic regions of N. America, Asia and Europe, including Britain. Essentially for lime-free soil. Prostrate mats and carpets of tangled woody stems clothed in tiny, hard, oval leaves and terminal heads of small pink flowers. It is almost invariably shy-flowering in gardens, although not difficult to grow in the right conditions.

LOTUS. *Leguminosae.* The classical Greek name *lotos*, which has been applied to a diversity of plants.

A fairly large genus of annual and perennial herbs and sub-shrubs widely distributed in temperate regions, only a few of which are of interest here. Sun-loving and summer flowering.

— **alpinus.** A form of *L. corniculatus*, which see.

— **becquetii.** From Kenya and resembles *L. corniculatus* in habit but has soft pink flowers. Almost certainly not in cultivation.

— **bertholetii.** From Teneriffe and only possible in an alpine house. Woody, straggling stems and intensely silvery-hairy leaves. Clusters of scarlet flowers.

— **corniculatus.** Our native Bird's-foot Trefoil, of which we cultivate the double-flowering form. Prostrate and spreading with heads of bright yellow flowers. *L.c.* 'Alpinus' is a Pyrenaean version with flowers which are tinted with red.

— **creticus.** From S. Europe. Procumbent and often densely felted with silver hairs but not invariably so. Clusters of yellow flowers.

— **hirsutus.** From the Pyrenees. Not an exciting plant but the purple and white flowers compensate for a somewhat weedy habit.

LUETKEA. (Spiraea.) *Rosaceae.* In honour of Feodor Lutke (1797-1882), a Russian admiral.

A genus of but one species, allied to **SPIRAEA**, from Western N. America. Prefers lime-free soil and light shade.

— **pectinata (Spiraea pectinata.)** Evergreen, with creeping stems and tufts of deeply cut leaves. It resembles a mossy saxifraga in growth and carries in summer short racemes of cream-white flowers. A good ground-coverer.

LUINA. *Compositae.* Origin unknown.

— **hypoleuca.** A dwarf, grey-leaved composite from the Rocky Mountains. It would be a good dwarf shrub for a hot, dry bank. The leaves are dark green above but felted beneath with snowy hairs. The creamy flowers are carried in terminal clusters.

LUPINUS. *Leguminosae.* The classical name, said to have derived from the Latin *lupus*, a wolf, because of a superstition that these plants destroyed the fertility of the soil. In fact, plants of this genus are valued since, like other leguminous plants, they are able to fix nitrogen, thus increasing the soil fertility.

Not many lupins are suited to the rock garden. I describe a few, but omit mention of several American species which, although they sound enticing and desirable, are certainly not in cultivation.

- lyallii. From N. America and a gem. It is probably more correctly named *L. lepidus var. lobbii*, but I retain the name by which it is best known. It is a good perennial, growing to a height of about 4 in. The silver filigree foliage makes neat rosettes and on the short stems are carried clusters of bright blue flowers, with hints of white and purple. It should be given alpine house treatment in gritty, lime-free soil rich in humus. There is a form, *L. l. var. danaus*, which is said to be even dwarfer and more silvery.
- ornatus. This comes from the mountains of California. It grows to a height of 9 in. or so, has silver leaves and short spires of intensely blue flowers. It is a more 'growable' plant than the preceding and similarly likes gritty, humus-rich, lime-free soil. It will succeed in the open.
- pilosus var. cosentinii. Although it is of no more than annual or biennial duration, this little Corsican is desirable, if obtainable. Rosettes of silver leaves close to the ground form a lovely base for the short spikes of bright blue flowers.

LUZULA. *Juncaceae.* From the Italian *lucciola*, a glow-worm. The application is dubious.

I hesitated before including this genus, but decided that three at least, of the woodrushes deserved mention, even if they are rather large for most rock gardens. They like semi-wild conditions in any good soil and will take some moisture. Summer flowering. All mentioned are European.

- lutea. Tufts of broad basal leaves and tall, slender stems carrying pale yellow flowers in clusters on a branching inflorescence.
- maxima. (L. sylvatica.) Bold clumps of broad, grassy leaves and erect stems carrying clusters of chestnut-brown flowerlets.
- nivea. One of the best. Loose tufts of wide, grassy leaves and elegant tall stems, with tufts of grey hairs in the leaf axils and clusters of snow-white flowers.
- sylvatica. See *L. maxima.*

LUZURIAGA. *Liliaceae.* Named in honour of Don Ignatio M.R. de Luzuriaga, a Spanish botanist.

A small genus of low-growing sub-shrubs, suitable for positions in shade and making good groundcover as they spread by underground stems.

- **marginata.** Dubiously in cultivation. From New Zealand and the extreme south of S. America. Woody, 6 in. stems in dense mats, pale green and with rolled margins. Small, solitary, heliotrope-scented flowers in the leaf axils, followed by white berries.
- **radicans.** Similar, usually about 4 in. high with quite large white, star-shaped flowers.

LYCHNIS. *Caryophyllaceae.* From the Greek *lychnos*, a lamp possibly referring to the ancient use of the leaves of a woolly species as wicks.

A genus which is much confused with other genera, such as MELANDRIUM, PETROCOPTIS, VISCARIA and AGROSTEMMA. See in particular MELANDRIUM and PETROCOPTIS. Easily grown, spring and summer flowering, sun-loving plants.

- **alpina.** (Viscaria alpina.) European, including, rarely, Britain. Neat, leafy tufts and short stems carrying heads of pale purple, rarely white, flowers. A selected clone with rich pink flowers is cultivated as *L.a.* 'Rosea'.
- **flos-jovis.** Central Europe and eastward. Tufts of leaves covered in grey hairs and 12 in. stems bearing heads of rather shrill, carmine-pink flowers. A clone named 'Hort's Variety' displays flowers of clearer pink.
- **lagascae.** See PETROCOPTIS glaucifolia.
- **pyrenaica.** See PETROCOPTIS pyrenaica.
- **viscaria.** (Viscaria viscosa.) The species is widely distributed in Europe, but has little garden value. The plant in commerce as *L.v.* 'Splendens Plena' is a boldly handsome subject, perhaps a little tall for small rock gardens, but a splendid 'front-row-of-the-border' plant. On 15 to 18 in. stems it bears close heads of intense crimson-magenta double flowers.

LYCOPODIUM. *Lycopodiaceae.* From the Greek *lykos*, a wolf, and *podion*, a foot, from a fancied resemblance to a wolf's foot.

- **alpinum.** The alpine Clubmoss is widely distributed throughout northern temperate and arctic zones, including Britain. Although not very easy to grow it can be tried in a cool, moist position. Prostrate stems and tufts of bright green forked, flat leaves.

LYCOPSIS. *Boraginaceae.* From the Greek *lykos*, a wolf, and *ops*, face. The flowers were supposed to resemble in shape the face of a wolf.

- arvensis. A Borage from Kashmir, with slender, erect stems and blue or white flowers in one-sided cymes in spring.

LYSIMACHIA. *Primulaceae.* From the Greek *lysimachos*, meaning to end strife, thus the English name of loosestrife.
A large family of plants from temperate and sub-tropical parts of the world. Few are suitable for the rock garden.

- anagalloides. See *L. serpyllifolia.*
- atropurpurea. (L. leschenaultii.) From the Balkans. Short, dense spikes of glowing purple-red flowers in August on 9 to 12 in. stems. Dubiously still in cultivation.
- henryi. A Chinese species with trailing stems becoming erect at the tips. Stems and leaves softly hairy and clustered yellow flowers at the branch ends. Confused in gardens with *L. pseudo-henryi*, which is very similar, but with more hairy stems and leaves.
- japonica. A Japanese species represented in gardens by the form *L.j.* 'Minuta' (sometimes labelled 'Minutissima'.) which makes a quite flat carpet of creeping stems beset with tiny green leaves and studded with innumerable small, starry, bright yellow flowers. It likes shade or a moist position and is not long-lived as a rule, benefitting from occasional dividing and replanting.
- leschenaultii. See *L. atropurpurea.*
- nummularia. This is our native Creeping Jenny, and not often a garden plant, but *L.n.* 'Aurea', its form with soft yellow leaves makes a pleasant carpet in cool places and is appreciated as an easy ground-coverer with no vices.
- pseudo-henryi. See *L. henryi.*
- serpyllifolia. (L. anagalloides.) From Eastern Europe. From a woody root rise erect, 6 in. stems clothed in small ovate leaves. In spring the whole plant is spangled with flowers like those of a bright yellow pimpernel.

LYSIONOTUS. *Gesneriaceae.* From the Greek *lysis*, loosening, and *notos*, the back, referring to its habit of opening the capsule away from the back suture.

- pauciflorus. From Japan and China. A rare sub-shrub with erect, woody stems to about 12 in. and long, rigid, narrow, dark green leaves, toothed at the margins and white beneath. From the leaf axils spring pendant tubular flowers some 2 in. long, lilac in colour with veinings of deeper colour. It is for the alpine house and likes to be planted over a piece of punky rotten wood and have a soil rich in humus. Summer flowering.

243

MAIANTHEMUM. *Liliaceae.* From the Greek *maios*, May, and *anthemon*, blossom.

A small genus of creeping plants for cool, shady positions. Closely related to, and sometimes included in the genera CONVALLARIA and SMILACINA.

— bifolium. Twin, ovate-cordate leaves and 3 to 4 in. stems carrying dainty racemes of small, fluffy white flowers. There are two N. American variants which are similar, but rather stronger in growth. The type inhabits most northern temperate regions, including Britain.

MALVASTRUM. *Malvaceae.* From the Latin *malva* and *aster*, indicating a resemblance to Malva, or mallow.

A genus, largely American, which only concerns us here in the case of one species.

— coccineum. Trailing stems and ash-grey leaves and short terminal racemes of scarlet flowers. For a warm, dry position, summer flowering.

MARGYRICARPUS. *Rosaceae.* From the Greek *margarites*, a pearl and *karpos*, a fruit.

— setosus. From the Chilean Andes. A valuable dwarf shrub, up to a foot in height, evergreen, with small, dark green and finely cut leaves. The flowers are inconspicuous but are followed by innumerable pure white fleshy berries. Any good soil and an open position.

MARRUBIUM. *Labiatae.* The classical Latin name.

A small genus of hoary-leaved plants, mostly from Central and Southern Europe and Mediterranean regions. They relish hot, dry positions with the maximum possible sunlight in any ordinary, well-drained soil. Few will attract the rock gardener, but *M. candidissimum, M. sericeum* and *M. velutinum* are worth consideration for the sake of the foliage, clothed with a dense pelt of fine white hairs. Their flowers are of no consequence. In habit they are dwarf, usually about 12 to 15 inches in height.

MATTHIOLA. *Cruciferae.* Named for Pierandrea Matteuci, 19th century Italian physicist.

A genus of annual and perennial herbs and sub-shrubs, containing *M. incana*, from which the garden Stocks have been derived. Natives of Western and Southern Europe and W. Asia, and all sun-lovers. Also related to CHEIRANTHUS, in which genus some species of Matthiola have sometimes been placed.

— fruticulosa. From S. Europe. Tufts of narrow grey leaves and six-inch scapes of purple flowers in spring and summer. It is variable, and the plants sometimes encountered as *M. perennis, M. valesiaca* and *M. varia* all belong here as subspecies, and are of similar appearance.

— scapifera. Would be a most desirable species, if it were obtainable. It comes from the High Atlas in N. Africa and makes cushions of crinkled grey leaves, hugging the rocks on which it grows, studded with stemless, fragrant, stock-like flowers. It would almost certainly require alpine-house treatment.

MAZUS. *Scrophulariaceae.* From the Greek *mazos*, a teat, because of the tubercles closing the mouth of the corolla.

Mostly prostrate herbs, related to MIMULUS and natives of Asia, New Zealand and Australia. Any good, well drained soil.

— pumilio. From New Zealand. Makes slowly spreading mats of dark green leaves, studded in spring and early summer with almost stemless flowers of blue and white.

— radicans. (Mimulus radicans.) New Zealand, usually in moist mountain meadows. Prostrate pads of bronzed leaves and pure white flowers marked with a striking blotch of violet in the centre. Early summer flowering.

— reptans. (M. rugosus.) Spreading 2 in. tufts of toothed green leaves and purple-blue flowers blotched with white and yellow in spring and summer. From the Himalaya.

— rugosus. See *M. reptans.*

— stolonifera. From Japan, and dubiously in cultivation. Low mats of green foliage with winged petioles and, probably, blue-purple flowers.

— surculosus. From the Himalaya and also doubtfully in cultivation. Spreads by rooting runners into carpets. Leaves coarsely toothed and short-stemmed purple flowers.

MECONOPSIS. *Papaveraceae.* From the Greek *mekon*, a poppy and *opsis*, like.

It is with some hesitation that I include a fairly comprehensive list of Meconopsis, so many of which are really too tall for rock gardens. On the other hand they are plants for which rock gardeners have a great affection and they can be grown in a rock garden environment and they are certainly 'alpine' in their natural environment, the majority of them being natives of the mountain regions of India, China and Burma.

- aculeata. From the Himalaya and perhaps not one of the most desirable species, although its blue flowers carried several to each 2 ft. stem, are not unattractive. It is monocarpic, in common with several other species.
- baileyi. See *M. betonicifolia* in addenda.
- bella. From the Himalaya, and the history of this beautiful dwarf species in cultivation is melancholy, for it has never really accepted captivity and is now very dubiously in cultivation at all. A perennial, it forms a deep tap-root and prefers a cool, north aspect. From the rosettes of leaves rise 4 to 6 in. stems each carrying one flower. The colour of the forms hitherto grown was an exquisite pale blue, but it can vary to pink or purple.
- cambrica. This, of course, is the Welsh poppy, native to Europe, including Britain and so well known that it scarcely needs a description from me. It can become a nuisance as it seeds with great profusion, but in semi-wild places it is very decorative. It is a deeply rooting perennial and from its tufts of deeply lobed leaves emits 15 in. stems carrying yellow flowers. There is a form with deeper orange flowers and another with double flowers, either yellow or orange.
- chelidonifolia. From Szechuan. A perennial, but sometimes short-lived species. Rosettes of deeply cut leaves and tall stems carrying cup-shaped yellow flowers.
- delavayi. From Yunnan, and only dubiously in cultivation at present. Rosettes of hairy, narrow to broad leaves, glaucous below and 9 to 12 in. stems carrying several large deep purple flowers.
- dhwojii. A monocarpic species from Nepal. Rosettes of lobed and bristly leaves and stems up to 18 in. or a little more carrying a branched inflorescence of yellow flowers.
- grandis. From Nepal, Tibet and Sikkim, and one of the most magnificent species. A sound perennial, it makes rosettes of narrow, toothed leaves with reddish hairs. The tall stems carry many purple buds which expand into enormous flowers of brilliant blue. Its finest manifestation is seen in the form introduced by the late G. Sherriff and usually marked 'G.S. 600'.
- horridula. Himalayan. Monocarpic. Leaves and stems rough and bristly with coarse hairs. The 2 to 3 ft. stems carry singly in the leaf axils flowers which may be blue, purple-blue or, rarely, white.
- integrifolia. Himalayan. Monocarpic. Handsome rosettes of wide leaves densely covered with golden hairs. The flower stem varies in

height from one to three feet and the very large flowers are carried in the leaf axils. The colour is normally yellow, but may be white. A very handsome and desirable species.

— latifolia. From Kashmir and monocarpic. Rosettes of coarsely toothed leaves felted with straw-coloured hairs. Tall, leafy stems and a long raceme of pale blue flowers carried singly on long petioles. A very desirable plant.

— napaulensis. (M. wallichii.) From the Himalaya. A variable and very handsome species. Fine rosettes of lobed, sometimes pinnatifid leaves densely hairy with reddish bristles. Tall candelabra-like, leafy stems carry multitudes of cup-shaped flowers which may be red, purple, blue or, occasionally, white. As with other monocarpic species the winter-persistent rosettes of foliage are extremely handsome.

— paniculata. Another tall, monocarpic species from the Himalaya, at times confused with *M. napaulensis*, but distinct from that species. Very large and handsome winter rosettes of softly hairy leaves and tall stems displaying a long inflorescence of cup-shaped yellow flowers.

— punicea. From the Himalaya. A species which has created great excitement but which clings only tenuously to cultivation. It is usually monocarpic but occasionally polycarpic. Loose rosettes of densely hairy leaves and pendant flowers which are borne singly on simple scapes and are of an intense poppy-red colour.

— quintuplinervia. From Tibet and W. China. Loose tufts of narrow, hairy leaves and lavender-blue flowers, pendant and carried singly on foot-high stems. It is a sound perennial and far from difficult.

— regia. From Nepal. Monocarpic. Very handsome winter rosette of narrow leaves, felted with silver or golden hairs. Tall, branching stems carry many large rich yellow flowers.

— simplicifolia. Nepal and Tibet. Monocarpic or polycarpic. Rather similar in some ways to *M. grandis*, but sufficiently distinct. Rosettes of irregularly-lobed leaves, mildly bristly and slightly nodding deep or light-blue flowers carried on long, simple scapes.

— superba. From Tibet and Bhutan. Monocarpic. Fine rosettes of leaves felted with silky white hairs. Branching 3 ft. stems carry many large white flowers.

— villosa. Already described on page 113 as CATHCARTIA *villosa*. It has always hovered uneasily between the two genera, and is variously listed under either name.

— wallichii. See *M. napaulensis*.

MEEHANIA. *Labiatae*. Probably named for Thomas Meehan (1826-1901), nurseryman and horticultural writer, London born but resident in Philadelphia.

— urticifolia. A fairly recent introduction from Japanese woodlands. A fine ground-cover for cool places in moist soil. Trailing, leafy stems and large, tubular rich purple flowers in summer.

MEGAPTERUM. See the genus OENOTHERA.

MELANDRIUM. See the genus SILENE.

MELITTIS. *Labiatae.* From the Greek *melissa*, a honeybee.
- melissophyllum. The Bastard, or Honey Balm, a native of Europe, including Britain. Runs modestly underground and emits foot-high stems dressed with hairy, aromatic leaves and many axillary clusters of pink and white, hooded flowers in summer. Good ground cover for light shade.

MENTHA. *Labiatae.* The Latin name of the genus.

Aromatic herbs, very popular in gardens and kitchens, very few of which fall within the scope of this Manual.
- pulegium. The common Pennyroyal and widely distributed in Asia, N. Africa and Europe, including Britain. Prostrate, freely branching and with whorls of pale purple flowers in summer and autumn.
- requienii. The Corsican mint. Absolutely prostrate films of soft green, intensely peppermint-scented tiny leaves, studded in spring and summer with small, stemless lavender flowers. Likes a cool position.

MERIOLIX. See the genus OENOTHERA.

MERTENSIA. *Boraginaceae.* Named for Francis Karl Mertens (1764-1831), Professor of Botany at Bremen.

A genus of perennial herbs, natives in the most part of E. Europe, Asia and N. America. Decorative, spring and summer flowering plants, mostly with a preference for positions where it is not unduly hot and dry.
- alpina. N. America. Dwarf, with short panicles of tubular blue flowers.
- bakeri. N. America. Similar to the above with perhaps slightly deeper blue flowers.
- coriacea. From N. America and it seems probable that to be strictly accurate this plant should be regarded as a form of *M. viridis*, but I adhere to the name by which we have come to know it. Low tufts of broad, rather leathery leaves, fringed with fine hairs and short-stemmed heads of bell-shaped clear blue flowers.
- echioides. From N. America. Nine in. stems carrying many-flowered racemes of deep blue flowers. The plant sometimes grown as *M.e.* 'Elongata' is correctly *M. elongata* (see below).

- elongata. From Kashmir. 6 in. stems, softly hairy and short racemes of bright blue flowers.
- maritima. N. Europe, including Britain. An inhabitant of sea-sands, not very easy to grow, but try it in almost pure sand. Tufts of glaucous-blue, rounded leaves and prostrate stems carrying terminal clusters of clear, soft blue flowers opening from pink buds.
- moltkioides. From Kashmir. Spreading tufts and brilliant blue flowers in clusters on short, leafy stems.
- oblongifolia. N. America. Fleshy, deep green leaves and clusters of blue flowers on 9 in. stems. It seems to prefer a fairly moist place.
- primuloides. From the Himalaya. Tufts of hairy stems and leaves and dense racemes of indigo-blue flowers on short stems.
- pterocarpa yezoensis. From Japan. This appears to be the correct name of the plant we have grown as *M. rivularis* 'Japonica'. It is a handsome plant with short, erect stems dressed with broad, pointed, grey-green leaves, softly hairy on the upper surface. Loose cymes of clear blue tubular flowers are carried terminally.
- rivularis. See *M. pterocarpa.*
- virginica. N. America. Tall, leafy stems ending in clusters of pendant, rather tubular flowers of clear blue. It can attain 18 in. There is a desirable form with pure white flowers.

In addition to the species briefly described above there are several other very desirable Mertensias, few of which appear to be in cultivation at present, mostly American. Watch out for, and obtain if possible, any of the following. *bakeri, brachycalyx, cusickii, horneri, linearis, lanceolata, longiflora, marginata, nutans, pulchella, tibetica, tweedyi* and *viridis.*

MEUM. *Umbelliferae.* Old Greek name, given by Dioscorides to this aromatic herb.

- athamanticum. Europe, including Britain, 12 in. tufts of finely dissected grey-green aromatic leaves. Compound umbels of many small, white to purple rayed flowers.

MIBORA. *Graminiae.*

- minima. (M. verna.) Native of Europe, including Britain. A tiny, neat emerald green grass which grows in the neatest of tufts. It is annual but seeds mildly, never becoming a pest and is invaluable for associating with alpine plants which like company, such as *Gentiana verna.* It seldom exceeds an inch in height.
- verna. See *M. minima.*

MICROMERIA. *Labiatae.* From the Greek *mikros*, small, and *meris*, a part. The flowers of these dwarf aromatic herbs are very small.

Sun-loving dwarf woody plants, mostly from Mediterranean regions. Most of them have to be protected from cats, which are irresistably attracted to them. Summer flowering.

- **amana.** A rare species from Turkish Kurdistan, probably not in cultivation and one for which I lack description, but it is praised by Dr. Peter Davis, an authority on the Turkish Flora.
- **barceloi.** From the Balearic Isles and probably synonymous with the N. African *M. inodora*, which see.
- **chamissonis.** (M. douglasii.) From N. America. Prostrate stems and highly aromatic leaves (which add piquance to any short drink based on gin!) and axillary purple flowers, singly or in clusters.
- **corsica.** Endemic to Corsica and Sardinia. Tiny thorny huddles of grey stems and leaves, pungently aromatic and small, rosy-lavender flowers.
- **croatica.** Similar in appearance to the above, but the flowers are carried in a contracted panicle.
- **douglasii.** See *M. chamissonis.*
- **flacca.** Like *M. amana*, this species comes from Turkish Kurdistan, is probably not in cultivation, but ought to be.
- **graeca.** Mediterranean. The variety *consentina*, from the Italian Alps is highly praised as making tufts of rich pink, but I have not seen it.
- **inodora.** Rigid erect branches forming a low bush and unusually large pink flowers. Said to be synonymous with *M. barceloi.*
- **microphylla.** Mediterranean. Nine in. bushes and dark green aromatic foliage, spattered with pink flowers.
- **piperella.** Stiff, 3 in. bushlets, rather thorny. Tiny grey leaves — highly scented, and reddish-purple flowers.
- **pygmaea.** See SATUREJA *montana.*
- **rupestris.** (Satureja rupestris.) From S. Europe. Fifteen in. stems ascend from a woody base and cymes of white or purple flowers.
- **varia.** (Thymus ericifolius.) Neat mounds of thyme-like and thyme-scented yellow-green leaves and lavender flowers. A good plant for crevices in paving.

MILIUM. *Gramineae.*

- **effusum.** This is a native grass, found in damp and shady woodlands, but the plant grown in gardens, often as 'Bowles' Golden Grass, is *M. effusum* 'Aureum' and this is a handsome grass with gracefully arching stems to a height of 18 in. or a little more and the whole plant is golden from bottom to top, leaves and flower heads alike.

MILLIGANIA. *Liliaceae.* A small genus, all natives of Tasmania. The two species described will thrive in warm, light soil and sheltered places.

- densiflora. From a short, thick rhizome rise tufts of long, pointed leaves, sparsely white-haired. The fairly tall, branching stems carry short, dense racemes of white, or occasionally lavender coloured flowers in midsummer.
- longifolia. Tufts of green, narrow leaves and ascending, branching stems bearing branched panicles of many small white flowers in summer.

MIMULUS. *Scrophulariaceae.* The Latin diminutive of· *mimus*, a mimic. The flower resembles the face of a monkey.

A large family of annual and perennial herbs and a few shrubs, widely distributed. Those appropriate to rock gardens are listed below, and will mostly prefer moist, cool conditions. Spring and summer flowering.

- alpinus. This is but one of the many forms of *M. luteus.* It is neat and dwarf, with bright yellow flowers.
- bigelovii. From California and Colorado. Six in. stems clothed in sticky leaves and crimson flowers, marked in the throat with purple.
- X burnetii. This is a hybrid between *M. cupreus* and *M. luteus.* It has the habit of the latter and copper-yellow flowers with yellow throats and the mouth of the flower spotted with deeper colour.
- cupreus. Close to, and possibly should be included under *M. luteus*, but of slightly more tufted habit. It has given rise to many named clones of brilliant colour, of which the following are good examples — 'Bees' Dazzler', 'Brilliant', 'Fireflame', 'Leopard', 'Red Emperor', and 'Whitecroft Scarlet'.
- langsdorffii. Yet another of the many variants of *M. luteus*, with bright yellow flowers.
- lewisii. N. American and Canada. Rather tall for the rock garden, but a pretty plant carrying many deep pink flowers on 18 in. stems. I like it best in its rare albino form, which is much dwarfer and displays snow-white flowers.
- primuloides. From N. America. A choice miniature making flat mats of threadlike stems clothed with rosettes of tiny, hairy leaves. The small but brilliantly yellow flowers are carried singly on short, fine stems. It must have a cool, moist place in gritty soil and be divided and replanted frequently.
- radicans. See MAZUS *radicans.*
- rupicola. A fabulous beauty, but it grows in Death Valley and is sure to be difficult, even if obtainable. It is a saxatile plant forming low tufts of widish, pointed, hairy leaves. The flower is rose-pink, with a yellow centre and there are vivid maroon blotches at the base of each petal.

251

MINUARTIA. *Caryophyllaceae.* Named in honour of Juan Minuart (1693-1768), of Barcelona.

A genus which has been much confused with ARENARIA and ALSINE. The latter name should disappear altogether, according to the *Flora Europaea.* All those mentioned below require similar conditions to those which would be given to Arenarias. Some which might be expected to appear below will be found under Arenaria in cases where I have adhered to a well-known, even if inaccurate, name.

- aretioides. Europe. Dense hummocks, white flowers.
- biflora. Described under ARENARIA.
- gerardii. See *M. verna.*
- graminifolia. Described under ARENARIA.
- imbricata. Supposedly European but I find no authority for the name. It forms pleasing grey-green cushions of crowded rosettes and the short-stemmed, quite large white flowers are attractive. Spring and summer flowering.
- juniperina. A cliff-dweller from Greece. Tufts of stiff, spiky leaves and few-flowered cymes of white flowers. Summer.
- laricifolia. Described under ARENARIA.
- parnassica. See *M. stellata.*
- pulvinaris. A rarity from Turkey, making tidy domes of congested pale green leaves studded sparsely with white flowers in spring.
- saxifraga. A great rarity from the Bulgarian mountains, dubiously now in cultivation. Dense, caespitose pads of congested rosettes of small, stiff leaves and white flowers in compact cymes on short stems in spring and summer.
- sedoides. From the European Alps. Like a tuft of *Silene acaulis* but the flowers are dingily greenish-yellow. Nice as a cushion plant if you ignore the blossoms.
- setacea. Another pleasant cushion-forming plant from the European Alps with quite good white flowers in small cymes on short stems in summer.
- stellata. (M. parnassica.) Eastern Europe. Flat, hard pads of green leaves in congested huddles and almost stemless white flowers in spring.
- verna. This has been *Arenaria verna* and *Alsine verna* but nestles correctly in this genus. Widely distributed in Europe, including Britain, as a rarity. The emerald, tiny narrow leaves form the neatest of tidily rounded domes, spangled in spring with white flowers on inch-high threadlike stems. A splendid sink or trough plant, or for the scree. The sub-species *gerardii* is similar, but much looser in growth.

MITCHELLA. *Rubiaceae.* Named for Dr. John Mitchell (1711-1768), physician of Virginia and a correspondent of Linnaeus.

- repens. From N. America and needs lime-free, peaty soil and a cool position. It is a neat evergreen with trailing, woody stems beset with pairs of glossy leaves. Small white flowers in pairs, followed by red berries.

— **undulata.** From Japan and similar to the above but a little larger in all its parts and requiring similar conditions.

MITELLA. *Saxifragaceae.* A diminutive of the Greek *mitra*, a cap. An allusion to the shape of the seed pod.

A small family, natives of N. America and N.E. Asia. They like cool, semi-shaded positions and are spring flowering, but valued more for their foliage than for floral beauty.

— **breweri.** From N. America and Canada. Dark green, lobed and kidney-shaped leaves in neat clumps and slender, leafless stems carrying many green flowers with fringed edges to the petals. An exception to my comments in the introduction above; these flowers have charm.

— **diphylla.** Lobed green leaves and slender, 9 in. stems carrying green-white flowers. From N. America and Canada.

— **nuda.** Also an American. Characteristic rounded or kidney-shaped leaves and thin spires of greenish flowers.

— **pentandra.** From Alaska to California. Wide, bluntly-lobed leaves and 12 in. leafless scapes carrying loose racemes of greenish flowers.

MOEHRINGIA. *Caryophyllaceae.* Named in honour of Paul Heinrich Gerard Moehring (1710-1792), German physician and author of *Hortus Proprius.*

A genus of mostly European plants, closely allied to ARENARIA and MINUARTIA. They mostly have more botanical interest than garden value. There is so much similarity between the species, which are mat-forming, with white flowers, that individual descriptions are pointless. Any of the following would be worth growing. *M. bavarica, M. ciliata, M. dasyphylla,* and its variety *sedoides, M. glaucovirens, M. muscosa* and *M. pendula.* They are all European.

MOLINIA. *Gramineae.* Named in honour of Juan Ignacio Molina (1740-1829), writer on the natural history of Chile.

A genus of only two species, one Japanese, the other widely distributed over Europe, Asia and Asia Minor.

— **caerulea.** Europe, including Britain. A tufted grass with slender leaves. The type has no particular garden value but the form 'Variegata' adorns its rather rigid leaves with white stripes and is attractive, but slightly invasive.

MOLTKIA. *Boraginaceae.* Named for Count Joachim Gadske Moltke (1746-1818), Danish statesman.

A genus, mostly European but some in Asia. Closely related to, and often confused with, LITHOSPERMUM. Sun lovers and summer flowering.

— **caerulea.** From Asia Minor. A foot-high bush with woody stems and narrow, pointed, rather silky leaves and short cymes of blue flowers.

— **doerfleri.** Eastern Europe. Erect, 15 in. bushes, narrow, slightly hairy leaves and short cymes of purple flowers.

— **X froebelii.** A hybrid between *M. petraea* and *M. suffruticosa* and intermediate between the parents in appearance.

— **graminifolia.** See *M. suffruticosa.*

— **X intermedia.** A hybrid of similar parentage to *M. froebelii* and a slightly taller plant with flowers of deep, clear blue.

— **petraea.** From Greece, and the Balkans. Neat, dwarf bushes of woody stems and grey-green leaves and abundant heads of soft blue flowers. One of the best.

— **speciosa.** A dubious name but a delightful plant. It comes from Kashmir and has been exhibited and grown as a Mertensia species but probably should be included in this genus. Very dwarf, with silvery, narrow leaves and heads of forget-me-not-blue flowers.

— **suffruticosa.** (M. graminifolia. Lithospermum graminifolium.) From S. Europe. Tufts of long, narrow, almost grass-like dark green leaves and terminal, drooping clusters of pale blue flowers.

MONARDELLA. *Labiatae.* A diminutive of Monarda, which these aromatic herbs resemble.

A small family of aromatic plants, natives of Western N. America. Hardy, summer and autumn flowering.

— **macrantha.** From creeping rootstocks grow tufts of ovate leaves and 9 in. stems carrying heads of tubular scarlet flowers.

— **nana.** Tufts of small grey leaves and heads of flesh-pink flowers.

— **odoratissima.** Decumbent, rather woody stems and narrow, heavily aromatic leaves. Short, ascending stems carry dense heads of pale purple flowers.

— **villosa.** The 9 to 12 in. stems with softly hairy, grey-green leaves and heads of small, tubular flowers varying in colour from pale purple to red.

MONESES. *Pyrolaceae.* From the Greek *monos*, single and *esis*, sending forth. An allusion to the solitary flower.

— **uniflora.** (Pyrola uniflora.) North and Central Europe, including Britain, Japan and N. America. A beautiful but difficult plant, asking for acid soil and a cool and shaded position. Best in the peat garden or for careful culture in an alpine house. Tiny tufts of rounded, leathery, toothed leaves and 3 in. stems offering one, cup-shaped, white or soft pink fragrant flower in May-June.

MONTIA. *Portulacaceae.* Named for Giuseppe Monti (1682-1760), Professor of botany at Bologna.

A genus allied to LEWISIA, summer flowering, for sunny positions.

— **chamissoi.** From N. America, where it usually grows in wet places. Leafy procumbent stems, rooting at the nodes and short racemes of pink or white flowers.

— **neopaxia.** From Australian mountains. Prostrate, succulent stems and leaves and substantial white, or soft pink flowers.

— parvifolia. (Sometimes wrongly named M. parviflora.) N. American. A short-lived perennial forming mats of crowded rosettes of fleshy leaves and many thread-like stolons. Loose heads of white, pink-flushed flowers on 4 in. stems. Nice, but slightly weedy.

MORISIA. *Cruciferae.* Named for Giuseppe Giacinto Moris (1796-1869), professor of botany at Turin and author of a flora of Sardinia.

— **hypogaea.** See *M. monantha.*

— **monantha.** A monotypic genus confined to Corsica and Sardinia, where it grows in the sand on the sea shore. Narrow, saw-edged leaves in tiny, prostrate tufts and an almost stemless corymb of large golden-yellow flowers. Spring. Full sun and essentially sharp drainage in sandy soil.

MUEHLENBECKIA. *Polygonaceae.* Named for Henri Gustave Muehlenbeck (1798-1845), a French physician.

A genus of creeping and climbing plants, mostly from Australasia and S. America. Of no floral beauty and only one species need concern us here.

— **complexa.** (M. nana.) From New Zealand. Dense carpets of tangled, thin stems clothed with many small, rounded, dark green leaves. Flowers inconspicuous but the small white berries occasionally produced are attractive. A useful ground-coverer for sun or shade.

MYOSOTIS. *Boraginaceae.* From the Greek *mus*, mouse and *ous* or *otos*, ear.

A large genus of annual and perennial plants, natives to temperate regions, mostly in Europe and Australasia. The common Forget-me-not is *M. scorpioides* (M. palustris).

— albida. A common coastal plant from New Zealand, with clusters of small white flowers.

— alpestris. Common in Europe, including Britain. Several named clones are, or have been, cultivated, notably 'Ruth Fischer', with crimped leaves and branching heads of light blue flowers.

- angustata. A New Zealand species, presumably white-flowered but it does not appear to be in cultivation.
- australis. Rosettes of greenish-brown leaves and short-stemmed heads of white or yellow flowers. New Zealand.
- azorica. From the Azores, the Canaries and N. Africa, and not quite hardy. A short-lived perennial carrying heads of intensely coloured violet-purple flowers on 9 to 12 in. stems.
- caespitosa. Closely related to *M. scorpioides*. European, including Britain. A good clone is *M.c. 'Rehsteineri'*, only a few inches high and of tufted habit, with clear blue flowers.
- colensoi. See *M. decora*.
- decora. (M. colensoi.) From screes of New Zealand mountains. Prostrate rosettes and shapely white flowers.
- hookeri. From the Himalaya and probably not in cultivation. It should make tufts of hoary leaves and carry solitary bright blue flowers on 3 in. stems.
- idaea. From Crete, and described by Dr. Peter Davis, who should know, as 'a thoroughly lousy plant'!
- keniensis. From Kenya and described as forming rock-hard cushions of dark green leaves. The flower colour is not quoted and it is surely, if regrettably, not in cultivation.
- lyallii. New Zealand. Tufts of leaves and short stems bearing small heads of white flowers.
- macrantha. From New Zealand. From tufts of hairy leaves rise foot-high stems carrying forked cymes of bronze-yellow flowers.
- pulvinaris. New Zealand. Cushions of soft grey hairy leaves and stemless solitary white flowers in profusion.
- rupicola. Probably only a mountain form of *M. alpestris*. Europe, including Britain and a treasure with small heads of azure flowers on 2 in. stems. Grow in impoverished, gritty soil.
- spathulata. Tufts of grey, hairy leaves and white, yellow-eyed flowers. New Zealand.
- traversii. New Zealand. Rosettes of pale green leaves and erect, 12 in. stems bearing heads of white or soft yellow flowers.

MYRTEOLA. See MYRTUS *nummularia*.

MYRTUS. *Myrtaceae*. The classical Greek name.

- nummularia. (Myrteola.) The only species which qualifies for inclusion in an alpine plant Manual. It hails from the Argentine, Chile and the Falkland Isles and is hardy, forming prostrate tangled mats of reddish woody stems set with tiny, leathery, rounded leaves. The small white flowers are carried terminally and are followed by nice pink berries.

NAMA. (ANDROPUS) *Hydrophyllaceae.* From *nama,* a stream of water. An allusion to the habitat of some species.

A genus of annual and perennial herbs, mostly natives of Western N. America but there are some tropical species. They are dubiously in cultivation and will probably need alpine house treatment if obtained.

- **carnosum.** From saline dunes in Mexico and sure to be difficult. Rosettes of sticky leaves and pyramidal spikes of many large, pearly bells flushed with mauve.
- **lobbii.** From California. Basal rosettes of dark green leaves and white-woolly stems and leaves. I have not seen it in flower and lack a description of the colour.
- **rothrockii.** This appears wrongly in the RHS Dictionary as 'rock-rothii'. From California. Erect, nine-inch bristly stems rise from a deep perennial root and carry dense terminal heads of lavender-coloured flowers.

NANDINA. *Berberidaceae.* The Latinized form of the Japanese name.

- **domestica.** The only species, and not an alpine. I include it only because of the recent advent into Europe of several delightful pygmy forms which are eminently suitable for the alpine house, and hardy enough to be grown on the rock garden in favourably sheltered places. The leaves are composed of elegant narrow, pointed leaflets and take on rich autumn tints. The type carries panicles of white flowers, followed by purple-red berries but I have not yet seen flowers or fruits on the pygmies.

NARDOPHYLLUM. *Compositae.*

- **bryoides.** From Patagonia, a fairly recent introduction which has as yet secured no more than a tenuous hold on cultivation. It grows in

NARDOPHYLLUM — *continued*

the form of a stiff, evergreen shrublet whose sparsely-branched stems are clothed in a woolly white tomentum with a few thick, blunt leaves densely felted on the undersides. It does not exceed a few inches in height. The small flowers are yellowish and inconspicuous.

NARTHECIUM. *Liliaceae.* A diminutive of *narthex*, a rod.

— ossifragum. This British bog plant is certainly not an alpine, but it has definite possibilities for moist positions in the rock garden for the sake of its racemes of yellow flowers which it carries above low tufts of short, rigid, iris-like leaves in summer.

NASSAUVIA. *Compositae.*

A genus of difficult composites, of which, as far as I know, only *N. revoluta* has been cultivated in this country and even so, with little success. It forms curiously shaped, squat columns of congested, diminished fat and fleshy grey-green leaves forming dense, low tufts. I do not think it has yet flowered in cultivation but I may be wrong as one or two clever cultivators in Scotland seem to be having some success with it. From Patagonia.

NECTAROSCORDUM. See ALLIUM *siculum.*

NEPETA. *Labiatae.* The Latin name for these plants.

There are very few in this genus which qualify for inclusion here. They are mostly herbaceous plants widely distributed through the Northern Hemisphere.

— discolor. A Himalayan species with spreading, leafy stems and cylindrical heads of flowers, pale blue, with a white lip. It should be worth growing if obtained.

— hederacea. This is correctly *Glechoma hederacea* but I retain the better known name. Europe, including Britain. An invasive ground-coverer, best grown in the form 'Variegata' which decorates its small leaves on the trailing stems with patterns of white. For a moist, shaded place.

— leucocyanea. This comes from the Hindu Kush and is described as having good blue flowers. It might be a trifle tall for most rock gardens.

— longibracteata. From the Himalaya, and I wish it were available. It inhabits stony screes, making tufts of grey, woolly leaves, aromatic when bruised. Flower stems are as woolly as the foliage and the blossoms are violet-blue, the lips marked with deeper colour.

— troodii. From Cyprus, and probably not too hardy. Leaves and stems are woolly-white, flowers are purple blue, dwarf.

NERTERA. *Rubiaceae.* From the Greek *nerteros*, lowly, from the habit of growth.

- **depressa.** See *N. granadensis.*
- **granadensis** (N. depressa.) This ought not to be included, but it is so often grown in alpine houses that I venture to include it. It comes from S. America, New Zealand and Australia and is far from hardy. Creeping mats of fleshy, frail stems root as they run and are clothed in tiny green leaves, over which are carried myriads of round, bright orange berries.

NIEREMBERGIA. *Solanaceae.* Named for Juan Eusebio Nieremberg (1596-1658), a Spanish Jesuit and author of a book on the marvels of nature.

- **caerulea** (N. hippomanica.) From the Argentine and hardy, or nearly so. Twelve in., erect leafy stems are crowned by many large, deep violet-blue flowers. Summer and on into the autumn.
- **hippomanica.** See *N. caerulea.*
- **repens.** (N. rivularis.) From S. America and hardy. Absolutely prostrate and spreading by creeping underground stems. Large, white, bell-shaped almost stemless flowers. Likes a sunny place in gritty soil, not too dry. Summer.
- **rivularis.** See *N. repens.*

NOCCAEA. *Cruciferae.* Named for Domenico Nocca, c.1790, Professor of botany at Padua.

Two rather inconspicuous European alpines, closely related to both Iberis and Thlaspi. *N. alpina* makes small tufts and 4 in. stems carrying white flowers. *N. stylosa* is of similar habit but the flowers are soft lilac in colour. Neither would stop any traffic. Spring flowering.

NONNEA. *Boraginaceae.* Named for J. P. Nonne of Erfurt (1729-1772) a German writer on botany.

Two rather obscure borages. *N. picta* is found in the Caucasus and has reddish-violet flowers and *N. pulla*, from Kurdistan has flowers of deep purple. Probably rather large for the rock garden but could have garden value if obtainable.

NORDMANNIA. See the genus TRACHYSTEMON in addenda.

NOTOTHLASPI. *Cruciferae.* From the Greek *notos*, southern and Thlaspi.

— rosulatum. The penwiper plant of high screes in New Zealand really qualifies to be regarded as one of the gardener's classic failures. As far as I know it has never been successfully grown for more than a very short time, although its pictures and descriptions continually tempt the experts to have 'one more try'. Upon a fleshy tap-root sits a symmetrical, flat rosette of felted grey leaves with lightly serrated margins. From the precise centre of the rosette rises a 9 to 12 in. tapered inflorescence crowded with fragrant cream flowers. it is monocarpic and I can offer no recipe for success other than the provision of perfect drainage and a considerable amount of luck, and, of course, alpine house treatment.

NOTOTRICHE. *Malvaceae.*

We may hear in the last syllable of the name of these Andean mallows what gardeners have to say of them, for they are very definitely 'tricky' and difficult to grow. Few have crept into cultivation and none, as far as I know, permanently. The invaluable Bulletins of the Alpine Garden Society enticingly list a dozen or more species, none of which is available commercially. They do not grow below an elevation of 14,000 ft. in the Andes, many being found in Southern Peru. They are enticing, many of them forming cushions of felted leaves and carrying brilliantly coloured flowers. As with many other Andean alpine treasures, we long to grow them and urgently seek the secret of success.

OAKESIELLA. *Liliaceae.* Named for William Oakes (1799-1848) a New England botanist.

— **sessilifolia.** (Uvularia sessilifolia.) So closely related to UVULARIA that I feel it might well be included in that genus. It likes partial shade and rich, moist soil, preferably, but not essentially lime-free. The foot-high, forked stems carry narrow, pointed leaves and the yellow, bell-shaped flowers are borne on axillary pedicels in summer. It comes from N. America and Canada. The particular form that I grow has nicely green and white variegated foliage.

ODONTOSPERMUM. See the genus ASTERISCUS.

OENOTHERA. *Onagraceae.* The derivation is from a Greek source but is obscure. It was almost certainly a name used by Theophrastus for a plant in no way related to these plants. A large genus of American plants, a few of which have become naturalized in Europe and elsewhere and absorbed into local floras. The few appropriate to rock gardens are described below. In America particularly botanists have divided them into several distinct genera, such as ANOGRA, MEGAPTERUM, MERIOLIX etc. These I have ignored, adhering to the familiar name.

— **acaulis.** (taraxacifolia.) A rather short-lived perennial from Chile. Tufts of dandelion-like leaves and stemless central clusters of large white, or soft yellow flowers.

— **caespitosa.** A splendid, but not too easy species from desert lands in N. America. Grow it in the alpine house or in a hot, dry position outside, in light, sandy soil. It spreads by underground runners, emitting tufts of narrow, jagged-edged leaves and immense white, fragrant flowers on short stems. Several forms showing slight variations have been distinguished, such as *glabra, montana, eximia, macroglottis* and *marginata.*

261

- eximia. See *O. caespitosa.*
- flava. Little more than biennial, from Utah, but a nice, tufty plant with narrow, serrated leaves and stemless flowers, rather 'square' in shape of light yellow.
- fremontii. From plains in Kansas and Texas and could be described as a refined version of *O. missouriensis.*
- glabra. See *O. caespitosa.*
- lavendulifolia. Again a species from the plains of N. America. Dense rosettes of softly hairy leaves and mahogany buds which expand into short-stemmed, large yellow flowers.
- macrocarpa. See *O. missouriensis.*
- macroglottis. See *O. caespitosa.*
- marginata. See *O. caespitosa.*
- mexicana 'Rosea'. See *O. speciosa.*
- missouriensis. Although demanding a fair amount of space this is a magnificent plant with a very long flowering season. Herbaceous in habit, it makes a spreading mat of decumbent leafy stems, ending in immense yellow flowers.
- montana. See *O. caespitosa.*
- speciosa. Slightly tender, from Mexico. Often grown as *O. mexicana* 'Rosea', but correctly *O.s.* 'Childsii'. Clusters of short, red stems and the rose-red, rather small, but decorative flowers are carried freely in the leaf axils from June until autumn.
- taraxacifolia. See *O. acaulis.*
- trichocalyx. A tap-rooting desert plant, perennial, but is capable of literally flowering itself to death. Tufts of long, tapering, grey-green leaves and large white or soft pink flowers on short stems.

OMPHALODES. *Boraginaceae.* From the Greek *omphalos,* a navel. The nut-like seed, hollowed on one side, resembles the human navel.

A small genus of annual and perennial, spring and summer flowering herbs, natives of Mediterranean regions, E. Asia and Mexico.

- aliena. From Spain, and, unfortunately, not in cultivation, some traveller please note. It grows on sun-baked cliffs near Grazalema. Tufts of heart-shaped leaves and exquisitely blue flowers in loose clusters on short stems.
- cappadocica. From the Caucasus. A common garden plant and invaluable for an early spring display of clear blue flowers above low clumps of heart shaped leaves. It prefers a cool position. A selected clone named 'Anthea Bloom' has slightly grey-green leaves and flowers of lighter blue.
- cornifolia. See *O. lojkae.*

OMPHALODES – *continued*

- X florairensis. A hybrid once raised by the late Henri Correvon on his nursery near Geneva between *O. lucilae* and *O. nitida*. It was intermediate between the parents, but I doubt if it still exists.
- lojkae. (O. cornifolia.) From the Caucasus, and similar to *O. cappadocica* but more robust in all its parts.
- luciliae. From Grecian cliffs and the aristocrat of the race, do not be misled by the *Flora Europaea*, which, in its botanical wisdom says, 'like *O. verna*'!! Loose, low tufts of glabrous grey leaves and loose racemes of sky-blue flowers. The buds are often pink. For sunny crevices or the alpine house and an avid lime-lover.
- lusitanica. See *O. nitida*.
- nitida. (O. lusitanica.) From Spain and Portugal. Not unlike *O. cappadocica* but with smoother leaves and lax racemes of clear blue flowers. For a cool position.
- rupestris. From the Caucasus, and very dubiously in cultivation, although it was once introduced by my late father. The heart-shaped leaves are felted with a white tomentum and the flowers, in loose racemes on short stems, are sky-blue.
- verna. From the European Alps. The earliest of all to flower, tufts of heart-shaped leaves and terminal clusters of bright blue flowers. There is also a nice albino form with pure white blossoms.

OMPHALOGRAMMA. *Primulaceae.* From the Greek *omphalos*, navel and *gramma*, letter or marking.

A small genus, closely related to PRIMULA, natives of China and Tibet. Few are in cultivation and they are not easy to grow, but succeed better in the cool and humid conditions of Scotland than they do in the southern counties of England.

- brachysiphon. From S.E. Tibet. Velvety black-purple bells pendant from very short stems. Probably not now in cultivation.
- delavayi. The rosettes of rounded leaves are softly white-haired. The flowers, carried singly before the leaves develop, are widely funnel-shaped and deep purple-blue in colour.
- elegans. Softly hairy leaves and 6 in. stems carrying tubular, deep purple flowers.
- elwesianum. Large, rich purple flowers on 6 in. stems.
- engleri. Probably not in cultivation but described as extremely lovely. Tufts of flannelly, dark green leaves and huge, pinguicula-like flowers solitary on short stems.
- farreri. From Upper Burma. Heart-shaped, hairy leaves and short scapes carrying large, funnel-shaped deep purple flowers.
- franchettii. From Burma, and described as having magenta flowers.
- rockii. See *O. vinciflorum*.

- souliei. Entire, hairy leaves and violet-blue flowers on short stems.
- vinciflorum. (O. rockii.) A variable, but lovely species, to which it is thought *O. engleri* may properly belong. It has been more successfully cultivated than most of the other species. Rosettes of blunt, hairy leaves and solitary, large, tubular flowers of rich violet-blue.

Omphalogrammas are mostly lime-lovers and require soil rich in humus and gritty enough to ensure perfect drainage and cool, north-facing positions. They are spring and summer flowering.

ONOBRYCHIS. *Leguminosae.* From the Greek *onos*, an ass, and *brychis*, branch, or possibly *bryche*, bellowing, asses were said to bray for it!

A genus of leguminous herbs and sub-shrubs, natives of Europe, N. Africa and W. Asia. Said to be easy to grow and some are certainly decorative, but little success has been achieved in their cultivation and I would be surprised if any are available commercially.

ONONIS. *Leguminosae.* The classical Greek name for these plants.

A race of shrubs and sub-shrubs and some annual, biennial and perennial herbs, a few of which are appropriate for rock gardens. They are sun-lovers and spring and summer flowering.

- cenisia. Alps of Europe and N. Africa. Tiny bushes of tangled stems with small, trifoliate leaves. Solitary rose-pink flowers in the upper leaf axils.
- minutissima. S. Europe and Algeria. Similar in habit to *O. cenisia* but with short, terminal racemes of golden flowers.
- natrix. From Europe and N. Africa and can eventually make a 20 in. bush. The solitary, pea-flowers are yellow, the standard streaked with red.
- rotundifolia. A low shrublet with woody stems and rounded leaflets. The relatively large flowers are carried in small clusters and are rose-pink, with red-streaked standards.
- stricta. From the Pyrenees. Dwarf, with bright yellow flowers.

ONOSMA. *Boraginaceae.* From the Greek *onos*, an ass and *osme*, smell. The roots of some species are said to smell like an ass.

A fairly large genus of plants, mostly natives of Mediterranean regions but spreading into Asia Minor and Central Asia. Sun-loving and summer flowering. Very few are cultivated and several have no garden value. Of the many known species I propose to describe only those which are, or have recently been, in general cultivation.

- **albo-pilosa.** From Asia Minor. Tufts of narrow, hairy leaves and white, rose-flushed tubular flowers.
- **albo-rosea.** (cinerea.) Tufts of narrow, silver-haired leaves and pendant heads of tubular, white flowers which flush pink as they age.
- **bourgaei.** From Armenia. Tufts of narrow, roughly hairy leaves and drooping heads of white, tubular, fragrant flowers.
- **caespitosa.** From Cyprus. Characteristic tufts of narrow, hairy leaves and pendant heads of fragrant, pale yellow tubular flowers.
- **cinerea.** See *O. albo-rosea.*
- **echioides.** See *O. taurica.*
- **sericeum.** From Asia Minor and Iran. Narrow leaves coated with silver hairs and drooping racemes of cream-yellow flowers.
- **taurica.** The most commonly grown species. It, and *O. echioides* are much confused in gardens. They are similar and the one usually grown under either name is *O. taurica.* It is a fine inhabitant of a sunny cleft or crevice and a splendid wall plant. Tufts of narrow, roughly hairy leaves and pendant croziers of fragrant, tubular yellow flowers.

ONOSMODIUM. *Boraginaceae.*

A small genus of N. American and Mexican plants, closely related to ONOSMA, few, if any of them are in cultivation and they are less garden worthy than the Onosmas in any case.

OPHIOPOGON. *Liliaceae.* From the Greek *ophis*, a snake and *pogon*, a beard. The allusion is obscure.

A small genus of Asian perennials, only one of which really qualifies for inclusion here.

- **planiscapus.** From Japan. The typical species is less garden worthy than the variety *nigrescens*, which forms creeping tufts of narrow, almost black leaves. The small, bell-shaped flowers open white and change to mauve and are borne in dense, erect racemes on short stems in summer and early autumn. They are followed by luscious black berries. It is hardy and easily grown in a not-too-hot position.

OPITHANDRA. *Gesneriaceae.*

- **primuloides.** The only species in its genus and native to Japan. It is very dubiously in cultivation at present. It has a plethora of synonyms, having at various times been genetically named CHIRITA, BOEA, DIDYMOCARPUS and OREOCHARIS. Short rhizomes and fleshy, cordate, grey-green, toothed leaves and tubular violet-purple flowers. If obtainable it will require, and deserve, alpine house treatment, in compost rich in humus.

OREASTRUM. See ASTER *pulchellus.*

OREOBOLUS. *Cyperaceae.*
A small genus of New Zealand Sedges, one or two of which would be of interest, even if no great beauty, if obtainable. *O. pectinata* and *O. impar* both form close, dense tufts and sound attractive.

OREOCHARIS. *Gesneriaceae.* From the Greek *oros*, a mountain and *charis*, beauty.
A small genus of Asian plants, a few species of which are occasionally grown under alpine house conditions, but they are not easy and demand great care and attention.
- aurantiaca. From Yunnan. Ramonda-like rosettes and short scapes carrying one or more tubular yellow flowers with red calyces.
- primuloides. From Japan. Flat rosettes of hairy leaves and pendant umbels of several, Streptocarpus-like flowers of lilac with a white throat.
- forrestii. From Yunnan. Coarsely-toothed, russet-haired leaves in rosettes and loose cymes of yellow, long-tubed flowers.

OREOCARYA. *Boraginaceae.*
A small genus, related to LITHOSPERMUM and mostly American. It is doubtful if any are in cultivation, certainly not commercially, but some of the species should be worth growing. Among those to seek would be *OO. confertiflora, flava, flavoculata, grahamii* and *nana.*

OREOPOLUS. See the Genus CRUCKSHANKSIA.

OREOSTYLIDIUM. *Donatiaceae.* From the Greek *oros*, mountain = mountain Stylidium.
- subulatum. Dense tufts of needle-like leaves, light green, sometimes mottled red. Very short stems carry singly small white flowers. From New Zealand and will demand alpine house treatment. The only species in the genus.

ORESITROPHE. *Saxifragaceae.* From the Greek *oresbios*, living on mountains.
- rupifraga. From China. From a thick and scaly rootstock spring wide, toothed leaves and a 6 in. stem carrying a loose panicle of white or pale rose, bell-shaped flowers. The foliage adopts good autumn tints. For a cool position.

ORIGANUM (Amaracus.) *Labiatae.* The classical Greek name *origanon*, for these aromatic plants.

A small genus of sub-shrubs or herbaceous perennials, mostly found in Mediterranean regions. All sun-lovers and summer flowering.

- **amanum.** A comparatively recent introduction, collected in Anatolia by Dr. Peter Davis. Tiny, compact bushes beset with pale green leaves and clusters of long-tubed flowers of lilac pink, sub-tended by pink bracts. The flowers have a long individual life. For the alpine house or sunny scree.

- **dictamnus.** From Crete. Ascending 8 in. branches clothed with rounded leaves heavily white-felted. Drooping heads of pink flowers among the showy bracts characteristic of the genus.

- **hybridum.** From the Levant. Decumbent, branching stems and heads of drooping pink flowers.

- **laevigatum.** From Anatolia. From woody rootstocks rise 8 in. stems, branching and graceful and mahogany red. Handsome heads of long-tubed pink flowers, enhanced by the red-purple bracts.

- **microphyllum.** From Crete. 8 in. stems, branches purplish. Flowers pink, in globose spikelets at branch tips.

- **pulchellum.** From S.E. Europe and a pretty, but sometimes invasive plant with crowded 8 in. stems crowned with heads of pink, hop-like flowers.

- **pulchrum.** See *O. scabrum.*

- **rotundifolium.** A recent and valuable introduction from Turkey. On woody, short stems are rounded, glabrous leaves in stem-clasping pairs. The drooping inflorescences consist of whorls of pale pink flowers between large papery bracts. Best in lime-free soil.

- **scabrum pulchrum.** From Greece. Compact, 6 in. bushes of wiry, branched stems clothed in smooth, pointed leaves covered with brown dots. The lilac-pink flowers, enclosed in purple bracts are carried in branching cymes at the branch tips.

- **tournefortii.** From Greece. 12 in. branching leafy stems terminating in heads of hop-like bracts from which protrude the mauve-pink flowers.

- **vulgare 'Aureum'.** I am slightly dubious of including this, the golden-leaved form of the common Marjoram, but it makes neat, dwarf, colourful bushes of bright foliage and is not without its uses in the rock garden.

ORNITHOPUS. *Leguminosae.* Resembling a bird's foot.

- **isthmocarpus.** From Morocco. Slender stems and few-flowered heads of quite pretty pink flowers. Summer. 12 in.

OROBUS. See the genus LATHYRUS.

ORPHANIDESIA. *Ericaceae.* In honour of Theordoros Georgios Orphanides (1817-1886), Professor of botany at Athens.

- **gaultherioides.** Until recently this was regarded as a monotypic genus, but the one species has now officially been included in the genus EPIGAEA. It has become so well known under this name however, that I retain it for convenience. A rarity from Lazistan and Transcaucasia. A prostrate shrub with hairy branches and broad evergreen leaves, bristly on both surfaces. The racemes carry from one to three sessile flowers, of considerable size, cup-shaped and clear rose-pink in colour during the spring. It is not an easy plant to please and demands full shade and lime-free soil. Regrettably twice described, see also p.162 under EPIGAEA.

OSTEOSPERMUM. See the genus DIMORPHOTHECA.

OURISIA. *Scrophulariaceae.* Named for Governor Ouris of the Falkland Islands.

A small genus, natives of New Zealand and Tasmania and S. America. Best in lime-free soil and cool, shaded or north-facing positions. Spring and summer flowering.

- **alpina.** There is considerable confusion in gardens between this plant and *O. coccinea* and *O. elegans.* The true *O. alpina* should have oval, dark green leaves, sometimes showing some variegation. Its pink flowers are inferior in quality to those of *O. elegans*, but I doubt if it is in cultivation at present in any case.
- **caespitosa.** This forms prostrate mats of small leaves decorated with small white flowers on very short stems. The var. *gracilis* is even more compact. Both are excellent peat garden plants.
- **coccinea.** I believe the plant in gardens under this name to be *O. elegans*, q.v.
- **elegans.** (*O. coccinea.*) Tufts of heart-shaped, light green, toothed leaves and 8 in. stems carrying loose racemes of tubular red flowers.
- **glandulosa.** Rhizomatous, with small, leathery leaves, hairy above and glabrous beneath. Short stems carry the white flowers.
- **macphersonii.** Large, dark green leaves and 12 in. stems carrying several good white flowers.
- **macrocarpa.** A robust plant with thick stems adorned by large, leathery rich green leaves and stems up to 20 in. carrying heads of large white, yellow-eyed flowers.
- **macrophylla.** Resembles a slightly smaller *O. macrocarpa.*
- **magellanica.** (*O. ruelloides.*) From Patagonia, where it is said to grow in very wet places. A straggling habit, with broad, crenate leaves and long-tubed scarlet flowers on short stems.
- **microphylla.** Mat-forming, with four rows of adpressed leaves. Each slender, short, branching stems carries several tubular pink flowers. For the alpine house.

- **pearcei.** Creeping, with broad leaves, toothed, and purple beneath. Short scapes carry several tubular, crimson flowers, streaked with blood-red.
- **ruelloides.** See *O. magellanica.*
- **sessilifolia.** Creeping, with rounded, overlapping leaves, toothed, and hairy on the upper side. Short scapes of quite large white, yellow-eyed flowers.
- **vulcanica.** Similar in habit and appearance to *O. caespitosa.*

OXALIS. *Oxalidaceae.* From the Greek *oxys*, sour or sharp. This enormous family has a world-wide distribution. It contains many good garden plants and some almost ineradicable weeds. The temptation is almost irresistible to include a long list of these often very beautiful plants, but common sense dictates mentioning only those really suitable for the rock garden or alpine house. Many that clamour for inclusion are not really hardy.

- **acetosella.** This is the Stubwort of our own woodlands and is best grown in the form *O.a.* 'Rosea', a modest creeper with tiny leaves and small flowers of glowing pink.
- **adenophylla.** From Chile. It forms a scaly, soft bulb-like tuber, from which rise, in the spring, crinkled, glaucous leaves in dense tufts, crowned by large, goblet-shaped rose-pink flowers, the petals lined with veins of deeper colour.
- **cernua.** See *O. pes-caprae.*
- **chrysantha.** The authenticity of this name appears to be doubtful, but it covers a delightful, rather spreading carpeter forming sheets of light green, trifoliate leaves, covered for weeks on end by innumerable soft yellow flowers. It is not completely hardy but a few rooted pieces lifted and kept in a frame for the winter assures continuity of a very decorative plant. It appears to have come from S. America.
- **corniculata.** No one who has been pestered by this fiendish weed would knowingly allow it to enter his garden, pretty though it is, especially in the form with bronzed leaves and tiny, bright golden flowers. Avoid it like the plague.

  deppei. A Mexican, and slightly tender. Curiously truncated leaves, often marked with purple bands and umbels of large, rich purple flowers on 6 in. stems.
- **depressa.** See *O. inops.*
- **enneaphylla.** A great treasure, introduced many years ago from cold and misty Falkland Islands, where it threads long chains of scaly tubers in peaty soil of narrow rock crevices. The crinkled leaves are silver-grey and are additionally decorated by short-stemmed, huge flowers, which may be glistening white, or pink flushed.

— **inops.** (O. depressa.) I am not sure which name is correct, but it is so well known as *O. inops* that I retain it. It can be invasive, but only moderately, and is pretty enough to be forgiven. Lobed, grey-green leaves and large flowers of bright rose-pink with lighter centres. A very cold winter will curb its activities as it appears to have been introduced by the late Mrs. Garnet-Botfield and I assume it came from S. Africa.

— **laciniata.** From Patagonia, whence it was introduced by Mrs. R. Tweedie in 1955. It has something of the habit of growth of *O. enneaphylla*, making slender chains of tiny, scaly tubers. The glaucous green leaves are divided into several narrow leaflets with purplish margins. The widely trumpet-shaped flowers on very short stems vary from almost white to vivid purple.

— **lobata.** A gem from Chile whose curious growth habits have to be understood. From tiny, fur-coated bulbs rise, in the spring, tufts of emerald-green leaves. These very soon disappear, often to the despair of the owner, but patience reveals that they reappear in the early autumn, this time accompanied by many short-stemmed flowers of purest gold. It is hardy, but so small and precious that many people harbour it in the alpine house.

— **magellanica.** From S. America. Absolutely prostrate mats of tiny, dark green leaves from scaly stolons and stemless, rounded, pure white flowers in profusion. It seems happier in a cool position, than in full sun.

— **obtusa.** I do not know where this comes from, nor am I sure that the name is valid, but it covers a desirable species with low tufts of trifoliate leaves and wide funnels of rich rose-pink on short stems.

— **oregana.** From N. America. Vigorous tufts of wide, three-cleft leaves and glowing purple flowers of goodly size just above the foliage.

— **pes-caprae.** (O. cernua.) This is another pest to be avoided. It came originally from Bermuda I believe, but is now widely naturalized in the warmer parts of Europe and elsewhere in the world. It spreads with astonishing rapidity in mild climates and has handsome yellow flowers on tall stems — but do not be tempted.

— **vespertilionis.** From Mexico and not hardy, but safe in an alpine house. Deeply cleft, two-lobed leaves and clusters of pink or purple flowers on short stems.

OXYRIA. *Polygonaceae.* From the Greek *oxys*, sharp, because of the acidity of the leaves.

— **digyna.** (reinformis.) A pleasant weed for an odd corner. Native of Europe, including Britain. Low tufts of fleshy, rounded, lobed leaves which take rich autumn colours. Short spikes of greenish flowers. The flat seedpods are conspicuous and coloured bronze-red.

OXYTROPIS. *Leguminosae.* From the Greek *oxys*, sharp and *tropis*, a keel. An allusion to the form of the flower.

A large genus of herbs and sub-shrubs, native to mountainous regions of Europe, Asia and N. America. There are many beautiful species but they do not appear to have accepted cultivation happily and are rarely grown. Their flowers may be white, violet, purple or pale yellow. Sun-loving and summer flowering. The names of a few desirable species are listed below:

- besseyi
- blankinshipii.
- campestris.
- lagopus.
- nana.
- sericea.
- triflora.

Any of these would be worth trying, if obtainable. They do not transplant happily and are best raised from seed and left undisturbed if and when established.

OZOMELIS. *Saxifragaceae.* Derivation obscure.

A rather obscure small family of N. American mountain plants. The only one which seems to have crept occasionally into cultivation is *O. diversifolia*, a creeping, rhizomatous plant with triangular, cordate leaves and short racemes of greenish-white (?) flowers. As a genus they appear to prefer rather moist situations.

PACHISTIMA. (Sometimes, but wrongly, PACHYSTIMA or PACHYSTIGMA). *Celastraceae.*

A genus of two species of dwarf, evergreen shrubs, both from N. America. They prefer light shade and lime-free soil. Summer flowering.

— canbyi. Woody, self-layering stems clothed in narrow, slightly toothed leaves. Small greenish flowers in the leaf-axils followed by white fruits. Seldom exceeds 8 in.

— myrsinites. Small, leathery leaves, toothed in the upper half. Short-stalked red flowers in the leaf axils and white fruits. A trifle taller than the preceding species.

PACHYCLADON. *Cruciferae.* From the Greek *pachys*, thick and *cladon*, a shoot.

A New Zealand genus of two species of alpine, tap-rooting crucifers. *P. crenata* and *P. novae-zelandae* are similar in appearance, the latter being slightly the larger of the two. Flat rosettes of narrow, toothed leaves and clusters of small white fragrant flowers on very short stems.

PANCRATIUM. *Amaryllidaceae.* The Greek name for a bulbous plant.

Although bulbs in general are excluded from this Manual, one or two exceptions cannot be denied, this being one I do not care to omit.

— illyricum. From Mediterranean regions, notably Corsica and Sardinia. Very large bulbs from which rise sheaves of broad, grey leaves of great substance. The large, white, intensely fragrant flowers are carried on 12 in. stems in summer. Requires a warm situation if grown outside.

PAPAVER. *Papaveraceae.* The Latin name for the Poppy family.

A large family, widely distributed, few of which concern us here, but among the few are some valuable rock garden plants. Spring and summer flowering and lovers of open, sunny positions in gritty soil.

- alpinum. The dainty alpine poppy is short-lived but very desirable, and readily and harmlessly perpetuates itself by seedlings. European alps. Tufts of tiny segmented leaves and solitary flowers on short stems, white or pink or, in the case of the variety *kerneri*, soft yellow and larger than those of the type.

- burseri. Mostly from the Eastern alps. Rather like *P. alpinum* but with pure white flowers.

- fauriei. See *P. miyabeanum.*

- mairei. From N. Africa. Vivid red flowers on rather tall stems.

- **myabeanum.** From Japan. This many be more correctly *P. fauriei*, but I retain the name by which it has become well known in gardens. A dainty creature with rosettes of wide, hairy, grey-green, serrated leaves and large soft yellow poppies on short stems. Not long-lived but very desirable.

- pyrenaicum. From the Pyrenees and very similar to *P. alpinum* but with less glaucous foliage.

- radicatum. A widely distributed, rather tall species and extremely variable. The most desirable form would appear to be the rare *P.r. hyperboreum* from Scandinavia which bears large, sulphur-yellow flowers on short stems.

- rupifragum. A Spanish species with good, brick-red flowers. It is most desirable in its shorter-stemmed forms.

- sendtneri. Central and Eastern Europe. Another of the *P. alpinum* persuasion. The rounded flowers are usually white.

- triniifolium. From the Caucasus and Asia Minor. A biennial or monocarpic species forming an exquisite rosette of finely cut silver filigree foliage. It should be relished as a foliage plant for the pyramids of purplish flowers are not inspiring. For the alpine house or sunny scree.

PARADISEA. *Liliaceae.* Named for Count Giovanni Paradisi (1760-1826).

- liliastrum. (Anthericum liliastrum). This, the lovely St. Bruno's lily, is the only species in its genus. European Alps. Tufts of narrow leaves and tall stems carrying heads of lily-like, white, fragrant flowers in summer.

273

PARAHEBE. *Scrophulariaceae.* From the Greek *para*, near and Hebe.

A genus of dwarf, mostly semi-woody plants nearly related to both HEBE and VERONICA, with both of which genera they are frequently confused in gardens. They are all natives of Australasia and are summer-flowering sun-lovers fit for any good soil. A number of species which ought to be included here will be found listed under the genus HEBE.

- X bidwillii. A hybrid between *P. decora* and *P. lyallii.* A tiny, neat shrublet with wee, rounded, glossy leaves and short racemes of white flowers veined with pink.

- canescens. This has been known as *Veronica liliputiana,* the specific epithet being very appropriate as it is a mere film of tiny stems and tiny grey leaves, spangled with short-stemmed blue flowers. Best in the alpine house as it is almost invisible when not in flower.

- catarractae. Erect bushes up to 8 in. with oval to narrow toothed leaves and white flowers with a central crimson zone. There is a plant grown in gardens as Hebe, or Veronica càtarractae which is quite distinct, with blue flowers on taller bushes.

- hookeriana. A small shrub of about 6 in. with narrow, leathery leaves and short racemes of white flowers streaked with pink.

- lyallii. The semi-prostrate branches root when they touch the soil. Thick, leathery and glabrous leaves and slender racemes of white flowers, often striped with pink.

PARAQUILEGIA. *Ranunculaceae.* From the Greek *para*, near and Aquilegia.

- anemonoides. (P. grandiflora. Isopyrum grandiflorum.) A rare delight from Kashmir eastward through the Himalaya. For careful cultivation in the alpine house, wedged into tight crevices between small pieces of stone. Tufts of delicate, grey, ferny foliage and rounded flowers, carried just above the leaves, singly on slender stems. They are rich lavender in colour with a central boss of golden stamens. It is a lime-lover.

- microphylla. (Isopyrum microphyllum.) Similar in many ways to the preceding but slightly dwarfer. It comes from Nepal among other Himalayan stations and has white flowers, centred by the characteristic boss of golden stamens. It requires similar treatment to *P. anemonoides.*

PARIS. *Liliaceae.* From the Latin *par*, equal, alluding to the regularity of its parts.

- polyphylla. From the Himalaya. This curious plant varies in height from a few inches to 2 ft. Its erect stems carry terminal whorls of rounded, pointed leaves, centred by the greenish flowers which are followed by red fruits.

— quadrifolia. Widely distributed, including Britain, where it is known as Herb Paris. 12 in. stems carry the characteristic whorl of terminal leaves and the yellow-green flowers are followed by black fruits. Both species like a lightly shaded position.

PARNASSIA. *Saxifragaceae.* A shortened version of the 16th century name *Gramen Parnassi*, referring to Mt. Parnassus in Greece. Plants for moist positions, summer flowering.

— fimbriata. From N. America and one of the handsomest of the genus. Slightly larger than our native *P. palustris*, it has white flowers, the petals delightfully and elegantly fringed.

— foliosa. From Japan, India and China. The 8 in. stems have leaves arranged in pagoda fashion and the white flowers are handsomely fringed.

— nubicola. From the Himalaya. Basal tufts of heart-shaped leaves and erect, wiry, branching stems carrying large white flowers, the petals veined with green lines.

— palustris. Our native Grass of Parnassus, which occasionally appears in gardens, where it deserves a place. From the small tufts of heart-shaped leaves rise stems up to 8 in. carrying several white, green-veined flowers.

— parviflora. From N. America. Rather like our native species but the veining of the white petals may be green or soft purple.

PAROCHETUS. *Leguminosae.* From the Greek *para*, near, and *ochetos*, a brook, because of its preference for moist soil.

— communis. The only species in the genus. It occurs in the Himalaya and in E. Africa. Prostrate, widely spreading stems and clover-like leaves. The gentian-blue pea-flowers are carried in profusion on short stems in late summer and on into the winter. It is slightly tender and should be protected in winter, or rooted pieces can be potted as an insurance.

PARONYCHIA. *Caryophyllaceae.* The Greek *paronychia*, a whitlow, from *para*, near and *onyx*, a nail. These herbs were said to effect a cure for whitlows.

Mat-forming, sun-loving plants with attractive foliage and showy silver bracts enclosing the inconspicuous flowers. Mostly from Mediterranean regions, but spreading into Tropical Africa and America.

PARONYCHIA — *continued*

- **argentea.** Grey mats and heads of silvery bracts. S. Europe.
- **capitata.** (P. nivea.) Similar to *P. argentea* but slightly bolder. Mediterranean.
- **cephalotes.** Europe. There is a strong family similarity between the species and this one is not unlike *P. kapela.*
- **nivea.** See *P. capitata.*
- **polygonifolia.** S. Europe. Not unlike *P. argentea*, but with smaller heads of silvery bracts.
- **pulvinata.** N. America. Tightly packed domes of grey, rather fleshy leaves and typical inflorescences.
- **serpyllifolia.** A specially compact sub-form of *P. kapela* from the Pyrenees.

PARRYA. *Cruciferae.* Named in honour of Capt. Sir William Edward Parry (1790-1855), an Arctic navigator.

A small genus of low-growing plants, natives of Arctic regions and N. America. Sunny positions in any good soil but they tend to dislike very wet winter conditions. A few species occur in the Himalaya.

- **lanuginosa.** Dwarf, tufted habit and hairy leaves. Short racemes of pink flowers. From the Himalaya.
- **macrocarpa.** Arctic regions. Low tufts of narrow, entire or toothed leaves and short spires of lilac flowers.
- **menziesii.** N. America. Short, woody stems and basal rosettes of very hairy leaves. Loose racemes of bright purple flowers.
- **microcarpa.** From the Altai mountains. Very dwarf with white or pink flowers in short racemes.
- **nudicaulis.** From the Hindu Kush. From tufts of basal hairy leaves rise 6 in. stems carrying short racemes of large, violet, dark-centred fragrant flowers.

PASSERINA. *Thymeliaceae.* From *passer*, a sparrow. The beaked seeds are said to resemble the head of a sparrow.

A genus of small, evergreen, heath-like shrubs, some from S. Africa, which are not hardy. The European species at least have been transferred to the genus THYMELAEA, which see.

PATERSONIA. *Iridaceae.* Named in honour of Col. W. Paterson (1755-1810), Scottish traveller in S. Africa during the 18th century.

- **glauca.** Tufted, narrow leaves. Short stems with several blue flowers, each subtended by a transparent bract. From Australia. For warm, moist soil.

PATRINIA. *Valerianaceae.* Named in honour of Eugene L. M. Patrin (1724-1815), French minerologist and botanist.

A small group of, mostly, Asian plants, herbaceous perennials for open, sunny positions in any good soil. Summer flowering.

- — gibbosa. Leafy, 8 in. stems rising from crowded, rounded leaves. Flat clusters of yellow flowers. From Japan.
- — palmata. See *P. triloba.*
- — sibirica. Siberian. From tufts of rather thick leaves rise glabrous, 8 in. stems terminating in heads of yellow, scented flowers.
- — triloba. (P. palmata.) From Japan. Tufts of deeply lobed, palmate leaves and 8 in. stems carrying loose, three-branched cymes of yellow flowers.

PEDICULARIS. *Scrophulariaceae.* From the Latin *pediculus*, a louse. The presence of this plant in a field was supposed to produce lice in sheep.

A large race of plants, many of them beautiful, widely distributed over the N. Hemisphere and very tempting to gardeners who see them in the wild. They are, however, parasitic, and are seldom grown with any success in gardens. The likelihood of growing them is so remote that, withal regretfully, I omit any specific descriptions, leaving it to individuals to 'have a go' with any of which they may be able to obtain seeds.

PELARGONIUM. *Geraniaceae.* From the Greek *pelargos*, a stork. The fruit has a beak not unlike that of a stork.

- — endlicherianum. The only hardy species, from Asia Minor. Loose hummocks of heart-shaped, lobed leaves and on 6 in. stems loose heads of bright pink flowers, the upper two petals much longer than the lower ones. For a warm and sheltered position.

PENSTEMON. *Scrophulariaceae.* From the Greek *pente*, five and *stemon*, a stamen.

A large genus, natives, with one exception in NE. Asia, of N. America and Mexico. They are represented in rock gardens by several species, which are sometimes ill-defined and merge one into the other, and by many clones and hybrids, of garden origin. They are invaluable summer flowering plants for open, sunny positions, and appreciate protection from cold east winds. I accept no responsibility for the accuracy of the names used. Even so I list only a tithe of the names to be found in the Indices of the Alpine Garden Society's Bulletins or in various text books. The genus is taxonomically confused, to say the least of it and urgently needs expert disentanglement. There is an American Penstemon Society, to whose publications I am indebted for much valuable information on the genus. They publish a list of Penstemons considered suitable for rock gardens, which I append at the end of my own alphabetical arrangement, omitting those which I have attempted to describe.

- **acaulis.** Mat-forming with large blue flowers on very short stems. Highly desirable but very dubiously in cultivation.

- **alpinus.** Usually less than 12 in. with good clear-blue, white-throated flowers.

- **X 'Amethyst'.** A hybrid, similar to *P. scouleri* in stature, with tubular amethyst flowers.

- **arizonicus.** 6 in. stems and loose heads of purple-blue flowers.

- **auribarbis.** Bushy habit and large lavender flowers in loose heads.

- **baccharifolius.** From Texas, and might not be hardy, but is handsome, with tall stems carrying many scarlet flowers well into the autumn.

- **barrettae.** Related to *P. rupicola*, but more erect. Lilac-purple flowers.

- **campanulatus.** The type is too tall for most rock gardens, but the variety *pulchellus* makes low mats and has small but brilliant blue flowers.

- **confertus** (P. procerus.) Prostrate habit and slender stems carrying cream-white or pale yellow flowers.

- **cristatus.** Probably correctly *P. eriantherus*, which see.

- **davidsonii.** A variable species, and confused in gardens with *P. rupicola*. In its best form it makes low bushes of woody stems and grey-green fleshy leaves and has surprisingly large flowers of glowing deep pink. According to some authorities a form of *P. menziesii*.

- **eriantherus.** Quite dwarf, with large reddish-purple flowers.

- **fruticosus.** Close to *PP. menziesii* and *scouleri*, fairly tall, with tubular purple flowers.

- **glaucus.** Up to 8 in. with compact spikes of purple flowers.

- **heterophyllus.** Rather tall and best grown in the form variously named 'True Blue', 'Blue Spire' or 'Blue Gem'. This is dwarfer and with clear gentian-blue flowers.

- **humilis.** Quite dwarf with hairy leaf stems. The flowers may be blue, or almost white.

- **linarioides.** Mat-forming with one-sided spikes of tubular blue flowers.

- **lyallii.** Neat, dwarf bushes and many clusters of large purple flowers.

- **menziesii.** Another very variable species of which several forms are grown. If there can be said to be a typical form it would be bushy, about 8 in. high and carry violet-blue to purple flowers. Possibly the most desirable form is that named *microphyllus*, which is very compact.

- **newberryi.** Of similar habit to *P. menziesii* but with pink or rose-purple flowers.

PENSTEMON — *continued*

- pinifolius. Low bushes of very finely cut foliage and loose spikes of narrowly tubular flowers, variously described as orange-crimson, scarlet or red. An excellent plant.
- procerus. See *P. confertus.*
- roezlii. The true plant is seldom seen. It should be a low bush with spreading panicles of dark blue or violet flowers. The plant commonly grown under this name, with rose-red flowers may be a form of *P. newberryi* — or not, nothing is certain in the world of penstemons.
- rupicola. One of the best. Almost prostrate, with thick, oval, grey-green leaves and clusters of rose-carmine flowers.
- scouleri. 12 in. bushes with narrow, leathery, toothed leaves and purple flowers. There is also a desirable albino.
- X 'Six Hills Hybrid'. Raised many years ago on a then famous nursery, possibly *P. davidsonii* X *P. eriantherus*, Dwarf, bushy habit and glaucous foliage, with clusters of large lavender-purple flowers.
- teucrioides. Very dwarf and desirable, with bright blue flowers.
- virens. I cannot trace this as a valid name, but the plant which it identifies is mat-forming with short stems carrying deep blue flowers.
- X 'Weald Beacon'. A hybrid of unknown parentage raised by the late A. G. Weeks in his Surrey garden. Similar in habit to *P. roezlii* of gardens but with more blue in the flower colour.

Here follows a list of names recommended by the American Penstemon Society as desirable for rock gardens. *Abielinus*, gentian-blue, *albidus*, white, *angustifolius*, violet-blue, *cardwellii*, light purple to pink, *coelestinus*, blue, rather tall, *coloradensis*, purple-blue, *exilifolius*, white, *hallii*, violet-purple, *linarioides*, lilac-purple, *montanus*, pink to purple, *paysonorium*, blue, *rudicosus*, blue dwarf, *tolmiei*, blue to bright purple, *watsonii*, chocolate-purple. I accept no responsibility for any of these names.

PENTACHONDRA. *Epacridaceae.*

- pumila. A tiny evergreen shrub with crowded branches and small, bronze-green leaves. Cylindrical white flowers are carried singly in the leaf axils and are followed by red berries. For shade and lime-free soil. From New Zealand, Tasmania and Australia.

PENTAPERA. *Ericaceae.* From the Greek *pente*, five and *pera*, a bag. The ovary is five-celled.

- sicula. The only species in the genus, from Sicily, Malta and Syria. A slow growing, dwarf evergreen shrub for lime-free soil. The erect, downy stems carry the heather-like leaves in whorls of four. Terminal clusters of white or soft pink pitcher-shaped flowers in early summer. Best in the alpine house.

279

PEREZIA. *Compositae.* Named for Lorenzo Perez, 16th century Spanish apothecary.

An all American genus of annuals and perennials. For sunny screes or the alpine house, summer flowering.

— linearis. Dense, low tufts of narrow, pointed leaves and short-stemmed, chaffy buds which open into blue daisies.

— megalantha. From Patagonia. Dwarf tufts and cream or lilac florets enclosed in a ruff of tawny bracts. Green, crenate leaves in a rosette.

— pinnatifida. From the Peruvian Andes and almost certainly not now in cultivation. It should be mat-forming, with scarlet and orange flowers on short stems.

PERNETTYA. *Ericaceae.* Named in honour of Antoine Joseph Pernetty (1716-1801), who botanised in S. America with Bougainville in the mid 18th century.

A race of, mostly, tall, evergreen shrubs for lime-free soil. Very few qualify for inclusion here.

— empetrifolia. See *P. pumila.*

— prostrata. Low mounds of arching, woody stems, rather bristly and clothed with narrow, glossy, bright green leaves. Pitcher-shaped white flowers in summer, followed by berries, usually black. From S. America.

— pumila. (P. empetrifolia.) Almost prostrate with wiry stems and tiny leaves. Flowers white and the following fruits may be white or pink.

— tasmanica. Mat-forming with very small, leathery, pointed leaves. Flowers inconspicuous but they are followed by large red berries.

PETROCALLIS. *Cruciferae.* From the Greek *petros*, a rock and *kallis*, beauty.

At one time the few species of Petrocallis were included in the genus DRABA but have now been separated and given generic rank.

— fenestrata. Similar in some ways to *P. pyrenaica* but of looser habit with longer flower stems carrying sprays of white flowers. Sun and gritty soil, spring flowering. Alps of Europe.

— pyrenaica. Alps of Europe. A treasure of the high screes. Neat, mounded cushions of downy shoots dressed in tiny wedge-shaped leaves, toothed at the apex. Very short stems carry innumerable white flowers, tinged lilac and very fragrant, in the spring. A good alpine house plant or for a choice scree or pocket of gritty soil. There is a form with white, yellow-eyed flowers known as *P.p. leucantha.*

PETROCOPTIS. *Caryophyllaceae.* From the Greek *petros*, a rock and *kopto*, to break.

- — **glaucifolia.** (Lychnis lagascae.) Pyrenees. Low tufts of blue-grey leaves and carmine, white-centred flowers on short stems in summer.
- — **pyrenaica.** (Lychnis pyrenaica.) Similar in habit to the preceding but the flowers are soft pink or occasionally white. From the Pyrenees.

PETROCOSMEA. *Gesneriaceae.* From the Greek *petros*, a rock and *kosmos*, ornament.

For north-facing positions or the alpine house, in soil which is well drained and rich in humus. Summer flowering. In leaf formation they much resemble Ramondas, and ask for similar treatment although not quite as hardy.

- — **flaccida.** Rather fleshy, pear-shaped leaves and blue or purple flowers carried in slender footstalks.
- — **kerrii.** Definitely for the alpine house. Rosettes of velvety leaves and white flowers with yellow centres. An exciting but not very easy plant.
- — **nervosa.** Fleshy and hairy leaves in rosettes and blue, two-lipped flowers.
- — **parryorum.** Tufts of fleshy leaves with waved margins and cymes of bell-shaped violet flowers.
- — **wardii.** The small leaves are white-haired and gathered into small rosettes. The flowers may be white, cream or yellow.

PETROMARULA. *Campanulaceae.* A Cretan vernacular name meaning 'rock lettuce'.

- — **pinnata.** This Cretan rock dweller was once included in the genus PHYTEUMA. Large rosettes of pinnate, deeply slashed leaves and tall spikes like a candelabrum of hundreds of small, starry mauve-blue flowers. Rather tall when in flower. Probably best in an alpine house.

PETROPHYTUM. *Rosaceae.* From the Greek *petros*, a rock and *phyton*, a plant.

A small genus of N. American alpines, closely related to SPIRAEA. Happy in rock crevices or sharply drained gritty soil. Hardy, summer flowering.

- — **caespitosum.** (P. elatius.) (Spiraea caespitosa.) Dense tufts of small, silkily hairy leaves and short, dense racemes of tiny white flowers.
- — **cinerascens.** Rather similar to the preceding, but with ash-grey leaves.

PETROPHYTUM — *continued*

- elatius. See *P. caespitosum.*
- hendersonii. Endemic to the Olympic Mountains of the State of Washington. Neat hummocks of dark green, often bronzed leaves and fluffy spires of cream-white flowers on very short stems. A confirmed crevice lover.

PHACELIA. *Hydrophyllaceae.* From the Greek *phakelos*, a bundle, from the bunched flowers of the original species.

A large genus of, mostly, annuals, nearly all from N. America.

- dalesiana. Perennial. Basal rosettes of oblong, long-petioled leaves and 3 in. stems with lax racemes of a few bell-shaped white flowers with purple anthers.
- platycarpa. A short-lived perennial. Flat rosettes like a silver-leaved Morisia and central clusters all summer of almost stemless mauve flowers, streaked with darker colour.
- sericea. The best of them all, but not an easy plant, demanding vigilance and gritty, preferably lime-free soil, and certainly best in an alpine house. A good perennial, it makes dense tufts of silver, deeply lobed leaves and the short stems carry dense terminal racemes of bright purple-blue flowers with protruding stamens.

PHAGNALON. *Compositae.*

- helichrysoides subsp. lanatum. From the Atlas mountains. Carpets of grey leaves and short-stemmed pompons of yellow flowers expanding from bronze involucres. For hot, dry positions. Summer.

PHALANGIUM. See the genus ANTHERICUM.

PHILESIA. *Liliaceae.* From the Greek *phileo*, to love, from the beauty of the flowers of this one Chilean species.

- buxifolia. See *P. magellanica.*
- magellanica. A much branched, evergreen dwarf shrub — it will scramble up an adjacent wall or into any convenient support — with narrow, leathery leaves inturned at the edges. The flowers, a few or solitary appear at the branch tips and are large, tubular in shape and crimson in colour. A very spectacular plant for peaty soil and a north aspect or light shade. Summer flowering.

PHLOX. *Polemoniaceae.* From the Greek *phlox*, a flame.

A large genus, confined in its distribution to the American continent with one exception, a species which is not in cultivation. The family ranges from tall border phloxes, with which we are not concerned, to many dwarf kinds, admirably adapted for rock gardens and, for the choicer ones, the alpine house. They are spring and summer flowering and, unless otherwise stated, easily grown in any good soil and open, sunny positions. For much of the information given below I am indebted to the admirable monograph of the genus Phlox written by Dr. Edgar T. Wherry, and published in 1955.

— aculeata. Probably a subspecies of *P. viridis*. Prickly mounds of compact habit, with several pink to purple flowers on short stems. Fragrant.

— adsurgens. Mats of entangled, creeping stems with glabrous and shining leaves. The rounded flowers, several to each short stem, are usually salmon-pink, but the colour is variable and distinct clones have been selected and given clonal names. It prefers a cool, lightly shaded position and soil rich in humus.

— albomarginata. Compact, caespitose habit and pink or white flowers.

— alyssifolia. Compact plant, up to 4 in. high. The flowers may be purple, pink or, more rarely, white. Slightly fragrant.

— amabilis. Up to 12 in., the petals of the starry, purple or pink flowers are deeply notched.

— amoena. Mats of tangled, woody stems and flower stems up to 8 in. bearing several large flowers. The colour is variable, ranging from pink to purple.

— andicola. Not from the Andes, as the name might suggest, but from the plains of Nebraska and adjacent foothills. Spreading mats connected by rhizomes and 5 in. stems carrying several white, or yellowish, occasionally purple flowers.

— austromontanta. Humps of closely packed growths and pink or lavender, rarely white, slightly fragrant flowers.

— bernardina. See *P. dolicantha*.

— bifida. Prostrate mats and lax stems carrying several flowers of good size which may be lilac, lavender or white. Mildly fragrant.

— 'Blue Ridge'. See *P. stolonifera*.

— borealis. A compact, mounded plant with lilac, lavender or, rarely, white flowers.

— brittonii. See *P. subulata*.

— bryoides. Crowded humps of stems set with closely packed tiny leaves. The short stems carry singly white flowers, sometimes lavender-flushed.

— buckleyi. Spreads by rhizomes into matted colonies. The rather tall stems bear thickish, sword-shaped leaves and the many flowered terminal inflorescences carry bright purple or pink blossoms.

— caespitosa. Mounded cushions of closely packed shoots and lavender to white, fragrant flowers on very short stems.

— 'Camla' (camlaensis.) This is usually listed as a form of *P. subulata* but appears to be a variant of a subspecies of *P. nivalis*. If first appeared in Britain in the garden of the late F. W. Millard, a great plantsman. It carries large salmon-pink flowers boldly on 4 in. stems.

— canadensis. See *P. divaricata*.

— canescens. See *P. hoodii*.

— carolina. An inhabitant mostly of open woodlands. Rather tall, leafy stems carrying heads of many pink to purple flowers. White forms are not unknown.

— caryophylla. From a woody base spring 8 in. stems with narrow leaves and heads of several clove-scented purple flowers.

— X 'Chattahoochee'. Possibly a hybrid between *P. divaricata* and *P. pilosa*. A recent introduction and a splendid plant which hesitated before accepting captivity but is now settling down. On the 12 in. leafy stems are loose heads of rounded deep violet, purple-eyed flowers. It appears to relish peaty soil and light shade.

— cluteana. Spreads by slender rhizomes. 8 in. stems bear compact heads of purple, pale-eyed flowers.

— covillei. Low mounds of narrow, concave leaves and short stems carrying a few lavender to almost white fragrant flowers.

— diffusa. Mounded humps of congested growths and several lilac, pink or white flowers on short stems.

— divaricata. (P. canadensis.) Spreads into clumps by rooting sterile shoots. Twelve in. stems and softly hairy, narrow leaves. Lax heads of many violet-blue flowers. A commonly grown form is *P.d. laphami* with flowers of deeper hue and with an even darker eye.

— dolicantha. (P. bernardina.) 6 to 8 in. stems display heads of long-petalled bright pink flowers. Appreciates light shade.

— douglasii. Of tufted habit with lavender, pink or white flowers on very short stems. It is confused with and has hybridised with other species in gardens.

Under the banner of *P. douglasii* in catalogues will be found such names as 'Boothman's Variety', mauve, 'Crackerjack', crimson-red, 'May Snow' (or, sometimes, 'Snow Queen'), pure white, 'Red Admiral', crimson, 'Rose Cushion', rich pink, and others. These are all excellent, tufted cushion-forming plants, small enough for stone trough and sink gardens and less vigorous and spreading than the innumerable forms of *P. subulata*.

— frondosa. A name occasionally found in catalogues. It is probably a hybrid between *P. subulata* and *P. nivalis*. The old favourite but now almost extinct *P*. 'Vivid' also belongs here.

— gladiformis. Cushion-forming, the very short stems carrying a few lilac or lavender flowers. The foliage of this species emits a curious musky odour, a characteristic rare in the genus.

— 'Gladwyne'. Probably a clone of *P. nivalis*. Cushion-forming with large, beautifully shaped cream-white flowers.

- **griseola.** Tufts of grey-green foliage and solitary, light purple, pink or white fragrant flowers on short stems. A subspecies named *P.g. tumulosa* is too similar to have individual garden merit.

- **X henryae.** A hybrid between *P. nivalis* and *P. bifida*, and intermediate between the parents in appearance.

- **hoodii.** Prostrate tufts and almost stemless flowers, commonly white, but occasionally pale or deep lavender, fragrant. I have seen it growing in profusion on the golf course at Calgary in Canada — and, indeed, once delayed an important match by gathering seeds on the fairway! A rather prickly-leaved form is identified as *P.h.* 'Canescens'.

- **kelsyei.** Rather thick, almost succulent leaves and 4 in. stems carrying several lilac, lavender or white fragrant flowers. The cultivar *P.k.* 'Rosette' is a dwarfer cushion with deep violet-pink flowers.

- **laphamii.** See *P. divaricata.*

- **mesoleuca.** (sometimes mesaleuca.) There is great confusion in gardens between this, *P. nana ensifolia* and *P. triovulata.* I emerge from much investigation not much wiser than when I began, but it appears reasonably certain that the plant grown in English gardens under any of these names is *P. triovulata.*

- **X 'Millstream'.** A new hybrid recently introduced from America. Probably a hybrid between *P. amoena* and *P. stolonifera.* Fine large rich pink flowers with a white eye ring and a central star of red on 6 in. stems.

- **missoulensis.** This has been confused with, and is similar to both *P. douglasii* and *P. caespitosa* but has been permitted to retain specific rank. Its good flowers are bright lavender or clear pink. As with almost all phloxes there is considerable variation in the flower colour.

- **muscoides.** This is but another subspecies of *P. hoodii*, with white, gently fragrant flowers.

- **nana ensifolia.** See *P. triovulata.*

- **nivalis.** Although the flowers of this cushion-forming species are described as being typically purple or pink or occasionally white, the clone in gardens invariably carries pure white flowers.

- **'Pink Ridge'.** See *P. stolonifera.*

- **procumbens.** See *P. stolonifera.*

- **reptans.** See *P. stolonifera.*

- **setacea.** See *P. subulata.*

- **stolonifera.** (P. reptans and P. procumbens of gardens.) Mats of leafy, semi-procumbent stems and erect, 6 to 8 in. stems carrying lax inflorescences of flowers. It is a variable plant, the colour ranging from lavender through violet to purple. Several named forms or clones exist in gardens, of which two of the best are 'Blue Ridge' and 'Pink Ridge' and there is also a fine albino named *P.s.* 'Ariane'.

- **subulata.** (P. setacea.) The moss phloxes are highly valued rock garden plants. It would not be possible to describe a recognisable fixed species in such a variable plant, of which a host of named varieties are cultivated, nor is it either feasible or desirable to enumerate a lengthy list of names in this Manual. Consult any alpine plant catalogue, or our price list and you will be able to choose from a dozen or more selected and named forms. *P. brittonii*, with white flowers and also its pink-flowered form, sometimes offered in catalogues, are forms of *P. subulata*.

— triovulata. Without being certain that I am correct in doing so I describe under this name the plant which has been variously identified in British gardens as *P. mesoleuca*, *P. mesaleuca* and *P. nana ensifolia* It is not an easily pleased plant and should be accorded alpine house treatment. It spreads by underground roots and is best accommodated in wide, not very deep pans, in light, sandy soil. From the running roots rise intermittently thin stems with a few narrow, hairy grey leaves and loose cymes of large, rounded flowers of great beauty and clear pink colour. It is an exciting but aggravating plant with more failures recorded than successes.

— tumulosa. See *P. griseola*.
— 'Vivid'. See *P. frondosa*.

This by no means completes the list of known Phlox species and subspecies. Even some of those included above may not be available, but it gives a good cross section of this invaluable genus.

PHUOPSIS. (Crucianella.) From Phu, *Valeriana phu*, and *opsis*, resembling. An allusion to the similarity between the plants.

— stylosa. The only species. Not really an alpine plant, but often grown as a carpeter on rock gardens. Mats of tiny slender green leaves and heads of small pink flowers in summer. The plant exhales a curious, musky scent, especially after rain. From the Caucasus.

PHYLLACHNE. *Stylidiaceae.*

A small genus of cushion-forming alpine plants from Tasmania, New Zealand and southern S. America. Rare in cultivation and not very easily grown, definitely for alpine house culture in gritty soil. The few likely to be occasionally encountered in gardens are *P. colensoi*, *P. clavigera* and *P. rubra*. They all grow as mats of congested rosettes, adorned by stemless white flowers.

PHYLLIOPSIS. *Ericaceae.*

— hillieri 'Pinnochio'. This extremely interesting bigeneric hybrid between *Kalmiopsis leachiana* and *Phyllodoce breweri* originated on Messrs. Hillier's nursery and is slowly creeping into cultivation. It is intermediate between the parents in appearance and will surely prove a highly valued addition to dwarf shrubs for the peat garden. Spring flowering.

PHYLLODOCE. *Ericaceae.* Named for a sea-nymph, in accordance with the custom of naming genera of *Ericaceae* after nymphs and goddesses initiated by Linnaeus.

A genus of hardy, dwarf, evergreen, heath-like plants for lime-free soil and cool positions or partial shade. Widely distributed in the northern hemisphere. They are very desirable peat-garden plants.

- aleutica. From N. E. Asia and Alaska. Eight in. erect stems forming dense mats. Rather pale green, tiny leaves and terminal heads of bell-shaped chartreuse-green flowers.
- X alpina. (P. hybrida.) From Japan and a hybrid between *P. nipponica* and *P. aleutica.* Similar in habit to the preceding, but the pendant, bell-shaped flowers are pink.
- amabilis. See *P. nipponica.*
- breweri. From N. America. Rather lax 10 to 12 in. stems and sub-erect terminal racemes of pink, open and not bell-shaped as in other species.
- caerulea. Widely distributed in alpine-Arctic regions and also a rare British native. Rather lax 10 in. stems and loose terminal clusters of light or dark purple urn-shaped flowers.
- empetriformis. N. American. Spreading mats of 6 in. stems and terminal clusters of pale or deeper pink, sometimes brownish-pink, flowers.
- glanduliflora. N. American. Straggly, erect 8 in. stems and chartreuse-green, slightly fragrant bell-shaped flowers.
- hybrida. See *P.X. alpina.*
- X intermedia. A variable set of hybrids between *P. empetriformis* and *P. glanduliflora.* At least two selections have been named, *drummondii*, with dark purple flowers, and 'Fred Stoker', pale purple.
- nipponica. (P. amabilis.) Japanese. A compact dwarf with erect, 8 in. stems and terminal nodding bells which may be white or soft pink. The plant often grown as *P. tsugaefolia* appears to be a slightly larger version of this species.
- tsugaefolia. See *P. nipponica.*

PHYLLOTHAMNUS. *Ericaceae.*

- erectus. An interesting and beautiful bi-generic hybrid between *Phyllodoce empetriformis* and *Rhodothamnus chamaecistus*, raised on a Scottish nursery about the middle of last century. Erect stems, up to 16 in. crowded with dark green, narrow, leathery leaves and terminal umbels in April and May of funnel-shaped rose-pink flowers. For lime-free soil.

PHYSARIA. *Cruciferae.*

A race of not very distinguished, mostly if not all N. American crucifers. The yellow flowers vary in size and attraction but they are often followed by inflated and spectacular bladder-like seed pods, sometimes displayed over rosettes of silver foliage. The species *PP. acutifolia, condensata, didymocarpa* and *floribunda* are occasionally in cultivation and will appreciate open, sunny positions.

PHYSOPLEXIS. *Campanulaceae.* See PHYTEUMA *comosum.*

PHYTEUMA. *Campanulaceae.* The ancient Greek name used by Dioscorides for another plant.

A race of European alpine and sub-alpine plants, from which I note with regret that our old friend *P. comosum* has been removed and given generic rank as PHYSOPLEXIS *comosa.* Consistently flouting authority I retain the name to which we have become so well accustomed. Those described are all sun lovers, for good, well drained soil and are spring and summer flowering.

- balbisii. See *P. cordatum.*
- betonicifolium. Rather tall, the oval heads of pale blue or lilac flowers being carried on stems up to 2 ft. high.
- carestiae. See *P. humile.*
- charmelii. Tufts of basal leaves, some heart-shaped, others long and pointed. Blue flowers on 8 in. stems in rounded heads.
- comosum. (Physoplexis comosa.) An almost legendary species from limestone crevices in the E. and S.E. Alps. For the alpine house or tight crannies outside. Tight tufts of kidney-shaped basal leaves, stem leaves lance-shaped. Heads of claw-shaped long-tubed flowers on short stems. The colour varies from deep to pale blue. It is aptly described by a writer in the Bulletin of the Alpine Garden Society as a plant which contrives to be both distinctly odd and remarkably beautiful.
- confusum. Very similar in appearance, and by some authorities considered synonymous with *P. globulariifolium.*
- cordatum. (P. balbisii.) Heart-shaped leaves and slender 8 in. stems and pale blue flowers in compact oval heads.
- globulariifolium. (P. pauciflorum.) Tufts of lance-shaped, often lightly toothed leaves and short stems bearing heads of violet-blue flowers. The plant grown as *P. pedemontanum* is now considered synonymous with this species.
- halleri. See *P. ovatum.*

- **hedraianthifolium.** Distinct long, narrow, toothed leaves, each tooth ending in a slender point. Six in. stems carry globular heads of blue flowers.
- **hemisphaericum.** Low, dense tufts of very narrow leaves and short stems carrying flattened globular heads of blue flowers.
- **humile. (P. carestiae.)** Small and tufted with narrow leaves and short stems displaying rather squat heads of purple-blue flowers.
- **michelii.** Basal leaves oval-triangular and sharply pointed. Tall stems carrying oval heads of lilac-blue flowers.
- **orbiculare.** Rounded basal leaves in a rosette and 12 to 16 in. stems bearing globular heads of blue flowers.
- **ovatum. (P. halleri.)** A robust species, maybe too tall for most rock gardens, but, like others of the taller species, excellent for an alpine meadow. Heart-shaped, ragged-edged leaves and a rather cylindrical head of purple-blue flowers.
- **pauciflorum.** See *P. globulariifolium.*
- **pedemontanum.** See *P. globulariifolium.*
- **scheuchzeri.** Flattened, spherical heads of blue flowers on 12 to 16 in. stems.
- **sieberi.** Tufts of lance-shaped leaves and short stems carrying globular heads of blue flowers.
- **spicatum.** An occasional British native and rather tall for most rock gardens. The stems can attain 30 in. and the flowers, in cylindrical heads may be greenish-white, yellowish, or pale or deep blue.
- **tenerum.** The round-headed Rampion of British and European chalk grasslands. Violet-blue flowers in globose heads.
- **vagneri.** Fairly short stems and rounded heads of violet-blue flowers.

PICRORHIZA. *Scrophulariaceae.* From the Greek *pikros*, bitter. and *rhiza*, a root.

- **kurrooa.** A not very distinguished herb from Kashmir. Leaves spoon-shaped and toothed, rather leathery. Short spikes of white or pale blue flowers in summer.

PICROTHAMNUS. See ARTEMISIA *spinescens.*

PIERIS nana. See ARCTERICA *nana.*

PIMELEA. *Thymelaeaceae.* From the Greek *pimele*, fat, from its richness in oil.

PIMELEA — *continued*

A genus of Australasian herbs and evergreen shrubs, few of which qualify for the rock garden, or are available. And many are too tender to be grown unprotected in the open. Some of the dwarf New Zealand species would be tempting. Probably happiest in lime-free soil, spring and summer flowering.

— **coarctata.** See *P. prostrata.*
— **prostrata.** The plant commonly grown as *P. coarctata* is probably a congested form of this species. It makes completely flat mats of tangled stems with tiny grey leaves. Waxy-white flowers are followed by fleshy white fruits. It is apt to suffer in severe winters and relishes light protection. It also appears to suffer occasionally from the same mysterious 'die-back' which afflicts some of the daphnes, to which it is related. Other species which would be of interest in the alpine house, if obtainable, are *P. buxifolia, P. drupacea, P. humilis, P. nivea* and *P. physodes.*

PINELLIA. *Araceae.* Named in honour of Giovanni Vincenzo Pinelli (1535-1601), an Italian botanist.

— **ternata.** (P. tuberifera.) From tiny tubers spring small, segmented leaves and typical but small green aroid flowers on short stems. For cool soil and light shade.
— **tuberifera.** See *P. ternata.*

PINGUICULA. *Lentibulariaceae.* From the Latin *pinguis,* fat, from the greasy appearance of the leaves of these insectivorous plants.

There are some 40 species of pinguicula widely distributed in the Northern Hemisphere, with a few in the Andes, extending as far as the Antarctic. Many of them are for greenhouse culture, but a few hardy species find much favour among alpine gardeners. They demand boggy conditions. May-June flowering. They over-winter as small, dormant buds.

— **alpina.** Europe, including Britain. Clusters of thick, sticky, yellow-brown leaves and short stems carrying singly yellow-throated white flowers.

— **grandiflora.** S.W. Europe and Ireland. Rosettes of wide, fleshy, glutinous leaves and 4 in. stems displaying large, open-mouthed flowers of rich violet-blue.

— **longifolia.** From the French and Spanish Pyrenees. Rosettes of large, rather flaccid, wavy-edged yellow-green leaves and long-spurred lilac-purple flowers with a white zone and yellow markings on the wide lower lip. It appreciates some winter protection.

290

PINGUICULA — *continued*

- **lusitanica.** An exception to the family rule in that it winters as a rosette of yellowish, sometimes purple-tinted leaves. The pale lilac flowers have yellow throats. From France, Spain, Portugal and Britain.

- **vulgaris.** Europe, including Britain. Oblong, succulent leaves with incurved margins. The short-stemmed flowers are violet in colour with a wide lower lip which bears a broad white patch in the throat.

PLAGIORHEGMA. See the genus JEFFERSONIA.

PLANTAGO. *Plantaginaceae.* The Latin name for these plants. Generally speaking not a family of particular beauty with the exception of a few species with rosettes of silver and grey-haired leaves.

- **argentea.** (P. serpentinicola.) Central Europe. Tufts of long, narrow leaves, densely felted with long, closely adpressed silvery hairs. As is common in the genus, the flowers have no value. For gritty soil and full sun.

- **cynops.** See *P. sempervirens.*

- **lanceolata.** Widely distributed in Europe. A not very exciting species but the long, narrow, sometimes lightly tooth-edged leaves are felted with grey hairs.

- **major.** The ubiquitous Plantain which we endeavour to eliminate from our gardens, but it has one or two amusing forms. The red-leaved Plantain makes lusty rosettes of beetroot-red leaves and is a coarse but colourful plant. The Rose Plantain is probably a form of *P. media*, and, instead of flowers bears a neat rosette of small green leaves in an array as orderly as a Victorian posy. There are two Rose Plantains, the other is a coarser plant and may be a mutant of *P. major.* It, too, displays a rosette of green leaves instead of flowers, but it is not so neat or amusing.

- **monosperma.** From the Pyrenees and another quite desirable species with long, flat leaves coated with fine silver hairs.

- **nivalis.** One of the best. Its neat rosettes of narrow leaves are thickly felted with a pelt of fine silver hairs.

- **sempervirens.** (P. cynops.) Europe, and one which forsakes the traditional rosette formation and makes low, twiggy bushes. It may not be beautiful but it is quaint and is enjoyed by those who appreciate the unusual.

- **serpentinicola.** See *P. argentea.*

PLATYCODON. *Campanulaceae.* From the Greek *platys*, broad and *kodon*, a bell.

A monotypic genus, native to China and Japan. Of the one species there are several cultivated and named forms. Summer flowering, for open, sunny positions, in any good soil.

— grandiflorum. Herbaceous, with stout, deeply-delving roots from which rise 12 in. stems. The lower leaves are toothed and whorled, the upper ones scattered. The flowers may be solitary or in few-flowered clusters. The buds are balloon-shaped and expand into large purple-blue flowers. Of the named forms the following are desirable. 'Apoyama', a dwarf; 'Mariesii', with large, soft blue flowers; 'Mother of Pearl' and 'Roseum', each with soft pink blossoms.

PLEIONE. *Orchidaceae.* Named for *Pleione*, the mother of the seven Pleiades.

A genus of near hardy Asian orchids which have become prominent during the past two decades. One or two of them have been successfully grown in the open but it is as cold greenhouse or alpine house plants that they excel. There have been many recipes for their cultivation but experience is proving that they can be grown to perfection in a good, humus-rich compost containing plenty of fine grit and that fussy composts and the use of sphagnum moss are quite unnecessary. It is important that they should be kept dry — but never parched — during their dormant stages. Their naming has become confused, especially by the too numerous variants of such species as *P. formosana*. It is now known that *PP. formosana, limprichtii, pricei, pogonioides, henryi* and *delavayi* must all be placed under the variable *P. bulbocodioides*, but, for ease of reference, I retain below the names by which they have now become so well known in gardens. With one or two exceptions they are spring flowering.

— bulbocodioides. See introduction above.
— delavayi. From Yunnan. A species near to *P. yunnanensis.* The pseudo-bulbs are globose and the leaves appear after the flowers. The flowers are bright rose-purple in colour with red-brown markings on the lips and the wide centre lobe is decorated with five crested 'keels'.
— formosana. Large green pseudo-bulbs and foliage which becomes almost aspidistra-like at maturity. It is infinitely variable and there are many named clones with variously coloured and variously marked flowers, including some fine albinos with handsome pure white flowers. I make no attempt to sort out the taxonomic confusion. They are all good and easily grown and very rewarding.
— forrestii. One of the rarest and best. It came from Yunnan many years ago and was almost lost to cultivation but has, fortunately, re-appeared and is now occasionally, but expensively, available.

292

The pseudo-bulbs are pear-shaped and the leaves develop after the flowers. The bright orange-yellow flowers are marked with brown on the lip, which is fringed and has seven wavy 'keels' down the centre.

— **henryi.** See *P. pogonioides.*

— **hookeriana.** From the Himalaya. Flask-shaped pseudo-bulbs. The, usually, solitary leaf appears after the flowers. The flowers are rose-purple with a pale — sometimes white — lip. There are some red-brown markings and from five to seven yellow crested 'keels'.

— **humilis.** From Nepal. Flagon-shaped pseudo-bulbs and lanceolate leaves which appear after flowering. The large flowers are almost white but there is a faint infusion of pink. The lip is marked with brown-purple stripes and blotches and is heavily fringed. A distinct form, collected by Kingdon Ward in Burma received an Award of Merit in 1971 under the name *P.h.* 'Frank Kingdon Ward'. It has long, conical pseudo-bulbs and the flowers are heavily suffused with pale mauve, the lip being decorated by numerous crimson spots between the 'keels'. Both this and the type form tufts of hair-like protuberances at the tip of the new pseudo-bulbs. These are embryonic pseudo-bulbs from which the plant can be increased.

— **lagenaria.** Rather flattened, green pseudo-bulbs are mottled with brown and have a solitary green leaf after flowering. The flowers are rose-lilac, the lip spotted with crimson on a white ground. There are five fringed 'keels'. It comes from the Khasia hills and is not one of the hardiest.

— **limprichtii.** One of the showiest and easiest, also one of the hardiest and will succeed in the open in a cool but protected position - a good peatbed plant. From Western China. Green, flask-shaped, pseudo-bulbs and dark green leaves after the flowers. Flowers brilliant red-purple, carried on pink stems. The white throat is heavily freckled with crimson and the lip has a white fringe.

— **maculata.** From Khasia and Sikkim, and not one of the hardiest species. The green, brown-mottled pseudo-bulbs are flattened on one side. The white flowers have a rounded lip, blotched with deep purple. There is a variety named 'Virginea' which has entirely white flowers with a yellow throat.

— **pogonioides.** (henryi.) From China. The pseudo-bulbs are narrowly oval in shape and carry a single leaf at the same time as the flowers, which are richly magenta-rose with deeper markings on the heavily 'keeled' lip. The dry pseudo-bulbs are said to be used medicinally by the Chinese as a drug called *Pen mu.*

— **praecox.** From N. India and Burma and one of the earliest to flower. The flattened pseudo-bulb is curiously 'warted', with a prominent central cone. The rather folded leaves appear when the flowers have faded. The flowers are rose-purple in colour, with a paler, sometimes almost white lip and several crested 'keels'.

— **pricei.** From Formosa. Dark, broadly flask-shaped pseudo-bulbs. It is a variable plant, the usual colour being purple, the lip marked with brown and heavily fringed. The 'keels' on the lip are yellow.

— X 'Versailles'. A hybrid between two subspecies of *P. bulbocodioides*, *P. formosana* and *P. limprichtii*. The plant was raised by the late Dr. Morel and is intermediate between the parents in appearance. Lately other, similar crosses have been made, differing in slight degree from the original hybrid.

— yunnanensis. From China, and first cultivated here in 1906, and exhibited then by Messrs. Sutton of Reading. Rather late-flowering. The pseudo-bulb is coloured deep olive-green and rather flat. The bright rose-red flower has a paler lip, blotched with dark purple on the heavily fringed front lobe and in the throat of the flower.

PLUMBAGO larpentae. See CERATOSTIGMA *plumbaginoides*.

PODOPHYLLUM diphyllum. See JEFFERSONIA *diphylla*.

POLEMONIUM. *Polemoniaceae Polemonion* was a name used by Dioscorides for a medicinal plant.

A small genus of mostly perennial herbs, natives of North and Central America, Asia and Europe. Few of them are cultivated and I list only those commonly or occasionally encountered in gardens. They are summer and late summer flowering, and succeed in any good, well-drained soil.

— brandegeei. From N. America, where it grows on shady volcanic cliffs. Hairy and sticky stems up to 6 in. with narrow leaflets. Terminal clusters of crowded straw-yellow flowers. All parts of the plant exude a vaguely unpleasant smell.

— caeruleum. Common in the Northern Hemisphere, including occasionally Britain. Really too tall for rock gardens but a good front-of-the-border plant. Commonly known as Jacob's Ladder it has stems up to 20 in. high with leaves cut into many leaflets. Terminal and axillary cymes of blue, or rarely white flowers.

— campanulatum. A species from the Arctic, said to have good blue flowers, but I have not seen it.

— carneum. N. American, and again rather too tall, especially for small rock gardens. Tall stems and much almost ferny foliage and carillons of flesh-coloured to cream bells. The variety 'Luteum' has larger flowers of rich yellow.

— confertum. From N. America and one of the most desirable. From almost woody stems spring tufts of sticky leaves cut into the finest leaflets. On short stems just above the pretty foliage are dense heads of saucer-shaped flowers of clear blue. It likes a sunny, but not arid situation.

— **eximeum.** From the high peaks of N. American mountains, and there named Sky Pilot. Tufts of sticky leaves composed of small, crowded leaflets which seem to be whorled. On short stems are carried crowded, rounded heads of flowers which may be blue or purple, often with white or yellowish tubes. The following names cover plants which are really in the *eximeum* group and are often regarded as variants or forms of that species. *P. chartaceum, P. elegans,* and *P. viscosum.*

— **mellitum.** Probably a form of *P. confertum* but slightly taller and with flowers of paler blue. Both plants emit a strong and rather 'beery' odour.

— **pulcherrimum.** N. American and a lusty, vigorous beauty, probably best in the front of a flower border where its blue, white or yellow throated flowers on 20 in. stems may receive their due meed of admiration.

POLYGALA. *Polygalaceae.* The Latin name, derived from the Greek word *polygalon,* from *polys,* much, and *gala,* milk. These plants were supposed to aid the secretion of milk, hence the common name Milkwort for the British *P. vulgaris.*

A very large genus of annual and perennial herbs, sub-shrubs and shrubs of world-wide distribution. The few species appropriate to this Manual are briefly described below.

— **alpestris.** This, and its subspecies *croatica* are desirable wee shrubs from Europe, but dubiously in cultivation. *Flora Europaea* tells us that the flowers are blue or white, but they are elsewhere described as red and blue?

— **boissieri.** From Spain. Leafy stems up to 12 in. and rose-pink flowers.

— **calcarea.** European, including occasionally in Britain. Prostrate, dark-leaved stems and lax racemes of blue flowers. A lime lover. The clone known as 'Bulley's Variety' has extra large flowers of deep, clear blue.

— **chamaebuxus.** From the mountains of Europe. Woody, 5 in. stems with hard, box-like leaves and short axillary racemes of yellow and cream flowers. It is even more spectacular in the form 'Grandiflora', which has carmine and yellow flowers and is sometimes seen under the names *rhodoptera* or 'Purpurea'. It appreciates peaty soil and light shade.

— **comosa.** From Spain and elsewhere in Europe. Rather lax stems adorned by plumes of crimson-purple flowers.

— **croatica.** See *P. alpestris.*

- lutea. From N. America. Stems to 8 in. rather spreading and rather globose, dense spikes of orange-yellow flowers.

- major. From Greece and also found in Italy and Austria. Rather tall, erect stems carrying loose spikes of clear rose-flowers. For a warm and sunny position.

- microphylla. By some botanists this is given generic rank as BRACHYTROPIS *microphylla*. It comes from Southern Portugal and is a gem which has not yet taken kindly to cultivation. Low bushlets of hard, woody stems, smothered in spring with myriads of gentian-blue flowers. For the alpine house or a sunny, rather spartan scree.

- nicaeensis. Mediterranean regions. Rather lax stems and pink, blue or white flowers. A form endemic to Corsica exists with flowers of sugar-icing pink.

- paucifolia. From N. America. Rather weak, trailing stems with large, rose-purple and white flowers clustered in the leaf axils. A lovely plant but temperamental. Best tried in lime-free soil and perhaps light shade.

- rhodoptera. See *P. chamaebuxus.*

- vayredae. From Spain, and like a diminished *P. chamaebuxus* with much narrower leaves, forming low mats and bearing flowers of reddish-purple with a yellow keel.

- vulgaris. This is our British Milkwort, and seldom cultivated, although it is perennial and not unattractive, the lowly stems bearing pretty blue, pink or almost white flowers.

POLYGONATUM. *Liliaceae.* From the Greek *polys*, many, and *gony*, the knee-joint, in allusion to the many joints of the rhizomes.

A small genus, including the well-known Solomon's Seal, widely distributed over the Northern Hemisphere. The few suitable for rock gardens or peat beds are described below. They appreciate soil rich in humus and light shade and are spring and summer flowering

- curvifolium. A Solomon's Seal from Nepal with pink flowers.

- falcatum. From Japan and Korea. Rhizomatous roots and ascending stems having narrow, sessile leaves. In the leaf axils appear several narrowly tubular, pendant flowers of greenish-white. Usually about 8 to 12 in.

- hookeri. From the Himalaya. Prostrate, producing tufts of crowded pointed leaves and many almost stemless, starry pink flowers with petals of good substance. Shade and humus-rich soil

- multiflorum. The common Solomon's Seal, native to Europe

(including Britain) and N. Asia. A beloved plant but too large for rock gardens.

— nanum. This name exists but I doubt if it has any authority or is more than a dwarf form of the Solomon's Seal.

— odoratum. (P. officinale.) Native in limestone woodlands. Much dwarfer than *P. multiflorum* and with fewer, scented flowers on the slightly arching stems.

— officinale. See *P. odoratum.*

— verticillatum. A rare native, and rather too tall for this Manual. The whorled leaves and greenish flowers are carried on stems up to 3¼ ft. tall.

POLYGONUM. *Polygonaceae.* From the Greek *polys*, many, and either *gonos*, offspring or seed, in allusion to the many seeds, or *gony*, knee-joint, an allusion to the swollen joints of the stems.

A large genus of annual and perennial herbs, rarely sub-shrubs, widely distributed throughout the temperate regions. Many are herbaceous border plants, and some are very definitely invasive. The few rock garden species are described below and are all easily grown in sun and any good soil.

— affine. (P. brunonis.) From the Himalaya, and usually regarded as a front-of-the-border plant, but dwarf enough for fairly large rock gardens. Mat-forming, with ascending 12 in. stems carrying spikes of red flowers. The foliage takes good bronze-red tints in winter. There are at least two good forms with more richly coloured flowers, 'Darjeeling Red' and 'Lowndes's Variety'.

— bistortoides. Related to and similar to *P. viviparum*, from N. America and usually lacking the bulbils characteristic on the stems of that species.

— brunonis. See *P. affine.*

— capitatum. From Northern India and not reliably hardy, but frequently grown for the sake of its attractive foliage. Where it flourishes it can become invasive. Trailing stems set with deep green, pointed leaves, each one conspicuously decorated with a plum-coloured, V-shaped mark. The short stems carry small, rounded heads of pink flowers.

— emodii. From Bhutan and similar to, but less hardy than *P. affine.* The leaves are narrower and the red flowers borne on more slender spikes.

— equisetiforme. From Mediterranean regions. Corsica in particular, and really too tall, but so unusual and interesting that I include it. The thin, wiry stems reach 2ft. in height and along their length bear myriads of small, white, honey-scented flowers. Never spectacular but always attracts favourable attention.

— **forrestii.** Collected several times in Yunnan but never successfully introduced. It is spoken of as beautiful and we can only long for a successful introduction.

— **paronychia.** From California and described as forming mats of dark green foliage. It might be good but I do not know the colour of its flowers.

— **tenuicaule.** From Japan and very small with slowly spreading rhizomes and small leaves. The white flowers are carried in cylindrical racemes on 4 in. stems in very early spring.

— **vaccinifolium.** From the Himalaya and an invaluable late-flowering plant. Woody stems form trailing mats and end in slender racemes of heather-pink flowers in late summer and autumn, when the small, pointed, leathery leaves take on rich autumn tints. Splendid in a wall or tumbling over a rock face.

— **viviparum.** The Arctic, and N. Europe, including Britain. Dwarf and not spectacular, but interesting because of its habit of carrying small purple bulbils among the pink or white flowers on the slender racemes.

POTENTILLA. *Rosaceae.* From the Latin *potens*, because of the reputed medicinal properties of some of these plants.

A very large genus of herbaceous plants and shrubs widely distributed throughout the Northern Hemisphere. Generally speaking they are sun-loving and summer-flowering and succeed in any good, well drained soil. Any exceptions will be noted. It is an important family, containing many good rock garden plants but there are some which are frankly weedy, and others unlikely to be obtainable and these have been omitted from the following already rather lengthy list. Others come on the border-line between rock garden and border plants and have been omitted for this reason.

— **alba.** From Central and Southern Europe. An invaluable ground-cover plant. Mats of leaves which are divided into sessile leaflets, silver-haired on the undersides. Heads of several large, white, yellow-eyed flowers on short stems.

— **alchemilloides.** Pyrenees and Northern Italy. Low tufts of palmate leaves divided into several leaflets, silvery beneath and compact corymbs of many white flowers. Rather late flowering.

— **alpestris.** See *P. crantzii.*

— **ambigua.** See *P. cuneata.*

— **anserina.** One might easily be tempted by the handsome silvered leaves of our wild Silverweed to transplant it into the garden, but it is a weed which is difficult to eradicate, so leave it by the roadside.

— apennina. The leaflets are silver-haired and the 8 in. stems carry white flowers. Not exciting, but worth growing. From the Balkans and the Apennines.

— argentea. Europe, Asia Minor and Siberia. Hairy stems and palmate foliage with many leaflets green above and silver beneath. Rather tall stems bear terminal cymes of sulphur-yellow flowers.

— argyrocoma. From California and would be treasured, if obtainable, for its foliage, composed of adpressed silver leaflets. Dense cymes of white flowers on short stems.

— aurea. European Alps, including Pyrenees. Spreading mats of green leaves with many leaflets and loose clusters, on procumbent stems, of rich yellow flowers. There is a form with semi-double flowers and another, *P.a. chrysocraspeda*, with flowers of rich orange-yellow.

— biflora. This beautiful species from the Karakoram I include with some hesitation for it is very doubtully in cultivation but it is a lovely cushion plant with massed pinnate leaves and sheets of bright yellow flowers. A form or subspecies, *P.b. inglesii* comes from Nepal and is similar but with paler-yellow blossoms.

— brauniana. (P. dubia.) European Alps. Prostrate tufts of leaves divided into wedge-shaped leaflets and flowers, usually solitary, of good size and good yellow colour.

— caulescens. From S. Europe. Tufts of five-cleft silver leaves and semi-trailing stems each carrying a few white flowers.

— chrysocraspeda. See *P. aurea.*

— cineria. (P. tommasiniana.) From the European Alps. Neat mats and tufts of grey, softly hairy leaves and clusters of clear yellow flowers.

— clusiana. From the Eastern Alps. Mats of leaves with several leaflets, silky-haired on the margins and undersides. Few-flowered cymes on short stems of large white flowers.

— comarum. This has already been described as COMARUM *palustre*, q.v., but is probably more correctly included in Potentilla.

— coriandrifolia. (P. meifolia.) From the Himalaya. Mats of glabrous, deeply cut leaves and short-stemmed white flowers, the petals crimson-blotched at the base. It has been cultivated but has not proved very easy to please. Probably best in the alpine house.

— corsica. See *P. rupestris.*

— crantzii. (P. alpestris.) From Arctic areas of Europe, Asia and N. America. Tufts of stalked, palmate leaves cut into leaflets, green on both sides, and loose clusters of yellow flowers, often orange-blotched at the petal base.

— crassinervia. Corsica and Sardinia. Varies in height from 4 to 12 ins. Palmate leaves, with thick, softly hairy leaflets and many-flowered cymes of white flowers. Rather late flowering.

— cuneata. (P. ambigua.) From the Himalaya. Low tufts of rather thick leaves divided into wedge-shaped leaflets, green above, glaucous beneath. Large yellow flowers solitary on 4 in. stems in mid to late summer.

— **curviseta.** From the Himalaya. Similar in habit to *P. eriocarpa* with an abundance of short-stemmed rich yellow flowers.

— **deorum.** From Greece. In habit it resembles *P. nitida* but with less silvery leaves and white flowers.

— **diversifolia.** From N. America. The basal leaves are silky, and on fairly tall stems appear pale yellow flowers.

— **dubia.** See *P. brauniana.*

— **eriocarpa.** From the Himalaya. Spreading mats of grey-green leaves with many very short-stemmed yellow flowers all summer. A fine carpeter for gritty soil.

— **fragiformis.** The plant often grown under this name in gardens is *P. megalantha*, q.v., I doubt if the true *P. fragiformis* is in cultivation.

— **frigida.** From the European Alps and very similar to *P. brauniana* but twice the height when in flower.

— **fruticosa.** In its many forms this species is widely distributed over the Northern Hemisphere, including Britain. In gardens it is represented by a host of selections, clones and hybrids which it would be tedious to enumerate and describe here. They may be found in many catalogues, including our annual price list, from which a selection can be made. The dwarfer kinds are eminently suitable for rock gardens and they associate well with such dwarf shrubs as the hardy heathers. The flowering season is prolonged and they should be regarded as indispensable garden plants, flourishing in sun or light shade and in almost any soil. Recent introductions of forms with pink and red flowers are particularly desirable but these should be given light shade as the rich colour is apt to fade quickly in full sunlight.

— **glaucophylla.** A dwarf N. American species with shining, blue-green leaves and soft yellow flowers.

— **grandiflora.** A rather late-flowering European species which can be dwarf but occasionally extends its flower stems to 16 in. Tufts of hairy, toothed leaves and erect, few-flowered cymes of yellow flowers.

— **hyparctica.** From Arctic areas of Europe and N. America. Hummocks of grey, softly hairy leaves and large yellow flowers on short stems. Small and neat enough for trough and sink gardens.

— **inglesii.** See *P. biflora.*

— **lanata.** See *P. nivalis.*

— **megalantha.** (P. fragiformis of gardens.) From Japan. Tufts of large palmate, softly hairy grey-green leaves and short stems carrying very large rich yellow flowers.

— **meifolia.** See *P. coriandrifolia.*

- montana. Related, and similar to, *P. alba*, from S.W. Europe. With several quite large white flowers to each semi-procumbent stem.
- multifida. Widely distributed, being found in Europe, Russia, Tibet and Korea. The deeply cut leaflets are silky-haired beneath. The 8 in. stems carry terminal corymbs of small yellow flowers.
- nevadensis. From Spain. Prostrate stems with pretty leaves, silvery beneath and axillary terminal yellow flowers.
- nitida. One of the glories of high screes in the European Alps. Flat mats of silver foliage and almost stemless pink flowers. *P.n.* 'Rubra' is a selected form with more richly coloured flowers and *P.n.* 'Lissadell' is particularly richly coloured. Forms also exist with white, or almost white flowers. Grow in a sunny scree and it flowers more freely on a starvation diet.
- nivalis. (P. lanata.) From S. France and Spain and varies in height from 4 to 12 in. Like a dwarfer *P. valderia*, stems and leaves silkily-haired and loose clusters of white flowers.
- nivea. Europe. A dwarf, with three-lobed silky-white leaves and large yellow flowers, solitary or in small clusters. It is a confirmed lime-lover.
- ochroleuca. A neat form of *P. fruticosa* with pale yellow flowers.
- palustris. See COMARUM *palustre*.
- pyrenaica. A species from the Pyrenees, very near to *P. aurea*.
- recta. S. Europe, N. Africa and Siberia. It can grow to 16 in. and is more properly a plant for the front of a border. The erect, leafy stems carry compact terminal corymbs of yellow flowers. It is most commonly grown in the form *P.r.* 'Warrenii' (often wrongly spelled 'Warrensii') with rich golden flowers.
- reptans. A British native and a weed, but there is a form which has double yellow flowers on the procumbent stems and is worth growing.
- X 'Roxana'. A garden hybrid and rather tall, but handsome, with loose clusters of rose-red, dark-centred flowers all summer.
- rupestris. (P. corsica.) A rare British native and a trifle weedy, but desirable in the form 'Pygmaea' from Corsica and Sardinia, which carries its clusters of white flowers on short, erect stems.
- salesoviana. From Tibet, and a dwarf shrub. Dark green, dissected leaves, silvery beneath, and cymes of large white flowers.
- salesovii, or salesowii. See *P. salesoviana*.
- saxifraga. European Alps. Low tufts of leaves with toothed leaflets and silvery beneath, and loose terminal cymes of white flowers.
- speciosa. From E. Europe and Asia Minor. Silver-leaved low tufts and many, rather small white flowers on short stems.
- tabernaemontani. (P. verna.) Europe, including Britain. Mat-forming, with wedge-shaped leaflets and semi-procumbent stems carrying

small yellow flowers. Not an exciting plant but worth growing.

— tommasiniana. See *P. cineria.*

— X 'Tonguei'. An invaluable, long-flowering, mat-forming hybrid, possibly between *PP. aurea* and *nepalensis.* Dark green, often bronzed leaves and low, spreading stems carrying innumerable flowers of soft apricot, suffused with crimson.

— valderia. From the Maritime Alps and the Balkans. Rather sprawling stems and leaves divided into wedge-shaped, toothed leaflets. Dense corymbs of white or very pale yellow to cream flowers.

— verna. See *P. tabernaemontani.*

— visianni. Eastern Europe. Pinnate leaves with many leaflets and loose panicles of large yellow flowers on fairly tall stems.

— warrenii. See *P. recta.*

— warrensii. See *P. recta.*

POTERIUM spinosum. See SARCOPOTERIUM *spinosum.*

PRATIA. *Campanulaceae.* Named for Ch. L. Prat-Bernon, French naval officer (d. 1817). Lobelia in part, this genus offers a few low growing carpeting plants for moist, cool positions.

Between the few cultivated species suitable for rock gardens there is a close similarity. They are all creeping plants, rooting at the nodes of the ground-hugging stems, with rounded, rather succulent green leaves. It is pointless to describe them individually in in detail, but *P. angulata* has white flowers followed by red-purple fruits. *P. arenaria* is similar, with slightly larger leaves, *P. begoniifolia* has blue flowers, comes from Nepal, is slightly larger than most of the other species and is not quite hardy. *P. macrodon* has white and purple flowers followed by good purple-red fruits. The white flowers of *P. repens* are marked with violet. Of *P. balfouriana* and *P. treadwellii (or tredwellii)* I can find no authentic record, although both names exist in gardens and cover plants similar to any of the above other than *P. begoniifolia.* They come, mostly, from Australasia and also from Asia and S. America.

PRIMULA. *Primulaceae.* A contraction of the medieval name *primula veris* for the daisy, meaning 'firstling of spring', a diminutive of the Latin *primus*, first, used for early-flowering plants.

A genus of more than 500 species, widely distributed throughout of the N. Temperate zone, but with some outliers in S. America, N. Africa and even Java. To describe in the detail such an important family undoubtedly deserves, all the species, forms and hybrids of interest to the rock gardener, would demand so much space that this Manual would need an additional volume. A recent publication of the Alpine Garden Society entitled 'A Gardener's Guide to the Asiatic Primulas', compiled by Mr. Roy Green so adequately covers this important group that I propose shamelessly to crib briefly from it and refer those desirous of more detailed information to the actual volume, which can be obtained from the secretary of the Society at Lye End Link, St. Johns, Woking, Surrey. To make reference easier I propose to deal first with the Asiatic Primulas and, separately in one group, with those from Europe, Asia Minor, the Caucasus and America. Botanically the genus is divided into 30 sections as follows.

(1) AMETHYSTINA. (2) AURICULA. (3) BULLATAE. (4) CANDELABRA. (5) CAPITATAE. (6) CAROLINELLA. (7) CORTUSOIDES. (8) CUNEIFOLIA. (9) DENTICULATA. (10) DRYADIFOLIA. (11) FARINOSAE. (12) FLORIBUNDAE. (13) GRANDIS. (14) MALACOIDES. (15) MALVACEAE. (16) MINUTISSIMAE. (17) MUSCARIOIDES. (18) NIVALES. (19) OBCONICA. (20) PARRYI. (21) PETIOLARES. (22) PINNATAE. (23) PYCNOLOBA. (24) REINII. (25) ROTUNDIFOLIA. (26) SIKKIMENSIS. (27) SINENSIS. (28) SOLDANELLOIDEAE. (29) SOULIEI. (30) VERNALES.

The section to which each belongs will be indicated by the bracketed number after its name. Unless otherwise stated it can be accepted that those in the Asiatic group prefer moist soil and are indeed, very often described as 'bog primulas'. Bearing this preference in mind it can be assumed that most of them will grow very well in other than 'bog' conditions.

PRIMULAS (ASIATIC)

Species, not now, or unlikely to be in cultivation have been omitted. Those in the PETIOLARES section (21) will be found mostly to be difficult in the southern counties, but many of them flourish in the cooler and more humid north.

— **agleniana.** (18) Widely distributed in the Himalaya. The 8 to 16 in. scape carries a single umbel of several fragrant flowers. They are bell-shaped and pale yellow, with a deeper-coloured eye showing farina. There are forms with white or rose-pink flowers.

— **algida.** (11) Moist alpine and sub-alpine meadows from the Caucasus to Turkestan, Iran and the Altai. Tufts of, usually, farinose leaves and short stems carrying heads of violet-pink or rarely white flowers.

— **alpicola.** (26) From Tibet and a widely variable species. The tall scape carries one, or occasionally two umbels of funnel- shaped flowers. The colour may be white, yellow, violet or purple. In gardens names such as 'Alba', 'Luna' and 'Violacea' have been given to selected forms.

— **anisodora.** (4) From China. The fairly tall stems support several superimposed umbels of narrowly funnel-shaped flowers of very deep crimson, almost black-crimson in some lights. The foliage and the roots are strongly aniseed-scented.

— **apoclita.** (17) From Tibet, Yunnan and Szechuan and dubiously in cultivation. From tufts of toothed, slightly hairy leaves rise 6 in. stems bearing spikes of fragrant flowers with reflexed segments and deep purple-blue in colour.

— **aurantiaca.** (4) From Yunnan. Rosettes of raggedly-toothed leaves, slightly farinose beneath and 12 in. stems carrying several super-imposed umbels of orange-red flowers.

— **aureata.** (21) A rare, and not easy species from Nepal. The winter rosettes are coated with silver farina, which disappears during the summer. The very short scape, mostly hidden in the leaves, carries several large, impressive flowers with rather fleshy, usually toothed lobes. The colour is cream-yellow with a flush of orange-yellow in the throat.

— **auriculata.** (11) Distributed in Iran and Turkey and north into the Caucasus. On the stout rhizomes are usually the withered remains of old leaves. The stems, of varying height carry compact umbels of reddish-purple, yellow-eyed flowers, but the colour too, is variable.

— **beesiana.** (4) Stout rosettes of largish, toothed leaves, only slightly farinose and tall stems carrying several umbels of rose-carmine flowers with orange tubes and a yellow eye.

— **bellidifolia.** (17) From Sikkim, Tibet and Bhutan. Rosettes of leaves very much like those of the common daisy and a 4 to 8 in. scape carrying a head of reflexed flowers. The colour ranges from mauve to violet and there is a ring of white farina in the throat. Rare and not very easy but occasionally available.

— **bhutanica.** See *P. whitei.*

— **boothii.** (21) From Bhutan. Rare, and happier in the north than the south. Winter tufts of leaves in loose clusters, pinkish-brown beneath. A very short scape displays many rather large purple-pink flowers with a yellow eye surrounded by a narrow band of white.

— **bracteosa.** (21) From the Himalaya. Rosettes of farinose, toothed leaves and a scape, short at first but later lengthening, carrying an umbel of few or many lilac-pink, yellow-eyed flowers, again with a ring of white. At the end of flowering it may produce vegetative buds at the top of the scape which, if pegged down into soil, will root.

— **bulleyana.** (4) From Yunnan. One of the popular Candelabra primulas, with several whorls of orange-red flowers on red petioles on the tall stems. It has been crossed with *P. beesiana* and produced strains of brightly coloured hybrids.

— **burmanica.** (4) From Yunnan and Burma and distinct from the related *P. beesiana* in that it is completely efarinose except for a dusting on the inside of the calyx lobes. The tall stems have whorls of red-purple, yellow-eyed flowers.

— **calderiana.** (21) From the Himalaya. This rather variable species makes clumps of fleshy roots and long, narrow, efarinose leaves. The stem, of varying height, carries an umbel of maroon-purple, yellow-eyed flowers.

— **capitata.** (5) From the Himalaya. Rosettes of short, broad, toothed leaves, usually heavily farinose and scapes of variable height carrying flattened, globose heads of many small, tubular flowers of blue-purple. There is an especially richly coloured form known as *P.c. mooreana.*

— **capitellata.** (11) From Iran and Afghanistan. A typical plant of the *Farinosae* section and often short-lived. Tufts of leaves which are farinose beneath and compact heads of pink flowers on stems of varying height.

— **cawdoriana.** (28) From Tibet. Flattened rosettes of coarsely-toothed leaves. Short stems carry heads of a few narrowly conical violet flowers, paler at the base and with a conspicuous white eye. A lovely but rather difficult plant.

— **chionantha.** (18) From Yunnan. The first leaves are heavily farinose but this disappears as the leaves adopt the typical long strap-shape of the section. The 12 to 20 in. scapes carry one or more umbels of milk-white, yellow-eyed fragrant flowers. Some authorities consider it to be no more than a white-flowered variety of *P. sinopurpurea,* which it resembles in all but colour.

— **chrysopa.** See *P. gemmifera zambalensis.*

— **chungensis.** (4) From the Himalaya. Tufts of efarinose leaves, the edges shallowly-lobed and toothed. The tall stems bear several whorls of red-tubed orange flowers.

— **clarkei.** (11) From Kashmir. A tiny plant forming tufts of small leaves with very short-stemmed pink flowers, either singly or in few-flowered umbels. It requires to be quite frequently divided and re-planted to keep it in good health.

— **cockburniana.** (4) From Szechuan and closely related to *P. chungensis* of which it might be regarded as a smaller version with rather more richly coloured flowers. It is usually rather short-lived.

— **concholoba.** (17) From Burma and Tibet. Rosettes of oblong. toothed leaves rounded at the apex. The scape, of variable height, carries a globose head of deep violet flowers, heavily powdered with white farina.

— **cortusoides.** (7) From Siberia. Short, lobed and softly hairy leaves. Umbels of pink or rose-violet flowers on 4 to 6 in. stems.

— **cuneifolia.** (8) Widely spread from Siberia to Japan, the Aleutian Islands and the coast of Alaska. Tufts of coarsely-toothed leaves and stems of variable height carrying umbels of up to ten rose-red flowers with a yellow eye.

— **cunninghamii.** (21) From Sikkim and Tibet. Low, compact rosettes of finely-toothed leaves with whitish-yellow farina. Many flowers on short petioles form a central tuft and are lavender-blue with a yellow throat. A very beautiful but tricky plant, demanding, particularly in the south, all the care and attention needed by the *Petiolares* primroses.

— **denticulata.** (9) From Afghanistan, throughout the Himalaya and into China. The ever-popular 'drumstick primula', easily grown and reliable. Tufts of strong foliage and 12 in. stems bearing large, globose heads of crowded flowers. The colour is variable from pure white to deep rose-red and there exist several garden named clones.

— **deuteronoma.** (21) From Sikkim and Nepal. Until recently doubtfully in cultivation but now occasionally seen. Thick rhizomes with long, fleshy roots and broad, efarinose leaves, finely-toothed. The purple, yellow-eyed flowers are clustered in the centre of the rosettes on very short stalks.

— **dickieana.** (1) From Nepal, and recently re-introduced, Tufts of short, narrow, efarinose leaves and a short scape carrying a single umbels of drooping flowers, of which the colour may be yellow, white, mauve, violet or purple, usually with a yellow eye to the blossom.

— **eburnea.** (28) From Bhutan. Very dubiously in cultivation, but a gem which should be re-introduced. It was described by Sherriff as 'the gem of the whole Eastern Himalaya'. Tufts of stalwart, oblong, sharply-toothed leaves and 6 in. stems carrying compact heads of large, ivory-white flowers.

— **edgeworthii.** (P. winteri.) (21) From the Himalaya. One of the most accommodating of the *Petiolares* section. The winter foliage forms a congested rosette of heavily farinose leaves but the foliage is green in summer. The very short scape is obscured by the foliage and displays clusters of soft mauve, yellow-eyed flowers. There is also a very good albino.

— **erratica.** (11) (P. loczii.) From the Himalaya. Tufts of small leaves, lightly farinose beneath and heads of pink flowers on short stems. The plant produces leafy stolons which root where they touch the ground and produce new plants.

— **fauriae.** (11) From Japan. Tufts of short, finely crenulated leaves. with yellow farina beneath and short stems carrying umbels of pink flowers.

— **florindae.** (26) From Tibet and a giant which delights in a really wet position and will even grow in a few inches of water although it will exist, less robustly, in drier soil. Large, rounded leaves cordate at the base and 3 ft. stems carrying great heads — or occasionally superimposed umbels of funnel-shaped sulphur-yellow flowers. There are also races of colour forms in orange and reddish shades.

— **forrestii.** (3) From Yunnan. An exception to most of the Asiatic primulas in preferring a dry site. It is a splendid subject for growing in the crevices of a dry stone wall, or in the alpine house. From woody rhizomes grow bold tufts of rugose, leathery, dark green leaves. The scape, of variable height, carries an umbel of rich golden, orange-eyed flowers.

— **gambeliana.** (25) Widely distributed in Tibet, Bhutan, Sikkim and Nepal. Tufts of rather rounded, cordate leaves, sharply toothed at the margins. The 4 to 8 in. stems carry one, or occasionally two superimposed umbels of violet-purple, yellow-eyed flowers.

— **gemmifera.** (11) From Kansu, Szechuan and Tibet. A short-lived plant which produces several basal buds, one or more of which persist and eventually replace the parent-stock. Tufts of rather rounded, toothed leaves and sturdy, erect 8 in. scapes carrying umbels of lavender-pink flowers. The variety *zambalensis* (P. chrysopa) is slightly larger in all its parts and usually of slightly richer colour.

— **geranifolia.** (7) From the Himalaya. Softly hairy, palmate, lobed leaves, sharply toothed and one, sometimes two, umbels of rose-purple flowers, semi-pendant, on 6 to 8 in. stems.

— **gracilipes.** (21) Distributed from Nepal and Sikkim to Bhutan and Tibet. From a branching rhizome grow compact tufts of efarinose leaves, contracting to a tight bud in winter. On thin pedicels appear singly, but in quantity, bright purple-pink flowers, yellow-eyed and with a zone of white around the eye.

— **helodoxa.** (4) From Yunnan and Burma. One of the best of the yellow-flowered *Candelabra* primulas Cn 2 ft. stems are many whorls of fragrant golden-yellow flowers.

— **heucherifolia.** (7) From Szechuan. Rounded, lobed, softly hairy leaves, bluntly toothed. The 8 in. stems carry a single umbel of nodding pink flowers.

— **hopeana.** See *P. sikkimensis.*

— **hyacinthina.** (17) From Tibet. In gardens its name is too often confounded with the European hybrid P. X 'Hyacintha'. Rosettes of rather long, toothed leaves, with farina on the undersides. The 8 to 12 in. scape bears compact heads of fragrant violet-blue flowers.

— **ianthina.** (4) From Sikkim. The long leaves are edged with small

307

teeth and the stem, up to 2ft. tall, carries several whorls of violet-blue flowers.

— **inayatii.** (11) From Kashmir. Rosettes of strap-shaped, entire leaves usually with cream or sulphur-coloured farina on the undersides. The 4 in. stems carry an umbel of purple-blue to lilac, yellow-eyed flowers.

— **involucrata.** (11) From the Himalaya. Leaves small, rounded at apex and usually without marginal teeth. The scape 4 to 8 in. tall, carries an umbel of a few pendant white, yellow-eyed flowers. Forms occur in which the flowers are faintly suffused with purple or lilac.

— **ioessa.** (26) From Tibet. Saw-edged, efarinose leaves and 8 in. scapes on which are loose umbels of pendant, funnel-shaped fragrant flowers. The colour varies from almost white to deep violet.

— **jaffreyana.** (11) Rosettes of small, farinose leaves, which lengthen as the season advances. The scape, at first short but lengthening, carries a small umbel of mauve to violet flowers. The eye is yellow or, occasionally, green. From Tibet.

— **japonica.** (4) From Japan and introduced in 1871, a time when so many plants were given this specific epithet that it became common practise to refer to working gardeners as 'Japonicas', or 'Ponicas'. I possess a very old plant catalogue which contains an advertisement for 'Japonica Aprons' (and a very useful garment it was too!). Really too well known to need a description. The tall stems carry tiers of red-purple flowers. It is more commonly grown in one or other of the several named forms, of which two of the best are 'Miller's Crimson' and 'Postford White' - both of which, curiously, come almost entirely true from seed.

— **jesoana.** (7) From Japan. Softly hairy, lobed and irregularly toothed leaves and a scape which can be short or tall and bears several umbels of rose-purple flowers with a white or yellow eye.

— **kingii.** (1) From Tibet, China and Burma. The species of this section are not accommodating themselves happily to cultivation and only this one and *P. dickieana* appear to have survived in gardens. The efarinose leaves have wide-winged petioles and almost entire margins. The scape, at first short, but lengthening, carries an umbel of semi-pendant deep wine-red, bell-shaped flowers.

— **kisoana.** (7) From Japan, as rare in nature as it is in gardens. Softly hairy, wavy edged leaves and one, occasionally two, umbels of pink or mauve-pink flowers.

— **lichiangensis.** See *P. polyneura.*

— **littoniana.** See *P. vialii.*

— **loczii.** See *P. erratica.*

— **macrophylla.** (18) From the Himalaya and has been confused with *P. nivalis.* The long, narrow, strap-shaped leaves are usually farinose beneath. The 10 in. stem carries a many-flowered umbel of lilac or violet flowers, each with an eye of deep purple, sometimes yellow-tinted.

— **melanops.** (18) From Szechuan. The foliage resembles that of *P. chionantha*, but is narrower. Each 12 in. scape carries one or two umbels of nodding deep violet flowers with dark eyes.

— **modesta.** (11) From Japan. From a congested winter bud come rosettes of small, rather rounded farinose leaves and the short scape bears an umbel of purple-pink flowers.

— **mollis.** (7) From Bhutan, and slightly tender and best given alpine house shelter. Rather broad, hairy and lobed leaves and short or tall stems carrying superimposed umbels of deep pink to crimson, yellow-eyed flowers.

— **muscarioides.** (17) From Tibet, Szechuan and Yunnan. Rosettes of spatulate, efarinose leaves and, on 12 in. stems short spikes of fragrant, reflexed deep purple-blue flowers.

— **nepalensis.** (21) Tufts of irregularly toothed, efarinose leaves and a stout 10 in. scape carrying an umbel of several yellow flowers. Collected in Nepal in 1930.

— **nutans.** (28) From Yunnan and Szechuan. A beautiful but sometimes short-lived species. Tufts of efarinose leaves tapering from a rounded apex to a winged petiole. An 8 to 12 in. scape carries a dense head of downward-pointing funnel-shaped flowers of lavender-violet.

— **obliqua.** (18) From Sikkim and Nepal, Bhutan and Tibet. Tufts of strap-shaped leaves, with yellow farina on the undersides and, on a tall, stout scape, an umbel of yellow or almost white flowers, with some petal lobes reflexed, a characteristic which gives the plant its specific epithet.

— **obtusifolia.** (18) From the Himalaya. Leaves oblong and rounded at the apex, with white farina below. Scapes of varying stature carry several umbels of purple-blue flowers with white or yellow eyes.

— X 'Pandora'. A hybrid between *P. edgeworthii* and *P. scapigera*.

— X 'Peter Klein'. A putative hybrid between *P. clarkei* and *P. rosea* whose authenticity remains uncertain.

— **petiolaris.** (21) From Nepal. Loose rosettes of efarinose leaves, contracted to a stout bud in winter. Short pedicels carry singly large flowers which may be soft blue or purple-blue.

— **poissonii.** (4) From Szechuan and Yunnan. Similar in habit and flower to both *P. anisodora* and *P. wilsonii*, but efarinose and non-aromatic.

— **polyneura.** (7) *(P. lichiangensis.)* From China. Tufts of lobed, smooth or hairy leaves, margins entire or toothed. The scape, of varying height, carries several umbels of flowers which may be pale rose, crimson or wine-purple.

— **prolifera.** (4) From Assam. Long, narrow, efarinose, sharply toothed leaves. 20 in. stems bearing whorls of yellow flowers.

— X 'Prospect'. A deliberate hybrid between *P. wollastonii* and *P. reidii*. Intermediate between the parents.

309

— **pulverulenta.** (4) From Szechuan. One of the nicest of the *Candelabra* section and most popular in one or other of the selected forms and strains. The flowers of the type are carried in whorls on tall stems and are deep pink — almost red, with a dark red or purple eye. The flowers of the 'Bartley Strain' are in shades of pastel pink.

— **pycnoloba.** (23) The only member of its section, from Szechuan. It is rare in nature and rarer still in cultivation. Broad leaves, felted with fine white hairs and short stems carrying dense racemes of curious, red and green flowers. It has been sterile in gardens but can be increased from root cuttings.

— **redolens.** (3) From Yunnan. Dwarf and shrubby and similar in general appearance and in needs to *P. forrestii*. The flowers are pale pink or mauve-pink and fade to a creamy colour.

— **reidii.** (28) From the Himalaya. A choice and beautiful species, essentially requiring moist conditions during the growing season. Ovate, efarinose leaves and coarsely toothed margins. The 4 in. scape carries a head of several pendant, bell-shaped flowers of ivory-white. The variety *williamsii* from Nepal, is slightly more robust and, if possible, even more beautiful with a delicate fragrance from the soft blue to white flowers.

— **reinii.** (24) From Japan. Rests in the winter as a bud, protected by brown scale-leaves. Cordate, lobed leaves sharply toothed and short stems with, usually, one, but occasionally a small umbel of rose-purple flowers with a yellow eye.

— **reptans.** (16) From the Himalaya. Few species of this section have ever been successfully cultivated, but *P. reptans* remains fitfully in gardens, especially in Scotland. It makes a dense, prostrate mat and carries, on short stems, surprisingly large violet-pink flowers. A partially shaded lime-free scree or the alpine house would seem to offer the best chances of success.

— **reticulata.** (26) From the Himalaya. Similar in many ways to *P. sikkimensis* but usually dwarfer and the flowers may be yellow or white.

— **rockii.** (3) From limestone cliffs in Szechuan. Dubiously in gardens now. Rather like *P. forrestii*, but a smaller plant with thin, woody rhizomes covered with the remnants of old leaves, and umbels of yellow flowers on short pedicels.

— **rosea.** (11) From the Himalaya and Afghanistan, and a lover of really wet soil. The flowers develop before the tufts of glabrous, efarinose leaves and begin to open as the scape thrusts through the soil in very early spring. The scape eventually lengthens to 12 inches or more. The rose-red flowers are borne in dense umbels. There are forms with deeper coloured flowers and one, which came from Holland with an unpronounceable name and was rechristened *P.r.* 'Delight' with blossoms of clear soft pink.

— **rotundifolia.** (25) From Nepal and Sikkim. The thick rootstock is covered with overlapping yellow-farinose bud-scales and the remains of old foliage. Rather triangular, toothed leaves, the upper surface shiny, the lower with cream-yellow farina. 12 in. scapes carry one or two umbels of pink flowers with yellow eyes.

— **saxatilis.** (7) From Korea and China. Hairy, lobed leaves, irregularly toothed. One, or sometimes two umbels of rose-violet or pink flowers are seen on 12 in. stems.

— **X 'Scapeosa'.** A hybrid between *P. scapigera* and *P. bracteosa*.

— **scapigera.** (21) From Sikkim and Nepal. Clumps of efarinose leaves and short scapes, almost hidden in the foliage, holding a many-flowered umbel of pink flowers, each with a yellow eye surrounded by a narrow white band.

— **secundiflora.** (26) From Szechuan and Yunnan. It resembles *P. sikkimensis* in all but the colour of the pendant flowers, which are wine-red.

— **serratifolia.** (4) From Yunnan, Tibet and Burma. Sharply toothed efarinose leaves and umbels of yellow, orange-barred flowers on 12 in. stems.

— **sessillis.** (21) From the Himalaya. Similar in growth habit to *P. petiolaris*. The soft mauve flowers are yellow-eyed and the eye is surrounded by a narrow band of white.

— **sherriffiae.** (28) A very distinct and striking species from Bhutan. It has never been an easy plant and should be cossetted in the alpine house. The efarinose leaves are oblanceolate, the margins toothed or entire and delicately fringed with white hairs. The 4 in. scape carries a head of horizontally arranged, very long-tubed flowers. The corolla is soft lavender-violet, with flecks of farina outside and in the throat.

— **sibirica.** (11) Similar in appearance to both *P. involucrata* and *P. yargongensis* of the same section with flowers of purple-pink and yellow-eyed. Oddly enough it has never been as easy to grow as the two species it resembles.

— **sieboldii.** (7) From Japan, Korea, Manchuria and N. Mongolia. It is very unfortunate that this species and its numerous splendid forms is not more widely known or grown. It was once popular, although thought not to be reliably hardy. This has been disproved and it is high time we sought it in all its variations. The rather wedge-shaped leaves are softly hairy, with lobed and toothed margins, It is deciduous. The height of the scape varies from 4 to 12 ins. and each one carries one or two umbels of large flowers. According to variety the colour can be white, pink, deep red or shades of lavender. It relishes light shade and soil rich in humus but well drained.

— **sikkimensis.** (26) From the Himalaya, where it is widely distributed. From the tufts of efarinose, toothed leaves rise fairly tall stems carrying umbels of slightly pendulous, fragrant yellow flowers. A geographic variation is known as *P.s. hopeana* and is a more slender plant with pale yellow flowers fading to almost white.

— **sinopurpurea.** (18) From Yunnan. Is much confused with *P. macrophylla*, but distinct. In appearance it resembles the other *Nivalid* primulas but the scape is short (but can occasionally lengthen) and carries purple-violet flowers, white or grey-eyed.

— **smithiana.** (4) From the Himalaya. Rather similar in appearance to *P. helodoxa* but usually taller and with heads of clear soft yellow flowers.

— **sonchifolia.** (21) From Yunnan, Szechuan, Tibet and Burma. An exciting species and amenable to cultivation, especially in the north of Britain. It winters in the form of a fat bud protected by overlapping yellow-brown scales. In early March the buds open to reveal the flowers nestling in the rosette of leaves. The scape slowly lengthens to perhaps 12 ins. and carries the umbels of lavender or clear blue, indigo-violet or, occasionally white flowers, each with an eye of rich yellow.

— **stenocalyx.** (11) From China. Tufts of daisy-leaves, efarinose above but often white or yellow farinose beneath. 6 in. stems carry heads of lavender or pink flowers.

— **strumosa.** (21) From Bhutan and Nepal. Very close to *P. nepalensis* but differing in its farinose leaves and by details of the calyx and corolla.

— **stuartii.** (18) From the Himalaya. Tufts of strap-shaped leaves with yellow farina beneath. 12 in. scapes carry one or more umbels of golden-yellow flowers. Rather dubiously in cultivation.

— **takedana.** (24) Tufts of rather broad, lobed and toothed hairy leaves and 6 in. scapes carrying one or more umbels of funnel-shaped white flowers. From Japan.

— **tosaensis.** (24) From Japan. Very close to *P. reinii*, from which it differs in only minor botanical details.

— **tsariense.** (21) Tibet and Bhutan. Dark green, efarinose leaves sometimes tinted with purple. The scape, also often purple-tinted, is some 6 ins. tall and carries a single umbel of blue-purple or occasionally white flowers, always with a yellow eye.

— **vialii.** (17) (P. littoniana.) Tapering, hairy, efarinose leaves and tall stems carrying dense spikes of flowers. The calyx of the flowers when in bud is crimson and the lower flowers in the spike open first, so that one is presented with a column of violet-blue flowers surmounted by the overlapping crimson calyces above. A very handsome primula. Yunnan and Szechuan.

— **waltonii.** (26) Tibet and Bhutan. Leaves raggedly toothed, smooth and without farina. The scape can be 2 ft. tall and carries an umbel of pink to wine-red flowers. Most of the plants grown under this name appear to be hybrids, possibly crosses with yellow-flowered species of the section.

- **wardii.** See *P. yargongensis.*

- **warshenewskiana.** (11) Do not be deterred by the name, this is a very delightful primula. It comes from Turkestan to the Himalaya and makes carpets of small, usually efarinose leaves, finely toothed at the margins. The very short scapes carry umbels of rose-pink, yellow-throated flowers. Like *P. clarkei*, which it in many ways resembles, it benefits from regular division and replanting.

- **whitei.** (21) (P. bhutanica.) From the Assam Himalaya, Bhutan and Tibet. Some authorities still contend that *P. bhutanica* is a distinct species, but the consensus of opinion indicates that it should be regarded as synonymous with *P. whitei.* The winter resting stage is spent as a fat bud, protected by overlapping, yellow-farinose scales. The leaves which develop are at first farinose but this largely disappears. On a short, but later elongating scape is an umbel of pale or deep blue, white-eyed flowers.

- **wigramiana.** (28) From Nepal and rather dubiously in cultivation. Spreading rosette of softly hairy leaves which are lightly toothed. The 12 in. scape carries a head of funnel-shaped, pendant white flowers.

- **wilsonii.** (4) From Szechuan and Yunnan. Rather long and narrow, finely-toothed leaves and tall stems carrying several whorls of purple flowers. Related to, and rather similar to, *P. poissonii.*

- **winteri.** See *P. edgeworthii.*

- **wollastonii.** (28) From Tibet and Nepal. Rosettes of leaves, white-haired on both surfaces. 8 in. stems bear heads of bell-shaped, pendant violet-blue flowers.

- **yargongensis.** (11) (P. wardii.) Thin rhizomes and efarinose leaves and 8 in. stems with umbels of mauve, pink, soft purple, or rarely, white flowers. From Szechuan, Yunnan and Tibet.

- **yuparensis.** (11) From Japan. Small tufts of leaves, minutely toothed efarinose above but with light farina beneath. 3 to 8 in. stems bear few-flowered umbels of purple flowers.

SPECIES AND HYBRIDS FROM EUROPE, AMERICA AND THE CAUCASUS

(Obscure species unlikely to be found in cultivation have been omitted).

PRIMULAS

- **abchasica.** See *P. vulgaris.*

- **acaulis.** See *P. vulgaris.*

- **X 'Aileen Chapman'.** See *P. X pruhoniciana.*

- **allionii.** (2) From the Maritime Alps. An alpine house gem. Dense domes of crowded rosettes of softly hairy leaves and almost stemless, rounded flowers with overlapping petals of rich pink. Several named clones exist, of which 'Bevan's Variety' (also known as 'Crowsley form') is a splendid example, with flowers of especially rich colour. There is also a good albino, and sundry slightly suspect hybrids, the best of which will be dealt with in their alphabetical sequence. A lime-lover.

— X **alpina.** A hybrid between *P. auricula* and *P. latifolia.* Flowers violet-purple with a creamy white eye.

— **altaica.** A name which has been applied to several primulas, such as *P. amoena,* a form of *P. vulgaris* and to *P. elatior,* but appears to have no authority.

— **amoena.** (3) From N.E. Turkey and the Caucasus. Rather polyanthus-like leaves and 6 in. stems bearing umbels of flowers which are commonly violet or lavender-blue, but may be yellow or white, always with a good yellow eye.

— **apennina.** (2) From the Apennines. Rosettes of small, softly hairy leaves, with an edging of brown hairs and lightly toothed at the apex. Short stemmed umbels of pink flowers. Possibly happier in lime-free soil.

— **archibaldii.** (11) From the Caucasus. Tufts of oblong leaves bluntly and remotely toothed and 6 to 8 in. stems bearing several lilac flowers with a pale green throat.

— **auricula.** (2) European Alps. Rosettes of rather fleshy leaves, with or without farina and heads of a few or many rather tubular bright yellow, white-throated flowers. It is extremely variable, with many geographic variations throughout its range of distribution. Noteworthy forms are *albocincta, ciliata, balbisii* (probably identical with *ciliata), monacensis, moschata, obristii, widmerae.*

— X **'Barbara Barker'.** This is probably a hybrid between *P. allionii* and *P. hirsuta.* As far as I can discover the parentage was never officially recorded. A handsome hybrid with good foliage and heads of large rose-red flowers.

— X **'Beatrice Wooster'.** A reputed hybrid between *P. allionii* and *P. marginata* 'Linda Pope'. Mats of rosetted leaves like those of *P. allionii* but larger and less sticky and hairy. The plant can be entirely obscured by the short-stemmed, well-shaped rose-pink, white-eyed flowers.

— X **berninae.** A hybrid between *P. hirsuta* and *P. latifolia.* Intermediate between the parents, with fine purple flowers. A selected form found by the late Paul Rosenheim named 'Windrush' is dwarfer with flowers of rich red-purple.

— X **biflora.** *P. minima* crossed with *P. glutinosa.* Similar to *P. minima* but two flowers of clear rose on each short scape.

— X **bileckii.** A hybrid between *P. minima* and *P. hirsuta.* Tufts of leaves like those of *P. minima* but wider, and more finely toothed and very large pink flowers with a solid white eye.

- 'Blairside Yellow'. The provenance of this delightful plant is uncertain. It may be a form of *P. auricula*, or, just possibly a hybrid. Neat rosettes of rather rounded, toothed leaves and heads of tubular rich yellow fragrant flowers on 4 in. stems.

- X bowlesii. A hybrid between *P. pedemontana* and *P. latifolia*. A variable hybrid, resembling a fine form of *P. latifolia*, with the typical russet edging to the leaves.

- carniolica. (2) From the Eastern Alps. Oval, dark green and glossy leaves and several rose-pink flowers to each short stem, each with a conspicuous mealy white eye. It appreciates a modicum of shade and soil rich in humus.

- clusiana. (2) From the Eastern Alps. Rosettes of leathery, glossy leaves. The 4 in. scape carries several flowers of rich rose-pink, the petals deeply cleft at the tips. A lime-lover in nature.

- columnae. See *P. veris*.

- commutata. See *P. villosa*.

- cottia. See *P. villosa*.

- X crucis. A hybrid between *P. marginata* and *P. latifolia*. Usually like a rather poor *P. marginata* with pinkish-mauve flowers, but a good form was once discovered by Reginald Farrer, which he named 'Blue Bowl'. I doubt if it still exists.

- cusickiana. (20) A rare N. American species which makes spasmodic appearances in British gardens but seldom lingers long. In nature it is saturated early in the year but subjected to a thorough baking later in the summer. Basal tufts of small, ovate leaves support a short scape carrying a head of velvety-violet, intensely fragrant flowers.

- daonensis. (2) (P. oenensis.) From the Rhaetian alps and its place in gardens has too often been taken by a condensed form of *P. hirsuta*. Rosettes of small, viscid leaves, edged with rusty hairs and few-flowered, short scapes carrying flowers which can be a rather shrill pink, but forms exist with clear pink flowers.

- darialica. (11) From the Caucasus. Like a *P. farinosa* with sharply toothed leaves and a 4 in. scape bearing rose-carmine, yellow-eyed flowers.

- davisiana. (12) A comparative newcomer collected in Turkey in 1954 by Dr. Peter Davis, after whom it has been named. Found in crevices of limestone cliffs, it has a very short stem carrying a small umbel of deep yellow flowers. Probably best in the alpine house.

- decipiens. (11) Very dubiously in cultivation. From Patagonia and like a *P. farinosa* with farina'd leaves and pink flowers.

- deorum. (2) From Bulgaria. Rosettes of long, narrow, rather leathery untoothed leaves and umbels of rose-purple flowers on 6 in. scapes Usually shy-flowering in gardens. It inhabits wet alpine meadows.

- X deschmannii. *P. wulfeniana* crossed with *P. minima*. Marriages between *P. minima* and *P. wulfeniana* have produced this hybrid and two others, *P. X serrata* and *P. X vochinensis*, all of them apt to be shy-flowering. Pads of short, bright green dentate leaves and several tubular pink flowers on very short stems.

— X 'Dianne'. A hybrid between *P. X forsteri* (already a hybrid) and a form of *P. X pubescens*, another hybrid. Tufts of thick, shining green leaves and very short stems carrying two or three large magenta-crimson flowers.

— X dinyana. A hybrid between *P. latifolia* and *P. integrifolia*. Long, shining green, untoothed leaves and loose scapes of wide-open purple-red flowers.

— X discolor. A hybrid between *P. auricula* and *P. daonensis*. A variable hybrid and, just possibly, owing something of its parentage to *P. spectabilis*.

— X dumoulinii. *P. minima* crossed with *P. spectabilis*. Rather rounded, finely-toothed, glossy green leaves and a one-flowered scape bearing a blossom like that of *P. minima*.

— elatior. (30) From Russia and Europe, including Britain, very widely distributed and with several subspecies recorded. Cowslip-like leaves and 8 in. stems carrying heads of slightly nodding, pale yellow flowers marked with orange in the throat.

— ellisiae. (20) From N. America. Tufts of fleshy, glabrous leaves and 6 in. stems carrying loose, one-sided umbels of mauve flowers, each lobe marked by a dark purple basal blotch.

— X 'Ethel Barker'. Reputedly a hybrid between *P. allionii* and *P. hirsuta*. Rosettes of broad, often silver-edged, toothed leaves and short stems bearing bold heads of large pink, white-eyed flowers.

— X fachinii. A hybrid between *P. minima* and *P. spectabilis*. A splendid plant displaying very large flowers of almost clear red on very short stems.

— X 'Fairy Rose'. Reputedly a hybrid between *P. allionii* and *P. marginata* 'Linda Pope'. Intermediate, some seedlings leaning towards one supposed parent and sometimes towards the other.

— farinosa. (11) Throughout Europe, including Britain. This is our own well-loved Bird's-eye primrose of moist northern meadows. Whilst not very long-lived it is a charmer, with tufts of farinose leaves and short stems bearing heads of pink, yellow-eyed flowers. It differs slightly in its various areas of distribution and some subspecies and forms have been named, such as *exigua*, *davurica* and *algida* and there is an occasional albino.

— X fladnitzensis. A hybrid between *P. minima* and *P. villosa*. Intermediate between the parents but leaning somewhat towards *P. minima*.

— X floerkeana. A hybrid between *P. minima* and *P. glutinosa*. This marriage has produced some of the most beautiful hybrids. Rosettes of wedge-shaped, toothed leaves and large flowers of glowing purple on very short stems.

- **X forsteri.** A hybrid between *P. minima* and *P. hirsuta.* Rosettes of small, glossy leaves and large pink, short-stemmed flowers often carried in pairs.
- **frondosa.** (11) From Bulgaria and like a robust *P. farinosa,* with farina on the undersides of the leaves. Stems up to 6 in. carry heads of rich rose flowers, frequently with a white eye.
- **X 'Garryarde'.** This name really represents a small group of primrose-polyanthus hybrids. Tufts of typical primrose leaves emit many 12 in. stems carrying bold heads of large polyanthus flowers. The colours may be pink, lavender, lilac or a suffusion of colours.
- **X 'Gladaline'.** A hybrid between *P. allionii* and *P. X pubescens* which may no longer exist. It formed rosettes of shiny, toothed, slightly farinose leaves and on short stems carried cherry-red, yellow-eyed flowers.
- **glaucescens.** (2) From the European Alps. A variable species, typically forming tufts of small, stiff, leathery leaves with a pronounced cartilaginous margin. The short, purple stems carry heads of several large lilac-purple flowers. Two subspecies sometimes encountered, differing only slightly from the type, are *P.g. calycina* and *P.g. long - obarda,* the first from Judicaria and the second from the Lombardy Alps.
- **glutinosa.** (2) A lovely and rare species from the southern and eastern Alps. Small tufts of strap-shaped, browny-green rather sticky leaves and 5 in. stems bearing violet-blue, fragrant flowers. It tends to be shy-flowering and is best in lime-free soil.
- **X goeblii.** A hybrid between *P. auricula* and *P. villosa.* This is what might be described as a 'central type' for hybrids between these two species and the name *P. X tauernensis* has been suggested for it, but is not widely used. Grey-green, toothed leaves and a scape rising just clear of the leaves. Rather dull-rose flowers with a clear white eye.
- **halleri.** (11) (P. longiflora.) From the Alps of Europe, especially in the east. Farinose leaves and short-stemmed heads of flowers rather like those of *P. farinosa,* but larger and with a markedly long tube.
- **X heeri.** *P. hirsuta* crossed with *P. integrifolia.* Narrow, entire , glaucous leaves and few-flowered umbels of rose-red flowers.
- **helvetica 'Alba'.** See *P. X pubescens.*
- **heterochroma.** (30) Really a subspecies of *P. vulgaris,* found in the Caucasus, Iran and Afghanistan - and probably also in Turkey. In all ways it resembles the common primrose except that its flowers range in colour from yellow to pink and red, and occasionally, white.
- **hirsuta.** (2) *(P. rubra)* This species is endlessly confused, both in gardens and in nature, with *P. latifolia* (P. viscosa). It is variable but typically forms rosettes of broad, obtuse, usually dentate and felted with fine, reddish hairs. On short scapes are umbels of flowers which vary from dingy pink to good clear pink or red. There is a fine albino, which resembles, and has been confused with *P. X pubescens* 'Alba' (P. helvetica 'Alba').

317

— **X huteri.** A hybrid between *P. minima* and *P. glutinosa.* Intermediate between the parents and with large red-purple flowers.

— **ingwerseniana.** (30) This was discovered in Greece by my late father and given specific rank by the botanists in Edinburgh. To all intents and purposes it is a primrose with pure white, yellow-eyed flowers. It would seem to me to be more correct to classify it as a subspecies of *P. vulgaris.*

— **integrifolia.** (2) From the Pyrenees, the Engadine and the Vorarlberg, on both granitic and limestone formations. Tufts of narrow, strap-shaped leaves but not so glutinous as those of *P. glutinosa,* which they in some ways resemble. On short stems are few-flowered umbels of reddish-lilac flowers.

— **intricata.** A subspecies of *P. elatior,* from which it scarcely differs.

— **X 'Joan Hughes'.** Reputedly a hybrid between *P. allionii* and *P. marginata* 'Linda Pope'. Compact pads of congested rosettes of soft, but not sticky leaves and umbels of magenta-pink flowers on short, slightly sticky scapes.

— **juliae.** An old garden favourite, introduced from the Caucasus many years ago, and the parent, with other members of the *Vernales* section of the many hybrids grouped under the collective name *P. juliana,* correctly *P. X pruhoniciana.* Mats of short rhizomes with rounded, toothed leaves and short-stemmed bright purple flowers. It prefers a cool rather than a hot position.

— **juliana.** See *P. X pruhoniciana.*

— **X juribella.** A hybrid between *P. minima* and *P. tyrolensis.* Intermediate between the two tiny parents and large rose-purple flowers on very short stems.

— **X kellereri.** A hybrid between *P. minima* and *P. hirsuta.* Very similar to *P. X. steinii* (of similar parentage) but slightly smaller in all its parts.

— **kitaibeliana.** (2) From the eastern Alps. Rather lax, viscid leaves, sometimes toothed, sometimes entire, and with a pelt of fine hairs, One or two rose-lilac flowers on very short stems.

— **latifolia.** (2) (P. viscosa). From the European Alps and widely distributed. A very variable species with sometimes long, lax, rather viscid leaves and sometimes, shorter, smaller leaves. The short stems carry many-flowered umbels of funnel, or bell-shaped purple or dark violet, usually fragrant flowers.

— **leucophylla.** A subspecies of *P. elatior.*

— **X loiseleuri.** This has been recorded as a hybrid between *P. auricula* and *P. allionii,* but this is an unlikely cross and it is more likely to be *P. auricula* crossed with *P. tyrolensis.* It is intermediate in appearance, between these two species.

— **longiflora.** See *P. halleri.*

318

— X 'Margaret'. A probable *P. allionii* - *P. pubescens* hybrid. Compact rosettes of grey-green leaves. Umbels of up to 20 large flowers of deep lilac-pink with a good white eye.

— **marginata.** (2) From the Maritime Alps. Usually a cliff and crevice dweller. It makes long, woody stems surmounted by rosettes of deeply jagged, silver-edged leaves and carries good heads of sizeable flowers. The colour is variable, ranging from pale lavender to shades of blue and purple. Selected forms have been given clonal names, such as 'Beamish Variety', 'Prichard's Variety', and best of all, 'Hycinthia' and 'Linda Pope'. The former occurred as a seedling from *P. m.* 'Beamish Variety' and carries bold umbels of deep mauve - blue flowers. The latter, whose origin is obscure, has splendid foliage markedly silver-edged and fine umbels of large soft lavender-blue flowers.

— X 'Marven'. A hybrid between *P. marginata* and *P. X venusta* and is a lovely plant with leaves like those of *P. auricula* and powdered stems carrying heads of rather funnel-shaped deep purple-blue flowers with a clear white eye.

— X 'Miniera'. A hybrid between *P. allionii* and, probably *P. marginata*. Rosettes of dull green leaves, without farina and non-viscid. Very short stems carry clusters of rosy-mauve flowers.

— **minima.** (2) From the European Alps. Tiny tufts of wedge-shaped leaves with toothed ends and very short stems carrying large clear pink flowers with a deep notch at the end of each petal.

— **mistassinica.** (11) From N. America. This is a dainty American and Canadian version of *P. farinosa* with tiny rosettes of crinkled leaves and 4 in. stems bearing dainty heads of pink or mauve flowers.

— X **muretiana.** A hybrid between *P. latifolia* and *P. integrifolia.* Several varying hybrids of this parentage exists, some verging towards one parent and others to the other. This leans towards *P. latifolia.*

— **oenensis.** See *P. daonensis.*

— X **oenipontina.** A name which has been suggested for one of the several hybrids between *P. auricula* and *P. latifolia.* Rather long, narrow leaves, devoid of farina and one-sided trusses of rose-purple flowers.

— **officinalis.** See *P. veris.*

— **palinuri.** (2) From a few limestone cliffs in the Province of Salerno. Stout rhizomes end in tufts of large, broad, lax leaves of bright green, serrated at the edges and efarinose. On 8 in. stems are one-sided umbels of small, cowslip-scented clear yellow flowers. It asks for, and deserves, a warm sunny crevice.

— **parryi.** (20) From N. America. Tufts of narrow, slightly serrated leaves and a 10 in. stem carrying a many-flowered umbel of rather tubular bright purple, yellow-eyed flowers. Best in lime-free soil and a not too hot position.

319

— **pedemontana.** (2) From the Graian and Cottian Alps. It resembles a smaller and neater *P. hirsuta* with rounder, more glossy leaves, conspicuously edged with russet hairs.

— **X penzoi.** A hybrid between *P. wulfeniana* and *P. tyrolensis*. It is found in the Dolomites and has small rosettes of narrow, more or less toothed leaves and a few lilac-purple flowers to each short stem.

— **X portenschlagii.** One of the numerous crosses between *P. clusiana* and *P. minima*, and intermediate between the parents.

— **X pruhoniciana.** This is the name which should replace the well-known *P. X juliana*, and represents a blanket name covering the many hybrids between *P. juliae* and other members of the *Vernales* section. The names of these are legion and it would be pointless to attempt any detailed descriptions, but here belong, for example, *P.* 'Wanda', *P. juliana* 'Gloria' and countless others of primrose or polyanthus type. All good garden plants.

— **X pseudo-forsteri.** A false name which usually covers a slightly smaller version of *P. X forsteri*.

— **X pubescens.** I have heard this name described as being more a cry of despair than a reasoned attempt to name any definite plant. It covers the crosses between *P. auricula* and *P. latifolia*, of which there are not only the natural hybrids found in the wild but a multitude of later garden seedlings and selections. Here, again, I swerve from any attempt at detailed descriptions, but bear in mind that here should belong — if it still exists, the lovely, pure white primula long known and loved as *P. helvetica* 'Alba'.

— **X rhaetica.** A hybrid between *P. auricula* and *P. hirsuta*, and more or less intermediate between the parents.

— **rubra.** See *P. hirsuta*.

— **rusbyi.** (20) From New Mexico and Arizona. Clumps of leathery, dark green leaves, serrate at the margins and 8 in. stems carrying one-sided umbels of curiously coloured flowers, best described in the words of the inimitable Reginald Farrer, who said "They are like an old bloodstain on faded velvet".

— **X salisburgensis.** A hybrid between *P. minima* and *P. glutinosa*. Unfortunately shy-flowering but when it does the blossoms are large and blue-violet in colour.

— **scotica.** (11) A rarity from the extreme north of Britain. Tiny tufts of farinose leaves and very short stems carrying small heads of violet-purple, yellow or white-throated flowers. Short-lived and definitely not to be collected except perhaps as seed.

— **X serrata.** A hybrid between *P. wulfeniana* and *P. minima*. This is often seen labelled *P. X serratifolia*, a name which should be abandoned since it already belongs to an Asiatic species. Tufts of tiny, rather narrow leaves and short-stemmed flowers resembling in colour those of *P. wulfeniana*.

— **sibthorpii.** See *P. vulgaris.*

— **spectabilis.** (2) Rosettes of brilliantly green, glossy leaves, hard and leathery, often slightly twisted and with a pronounced cartilaginous margin. There is also a characteristic pitting on the upper surface not seen in any other species. Rather shy-flowering but when it does the large flowers are clear rose-pink, often with a definite white eye.

— **specuicola.** (11) From N. America. Like a rather frail *P. farinosa*, with farinose leaves and violet flowers.

— **X steinii.** *P. hirsuta* crossed with *P. minima.* Intermediate in leaf between the parents but with fine crimson, white-eyed flowers of wide funnel shape.

— **stricta.** (11) This is a rather poor version of *P. farinosa* from sub-arctic Europe.

— **suffrutescens.** (8) From California. Best regarded as an alpine house plant. Of shrubby habit, the stiff, thick stems carry narrow, leathery yellow-green leaves, sharply serrated and from the terminal clusters of leaves appear short stems carrying fragrant flowers of rich pink and with a yellow eye.

— **X tauernensis.** See *P. X goeblii.*

— **X thomasiana.** Of the same parentage and very similar to *P. X heeri.* Not to be confused with *P. tommasinii*, which is an obscure subspecies of *P. elatior.*

— **tyrolensis.** (2) From the Dolomites. Rosettes of small, sticky leaves. Very short stems carry two or three large wine-red, white-eyed flowers.

— **X venusta.** A hybrid between *P. auricula* and *P. carniolica.* A fertile hybrid which has produced several fine children. The leaves are intermediate between the parents and farinose and there are loose umbels of soft pink flowers.

— **veris** (30) (P. officinalis.) The common cowslip, widely distributed in Europe, including Britain. In its several geographical locations it has subspecies, such as *macrocalyx, canescens* and *columnae.*

— **villosa.** (2) (P. commutata.) From the Eastern Alps and resembling a condensed, narrower-leaved *P. latifolia.* It has also been confused with *P. hirsuta.* The broad, sticky leaves are serrate and covered with minute reddish glandular hairs. The stem carries a head of small, rose-red flowers. The more lax-leaved form from Styria which was regarded as a subspecies and named *commutata*, is now regarded as indistinguishable from the type.

— **viscosa.** See *P. latifolia.*

— **X vochinensis.** A hybrid between *P. wulfeniana* and *P. minima.* Dense rosettes of stiff, dark green leaves and deep red flowers on short stems. It flowers more freely than others of the same parentage.

— **vulgaris.** (30) (P. acaulis.) Our own beloved primrose of which there are numerous geographic variations, one of the best being

P.v. sibthorpii, which has typical primrose flowers of clear pink.
— **wulfeniana.** (2) From the Eastern Alps. Rosettes of hard, narrow, glossy, acutely-pointed dark-green leaves and umbels of three or more large ruby-purple flowers.

The Asiatic, American and European primulas are grouped into sections, which I have indicated by the numbers in brackets after their names, but they are also subdivided into many sub-sections, which I have ignored, this not being a botanical treatise.

PRUNELLA. *Labiatae.* Early German herbalists used the names Prunella and Brunella interchangeably. They could be derived from the German word *braun* (from the Latin *prunum*) meaning purple, or from the German word *braune,* meaning quinsy, a disease these herbs were thought to cure.

A small genus of plants which are not truly alpine, but are dwarf enough and, in a few instances, decorative and sufficiently non-invasive to be used on the rock garden. A few species are widely distributed over Europe. They are easily grown and summer flowering, and, whilst sun-lovers, appreciate a not too scorching position.

The common Self Heal, (*P. vulgaris*) is a British native without garden value, but the two forms *P.v. laciniata,* with deeply cut foliage and white flowers and *P.v. pinnatifida, P. incisa* 'Rubra' of some catalogues, with rose-red flowers, both neat and dwarf, are well worth growing. Additionally there are some clonally named forms, such as *P.* 'Lilac Loveliness', 'Pink Loveliness', 'White Loveliness' and 'Red Riding Hood', which are desirable and decorative and useful as ground-cover plants.

PRUNUS. *Rosaceae.* The Latin name.

Although, generally speaking, shrubs are not included as such in this Manual, space must be found for a few of the true dwarfs which find an appropriate place on rock gardens, and one species of Prunus certainly qualifies in this context.

— **prostrata.** This hails from mountainous Mediterranean regions and is a compact, rock-hugging shrub with woody stems which twine into intricate tangles and display, before the leaves develop, small, bright pink flowers. It asks for, and deserves, a warm sunny position in a rocky environment.

322

PTERIDOPHYLLUM. *Papaveraceae.* From the Greek *pteris*, a fern and *phyllon*, leaf.

— **racemosum.** The only species in its genus, from coniferous woodlands in Japan. From tufts of deeply cut, fernlike leaves rise 6 to 8 in. stems carrying an elegant raceme of tiny white flowers. It flowers in summer and appreciates humus-rich soil and some shade.

PTEROCEPHALUS. *Dipsaceae.* From the Greek *pteron*, a wing and *kephale*, a head.

The fruiting heads of these plants appear to be covered with feathers. A small genus distributed in Mediterranean regions and and in Asia, related to and in part synonymous with SCABIOSA. They are sun-lovers, and spring and summer flowering.

— **depressus.** From Morocco. Flat mats of crinkled, grey-green leaves and mushroom-pink scabious flowers on very short stems. The seed heads are silvery-pink and almost equally attractive. Best in the alpine house.

— **hookeri.** From China and Bhutan. Hairy, pinnatifid leaves and 12 in stems carrying heads of small yellow or violet flowers with purple anthers.

— **parnassi.** From Greece. Low mats of grey, hairy crenate leaves and on short stems heads of purple-pink flowers. This is now correctly *P. perennis*, subspecies *perennis*, but I retain the more familiar name. Subspecies *bellidifolius* has equally hairy, but usually green leaves.

— **perennis.** See *P. parnassi.*

— **pinnardii.** From Anatolia. Rather like *P. parnassi*, but even more silvery.

— **spathulatus.** From Spain, Prostrate mats of woody stems and intensely hairy silver-grey leaves and pink scabious flowers on short stems.

PTILOTRICHUM. *Cruciferae.* From the Greek *pteron*, a wing and *thrix*, a hair.

A genus closely related to ALYSSUM, with which, in gardens, it is often confused, but always with white or pink flowers. No true ALYSSUM has white flowers. Avid sun-lovers. Widely distributed in the warmer parts of Europe. Spring and summer flowering.

— **halimifolium.** (Alyssum halimifolium.) From Italy and Spain. An 8 in. shrublet with lanceolate silvery leaves and corymbose heads of white flowers.

— **purpureum,** (Alyssum lagascae.) From Spain. Tufts of small silvery leaves and dense corymbs of pink and purple flowers.

323

PTILOTRICHUM — *continued*

- **lapeyrousianum.** (Alyssum lapeyrousianum.) From the Pyrenees. 10 in. bushes of tortuous stems and silver leaves. Heads of quite large white flowers.

- **longicaule.** (Alyssum longicaule.) Prostrate, spreading stems and rosettes of hairy silver leaves. Loose corymbs of white flowers.

- **pyrenaicum.** (Alyssum pyrenaicum.) 8 in. woody stems and small leathery silver-grey leaves and dense spikes of white flowers with chocolate anthers.

- **reverchonii.** (Alyssum reverchonii.) From Spain. Rather like *P. pyrenaicum* but with broader leaves.

PULSATILLA. (ANEMONE.) *Ranunculaceae.* From the Latin *pulso,* to strike, or set in violent motion. The relevance is uncertain. Better known to most gardeners as Anemones, but there are sufficient botanical differences for the following to have been separated from that genus. They are spring-flowering, sun and mostly, lime-loving plants.

- **alpina.** (Anemone alpina.) The glory of European alpine meadows. Bold tufts of ferny foliage and tall stems displaying large, snow-white flowers, followed by the seed heads, which Reginald Farrer so graphically describes as 'wildly whirling struwelpeter balls of twisting silver-fluffy seeds'. The subspecies *sulphurea* is equally beautiful, with rich yellow flowers. The latter is said to be a calcifuge, but I have always found it to be lime-tolerant in gardens. Neither plant likes root disturbance and should be planted as young, pot-grown, seedlings and thereafter never disturbed.

- **cernua.** (Anemone cernua.) From Japan. Silky-pubescent foliage and claret-coloured flowers nodding on fairly tall stems.

- **halleri.** (Anemone halleri.) From Europe. Broad, flat leaves shaggy with silky hairs and 6 in. stems carrying large, rich violet flowers.

- **montana.** Tufts of green, ferny leaves and tall stems bearing nodding red-purple flowers which are narrowly bell-shaped.

- **occidentalis.** (Anemone occidentalis.) From N.W. America, where it more or less takes the place of the European *A. alpina,* and is equally sumptuous. It breaks through the ground as the snow melts with foliage finely cleft into narrow segments. The large flowers are white but the backs of the petals are suffused with purple-blue. Eventually the stems elongate to carry proudly aloft great heads of long-awned tawny silken seeds.

- **patens.** From N. Europe and Siberia. Palmately-lobed leaves and violet-blue to lilac flowers centred by golden stamens.

- **pratensis.** (Anemone pratensis. Anemone albana.) From Europe and into S. Russia. Leaves pinnately-divided and nodding flowers of very

324

dark reddish-purple — sometimes almost back-purple.

— **vernalis.** Alps of Europe. This has been acclaimed the most lovely of all alpine flowers, with some justification. Low tufts of carroty leaves and short stems, shaggy with golden-bronze hairs and upturned goblet-shaped flowers, irridescent and opal-white within and with a tassel of golden stamens. The outside of the flowers shimmer with silky gold and violet hairs.

— **vulgaris.** (Anemone pulsatilla.) The Pasque Flower of some English chalk hills and, in greater splendour, of the chalk downs of Normandy and Brittany and elsewhere in Europe. The British version is a rather precious pygmy in comparison with its more majestic cousins across the channel, making tiny tufts of carroty leaves and displaying rich purple, crocus-like flowers on very short, hairy stems. Too rare to collect and diminishing yearly in numbers. There do exist nursery-grown stocks. Otherwise, what can one say of this ever popular and beautiful plant, which exists in numerous named or anonymous clones and variations? There are white ones, crimson ones, purple ones, all large-flowered and shaggy with fine hairs. Like *A. alpina*, they all resent root disturbance and, once established, should be left to increase each year in splendour.

PUTORIA. *Rubiaceae.* From the Latin *putor*, a strong smell. A small genus of sun-loving Mediterranean shrubs, of which only one need concern us here.

— **calabrica.** An evergreen, low, straggling shrub with lanceolate leaves and terminal clusters of several purple-rose flowers followed by juicy red berries. If roughly handled, and sometimes on hot days, the plant emits a strong and slightly unpleasant aroma.

PYGMEA. *Scrophulariaceae.* The name refers to the habit of these small plants. A small group of alpine cushion plants, endemic to New Zealand. They demand much patience and skill if they are to be grown successfully and must be regarded as alpine house plants and given the same gritty soil and treatment that would be meted to other high alpine cushion plants. Any of them would be exciting to try but they are seldom available. Those which may be chanced upon are *P. armstrongii*, *P. ciliolata*, *P. myosotoides*, *P. pulvinaris* and *P. thompsonii*, all with stemless white flowers studded over the dense cushions of tiny, softly hairy leaves.

PYROLA. *Pyrolaceae.* The Latin diminutive of *Pyrus*, (pear) from the pear-shaped leaves of these herbs.

Natives of Europe, Asia and N. America. Few species are successfully cultivated, the best prospects of success are in light woodland soil and semi-shade or in the peat garden. They are summer flowering and should not be disturbed once established. They spread by means of long, white, underground stolons.

— **asarifolia.** From N. America. Leathery, shining, kidney-shaped leaves and bell-shaped white flowers on 5 in. stems. *Var. incarnata* has pink flowers.

— **carpatica.** From the Carpathians. Rather like *P. rotundifolia* but the white bells are sometimes tinged with pink.

— **chlorantha.** See *P. virens.*

— **grandiflora.** From Iceland and Arctic Russia. Round, entire, shining green leaves and loose racemes of white, greenish-white or faintly pink flowers.

— **incarnata.** See *P. asarifolia.*

— **media.** Europe, including Britain. Like a smaller *P. rotundifolia* with lax racemes of white bells, sometimes flushed with soft pink.

— **minor.** The common Wintergreen. A British native and widely spread in Europe, Asia (Japan) and N. America. Small, leathery, rounded leaves, and short stems carrying white, usually rose-flushed flowers.

— **norvegica.** Typical rounded leaves and widely campanulate bells of white, often pink-flushed. From Scandinavia.

— **picta.** From N. America. Not one of the beauties of the race, the bells are greenish-white. The round leaves are blotched white above and purple beneath.

— **rotundifolia.** The larger of the British native species and also widely distributed throughout the Northern Hemisphere. Slightly crenulate, rounded glossy green leaves and short racemes of pendant white bells. There is a subspecies, *P.r. maritima* which occurs on sea coasts in the north of England and on the coasts of Germany and France. It is found growing in almost pure sand.

— **secunda.** This should now be known as ORTHILIA *secunda* but I retain the better known name. To make confusion worse confounded, some authorities refer it to the genus RAMISCHIA. A British native, it also occurs in Europe, Japan and N. America. It resembles other species and the flowers are greenish-white, carried in dense racemes.

— **uliginosa.** Another N. American species with flowers of bright red-purple or rose.

— **uniflora.** See MONESES *uniflora.*

— **virens.** (P. chlorantha.) N. American. The bell-shaped flowers are greenish-yellow.

PYRETHRUM alpinum. See CHRYSANTHEMUM *alpinum*.

PYXIDANTHERA. *Diapensiaceae.* From the Greek *pyxis*, a box and *anthera*, anther. The anthers open like the lid of a box.
- **barbulata.** The pixie moss of Pine Barrens in the E. United States. Not an easy plant to grow and demands much care and even then seldom persists in cultivation. Give it alpine house treatment, in acid, peaty, moist soil. Evergreen and as small as a moss with tufts of tiny green leaves and almost stemless white or pink flowers in early spring.

RAFFENALDIA. *Cruciferae.* Named in honour of Alire Raffeneau Delile, 19th century Professor of Botany at Montpelier.

- **primuloides.** (Cossonia africana.) From Morocco and Algeria. An avid sun-lover forming rather untidy tufts of narrow, jagged-edged leaves and flowering throughout the summer with yellow, four-petalled blossoms on 4 in. stems. In appearance it much resembles a larger, coarser *Morisia monanthos.*

RAMONDA. *Gesneriaceae.* Named for Louis Francis Ramond, Baron de Carbonniere (1753-1827), botanist and traveller in the Pyrenees.

A genus of three species, natives severally of southern and eastern Europe. They all make flat rosettes of dark green, corrugated and tooth-edged leaves and should be planted in north-facing or shaded crevices between rocks or in a wall, and given soil well provided with humus, but sharply drained. They are all spring and early summer flowering.

- **myconi.** *(Ramonda pyrenaica.)* From the Pyrenees. The 4 in. stems bear one or several flat, rounded, wide-petalled flowers of purple-blue, but white and pink-flowered forms appear amongst seedlings.

- **nathaliae.** From Bulgaria and Serbia. Similar to *R. myconi* but with more glossy green leaves, edged with dark hairs.

- **X permixta.** A hybrid between *R. myconi* and *R. serbica* and intermediate between the parents.

- **pyrenaica.** See *R. myconi.*

- **serbica.** From the Balkans. Again similar in general appearance to *R. myconi*, but the flowers are slightly cup-shaped and smaller.

There does exist — just, a very rare bi-generic hybrid between *Ramonda serbica* and *Jankaea heldreichii* which was raised by a Mr. Van der Dem and distributed by the Correvon nursery in Geneva many years ago as *Ramonda X Van der Demii.* I know of at least one enthusiastic amateur who has plants of it and one dares to hope that it may once again, if slowly, be distributed. A hybrid has also been recorded between RAMONDA and HABERLEA, but I do not know if this still exists.

RANUNCULUS. *Ranunculaceae.* The Latin name from the diminutive of *rana,* a frog, because many of the species grow in damp places.

A large and important family, widely distributed over the world but more numerous in temperate and cold regions of the Northern Hemisphere. Some obscure species, which may have made only tentative appearances in cultivation, have been omitted.

- **abnormis.** A rare species from Spain and Portugal. On 8 in. stems it displays rich yellow flowers of good size and substance.

- **acetosellifolius.** From Spain, Basal tufts of blue-green, arrow-shaped leaves. On 4 in. rather purplish stems the cup-shaped white flowers are carried singly, the overlapping segments being slightly notched at the tip. It appreciates cool, slightly damp conditions and is beloved by slugs.

- **acris.** One of the common, tall, field buttercups, best kept out of the garden, but the form with perfectly double flowers is worth growing in the border.

- **adoneus.** From N. America, where it grows on limestone screes. On quite short stems it carries good yellow flowers of excellent solidity.

- **alpeophilus.** Also from N. America and very similar to *R. adoneus.*

- **alpestris.** A precious little white-flowered alpine buttercup from the European Alps. Tufts of small, roundish and heart-shaped lobed leaves, toothed at the margins and neat white saucers on very short stems. The variety *traunfellneri* comes from the eastern Alps and is smaller, with more finely cut leaves and similar blossoms.

- **amplexicaulis.** From the Pyrenees. Slender, pointed, stem-clasping glaucous leaves and 6 in. stems carrying several large, pure white flowers. Occasional forms with semi-double flowers occur and an especially large-flowered clone has been selected and named *grandiflora.*

- **andersonii.** From N. America. Tufts of glaucous, pinnatifid leaves. The flowers are said to be 'pinkish', but I have not seen them.

— **anemoneus.** An outstandingly beautiful species from Australia. It may not be in cultivation, but I include it in the hope that someone may send seeds. It should produce very large, pure white flowers as the leaves unfold.

— **anemonoides.** See CALLIANTHEMUM *anemonoides.*

— **bilobus.** From the alps of Europe. Similar to *R. alpestris* but with dark green, kidney-shaped crenate leaves. The numerous white petals are deeply notched at the apices.

— **brevifolius.** From Asia Minor. Similar to *R. thora*, but dwarfer, with grey-green leaves wider than long. The short stems carry solitary yellow flowers.

— **buchananii.** From New Zealand. Deeply cleft grey-green leaves in tufts and several 8 in. stems each carrying one or more spectacular white flowers.

— **bulbosus.** (R. speciosus.) A British native and only worth garden space in its handsome double-flowered form. The flowers, on 12 in. stems are perfect golden pompoms.

— **bullatus.** From Cyprus. Wee tufts of shiny, toothed leaves and short-stemmed rather small flowers of brilliant yellow.

— **bupleuroides.** From Portugal. Much like *R. pyrenaeus* in habit but the branching stems carry many pale yellow flowers.

— **calandrinioides.** From the Atlas mountains of N. Africa. From thick, fleshy roots spring wide, lanceolate grey leaves and, in earliest spring, or even in February, 6 to 8 in. stems carrying from one to three large flowers, usually white, but often flushed pink. It is hardy but is seen at its best in the alpine house, where the paper-thin petals do not get damaged by wind and rain.

— **carpaticus.** This comes from the Carpathians and is similar to — and sometimes thought to be synonymous with — *R. gouanii*, which is found in the Pyrenees.

— **chordorhizos.** From New Zealand. Pewter-coloured, deeply cleft foliage and large, short-stemmed yellow flowers, green in the throat.

— **crenatus.** From the alps of Europe. Small tufts of rounded, heart-shaped, dull green leaves, toothed at the apex. The white flowers are as large as, and similar to, those of *R. bilobus.*

— **creticus.** From Crete. A boldly handsome, rather tall buttercup with tufts of lobed, crenate leaves and heads of numerous large, richly golden flowers.

— **cupreus.** From Crete. A rarity with finely segmented leaves, not unlike that of the alpine poppy and short, almost leafless stems each carrying one large flower of coppery-orange colour. Very dubiously in cultivation but if obtained would probably need alpine house cultivation.

— **cymbalaria.** From N. America, but naturalized in parts of N. Europe. Ascending stems from creeping stolons. Leaves dentate and erect 10 in. stems carrying bright yellow flowers.

— **erriorhizus.** From the mountains of Iran. A rarity, but may shortly be available in view of the collecting now going on in the area. Small tufts of deeply divided leaves and golden flowers on short stems.

— **eschscholzii.** From N. America and British Columbia. Low tufts of smooth, fleshy, deeply cut leaves and several large, pale yellow flowers on 4 in. stems.

— **X 'Essex'.** An interesting garden hybrid between *R. amplexicaulis* and *R. parnassifolius*. It was exhibited in 1957 by the late Mr. Hammer, in whose Essex garden it occurred spontaneously. It may no longer exist. It was intermediate in appearance between its handsome parents.

— **ficaria.** This is the common British wild plant known as the Lesser Celandine, and not to be trusted in the garden, but it has several variants which are well worth growing in soil which does not dry out too severely, and are trustworthy. They are all either colour variants or double-flowered forms of the type which have been collected in the wild and brought into cultivation. Some of the best are 'Albus', with white single flowers. 'Aurantiaca' (one of the best) with single, coppery-orange flowers. 'Flore Plena', rich yellow and double, 'Major', a giant with very large golden flowers on 8 in. stems, and 'Primrose', which is single and creamy-yellow.

— **geranifolius.** See *R. montanus*.

— **glaberrimus.** From N. America. It makes a few fleshy, three-cleft leaves close to the ground and displays large golden flowers on very short stems early in the year.

— **glacialis.** From the high Alps of Europe and the delight and despair of alpine gardeners, for it is a species which has never taken kindly to captivity and, apart from occasional, isolated successes, resists all attempts to persuade it to display in gardens the beauty which is breathtaking in its natural habitats, where it chooses for preference non-calcareous areas. Prostrate tufts of fat, fleshy, grey-green cleft leaves and short, branching stems carrying enormous rounded flowers of dazzling whiteness. After fertilisation the petals change colour to pink, deepening to rich rose-red. If you try it, give it grit mixed with humus and a lot of water as soon as it begins to grow in the spring, and keep it in the alpine house.

— **gouanii.** From the Pyrenees. Tufts of large, rounded, lobed leaves and stout but short stems carrying several large, handsome golden buttercups.

— **gramineus.** From the mountains of S. Europe, where it is locally abundant. Tufts of narrow, grassy leaves and 8 in. stems carrying many large, saucer-shaped rich yellow flowers.

— **haastii.** I have omitted most of the New Zealand species because they are unfortunately not in cultivation in this country, but *R. haastii* does occasionally make a shy appearance and is to be treasured for its glaucous, blue-grey leaves and yellow flowers with thick, waxy petals. It will need alpine house treatment and scree soil rich in humus.

— **histriculus.** A rarity from N. America which has wide, scalloped leaves and carries white flowers loosely on short stems.

— **insignis.** From New Zealand. Thick, undivided leaves with toothed leaves margined with brownish hairs. Branching stems carry many large golden flowers.

— **kochii.** From Turkey, and has been in cultivation but I am uncertain of the present situation. Low tufts of entire, rounded leaves and on short stems very large richly golden flowers, the petals as glossy as those of the Lesser Celandine.

— **lappaceus.** A treasure from Tasmania, dubiously in cultivation. Neat tufts on dry hillsides surmounted by mounds of glossy, brilliantly golden flowers.

— **lobulatus.** From New Zealand. Bright green, thick, kidney-shaped leaves on short brown petioles and racemes of large lemon-yellow flowers on 8 in. stems.

— **lyallii.** The king of New Zealand buttercups, perhaps over-large for the average rock garden but a plant which every alpine plant enthusiast longs to grow — although success is often elusive. It likes to delve its roots deeply into moist soil. In British gardens we seldom see it assume the proportions it can attain in alpine New Zealand, where the glossy green, saucer-shaped leaves can be 8 in. or more in diameter and the stately, branching stems can reach a height of 40 in. carrying panicles of huge white flowers. My own solitary success came when I grew it near to a water-tub, in rich, deep soil and everyone who passed the tub during spring and summer had instructions to splash water over the ranunculus.

— **millefoliatus.** From Southern and Central Europe. Tufts of finely dissected leaves and 6 in stems carrying rounded yellow flowers.

— **montanus.** (R. geranifolius.) Botanically a divergent group, scattered throughout the mountains of Europe. The few which concern us have been dealt with under their better known names, of which *R. gouanii* is an example. What may be regarded as the type species makes neat, low tufts of glabrous or lightly haired leaves, sometimes stem-clasping. The bright yellow flowers are carried on short stems. A garden cultivar named 'Molten Gold' is of particular neatness. floriferousness and merit.

— **monroi.** From New Zealand and similar to, and possibly identical with, *R. insignis.*

— **parnassifolius.** From the Alps of Europe and, in its best form, a treasure, but it can be disappointing. Tiny tufts of leathery, dark green, heart shaped pointed leaves and short stems which carry, snow-white flowers which ought to have wide, overlapping petals, but are sometimes rather squinny and narrow-petalled. For sunny places and gritty soil.

— **paucifolius.** From New Zealand and very similar to, and possibly synonymous with *R. crithmifolius* and *R. chordorhizos*. The latter is described, *q.v.*

— **pygmaeus.** From Arctic Europe. The smallest of buttercups with tufts of tiny leaves and short-stemmed yellow flowers.

— **pyrenaeus.** From the European Alps, including Spain and Corsica. Narrow, ribbed leaves and fine white flowers on 8 in. stems, but there are poor forms which should be avoided. At its best, it is a splendid plant.

— **repens.** A British native and included, partly as a warning for it is a running, pernicious weed, and partly to praise the occasional colour forms which are found. I have a delightful lemon-yellow form which really does stay at home.

— **rutifolius.** See CALLIANTHEMUM *anemonoides.*

— **sartorianus** (or sometimes *sartori*). A rather undistinguished species with yellow flowers from the Balkans and Italy.

— **seguieri.** Scattered in widely separated areas of the European Alps, usually on limestone. Tufts of finely cut, smooth, grey-green leaves and rounded milk-white, golden-eyed flowers like small moons on very short stems. A scree or trough plant *par excellence.*

— **speciosus.** See *R. bulbosus.*

— **sulphureus.** From sub-Arctic Europe. Rather tall but it has nice sulphur-yellow flowers.

— **thora.** European Alps. Wide, slightly scalloped and toothed leaves which tend to clasp the flower stems which carry numerous, but rather small, shrill yellow flowers. Interesting in leaf but not a floral beauty.

— **traunfellneri.** See *R. alpestris.*

— **wettsteinii.** From the Eastern Alps. Deeply divided leaves at ground level, and handsome, snow-white flowers on short stems.

RANZANIA. *Berberidaceae.* Named for Ono Ranzan (1729-1810), a celebrated Japanese naturalist.

A genus of one Japanese mountain woodland species.

— **japonica.** For cool, lime-free soil. Best in the peat garden or alpine house. The flowers, which precede the leaves in spring are nodding. saucer-shaped, of good size and soft lilac in colour and carried on

12 in. stems. The flowers may be followed by white fruits. The leaves are divided into lobed leaflets.

RAOULIA. *Compositae*. Named for Edouard Raoul (1815-1852), a French naval surgeon who collected plants in New Zealand.

An entirely Australasian genus, mostly in New Zealand. A few carpeting species have long been cultivated and are easily grown in well-drained soil and open, sunny positions. Others are difficult but rewarding alpine house plants. Of the twenty or so New Zealand species, I include those which make occasional, often only too brief appearances in British gardens. There are others, equally enticing, but they are seldom, if ever, available. The temperamental, cushion-forming alpine house species demand the utmost care in very gritty soil or tufa rocks. They appear not to object to lime. Many perish through injudicious overhead watering.

— **australis.** The best known species. Flat carpets of crowded, tiny, intensely silver leaves in wee rosettes and spatterings of minute yellow flowers in dense heads. It grows well outside, but may suffer in very wet and cold winters.

— **bryoides.** Although they are distinct species I lump this together with *R. buchananii*, *R. eximia* and *R. mammilaris*. They are equally difficult and of similar appearance. The congested rosettes form grey and silver humps, almost like hardened lumps of silvery frogspawn. They are exciting and exasperating. To grow them well represents a great triumph.

— **buchananii.** See *R. bryoides*.

— **eximia.** See *R. bryoides*.

— **glabra.** One of the easiest. Flat green mats and tiny stemless heads of cream-white flowers.

— **goyenii.** This might well have been included with the other species mentioned under *R. bryoides*, it falls into a similar classification.

— **grandiflora.** Rather loose mats of tiny, pointed silver leaves and quite large, stemless white, golden-centred flowers. Not as difficult as some and benefits from fairly frequent division.

— **haastii.** This emulates other cushion-forming species in light green leaves packed into densely crowded rosettes.

— **hectori.** Hard, silver-green hummocks.

— **hookeri.** A comparatively new introduction which is fast becoming a very popular alpine house plant, and may well succeed as happily in the open as *R. australis*, of which it is a slightly larger, even more silvery counterpart.

— **lutescens.** This has been grown under the name *R. subsericea*. It is a mere film of wee, tightly packed rosettes of minute grey-green leaves. The mats are liberally studded with tiny stemless clusters of yellow flowers in spring. A fine tufa plant.

— **mammilaris.** One of the most typical of the New Zealand 'Mountain Sheep', forming hard mounds of silvered rosettes. It is as intractable as others of its kind.

— **rubra.** Another silver hummock but with clusters of crimson florets almost concealed among the tightly packed rosettes.

— **subsericea.** See *R. lutescens.*

— **tenuicaulis.** A very easy grey-green carpeter, useful as ground cover for small alpine bulbs in gritty soil and sunny positions.

REAUMURIA. *Tamaricineae.* Named for Rene A. Ferchault de Reaumur (1683-1757), a French entomologist.

— **vermiculata.** A very dwarf, compact shrub, native to N. Africa and Sicily. The woody stems carry whorls of narrow, blue-green leaves and single flowers like those of a white Saxifraga. It will demand alpine house treatment or a warm and sheltered position in the open.

REINECKIA. *Liliaceae.* Named for Johann Heinrich Julius Reinecke (1799-1871).

— **carnea.** (Liriope hyacinthiflora.) From China and Japan. For light shade and, preferably, lime-free soil. Spreading rhizomes and long, narrow, rather thick leaves and loose spikes of flesh-pink flowers in spring on 8 in. stems.

RHAMNUS. *Rhamnaceae.* The ancient Greek name for various spiny shrubs. A genus of, mostly, tall shrubs but there are one or two dwarf species suitable for the rock garden.

— **procumbens.** From the Himalaya. A low mound of entangled branches with small, shining green leaves. The inconspicuous flowers are followed by black fruits. It is dubiously in cultivation.

— **pumilus.** From the Alps of S. Europe. Usually prostrate with, spreading, woody stems and blue-black fruits. Very appropriate to the rock garden.

RHEXIA. *Melastomaceae.* Name used by Pliny, of uncertain origin, for some other plant.

A small genus of herbs or sub-shrubs, natives of N. America. They appreciate lime-free soil and warm positions. *R. ciliosa* and

R. mariana are sometimes cultivated but are rather tall for most rock gardens. The species described below is the most appropriate to this Manual.

— **virginica.** Erect, bristly, 8 in. stems with lanceolate leaves and crowned with quite large red-purple flowers in summer.

RHODIOLA. *Crassulaceae.*

— **rosea.** (Sedum rosea. Sedum rhodiola.) After shuffling uneasily between the genera SEDUM and RHODIOLA, this British native appears to have come to rest as *R. rosea*. It makes a thick, fleshy rootstock from which rise in spring erect stems bearing many narrow, alternate leaves to a height of 8 to 10 in. and ending in heads of greenish-yellow flowers. It is an attractive plant in the early year, but cannot claim great floral beauty. The variety *R.r. heterodonta* is more spectacular. The young stems and leaves are rich purple and the flowers are rich rust-red in colour.

RHODOHYPOXIS. *Hypoxidaceae.* From the Greek *rhodo*, red and *Hypoxis*, the genus to which this is related.

A small genus of S. African plants with tiny, corm-like roots. They occur at high elevations in the Drakensberg mountains and may be regarded as hardy, although it is not unknown, in very wet and cold situations for them to suffer loss during the winter. They should be given a soil mixture rich in peat and unlikely to dry out in the summer. They flower continuously throughout the summer.

— **baurii.** The best-known species and the one from which the many named cultivars have been raised. The colour varies according to variety from white, through shades of pink to deep red. The choice is wide and a selection should be made from catalogues listing the numerous cultivars. They seldon exceed 2 in. when in flower.

— **milloides.** Almost sessile, rose-pink flowers. Very rare in cultivation and probably not as hardy as *R. baurii.*

— **rubella.** Quite diminutive, bright pink flowers. A charming sink or trough plant.

RHODOTHAMNUS. *Ericaceae.* From the Greek *rhodo*, red, and *thamnos*, a shrub.

— **chamaecistus.** The only species in its genus and a native of limestone areas in the Alps of Europe. A neat, dwarf shrub, slow-growing, with erect 10 in. stems clothed in small, narrow, dark green leaves and terminal clusters of saucer-shaped rich pink flowers in spring. It appreciates a humus-rich, gritty soil and a sunny, but not scorching, position.

RICOTIA. *Cruciferae.* Named for Ricot, a little-known French botanist.

— **davisiana.** A pleasant little crucifer from Crete, for which I have a particular affection as it is named in honour of its discoverer. Dr. Peter Davis, who began his horticultural career on this nursery many years ago, and is now one of our leading botanists and responsible for writing a monumental Flora of Turkey. From a woody base rise brittle stems bearing fleshy, blue-grey leaves and carrying rounded heads of pink flowers. It does not usually exceed 5 in. in height. For the alpine house.

ROETTLERA. See the genus OREOCHARIS.

ROHDEA. *Liliaceae.* Named for Michael Rohde (1782-1812), a physician of Bremen.

— **japonica.** From Japan. For peaty woodland soil and light shade. Stout, creeping rhizomes and tufts of lanceolate leaves and slender, many-flowered spikes of white flowers, followed by red or yellow fruits. Usually about 12 to 16 in. Spring and summer flowering.

ROMANZOFFIA. *Hydrophyllaceae.* Named for Prince Nicholas Romanzoff, who financed a round-the-world expedition in 1816-17.

A small genus of plants, similar in appearance to some Saxifragas, from Western N. America and N.E. Asia. They have a liking for cool positions in moisture-holding soil. Spring and summer flowering.

— **sitchensis.** Tufts of small, round, scalloped, bright green leaves and loose, short-stemmed sprays of white flowers, centred with golden stamens.

— **tracyi.** A rather dim and disappointing species from wet and mossy rocks of the Californian sea coast. The white flowers are too small to be significant.

— **unalaschkensis.** From the Aleutian Islands, and not unlike *R. sitchensis* with short-stemmed, attractive waxy-white flowers.

ROSA. *Rosaceae.* The Latin name of these plants.

In spite of their importance as garden plants, there is little to be said about roses in this Manual. I deplore the use of the many miniature roses on rock gardens, where they are entirely out of context with their surroundings. Even *R. pendulina* (R. alpina), the alpine rose of European mountains, is too vigorous for small rock gardens, although it is to be valued for the sake of its large pink flowers. The variety *pyrenaica* is dwarfer and more suitable and the single, deep rose-red flowers are beautiful.

ROSCOEA. *Zingiberaceae.* Named in honour of William Roscoe (1753-1831) of Liverpool, a founder of the Liverpool botanic garden and author of a Monograph on the Natural Order *Zingiberaceae.*

Plants from China and the Himalaya for cool, deep soil and light shade, summer flowering. They scarcely qualify as alpines, but are grown on many rock gardens.

- **alpina.** Not one of the most showy, but the dwarfest, and quite attractive, with short spikes of pink flowers. It seldom exceeds 8 in.
- **auriculata.** Probably a form of *R. purpurea* 'Procera', from which it differs only in the leaves being auriculate at the base.
- **cautleoides.** A robust and handsome plant with strong tufts of glossy, lanceolate leaves from which rise 12 in. stems carrying hooded, soft yellow flowers.
- **humeana.** As vigorous as the preceding species, but the orchid-like flowers are purple with a yellow throat to the long corolla tube.
- **purpurea.** Another strong-growing plant which is overtaken in beauty by the form *procera*, whose hooded, large flowers of rich lavender-purple have a strikingly prominent white lip.

ROSMARINUS. *Labiatae.* From the Latin *ros*, dew, and *marinus*, maritime. It is wild on sea cliffs in S. Europe.

Dearly loved garden plants, but not for most rock gardens, with the sole exception of the prostrate plant long known as *R. officinalis prostratus*, but now said to be correctly *R. lavandulaceus*, although I observe that *Flora Europaea* does not appear to recognise this name. Not reliably hardy, especially in cold districts, but splendid when draped over a dry, hot wall. Its trailing stems, clothed in aromatic leaves carry many clusters of blue flowers in summer.

ROSULARIA. *Crassulaceae.* From *rosula*, a little rose, a reference to the characteristic leaf-rosettes.

A small genus from Asia and Asia Minor, much confused in the past with the genera COTYLEDON, UMBILICUS and even SEDUM. For warm situations in the open or for the alpine house, spring and early summer flowering.

— **libanotica.** Occasionally grown in the form *steudetii* from Iran. The large rosettes of fleshy leaves support loose cymes of dainty pink flowers. Definitely for the alpine house.

— **pallida.** Long grown as COTYLEDON chrysantha. Rosettes like those of a small, softly grey-haired Sempervivum and short spikes of soft yellow tubular flowers.

— **platiphylla.** Rosettes of smooth, fleshy leaves and short spikes of white flowers.

— **serrata.** Rosettes of fleshy leaves, toothed at the margins. The white flowers have red markings.

RUBUS. *Rosaceae.* The Latin name for the genus.

An enormous family, of more than 400 species with a world-wide distribution in the tropical, sub-tropical and temperate world. Very few are of interest to rock gardeners. rs.

— **arcticus.** A creeping species from the Northern Hemisphere and Arctic regions. It spreads by underground stems, emitting tufts of small, trifolate leaves and frail, short stems each carrying one quite large rich pink flower. A fine peat-garden plant or for similar situations.

— **calycinoides.** (R. fockeanus of gardens.) Absolutely prostrate, rough hairy stems which root at the joints. Mallow-like, three-lobed leaves are glossy green and matt-surfaced. White flowers borne in small clusters between the foliage.

— **chamaemorus.** A native of moors and bogs in northern Britain. Not an easy plant to cultivate, but worth attempting in a peat bed where the creeping stems might produce the good white flowers, followed by the bramble-fruits with red and orange drupes.

— **fockeanus** of gardens. See *R. calycinoides.*

RUPICAPNOS. *Fumariaceae.* Derivation obscure.

— **africanus.** A rarity from the Riff Mountains where it grows in Tufa cliffs. Fleshy, blue-green leaves in low mounds and rose-pink flowers shaped like those of a Corydalis. Definitely for the alpine house. Spring Flowering.

RUTA. *Rutaceae.* The Latin word, meaning bitterness.

The common Rue, *R. graveolens* is no rock garden plant, but one or two of the dwarfer species are admissible. They are all avid sun-lovers, aromatic and summer flowering although grown mainly for their foliage.

- **corsica.** A dwarf, spiny, grey-leaved shrub with white flowers but curious rather than beautiful. From Corsica and Sardinia.
- **montana.** From S.W. Europe. Low mounds of finely dissected silver-grey leaves. A delightful foliage plant.
- **patavina.** This comes from the Balkans and is now correctly HAPLOPHYLLUM *patavinum*. Low bushes of grey, bitterly aromatic leaves and yellow flowers.

RYDBERGIA grandiflora. See HYMENOXIS *grandiflora.*

SAGINA. *Caryophyllaceae.* From the Latin *sagina*, fodder, because of the fattening qualities of spurrey *(Spergula sativa)* which was once contained in this genus.

A small genus of, often, rather weedy plants but containing a few desirable rock garden and alpine house plants.

- **boydii.** The choicest of its race and of interest since it was once discovered in Scotland in 1878, or thereabouts, and has never since been found as a wild plant. For the alpine house, scree, or sink and trough gardens. Tightly compressed rosettes of small, highly glossed, deep-green leaves in neat, domed hummocks. The flowers are greenish and inconspicuous. It suffers frequently from attack by red spider mites against which precautions should be taken.
- **glabra.** (ARENARIA caespitosa, hort.) A common and useful plant, more specially in the form 'Aurea', which makes low mats of thread-like golden shoots starred with short-stemmed white flowers in spring and early summer. For any soil or sunny position. The type is native to northern and Arctic Europe.
- **linnaei.** See *S. saginoides.*
- **pilifera.** From Corsica and Sardinia and not unlike *S. glabra* and a useful carpeter.
- **saginoides.** (S. linnaei.) From Spain, Greece and into Arctic Europe. A rather spindly mat-forming plant from the Alps of Europe. Not exciting but can be used as an easy ground carpeter.

SALIX. *Salicaceae.* The Latin name for the genus.

A very large genus of deciduous trees and shrubs, ranging from tiny, ground-hugging plants to tall trees. They are widely distributed throughout the Northern Hemisphere. Although shrubs, as such, are largely excluded from this Manual, there are certain exceptions, of which this is one, for the dwarf willows are too important to be omitted from any list of rock garden plants. They are

341

easily grown, tolerant of most soils and sun-lovers in general, although they do not appreciate situations which are too sunscorched. With the exception of one species, *S. bockii*, which bears its catkins in the autumn, but is too tall a shrub for inclusion here, they display their decorative male catkins in the spring. Written descriptions of some of the dwarf species would convey little and therefore the majority of individual descriptions are brief, but all those listed are very desirable dwarf or creeping shrubs for rock gardens and even for sink and trough gardens.

— alpina. (S. jacquinii.) From the E. Alps. Spreading, procumbent stems, small rounded leaves with entire margins and slender grey catkins.

— angulorum. From the Rocky Mountains of N. America, and has appeared in gardens in the form of the variety *antiplasta*, which is an extremely desirable rock-hugging shrublet with 1 in. catkins which appear red because of their brightly coloured stamens. The smaller female catkins are silver.

— apoda. From the Caucasus, and introduced about 1937 by the late Walter Ingwersen. Prostrate, vigorous, spreading stems clad in glossy green leaves. The male catkins are long and at first silver, becoming flushed with glowing orange and pink as they mature. The female catkins, as always on separate plants, are grey and much less conspicuous.

— arbuscula. (S. formosa.) A rare British native and from many other European stations. Creeping woody stems and dense mats of deep-green leaves, glaucous beneath. Long, slender grey catkins.

— arctica. From the Rocky Mountains. An attractive, very dwarf species but very dubiously in cultivation.

— X boydii. A treasured pygmy tree which commemorates the late William Brack Boyd, a Scottish farmer and botanist. It was discovered by him, somewhere in Perthshire sometime during the 1880's and is a supposed hybrid between *S. lanata* and *S. reticulata*, but it has never been found since and the parentage is conjectural. Stiff, erect, gnarled branches form a very slow-growing tiny tree. After many years it can attain a stature of approximately 16 to 20 ins. The rounded, leathery leaves are reticulated and grey-green and the stubby catkins are silver, maturing to cream. It is one of the best dwarf shrubs for sink and trough gardens.

— X finnmarchica. A natural hybrid between *S. myrtilloides* and *S. repens*. A wide-spreading prostrate shrub with small leaves and small grey catkins.

— formosa. See *S. arbuscula*.

— glaucosericea. From the European Alps. Prostrate woody stems and silver-haired leaves and typical grey catkins.

— X grahamii. A hybrid between two British and European species, *S. herbacea* and *S. myrsinites*. Mats of entangled woody stems with shining green leaves and erect, showy catkins.

— **hastata wehrhahnii.** (S. wehrhahnii.) I hesitated before including this handsome willow as it will eventually become too large for most rock gardens, but in its younger stages it is a useful dwarf shrub with a splendid display of large, cream-white catkins on the still leafless stems in eary spring.

— **helvetica.** European. A small, bushy, erect shrub with grey-green, softly hairy leaves. The catkins are silver at first, becoming yellow as they mature.

— **herbacea.** Abundant in northern British mountains, and elsewhere in Europe. One of the smallest, forming mats of creeping stems. The tiny leaves are glossy and reticulated. The grey catkins appear together with the leaves in spring.

— **jacquinii.** See *S. alpina.*

— **lanata.** A rare British native and also found in Arctic and sub-arctic Europe. Lusty bushes of woody stems up to 20 in. or more in height. The oval or rounded leaves are thickly felted with silver hairs and the robust yellow-grey catkins are very conspicuous. Too large for very small rock gardens.

— **lapponum.** A nice dwarf willow and a British native and also from as far away as Siberia. Tangles of woody stems, downy grey leaves and silky silvery catkins.

— **X moorei.** A hybrid between *S. herbacea* and *S. phylicifolia* (which itself is too tall for most rock gardens). Low, spreading mats of entwined stems, shining green leaves and pretty grey catkins.

— **myrsinites.** A prostrate species from Britain, N. Europe and N. Asia. Carpets of short, ascending stems, glossy green leaves and catkins on the leafless stems in early spring.

— **myrtilloides.** A low shrub, spreading by underground stems. Leaves dull green above, grey-green beneath and short grey catkins. The selected form 'Pink Tassels' has pretty, soft pink catkins.

— **nivalis.** A tiny shrublet, barely 1 in. high. The stems are clothed in tiny, dark green leaves and the catkins, which I have not seen, are described as red!

— **polaris.** From Arctic Europe. Creeping stems and small, glossy leaves and characteristic catkins.

— **pygmaea.** I cannot trace an authentic reference to this name but the plant it covers is a 12 in. shrublet with woody stems and handsome silver grey catkins before the leaves appear.

— **pyrenaica.** A low, spreading shrub with reddish-brown twigs, shiny leaves and rather lax catkins appearing with the leaves. From the Pyrenees.

— **repens.** Widely distributed in Britain, elsewhere in Europe, Siberia and west and central Asia. Too vigorous and spreading for small rock gardens, but a pretty, low shrub with far-flung branches, grey leaves and grey catkins. A form occasionally cultivated and known as

'Boyd's Pendulous' forms an erect stem which later droops pendulous branches, creating a weeping willow in minature.

— **reticulata.** A British native and widely distributed elsewhere, even into N. America. Prostrate stems in dense mats and rounded, leathery, net-veined leaves and erect catkins appearing after the leaves.

— **retusa.** From the European Alps. Carpets of thin, creeping stems and tiny, glossy, notched leaves. The grey catkins are small and erect.

— **X saddleri.** Probably a hybrid claiming *S. lanata* as one of its parents and in appearance a smaller version of that species.

— **saximontana.** From N. America and almost a replica of *S. reticulata.*

— **serpyllifolia.** This has usually been regarded as a miniature form of *S. retusa,* but *Flora Europaea* now gives it specific rank. Absolutely prostrate, with tiny leaves and small but likeable catkins.

— **X stephaniae.** This is another probable *S. lanata* hybrid and is more suitable than that species for small rock gardens.

— **stuartii.** Probably a form of *S. lanata* and robust. The shoots have orange buds and the leaves are silver-haired. The catkins are large and handsome.

— **subopposita.** From Japan and Korea. A very rare dwarf species with short, erect stems forming bushes which have been likened to a dwarf Hebe. The silvery catkins appear before the leaves.

— **uva-ursi.** From N. America and one of the best absolutely prostrate willows. Creeping woody stems and small, rounded, glossy leaves and catkins which appear with the young leaves.

— **wehrhahnii.** See *S. hastata.*

— **yezoalpina.** A rare Japanese species with long, slender, trailing stems and reticulated glossy leaves.

SALVIA. *Laviatae.* The Latin name, derived from *salvus,* safe, or sound, from the supposed medicinal virtues.

An enormous family of more than 500 species, scattered over the temperate and warmer parts of the world. Few are of interest to alpine gardeners. A few from N. Africa and Turkey which sound enticing I omit because they are not likely to be available. They are all avid sun-lovers and summer flowering.

— **argentea.** An inhabitant of cliff faces and rocky crevices in E. Europe. Large rosettes of large, irregularly toothed and lobed leaves which are felted with a mat of silver hairs. The inflorescence is a candelabrum of branching, horizontal stems radiating from the central, tall spike and carrying innumerable white, hooded flowers. Probably best in the alpine house, or for sunny crevices in the open.

— **caespitosa.** From the mountains of Turkey. From a short, woody trunk spring stems carrying entire or pinnate intensely silver-haired leaves. The leaves are aromatic. The flowers are carried in short-stemmed clusters and have wide tubes and a broad lower lip. In the wild the colour is variable, but the form in cultivation has lilac-pink blossoms. It is happiest in the alpine house.

SAMOLUS. *Primulaceae.* The Latin name, possibly of Celtic origin for a plant gathered by Druids.

— **repens.** From Australia and New Zealand. A rather frail plant for moist soil, making slender, erect stems some 4 to 6 in. high and ending in clusters of starry pink flowers in spring and summer.

— **spathulatus.** From the sea-coast meadows of Patagonia. It has been in cultivation, fitfully. It is low-growing with good pink flowers, but is now only dubiously available.

SANGUINARIA. *Papaveraceae.* From the Latin *sanguis*, blood. All parts of the plant exude a copious red sap.

A genus of a single species from N. America. Spring flowering, and for cool or shaded positions in sandy-peaty soil. A fine peat-bed plant.

— **canadensis.** From thick, rhizomatous roots spring scalloped grey leaves enclosing the flower buds, which expand into solitary, wide, snow-white flowers. A form has existed with larger flowers which was dignified as 'Grandiflora' and there is an entrancing double-flowered form which is rare, but no more difficult than the type. It does not exceed 6 in. when in blossom.

SANTOLINA. *Compositae.* From the Latin *sanctum-linum*, holy flax, an old name for *S. virens*.

A race of shrubby plants of which only one is really suited to the rock garden.

— **chamaecyparissus corsica.** (C. incana.) Often catalogued as *S. incana* 'nana', this is a neat, 6 to 9 in. bush of silver stems and foliage. It has lemon-yellow heads of flower but these are less important than the foliage. A sun-lover for any soil. Summer flowering

— **incana.** See *S. chamaecyparissus.*

SAPONARIA. *Caryophyllaceae.* From the Latin *sapo*, soap. The roots of *S. officinalis* were used to make soap.

Spring and summer flowering, sun-loving plants.

— **bellidifolia.** From the Pyrenees and eastward into the Balkans. Allied to *S. lutea*, but taller, with heads of straw-yellow flowers.

- **X boissieri.** A hybrid between *S. caespitosa* and *S. ocymoides.* Neat 3 in. cushions of clear pink flowers. A good scree or trough plant.
- **X 'Bressingham Hybrid'.** A hybrid between a selected form of *S. ocymoides* and *S.X. olivana,* (itself a hybrid between *S. caespitosa* and *S. pumilio.)* Mats of red stems and small, softly hairy leaves. The tip of each stem ends in a cluster of deep pink flowers.
- **caespitosa.** From the Pyrenees. Humps of congested, narrow, thick leaves from which rise 4 in. stems carrying two or three bright pink flowers.
- **cypria.** From Cyprus and usually happier in an alpine house if a sunny crevice is not available. Cushions of glaucous, blue-green leaves, and bright pink flowers on short stems.
- **depressa.** Differs only in small details of foliage and other minor points from *S. cypria.*
- **lutea.** From the European Alps. Small tufts of tiny leaves and short-stemmed heads of straw-yellow flowers. Not a beauty, but interesting.
- **ocymoides.** From the Alps of Europe and especially the Pyrenees. Good for walls or crevices, from which its leafy stems cascade and offer sheets of bright pink flowers. There is a rather rare albino, and a very charming, compact plant grown as *S.o* 'Rubra Compacta', which I suspect may be a hybrid. It forms flat mats of creeping stems sheeted with rich red flowers.
- **X 'Olivana'.** A delightful hybrid between *S. pumilio* and *S. caespitosa.* Cushions of green stems and leaves and short, radiating stems carrying many quite large pink flowers.
- **pulvinaris.** From the Eastern Mediterranean. A lovely plant for screes or trough and sink gardens. Mats as compact as those of *Silene acaulis* of tiny, bright green leaves and radiating, prostrate stems each carrying several rich pink flowers. It is seen at its best if given a somewhat austere diet.
- **pumilio.** (Sometimes listed as *S. pumila.)* From the Eastern Alps. Cushion and mat-forming. It makes a deeply delving tap root requiring a good depth of soil. Sometimes shy-flowering unless starved and mature. Solitary, almost stemless pale or deep pink flowers with rather widely separated petals.

SARCOCAPNOS. *Papaveraceae.* From the Greek *sarkos*, fleshy and *kapnos*, the Greek name for fumitory.

- **crassifolia.** (S. speciosa.) From Spain and Morocco. It commonly inhabits rather shady rock crevices. Fleshy stems and grey leaves in low tufts and short racemes of pale pink flowers in spring. For the alpine house.
- **enneaphylla.** From Spain and the E. Pyrenees. Tufts of freely branching stems, woody at the base, leaves often pinnatisect, with oval segments, the short-spurred flowers may be white or yellowish, with purple tips. Also best in the alpine house.

— **speciosa.** See *S. crassifolia.*

There are one or two other species, dubiously in cultivation, such as *S. baetica* and *S. integrifolia*, which differ little from the preceding.

SARCOPOTERIUM. *Rosaceae.* From the Greek *sarkos*, fleshy and *Poterium.*

— **spinosum.** (Poterium spinosum.) From Sardinia and other Mediterranean regions. A lover of hot, dry positions or the alpine house. A dwarf, much branched spiky shrub, the stems tomentose and the lateral branches forming leafless spines, and, in summer, tiny clusters of small red flowers. It is said to be the plant from which the Crown of Thorns was made.

SARMIENTA. *Gesneriaceae.* Named for Mart. Sarmiento, a Spanish botanist.

— **repens.** From Chile, where it is partially epiphytic, also growing among mosses in damp places. It is the only species in its genus and makes a small, creeping, wiry-stemmed shrub with opposite, fleshy, entire or slightly toothed leaves and pendant, solitary crimson flowers in the leaf axils. For the sheltered peat bed or the alpine house in lime-free, peaty-soil.

SAROTHAMNUS. A genus of Leguminous plants now included in CYTISUS.

SATUREJA. (Commonly rendered in gardens as SATUREIA .) *Labiatae.* The Latin name for this herb which was well known to the ancients and was recommended by Virgil for planting near bee hives.

A genus of aromatic herbs and sub-shrubs. Sun-lovers and summer flowering.

— **alpina.** Now correctly ACINOS *alpinus* but described in this Manual under its better known name of CALAMINTHA *alpina*, which see.

— **ashei.** A rarity, dubiously in cultivation, from sand dunes in Georgia. Erect stems, aromatic foliage and pink flowers.

— **montana.** (MICROMERIA pygmaea.) From S. Europe. Short-stemmed semi-prostrate or erect bushes of aromatic foliage and short spikes of pale pink flowers.

SATUREJA — *continued*

- **rupestris.** See MICROMERIA *rupestris.*
- **spicigera.** From Asia Minor and dubiously in cultivation. Dies down in winter to a thick, fleshy root. In late summer new, prostrate stems appear, and, in September, many snow-white flowers.
- **spinosa.** A 9 in. spiky shrub from Crete with white or pale lilac flowers.
- **subspicata.** This is *S. montana* subspecies *illyrica* and differs from the type only in minor details and geographical location.

SAUSSUREA. *Compositae.* Named for Horace Benedict de Saussure (1740-1799), Swiss philosopher and scientist.

A family of sometimes weedy but occasionally exciting composites from Europe, Asia and N. America. The few most likely to interest the alpine gardener are rarely in cultivation and seldom endure for more than a year or two. If any of the following were to be obtained they are worth attempting. *S. alpina. S. candolleana. S. gossipiphora. S. sorocephala.* Alpine house treatment would be advisable.

SAXIFRAGA. *Saxifragaceae.* From the Latin *saxum*, a rock, and *frango*, to break. Growing in rock crevices this herb was supposed to be capable of breaking rocks and, was accorded a medicinal quality of breaking up stones in the bladder.

A large and important family of more than 300 species and countless hybrids and forms. Usually in alpine locations in the north and south temperate regions, in Asia and, rarely in S. America but entirely absent from Australia and S. Africa.

To do full justice to such a family would demand a separate volume and I propose to deal with it much in the manner that I employed with the genus PRIMULA. For more detailed information there is no more convenient source than the monograph on the genus written by Mr. Winton Harding and published by the Alpine Garden Society in 1970. I would suggest that both these valuable publications be used in conjunction with this Manual by those seeking more detailed information than it is possible to print in this Manual.

The genus is divided botanically into a number of sections, listed below. Where relevant, the number of the section to which a particular plant belongs will be found in brackets after its name in the alphabetical sequence.

(1) MICRANTHES (Formerly BOROPHILA.) (2) HIRCULUS.
(3) ROBERTSONIANA. (4) MISCOPETALUM. (5) CYMBAL-
ARIA. (6) TRIDACTYLITES. (7) NEPHROPHYLLUM.
(8) DACTYLOIDES. (9) TRACHYPHYLLUM. (10) XANTH-
IZOON. (11) EUAIZOONIA. (12) KABSCHIA.
(13) PORPHYRION. (14) TETRAMERIDIUM. (This section is
now usually merged with section 12.) (15) DIPTERA.

The sections are also sub-divided in various subsections, which, on
the whole, I shall ignore as they are of little more than botanical
interest. Many of the species in the genus have been omitted from
this Manual, because of their unavailability. Unless otherwise stated
those included will relish open, sunny positions in sharply drained
soil. By and large they are lime-lovers tolerant of neutral conditions.
Exceptions will be noted. The principal flowering season is during
spring and early summer but there are a few late-flowering species.
This quality will be noted where relevant.

In the case of hybrids described the reference to sections is usually
omitted. This is because, in some cases the parents are in separate
sections. Where the parentage is known and quoted, the sections
can be traced by reference to the species involved. In all cases, as
elsewhere in this Manual, a hybrid is indicated by a X preceding
the name.

— X 'Ada'. A hybrid between *S. tombeanensis* and a form of
S. burseriana (now correctly *S. burseiana.*) Very compact cushions
and the short-stemmed flowers should be white, but there is a
plant in cultivation under this name which has pale pink blossoms.

— adscendens. (6) Widely distributed throughout Europe. Biennial, up
to 12 in. in height, with spikes of good white flowers. It appreciates
light shade.

— aizoides. (10) The only species in its section. It occurs throughout
Europe, including Britain and is also found in N. America and Asia.
Low mats of stems clothed in narrow, fleshy, light green leaves. The
yellow, red-spotted flowers are carried in short terminal cymes. It
appreciates moisture and a cool position. There are two forms, one
with orange flowers and the other dark red, which are identified as
aurantia and *atrorubens* respectively.

— aizoon. (11) According to the latest classification this is now
correctly *S. paniculata*, but I retain the well known name. It is a very
variable species widely distributed throughout southern and central
Europe and extending into Arctic regions. It would be difficult to
point to any one plant and say with authority "that is typical
S. aizoon". Lengthy lists of named forms exist in catalogues, to which
you are referred to make a selection. I will confine myself to
mentioning, as being of special merit, *S.a.* 'Rosea', with soft pink
flowers, *S.a.* 'Lutea', clear yellow, and *S.a. minutifolia*, the smallest
and most compact of all. This last one is occasionally listed as
S.a. baldensis.

- **ajugifolia.** See *S. praetermissa.*
- **X 'Amitie'.** A hybrid between *S. lilacina* and a form of *S. marginata.* Grey hummocks and deep lilac buds which expand into flowers of paler colour.
- **andersonii.** (12) A comparative newcomer from Nepal, now established in cultivation. Cushions of lime-encrusted leaves in tight rosettes and 1 to 2 in. stems each carrying several white or soft pink flowers. So far it is not inclined to flower with great freedom and I suggest a modicum of austerity in very gritty soil.
- **X andrewsii.** A hybrid whose parentage is open to question. It was discovered growing wild in eastern Ireland and one of its parents is almost certainly *S. hirsuta*, a native of Ireland, where the plant was originally found. The other parent might well be *S. aizoon*, with pollen blown or bee-carried from an adjacent garden. A sturdy ground-coverer best in partial shade. Tightly clustered rosettes of toothed leaves and 10 in. red stems carrying many white, pink or red-spotted flowers.
- **androsacea.** (8) From high elevations in the European alps. Usually in acid conditions and with a liking for moisture and light shade. Tufts of leaves which may be entire or three-toothed. A few quite large white flowers of good substance are borne on short stems.
- **apiculata.** A hybrid, probably between *S. sancta* and a form of *S. marginata.* It is one of the easiest and most popular early flowering hybrids, making cushions of bright green, closely packed narrow leaves, freely studded with an abundance of yellow flowers carried in heads of ten or more on 3 in. stems. There is a white-flowered sport, *S.a.* 'Alba' which is also desirable.
- **aquatica.** (8) From streamsides and moist places in the Pyrenees . A robust plant, forming lush mounds of large, leathery, deeply cleft leaves of shining green. Branching, foot-high stems carry loose panicles of white flowers.
- **arachnoidea.** (7) A rarity, interesting but not very beautiful, which grows in dry limestone caves near Lake Garda. Of annual or biennial duration, it makes lax cushions of oval, toothed, hairy leaves and produces rather nondescript pale yellow flowers.
- **X 'Arco-Valleyi'.** An old but still valuable hybrid between *S. lilacina* and *S. burserana* 'Minor'. Pads of crowded rosettes on which rest almost stemless soft pink flowers of good substance.
- **aretioides.** (12) From the Pyrenees. Hard hummocks of congested rosettes and, on very short stems, few-flowered clusters of golden flowers. Best out of direct sunlight, in gritty soil. A good sink or trough plant.
- **aristulata.** (2) From the Himalaya and dubiously in cultivation. Dense tufts of leaves in small rosettes and large yellow solitary flowers on 2 in. stems. If obtained it is sure to prefer a cool, moist position.
- **aspera.** (9) From the European alps, usually in lime-free conditions. Dense mats of small, stiff, bristle-edged leaves and short stems

carrying a few soft yellow flowers, spotted with orange. The plant often grown as *S.a. bryoides* has now been given specific rank.

— **X assimilis.** A hybrid of uncertain parentage, but possibly *S. burserana* and *S. tombeanensis.* Firm grey cushions and short-stemmed large, pure white flowers.

— **austromontana.** See *S. bronchialis.*

— **'Ballawley Guardsman'.** This is one of the many 'Mossy' selections or hybrids and has velvety crimson-scarlet flowers.

— **X bellunensis.** A hybrid between *S. aizoon (paniculata)* and *S. hostii.* Resembles a robust *S. aizoon* with white flowers on fairly tall stems.

— **biasolettii 'Crystalie'.** A handsome hybrid between *S. grisebachii* and *S. sempervivum* (S. porophylla thessalica.) Intermediate between the parents, and a decorative crimson inflorescence.

— **biflora.** (13) From high altitudes in the European alps. Usually rather difficult and best given alpine house treatment in gritty but moisture-holding soil. It is shy-flowering and when in blossom resembles an inferior form of *S. oppositifolia.*

— **X bileckii.** A hybrid between *S. ferdinand-coburgii* and *S. tombeanensis.* Firm, silvery-grey cushions of small, incurved leaves and several soft yellow flowers on 2 in. stems

— **'Bob Hawkins'.** A new hybrid or selection in the 'Mossy' group forming compact hummocks of deeply-cleft leaves variegated in silver and green, in contrast with crimson tints seen in the older leaves. Good white flowers on 6 in. stems.

— **blepharophylla.** A form of *S. oppositifolia,* which see.

— **X boekleri.** A hybrid between *S. ferdinand-coburgii* and *S. stribrnyi.* Rosettes of silver-grey leaves and 3 in. stems carrying many orange. or red, yellow-tinted flowers in early spring.

— **X borisii.** A hybrid between *S. ferdinand-coburgii* and *S. marginata.* Pads of pointed, blue-grey leaves and 3 in. reddish and hairy stems carrying a few large, citron-yellow flowers.

— **boryi.** (12) Nearly related to, and almost indistinguishable from, *S. marginata.*

— **X 'Boston Spa'.** A good hybrid of uncertain origin. Mat-forming with flowers resembling those of *S. apiculata,* but of a rather richer yellow.

— **X boydii.** One of the oldest hybrids, raised in 1890 and now becoming a little exhausted with age. The parentage was probably *S. aretioides* and a form of *S. marginata.* Worth struggling with for the sake of its rich yellow flowers on short, red stems over tight cushions of rosettes. A rare sport with white flowers exists, but is seldom seen.

— **X 'Bridget'.** A hybrid between *S. stribrnyi* and a form of *S. marginata.* Tight rosettes of silvery leaves and short inflorescences of mauve - pink flowers.

— **bronchialis.** (9) From sub-Arctic Europe, Asia and N. America. Like a compressed version of *S. aspera* and of little horticultural merit, the form *austromontana* is the one most commonly grown.

— **brunoniana.** (2) From the Himalaya. Rosettes of bristle-margined leaves from which spring innumerable frail, red, strawberry-like runners ending in new rosettes which root where they touch the ground. The yellow flowers are carried in loose panicles on 4 to 6 in. stems in mid-summer. A plant for a cool position in moist but gritty soil, or the alpine house — it can be injured by a severe winter.

— **bryoides.** (9) Like *S. bronchialis*, this resembles a compressed *S. aspera*. It is commonly grown as a form of that species.

— **bulbifera.** (7) From Central and Southern Europe and rather like a gaunt and less garden-worthy *S. granulata*, to which species it is closely allied.

— **X burnatii.** A hybrid between *S. aizoon* and *S. cochlearis*, a natural hybrid originally found in the Maritime Alps. Intermediate between the parents, and loose sprays of white flowers on 6 in. reddish stems.

— **burserana.** (12) (S. burseriana.) Mostly from the Eastern Alps and very variable in its geographic distribution. Typically it makes hard cushions of glaucous, grey-green spiky leaves and carries pure white flowers on 3 in. reddish stems. It is one of the gems of its section, in all of its many cultivated forms or hybrids, to which the following names are a reference without detailed descriptions. They are all good. 'Brookside'. 'Crenata'. 'Gloria'. 'His Majesty'. 'Major Lutea'. 'Sulphurea', plus the forms *major, minor* and *tridentata*. These are all splendid plants for screes, trough or sink gardens, or the alpine house.

— **caesia.** (12) Widespread in the European alps, and a lover of deep rock crevices. It is an ideal plant for growing in Tufa rock. Tiny rosettes of hard grey leaves compress into tight hummocks. 3 in. stems carry several surprisingly large pure white flowers, usually in June. It is happiest when accorded a measure of austerity. For *S. caesia of St. Johns* see *S. stricta*.

— **caespitosa.** (8) A rare British native and also found in Arctic Europe and N. America. Of little garden value but interesting as being one of the original parents of the many 'Mossy' hybrids. Compact tufts of three-lobed soft green leaves and 'off-white' small flowers on 3 in. stems.

— **callosa.** (11) (S. lingulata.) A very variable, but invaluable species from Spain, S. France and Italy. Its rosettes are composed of silver leaves, narrow in most cases but broader in some geographic forms, and the white flowers are carried in gracefully arching panicles. Although they like the sun they appreciate positions where they receive light shade for part of the day. Catalogues may list several named varieties, such as *albertii, australis, bellardii* and *lantoscana*.

— **camposii.** (8) (S. wallacei). From the limestone mountains of

S. E. Spain. Tidy, rather hard cushions of narrowly divided, sticky leaves. The leaf segments are grooved on their upper surfaces. The white flowers are carried in loose trusses on 9 in. stems. It is a handsome plant, a sun-lover and not absolutely hardy in severe winters.

— X canis dalmatica. A hybrid between S. cotyledon and a form of S. aizoon. Rosettes of green incurved leaves and 15 in. spikes of white flowers heavily spotted with purple.

— cardiophylla. (2) From Western China, originally in 1869 and recently re-introduced. For moist and peaty soil — a good peat-garden plant, where it should make wide, low mats of foliage and on 4 in. stems carry several flowers of rich orange-yellow.

— X 'Carnival'. A 'Mossy' with good crimson-rose flowers on short stems over neat foliage.

— cartilaginea. This is one of several sub-species of S. aizoon (paniculata).

— caucasica. (12) From the Caucasus, and not highly rated, but the variety desoulavyi is frequently grown and is not undeserving of a place. It forms dense, hard pads of congested dark green rosettes and carries yellow flowers singly on 2 in. stems.

— cebenensis. (8) Confined to the Cevennes in S. France. Hard, domed cushions of three-cleft, very sticky, hairy leaves. The 2 in. stems carry several good white flowers with overlapping petals. Best in the alpine house or in a trough or sink garden. Good for a hole in a Tufa rock.

— X 'Cecil Davis'. A good hybrid of uncertain parentage. It could be S. longifolia crossed with either S. aizoon or S. cochlearis. Splendid rosettes of silvered leaves and 9 in. red stems carrying plumes of white flowers.

— ceratophylla. See S. trifurcata.

— X 'Cherry Trees' The constitution of this fine, and very old hybrid is unfortunately weakened. It can certainly claim S. burserana as one of its parents. Tight domes of neat rosettes emit short-stemmed flowers of rich yellow.

— X churchillii. A natural hybrid between S. hostii and S. aizoon. Rosettes of conspicuously toothed leaves beaded with silver and 9 in. spikes of white flowers.

— cochlearis. (11) From rather restricted areas in the Maritime Alps on either side of the French-Italian frontiers. It is one of the most desirable of the encrusted saxifragas, forming compressed domes of huddled silver-grey, spoon-shaped leaves. The white flowers are carried plentifully in elegant plume-like sprays on 6 to 9 in. stems; they are set off by the reddish flowering stems. There are one or two forms in cultivation, S.c. 'Minor' differs only in being an even smaller and more tightly compressed cushion. The so-called S.c. 'Major' is larger and looser growing and is possibly a hybrid with S. callosa. A plant in cultivation as S. probinii, I am unable to separate in any detail from typical S. cochlearis.

- conifera. (8) From Northern Spain. A tiny 'mossy' which spends the summer in the form of oat-like, dried buds. These expand into compact cushions of tiny silvery-green leaves in the spring and several quite large white flowers are carried on 3 in. stems. It requires alpine house treatment, or a corner in a stone trough or sink garden, and a watchful eye during its dormant, and apparently moribund period.

- corsica. (7) This species from Corsica, Sardinia, the Balearic Isles and Spain is closely related to *S. granulata*, our native meadow saxifrage but the basal leaves are three-lobed and the sprays of white flowers are elegant and of good size.

- cortusifolia. (15) From Japan and related to *S. fortunei*, of which it resembles a diminished version and is several weeks earlier in blossom. It can be distinguished from *S. fortunei* also by the fact that one or more of its characteristically long lower petals are untoothed. There is a form in cultivation with pink flowers, known as *S.c.* 'Rosea' which is desirable, but rare. A cool situation in rich soil is best.

- cotyledon. (11) A variable species with a wide distribution in the European alps, extending into Scandinavia and N. America, it is more often than not found on granitic formations but, on the whole, is tolerant of lime in cultivation. Typically the species makes wide, flat rosettes of broad, strap-shaped leaves, usually toothed and lime-encrusted on the edges. The tall, pyramidal inflorescences carry myriads of white flowers in summer. On this basic theme there are many variations and several named forms or hybrids are grown. These are sometimes geographic variants, in other cases they are garden selections. Descriptions of these will be found in catalogues, but mention ought to be made of one or two of special merit. *S.c.* 'Caterhamensis' has largely been superseded by *S.c.* 'Southside Seedling', in which the white flowers are so heavily spotted with red as to appear pink at a short distance. *S.c.* 'Norvegica' is a northern form and the leaves differ from those of the type by narrowing abruptly to a sharp point. *S.c.* 'Pyramidalis' is an especially fine form from the Pyrenees with a large, broad and pyramidal inflorescence and rather narrower leaves.

- X 'Cranbourne'. A hybrid of unknown parentage in the Kabschia section, and one of the best. Almost flat tufts of dark green foliage in huddled rosettes and almost stemless large pink flowers.

- crustata. (11) From the Eastern Alps. A not very exciting species and one which, unusually, seems to enjoy a modicum of shade. Silver-beaded leaves crowd into low mats and the rather off-white flowers are borne on 6 in. reddish stems.

- cuneifolia. (3) From sub-alpine woodlands of S. Europe. It, and its two varieties, *capillipes* and *subintegra*, are neat carpeters for shady places. In appearance they are not unlike a miniature London Pride, with 6 in. panicles of cream-white flowers.

- cuscutiformis. (15) Presumably from China, although I believe it is not known as a wild plant. From its rosettes of rounded, often bronzed leaves spring many threadlike red runners ending in small rosettes which will root and spread the colony. Short panicles carry several white flowers in which the irregularity of the petals is not as noticeable as in other members of the Diptera section. Dubiously hardy and best given alpine house treatment.

— **cymbalaria.** (5) An annual, native to Eastern Europe and Asia Minor, and one of the exceptions I have permitted myself in the general exclusion of annuals. I like to allow it to inhabit crevices in cool, shaded places and enjoy its tufts of green, toothed leaves and short, leafy spikes in the axils of which appear the clear yellow flowers.

— **decipiens.** See *S. rosacea.*

— **demnatensis.** (8) A rarity from cliffs in the High Atlas mountains of Morocco. From a thick rootstock rise short stems bearing rosettes of green, aromatic and sticky leaves, deeply segmented. The white, green-veined flowers are carried in short panicles. For the alpine house preferably.

— **'Diana'.** A 'Mossy' with pale pink flowers on 6 in. stems.

— **diapensioides.** (12) From the European alps. Tiny rosettes of small grey leaves huddled into dense, hard tufts and several pure white flowers on 2 in. stems. It is slow-growing and not one of the easiest, best cosseted in a crevice between rocks in a stone trough or sink, or in the alpjne house. The so-called *S.d.* 'Lutea' is almost certainly of hybrid origin. It is slightly larger, easier and has nice yellow flowers.

— **X engleri.** A reputed hybrid claiming *S. hostii* as one parent. Rosettes of narrow, blue-green leaves encrusted with silver edges and yellow-green flowers on short, branching stems.

— **'Dubarry'.** A 'Mossy' with large, rich crimson flowers. Later flowering than others of its group.

— **X 'Dr. Ramsey'** A hybrid between *S. longifolia* and *S. cochlearis.* Handsome silvered rosettes of spoon-shaped leaves and 9 in. sprays of white flowers.

— **'Elf'.** A miniature 'Mossy' with carmine flowers on very short stems, and late flowering.

— **X 'Elizabethae'.** A hybrid between *S. burserana* and *S. sancta.* An easy and popular hybrid forming green mats smothered in short-stemmed heads of clear yellow flowers.

— **erioblasta.** (8) A rare, sun-loving 'Mossy' species from Southern Spain forming cushions of small rosettes which, in the fiercest heat of summer become tight dormant buds. These buds, known to the Spanish as 'Virgin's Pearls', if crushed, disclose a tiny green spark of life in the centre. The short-stemmed flowers are pure white. It appreciates, and deserves, alpine house treatment.

— **X 'Esther'.** A hybrid between *S. aizoon* 'Lutea' and *S. cochlearis.* A deservedly popular hybrid, easily grown and decorative with heads of cream-yellow flowers on 6 in. stems.

- exarata. (8) From Southern Europe. A neat 'Mossy' species forming low tufts of, usually, three-lobed leaves and bearing several cream-white flowers on very short stems. For the alpine house.

- X 'Faldonside'. A hybrid between *S. aretioides* and a form of *S. marginata.* Best not exposed to hot sunshine. Hard hummocks of grey rosettes and large, rich yellow flowers on 2 in. stems.

- 'Federici-Augustii'. This may be a hybrid, of uncertain parentage, or a form of *S. sempervivum*, the latter being the more probable. Rosettes of rather broad, silvered leaves and short stems with rose-red flowers.

- ferdinandi-coburgii. (12) From the Pirin mountains of Bulgaria. Congested rosettes of small leaves and golden-yellow flowers carried in cymes on 2 in. stems.

- florulenta. (11) A lime-hating rarity from a restricted area of the Maritime Alps, where it grows on the shady sides of granitic rocks in tight crevices. An ancient species, known originally to fossil botanists and, as might be expected, not an easy plant to grow. If obtained it should be given royal alpine house treatment. Flat rosettes of regularly arranged deep green leaves, spine-pointed at the tips. The rosette is magnificent but the inflorescence disappointing, the muddy purple flowers being carried in narrow panicles.

- 'Flowers of Sulphur'. A 'Mossy' which is unique in the colouring of its soft lemon-yellow flowers.

- X forsteri. An inter-sectional hybrid between *S. caesia* and *S. mutata.* It is of considerable interest but has little horticultural value. It has small rosettes of thick, green leaves and carries pink flowers on fragile stems.

- fortunei. (15) From China, Japan, Korea and Manchuria. A valuable late-flowering species, often at its best in the late autumn. For cool soil and out of full sunshine. It is wise to regard it as a lime-hater although I have known it to tolerate some alkalinity. Large, rounded, lobed and glossy leaves have petioles embracing the stems. Bright green at first, the foliage becomes tinted with reddish-bronze and there are forms, such as 'Rubrifolia' and 'Wada' which carry this rich colour throughout the year. The graceful, 15 to 18 in. stems carry panicles of many white flowers, of which the bottom one or two petals are toothed and much longer than their upper fellows. This characteristic feature of the Diptera section is strongly pronounced in this species.

- 'Four Winds'. A 'Mossy' of outstanding merit with flowers of brilliant deep crimson in clusters of four or five on 9 in. stems.

- X 'Francis Cade'. Various parentages have been suggested for this hybrid but it is probably *S. cochlearis* crossed with *S. callosa.* Rosettes of narrow, grey, pointed leaves and one-sided sprays of white flowers on reddish 9 in. stems.

- X franzii. A hybrid between *S. aretioides* and *S. ferdinandi-coburgii.* Hard, compact domes and rich yellow flowers on 3 in. stems.

- 'Gaiety'. An early flowering 'Mossy' with deep pink flowers, short stems and a neat habit.

- X gaudinii. A natural hybrid found in the Pyrenees between *S. aizoon* and a *S. cotyledon* form. Rosettes of leathery, strap-shaped leaves and short, branching stems with many white, red-spotted flowers.

- X 'Gem'. A hybrid between *S. burserana* and *S.X* 'Irvingii'. Dense cushions and large, short-stemmed soft pink flowers.

- geoides. A species of somewhat doubtful authenticity which grows on the Picos de Europa in Spain, on shady cliffs. It has tufts of ivy-shaped, small leaves, purple on the undersides and short stems carrying white flowers. Dubiously in cultivation.

- geranioides. (8) From the Pyrenees. Tufts of much divided leaves and compact heads of pure white flowers. It likes shade and moisture.

- X 'Geuderi'. A hybrid of uncertain parentage within the Kabschias group. Pads of grey, spiky, tiny leaves and yellow flowers on short stems.

- X geum. (3) Although long thought to be a species this plant is now determined as a hybrid between *S. hirsuta* and *S. umbrosa.* It is occasionally found between the parents in the Pyrenees and is intermediate between them in appearance with showers of pretty, white or soft pink flowers on 6 to 9 in. stems. It appreciates shade and is a good ground coverer. Several variants have been selected and are sometimes offered under individual names.

- X girtanneri. A monocarpic hybrid between *S. mutata* and *S. aizoides.* Rosettes of small, broad, fleshy leaves and short spikes of starry orange-copper flowers.

- globulifera. (8) A rather obscure species from limestone cliffs in Spain. Spreading mats of small, deeply lobed leaves and a short stem carrying a few small white flowers. Of no great garden value and best treated as an alpine house plant if grown.

- 'Gnome'. A rather nice 'Mossy', very dwarf and late-flowering with good crimson flowers.

- granulata. (7) This is our native meadow saxifrage with an immense distribution in northern and southern Europe, N. America and Asia. Tufts of crenulated leaves and characteristic root bulbils. The white flowers are carried in elegant 9 in. sprays. It is most commonly grown in the form with double flowers, but the type is well worthy of garden space. It likes moisture-retentive soil and dies back to rest quite soon after flowering.

- X 'Grace Farwell'. A hybrid of uncertain parentage within the Kabschia group. Mats of dark green leaves and wine-red flowers, singly or in pairs on short stems. The colour is good but the flowers often do not open widely.

- grisebachii. (12) The type species is to be found in the Balkans and E. Europe, but the form more commonly grown is the selection known as 'Wisley', which is more vigorous and more brightly coloured. The handsome, symmetrical rosettes of silvered leaves form a startling base for the crimson inflorescence which emerges in the spring, carrying the small flowers between colourful bracts. Not a difficult plant but happiest in the alpine house.

— **X gusmussii.** A hybrid between *S. sempervivum* and *S. luteoviridis.* Silvered rosettes and 6 in. stems carrying flowers of pale orange-red.

— **X guthreana.** A hybrid between *S.X andrewsii* and *S. aizoon* and resembling a similar, but smaller *S.X andrewsii.*

— **X haagii.** An old hybrid between *S. ferdinandi-coburgii* and *S. sancta.* Still a good and very amenable plant, forming cushions of dark green leaves with 3 in. stems carrying small but rich golden flowers.

— **X 'H. Marshall'.** A hybrid of similar parentage and appearance to *S.X* 'Gem' but with deep coloured flowers.

— **hartii.** (8) A rare species, confined in nature to the maritime cliffs of Arranmore Island in Ireland. Neat tufts of green, hairy, sticky leaves and compact heads of good white flowers on 2 to 3 in. stems.

— **X 'Heinrichii'.** A hybrid between *S. aretioides* and *S. stribrnyi.* Tufts of inch-wide rosettes and short, branching stems carrying heads of several yellow flowers with red-purple sepals, giving a bicolored effect.

— **heucherifolia.** See *S. rotundifolia.*

— **hirculus.** (2) Widely distributed over the Northern Hemisphere and a rare British native in damp places. The form from the Himalaya, in spite of only minor botanical difference, has been given specific rank, as *S. montana.* Grow it in sandy peat which is always moist. Narrow, bright green leaves and 6 in., leafy stems carrying one or a few yellow, red-spotted flowers. In central Europe exists a form *S.h.* 'Major'. which is larger in all its parts.

— **hostii.** (11) From the Eastern limestone alps. Loose rosettes of strap-shaped leaves, toothed at the margins. Erect, foot-high stems carry branching panicles of cream-white flowers, sometimes spotted with red. A form, *S.h. altissima,* which occurs in the wild, is larger in all its parts and is the form most often cultivated.

— **hypnoides.** (8) Widely distributed in Europe and into sub-arctic regions, also a British native, known as 'Dovedale Moss'. It is a pleasant, but not exciting 'Mossy' for cool places; of prostrate habit with 6 in. stems bearing pendant buds which expand into starry white flowers.

— **imbricata.** (12) A desirable rarity, dubiously in cultivation, from Kashmir. Tight wads and pads of imbricated grey leaves and stemless white flowers.

— **incrustata.** Either a garden name or a slightly varying form of *S. crustata.*

— **X 'Iris Prichard'.** A hybrid between *S.X godroniana* and *S. lilacina.* Rosettes of lime-encrusted, tiny leaves in compact humps and 2 in. stems carrying from one to three buff-apricot flowers. Very early flowering.

- **irrigua.** (7) A usually monocarpic, but occasionally perennial species from Asia Minor. Loose rosettes of pale green, sticky and deeply cleft leaves from which rise branching, foot-high stems carrying many quite sizeable white flowers. Best in the alpine house.
- **X 'Irvingii'.** A hybrid between *S. burserana* and *S. lilacina*. Old, but still one of the best early flowering Kabschias. Tight and tiny mounds of glaucous-grey rosettes and almost stemless blush-pink flowers.
- **X 'James Bremner'.** A robust 'Mossy', possibly claiming *S. granulata* as one parent. The foot-high stems carry heads of large, solid, pure white flowers.
- **X 'Jenkinsae'.** A hybrid similar in parentage and appearance to *S.X* 'Irvingii' but somewhat looser in habit and with definite, but very short stems.
- **juniperifolia.** (12) A Caucasian species forming dense, dark green humps of tiny, spiny leaves. The flowers, on short stems, are yellow, but not spectacular and the protruding stamens are the most prominent feature. The sub-species *S.j. sancta* is more garden worthy. In austere conditions it makes a bright display of golden-yellow flowers.
- **X 'Kathleen Pinsent'.** A hybrid claiming *S. callosa* as one parent. Rosettes of silver, spathulate leaves and erect, 9 in. stems carrying many soft pink flowers.
- **X 'Kellereri'.** A hybrid between *S. burserana* and *S. stribrnyi* and one of the first to flower, often opening its blossoms in January. The small, silvered rosettes produce 4 in. stems carrying several small, rather tubular pink flowers.
- **X 'Kewensis'.** A hybrid between *S. porophylla* and a form of *S. burserana*. Neat tufts of narrow, spiny grey leaves and short sprays of lilac-pink flowers on reddish stems.
- **kotschyi.** (12) From Asia Minor. A not very spectacular species but of neat, mat-forming habit and a short inflorescence of small pale yellow flowers.
- **X 'Lady Beatrix Stanley'.** Of the same parentage as *S.X* 'Iris Prichard' and of similar appearance but with freely borne rich red flowers.
- **latepetiolata.** (7) From a small area of Eastern Spain. A biennial which dies after flowering. Symmetrical, handsome rosettes of long-stemmed, kidney-shaped leaves, hairy, and sticky to the touch. The handsome pyramid of white flowers is a foot or more in height, and almost as wide at its base. It flowers in late May or June and, although hardy, is usually given alpine house treatment.
- **latina.** See *S. oppositifolia*.
- **lilacina.** (12) A Himalayan species which has been concerned in the parentage of many fine hybrids. Its own merits are considerable. It makes flat pads of rosettes with tiny leaves in quadrangular arrangement and the almost stemless flowers are pure lilac in colour. It likes gritty, lime-free soil and a modicum of shade.

- lingulata. See *S. callosa.*

- longifolia. (11) From the French and Spanish Pyrenees. A cliff dweller, making splendid, large, symmetrical rosettes of narrow, lime-encrusted leaves and emitting huge panicles of innumerable white flowers. Its most splendid manifestation is seen in *S.* 'Tumbling Waters', which is a selection or hybrid.

- lowndesii. (12) A Himalayan species which has made one or two shy appearances in cultivation but has not, so far persisted. Prostrate mats and stemless mauve-pink flowers excited very favourable comment on the few occasions they were seen.

- luteoviridis. (12) From the Eastern Alps and Asia Minor. Crowded rosettes of entire, glaucous leaves, often slightly purple beneath. Short stems and terminal panicles of flowers whose yellow petals are enclosed in a green corolla.

- X 'Macnabiana'. A hybrid between *S. cotyledon* and *S. callosa.* It received an Award of Merit as long ago as 1885 and it is rather doubtful if the original plant survives. It should form rosettes of broad, dark green leaves and carry an 18 in. spire of white flowers, heavily spotted with red.

- marginata. (12) A very variable species ranging in its distribution from the Southern to the Eastern alps. Compact and mat-forming it carries on its 2 in. stems several large, slightly funnel-shaped white flowers of good substance. Named varieties in cultivation are *rocheliana, coriophylla* and *karadzicensis.* The first has longer leaves in a very flat rosette, and second arranges its leaves as a distinct column and the last is the smallest of all, with very tiny leaves and flowers on 1 in. stems. There is a yellow flowered plant, sometimes named *S.m. rocheliana* 'Lutea' which is certainly a hybrid.

- X 'Marie Theresiae'. A hybrid between *S. grisebachii* and *S. burserana.* Distinct and attractive with rosettes of grey-green, pointed leaves and several small pink flowers on red stems.

- media. (12) From the Pyrenees. Rosettes of lime-encrusted, broad, sharply pointed leaves and a compact spike of pink flowers enclosed in large, red-haired calyces.

- X 'Megasaeflora'. A hybrid probably claiming *S. burserana* as one of its parents, with foliage resembling that species and large flowers of rose-pink with separated petals.

- montana. See *S. hirculus.*

- moschata. (8) A widely distributed European species, mat-forming and not unattractive but seldom grown except in the form of one of its many variants and even more numerous hybrids, a very popular form is *S.m.* 'Cloth of Gold', with rich yellow foliage.

- X 'Mother of Pearl'. A hybrid of obscure parentage, but almost certainly claiming *S. lilacina* as one parent. Tight pads of spiny grey tiny leaves and large, rounded flowers of silvery-pink on very short stems.

- X 'Mrs. Piper'. A 'Mossy' with good red flowers and of neat habit.
- muscoides. (8) A European species of compact, mat-forming habit which has been much confused with *S. moschata*. Entire leaves, which adopt a silvery tone as they die and dry, and white or yellow flowers on very short stems.
- mutata. (11) Widely distributed through Europe. Rosettes of strap-shaped shiny dark green leaves without lime encrustation. The erect, foot-high stem carries many narrow-petalled coppery-orange flowers. The rosette which blossoms dies after flowering.
- 'Myra'. A hybrid between *S. scardica* and *S. lilacina*. A very early but still vigorous hybrid, resembling *S.X* 'Cranbourne' in foliage but with flowers of even deeper, richer pink.
- nivalis. (1) A species of little garden value, but interesting as a rare British native, also found in arctic and sub-arctic Europe and N. America. It inhabits wet, rocky positions and over the ground-hugging tufts of rather leathery leaves displays heads of greenish-white flowers.
- X 'Obristii'. A hybrid between *S. burserana* and *S. marginata*. Intermediate between the parents and with large white flowers on 2 in. stems.
- X 'Ochroleuca.' A hybrid between *S. sancta* and a minor form of *S. burserana*. Like *S. burserana* but with rather starry, pale yellow flowers.
- oppositifolia. (13) A species of immensely wide distribution throughout Europe, including Britain, N. America and the Himalaya. It varies as widely as its distribution would suggest. In its typical form it makes prostrate mats of thin stems clothed in tiny leaves arranged in opposite pairs. The purple-red flowers are borne at the ends of the shoots. There is an albino form with rather squinny white flowers, and selected forms under such names as 'Splendens' and 'Grandiflora' are the usually preferred garden plants. Especially richly coloured are two old selections, now rarely available, named respectively 'W.A.Clark' and 'Wetterhorn'. *S.o. blepharophylla* is a form from the granites of the Central Alps and *S.o latina* comes from Italy and is desirable. In any of its manifestations it is a good plant, usually preferring a rather cool situation, all are very early flowering.
- oranensis. (8) A very distinctive 'Mossy' from N. Africa, best given alpine house treatment. Domes of fleshy, wedge-shaped leaves, usually three-cleft at the tips. On 3 in. stems in summer it carries large white flowers, at which time the foliage adopts reddish tints. During dry summer months the rosettes may shrink into tight protective buds.
- paniculata. See *S. aizoon*.
- X paradoxa. A natural hybrid between *S. hostii* and *S. crustata*. found in the Eastern Alps. Narrow, silvery leaves and 6 in. brownish stems carrying cream-white flowers. There is a species in Section (6)

bearing the same name, but it is of no horticultural significance and is sometimes referred to the genus ZAHLBRUCKNERA.

— X patens. A rare natural hybrid between *S. caesia* and *S. aizoides.* It is like a loose-growing, less silvery *S. caesia.* The short, branching stems carry butter-yellow flowers in summer. The same hybrid has appeared in gardens and has been distributed as *S.X. patens* 'Elliott's Variety' and *S. sulphurea.*

— X 'Paulinae'. A hybrid between *S. ferdinandi-coburgii* and *S. burserana.* Tightly tufted habit of grey-green rosettes and rounded, primrose-yellow flowers on very short stems.

— X 'Pearly King'. A very dwarf and neat 'Mossy' with clear white flowers.

— X pectinata. A hybrid between *S. aizoon* and *S. crustata.* A natural hybrid from Carniolia with heavily lime-encrusted narrow leaves and cream flowers on 6 in. stems.

— pedemontana. (8) A widespread and variable species in the European alps. Rather thick and fleshy leaves, three-cleft and again divided. Good white flowers on short stems. Best in lime-free soil and light shade.

— pentadactylis. (8) From Spain and the Pyrenees. Tufts of smooth, sticky and aromatic leaves and short, branching stems carrying many small, white, starry flowers with a hint of cream in the colour. Several sub-forms are recognised and *var. wilkommiana,* from Central Spain is said to be a more robust and decorative plant.

— X 'Peter Pan'. A neat, dwarf 'Mossy' with crimson flowers.

— X petraschii. A hybrid between *S. tombeanensis* and a form of *S. marginata.* Firm grey hummocks and several large white flowers on 2 in. stems.

— X 'Pixie'. A very neat, dwarf 'Mossy' with rose-red flowers.

— X polita. A hybrid in the *S. umbrosa* group.

— X 'Pompadour'. A very old 'Mossy' but still one of the best. Dusky Crimson flowers on 9 in. stems.

— porophylla. (12) From the Apennines, and the Abruzzi mountains. Small rosettes of spreading, spathulate leaves. The 6 in. stems are clad in similar leaves, and hairy. The upper third is beset with sessile pink flowers encased in baggy purple calyces. There are several forms known, one of which, previously known as *S.p. thessalica,* is now given specific rank as *S. sempervivum,* which see.

— X 'Portae'. A hybrid between *S. crustata* and *S. aizoon.* Very similar to, and often confused with, *S.X. pectinata.*

— portosanctana. (8) From the island of Porto Sancta in the Madeiras. Mats of fleshy, light green leaves, slightly three-cleft. 6 in. stems carry several large, pure white flowers. For the alpine house.

- **praetermissa.** (8) (S. ajugifolia.) From moist places in the Pyrenees. Tufts of spreading shoots with deeply cut leaves. From the axils of these rise 4 to 6 in. stems carrying from one to three white flowers.
- **pravislavii.** (12) From Macedonia. Rounded domes of dark green spiny leaves and rich yellow flowers on 2 in. stems.
- X **'Primrose Bee'.** A hybrid of similar parentage, and very similar to *S.X apiculata.*
- X **'Primulaize'.** A hybrid between *S. aizoides* and a minor form of *S.* urbium. Low mats of tangled stems clad in narrow, slightly notched leaves and dainty sprays of carmine, red or salmon flowers. It likes light shade and moist conditions.
- X **'Priory Jewel'.** A hybrid claiming *S. lilacina* as one parent. Compact silver-grey cushions and pink flowers on 1 in. stems.
- **probinii.** See *S. cochlearis.*
- X **prosenii.** A hybrid of unknown parentage with distinct flat, grey rosettes and orange-red flowers on short, branching stems.
- X **pseudo-borisii.** A hybrid between *S. ferdinandi-coburgii* and a form of *S. marginata.* Dense tufts of silver-grey rosettes and 3 in. stems carrying corymbs of pale yellow flowers. This and the two following 'pseudo's' are rather dubiously named hybrids, but worth growing.
- X **pseudo-forsteri.** A hybrid between *S. crustata* and *S. cuneifolia.* Neat rosettes of round, glossy leaves and dainty sprays of starry white flowers.
- X **pseudo-kotschyi.** A hybrid with the growth habit of *S. marginata* and pale yellow flowers.
- X **'Red Admiral'.** A tidy 'Mossy' with rounded, bright red flowers on 4 in. stems.
- **retusa.** (13) From the European alps and rather like a very compact and prostrate form of *S. oppositifolia* but easily distinguished by the short, erect corymbs of several small, but rich red flowers with prominent purple stamens and orange anthers. Often grown in the alpine house, it is happy enough in the open in gritty, preferably lime-free soil, rich in humus and in light shade or with a northerly aspect.
- **rigoi.** (8) A rare species from Spain. In high summer its leaves share the characteristic of this group by shrinking to scaly buds. Large white flowers on 4 in. stems.
- X **'Riverslea'.** A hybrid between *S. ferdinandi-coburgii* and *S. lilacina.* Dense silver-grey hummocks of congested rosettes and rose-purple flowers on 2 in. stems.
- **rosacea.** (8) (S. decipiens.) A species widely distributed in Europe, including Britain. Very variable but desirable in its most compact forms with white flowers on stems of varying height. It appreciates shelter from hot sunshine.

— rotundifolia. (4) From central and southern Europe and Russia and a variable species of which several named forms are grown. Typically it is a lover of shade and moist soil with tufts of fleshy, kidney-shaped leaves on long stems. The tall, leafy stems carry loose panicles of starry white flowers, often freckled with red or pink spots. The form *heucherifolia* is the most deserving, having an especially neat and tidy habit and flowers heavily pink-spotted.

— X 'Rubella'. A hybrid of similar parentage and appearance to *S.X irvingii.*

— rudolphiana. This is yet another form or sub-species of *S. oppositifolia.*

— rufidula. (1) From N. America. Neat rosettes of leathery, oval, toothed, dark green leaves and short, stiff stems carrying starry white flowers with noticeably red anthers. Appreciates light shade and lime-free soil.

— X salomonii. A hybrid between *S. burserana* and a form of *S. marginata.* Spiny, silver-grey cushions and 3 in. reddish stems carrying pink buds which expand into good white, wide-petalled flowers.

— sancta. See *S. juniperifolia.*

— X 'Sanguinea Superba'. One of the oldest and still one of the best 'Mossy's'. Deep crimson flowers which do not fade in bright sunlight.

— sarmentosa. See *S. stolonifera.*

— scardica. (12) From the Eastern Alps. Rosettes of broad, spiky leaves gathered into hard domes. On each 4 in. reddish stem are several pure white flowers. The plant grown as *S.s. obtusa* is probably a hybrid. It has green stems, narrower, not so spiny leaves and flowers similar to those of the species. Forms are grown with pink-flushed flowers and appear as *S.s. erythrantha*, or *rosea.* They are not officially given separate status.

— X schleicheri. A hybrid between, probably, *S. burserana* and *S. stribrnyi.* Similar to *S.X. kellereri*, but dwarfer in all its parts with neat pink flowers on 2 in. stems.

— X schottii. A hybrid between *S. luteoviridis* and *S. stribryni.* Flat, silvered rosettes and short, branching stems carrying small yellow flowers.

— sedoides. (8) A rather dowdy species from the eastern limestone alps. Loose, low mats of rosettes and greenish-yellow flowers on short stems.

— sempervivum. (12) This is the plant usually grown as *S. thessalica*, or *S. porophylla var. thessalica.* Neat domes of spiny-leaved, silver-grey rosettes. Short stems clad in spathulate leaves and fine hairs, the upper third set with pink flowers enclosed in baggy purple calyces.

— **sibirica.** (7) Tufts of ivy-shaped green leaves and 6 in. leafy stems bearing several quite large white flowers. It will appreciate light shade and moisture.

— **sibthorpii.** (5) Little more than an annual, but nice when allowed to colonise cool crevices. It comes from Greece and the orange-yellow flowers freely carried on short stems are attractive.

— X 'Southside Seedling'. See *S. cotyledon.*

— **spathulata.** (8) From N. Africa and needs alpine house treatment. Tufts of narrow, entire, smooth leaves and 9 in. sprays of smallish white flowers.

— X 'Splendens'. A garden hybrid owning a form of *S. callosa* as one parent, the other being unkown. Decorative rosettes of narrow, silvered leaves and short, arching sprays of white flowers.

— **spruneri.** (12) From the Eastern Alps. The small leaves in compressed rosettes are felted with fine hairs. Flat heads of white flowers on 3 in. stems.

— **squarrosa.** (12) The smallest of all the Kabschia group. It forms grey, almost lichen-like scabs on the limestone cliffs of Southern and Eastern Europe. On 3 in. branching stems it carries several good white flowers.

— 'Stansfieldii'. A very old 'Mossy' with white flowers, now superseded by superior white-flowered forms.

— X **steinii.** A hybrid between *S. aretioides* and *S. tombeanensis.* Minute silver rosettes in firm hummocks and cream-white flowers in loose corymbs on short stems.

— **stellaris.** (1) A widely distributed and very variable species, native to Britain among other European stations. Leathery, dark green leaves with jagged margins and branching, 6 in. stems carrying starry white flowers. It likes a moist position.

— **stolonifera.** (15) (S. sarmentosa.) An old 'windowsill' favourite, known as 'Mother of Thousands' 'Wandering Jew' or 'Roving Sailor'. From China and Japan and not completely hardy. Rounded, veined and marbled leaves and strawberry-like runners bearing plantlets at their tips. Foot-high branching stems carry a profusion of white flowers spotted with red and yellow. The lower petals are characteristically several times as long as the upper ones. The form 'Tricolor' is less hardy than the type and has deeply cut leaves patterned in green, red and white.

— X 'Stormonthii'. A garden hybrid of unkown parentage forming spiny, dark green cushions decorated with 3 in. leafy stems carrying a few pale yellow flowers.

— **stribrnyi** (12) From Greece and Bulgaria. Handsome, broad-leaved, silver-grey rosettes and short, branching stems carrying small pink flowers which are enveloped in baggy red-purple calyces.

— X **stricta.** A hybrid of *S. crustata* which has borne various names in gardens and was long known as *S. caesia of St. Johns.* Nice, compact huddles of small silvered rosettes and short-stemmed white flowers.

— strigosa. (2) From the Himalaya. Although Reginald Farrer dismissed this rare species as almost a 'floral delinquent' it is well worth growing, if available. Rosettes of soft green leaves and showers of buttercup-yellow flowers with scarlet-tipped stamens. For a cool, slightly shaded position.

— S. 'Stuartii'. A hybrid between *S. aretioides* and *S. media X. stribrnyi.* Like *S. media* in its rosettes and with 4 in. stems carrying soft yellow flowers.

— X 'Suendermannii'. A hybrid between *S. burserana* and *S. stribrnyi.* There are several slightly different clones of this hybrid, which have had such names as 'Major' and 'Purpurea' appended to them. All are good, with crowded rosettes of spiny grey leaves and short, branching stems bearing several rounded, rose-red flowers. I believe the form *S.X s.* 'Purpurea' was once given an Award of Merit under the erroneous name of *S.X* 'Hedwigii'.

— taygetea. (4) A dainty species from Greece and Albania and, possibly, southern Italy. It resembles a refined *S. rotundifolia* with paler green leaves and shorter stems carrying delicate showers of white, pink-spotted flowers.

— X 'Tazetta'. A rare natural hybrid between *S. taygetea* and *S. cuneifolia,* known, and then lost until rediscovered by my late father in the Balkans. Small tufts of leathery, spoon-shaped leaves and leafless, short stems bearing loose showers of white flowers dotted with soft pink markings.

— tenella. (8) A species of 'Mossy' from the Eastern Alps. Mats of emerald-green, narrow, pointed and keeled leaves in close columns. The dainty white flowers are carried on 3 in. stems. It appreciates some shade and a cool soil.

— thessalica. See *S. sempervivum.*

— X 'Timbalii'. A hybrid between *S. aizoon* and a form of *S. cotyledon.* Rather loose rosettes of broad leaves with serrated edges and narrow, pyramidal spikes of white, rather pink-spotted flowers.

— tolmiei. (1) A species from N. America, extending into Alaska, which resembles a sedum more than a saxifraga. Spreading mats of crowded, pale green fleshy leaves and 2 in. stems each carrying a few white, or cream-white flowers. Gritty soil and moisture may please it, but it is not an easy plant.

— tombeanensis. (12) A species localized in the Italian Alps. Dense, hard domes of congested rosettes of tiny grey leaves. On 2 in. stems appear several quite large white flowers of good substance.

— tricuspidata. (9) From Arctic Canada and N. America. Humps of woody stems set with wedge-shaped leaves three-toothed at the apices. Branching 6 in. stems carrying white, yellow-spotted flowers.

— trifurcata. (8) (S. ceratophylla.) From Spain. Tufts of woody stems set with three-cleft and then re-divided leaves which are gummy and aromatic in summer. 6 in. branching stems carry many white flowers.

— X 'Triumph'. A good 'Mossy' with unfading, large, blood-red flowers.

SAXIFRAGA — *continued*

- 'Tumbling Waters. See *S. longifolia.*

- X tyrolensis. A natural hybrid between *S. caesia* and *S. squarrosa*, and intermediate between the parents in appearance and often more amenable to cultivation than either.

- umbrosa. The true species does not appear to be in cultivation, but see *S.X urbium.*

- X urbium. A hybrid between *S. spathularis* (see addenda) and *S. umbrosa.* This is the plant universally known in gardens as *S. umbrosa,* or, more affectionately, 'London Pride'. It is of obscure garden origin and has certainly been cultivated and loved since the 17th century or even earlier. The typical plant is too well known to need any description from me but it has several cultivars of sterling merit. There is one with golden variegated foliage and several, smaller, under the group name *primuloides.* Two of these, respectively 'Clarence Elliott' and 'Walter Ingwersen', were the discoveries, almost simultaneously, of these two great plantsmen, each of whom staunchly supported the right of his 'baby' to be regarded as the smallest and the best. Neither Joe Elliott or I, or anyone else, can detect the slightest difference between them!! They are — or it is — a charming miniature of the 'London Pride' with rich pink flowers on 6 in. stems. There is also a variegated form in this group.

- X 'Vahlii'. A hybrid probably claiming *S. tombeanensis* as one parent. Firm, silver-grey, domed hummocks and pure white flowers on 1 in. stems.

- valdensis. (11) A species which looks like a member of the Kabschia group and has been included in that section by some authorities. From the French/Italian Alps, and a lover of rock crevices, where it makes hard tufts of silvered leaves. It closely resembles *S. cochlearis* in one of its minor forms and, in fact, that plant often does duty for it in gardens. On reddish, 3 in. stems are borne a number of good white flowers in clusters.

- X 'Valerie Finnis'. A hybrid obviously claiming *S. burserana* as one parent and certainly one of the best yellow-flowered Kabschia hybrids. Dense hummocks of grey-green spiky leaves smothered with broad-petalled yellow flowers carried singly on short pink stems.

- **vayreana.** (12) (S. vandellii.) From the Lombardy Alps. Rigid, spiny hummocks of grey-green leaves and flattish heads of white flowers on 3 in. stems.

- veitchiana. (15) From China. Fleshy rounded leaves and sometimes, long stolons. Panicles of white flowers with petals of unequal lengths. Some shade, flowers in late summer.

- wallacei. See *S. camposii.*

- X wildiana. A pretty hybrid between *S. aizoon* and a form of *S.X geum* Basal rosettes of glossy, leathery leaves with markedly toothed. margins. Red flower stems and white, red-spotted flowers on 9 in. stems in loose showers. Now rare, although known since its discovery in the Botanic Garden at Dresden in 1836.

SAXIFRAGA — *continued*

- X 'Winifred'. A fine Kabschia hybrid claiming *S. lilacina* as one known parent. Similar to *S.X.* 'Cranbourne', but with flowers of deep, rich crimson.
- X 'Winston Churchill'. A good 'Mossy' with large flowers of clear pink.
- X zimmeteri. A hybrid between *S. aizoon* and *S. cuneifolia.* Neat carpets of rosetted, glossy, leathery leaves showing a distinctly grey leaf-margin. Starry white flowers with orange anthers on 4 to 6 in. lightly branched stems. Found wild in Austria in 1870, but remains a rarity in gardens.

SCABIOSA. *Dipsaceae.* From the Latin *scabies,* the itch, which, because of the roughness of its leaves, the plant was supposed to cure.

A family of sun-loving plants, mostly too tall for rock gardens, but with a few acceptable exceptions. They are natives of Europe, Asia and N. Africa with the greatest concentration in Mediterranean regions. They are summer flowering.

- alpina. According to authority, this should be *Cephalaria alpina,* a giant growing to 6 ft. but the plant in gardens under this name is a neat mat of greyish, cut foliage displaying lavender flower heads on 6 in. stems. There is a *nana* form which is even dwarfer. Whatever the correct name should be, it is a very desirable plant.
- atropurpurea. (S. maritima.) From dry places in S. Europe. Although a biennial it is an attractive plant, carrying heads of lilac to dark purple flowers gaily on 9 to 12 in. stems.
- cretica. From the rocky cliffs of Crete and Majorca, where it makes wide, low mounds of oval leaves felted with silky grey hairs. The flowers may be pink or blue and are carried in flattish heads on short stems. For the alpine house.
- graminifolia. Tufts of long, narrow grey leaves and on slender, 9 in. stems, heads of soft lavender flowers. An easy and pleasant plant.
- holosericea. (S. pyrenaica.) From the warmer European Alps. Tufts of lanceolate, silvery leaves, the upper leaves pinnatisect and heads of reddish-purple flowers on fairly tall stems.
- hookeri. A rare species from the Himalaya. Tufts of basal lanceolate, entire leaves and short stems carrying a flat head of yellow flowerlets from which protrude black anthers. It may well be more rightly included in the genus PTEROCEPHALUS.
- lagodechiana. A species from the Caucaus, possibly not at present in cultivation. Tufts of finely cut leaves and short, branching stems bearing heads of clear lavender flowers.

368

- lucida. Widely distributed in Europe. Tufts of oval, glabrous leaves, gently lobed at the margins. On 8 in., unbranched stems appear heads of rose-lilac to deep mauve flowers.
- maritima. See *S. atropurpurea.*
- pterocephalus. See PTEROCEPHALUS parnassii.
- pulsatilloides. From Spain. A desirable rarity. Deeply shredded, very hairy foliage and short stemmed heads of lavender flowers. Probably an alpine house plant.
- silenifolia. From Central and Southern Europe. Basal leaves entire, upper and stem leaves segmented. Heads of lilac flowers on 9 in. stems.
- sphaciotica. A gem from Cretan mountains, dubiously in cultivation. Tight hummocks of pinnate, silvery leaves and heads of clear pink flowers on 4 in. stems.
- tomentosa. See *S. turolensis.*
- turolensis. Dense tufts of intensely silver pinnatisect leaves and short stems carrying heads of red-purple flowers. From Spain and for the alpine house.

SCHIVERECKIA. *Cruciferae.* Named for S.B. Schivereck (1782-1815) of Krakow, Poland.

A genus closely related to ALYSSUM. Sun-loving, spring and summer flowering.

- doerfleri. From the Balkans and Asia Minor. Rosettes of leaves covered with silver stellate hairs. White flowers on 2 in. stems.
- podolica. (Alyssum podolicum.) From E. Europe. Tufts of grey, lanceolate leaves, margins two-toothed. Corymbs of white flowers on short, leafy stems.

SCHIZOCODON. A genus now included in SHORTIA, which see.

SCHIZOSTYLIS. *Iridaceae.* From the Greek *schizo*, to divide, and *stylis*, a column.

The style of the flowers is divided into three parts. A genus of two species of S. African plants. Not alpine, or really suited to the rock garden. Those cultivated are forms of *S. coccinea*, in varying shades of pink or deep red. Late summer and autumn flowering.

SCLERANTHUS. *Caryophyllaceae.* From the Greek *skleros*, hard, dry, harsh and *anthos*, flower.

 — **biflorus.** New Zealand and Tasmania. Compact cushions of minute, pubescent leaves. The flowers are tiny and inconspicuous but it makes a very good cushion plant for screes or sink and trough gardens. It is hardy and grows in any good gritty soil.

SCOLIOPUS. *Liliaceae.* From *scolios*, tortuous, and *pous*, a foot. Referring to the shape of the rhizome.

 — **bigelovii.** From California. Treat as for Trilliums. Handsome green leaves, patterned with brown markings and solitary, upward-facing flowers whose inner segments are purple and the outer ones green with purple lines. It flowers in early spring.

SCUTELLARIA. *Labiatae.* From the Latin *scutella*, a small dish, from the pouch on the fruiting calyx.

A large genus, widely distributed in temperate and tropical regions, a few of which are appropriate to rock gardens. Any good ordinary soil is suitable and they are sun-lovers and summer flowering.

 — **alpina.** From Central and southern Europe and extends also into Russia. A neat, rather mat-forming plant with ovate, sometimes toothed leaves and short, erect stems carrying a dense short raceme of the cream and purple flowers which are arranged in close pairs. It seldom exceeds 6 in. in height.

 — **ariana.** A species from the Hindu Kush which we would enjoy but which is very dubiously in cultivation. It is akin to *S. indica* and has flowers of soft lavender blue.

 — **baicalensis.** (*S. macrantha.*) An Asiatic species attaining a foot or so in height and racemes of blue or purple-blue typically hooded flowers in late summer.

 — **brittonii.** From the western States of N. America. Rather tuberous roots and ascending, 9 in. stems carrying singly in the leaf axils attractive blue and white flowers.

 — **goulimyi.** A species found in Greece by Dr. Goulimy, after whom it is named. I doubt if it is in cultivation but it is described as bearing rather large pure white flowers and should be sought. It may be no more than a subspecies of *S. velenovskyi.*

 — **hastata.** A plant in gardens under this name bears short spikes of lavender-blue to purple flowers. I can find no authority for the name

370

SCUTELLARIA — *continued*

and feel that it may possibly be a misspelling for *S. hastifolia*, a widely distributed species with an occasional escape station in Britain. Information of a genuine *S. hastata* and its provenance would be gratefully received.

— hirta. From the Balkans. Mat-forming, with branching stems from a woody base, and rounded, crenate leaves. At the ends of the trailing stems are cream, purple-hooded flowers of good size.

— indica. A Chinese and Japanese species which is seldom seen in gardens, where it is replaced by the wholly Japanese *S.i. japonica*, whose 6 in. stems are clothed in grey-green leaves and carry racemes of long, hooded lavender-purple flowers.

— macrantha. See *S. baicalensis*.

— macrochlamys. (Ajuga vestitum.) Another species from the Hindu Kush with trailing stems, both stems and leaves felted with long grey hairs. On short stems are racemes of salmon-pink flowers, veined with red-purple sitting in purple calyces.

— orientalis. From Spain. Decumbent stems bearing grey leaves. The flowers are commonly yellow but occasionally pink, the lower lip often being flushed with red.

— scordifolia. From Korea. A handsome plant spreading by underground roots. The erect, 9 in. stems bear many indigo-blue flowers.

— virens. A species from the Middle East with upright stems and long yellow flowers. The crenate leaves are smooth, lacking the hairs apparent on other species.

SEDUM. *Crassulaceae.* Name used by the ancients for various succulent plants, from *sedo*, to sit, from the manner in which some species grow on rocks.

A very large genus of, mostly, fleshy stemmed and leaved plants, ranging from prostrate plants to sub-shrubs. Widely distributed in the Northern Hemisphere and also spreading into Central Africa and Bolivia. In general they are lovers of sunlight and warmth — the few exceptions will be noted. The majority will flourish in any good, well drained soil and a minority will endure conditions of considerable austerity — and be all the better for a starvation diet. They flower during summer and some continue on into the autumn months.

— acre. The common Wall-pepper and widely distributed in Europe and also a native of Britain. It is seldom safe to admit it to gardens as it is an avid spreader, but it has several variants which are well worth growing, of which the best are *S.a.* 'Aureum', with golden-tipped stems, *S.a.* 'Elegans' which is similar but silver-tipped and, best of all, *S.a.* 'Majus', also known as 'Maweanus', which is larger and more robust than the type and is not invasive.

371

- **aizoon.** Really an herbaceous perennial, but its foot-high stems are not too tall for most rock gardens. Erect stems with irregularly toothed leaves and heads of golden flowers. It inhabits Asia, from Japan to Siberia.
- **album.** A widely distributed and very variable species, occuring in Europe, Asia and N. Africa. It is an occasional naturalized native of Britain, and is too invasive in its typical form for use in rock gardens — but I have seen it used to great effect as ground-cover in rose-beds. Its several selected and named forms however, are decorative, easily grown mat-forming plants and such forms as *micranthum*, *murale* and *murale* 'Coral Carpet' can be admired without fear. They rely largely on foliage for their effectiveness although the tiny white, or soft pink flowers are not without value.
- **alpestre.** From Central and Southern Europe and Asia Minor. Fleshy green leaves and short, leafy stems bearing heads of greenish-yellow flowers.
- **alsinefolium.** From S. France and N. Italy. Flat rosettes of dark green, rather sticky leaves and 6 in. stems bearing few-flowered heads of white flowers.
- **altissimum.** See *S. sediforme*.
- **amplexicaule.** See *S. tenuifolium*.
- **anacampseros.** S.W. Europe. Long procumbent, brown, snaky stems with thick, blue-grey leaves and heads of purple-pink flowers.
- **anglicum.** Europe, including Britain. Low carpets of fleshy green leaves, tinted with red in full exposure and short-stemmed heads of starry pink flowers. Best in spartan conditions.
- **anopetalum.** See *S. ochroleucum*.
- **asiaticum.** See *S. crassipes*.
- **bithynicum.** A name of doubtful authenticity, some authorities placing it under *S. hispanicum*, or *S. glaucum*. Its provenance is also uncertain, but it may come from the Caucasus. It is a pleasant carpeter with glaucous foliage and pink or white flowers.
- **borissovae.** From the Caucasus and rather like *S. lydium* but with grey-green leaves and pale yellow flowers. Dubiously in cultivation.
- **bourgei.** From Central Mexico. A curious plant with flattened brown stems, fleshy leaves and heads of white flowers, sometimes with red-tipped petals. For the alpine house.
- **brevifolium.** From S.W. Europe and rather like a more glabrous *S. dasyphyllum* with short, wiry stems.
- **caeruleum.** From several Mediterranean Islands, including Corsica and Sardinia. An annual, but permissible for the sake of its clouds of soft blue, tiny, starry flowers on 3 in. stems.
- **cauticolum.** From Japan. An invaluable, late summer and autumn flowering species. In some ways it resembles *S. sieboldii*, but is a hardier plant. Herbaceous in habit, it erupts into myriads of drooping, woody stems set with glaucous, blue-grey leaves ending in large heads of crimson flowers. Lovely in a sunny crevice.

- chanetii. From China, and it has been included in the genus OROSTACHYS and is, according to some authorities, a form of *S. fimbriatum*. Rosettes of narrow, fleshy, blue-grey leaves, reddish beneath, each tipped with a spine and varying from 1 to 3 in. in length. In September the leaves die away and a flower stem appears, from 6 to 9 in. high with many tiny leaves, in the axils of which are small white flowers, tinged pink and with purple anthers. The flowering rosettes die, but, before doing so, produce offsets.

- crassipes. (S. asiaticum.) From the Himalaya and China. Herbaceous, producing erect, foot-high stems dressed in bright green, flat, toothed leaves and crowned with heads of curiously coloured and attractive whitish-yellow flowers in late summer.

- cupressoides. From Mexico. Tiny tufts of Cypress-like growths and heads of bright yellow flowers.

- dasyphyllum. Mediterranean regions and naturalized here and there in Britain. Short, wiry, branched stems in dense tufts with tiny crowded leaves, sometimes pink-flushed. Small cymes of white, pink-flushed flowers.

- divergens. From N. America. Prostrate, rooting red stems and fleshy, green, egg-shaped leaves. The stems terminate in heads of bright yellow flowers.

- douglasii. From N. America. Short, erect stems and foliage colouring to bronze and crimson and compact heads of yellow flowers. Proliferous shoots form on the flower stems, become detached, and take root.

- ellacombianum. The plant grown under this name is a Japanese native, either a form of, or synonymous with *S. kamtschaticum*, which see.

- ewersii. From the Himalaya to Mongolia. Many trailing, rather woody stems with opposite, stem-clasping rounded fleshy leaves, sometimes faintly toothed. Dense cymes of small pink or pale violet flowers. A condensed form named *S.e. homophyllum* is neater, and is sometimes grown under the name *S. hayesii*.

- farinosum. A species from Madeira, and not quite hardy. It is similar to *S. anglicum*, with white flowers. In gardens its name is often wrongly given to *S. brevifolium*.

- fimbriatum. A Chinese species, dubiously hardy with dense panicles of white flowers mottled red and green on the backs of the petals.

- floriferum. Dubiously a true species and possibly intermediate between *S. kamtschaticum* and *S. middendorffianum*. Low, sprawling, leafy stems and many heads of golden flowers, beloved by bees, in late summer.

- glaucum. See *S. hispanicum*.

- gracile. From Iran and the Caucasus. Neat, bright green carpets of reddish, densely leafy shoots and on 2 in. stems small heads of white, red-spotted flowers.

SEDUM — *continued*

- hayesii. See *S. ewersii.*
- heterodontum. A form of RHODIOLA *rosea*, which see.
- hillebrandtii. See *S. sartorianum.*
- hirsutum. From S.W. Europe. Compact cushions of fleshy, hairy incurved rosettes. 2 in. stems and white flowers sometimes tinted pink. The plant often grown as *S. winkleri* is correctly subspecies *baeticum* of *S. hirsutum.* It is a magnified version of the type with large, glistening white flowers.
- hispanicum. (*S. glaucum.*) From S.E. Europe. The type is usually of no more than annual duration, but the form commonly grown as *S.h.* 'Minus' is perennial and makes pretty carpets of blue-grey, tiny fleshy leaves starred with white, pink-flushed flowers on 1 in. stems.
- hobsonii. (*S. praegerianum.*) From Tibet. An herbaceous species, it makes a central rosette of narrow, shining green leaves from which radiate prostrate stems with alternate, sessile leaves ending in clusters of a few urn-shaped rose-pink flowers. It usually flowers during July and August and is probably happiest in an alpine house in very gritty compost.
- humifusum. From Mexico and happier in an alpine house. It forsakes the family sun-loving tradition and likes cool, gritty, moist soil and some shade. Almost mossy carpets of tiny rosettes of bright green leaves, tinted red in winter, studded with surprisingly large clear yellow flowers on very short stems.
- hybridum. From the Ural mountains but naturalized here and there in Europe as a garden escape. Mats of neatly notched foliage and flat cymes of yellow flowers.
- jepsonii. See *S. rubroglaucum.*
- kamtschaticum. (*S. ellacombianum.*) From N. Asia. Low mats of dark green leaves and heads of bright yellow flowers. More spectacular is the form 'Variegatum' with handsomely variegated foliage and flower-heads turning to crimson in the autumn. A sub-species is *S. middendorffianum*, from Manchuria. Low tufts of erect stems clothed in narrow, reddish-brown leaves forming a pleasing contrast to the many cymes of bright yellow flowers.
- kirilowii. From China, Burma and Tibet. Rather tall, but handsome. 18 in. unbranched stems with toothed leaves and flat heads of reddish-bronze flowers in late summer.
- lampusae. Endemic to the limestone mountains of Cyprus. Flat rosettes of overlapping leaves, pale green, spotted with pink. From the exact centre of the rosette rises a flower stem reaching a height of a foot or more bearing dense spires of starry pale pink flowers flecked with rusty-red, yellow eyes and white anthers. A quite spectacular but monocarpic species, best grown in the alpine house.
- linearifolium. From China and the Himalaya. Erect, slender, 9 in. stems, unbranched and light green, deeply cut and toothed leaves. Flat cymes of purple-red flowers in August and September.

374

— **lydium.** From Asia Minor. Compact tufts of crowded stems and small green leaves which become bronze-red in summer, 3 in. stems carry dense heads of white flowers.

— **magellense.** From S.E. Europe. Low tufts of bright green, flat leaves and short racemes of pure white flowers.

— **micranthum.** See *S. album.*

— **moranense.** From Mexico and not entirely hardy. Short, branched, wiry stems in 3 in. tufts with triangular, sessile leaves. The flowers are white, tinted red on the back of the petals. A form known as *arboreum* is more robust and is like a tiny shrub.

— **multiceps.** From N. Africa. Rather like a neat version of a non-invasive *S. acre*, with tiny dark green leaves arranged in spiral rows. Bright yellow flowers.

— **nicaense.** See *S. sediforme.*

— **oaxacanum.** From Mexico and definitely for the alpine house. Prostrate, branching stems with blunt, overlapping leaves. Small clusters of yellow flowers are carried at the branch tips.

— **obtusatum.** See *S. oreganum.*

— **ochroleucum.** (S. anopetalum.) Europe and Asia Minor. Slender, 6 in. stems with ranks of crowded linear leaves forming spreading mats. The cymes of flowers are whitish or pale yellow.

— **oreades.** From the Karakorum. Rosettes of bright green fleshy leaves, strongly reminiscent of a species of saxifraga and each rosette centred by a stemless cream-yellow flower.

— **oreganum.** (S. obtusatum.) From N. America. A deservedly popular sedum. Its 2 in. erect stems carry fat, paddle-shaped leaves which turn rich bronze-red and end in small, flat cymes of bright yellow flowers.

— **palmeri.** From Mexico, and best in an alpine house. Branching, foot-high stems with glaucous, fleshy leaves and pendant racemes of yellow flowers. A very decorative plant with a long flowering season.

— **pilosum.** From Asia Minor and the Caucasus. Biennial or mono-carpic. Very much like a grey-haired sempervivum in appearance carrying on the short, thick, leafy stems branched cymes of waxy, rose-red flowers.

— **populifolium.** From Siberia. Erect, woody, branching stems carry leaves shaped like those of a small poplar. Freely branching corym-bose cymes carry many small, white or soft pink, hawthorn-scented flowers in late summer. It can attain a height of 18 in.

— **praealtum.** From Mexico. Really a small shrub, with erect, branching stems up to 18 in. The entire, shining green leaves are fleshy, flat on face and rounded at back. Lax, much-branched panicles carry many rich yellow flowers in spring. Not always fully hardy.

— **praegerianum.** See *S. hobsonii.*

— **primuloides.** From Yunnan. Prostrate mats of dark green fleshy leaves and surprisingly large, white, bell-shaped flowers on short stems in late summer.

— **pruinatum.** From Portugal, Loose mats of light green stems and rather fine leaves and short, branching inflorescences carrying straw-yellow flowers.

— **pulchellum.** From N. America. Another odd-man-out in the genus in its preference for moist soil and a not too hot position. Reddish, sprawling stems with narrow, rich green leaves and star-fish shaped heads of rose-pink flowers in mid to late summer.

— **purdyi.** From N. America. Rosettes of bright green, glossy leaves connected by red stolons into domed hummocks. The golden yellow flowers are borne on 3 in. stems.

— **quinquifarium.** This is really a form of *S. brevifolium*, slightly larger, and with its small, globular leaves arranged in five spiral rows.

— **reflexum.** (S. rupestre.) A European species forming low mats of tangled stems and rather blue-grey leaves and cymes of yellow flowers.

— **retusum.** A Mexican species growing in the form of a tiny shrub, the small, flat leaves have notched tips. Neat heads of white flowers, the petals often red at the base.

— **rhodanthum.** From N. America. An herbaceous species with erect, foot-high stems and fleshy green leaves, toothed near the apex. The rose-pink flowers are carried in dense racemes.

— **rhodiola.** See RHODIOLA *rosea.*

— **roseum.** See RHODIOLA *rosea.*

— **rubroglaucum.** A N. American plant which the American botanists now include in the genus GORMANIA but which European botanists retain in the genus SEDUM. This has rounded, blue-grey leaves in huddled clumps. Small heads of yellow flowers on 3in. stems. Very similar, if not synonymous are SS. *jepsonii* and *watsonii.*

— **rupestre.** See *S. reflexum.*

— **sartorianum.** A confused species which *Flora Europaea* has now given specific rank. It has previously dithered uncertainly between *S. acre*, *S. stribrnyi* and *S. hillebrandtii*. The latter two are regarded as subspecies of the type. Mat-forming, bright green tiny leaves and heads of bright yellow flowers.

— **sediforme.** (S. nicaense. S. altissimum.) From Mediterranean regions. A rather robust species with ascending stems of a foot or more and thick, rather narrow leaves, closely imbricated in spiral rows on non-flowering shoots. Heads of greenish-white or straw-yellow flowers.

— **semenovii.** From Turkestan. 12 in. stems thickly set with fleshy leaves and bottle-brush racemes of white flowers.

— **sempervivoides.** From the Caucasus. Sempervivum-like rosettes of green leaves basally red-flushed. It is biennial and monocarpic. In the second year the centre of the rosette rises in the form of a small pagoda topped by a head of scarlet flowers.

- serpentinii. From E. Europe and Asia Minor. Rather like *S. album*, but with a more lax and corymbose inflorescence and pink-petalled flowers.

- sexangulare. Europe. Close mats of short stems on which are densely arranged several spiral rows of tiny green leaves, turning bronze in summer. 2 in. stems carry heads of bright yellow flowers.

- sieboldii. From Japan, and long cultivated as a window-sill plant in cottages, but hardy enough to survive outdoors in all but extremely cold conditions. Fleshy, rounded leaves in threes on trailing stems, which end in heads of rich reddish-purple flowers late in the summer. There is a form with handsomely variegated foliage.

- spathulifolium. From N. America and one of the most widely grown and deservedly popular sedums. Mats and carpets of short, fleshy stems set with rounded, fleshy leaves of purple-green, often dusted with white farina, and short stems carrying branched heads of clear yellow flowers. There are numerous named forms in cultivation, notably 'Cappa Blanca', with leaves so heavily powdered as to appear white, and 'Purpureum', whose leaves are larger and richly purple. A distinct but often weakly form is 'Aureum' whose leaves are tinted yellow.

- spurium. A Caucasian species which has naturalized from gardens in many parts of Europe. A creeping plant with broad leaves and heads of starry pink flowers in a lax inflorescence. A good ground-cover plant for places where the soil is poor. There is a form with white flowers and an improved clone bearing the cumbersome name of 'Schorbusser Blut' which bears deep red flowers.

- stahlii. A Mexican species and hardy only in the alpine house. The bronzed, berry-like leaves are borne in four vertical rows on the short stems and the yellow flowers are carried in a terminal cyme.

- stenopetalum. From N. America. Mats of dark green leaves and a forked inflorescence on short stems bearing bright yellow flowers.

- stoloniferum. From the Caucasus, and has been confused with *S. spurium*, from which it is quite distinct. Creeping stems and pairs of broad green leaves and three-branched, lax, leafy cymes carrying pink flowers.

- stribrnyi. See *S. sartorianum*.

- tatarinowii. From China. An herbaceous perennial throwing up erect annual stems set with fleshy, blunt, grey-green leaves toothed at the apex. About 6 in. tall it carries flat corymbs of white, pink-flushed flowers in late summer. It is hardy but is also a good alpine house plant.

- telephium. A polymorphic complex, European in distribution, including Britain. Most of the forms are rather too tall for any but a large rock garden. Characteristically it grows with erect, leafy stems from carrot-like tuberous roots, the stems being headed by corymbs of red-purple flowers.

- **tenuifolium.** (S. amplexicaule.) From S. Europe, Asia Minor and N. Africa. Related to, and not unlike the Portugese *S. pruinatum*, but, in summer the leaves die away leaving only broad basal protective sheaths. On short stems are lax, branched, few-flowered inflorescences carrying yellow flowers.

- **ternatum.** From N. America. Broad, entire leaves arranged in threes and, on short stems, branched cymes of white flowers.

- **X 'Vera Jameson'.** A splendid hybrid, probably claiming the rich purple-leaved form of *S. maximum* as one parent. *(S. maximum* is not included in this Manual as it is frankly a plant for the flower border.)* 9 in. stems arch gracefully, clothed in rounded, fleshy purple leaves and end in flat heads of dusky-pink flowers in late summer.

- **virens 'Monstrosum'.** This is really a cristate form of *S. reflexum*, curious rather than beautiful and of interest to plant collectors.

- **winkleri.** See *S. hirsutum*.

- **yosemitense.** From N. America. Mat-forming after the manner of *S. spathulifolium* but with bright green leaves in compact rosettes. The 4 in. stems carry flat, branched heads of clear yellow flowers.

SELAGINELLA. *Selaginellaceae.* A diminutive of SELAGO, the name of another moss-like plant.

A vast family of, mostly, greenhouse plants, widely distributed in Tropical America, S. Africa, S. America and Australia, with, I believe, only two species native to Europe. The two species described below require cool, shady or north-facing positions and appreciate soil which is retentive of moisture.

- **helvetica.** Widely distributed from Central Europe to Japan. Mossy mats of vivid green 'club-moss' foliage, changing to rusty-red in the autumn.

- **kraussiana.** This S. African species is usually regarded as a greenhouse plant but I have found it to be more than tolerably hardy if grown in similar conditions to *S. helvetica*. It is slightly taller than that species with copiously pinnate fronds.

SELAGO. *Selaginellaceae.* This appears to be an old Latin name used by Pliny for a plant which the Druids gathered, connected with their mysterious ceremonies.

A genus of, mostly, S. African evergreen shrubs and sub-shrubs. Only one species makes any pretence of hardiness and is a valuable plant for the alpine house.

- **sandersonii.** From S. Africa. A dwarf, dense, freely branching shrub. The narrow leaves are at first softly hairy but become glabrous as they age. In late summer it carries compact panicles of lilac to pale purple flowers.

SELLIERA. *Goodeniaceae.* Named for Francois Noel Sellier (1737 - c.1800) of Paris, an engraver of botanical illustrations.
— radicans. (Goodenia radicans.) From Australasia. Spreading mats of creeping, fleshy stems with fleshy leaves of varying size and one or two small white flowers on each short stem, spring from the leaf axils. It likes a not too hot and dry position and moisture-holding soil.

SEMIAQUILEGIA. *Ranunculaceae.* From *semi*, half, and AQUILEGIA, from its relationship to AQUILEGIA.
— adoxioides. (Aquilegia ecalcarata.) Also sometimes named SEMI-AQUILEGIA *ecalcarata.* From China. A dainty plant of about 12 in. height with typical aquilegia foliage and slightly purple stems bearing flights of purple-brown, spurless flowers in spring.

SEMPERVIVELLA. *Crassulaceae.* A diminutive of SEMPERVIVUM.
— alba. From the Himalaya. Crowded rosettes of green, pink-flushed fleshy leaves and short sprays of large white flowers carried in early summer. It likes the same treatment that would be given to sempervivums. Quite hardy but a good alpine house plant also.

SEMPERVIVUM. *Crassulaceae.* From the Latin *semper*, always and *vivus*, living.

A very large family of invaluable garden plants, consisting of a fairly small number of true species and countless hybrids, clones, forms and selections bearing a multitude of names. The nomenclature of the genus has always been confused, much of the confusion arising from the naming of selected seedlings by those who raised them and considered them worthy of individual recognition. Characteristically they form mounds of congested rosettes of fleshy leaves, varying greatly or slightly in shape and colouring. They are avid sun-lovers and will succeed in any ordinary soil but, although they will endure austerity with composure, they also respond favourably to better living conditions which they repay by more vigorous and colourful rosettes. Their flowers, on the whole, are unimportant although such species as *S. arachnoideum* are by no means to be despised florally. Any attempt to provide detailed individual descriptions for them all would be an unrewarding task and would convey little to the reader. Many, although distinct and worthy of separate recognition, so closely resemble others that a word picture would fail to differentiate between them adequately. In this Manual I propose to describe the true species and some of the authenticated hybrids. A more lengthy list of the names of all those we grow will be found in our annual price-list, which will be designed to use in conjunction with the Manual. Botanically, certain species have now been placed in the genus JOVIBARBA and these are indicated in the following text by that name being given in brackets.

- allionii. (JOVIBARBA.) Maritime Alps. Globular rosettes of hairy, yellow-green incurved leaves which are sometimes tipped with pink. The sparsely produced flowers are yellow in colour.

- altum. Caucasus. Large, lax rosettes of slightly pubescent leaves of light green, showing red colouring when grown fully exposed to sun. The flowers are red, with yellow anthers.

- andreanum. Found in N. Spain by Mrs. Andre Giuseppi, in whose honour it is named. The rosettes have few leaves and the central ones are usually in the form of a tight conical bud. The leaves are dull green in colour. The flower stem carries light-red, small leaves and a head of bright pink flowers with yellow anthers.

- arachnoideum. One of the most popular species and commonly known as the Cobweb Houseleek. It has probably been cultivated since the beginning of the 17th century. The crowded, green and pink-leaved rosettes are netted overall by a dense web of fine white hairs. The flowers are of a bright rose-red. There are numerous collected and cultivated forms, several of which have been separately named but they are all variations on the main theme of habit and colouring. It is widely distributed in the European Alps. There is a rare and lovely form with pure white flowers.

- arenarium. (JOVIBARBA.) From Eastern Europe. Crowded small rosettes of green and red glabrous leaves. The slender stem carries a head of yellow flowers.

- armenum. From Asia Minor. Rather similar in general appearance to *S. tectorum* but with smaller leaves and rosettes. The leaves are green and glabrous with purple tips. Yellow flowers and it is an avid sun-worshipper.

- atlanticum. From the Atlas Mountains of N. Africa and the only species known from that area. Originally regarded as a form of *S. tectorum*, it is sufficiently distinct from that species. Loose, medium-sized rosettes, often lop-sided and asymmetrical. Leaves pale green, lightly stained with red. It is sparse flowering, which does not matter as the lax stems carry only a few light pink flowers. It is slightly tender and may suffer in a severe winter.

- balcanicum. From Bulgaria and differs so slightly from several other species that it may rightly be no more than a form of either *S. erythraeum, S. ballsii* or *S. marmoreum*. It has more or less glabrous leaves and pale lilac flowers.

- ballsii. From Greece. Similar too, but smaller in leaf and rosette than *S. marmoreum*, and lacking the purple leaf tips of that species.

Semi-open rosettes of glabrous leaves, green in the type form but showing bronze shading on forms from other localities. Flowers dull pink.

— **X barbulatum.** This is a hybrid between S. *arachnoideum* and S. *montanum* and intermediate in appearance between the parents.

— borisii. See S. *ciliosum.*

— **borissovae.** Found in the Caucasus by Walter Ingwersen in 1935. Semi-open rosettes of glabrous, green, red-brown-tipped leaves. The slender stems bear compact heads of bright pink, fleshy-petalled flowers.

— **calcaratum.** (S. comollii.) Almost certainly a hybrid owing its origin in part to S. *tectorum*, but its provenance is uncertain. It has also gone under the name of S. *giganteum*, without authority. A magnificent, green and purple-leaved sempervivum of great size and extremely decorative.

— **cantabricum.** From Spain. Rosettes of rather lax green, brown-tipped leaves clothed with a dense pile of soft hairs. Short, stout, leafy stems carry heads of rich pink flowers, displaying longitudinal green lines on the petals.

— **caucasicum.** From the Caucasus. Similar in some ways to S. *marmoreum* but differing in having rather less leaves to each rosette. The leaves have a distinct terminal tooth and a brown apex. The flowers are red.

— **ciliosum.** Confined to Bulgaria with the exception of one distinct form from Macedonia. Globose rosettes of incurved, grey-green leaves and yellow flowers on short, stout, leafy stems. The most distinct form is S.*c. borisii* which is so freely covered with long white hairs as to appear almost white. A form from Ali Botusch has bright red leaves and another, from Mali Hat has tightly closed rosettes of plum-coloured leaves. There is also known a hybrid between this species and S. *erythraeum*, intermediate between the parents.

— **comollii.** See S. *calcaratum.*

— **dolomiticum.** From the Eastern Alps. Small, semi-open rosettes of pointed, upstanding leaves, bright green, the outer edge of old leaves richly red. On leafy stems are small heads of rich carmine-red flowers.

— **erythraeum.** From Bulgaria. Rosettes of green and red leaves covered with a dense indumentum of fine hairs. The stems carry rather large leaves and terminate in a head of wide-petalled bright pink flowers. The type grows on limestone but a form from the Pirin mountains occurs only on granite and has smaller rosettes of wholly green leaves.

— **X fauconettii.** A natural hybrid between S. *arachnoideum* and S. *tectorum.*

— **X fimbriatum.** Apparently two natural hybrids have borne this name. One is said to be a hybrid between S. *arachnoideum* and S. *montanum* and the other claims as parents S. *arachnoideum* and S. *wulfenii.* As with so many of the semperviva, both name and parentage are dubious.

— **X funckii.** This too, is of doubtful origin but there is support for the theory of a triple hybrid between *S. arachnoideum, S. montanum* and *S. tectorum,* which its appearance would well support.

— **giuseppii.** Known only from a restricted area in Spain, where it was found by the late Dr. P.L. Giuseppi in 1934. Dense clumps of small rosettes composed of bright green leaves each with a small dark tip, the central leaves of the rosette being fluffy with white hairs. Slender stems carry heads of rose-red flowers.

— **globiferum.** From the Caucasus and described a hundred years ago but only introduced in 1935. Large rosettes of yellow-green leaves, densely hairy on both surfaces and a compact inflorescence of greenish-yellow flowers with faint purple lines at the base of the petals.

— **grandiflorum.** From the Alps of Europe. Slightly lop-sided rosettes of dull green leaves with brown apices and enveloped in a soft down of fine, sticky hairs. It emits an unmistakable identification smell of goats. Yellow flowers, each petal with a purple spot at the base. In nature it meets other species and is responsible for many of the confused hybrids in the genus.

— **heuffelii.** (JOVIBARBA). Widely distributed in the Balkans and immensely variable. It differs from the majority of the semperviva in producing no offsets but the rosette divides into a number of individual rosettes with a common rootstock, forming hard, dense mounds. What might be regarded as the type has hard, pointed, hairy leaves but most of the numerous variants are glabrous. The short, stiff stems carry a head of, usually, yellow flowers, but forms with white flowers are known. Many of the variants have richly coloured leaves.

— **hirtum.** (JOVIBARBA hirta.) From the Eastern Alps. Another extremely variable species, differing in the several geographical stations, as do so many of the species. Typically the rosettes are semi-open and small, with sharply pointed, yellow-green leaves, often reddish brown on the outside. Stout stems carry bold heads of bright yellow flowers.

— **ingwersenii.** Found by Walter Ingwersen in the Caucasus in 1935. Compact, rather flat rosettes of bright green, brown-tipped leaves and small heads of pink, red-keeled flowers, which sometimes open only partially. Young rosettes are carried on thread-fine bright red stolons.

— **iranense.** A new species recently discovered in Iran, and scarcely known as yet in British gardens. Bold, handsome rosettes and a magnificent leafy stem carrying heads of large bright pink flowers.

— **kindingeri.** From Macedonia. Large rosettes of rather lax, hairy leaves, ciliate, light green with red tips. The flower stem is also hairy and well clothed with leaves and carries a head of good yellow flowers, the petals red-lined at the base, but it is apt to be shy-flowering.

- kosaninii. From the limestones of the Eastern Alps. Large, open rosettes of hairy leaves, sombre green in colour and with a dark tip. The rather tall, leafy stems have heads of red flowers, the backs of the petals being green. There are several slightly differing forms from different mountains.

- leucanthum. A species with a limited distribution in Bulgaria. Medium-sized rosettes, the inner leaves closed, the outer ones more or less erect or spreading. The slender stems carry heads of pale, but bright yellow flowers. Unlike S. *kindingeri* it is inclined to flower almost too freely and, of course, the flowering rosette dies.

- macedonicum. As its name implies, from Macedonia in several localities. Crowded, small flat rosettes with the central leaves closed and the outer ones more loosely arranged. The flowers are a good red colour.

- marmoreum. (S. schlehanii.) From the Balkans. A species which appears to replace S. *tectorum* in the Balkans but is a smaller, neater plant. It is variable, as are so many of the species, but in what may be regarded as its typical form it makes medium-sized rosettes which are hairy when young, becoming glabrous as they age. The light green leaves have well marked deep brown apices. The tall stems are leafy and bear large heads of crimson flowers, the petals white at the edges. An especially fine form, which appears to have originated in the Belvedere Botanical Garden in Vienna has leaves of glowing ruby-red with green tips and white marginal hairs. It is often grown as S. *ornatum* but should correctly be more cumbersomely named S.m. *rubrifolium ornatum*.

- michaelis-borsii. Probably from Rumania. Rosettes of apple-green leaves, covered with fine hair and with a pronounced mucronate tip. The outer leaves assume red coloration, especially on their margins and tips. I have not seen it in flower.

- minus. From Anatolia. Very small, crowded rosettes of globular shape, the central leaves closed, the outer ones spreading. The leaves are olive-green in colour with a bronze tint on the outer side when fully exposed to sun. Short, fleshy, leafy stems carry heads of yellow-green flowers. Very often the bases of the leaves are noticeably purple in colour. There are at least two distinct geographical forms known and in cultivation.

- montanum. Widespread in Europe, and extremely variable. At least a dozen names have been given to it in gardens, names which it would be pointless to particularize. Typically it forms small rosettes, hairy and dull green in colour and in some forms there is a distinct dark tip to the leaves. Short stems carry flowers of reddish-purple. It interbreeds freely with other semperviva and there are many hybrids claiming it as one of their parents. Possibly the most distinct of all its forms is *braunii* from Carinthia and Styria, which has white flowers, a rare occurence in the genus.

- nevadense. First found in Spain in 1934 by the late Dr. P.L. Giuseppi Dense, rather flat rosettes with leaves which tend to incurve. The green leaves are glabrous and often red on the outside. The short stems bear compact heads of rose-red flowers. The late Dr.Wale, an authority on the genus, separated a distinct form as *S.n. hirtellum* which has larger, hairy leaves lacking the red coloration but otherwise it is a similar to the type.

— octopodes. From Macedonia, where it is rare and only locally abundant. Rosettes of small, incurved leaves, blunt and hairy, green, with brown tips. There is an abundance of offsets on long, thin stolons. The slender stems have heads of good yellow flowers, the petals with a red spot at the base. The form *S.o. apetalum* differs from the type in having slightly larger rosettes, with a less well defined dark tip to the leaves and the flowers have no petals, these being replaced by numerous petaloid organs which are sterile.

— ossetiense. Found by the late Walter Ingwersen in the Caucasus in 1935. Rosettes of rather long, narrow leaves, very fleshy and green with a small brown tip. The short stem carries a few large flowers whose petals are white, with a purple base and lined with purple.

— pittonii. From the Eastern Alps. Small, neat rosettes of dull green, very hairy, dark-tipped leaves. The good yellow flowers appear in small heads on slender, leafy stems.

— pumilum. From the Caucasus and introduced in at least four distinct forms by Walter Ingwersen and Dr. Giuseppi in 1935. Characteristically it makes small rosettes of neat, green, pubescent leaves, becoming red-stained when grown in full exposure. The flowers are purple-blue in colour. The most desirable form is that collected on Mt.Elbruz at 9000 ft. which is a pygmy, with almost glabrous leaves and more richly tinted colouring.

— reginae-amaliae. Confined almost entirely to the mountains of Greece, with one intrusion into Albania. It is variable, differing slightly from separate localities. Packed rosettes, of medium size with pubescent dull green leaves, colouring on the outside when fully exposed, when the entire leaf may become purple. The tapering stem carries an open inflorescence of red flowers, the petals white-edged and marked with a central crimson band.

— ruthenicum. See *S. zeleborii.*

— schlehanii. See *S. marmoreum.*

— soboliferum. (JOVIBARBA sobolifera.) Linnaeus planted this species on his house in Sweden where, at least until a few years ago, it survived. Often confused in gardens with *S. globiferum*, which is rightly a Caucasian species and does not belong in the JOVIBARBA group. From Europe,with very globular rosettes, and offsets on short stolons which easily detach and fall to the ground. Leaves light green and incurved, turning to coppery red in full exposure. It seldom flowers and, when it does, resembles *S. arenarium* in blossom.

— tectorum. The commonest and best known of all the semperviva and cultivated by man since early days. The Greeks and Romans knew it and it was illustrated in the manuscript of the *Materia Medica*, written by Dioscorides in the 6th century. It is very variable but the most typical form is the one originally grown on house roofs as a charm against damage by lightning. No less than seventy synonyms have been given to this species and its innumerable forms. It is too well known to require a detailed description. It is widely distributed in Europe, from the Pyrenees to the Balkans and hybridises freely with other species where they meet in the wild. One or two of the more distinct forms are, *var. alpinum*, with smaller, neater rosettes, the base of the leaves stained red. *var. calcareum*, from the French Alps and once used extensively as a bedding plant. Rosettes of large leaves, sharply pointed and brown at the tip. *var. glaucum*, large rosettes of glaucous leaves, whitish at the base and *var. triste*, which is not authoritatively recognised but has been grown for many years under this name. Neat and compact with leaves of uniform red-brown colour.

— **thompsonianum.** From the limestones of Austria. Small, sub-globular rosettes, semi-open, of yellow-green leaves, rather lanceolate in shape and flushed red on the outside under full exposure. The small inflorescence consists of flowers yellow at the apex, with a pale purple band in the middle and whitish margins. Easily grown but usually shy-flowering.

— **X versicolor.** Not known as a wild plant and reputedly a hybrid between *S. zeleborii* and *S. marmoreum*. The rosettes are like those of *S. tectorum* but the flowers open yellow, fading to pale purple.

— **wulfenii.** From the Austrian and Swiss Alps. Glaucous, hard, fleshy leaves closed to a conical bud in the centre. The flowers are yellow and crimson-lined at the base of the petals.

— **zeleborii.** (S. ruthenicum.) From Serbia and Bulgaria. Large rosettes of pubescent leaves, almost velvety on the surface, often with a dark brown apical point. Tall, tapering stems carry yellow flowers, usually with a well marked crimson base.

In addition to the above there is a host of hybrids, many of fairly recent introduction from America, some of which are of outstanding beauty with large, richly coloured leaves. Their names would convey little and many of them are not yet fully proven, but they hold great promise.

SENECIO. *Compositae*. From the Latin *senex*, an old man, referring to the hoary pappus.

One of the largest of all genera, containing some 1200 species, varying from compact alpine plants to giant herbs and tall shrubs. Although the genus is cosmopolitan, most species are to be found in temperate regions. The few which concern us here are largely natives of European mountains. They are sun-loving, summer-flowering and, with one or two exceptions, easy to please.

- abrotanifolius. From the Southern and Eastern Alps and rather too tall for most rock gardens. It has woody stems up to 15 inches high, clad with dark green leaves deeply divided into segments and loose heads of orange to orange-red flowers. A good colour but a sprawling, untidy plant. The plant often grown as *S. tiroliensis* is no more than a subspecies of this, with no special merit.
- adonidifolius. From Central Europe and another rather tall, often sprawling plant with bright yellow flowers. Both this and the preceding species can be regarded as useful ground-cover for sunny places even in poor soil.
- flettii. From the Olympic mountains in the State of Washington. It is not a traffic-stopper, but a quite pretty dwarf with bright golden flowers.
- incanus. An alpine species widely distributed in Europe and with several slightly varying forms or subspecies. The typical plant makes low tufts of grey leaves divided into rounded segments. Small, neat heads of yellow flowers. The best of the subspecies is *carniolicus*, which asks for choice quarters in a sunny, gritty scree, or the alpine house. Its foliage is intensely silver and the orange-yellow flowers are attractive.
- leucophyllus. Perhaps the best of the European species. From the Pyrenees and Spain. Akin to, and possibly another geographical subspecies of *S. incanus*, with intensely silver divided foliage and tight heads of golden flowers on short stems. Scree or alpine house.
- tiroliensis (or tyrolensis.) See *S. abrotanifolius.*
- uniflorus. Local, in the Southern and Central Alps. Tufts of spoon-shaped, lobed leaves and very short stems carrying usually, one head of orange-golden tiny flowers.
- websteri. Endemic to the Olympics of Washington. I brought this back, many years ago, and treasured it but I doubt if it survives in British gardens. Bold clumps of large, deep green leathery leaves, crimson beneath, and large golden flowers on foot-high stems.

SERRATULA. *Compositae.* From *serrula*, a little saw, a reference to the saw-edged leaves.

- seoanei. This is the plant which has long been grown wrongly under the name *S. shawii*, the error probably arising from an original misspelling of a partially obliterated label. It comes from Portugal, Spain, and S.W. France, and is possibly only a subspecies of *S. tinctoria.* A valuable summer and autumn-flowering plant, it forms neat bushes up to 9 in. with dark green, deeply-cut leaves and branching stems carrying many thistle-like heads of pink flowers. It is an avid sun-lover.

SESELI. *Umbelliferae.* The ancient Greek name for an umbelliferous plant. A seemingly rather obscure genus which may yet be relegated elsewhere.

- **caespitosum.** From Greece. Hard hummocks of densely tufted rigid, pinnately-cut apple-green leaves. The low heads of greenish flowers are unimportant but it is an admirable cushion-plant for a sunny scree or the alpine house.

SHORTIA. *Diapensiaceae.* Named for Dr. Charles W. Short (1794-1863), Kentucky botanist.

The monotypic genus SCHIZOCODON has now been absorbed into the genus SHORTIA. Plants for woodland, lime-free soil and cool or shaded positions. They are slow to establish. Spring and early summer flowering.
- **galacifolia.** From N. America. Tufts of evergreen, rounded, glossy and leathery leaves, bright green but becoming bronzed in autumn. On each short stem appears one funnel-shaped, elegant white flower, the petals flushing pink as they age.
- **soldanelloides.** (SCHIZOCODON soldanelloides.) From Japan. Mats of woody stems and evergreen, ovate to wedge-shaped, glossy, toothed leaves. On short stems are racemes of open bell-shaped flowers with fringed petals, rose-red in the centre and fading to white at the margins. Three forms are cultivated, *alpinus*, a diminished form of the type, *ilicifolius*, with leaves more holly-like, and *magnus*, which is larger in all its parts.
- **uniflora.** From Japan. Running mats of woody stems and rounded, toothed leaves, less leathery than those of *S. galacifolia*, and larger. Carried singly on naked stems are large pink flowers with fringed petals.

SIBBALDIA. *Rosaceae.* Named in honour of Sir Robert Sibbald (1641-1722). First professor of medicine in the University of Edinburgh and author of *Scotia Illustrata.*

A small genus, distributed in Europe, N. Asia and N. America.
- **procumbens.** Extended over the whole range of the genus, including Britain. An unexciting creeping perennial for lime-free soil and shady places, quite a pleasant carpeter with small cymes of yellow flowers but it is sometimes apetalous.

SIBTHORPIA. *Scrophulariaceae.* Named for Humphrey Sibthorp (1713-1797), professor of botany at Oxford and father of the more famous botanist, John Sibthorp.
- **europaea.** Europe, including Britain. A perennial, creeping plant, rooting at the nodes, usually cultivated in the variegated forms, whose golden-green or silver leaves are attractive. For moist, cool positions. The flowers are minute and unimportant.

SIEVERSIA. See GEUM.

SILENE. *Caryophyllaceae.* The Greek name for *Viscaria,* now applied to this genus. A large family of annual and perennial herbs and, occasionally, sub-shrubs, natives of the Northern Hemisphere and S. Africa. The genus contains a number of valuable rock garden and alpine house plants. In general, and unless otherwise stated, they are sun-lovers and will grow in any good, ordinary, well drained soil. Unless otherwise described they are spring and early summer flowering.

- acaulis. One of the most typical and well loved alpine plants with an immense distribution in the Northern Hemisphere from Arctic America to Southern Europe, including Britain. Of densely tufted habit it forms wide mats of congested shoots clothed in small bright green leaves. In nature it is sheeted with almost stemless pink flowers but it is not quite so generous in gardens, where it may prove shy-flowering. It is more likely to blossom in abundance if given a spartan, gritty diet. There are numerous named forms of which one, *pedunculata,* has slightly taller stems and usually flowers very freely There is an albino and one or two others varying modestly from the type.

- alpestris. From the limestones of the Eastern Alps and a charming and easy plant. Low tufts of branching stems with narrow, glossy leaves and showers of white flowers with fringed petals. There is also a double-flowered form of equal merit which has lost nothing of grace by the multiplication of the petals.

- armeria. Although this species from Southern Europe is little more than an annual, it has merits and makes a pleasant display of grey-green leaves and compound heads of crimson-carmine flowers. It should be given a spartan diet to keep it to a neat and tidy habit.

- asterias. From the Balkans and similar to *S. armeria,* but a good perennial.

- boryi. From Spain and Portugal. Tufts of softly hairy foliage and nocturnal pink or white flowers peeping from curiously elongated calyx tubes. Interesting but not exciting, possibly best in the alpine house.

- californica. From California and Oregon. Erect, leafy stems up to a foot or so in height and many scarlet flowers of good size, the petals deeply cleft. It asks for, and deserves, a warm and sheltered position.

- echinus. From Asia Minor, and possibly a subspecies of *S. caryophylloides.* Although dubiously in cultivation it is much to be desired, forming compact tufts of spiny, sticky-leaved rosettes of darkest green and magenta-pink flowers on 1 inch stems. For the alpine house.

- ciliata. From the mountains of Southern Europe. From a woody root it makes compact mats of small roughly hairy leaves. On 6 in.

stems it bears one-sided racemes of flowers, white inside but green or reddish outside.

— cretica. From the Grecian islands and probably only biennial. On rather tall stems it carries many large white flowers.

— elisabetha. Often grown as MELANDRIUM *elizabethae*. From the Southern and Eastern Alps. On rather lax, spreading stems it carries enormous ragged flowers of brilliant magenta-crimson, rising from tufts of narrow, glossy leaves. For a sunny scree or the alpine house.

— hookeri. From California. Radiating, procumbent stems clothed in narrow, hairy leaves and axillary flowers of great size, the soft pink petals having narrow white rays from the throat, and deeply cleft at the tips. Not an easy plant and best accommodated in the alpine house, in gritty, lime-free soil which is nevertheless rich in humus.

— ingramii. From N. America, and similar to *S. hookeri* in appearance, but with red flowers. It is an easier plant to grow but deserves alpine house treatment.

— keiskei. From Japan, and Japanese botanists refer it to the genus MELANDRIUM but I retain the name by which it is now well known in our gardens. The form we have in Britain appears to be the one which is identified as *minor*. It makes neat tufts of erect, 4 in. stems with narrow, glossy leaves and small heads of rose-pink flowers.

— laciniatum. From Mexico and California and another wanderer from the genus MELANDRIUM. Erect, branching stems and narrow, hairy leaves. The drooping flowers are solitary and crimson. For the alpine house.

— macropoda. A Bulgarian plant of dubious specific rank, but worth garden room. It makes low tufts of glossy leaves from which rise thin, wiry, branching stems carrying small white flowers in profusion.

— maritima. Although commonly accorded specific rank this native plant is probably correctly regarded as a form of *S. vulgaris (S. cucubalus.)* In its single-flowered form it is scarcely worth considering as a garden plant, although pretty enough on the sea cliffs it adorns, but the form with large, fully double white flowers is splendid when trailing down the face of a sunny wall or spreading over a sunny rock.

— mollissima. From Morocco, a cliff dweller forming tufts of grey, hairy leaves from which spring short stems with clusters of cream-white flowers.

— monachorum. From the Balkans and near to *S. pusilla*. Short-lived but worth growing for its clouds of dainty white flowers on short stems. It will seed harmlessly and charmingly in a sunny spot in gritty soil.

— odontosepala. Although probably not in cultivation, there is reason to hope that this Iranian cliff-dweller may soon make its appearance in our gardens. It should form close mats of shiny green, sticky leaves with 4 in. stems carrying large white flowers, tinted with apple-blossom pink.

- pindicola. From Greece. A mountain-dweller forming tufts of caes-pitose leaves and with short, sticky stems carrying not very note-worthy white flowers, but a good cushion plant.
- plankii. Although not yet cultivated in this country, to my knowledge, I do know that it exists in one or two American gardens and am hopeful that it may wing its way across the Atlantic. It comes from New Mexico, and will insist upon alpine house treatment in order to display its clumps of caespitose foliage and scarlet flowers.
- pumilio. See SAPONARIA *pumilio.*
- pusilla. (S. quadrifida.) From Central and Southern Europe, north-wards. Not a very distinguished species and one which has wandered uneasily among several genera and specific epithets. Quite neat tufts of glossy small leaves from which rise rather weak, branching stems carrying small white or, rarely, pink flowers.
- quadrifida. See *S. pusilla.*
- saxifraga. Southern Europe and northward to the Carpathians. Widely distributed and variable. Usually appearing as dense tufts of caespitose leaves with short-stemmed white flowers, green or reddish on the undersides.
- schafta. An invaluable, late-flowering species from the Caucasus. Not an aristocrat, but easy and colourful. On 6 to 9 in. stems, usually unbranched, it carries rose-magenta flowers, singly or in twos from June until October.
- schmuckeri. Dense green cushions and small white flowers on short stems. The only reference I can find to its habitat is, that it comes from the mountains of N.W. Makedonija! — presumably Macedonia?
- suksdorfii. From the Cascade mountains of N. America. On 3 in. stems it displays inch-wide pale pink flowers with large inflated calyces.
- vallesia. From the Western Alps. Tufted hummocks of grey-green leaves and clammy, 6 in. stems carrying flowers which are pink with-in and blood-red outside. It only expands its flowers during the evening.
- virginica. Although it is a trifle tall, this N. American species is worth growing for the sake of its brilliant crimson-red flowers carried on stems which may be 18 in. high. It flowers from June to August.
- vulgaris. See *S. maritima.*
- wherryi. From N.W. America. Rather sprawling, leafy stems and large white or rose-pink flowers.
- zawadskii. From the Balkans. Rosettes of rather stiff, glossy leaves and 6 to 9 in. stems each carrying a few large white flowers with swollen calyces.

SIMETHIS. *Liliaceae.* Named for the nymph Simethis, mistress of Acis.

— **bicolor.** The only species in its genus, native of N. Africa, where it inhabits pine woods and will, therefore, like a peaty soil and some shade. From fibrous roots spring tufts of grassy leaves and erect, 9 to 12 in. stems carrying panicles of flowers which are white inside and purple on the outside. Summer flowering.

SISYMBRIUM. See HUGUENINIA.

SISYRINCHIUM. *Iridaceae.* Ancient Greek name used for another plant. A large family of annual and perennial plants, native of North and South America. It is a genus of some diversity and one or two of the commoner species have earned themselves a rather poor reputation by their eagerness to spread themselves by means of self-sown seedlings. These are the exceptions in a generally very acceptable race. Unless otherwise stated they thrive in full sun and any good soil and are spring and summer flowering.

— **angustifolium.** Commonly known as Blue-eyed grass. Tufts of grassy leaves and on 6 in. stems clusters of blue flowers. It is one of the spreaders and has naturalized itself here and there in Britain.

— **bellum.** Similar to *S. augustifolium.* The flowers are more violet-blue and of ten display a faint yellow throat.

— **bermudianum.** (S. iridioides.) A taller plant than either of the preceding. The winged, foot-high stems bear clusters of violet-blue flowers, yellowish in the throat.

— **californicum.** The flower stems can attain a height of more than one foot. Many-flowered clusters of large yellow flowers which open in steady succession.

— **chilense.** Characteristic tufts of narrow leaves and 9 in. stems carrying purple flowers, yellow in the throat.

— **convolutum.** From semi-tropical. S. America and sometimes considered rather tender. The 12 in. winged stems bear clusters of yellow, brown-veined flowers.

— **depauperatum.** From Patagonia and very dubiously in cultivation, but needs reintroducing. Tufts of rush-like leaves and 9 in. stems carrying white flowers vividly marked by a maroon eye.

— **douglasii.** (S. grandiflorum.) Very different, and very lovely. Entirely herbaceous, it erupts in early spring with frail tufts of narrow leaves and 6 to 9 in. stems carrying pendant bells of wine-red. There is also an equally pleasant albino. It dies down very soon after flowering and its position should be carefully marked.

— **filifolium.** From the Falkland Isles. Tufts of rush-like leaves and fairly tall stems each carrying several bell-shaped pendant flowers of white, veined with reddish purple lines.

— **gramineum.** See *S. angustifolium.*

- **graminifolium.** Clumps of narrow leaves and erect, branching, 9 in. stems bearing yellow flowers.
- **grandiflorum.** See *S. douglasii.*
- **idahoense.** The erect stems can vary in height from 6 to 17 in. and carry deep blue flowers.
- **iridifolium.** The narrow leaves are roughly ciliate at the margin and the tip usually incurves. The flowers are yellowish-white.
- **iridioides.** See *S. bermudianum.*
- **lutescens.** See *S. striatum.*
- **macounianum.** A newcomer from N. America and an invaluable plant. Fans of small, iris-like leaves and stems carrying many large white flowers. The form in cultivation is the albino. I am told the type has blue flowers.
- **macrocarpum.** Another newcomer from S. America. Low tufts of leaves like those of a small iris and short, erect stems carrying very large flowers of rich golden-yellow.
- **odoratissimum.** See SYMPHYOSTEMON *biflorus.*
- **striatum.** I may get into trouble for including this in an alpine plant Manual, but it is suitable for large rock gardens or the environment surrounding a small one — and, in any case, I like it too much to omit it. Strong fans of iris-like leaves and erect, 2ft. stems studded along their length with cream or pale yellow flowers. There is a handsome form with green and white variegated foliage.
- **tenuifolium.** From Mexico and its hardiness is suspect. Rather scanty, narrow leaves and yellow flowers on 9 in. stems, one to several on each stem.

SMELOWSKIA. *Cruciferae.* Obviously named for a Mr. Smelowsk, of whom I can find no record.

A small race of crucifers from N. America which would seem to be of some promise for rock gardens. *S. americana*, *S. calycina* and *S. ovalis* all make low mats of grey, dissected leaves and carry white or yellow flowers.

SMILACINA. *Liliaceae.* A diminutive of *Smilax.*

A small genus of hardy perennials, only one of which qualifies for inclusion in this Manual. Light shade and humus-rich soil will be appreciated.

- **stellata.** From N. America. From spreading roots spring glaucous, stem-clasping lanceolate leaves and racemes of small, starry white flowers on 12 in. stems in May and June.

SOLDANELLA. *Primulaceae.* A diminutive of *soldo*, a small coin, an allusion to the shape of the leaves.

A small genus of choice alpine plants from the Alps of Europe containing a few species and several natural hybrids. They have a not altogether deserved reputation for being temperamental. If given gritty soil, rich in humus and a cool position, they are not difficult. They are also often accused of being shy-flowering, but this is, as often as not, due to the fact that their flower buds, produced in early winter, nestle almost at ground level, concealed by the leaves, and are frequently devoured by slugs and snails. They are spring flowering.

- alpina. From Central and Southern Europe. Wee tufts of rounded, leathery leaves and, on very short stems, deeply fringed pendant lavender bells.
- X aschersoniana. Is *S. austriaca* crossed with *S. montana* and is intermediate between the parents.
- austriaca. From the Austrian Alps. Tufts of rounded, orbicular, entire leaves and stems carrying singly pendant, tubular flowers of lilac-blue lined with stripes of deeper colour and deeply fringed.
- carpatica. From the Tatra Mountains. A slightly controversial, but pretty species, intermediate in appearance between *S. alpina* and *S. montana.* The leaves are often reddish on the undersides. The purple-blue flowers are deeply fringed. There is also a handsome albino form.
- dimoniei. From Eastern Europe and the Balkans. Rather like *S. hungarica* but with the corolla lobes of the purple-blue flowers divided into three lobules.
- X ganderi. A natural hybrid between *S. alpina* and *S. minima.* It is nearest in appearance to *S. minima*, but it carries three flowers to a stem and the bells are wider and paler in colour.
- X handel-mazzetii. A natural hybrid between *S. austriaca* and *S. montana.*
- hungarica. From the Eastern Alps. Leathery, kidney-shaped leaves, purple beneath and from one to three widely bell-shaped purple-blue flowers on 4 in. stems.
- X hybrida. Is a natural hybrid between *S. alpina* and *S. pusilla.*
- X janchenii. An obscure natural hybrid between *S. minima* and *S. pusilla.*
- minima. Widely distributed in the European Alps. Tiny, round, spoon-shaped leaves and, on 2 in. stems narrow bells of pale blue streaked with violet within.
- X mixta. A natural hybrid between *S. austriaca* and *S. pusilla.*
- montana. Widely distributed in Europe. Rounded, leathery deep green leaves, cordate at the base, the margins often slightly scalloped Several widely bell-shaped, fringed purple bells on 6 in. stems.
- X neglecta. A natural hybrid between *S. minima* and *S. pusilla.*

- **pindicola.** From the mountains of Greece. The leathery, rounded leaves are dull green above and ash-green beneath. Funnel-shaped, deeply-cleft rose-lilac flowers, up to three on each 4 in. stem.
- **pusilla.** Widely distributed in Europe. Glossy, dark green cordate, leathery leaves in tiny tufts and narrowly bell-shaped pale violet flowers.
- **villosa.** From the Pyrenees. One of the largest and most easily grown. Leaf-stalks and flower stems densely felted with fine hairs, heads of purple-blue flowers, like those of *S. montana*, on 9 in. stems.
- **X wettsteinii.** A natural hybrid between *S. alpina* and *S. montana*.
- **X wiemanniana.** A natural hybrid between *S. alpina* and *S. austriaca*.

SOLEIROLIA. *Urticaceae.* Named for Joseph Francois Soleirol (d.1863) who botanized extensively in Corsica.

- **solierolii.** (HELXINE *solierolii.*) A creeping and almost ineradicable weed making flat mats of bright green, tiny, rounded leaves on rooting stems. The flowers are inconspicuous and its only use is to cover shady cool areas where nothing else will grow. Avoid it like the plague in rock gardens.

SOLIDAGO. *Compositae.* From *solido*, to make whole, referring to the reputed healing qualities of these plants.

A genus of mostly tall growing herbaceous plants, mostly natives of N. America, with outliers in temperate Europe and Asia. Easily grown and sun-loving and mid to late summer flowering.

- **brachystachys.** See *S. virgaurea*.
- **cutleri.** From N. America and comparable to the dwarf forms of *S. virgaurea*, which see.
- **minutissima.** See *S. virgaurea*.
- **virgaurea.** Europe, including Britain. The only forms of this variable species which are of interest to rock gardeners are *brachystachys*, a six-inch Golden Rod of densely tufted habit with yellow flowers, and the Japanese *minutissima*, which is similar in appearance.

SONCHUS. *Compositae.* The Greek name *sonchos*.

- **spinosus.** According to the latest classification this should now be known as LAUNAEA *cervicornis*. It is the plant which, in the dim and distant past was to be found in a few catalogues as ACANTHO-SONCHUS *cervicornis*. I retain one of its inaccurate but better known names. It comes from the hot hills of Spain and is a tangled dome of thorny stems, with a few narrow, toothed grey-green leaves and many small yellow flowers in summer. It demands alpine house treatment or a hot, dry corner in the open.

SORBUS. *Rosaceae.* From the Latin *sorbum*, the fruit of the Service Tree, *S. domestica.* Although shrubs, in general, are excluded from this Manual, it is essential to include *S. reducta*, from Burma and China, which makes low, gnarled bushes of woody stems with serrate, shining green leaves, heads of whitish flowers and handsome clusters of red berries. Even smaller, but unobtainable is the Himalayan *S. pygmaea.*

SPEIRANTHA. *Liliaceae.* From *speira*, a wreath and *anthos*, a flower.
— gardenii. The only species in its genus. A native of China. Basal rosettes of narrow, evergreen leaves and 4 to 6 in. stems carrying racemes of many starry white flowers in summer. A good peat garden plant as it appreciates shade and lime-free soil.

SPENCERIA. *Rosaceae.* Named for Spencer Le Marchant Moore (1850-1931). A botanist at Kew.
— ramalana. From China. Handsome, glossy, potentilla-like leaves in basal rosettes and 6 in. spikes of large golden flowers. Summer flowering and a sun-lover.

SPHAERALCEA. *Malvaceae.* from the Greek *sphaira*, a globe and, *Alcea*, mallow, an allusion to the globose fruits of these plants.
— munroana. From N. America. Spreading, semi-prostrate stems with lobed, grey-green leaves and axillary and terminal panicles of orange-scarlet flowers in summer. For a hot, dry position.

SPIGELIA. *Loganiaceae.* Named for Adrian van der Spiegel (1578-1625) Professor of anatomy and botany at Padua.
— marilandica. From N. America. Erect, 9 in. stems with narrow, sessile leaves on simple or forked spikes of showy flowers, red outside and yellow within. Summer flowering.

SPIRAEA. See the genera LUETKIA and PETROPHYTUM.

SPRAGUEA. See the genus CALYPTRIDIUM.

STACHYS. *Labiatae.* The Greek name for various genera of Labiatae.
A race of, mostly, tall perennials, rarely sub-shrubs or shrubs. Widely distributed in north temperate and oriental regions. Sun-

lovers and, unless otherwise stated, contented in open positions and any good soil. Summer flowering.

— **candida.** From Greece. Short, brittle stems clothed with thick, rounded leaves heavily felted with silver hairs make this an attractive foliage plant. The flowers, although less important, are not without charm. They are characteristically hooded, white, heavily veined with pink. It is best in the alpine house.

— **corsica.** From Corsica and Sardinia. Mats of shining emerald-green leaves upon which rest very short-stemmed creamy-pink flowers. Not very long-lived and should be divided and replanted every now and then.

— **cretica.** (S. italica.) S. Europe from S. France eastward. A species of dubious authenticity, it is probably a subspecies of *S. germanica*, which is a group species. Fairly tall tomentose stems and ovate leaves, grey-green above and densely silver-haired beneath. Loose spikes of purple flowers. Probably best in the alpine house.

— **discolor.** See *S. nivea.*

— **floribunda.** From Turkey and only dubiously in cultivation. Stems and leaves felted with yellow-green tomentum and spikes of sulphur-yellow flowers.

— **glutinosa.** Mediterranean regions. A stiffly shrubby bushlet with strongly aromatic foliage and small white flowers.

— **italica.** See *S. cretica.*

— **lavendulifolia.** From Asia Minor. Rather tall stems clothed with narrow, grey-green leaves and short spikes of pink flowers.

— **nivea.** (S. discolor.) Mats of crimpled green leaves and short spikes of white flowers. From the Caucasus.

— **saxicola.** From N. Africa. Lovely when starved in a narrow crevice, along which it spreads silver stems and leaves in dense mats. The cream flowers are borne in small clusters and are less important than the foliage. For the alpine house.

— **spinosa.** From Greece. Tangled tufts of spiny, spiky stems and leaves all clothed in silver hairs. The white flowers are sometimes suffused with pink and brown veins.

STACKHOUSIA. *Stackhousiaceae.* Named for John Stackhouse (1740-1819), British botanist.

— **pulvinaris.** An Australian alpine much to be desired. Mats of green, succulent leaves and almost stemless, fragrant cream-yellow flowers. Treasure it, if obtained, in the alpine house.

STATICE. See the genus LIMONIUM.

STELLERA. *Thymelaeaceae.* Named for Georg Wilhelm Steller (1709-1746) German naturalist and traveller.
- chamaejasme. From Central Asia. A seldom seen but very beautiful plant. The erect, 12 in. stems are clothed in small glaucous leaves and end in dense, globose heads of fragrant, pearl-white flowers. The unopened buds are crimson. It appears to be not too difficult to grow under the conditions that one would accord to the related daphnes, but it is not easy to propagate.

STENANDRIUM. *Acanthaceae.* From the Greek *stenos*, narrow, and *aner*, a man. The stamens of these plants are narrow.
- barbatum. Not an alpine, as it comes from desert lands in Texas and New Mexico, but could be an attractive alpine house plant. Mats of silver-haired leaves and short-stemmed, mimulus-like flowers of vivid cerise-crimson.

STREPTOPUS. *Liliaceae.* From the Greek *streptos*, twisted, and *pous*, a foot. A reference to the twisted flower-stems.
- roseus. From N. America, and sometimes known as UVULARIA *rosea*. The 9 in. arching stems carry oval, ciliate leaves and sprays of pink flowers in late spring or early summer. It enjoys peat garden conditions.

STYLIDIUM. *Stylidiaceae.* From the Greek *stylos*, a column. The stamens unite with the style to form a column.

A small genus of, mostly, Australasian plants. They prefer alpine house treatment here. Summer flowering and with a probable preference for limefree soil. The flowers of these plants have a green style which, when touched at a moment when fertilisation is due, fires like a trigger, striking any intruding insect and so exploding the ready-to-burst anthers and depositing the pollen.
- adnatum. Low bushes with short, needle-like leaves and 9 to 12 in. stems carrying sessile clusters of pink flowers.
- caespitosum. Cushions and tufts of short, fine leaves from which rise thin, wiry, branching stems of 6 in. or so, carrying white flowers with red markings at the base of the petals.
- graminifolium. Long, narrow, stiff and sharply pointed leaves in loose tufts and a stem, varying in height from 6 to 12 in. bearing many white and pink flowers.

STYLOPHORUM. *Papaveraceae.* From the Greek *stylos*, style and phoros, bearing, referring to the long, columnar style.
- diphyllum. From Eastern N. America. The basal leaves are deeply cut

into lobed divisions and the erect, downy, foot-high stems carry terminal clusters of inch-wide clear yellow flowers. For shady places, open woodland or the peat garden. Spring flowering.

STYPANDRA. *Liliaceae.* From *stype*, tow, and *andros*, anther. The stamens are downy.

— **caespitosum.** From Greece. Hard hummocks of densely tufted, rigid, stems carrying white, starry flowers. It may need alpine house protection.

SUTTONIA. *Myrsinaceae.* Named for the Rev. Charles Sutton (1756-1846), an amateur botanist.

— **nummularia.** This is probably more correctly included in the genus MYRSINE. A prostrate shrub from New Zealand with tangled, wiry stems and many small, brown-green leaves. The tiny flowers are often followed by purple berries on the female plants. For the peat garden or alpine house.

SWERTIA. A genus allied to GENTIANA of which few species are in cultivation and those few seldom successfully grown, even if hardy, which many of them are not. Many of them are annuals, others adopt a semi-climbing habit. They are of interest to try if obtainable, but do not merit detailed description here.

SYMPHYANDRA. *Campanulaceae.* From the Greek *symphuio*, to grow together and *aner*, anther. The anthers are joined.
A race closely related to Campanula, mostly from the Orient. Some are rather tall for the small rock garden but they are good summer-flowering plants of considerable decorative value. They flourish in any ordinary soil and sunny positions.

— **armena.** From the Caucasus. Deeply toothed, hoary foliage and branching 15 in. stems carrying many lavender-blue, bell-shaped flowers.

— **cretica.** From Crete. Tufts of rounded and pointed, smooth green leaves, coarsely serrate. The stems, up to 18 in. in height, are unbranched and offer several pendant bells more than an inch long and either pale blue or almost white.

— **hofmannii.** From Bosnia. Monocarpic or biennial. A large basal rosette of broad, regularly toothed leaves emits a bold central, leafy stem from the leaf-axils of which spring clusters of drooping large, bell-shaped flowers of creamy-white.

— **lazica.** (or, possibly, CAMPANULA *finitima.)* From Turkey, where it inhabits crevices on cliff faces. The pendant, branching stems carry many white or pink-flushed bellflowers.

— **ossetica.** From the Caucasus. A biennial, with large rosettes of toothed leaves and, on foot-high stems, racemes of silvery-lilac tubular flowers.

— **pendula.** From the Caucasus. Rosettes of ovate, toothed leaves and long, branching stems carrying panicles of pale yellow pendant flowers.

— **wanneri.** The Alps of Europe. Many-leaved rosettes, the leaves broad and regularly and deeply toothed, dark green and hairy on the upper surface. Tall stems carry racemes of violet-blue flowers.

SYMPHYOSTEMON. *Iridaceae.*

— **biflorus.** (SISYRINCHIUM *odoratissimum.*) From Patagonia. On rather lax stems appear several large, cream, maroon-striped lily-shaped flowers which are fragrant. Best in an alpine house. Spring flowering.

SYNTHYRIS. *Scrophulariaceae.* From the Greek *syn*, together, and *thyris*, a small door, alluding to a characteristic of the fruits.

A small, interesting genus confined in its distribution to N.W. America. They like cool rich soil, with plenty of humus and good drainage and do not relish burning hot positions although they like sun in moderation. Lime-free soil is preferable and they are spring flowering. They are closely related to the genus BESSEYA, which see. Of the known species of Synthyris few are in general cultivation, unfortunately.

— **cymopteroides.** (S. paysonii.) Tufts of pinnate leaves, with white tomentum when young and dense, 6 in. racemes of violet-blue flowers.

— **laciniata.** This species occurs on limestone ridges in Utah. Its leaves are bronze-green and the flowers are deep blue in a short, dense spike.

— **missurica.** Dark green, leathery, slightly lobed leaves and erect, 9 in. stems carrying many-flowered racemes of violet-blue flowers.

— **paysonii.** See *S. cymopteroides.*

— **pinnatifida.** Dense hummocks of pinnate, silver leaves. On 6 in. stems are racemes of blue flowers protruding from large silvery calyces. Not an easy plant and best given alpine house treatment, but utterly desirable.

— **ranunculina.** A rarity from the State of Nevada. Mats of tiny, scalloped leaves of rounded shape and short spikes of blue flowers.

— **reniformis.** (S. rotundifolia.) Bluntly-toothed, kidney-shaped leaves in dense tufts and short racemes of purple-blue flowers. The plant grown as *S. sweetzeri* is probably *S. reniformis var. cordata.*

— **rotundifolia.** See *S. reniformis.*

— **stellata.** Fine-haired leaves cut into several pairs of dentate lobes

SYNTHYRIS — *continued*

and, just above the foliage, short spikes of purple-blue flowers.
— sweetzeri. See under *S. reniformis.*

TALINUM. *Portulacaceae.* Derivation obscure.

A small genus, related to LEWISIA and those described below require similar treatment. Best regarded as alpine house plants. Spring flowering.

— **guadalupense.** From the island of Guadalupe, which lies off the coast of Baja California. There it grows in the fissures of black volcanic cliffs, the perfect setting for its white, fleshy leaves. I have not seen it in flower but it is said to display small panicles of lavender-blue blossoms.

— **okanoganense.** From the Okanogan mountains of the State of Washington. Absolutely prostrate, with fleshy stems and grey-green, needle-shaped fleshy leaves forming mats upon which sit almost stemless saucer-shaped flowers of satin-white with prominent central clusters of stamens. Not very long-lived but seeds generously. The seed should be sown as soon as convenient after ripening — and it very quickly falls from the pod.

— **spinescens.** Also from the State of Washington, in dry and sterile areas. From a short, thick trunk grow almost woody branchlets clothed with fat needle-like leaves. The stiff, straight flower stems branch into twigs which carry many wine-red flowers, again centred by attractive stamens. A form has been recorded with semi-double flowers.

— **wayae.** Although recorded as a new species more than thirty years ago after its discovery in the mountains in the vicinity of the Thompson River in N. America, this choice plant is dubiously in cultivation. Mats of fleshy stems adorned with fleshy, club-shaped blue-grey leaves and starred with many half-inch flowers. The petals are at first cream but become pure white. The whole plant may appear dead after flowering but if not over-watered during this period of rest resurrects in the spring.

— **X 'Zoe'.** Although it does not appear to have been recorded anywhere, this is a plant worthy of recognition. It almost certainly claims *T. okanoganense* as one parent and is of similar appearance, but

401

larger in all its parts, although remaining a mat-forming plant. I believe it to have been raised by the late Mr. Peacock, an enthusiastic member of the Alpine Garden Society who named it after his wife.

TANACETUM. *Compositae.* From the medieval Latin *tanazita,* a name still used in E. Europe. Ultimately from the Greek *athanasia,* immortality. It has been used in Europe, and in New England in funeral winding sheets as a discouragement to worms.

A genus of aromatic plants, natives of Europe, N. Africa, Asia and N. America. Very few are of interest to rock gardeners. They are sun-loving and grown more for their foliage than for their flowers.

— **capitatum.** From N. America and dubiously in cultivation, but ought to be. Low hummocks of intensely silver, dissected foliage and globular heads of small yellow flowers.

— **compactum.** Another desirable N. American. As compact and silvery as one of the hummocky Artemisias. It should be a superb silver-foliage plant for alpine houses.

— **densum** subspecies **amani.** From Asia Minor. Low mounds of delicately dissected leaves felted with white tomentum. For once the flowers have value and consist of flat corymbs of bright yellow disk florets, surrounded by an involucre of white and woolly bracts.

— **herderi.** From Turkestan. Thick, short, branched stems and rosettes of silvered leaves. Small heads of yellow flowers on 8 in. stems.

— **leucophyllum.** Another silky-silvery bushlet of about 9 in. from Turkestan, carrying small corymbs of yellow flowers.

— **pallidum.** This Spanish species, especially in the form of its subspecies *spathulifolium* is a very desirable plant, forming dense, low tufts of silver-haired leaves. On the 9 to 12 in. stems occur solitary flower heads having a central golden disk surrounded by a ring of sulphur-yellow ray florets.

TANAKAEA. *Saxifragaceae.* Named for Yoshio Tanaka (1838-1916). A Japanese botanist.

— **radicans.** The only species in its genus and a native of Japan. It relishes sandy, peaty, lime-free soil and a cool or shaded position. A good peat garden plant. Woody rhizomes give forth numerous short running stems with evergreen, leathery, rounded or heart-shaped leaves, toothed at the edges. The small white flowers are carried in paniculate cymes in late spring and early summer.

TARAXACUM. *Compositae.* From an ancient name, traceable through Latin and Arabic to the Persian *talkh chakok*, meaning bitter herb.

The *Flora Europaea* lists half a dozen closely written pages of Taraxacums, with which Heaven forbid that I should become involved, but there are one or two desirable dandelions which are not, sad to relate, in cultivation.

TEESDALIOPSIS. *Cruciferae.*

— conferta. A rare Spanish crucifer forming neat, crowded rosettes of narrow, entire leaves and short-stemmed corymbs of white flowers. If in cultivation it deserves alpine house treatment.

TELESONIX. *Saxifragaceae.* A genus into which American botanists have placed the plant we know as BOYKINIA *jamesii*, which see

TEUCRIUM. *Labiatae.* Probably named for Teucer, first king of Troy, who used the plant medicinally.

A widely distributed race of, mostly, shrubby plants, sun-lovers and summer flowering. A few of the dwarfer kinds are good rock garden plants. Their foliage is aromatic and their flowers often attractive.

— ackermerum. Provenance uncertain, but possibly Asia Minor, Low, spiky tufts of aromatic grey foliage and small heads of violet-purple flowers.

— arduinii. From S.E. Europe. Woody, erect stems 9 to 12 in. Coarsely-toothed leaves, grey beneath and spikes of whitish flowers in dense racemes.

— aroanium. From Greece. Huddled mats of entangled woody stems. silvery leaves and small heads of soft purple flowers. Small enough to use in sink and trough gardens.

— arvense. I can find no authority for the name but it is, as I grow it, a neat dwarf bush with deep pink flowers in late summer.

— aureum. See *T. polium*.

— chamaedrys. From Central and Southern Europe, the Orient and Morocco, and an introduced native to Britain. The typical species, although handsome enough, with erect stems clothed in glossy dark green leaves and ending in heads of pink flowers, is rather too large for most rock gardens. There is a more desirable dwarf form, and another with variegated foliage in stripes of green and cream.

403

- cyprium. From Cyprus. Prostrate mats like a silver-grey moss and globular heads of small white flowers on short stems.
- lithospermifolium. From Cyprus. For the alpine house. Congested low bushes of erect stems clad in narrow green leaves and good heads of crimson-red flowers.
- marum. From Mediterranean areas. A low, much branched silver-grey shrub with racemes of purple flowers.
- montanum. From S. Europe and the Orient. A foot-high shrub with small, entire leaves grey-haired beneath and heads of white flowers which become cream-coloured as they age.
- polium. (T. aureum.) From S. Europe. Mats of grey foliage and good heads of yellow flowers.
- pyrenaicum. From Spain and S.W. France. Spreading, 4 in. mats of woody stems clothed in rounded, softly hairy leaves and heads of hooded cream and lavender flowers.
- scordium. The common Water Germander is a British native and does not claim garden space, but the form known as 'Crispum' is amusing and has value. It makes clumps of erect, foot-high stems clothed in curiously crimpled fleshy leaves of soft green. It has no floral beauty but never fails to attract admiration.
- subspinosum. Prickly mats of spiky stems only an inch or two in height with small, silver leaves and many small crimson-red flowers. It is intensely aromatic and beloved by cats.

THALICTRUM. *Ranunculaceae.* A name used by Dioscorides for a plant which may have been a member of this genus.

A large and widely distributed family of plants which are mostly valued as border flowers but there are a very few delightful dwarfs. They are summer flowering.

- kiusianum. A neat plant from Japan with short, wiry stems usually about 6 to 9 in. high and loose heads of tiny purple flowers over and amongst the pretty, adiantum-like foliage.
- minus. The type is too tall for rock gardens. It is a native of Britain and, in its form *arenarium* is a dainty-leaved dwarf of about 9 in. Of value as a foliage plant.
- orientale. The gem of the dwarfs but something of a mystery. *Flora Europaea* describes its flowers as white and says that it comes from Greece and Asia Minor. Farrer says it comes from the Caucasus. Whatever may be the truth it provides us with a slow-growing but extremely desirable pygmy with erect, wiry stems of about 6 in. with adiantum-like leaves and branched stems carrying large, rich pink flowers. It spreads, very slowly, by means of underground stems.
- tuberosum. From the Pyrenees and Spain and, in its dwarfest form, an acceptable rock garden plant. The foliage is pretty and it gives showers of small white flowers. The roots are tuberous.

THEROPOGON. *Liliaceae.* From *theros*, summer and *pogon*, a beard.

- **pallidus.** From the Himalaya and the only species in its genus. It likes sandy, peaty soil and a cool position. Tufts of narrow, rather grass-like leaves and short racemes of lily of the valley-like white flowers, sometimes pink-tinted.

THLASPI. *Cruciferae.* The Greek name for a cress.

A race of mostly weedy, but a few aristocratic plants. Spring flowering and sun-loving.

- **alpinum.** Tufted, mat-forming perennial from the European Alps, and 4 in. stems carrying small white flowers.
- **bellidifolium.** From Eastern Europe. Densely caespitose and small heads on very short stems of purple, yellow-anthered flowers.
- **bulbosum.** From Greece. Neat rosettes of thick, spoon-shaped leaves and rose-purple flowers on 4 to 6 in. stems.
- **cenisium.** See *T. rotundifolium.*
- **kerneri.** This may be no more than a sub-form of *T. alpinum*, which it resembles, but it is more densely tufted in habit, with shorter stems and good white flowers. It comes particularly from the Eastern Alps.
- **limosellifolium.** See *T. rotundifolium.*
- **montanum.** A species from Central Europe extending to the Eastern Alps. Matted rosettes of rounded, glaucous leaves and short stems carrying heads of white flowers with yellow anthers.
- **nevadense.** Although given specific rank by *Flora Europaea* this is usually regarded as a geographic variant from Spain of *T. rotundifolium*, which it much resembles.
- **praecox.** From the Austrian Alps eastward. Tufts of erect, usually 6 in. stems and heads of small white flowers.
- **rotundifolium.** One of the gems of the European Alps and a plant which has won its way into the affections of alpine gardeners. From a deep tap root spread underground stems in the shingles and screes that it loves, emerging as tufts of rosettes of thick, fleshy wax-smooth dark green leaves, covered in spring and early summer with flat heads of intensely fragrant rosy-lavender flowers. Not one of the easiest plants to grow but it will succeed in a scree and in the alpine house. There are several geographic variants, rather similar in appearance but none with quite the glory of the type; *cenisium* is one of these, and *limosellifolium* another.
- **stylosum.** From the European Alps and rightly described by Farrer as 'an impermanent tuffet of green leaves with spidery heads of lilac-rosy blossoms'.

405

THYMELAEA. (PASSERINA) *Thymeliaceae.* From *thymos*, thyme and *elaia*, olive, referring to the thyme-like foliage and small, olive-like fruits.

— nivalis. From the Pyrenees and probably a subspecies of *T. dioica.* Like a prostrate Daphne which hugs the ground with tangles of woody stems, clothed in tiny, pointed leaves and smothers itself with myriads of small, fragrant yellowish flowers. It can be hardy but is more often accorded alpine house conditions, which it deserves. Slow-growing and early summer flowering.

THYMUS. *Labiatae.* The ancient Greek name used by Theophrastus for a plant of this genus.

A race of 100 or more species, widely distributed in temperate regions of the Old World, with concentrations in Mediterranean regions and Western Asia. Bushy or prostrate plants, strongly aromatic, and sun-lovers to a plant.

— adamovicii. Although I can discover nothing of the provenance of this plant it is one which I grew some years ago and admired. It formed mats of small, dark green leaves and gave a carpet of pink flowers. It may possibly be a form of *T. longicaulis,* and come from Jugoslavia.

— antoninae. From Spain, and sometimes thought, without good evidence, to be a hybrid between *T. longiflorus* and *T. zygis.* Erect, woody stems and small caespitose leaves and heads of purple flowers emerging from conspicuous bracts.

— azoricus. Highly aromatic tufts of very dark green leaves and rich pink flowers.

— bleicherianus. From Morocco. Low tufts of stiff stems with very narrow leaves and surprisingly large heads of individually large rich pink flowers.

— boissieri. See *T. cherlerioides.*

— broussonetii. From Morocco. Erect, foot-high stems and many narrow, glabrous leaves. The reddish flowers protrude from large purple bracts in dense heads.

— caespititius. From Spain and Portugal. Tidy tuffets of dark green leaves and short-stemmed heads of lilac-pink flowers. Small and neat enough for aristocratic companionship.

— capitatus. From Mediterranean regions. Low bushes of almost spiny stems with clustered, tiny leaves and heads of rose-pink flowers.

— capitellatus. From Portugal. Branching, woody stems in loose tufts, the whole plant camphor-scented. Heads of white flowers.

— carnosus. From Portugal. Erect, woody stems up to 12 in. with many small clusters of rather fleshy leaves and heads of white flowers.

— cephalotos. From Portugal. Related to, and similar to *T. membranaceus.* Low bushes with clustered, tiny leaves and large heads of showy, violet-purple bracts from which protrude the tubular soft violet flowers. Best in the alpine house.

— **cherlerioides.** (T. boissieri, T. hirsutus.) From the Balkans. Hairy, creeping stems with hairy leaves in axillary clusters and short, erect stems bearing small heads of pink flowers.

— **cilicicus.** A comparatively recent introduction, having been found by Dr. Peter Davis in Anatolia in 1947. It is a gem but should be given alpine house treatment, or light winter protection in the open. Over mats of soft green, not very aromatic leaves are huge, short-stemmed clusters of vividly lilac-pink flowers.

— **X citriodorus.** A natural hybrid between *T. vulgaris* and *T. pulegioides.* Short, erect stems forming low, neat bushes and strongly lemon-scented. It occurs in several named forms, notably 'Silver Queen', with handsomely silver and green variegated foliage, and 'Aureus', similarly variegated but in gold.

— **comosus.** From Eastern Europe and Asia Minor. Creeping stems and rounded, hairy leaves and large heads of good pink flowers. A form in gardens is known as *T.c.* 'Hirsutus' and is particularly hairy.

— **comptus.** From E. Europe, and near to *T. striatus.* Sprawling mats of 4 to 6 in. hairy stems and small, glaucous leaves. Hemispherical heads of rose-pink flowers.

— **doerfleri.** See *T. praecox.*

— **X 'Doone Valley'.** A lovely mule of uncertain parentage. The mats of olive green leaves are freckled with golden markings. Crimson buds expand into lavender flowers borne in rounded heads on 5 in. stems.

— **drucei.** See *T. serpyllum.*

— **'E.B. Anderson'.** See ACINOS in Addenda.

— **ericifolius.** See MICROMERIA *varia.*

— **funkii.** See *T. longiflorus.*

— **herba-barona.** From Corisca and Sardinia. Matted tangles of thin stems and dark green, strongly caraway-scented leaves. Heads of soft purple flowers.

— **hirsutus.** See *T. cherlerioides.*

— **hyemalis.** Really a Spanish version of *T. vulgaris* but with very short leaves. Flowers purple.

— **integer.** A mat-forming sub-shrub from Cyprus. Prostrate, woody shoots with dense tufts of leaves and white-haired stems carrying a globose head of rose flowers from wide purple bracts.

— **lanuginosus.** Although this is commonly listed among the forms of *T. serpyllum* it is probably correctly named *T. pannonicus* but I retain the name by which it is so well known in gardens. It is a grey-leaved flat carpeter with pretty pink flowers. A selected clone, named 'Hall's Variety' has purple buds and is even more free-flowering than the type.

— **leucotrichus.** From Greece, and a splendid plant. Mature plants build themselves into low mounds or cushions of twiggy stems clothed in small leaves margined with white hairs. The purple-pink flowers are crowded in dense heads. It appears to be fully hardy.

— **longicaulis.** Widely distributed in Europe. Woody, creeping stems with basal clusters of small leaves. The purple flowers are carried in small, dense heads.

— **longiflorus.** (T. funkii.) From Spain. In many ways similar to *T. membranaceus* and forms dense, low bushes of woody stems with narrow grey leaves and terminal heads of long-tubed purple flowers which emerge startlingly from green and purple bracts. For the alpine house or a warm, dry position in the open.

— **marschallianus.** See *T. pannonicus*.

— **mastichina.** From Spain and Portugal. Erect, 9 in. stems with sage-green, intensely aromatic leaves and heads of lilac flowers emerging from leafy calyces.

— **membranaceus.** From Spain. The woody stems form low domes of dark green foliage and the pink flowers are surrounded by spectacular, white, papery bracts. Both this and *T. mastichina* should be given the same treatment as *T. longiflorus*. *T. murcicus* is very similar and is probably a subspecies of this or *T. longiflorus*.

— **micans.** See *T. caespititius*.

— **murcicus.** See *T. membranaceus*.

— **necefferi.** From Anatolia. Introduced by Dr. Peter Davis and has short, wiry stems and leaves as tiny as the needles of a larch. It smothers itself with soft pink flowers and seems specially attractive to bees.

— **nitidus.** The plant commonly grown under this name is *T. carnosus*. The true plant is a subspecies of *T. richardii*, which see.

— **nummularius.** From the Caucasus and Asia Minor. A low bushy sub-shrub with notably broad leaves and hemispherical heads of mauve-pink flowers.

— **pallasianus.** From the Caucasus. Prostrate non-flowering shoots, flowering stems erect to 6 in. and hairy. Small, glabrous leaves lightly hair-fringed and round, compact heads of purple flowers.

— **pannonicus.** (T. marschallianus.) This is the plant already described as *T. lanuginosus*.

— X **'Porlock'.** Neat, low mounds of dark green, very aromatic foliage and heads of pink flowers. A very good hybrid of uncertain parentage.

— **praecox.** A species widely distributed in Europe, with several slightly divergent forms. Typically it has woody, creeping stems, those which flower carrying a terminal inflorescence of crowded purple flowers. The plant commonly grown as *T. doerfleri*, with very hairy leaves should belong here.

— **pulegioides.** A species widespread in Europe, including Britain, with a great many variants, some of which have been distinguished as sub-species. The flowers, in small heads, may be mauve, white or crimson.

- **richardii.** From the Balearic Isles to Jugoslavia. A species seldom grown but its subspecies *nitidus* is a tidy little plant with tufts of aromatic, dark green leaves and heads of pink flowers.
- **serpylloides.** A Spanish species with procumbent, woody stems and axillary clusters of small leaves, which are absent from the stems which carry the rather lax heads of purple flowers.
- **serpyllum.** A widely distributed species, including Britain. It is often confused with the somewhat similar *T. drucei* and is a widely variable plant, of which many clutivars are grown in gardens. It is a creeper, making dense mats of entangled threadlike stems clothed with small aromatic leaves. The flower colour, according to the particular form ranges from white, through shades of pink and purple to rich red. It is pointless to describe the forms in detail. They will be found listed in our price list, and in most alpine plant catalogues. The foliage is also variable and may be felted with grey hairs or glabrous and green. A newcomer to the selection is *T.s.* 'Elfin', which makes tight domes or 'buns' of tiny leaves and is an admirable, and stay-at-home cushion plant.
- **thracicus.** From Greece and the Balkans. Creeping, woody stems and purple flowers.
- **villosus.** From Spain and Portugal. Erect, woody stems clothed with axillary leaf clusters and heads of purple flowers. Up to 6 in. in height.
- **vulgaris.** The common culinary thyme with one or two selected forms, such as *T.v.* 'Aureus', with golden tinted leaves and another, sometimes named 'Silver Queen', with green and silver variegation.
- **zygis.** From Spain and Portugal. Erect, hairy, woody stems to 9 in. and clusters of white or pale pink flowers.

TIARELLA. *Saxifragaceae*. The Greek diminutive of *tiara*, a small crown. A reference to the shape of the seeds.

A small genus for cool positions. Apart from one species in Asia they are all N. American. Spring and early summer flowering.

- **californica.** Very near to *T. unifoliata* with panicles of white flowers on 12 in. stems.
- **collina.** Low carpets of elegant, cordate leaves and dense, feathery panicles of pink and white flowers. 12 in. or a little more.
- **cordifolia.** The leaves are softly hairy and take on pleasant bronze tints. The fluffy spires of cream-white flowers are borne on 9 to 12 in. stems. Forms with pure white flowers and another with more deeply bronzed foliage have been separated as 'Albiflora' and 'Purpurea' respectively.
- **laciniata.** Deeply cleft leaves and many small white flowers in a loose, narrow panicle.
- **menziesii.** See TOLMIEA *menziesii*.
- **polyphylla.** From the Himalaya, China and Japan. Three-lobed,

toothed leaves and a simple raceme of small white flowers on a 12 in. stem.

— trifoliata. Small green leaves divided into three leaflets, the middle one three-lobed, the laterals two-lobed and short stems carrying narrow panicles of small white flowers.

— unifoliata. Quite large, lobed leaves and elegant foot-high spires of creamy flowers.

— wherryi. Cordate, sharply three-lobed leaves becoming red in autumn and innumerable white or rose-tinted flowers in dense racemes on 15 in. stems.

TOFIELDIA *Liliaceae.* Named for Thomas Tofield (1730-1779), a Yorkshire botanist. A small family of perennial plants of small garden value. They have short or creeping rhizomes and grow best in light moist soil. They are spring and early summer flowering.

— alpina. Europe. Small tufts of flattened, grass-like foliage and 6 in. stems carrying tight racemes of small cream-coloured flowers.

— borealis. See *T. pusilla.*

— calyculata. Europe. Similar to *T. alpina* but slightly larger in all its parts and with spikes of greenish-yellow flowers.

— coccinea. A species from Greenland which sounds as if it might be worth growing for the sake of its purple-tinted flowers, which are almost sessile on tufts of short, grassy leaves.

— glutinosa. From wet meadows in N.W. America. Tufts of long, narrow leaves and 6 to 9 in. stems displaying racemes of cream-coloured flowers. Quite a pleasant bogling.

— gracilis. I know not from whence it comes, but it is a neat tuft of evergreen narrow leaves with short spikes carrying green and buff flowers.

— occidentalis. N.W. America. Rather similar in general appearance to *T. glutinosa.*

— palustris. See *T. pusilla.*

— pusilla. A British species and really with no merit for gardens. Small tufts, in marshy places, of narrow, pointed leaves and short spikes of greenish white small flowers.

— racemosa. Another American species with rather rigid, narrow leaves and stems up to 12 in. carrying loose racemes of whitish flowers.

TOLMIEA. *Saxifragaceae.* Named for Dr. William Fraser Tolmie (1830-1886), a Scottish physician and botanist.

— menziesii. (Tiarella menziesii.) From N.W. America and the only species in its genus. In cool places it makes tufts of handsome, Tiarella-like foliage and carries thin, tall racemes of greenish-yellow flowers in early summer. Worth growing only for its foliage.

TOWNSENDIA. *Compositae.* Named for David Townsend (1787-1858), of Pennsylvania. A small genus of dwarf, aster-like plants natives of N. America. Sun-loving and summer flowering.

- exscapa. Tufts of narrow, stemless leaves amidst which appear short-stemmed aster-like flowers, white or pale purple.
- florifer. An authoritative Flora of N. America describes this species as of no more than annual or biennial duration, but a plant growing under the same name in this country is a 3 in. mat of prostrate stems with leaves silver-grey leaves and large, flat, white flowers on very short stems. The plant we have here is certainly well worth growing although still a rarity.
- formosana. One of the best species. Large violet flowers, each with an orange centre on 4 in. stems.
- grandiflora. Tufts of paddle-shaped leaves and, on 6 in. stems, large violet-blue aster flowers.
- minima. For those who seek the miniature this is the smallest species, forming tiny tufts of green leaves, but the flowers are comparatively insignificant.
- parryi. Sometimes acclaimed the best of all, although not long-lived. From the tufts of small leaves emerge large lavender-blue flowers on very short stems, which elongate to 6 in. or so as the season advances.
- sericea. Is very close to, and may even be synonymous with *T. exscapa.*
- wilcoxiana. Small rosettes of neat leaves centred by large, aster-like flowers of lavender-violet. Seed should be saved as it is not long-lived.

TRACHELIUM. *Campanulaceae.* Already, if wrongly, dealt with under DIOSPHAERA, which see.

TRADESCANTIA. *Commelinaceae.* Named for John Tradescant (1608-1662), gardener to King Charles I.

Most of the many species are border rather than rock garden plants, but there are at least two desirable dwarfs.

- bracteata. From N. America. The typical, narrow, fleshy leaves of the genus and slightly branched, 9 in. stems carrying deep blue flowers in summer.
- brevicaulis. Also from N. America and similar in general appearance but the flowers are rose-red.

TREMACRON. *Gesneriaceae.* From the Greek *trema*, aperture and *macron*, large, a reference to the dehiscence of the anthers.

A genus of only two species, related to RAMONDA and to be regarded as alpine house plants. They are fitfully in cultivation but are seldom listed in catalogues. *T. forrestii* has rosettes of broad, coarsely hairy leaves and nine-inch stems on which are pendulous, bell-shaped cream-white flowers. *T. mairei* is similar but has thicker, more leathery leaves.

TRICHINIUM. *Amaranthaceae.* From the Greek *trichos,* a hair, referring to the shaggy inflorescence.

— **manglesii.** From Australia and not really hardy but will survive in an unheated alpine house. Sprawling, decumbent, leafy stems and heads of pink and white flowers shaggy with long white hairs. Grow in fairly rich soil and water freely when in full growth but sparingly after flowering.

TRICYRTIS. *Liliaceae.* From the Greek *tri,* three and *kyrtos,* humped. The bases of the three outer petals are swollen.

A small genus from Formosa, Japan and the Himalaya. They appreciate the same conditions accorded to Trilliums and are ideal peat-garden plants. Their stems are erect or arching and leafy and the curious flowers are carried terminally or in the leaf axils during the summer. They vary in height from one foot to two feet.

— **bakeri.** Flowers yellow, veined and spotted with red. From Japan.
— **formosana.** From Formosa. The white and purple flowers are spotted with deeper colour.
— **hirta.** From Japan. The white flowers are heavily marked with purple dots.
— **latifolia.** One of the tallest, from Japan. The white flowers are flecked freely with small purple spots.
— **macrantha.** Another tall species, from Japan. The primrose-yellow flowers are freely flecked with chocolate markings.
— **macropoda.** From China and Japan. On 2 ft. stems are many white, purple-spotted flowers. The variety *striata* has leaves striped with white lines.
— **maculata.** From the Himalaya. Loose terminal corymbs of white, purple-marked flowers.
— **stolonifera.** From Formosa and spreads by running roots. The mauve flowers are heavily marked with deeper colour.

TRIENTALIS. *Primulaceae.* The Latin word meaning one-third of a foot in height. Two species only, for shade and cool conditions. Ideal peat garden plants, spring-flowering.

— **borealis.** From N.W. America. From creeping rhizomes spring wiry, 9 in. stems with a whorl of small leaves at the top from which spring short pedicels, carrying starry white flowers.

— **europaea.** Europe, including Britain. Rather similar to the preceding but smaller and more delicate in all its parts.

TRIFOLIUM. *Leguminosae.* From the Latin *tri*, three and *folium* a leaf.

A large genus, widely distributed all over the Northern Hemisphere and also occurring in Tropical Africa and S. America. There are but few likely to entice the alpine gardener, but among the few are some very desirable plants. They are all sun-lovers, summer flowering and in no way difficult to grow.

— **alpinum.** Alps of Europe. From thick roots spring leaves composed of three narrow leaflets. Heads of pink and purple flowers on 4 in. stems.

— **badium.** From S. Europe and possibly rather coarse for small rock gardens, but an attractive plant throwing leafy stems from a massive root and displaying heads of golden flowers which become chestnut-brown as they age.

— **ottonis.** From Greece. Caespitose tufts of trifoliate leaves and short stems carrying heads of deep purple flowers.

— **pallescens.** From Central and Southern Europe. Procumbent or ascending foot-high stems and heads of yellowish-brown to pink flowers changing to chocolate with age.

— **pannonicum.** From S.E. Europe. 12 in. leafy stems in tidy tufts. The leaves are softly hairy and the clover flowers are creamy-white.

— **uniflorum.** European Alps. Low tufts of green trefoil leaves centred by clusters of pink pea flowers, each on a short stalk. Very desirable indeed and a good scree plant. There is also a nice form with pure white flowers.

TRILLIUM. *Liliaceae.* From the Latin *tri*, three. The leaves and other parts of these plants are in threes.

Rhizomatous, almost tuberous-rooted plants from N. America and also from Japan and the Himalaya. They like cool positions in moisture-holding soil and, once established are long-lived, very beautiful plants. Although peaty soil is often recommended, they will flourish in a much heavier medium as long as they do not become dried out in the summer. They flower in the spring. The flowers have three outer sepals and three inner petals.

— **cernuum.** From E. North America. Broad leaves, abruptly narrowing at the tip. On 12 to 15 in. stems are small flowers with white, slightly recurved segments.

— **chloropetalum.** N. America. A species often confused with *T. sessile.* Rather rounded, large leaves and tall stems carrying sessile greenish or purple flowers.

— **declinatum.** N. America. Rather similar to *T. erectum* but the white flowers tend to drop on long peduncles.

— **discolor.** (T. sessile var. wrayi.) The broad leaves are often marked with brown or purple on the upper sides. The terminal flowers have erect, narrow purple-green segments.

— **erectum.** (T. foetidum. T. obovatum.) From the circle of three wide leaves on foot-high stems rise red-purple flowers with erect segments. The colour varies to white and yellowish and there is a faintly unpleasant odour.

— **erythrocarpum.** A name of dubious authenticity for a plant which is very similar to *T. grandiflorum* but is rather later flowering, usually beginning when *grandiflorum* is fading.

— **foetidum.** See *T. erectum.*

— **grandiflorum.** From N. America and the most commonly grown and certainly one of the handsomest species. It is a real herald of spring, making bold clumps of the broad leaves on erect stems and carrying large, snow-white flowers, which frequently take on soft pink shades as they age. There is a rare and lovely form with perfectly double flowers, and occasional mutants in which the petals and sepals are streaked and striped with green in various shades.

— **luteum.** From the Eastern United States. Mottled green and brown leaves and lemon-yellow, fragrant flowers on foot-high stems.

— **nervosum.** (T. stylosum.) Eastern United States and southwards. Oval leaves and white, often pink-flushed flowers the petals with gently undulating margins.

— **nivale.** S.E. United States. A dwarf species with upturned, white flowers.

— **obovatum.** See *T. erectum.*

— **ovatum.** From W. North America. Bold leaves on tall, slightly reddish stems and white flowers. Very early, with or even before *T. grandiflorum.*

— **pictum.** See *T. undulatum.*

— **recurvatum.** N. American. Handsome, dark green foliage and sessile, red-purple flowers on tall stems.

— **rivale.** From California and Oregon. Even smaller than *T. nivale* with pretty pink and white flowers. A very distinct form, possibly to bear the clonal name 'Verne Ahiers', bears cup-shaped, shell-pink flowers. It is a rarity, dubiously in cultivation in Britain.

— **sessile.** N. America. Strong tufts of broadly oval leaves, often marbled with deeper colour and large, sessile flowers, usually deep mahogany-red but sometimes cream-white to pale yellow with erect segments. Forms have been selected and named, as *'Rubra', californicum,* and one, *'Wrayi'* is synonymous with *T. discolor.*

TRILLIUM — *continued*
- stylosum. See *T. nervosum.*
- undulatum. (T. pictum.) E. North America. A beauty, with short-stemmed white flowers painted with a rose-red blotch at the base of the petals.

TRIPTILION. *Compositae.* From the Greek *tri,* three, and *ptilon,* a wing, because of the three divisions of the pappus.
- spinosum. From Chile. A perennial with pinnately-lobed leaves on erect, 9 in. stems and heads of blue flowers in summer. Not very long-lived but easily grown in an open, sunny position and any good soil.

TROCHOCARPA. *Epacridaceae.* From the Greek *trochos,* a wheel, and *karpos,* fruit.
An allusion to the radiating cells of the fruits.
- thymifolia. Although this is undeniably a shrub, it is such a desirable plant for the rock garden or alpine house that I venture to include it, although shrubs, as such, are mostly excluded from this Manual. From Tasmania and a slow growing shrublet seldom exceeding a foot in height. The erect, stiff and woody stems are densely clothed in tiny, pointed, narrow, dark green leaves. The new shoots in spring are pinkish before darkening to the typical deep green. In early spring the flower buds appear as bunches like minute red grapes and eventually expand into red, yellow-rimmed bell-shaped flowers in slightly pendant clusters. For peaty, lime-free soil and, in the open, a warm and sheltered place.

TROLLIUS. *Ranunculaceae.* From the German *Trollblume,* or globe flower.
Most of the Trollius are border and bog plants but there are a few small species admissible to the rock garden. They are spring flowering and have the family liking for moist soil and cool conditions.
- acaulis. From the Himalaya and the smallest of all. Divided leaves in tiny tufts and short stems carrying rounded, golden-yellow flowers. Not more than 4 in. high.
- europaeus. Our native Globe Flower and rather too large for most rock gardens, but useful by a stream or pond-side. Many cup-shaped, lemon-yellow flowers on 12 to 18 in. stems.
- pumilus. Five-parted leaves and 6 to 9 in. stems bearing rounded yellow flowers. From N. India and China.
- yunnanensis. From China and Yunnan. Rather taller and can attain a foot or so in height, the stems carrying nice, flat and rounded bright yellow flowers.

TROPAEOLUM. *Tropaeolaceae.* Named by Linnaeus from the Greek *tropaion*, trophy, or the Latin *tropaeum*.

There is really only one species firmly in cultivation which can be included here, although there are exciting species, particularly in South America, which would be welcomed by rock gardeners. A few of these have trickled into Britain during recent years but are as yet not readily available, or proven for hardiness.

— polyphyllum. A tuberous-rooted species from Chile which should be planted at least a foot deep in a sunny position, preferably where it can hang down its long, trailing shoots over the face of a wall. The long stems carry lovely, lobed intensely silver leaves. From the leaf axils in the terminal half of the stem spring countless large, richly yellow flowers in early to mid-summer.

TROXIMON glaucum. See AGOSERIS *glauca.*

TSUSIOPHLLYUM. *Ericaceae.* Modified from the Japanese vernacular name *Tsutsuji*, and *phyllon*, a leaf.

— tanakae. Another admitted shrub which claims admission to the rock garden. From Japan, making a dwarf bush of tangled, woody stems, partially evergreen. The small leaves are hairy and have slightly recurved margins. The small white flowers are carried in dense terminal clusters in early summer. For the peat bed or cool, lime-free conditions.

TUBERARIA. *Cistaceae.*

— lignosa. (HELIANTHEMUM tuberaria.) From Mediterranean regions. Flat rosettes of narrow, hairy-edged leaves and 9 in. stems carrying loose sprays of yellow flowers over a long summer period. For a warm and sunny position.

TULBAGHIA. *Liliaceae.* Named for Rijk Tulbagh (1699-1771) Dutch Governor of the Cape of Good Hope.

A race, mainly S. African, of tuberous-rooted plants, few of which are truly hardy, but the undermentioned two species have every chance of success in a warm border at the foot of a south or west wall, or in the alpine house.

— natalensis. From Natal. Small clusters of narrow, garlic-scented leaves and erect, 9 to 12 in. stems carrying umbels of small, tubular flowers curiously shaded in white, pink and pale yellow. Summer flowering.

 — violacea. Widely distributed in the Cape Province. A taller plant with 15 in. stems bearing showy umbels of violet-purple flowers from August to September.

TUNICA. *Caryophyllaceae. Tunica,* an undergarment, referring to bracts at the base of the calyx.

The genus TUNICA has been abandoned in favour of PETROR-HAGIA, but I retain the generic name under which at least one valuable rock garden plant has become so well known.

 — saxifraga. From Central and Southern Europe. An easy and delightful summer-flowering, sun-loving alpine. Clouds of small pink flowers in lax sprays. Usually about 6 in tall. There is a form with double, pure white flowers and another, named 'Rosette' with double pink flowers.

UMBILICUS. Species in this genus likely to be of interest to rock gardeners have been relegated to other Genera, such as CHIASTO-PHYLLUM, ROSULARIA and OROSTACHYS.

UROSPERMUM. *Compositae.* From the Greek *oura*, a tail and *sperma*, a seed. The achenes are beaked.

- **dalechampii.** From S. Europe. Mats of crinkled, grey foliage and heads of soft yellow flowers with dark anthers. 12 in. Summer flowering. A sun-lover.

UVULARIA. *Liliaceae.* From the anatomical term *uvula* (the lobe pendant from the back of the soft palate in man) a reference to the hanging blossoms. A small genus of N. American plants. For cool soil and light shade.

The genus is in part often confused with OAKESIELLA.

- **caroliniana.** From the typically rhizomatous roots rise clusters of glossy green, sessile leaves and solitary or twin greenish-yellow tubular flowers pendant at the branch ends.
- **grandiflora.** The leaves are perfoliate and tall stems carry large, pendant bells of lemon-yellow.
- **perfoliata.** Very similar indeed to and possibly synonymous with *U. grandiflora*, but slightly smaller as a rule.
- **sessilifolia.** See OAKESIELLA *sessilifolia*.

VACCINIUM. *Ericaceae.* A Latin name of disputed origin. An invaluable large genus of shrubs, widely distributed in the Northern Hemisphere and in S. America. They are lime-haters and those described below are ideal peat garden plants. In a race of tall shrubs only the dwarfest have been included.

- caespitosum. From Canada and N. America. A low-growing deciduous shrublet which spreads into wide mats of woody stems with smooth, toothed leaves. The bell-shaped flowers, solitary in the leaf axils, are soft pink and are followed by sweet, blue-black fruits.
- floribundum. (V. mortinia.) From Ecuador. A low, evergreen shrub. The young shoots are pink and the dark green leaves, purple when young, are densely crowded on the sprayed branches. Close racemes of cylindrical, rose-pink flowers and red, edible berries.
- X intermedium. A hybrid between *V. myrtillus* and *V. vitis-idaea.* Low bushes, semi-evergreen. Bright green leaves and in short terminal racemes, or occasionally solitary in the leaf axils, bell-shaped pink flowers, followed by violet berries. Native of Europe, including Britain.
- modestum. A fairly recent introduction from the Himalaya. Mats of slender, creeping stems with tufts of small, smooth, leathery leaves at their ends. The flowers, solitary in the leaf axils, are long-stalked, campanulate and rose-pink in colour and are followed by edible violet berries.
- mortinia. See *V. floribundum.*
- moupinense. From China. A neat, dwarf evergreen of dense habit, leathery, untoothed leaves crowd the stems and racemes of mahogany-red flowers. The rounded berries are purple-black in colour.
- myrsinites. From N. America. A low, spreading evergreen with small, oval, finely-toothed leaves. Terminal and axillary clusters of soft pink flowers and blue-black berries.
- myrtillus. This is our native whortleberry or bilberry, forming dense mats of suckering stems. Oval, finely-toothed leaves and rounded, pink or greenish flowers singly or in pairs in the leaf axils, followed by the familiar 'blueberries'. It is widespread in Europe and extends to the Caucasus and Asia.

419

- **nummularia.** One of the best, from the Himalaya. Evergreen, with arching, hairy stems and double rows of leathery, glossy-green leaves. Dense clusters of rose-red cylindrical flowers occur at the end of the shoots and are followed by glossy black edible fruits.
- **oxycoccos.** Our native Cranberry. Widely distributed in Europe, N. America and eastward to Japan. Prostrate and evergreen, the wiry stems clothed in tiny, silver-backed leaves. The small pink flowers have reflexed petals and are followed by the characteristic rounded red berries.
- **praestans.** From N.E. Asia and Japan. Quite prostrate and deciduous. The bell-shaped white flowers are carried singly or in small clusters. The berries are large, glossy-red and sweetly flavoured.
- **vitis-idaea.** From Europe (including Britain), N. America and Asia. Dwarf, spreading evergreen with glossy, box-like leaves and bell-shaped white flowers often flushed pink and globular bright red berries.

VALERIANA. *Valerianaceae.* The medieval Latin name, derived from *valere*, to heal, an allusion to their medicinal qualities. A large family of herbs, sub-shrubs and shrubs, widely distributed. A few of the dwarfer species are enjoyable in the rock garden, although none is of startling beauty. They are sun-loving and summer flowering.

- **alpestris.** From the Caucasus. 6 in. leafy stems surmounted by heads of pinkish flowers.
- **arizonica.** From N. America. Creeping rhizomes and 3 in. erect stems with fleshy leaves and corymbs of pink flowers.
- **asarifolia.** From Crete. Of compact habit with foot-high stems and umbels of bright red flowers.
- **celtica.** From Europe. This is the Spikenard, valued for its aromatic qualities. Creeping rhizomes and small leaves. Loose panicles of yellowish flowers on quite short stems.
- **globulariifolia.** From the Pyrenees. Another aromatic species. Tufts of short stems with oval leaves and 4 in. stems with pinnatifid leaves and heads of good pink flowers.
- **montana.** Europe and the Caucasus. Erect, 6 in. stems, sometimes slightly hairy with blunt, lightly toothed leaves. Corymbs of lilac, pink or nearly white flowers.
- **saliunca.** Europe. Tufts of small, dark green leaves and neat corymbs of fragrant pink flowers on 4 in. stems.
- **saxatilis.** Europe. Tufts of neat green leaves and dainty spikes of white flowers on short stems.
- **supina.** From Central Europe. Carpeting, with dark green, shining leaves and loose corymbs of white, pink-flushed fragrant flowers on 6 in. stems.

— tuberosa. From S. Europe and Morocco. Rather weedy, but not without attraction when carrying the corymbs of small soft purple flower on 9 in. stems.

VANCOUVERIA. *Berberidaceae.* Named for Captain George V Vancouver (1758-1798).

A small genus, related to EPIMEDIUM and natives of N. America. For cool positions or light shade. Good peat garden plants, spring-flowering. Two of the three species are evergreen but *V. hexandra* is deciduous.

— chrysantha. The foot-high stems carry firm leaves divided into several leaflets. Loose sprays of small yellow flowers.

— hexandra. Graceful soft green leaves and panicles of white flowers on 9 in. stems.

— planipetala. Wiry stems and hard leaves cut into leaflets. Panicles of white, sometimes pink-tinted flowers on 9 in. stems.

VELLA. *Cruciferae.* From *veller*, the Celtic name for cress.

— spinosa. From Spain, and requires a hot, dry position or the alpine house. Low rounded bushes of dense habit and spiny growths. The rigid stems carry terminal corymbs of sulphur-yellow, four petalled flowers in summer.

VERBASCUM. *Scrophulariaceae.* The ancient Latin name for these plants.

Few of these widely distributed plants are appropriate to the rock garden but those few are highly desirable. They are avid sun-lovers with a prolonged summer flowering period.

— dumulosum. From Mediterranean regions. Rigid, foot-high stems form a low, humped bush. The leaves are grey-white and softly hairy on both surfaces. Each woody stem ends in a short raceme of rounded flowers with over-lapping petals of clear yellow and each flower has a rich purple 'eye'.

— X 'Golden Wings'. See CELSIOVERBASCUM 'Gold Wings'.

— X 'Letitia'. A natural hybrid between *V. dumulosum* and *V. spinosum.* It was the knowledgeable eye of Mr. K. Aslet at Wisley that observed and preserved this chance seedling, which has now become a deservedly popular plant. The upright, woody stems, branching at ground level carry lobed, velvety, grey-green leaves. The tips of the stems carry short racemes of inch-wide clear yellow flowers in profusion and for a prolonged summer period. There is a brown blotch at the base of each petal.

- **letourneuxii.** I doubt if this Medeterranean species is at present in cultivation. If only it were it would be a pleasant companion for the trinity of dwarf, spiky species, *V. dumulosum, V. pestalozzae* and *V. spinosum.* It is of similar habit, with yellow flowers, purple on the reverse.
- **pestalozzae.** From the Mediterranean. Felted yellow-tinged grey-haired leaves adorn the low, rigid woody stems and spikes of brilliant yellow flowers.
- **spinosum.** From Crete. Intricate tufts of spiky, woody stems and grey, toothed leaves and twiggy panicles of clear yellow flowers. At maturity about 12 in. tall.
- **wiedmannianum.** From Asia Minor. Flat rosettes of felted leaves from which rise spires of violet-purple flowers. Although it is said to be capable of a height of several feet it has never exceeded 2 ft. with me and is usually less.

VERBENA. *Verbenaceae.* The Latin name for the Vervain, *V. officinalis.*

- **chamaedrifolia.** See *V. peruviana.*
- **peruviana.** From S. America. Not really a rock garden plant, although some find its corymbs of vivid scarlet flowers irresistible. It is not fully hardy. I welcome it as little on the rock garden as I do miniature roses.

VERONICA. *Scrophulariaceae.* Named in honour of Saint Veronica. Immense confusion has existed — and still persists as to what is really a Veronica and what is a Hebe, a Parahebe or even a Veronicastrum. I take the coward's way out and include here only those which I like to think of as true Veronicas, having elsewhere described a few of the Hebes and Parahebes. Those listed below are sun-lovers and, unless otherwise stated, easy to grow in any good soil and are spring and summer flowering.

- **allionii.** European Alps. A creeping plant with somewhat blue-grey leaves, which are slightly leathery and rounded to oval in shape. Compact, short spikes of blue flowers.
- **alpina.** Not exciting, but worth growing in an unimportant place. Native to Europe (including Britain), Asia and N. America. Erect, rather hairy 6 in. stems and short terminal spikes of dull blue flowers.
- **aphylla.** European Alps. Rosettes of oval to round leaves and short, erect stems carrying loose heads of fairly large lilac-blue flowers, often veined with pink.
- **armena.** From Armenia. From a woody stock rise short stems clothed in finely cut leaves and short, loose spikes of bright blue flowers.

— austriaca. Europe. The plant commonly grown as *V. teucrium* is a subspecies of this and exists in gardens as several named clones, all good rock garden plants. The type forms low tufts of dark green foliage and bears short spikes of blue flowers. Worthy clones are 'Rosea', with pink flowers, 'Royal Blue', taller spikes of rich blue blossoms and 'Trehane', which has yellow foliage and bright blue flowers.

— X baileyana. A name of dubious authenticity, covering a neat hybrid, probably claiming *V. fruticans* as one parent. Like a tiny Box bush with bright blue flowers. We grew this many years ago but have lost it and if exists elsewhere I would greatly appreciate information.

— bellidioides. Europe. Small rosettes of rounded, shining green leaves and dainty spikes of soft blue flowers. 6 in.

— bidwillii. See the genus PARAHEBE.

— bombycina. From the Lebanon and a gem for the alpine house. 2 in. mats of frail stems and silvery-white rounded tiny leaves and very short stems carrying china-blue flowers. Very gritty soil and do not overwater.

— bonarota. See the genus PAEDEROTA in the Addenda.

— caespitosa. From the Levant and Lebanon. Dense tufts of grey, hairy leaves and almost stemless starry pink flowers. For the alpine house, or stone trough or sink.

— canescens. See the genus PARAHEBE.

— circaeoides. Provenance uncertain, and now rare in gardens. From a central root stock radiate prostrate stems carrying pleasant mauve-blue flowers.

— X corallii. The name is doubtful and the origin unknown, but this is a pleasing hybrid with mats of leaves, rather like those of *V. spicata* and 6 in. spikes of good pink flowers.

— dillenii. Another species about whose origin and authenticity I am very doubtful, but the plant sometimes grown under this name is of trailing habit, with finely cut leaves and short spires of lavender-blue flowers.

— filifolia. From New Zealand. Lax mats of fine stems smothered in finely cut green leaves and galaxies of soft blue flowers. 9 in.

— filiformis. It is with some temerity that I include this European species, for it can be an almost inerradicable weed, but it can also be extremely decorative - in the right place, possibly as ground cover beneath and between shrubs. Prostrate, frail, creeping stems and sheets of soft blue flowers.

— fruticans. (V. saxatilis.) Widespread in Europe. A neat, prostrate evergreen. Similar to, and may be a subspecies of *V. fruticulosa*. Deep blue flowers centred by a ring of red.

— fruticulosa. Europe. Erect, woody, 12 in. stems and oval, toothed leaves. The flowers may be pink, or blue with reddish markings, either solitary in the leaf axils or in loose clusters.

- **gentianoides.** From E. Europe and S.E. Asia. Possibly better at the front of a flower border, but useful on the larger rock garden. Tufts of fleshy green leaves from which rise 15 in. stems carrying many pale blue flowers. There is a dwarfer form, 'Nana' and another with handsomely silver and green variegated foliage.
- **X guthriana.** Another hybrid of doubtful parentage but with *V. fruticulosa* probably implicated. Tiny evergreen bushlets and short spikes of deep blue flowers.
- **kellereri.** From E. Europe. Mats of deep green leaves and 3 in. spikes of rich blue flowers.
- **lutea.** See the genus PAEDEROTA.
- **multifida.** From Russia and probably another subspecies of *V. austriaca.* Finely cut foliage in low mounds and dainty sprays of light blue flowers.
- **nummularia.** (V. numularifolia. V. nummularioides.) Mats of rounded light green leaves and small sprays of blue flowers. Small enough to use as a plant for crevices between paving stones. From the Pyrenees.
- **orientalis.** (V. taurica.) From Asia Minor. Tufts of leaves which may be entire or irregularly pinnatisect. Racemes of blue, occasionally pink, flowers on 9 to 12 in. stems.
- **pectinata.** From the Balkans and Asia Minor. Prostrate mats of trailing stems densely set with small, grey, very hairy leaves. The type, which is rarely seen in gardens has short spikes of blue flowers. The form commonly grown, and a good ground-cover plant, is 'Rosea', with rich pink flowers.
- **peduncularis.** From the Caucasus. The type carries clouds of pearl-white flowers on 6 in. stems but the form more commonly grown is 'Nyman's Variety' with larger, soft blue flowers.
- **perfoliata.** From Australia, where it is known as 'Digger's Speedwell'. A very unusual and interesting species and hardy. The long, arching stems are set with pairs of waxy, grey, oval, clasping leaves which encircle the stem on which they grow. Erect, axillary racemes carry violet-blue flowers, lined with dark colour.
- **prostrata.** (V. rupestris.) From Europe, including Spain, to North Central Russia. A useful, easy and showy species represented mostly in gardens by its named clones, such as 'Spode Blue', with light blue flowers, 'Royal Blue', much darker, 'Alba', pure white, 'Mrs. Holt', soft pink, 'Silver Queen', silvery-blue and 'Nana', a very dwarf, blue-flowered form. V. 'Kapitan', is also probably a form of this species, neat in habit and with good blue flowers.
- **pulvinaris.** See the genus PYGMAEA.
- **pyrolaefolia.** An introduction of Reginald Farrer's from China which is very dubiously in cultivation now. It is a treasure, with soft, rounded leaves and arching sprays of large, soft lavender-blue flowers , 6 in.
- **repens.** From Corsica and Spain. Close mats of prostrate stems with vivid green leaves, slightly toothed at the margins. The white, or pale

blue flowers are carried singly in the leaf axils.

— rosea. From Spain and N. Africa. Woody, 9 in. stems and hairy leaves which are pinnatifid. Slender racemes of soft pink flowers.

— rupestris. See *V. prostrata.*

— saturejoides. (V. satureoides.) From Dalmatia. Mat-forming, with slightly fleshy leaves hairy at the margins and short racemes of blue flowers, the petals marked red at the base.

— saxatilis. See *V. fruticans.*

— schmidtiana 'Nana'. I don't know where it comes from, maybe Japan, but it is a pretty little thing forming mats of huddled, deeply-cleft foliage and carrying short spikes of soft blue flowers in mid-summer. Good for stone sinks and troughs.

— stelleri. This is probably the plant which has been known as *V.selleri.* It comes from Japan. Mats of creeping rhizomes and pubescent stems with rounded, toothed leaves. On the short stems are racemes of purple-blue flowers.

— spicata. Widely distributed in Europe, including Britain. The type is not generally grown but there are many named forms which are very decorative, although rather tall for most rock gardens as their erect stems may reach 15 inches in height. The cultivated forms will be found in many catalogues, the colour of their flowers ranging from white, through blue and purple to deep red.

— sumilensis. A species rather similar to, but smaller than *V. gentianoides,* forming carpets of fresh green, rather narrow leaves from which rise 9 in. stems carrying in loose array flowers of clear blue.

— surculosa. From Asia Minor. Dense carpets of hairy, toothed leaves and short racemes of deep blue flowers.

— taurica. See *V. orientalis.*

— telephifolia. A choice species from Asia Minor. Best in the alpine house. Creeping stems carry small, waxy, silver-grey leaves and short-stemmed sheets of china-blue flowers. Very gritty soil and careful use of the watering can.

— teucrium. Is a subspecies of *V. austriaca,* which see.

— thymifolia. From Greece and adjacent countries. Carpets of matted, woody stems and small, narrow leaves, lightly hairy. On very short racemes are flowers which may be blue, lilac or pink.

VESICARIA. *Cruciferae.* From the Latin *vesica,* a bladder, because of the inflated seed pods.

— graeca. See ALYSSOIDES *utriculata.*

VICIA. *Leguminosae.* The Latin name for these herbs.
A large, widely distributed genus, of which a few are useful, summer-flowering rock garden plants. Sun lovers.

— argentea. From the Pyrenees. Semi-trailing stems set with pairs of silver-haired leaves and one-sided racemes of white flowers with violet markings.

— **cypria.** From the Middle East. Compact tufts of clover-like leaves and short racemes of cream flowers stained with blue at the apex of the standards.

— **onobrychioides.** From the Pyrenees and Maritime Alps. Rather tall, but quite spectacular. Like an enlarged and more richly coloured version of our native *V. cracca*.

— **orobus.** From the Pyrenees and elsewhere in Europe. Rather tall stems with many leaflets in pairs and racemes of white, violet-veined flowers.

— **persica.** Short, leafy shoots clothed in silver-haired leaves and bunches of blue, purple-tinted flowers.

— **pyrenaica.** Spain and S. France. Semi-procumbent stems with leaflets in pairs and solitary flowers of rich violet-purple.

— **unijuga.** From Asia. Erect, wiry stems and dense racemes of violet-purple flowers.

VINCA. *Apocynaceae.* Contracted from the Latin *vincapervinca*, to bind, or wind around, an allusion to the use of the flexible shoots in making wreaths. The periwinkles are scarcely rock garden plants, but are admired and constantly used as invaluable ground-cover plants for positions in light shade. *V. major* I omit from the list as it is altogether too large and rampant, but, especially in its handsomely variegated form, it is a very popular plant and much in request by flower arrangers. They flower in winter, spring and summer. All evergreen except *V. herbacea.*

— **acutiflora.** See *V. difformis.*

— **balcanica.** From the Balkans and dubiously in cultivation. Similar in general appearance to *V. major*, with rather more rounded leaves and blue flowers.

— **difformis.** (V. media. V. acutiflora.) From Mediterranean regions. Prostrate, leafy shoots and solitary pale blue flowers, usually in late summer.

— **herbacea.** From E. Europe and Russia. A trailing, herbaceous species with glabrous, rather blunt-ended leaves and purple-blue flowers.

— **libanotica.** From the Lebanon, and said to be similar to *V. herbacea*, but I doubt if it is at present in cultivation.

— **media.** See *V. difformis.*

— **minor.** Widely distributed in Europe and doubtfully a native of Britain — almost certainly an escape from gardens. This excellent plant exists in the form of many named clones. It creeps, crawls and spreads widely with vigorous, wiry, leafy stems and the flowers, according to the particular form may be snow-white, blue, purple or lavender and there are double forms of almost all the clones. The foliage too, exhibits silver or golden variegation in some of its many forms.

VIOLA. *Violaceae.* The Latin name for various fragrant flowers, a variant of the Greek *ion.*

A large and important family of very popular plants. There are some 400 known species, widely distributed throughout the north and south temperate zones. From the Andes come numerous species of rosulate violas, much resembling species of Sempervivum in their leaf formation. These have not yet been successfully cultivated, in spite of numerous attempts, and are excluded from the following lengthy, but still far from exhaustive list. All pansies and violettas are also excluded, for obvious reasons, as are the double Parma violets, once such popular plants but now regrettably scarce.

- **adunca.** Widespread in N. America. Compact tufts of short, rather woody, leafy stems. Small ovate leaves, sometimes toothed, sometimes entire and violet or lavender, white-eyed violets.
- **aetiolica.** From E. Europe. This is often listed as *V.a. saxatilis,* sometimes even *V. saxatilis aetolica.* It is a dainty and delightful plant with neat tufts of toothed leaves and short-stemmed clear yellow flowers - very occasionally with the upper petals violet.
- **alba.** From Central and Eastern Europe. Creeping rhizomes and rosettes which produce slender, non-rooting stolons. The white or violet flowers are very gragrant.
- **albanica.** See *V. magellensis.*
- **allchariensis.** From Macedonia. Mats of rhizomes and 4 in., leafy stems felted with fine grey hairs. The flowers are large and usually violet-blue.
- **alpina.** From the European Alps. Tufted, not creeping. Heart-shaped leaves, slightly toothed. The violet-coloured flowers have a golden throat and the lower petals are lined with deeper colour.
- **arborescens.** Mediterranean regions. Almost shrubby, up to a foot in height. Loose-growing woody stems with narrow leaves and long, stalked, short-spurred lilac-blue flowers.
- **arenaria.** See *V. rupestris.*
- **arsenica.** From Macedonia. Six-inch, leafy stems and bright green, rounded, toothed leaves. The large flowers are deep yellow, the petals marked with dark lines.
- **athois.** From Greece. A neat, cliff-dwelling violet with lilac flowers.
- **beckwithii.** From N. America. Neat tufts of lobed, densely hairy leaves and short-stemmed flowers. The upper petals are deep violet, the lower ones paler in colour with a yellow base. In nature it favours rather moist positions. It is very similar to *V. triternata,* but the latter appears to prefer drier conditions.
- **bertolonii.** (V. heterophylla.) From Italy and the Balkans. Compact, non-running root system and 9 in. stems carrying flowers similar in shape to those of *V. calcarata.* In different localities it varies in colour and may be lilac, yellow or white. The subspecies *corsica* appears to be consistent in bearing violet-blue flowers.

427

— **betonicifolia.** From Australia and dubiously in cultivation but to be hoped for. Tufted habit and deep purple, short-stemmed flowers.

— **biflora.** Widely distributed in the Northern Hemisphere, from Europe across N. Asia to N. America. Creeping stems and small, kidney-shaped leaves and, usually, pairs of small, bright yellow flowers, the petals veined with dark stripes. For a cool position in very gritty soil. A typical and well loved alpine plant.

— **blanda.** From N. America. Neat tufts of small leaves and many short-stemmed white, purple-veined violets.

— **bosniaca.** See *V. elegantula.*

— **calcarata.** European Alps. From frail, creeping rhizomes rise lance-olate leaves and 4 to 6 in. stems carrying rich violet. viola-shaped flowers. The subspecies *zoysii,* from the Eastern Alps, is a delightful form with clear yellow flowers and rather dark foliage.

— **canadensis.** From N. American mountain woodlands. Rather tall, lax stems with long-stalked, toothed leaves and flowers which are usually white, but are often tinged with violet, the lower petals being dist - inctly purple-veined.

— **canina.** This is our own beloved native Dog Violet, seldom cultivated but cherished in the wild. It is also known, incorrectly, as *V. flavicornis.*

— **cazorlensis.** From Spain. A very distinct and delightful species, and one of a treasured trinity of shrubby violas, the others being *V. delphinantha* from Greece and *V. kosaninii* from Albania. Tufts of soft stems clothed in small, needle-fine leaves rising from a woody base. The numerous flowers are long-spurred and rich pink in colour. Give it a narrow crevice in which to grow, either in the open or in the alpine house. It is not easy.

— **cenisia.** European Alps and especially Mt.Cenis. An alpine treasure, and not easy to please. It likes gritty scree, in which it rambles with underground stems which emit neat tufts of small leaves and short-stemmed, large pinky-purple flowers. Probably best in the alpine house.

— **chaerophylloides.** From S.E. Asia. From short rhizomes rise 5 in. stems with segmented leaves, the segments lobed and toothed. Large, violet or whitish, fragrant flowers.

— **chrysantha.** See *V. douglasii.*

— **collina.** Europe. Rather similar to *V. hirta,* but the flowers are pale blue and fragrant.

— **comollia.** Very dubiously in cultivation. It is closely related to *C. cenisia,* of which it may be a subspecies and is confined to the Bergamask Alps.

— **cornuta.** From the Pyrenees, and sparingly elsewhere in the Alps. An invaluable, long flowering, easily grown species, the flowers of the type being a good rich purple. It gives rise to several variations, notably one with pure white flowers and, when hybridized with the garden pansy, has been instrumental in the parentage of some good tufted pansies, violas and violettas.

— **corsica.** See *V. bertolonii.*

— **crassa.** From Japan. A very neat, tufted plant with deep green, heart-shaped leaves often suffused with red-brown stains. The short-stemmed flowers are deep yellow, the lower petal having dark striations. It prefers rather cool situations. ns.

— **crassiuscula.** From Spain. Tufts of slightly caespitose leaves and 9 in. stems bearing, usually, violet-coloured flowers but they may occasionally be pink or almost white. The lower petal is stained with gold.

— **cucullata.** N. America. There is obviously confusion in gardens between this species and *V. septentrionalis* and I am slightly dubious about either of them being true to name. *C. cucullata* forms mats of scaly rhizomes and has broad, pointed, toothed leaves. The flowers should be violet with a deeper throat and a white base. The plant commonly grown under this name has white flowers, the petals veined with thin purple lines. It is for a cool position. An authoritative American publication describes a variety 'Bicolor' which aptly fits this description.

— **cunninghamii.** From New Zealand. Small, neat tufts of rounded, toothed, rather thick leaves and many small white violets with lilac or yellow veining on the petals. It would like scree conditions or the alpine house.

— **dehnhardtii.** A subspecies of *V. alba* from Mediterranean regions with lilac flowers.

— **X 'Delmonden'.** A chance hybrid which occurred in a Kentish garden, possibly between *V. pedata* and *V. septentrionalis.* Deeply cleft leaves and charming deep lavender violets of goodly size on 4 in. stems.

— **delphinantha.** Another of the trinity of shrubby species, this time from Greece and, I believe, also found in Bulgaria. That great plantsman, Wilhelm Schacht, once described this viola as 'the finest alpine I have ever seen'. It is a crevice dweller and not easy, forming gnarled, woody stems and the short, wiry stems have thin leaves and end in rose-pink, twin-spurred flowers. Definitely for the alpine house or a choice tufa hole or crevice in a stone trough or sink garden.

— **delphinifolia.** See *V. pedatifida.*

— **doerfleri.** From the Eastern Alps. Tufts of crenate leaves felted with fine hairs on stems woody at the base. The deep violet flowers have a long, reflexed spur.

— **domestica.** See *V. papilionacea.*

— **douglasii.** (*V. chrysantha.*) From N. America. Leafy stems rise from creeping rhizomes, leaves cut into narrow segments. The orange-yellow petals are veined purple and the upper ones are purple-nrown on the reverse.

— **dubyana.** From the Italian Alps. Neat tufts of glabrous, or slightly hairy leaves and short stems carrying deep violet flowers, the lower petal with a yellow spot.

— **eizanensis.** From Japan, and probably more correctly regarded as a form of *V. chaerophylloides*, but I retain the name under which it is better known in gardens. Dissected leaves and purple violets on 4 in. stems.

— **elatior.** From Central and Eastern Europe, and Western Asia. The erect. 12 in. leafy stems carry many soft lavender violets from early summer on into the autumn.

— **elegantula.** (V. bosniaca.) From E. Europe. A particularly neat, tufted plant with flowers which are described botanically as being violet, yellow, or part-coloured, but the plant in cultivation consistently carries crimson-red flowers.

— **flettii.** Endemic to the Olympic mountains of the State of Washington, where it inhabits shady crevices. Reniform, scalloped and prominently veined leaves in tiny tufts and large flowers of reddish-violet, veined with deeper colour, yellow at the base of the petals.

— **X florariensis.** A hybrid raised in Switzerland by the late Dr. Henri Correvon between *V. cornuta* and *V. tricolor*. The purple flowers have short spurs and the petals are yellow at the base.

— **fragrans.** From Greece. Tufts of rather narrow leaves and short stems carrying one, or occasionally two, yellow or pale violet flowers.

— **glabella.** From N. America. Foot-high leafy stems with heart-shaped leaves and short-spurred yellow flowers, the petals veined purple.

— **gracilis.** From Eastern Europe and the Balkans. I doubt if the true species now exists in cultivation. Many plants distributed under its name are hybrids. The true plant is a gracious species with toothed leaves and fine, rich violet flowers. It should certainly be reintroduced.

— **grisebachiana.** From the Balkans. A choice and rare species. Small oval, faintly notched leaves, often with a purple shading on the green and 2 in. stems bearing rounded flowers of soft, clear blue. Scree, trough or alpine house.

— **hallii.** From N. America and akin to *V. beckwithii*. Leaves cleft into narrow segments and 6 in. stems carrying flowers whose upper petals are deep violet and the lower ones either yellow or white.

— **hederacea.** (ERPETION reinforme.) From Australia and slightly tender. For a cool place in moisture-holding soil. Creeping stems and small, cordate leaves and many short-stemmed white-tipped, violet-blue flowers.

— **heterophylla.** See *V. bertolonii*.

— **jooi.** (V. transylvanica.) From the Carpathian mountains. Basal rosettes of small but broad, cordate leaves and many pale violet flowers on short stems.

— **kosaninii.** The third of the rare, shrubby trinity of treasures. From Albania and Macedonia. Similar to *V. delphinantha* in some ways, but the flowers are lilac pink, with shorter spurs. It demands, and deserves as much special care as the others of its group.

— **labradorica.** A N. American species allied to *V. adunca* and most commonly grown in British gardens in the form 'Purpurea', whose heart-shaped leaves are dark green, suffused with purple. It is not long-lived but seeds itself and is too pretty to be regarded as a nuisance — in fact it makes good ground cover between shrubs. The innumerable flowers are dark violet in colour.

— **lanceolata.** N. America. The leaves are narrow and slightly toothed and the 6 in. stems carry white flowers.

— **lobata.** From N. America. Distinct leaves cut into several unequal lobes and carried at the top of purplish stems. The yellow flowers are veined with dark lines and flushed purple on the outside.

— **lutea.** Widely distributed in Europe, including Britain. A charming dwarf violet, plentiful in limestone pastures of our more northern counties. The flowers of the form usually most appreciated are clear yellow, but they run the gamut of forms with violet petals and, rarely, pure white.

— **macedonica.** See *V. tricolor.*

— **magellensis.** (V. albanica.) From E. Europe, rare and beautiful. Neat, tufted habit and clear pink flowers on short stems.

— **mirabilis.** Europe, mainly in alpine woodlands. Basal rosettes of small, cordate leaves and short, erect stems carrying pale violet flowers with a whitish spur.

— **mumbyana.** From Spain and N. Africa. Mats of crowded rosettes and erect stems carrying rounded, deep violet-purple, or occasionally yellow flowers.

— **nummulariifolia.** A rarity from the Maritime Alps and Corsica. From a central crown with a deep taproot radiate creeping stolons, emitting here and there tufts of tiny, untoothed, rounded, cordate leaves. Short-stemmed bright blue flowers are scattered over the mats it forms. For gritty scree, trough or alpine house.

— **nuttallii.** From N. America. A very distinct species forming clusters of softly hairy leaves. On 4 in. naked stems appear clear yellow violets. The form *praemorsa* has shorter, wider, more hairy leaves and the same golden blossoms.

— **odorata.** This is our own well loved sweet violet of which several named varieties are grown.

— **olympica.** A name sometimes, but probably erroneously, given to *V. gracilis.*

— **orphanidis.** From E.Europe. Low tufts of softly hairy leaves and flowers of soft mauve with a golden eye.

— **palustris.** This is the bog violet of many parts of Europe, including Britain. Seldom cultivated but could be used in a moist position. Rather rosetted glabrous leaves and pale lilac violets on short stems.

— **papilionacea.** (V. domestica.) From N. America and closely akin to *V. cucculata.* The typical flowers are of a deep violet colour but there are albino forms.

— **pedata.** From N. America. Appreciative of light shade. The palmate leaves are deeply cleft and the short-stemmed large flowers are typically dark violet in the upper petals and paler in the lower ones, but there are many colour variations, some having uniformly violet-blue petals, other have pinkish or almost white flowers. The plant commonly grown here as *V.p.* 'Bicolor' is characteristic of the type plant.

— **pedatifida.** N. America. Leaves cut into narrow segments and short-spurred pale violet flowers.

— **pedunculata.** Leafy stems rise from a stout rhizome. The leaves are rounded and coarsely-toothed. The stems can attain a foot or more and carry orange-yellow flowers, the petals veined with purple lines.

— **perinensis.** From E. Europe. Glabrous, obtuse, rather thick leaves and yellow, or occasionally white flowers on 4 to 6 in. stems.

— **persicifolia.** A European species related to, and similar to, *V. elatior.*

— **pinnata.** From Europe and N. Asia. Small tufts of segmented leaves and 4 in. stems bearing fragrant violet-blue flowers.

— **poetica.** From Greece and rather like *V. fragrans,* but with more glabrous foliage. The flowers may be yellow or soft violet.

— **praemorsa.** See *V. nuttallii.*

— **pumila.** From Europe and W. Asia. Similar to *V. elatior,* but a dwarfer plant.

— **rostrata.** A N. American species with rather tall, leafy stems and cordate leaves. The long-spurred flowers are lilac, with darker petal markings.

— **rugulosa.** This is properly a form, or subspecies of *V. canadensis,* which it closely resembles.

— **rupestris.** (*V. arenaria.*) Widespread in Europe. Tufty rosettes of cordate, obtuse leaves and short stems offering flowers which vary in colour from white, through pale blue to reddish-violet. The form most commonly grown is var *rosea,* with clear pink flowers.

— **sarmentosa.** See *V. sempervirens.*

— **saxatillis.** See *V. aetolica.*

— **sempervirens.** N. America. Makes stolons from short rhizomes, round-cordate, toothed leaves and many small, yellow, dark-spotted flowers on 3 in. stems.

— **scorpiuroides.** From Crete, Greece and N. Africa. A semi-shrubby species with foot-high stems and yellow flowers.

— **septentrionalis.** N. America. Like *V. cucculata* in habit. The flowers should be violet-purple, but are occasionally white.

— **sheltonii.** N. America. Glabrous leaves split into three lobes, these lobes further dissected. The flowers are yellow, the petals marked with purple.

— **sororia.** According to American botanists this is the correct name for *V. papilionacea.*

- **thomasiana.** European Alps. 6 in. stems rise from woody rhizomes. Heart-shaped leaves and fragrant, light violet-blue flowers with a thin, pointed spur.
- **transylvanica.** See *V. jooi.*
- **tricolor.** We need not concern ourselves with the annual or biennial wild tricolor violet, charming though it is, but the plant now considered to be a subspecies, *V.t. macedonica* is a must for any garden. It flowers from spring until autumn with innumerable glowing red-violet flowers on 6 in. stems. Not long-lived but replaces itself.
- **triternata.** See *V. beckwithii.*
- **valderia.** Close to *V. cenisia* but more hairy leaves. Flowers lilac-purple. From the Maritime Alps and difficult.
- **verecunda yakusimana.** It must be the smallest violet in the world. From Japan, and makes wee tufts of minute, rounded, glabrous leaves and on half-inch stems bears wee white violets with purple veins on the tiny petals. Ideal for stone troughs and sink gardens.
- **yakusimana.** See *V. verecunda.*
- **zoysii.** See *V. calcarata.*

So much for Viola. It is far from being a complete list of the known species but, even so, I have included some which are very dubiously, or not at all, in cultivation, for there is no good reason why they should not be re-introduced.

VISCARIA. A genus now discarded and its species referred to other genera, largely to LYCHNIS, which see.

VITTADENIA *triloba.* See ERIGERON *mucronatus.*

VITALIANA. See the genus DOUGLASIA.

WAHLENBERGIA. *Campanulaceae.* Named for Georg Wahlenberg (1780-1851), Swedish botanist.

With few exceptions the plants we have known in gardens as WAHLENBERGIA have been transferred to the genus EDRAI-ANTHUS, which see.

- hederacea. (Campanula hederacea.) Widely distributed in Europe, including Britain. A frail wanderer in moist places, with slender stems beset with tiny, ivy-shaped leaves and solitary, axillary flowers of soft blue. Spring and summer flowering.

- serpyllifolia. This is now correctly EDRAINATHUS *serpyllifolius* but I retain the name under which it has become so well known in gardens for many decades. The form usually grown is clonally named 'Major' and is an improved form of the type, with very large, rich violet-blue flowers, bell-shaped, over mats of rather dark green foliage. Unfortunately it is losing its constitution after generations of vegetative propagation and is not the vigorous plant it once was. Its best chance of survival seems to be when grown in rich scree and in full sun. It flowers in spring and early summer.

WALDHEIMIA. *Compositae.*

A small genus with several species to be found in Karakorum mountains of what is now Pakistan. They would be treasured if available but I doubt if any are at present in cultivation, but seek *W. nivea, W. tomentosa* and *W. tridactylites.*

WALDSTEINIA. *Rosaceae.* Named for Count Franz Adam Waldstein-Wartenburg (1759-1823) Austrian botanist.

Two species of usually creeping, but sometimes modestly erect plants from Europe, but also extending into E. Asia. They are easily grown, in sun or light shade and are summer flowering with a long season of blossom.

434

WALDSTEINIA — *continued*

— geoides. Lobed, cordate, toothed leaves and loose sprays of yellow flowers.

— ternata. (W. trifolia.) Creeping and rooting rhizomes with toothed. lobed leaves and showers of saucer-shaped golden flowers.

— trifolia. See *W. ternata.*

WARDASTER. *Compositae.* The generic name commemorates the first finding in Szechwan of this aster-like plant by the late Kingdon-Ward. *W. lanuginosus* has been cultivated, but proved temperamental and may not now exist in gardens. It forms tufts of woolly, aromatic leaves and the blue-violet flowers are surrounded by a woolly tomentum.

WELDENIA. *Commelinaceae.* Named in honour of Ludwig van Welden (1780-1853), master of ordnance in the Austrian army.

— candida. The only species on its genus, from the craters of extinct volcanoes in Mexico and Guatamala. For the alpine house. Deep-delving, fleshy, almost tuberous roots from which rise annually strong tufts of thick, broad and pointed dark green leaves. From the centre of the rosette rise short, erect scapes of dazzlingly white, cup-shaped flowers in long succession. The Guatemalan form appears to be almost identical but can be recognised by characteristic tufts of white hairs on the leaf surface. It should be kept well on the dry side during dormancy.

WERNERIA. *Compositae.* Named for Abraham Gottlob Werner (1750-1817). Dwarf, tufted perennial herbs, natives of the Andes of S. America. Only two species appear to have been cultivated, *W. nubigena* and *W. rigida.* Both are recommended for the alpine house. *W. nubigena* forms rosettes of narrow leaves and displays a few, almost stemless large white flowers - like those of a single chrysanthemum - the ray florets being red on the undersides. *W. rigida* makes loose cushions up to 9 in. of narrow leaves and has solitary yellow flower-heads with violet involucral bracts.

WITTSTEINIA. *Ericaceae.* Named for George Christian Wittstein (1810-1887). Author of books on plant nomenclature.

— vacciniacea. From Australia, but hardy. Really a shrub but eminently suitable for peat beds. Dwarf evergreen, gaultheria-like with leathery leaves and axillary clusters of bell-shaped greenish-white or reddish flowers.

WULFENIA. *Scrophulariaceae.* Named for Franz Xavier Freiherr von Wulfen (1728-1805). Austrian botanical author.

A small genus of tufted perennial, rhizomatous herbs, natives of Europe, W. Asia and the Himalaya. They ask only for good, moisture-holding soil and an open but not arid position. Summer flowering.

— amherstiana. From the Himalaya. Tufts of long, narrow leaves, slightly toothed and modestly hairy on both surfaces. 12 in. stems carry a loose, many-flowered inflorescence of handsome, purple-blue flowers.

— baldacii. From Albania. Similar foliage to above and elegant spikes of lilac-blue flowers.

— carinthiaca. From the S.E. Alps and the most commonly grown species. Not a great beauty, but useful. Leaves similar to those of the above species, the erect 12 in. stems have small, scale-like leaves and a raceme of blue flowers, pink and white forms are known.

— himalaica. A rare Himalayan species which appears to exist in Europe only as herbarium specimens. It should be similar to *W. baldacii* and is described as graceful and beautiful.

— orientalis. From Asia Minor. Long, narrow, toothed leaves, glabrous and a long, loose spray of heliotrope flowers.

Two hybrids have been identified, one between *W. baldacii* and *W. orientalis* and another (*W.X. suendermannii*) between *W. carinthiaca* and *W. baldacii.*

XYRIS. *Xyridaceae.* A name used by Dioscorides for IRIS *foeti-dissima.*

— brevifolia. From N. America. Tufts of rushlike leaves and cylindrical spikes of small bright yellow flowers.

ZAHLBRUCKNERIA. See SAXIFRAGA *paradoxa.*

ZAUSCHNERIA. *Onagraceae.* Named for Johann Baptist Zauschner (1737-1799) a professor at Prague.

A small genus of late-flowering, sub-shrubby plants from N. America. For hot-dry positions and invaluable for late summer and autumn colour in the rock garden.

- californica. Herbaceous, with annual stems which become woody and form rounded hummocks a foot or so in height, clad with small toothed hairy grey leaves. The branches end in loose sprays of tubular scarlet flowers. There is a very rare pure white form and one or two slightly varying forms have been named.
- cana. (Z. microphylla.) Of similar habit but notable for its very narrow silver-haired foliage.
- garrettii. Again similar in habit but with broader, rather leathery and veined leaves.
- mexicana. Often tacked onto the end of *Z. californica*, but no more than a synonym.
- microphylla. See *Z. cana.*
- septentrionalis. Remarkable for its particularly dwarf and tufted habit.

ZYGADENUS. *Liliaceae.* From the Greek *zygos*, a yoke and *aden*, a gland. The glands are in pairs at the base of the perianth.

As these plants from N. America and Asia are rhizomatous rather than bulbous they just squeeze in here. The three species, all N. America, sometimes grown are *Z. elegans*, *Z. glaucus* and *Z. nuttallii.* They are of similar appearance, with long narrow leaves in loose tufts and erect stems carrying racemes of starry flowers which are white, cream or greenish-white. They are more elegant than they may sound and like a cool, moisture holding soil and flower in summer.

ADDENDA

ACANTHOSONCHUS cervicornis. See SONCHUS *spinosus* in main text.

ACINOS. For A. alpinus see CALAMINTHA alpina in main text. The plant in circulation as THYMUS 'E.B. Anderson' is correctly *A. alpinus meridionalis.* Over carpets of green foliage it displays short spikes of violet-blue flowers over a long summer period.

AETHIONEMA thomasianum. A species of dubious authenticity from the Valle d' Aosta in Italy. Low tufts of straggling stems with small, fleshy, blue-grey leaves and heads of pink flowers.

ALCHEMILLA erythropoda. From E. Europe. A neat plant with tufts of grey, hairy leaves and loose sprays of soft yellow flowers on short stems. Not unlike a very refined and condensed *A. mollis.*

ANCHUSA undulata. From Greece. Tufts of narrow, softly hairy leaves and erect 9 in. stems carrying loose clusters of gentian-blue flowers in late summer and early autumn.

ARABIS flavescens. (A. caucasica.) European Alps. Compact habit and heads of soft yellow flowers in spring.

ASTELIA nivicola. From New Zealand. Handsome rosettes of bronzed silver leaves and spikes of greenish-white flowers which are followed by orange-yellow fruits. For peaty soil and a sunny position.

ASYNEUMA limonifolia. An exception to the rather scathing remarks in the main text. On 12 to 15in. wiry stems are showers of starry blue flowers. For scree or alpine house, summer flowering.

AZALEA procumbens. See LOISELURIA *procumbens* in main text.

BAHIA lanata. See ERIOPHYLLUM *lanatum* in main text.

439

BALLOTA frutescens. From S.W.Europe. A tiny shrub of tangled, spiny branchlets admist which appear heads of fluffy white flowers. For a hot, dry position.

BOLAX (azorella) gummifera. There is reason to believe that this plant is inseparable from *B. caespitosa*, which see in main text

— trifurcata. Wide, hard matts of congested rosettes of apple-green leaves and innumerable stemless clusters of yellowish tiny flowers.

CAMPANULA primulifolia. From Spain and Portugal, usually in damp and shady positions. Bold rosettes of softly hairy, toothed leaves and tall, erect stems carrying axillary and terminal bell-shaped blue flowers, often white at the base of the corolla.

CAMPHOROSMA perennis. From the mountains of Iran. Congested mats of procumbent stems clothed densely with tiny, pointed grey leaves. A good cushion plant with inconspicuous flowers. For a hot, dry scree or the alpine house.

CHRYSANTHEMUM (Leucanthemum) weyrichii. From Kamschatka and adjacent islands. From a woody rootstock rise many leafy stems forming a dense carpet of green, pinnatifid leaves with toothed leaflets. The 6 in. stems carry large composite flowers with pink ray-florets and a central disk of yellow florets. For a sunny place or the alpine house.

COLLOMIA. *Polemoniaceae.*

— rawsoniana. A rarity from a limited locality in N.W. America's Sierra Nevada. Tufts of soft green, glandular leaves and loose sprays of rather flimsy orange flowers. For shade and moisture.

CONVOLVULUS nitidus. This is now correctly *C. boissieri* **sub. species** *boissieri*

CORYDALIS ferouzii. A newly discovered species from the mountains of Iran, not yet firmly in cultivation but we live in hope. Low tufts of glaucous leaves and clusters of large, rich yellow flowers on very short stems. Definitely for the alpine house when available.

COSSONIA africana. See RAFFENALDIA *primuloides* in the main text.

COTULA atrata luteola. From New Zealand. Not 100 percent hardy, but a most attractive plant. Mats of dark, purple-tinted leaves and powder-puff heads of cream and pink flowerlets with a startling central boss of red and black.

CYNOGLOSSUM wallichianum. See ERITRICHIUM *strictum* in main text.

DAPHNE. For species and others omitted from those listed in the main text see the admirable Monograph published by the Alpine Garden Society.

DIANTHUS gelidus. Really a subspecies of *D. glacialis* from the Carpathians. Tufts of green leaves and short-stemmed showy pink flowers.

DISPORUM. *Liliaceae.* From the Greek *dis*, two and *spora*, seed. An allusion to the two ovules in each chamber of the ovary. Originally omitted from the Manual because they can make shrubby bushes of a foot or more in height, but I have relented as they are so decorative and useful for the larger rock garden, in line-free soil, preferably not in full sunlight. They are distributed in N. America and tropical Asia. Those briefly mentioned below are hardy. Of the 20 or more species those likely to be encountered are:
D. hookeri, 18 in. with small, greenish flowers and fine red berries.
D. lanuginosum is dwarfer, with yellowish flowers and red fruits.
D. oreganum is a form of D.hookeri and dwarfer but otherwise similar.
D. sessile from Japan (the others are all N. American) has white flowers and a form is known with variegated foliage.

EUPHORBIA capitulata. From the Balkans. Carpets of rounded. blue-green leaves on stems crowned by small heads of yellow flowers among orange bracts. 3 in.

GEUM triflorum. (Sieversia triflora.) From N. America. Clusters of basal, pinnate leaves and tallish stems carrying small groups of cream, purple-tinted, or white with reddish margined flowers in deep purple calyces.

GORMANIA. Included in SEDUM in main text.

HIERACEUM mixtum. From Spain. Rosettes of woolly white leaves and large yellow flowers on 6 in. stems.

HYPERICUM adenotrichum. From Mediterranean regions. Prostrate, radiating stems bearing many pairs of leaves edged with black hairs. The stems terminate in small clusters of rounded yellow flowers with calyces as black-haired as the foliage.

— hyssopifolium. Widely distributed in the Caucasus, S. Europe, Asia Minor and Siberia. Almost a sub-shrub of a foot or more in height. Cymes of yellow flowers in long panicles from June to August.

JASIONE jankae. Described in the main text but it is now correctly *J. heldreichii.*

LAUNAEA cervicornis. See SONCHUS *spinosus* in the main text.

LEWISIA rediviva 'Jolon'. A remarkable form of the type recently introduced with large flowers of icing-sugar pink.

LIRIOPE hyacinthiflora. See REINECKIA *carnea* in main text.

LITHODORA. See the genus LITHOSPERMUM in main text.

MYRSINE nummularia. See the genus SUTTONIA in main text.

MECONOPSIS betonicifolia. (M. baileyi.) Inexcusably missed in the main text. This is probably the best-known and most popular meconopsis. It can be short-lived or a good perennial. Handsome rosettes of leaves and tall stems bearing many large clear blue flowers.

MIMULUS luteus. Native from Alaska to New Mexico and widely naturalised elsewhere, including Britain. This is the common Monkey Musk, and not really a garden plant although it is decorative in marshy, semi-wild areas.

ORTHILLA secunda. See PYROLA *secunda* in main text.

OURISA X 'Snowflake'. A natural hybrid between *O. macrocarpa* and *O. caespitosa* 'Gracilis'. Compact tufts of purple-backed leaves and short, dark stems each bearing several large white flowers.

PAEDEROTA. *Scrophulariaceae.* A genus confused with, and sometimes included in VERONICA.

- ageria. See *P. lutea.*
- bonarota. (VERONICA bonarota.) From S. Europe. Short, hairy, twiggy stems and toothed leaves and terminal spikes of blue flowers in summer. A good crevice plant, or for the scree in sun.
- lutea (P. ageria. VERONICA lutea.) From the Eastern Alps and not unlike *P. bonarota* but slightly larger in all its parts and a short, terminal spike of yellow flowers.

PARTHENIUM *Compositae.* Modern classification appears to have submerged this genus into CHRYSANTHEMUM.

PETRORHAGIA. See the genus TUNICA in main text.

PTILOTRICHUM. (Alyssum.) The two species described below were unfortunately omitted from the main text.

- rupestre. From Greece. Dense tufts of woody grey-leaved stems and small heads of white flowers 6 in.
- spinosum. Better known, if incorrectly, as ALYSSUM spinosum. Domed bushes of wiry stems and small grey leaves and many heads of white flowers. There is a form having flowers of soft pink.

RANUNCULUS obesus. From Turkey. Tufts of finely cut, almost fernlike foliage and large yellow flowers very early in the year on stems about a foot in height.

SCHIVERECKIA bornmuelleri. See *S. doerfleri* in main text.

STACKHOUSIA. *Stackhousiaceae.* Named for John Stackhouse (1740-1819), Botanist.

- minima. From New Zealand. Tufts of congested stems dressed with small yellow-green leaves and short racemes of yellow flowers in summer. For a sunny scree or the alpine house.

STREPTOPUS amplexifolius. From Europe and N. America. 18 in. stems with smooth, glaucous, stem-clasping leaves and sprays of greenish-white flowers carried like those of the Solomon's Seal. For a cool, shady position.

SYMPHYANDRA. For a more detailed list of species in this genus see an excellent and comprehensive article, based on the work of the late Clifford Crook, in Bulletin No. 45 of the Alpine Garden Society, pages 246-254.

TRACHYSTEMON. *Boraginaceae* From the Greek *trachys*, rough, and *stemon*, a stamen.

— orientalis. (NORDMANNIA cordifolia.) Really too tall, and often invasive for the rock garden, but a useful ground coverer for half-shade in semi-wild places. Hairy stems and large leaves. On 18 in. stems are loose showers of blue borage flowers in spring and early summer.

BIBLIOGRAPHY

Listed below are the major books which have been consulted in the production of the Manual. Many others have also been used, too numerous to mention in detail.

The Royal Horticultural Society's Dictionary of Gardening.

Journals and Indexes of the Royal Horticultural Society.

The Bulletins of the Alpine Garden Society.

The Journals of the Scottish Rock Garden Club.

Flora of the British Isles, by Clapham, Tutin & Warburg.

Hortus Third.

Alpine Flowers of New Zealand, by A.F. Marks & Nancy M. Adams.

Flora of Japan, by Jisaburo Ohwi.

Mountain Flowers, by Anthony Huxley.

The Flowers of Europe, by Oleg Polunin.

Flowers of the Mediterranean, by Anthony Huxley & Oleg Polunin.

Index Londinensis.

Index Kewensis.

Flora Europaea.

The English Rock Garden, by Reginald Farrer.

The Present Day Rock Garden, by Dr. Sampson Clay.

Saxifragas, by Winton Harding.

Daphne, by C.D. Brickell & B. Mathew.

Asiatic Primulas, by Roy Green.

The Genus Phlox, by Edgar T. Wherry.

Campanulas, by Clifford Crook.

NOTES

NOTES